osophic Classics
Volume II

MEDIEVAL PHILOSOPHY

Walter Kaufmann
Late, of Princeton University

Forrest E. Baird, Editor
Whitworth College

Prentice Hall, Englewood Cliffs, New Jersey 07632

Library of Congress Cataloging-in-Publication Data
(Revised for volume 2)

Philosophic classics.

Includes bibliographical references.
Contents: v. 1. Ancient philosophy—v. 2. Medieval
philosophy—v. 3. Modern philosophy.
1. Philosophy. I. Kaufmann, Walter Arnold. II. Baird,
Forrest E.
B21.P39 1994   100   93-34534
ISBN 0-13-091316-2 (v. 1)
ISBN 0-13-091324-3 (v. 2)
ISBN 0-13-097551-6 (v. 3)

Acquisitions editor: Ted Bolen
Editorial assistant: Nicole Gray
Editorial/production supervision and
    interior design: Linda B. Pawelchak
Art supervision: Anne Bonanno
Chapter introduction sketches: Don Martinetti
Cover design: Donna Wickes
Photo editor: Lori Morris-Nantz
Photo research: Joelle Burrows
Production coordinator: Peter Havens

Cover art: *Head of Oriental Kings,*
    Fragment of the fresco. IX–X c.
    Rome, San Saba/Art Resource, NY

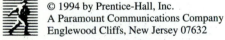

© 1994 by Prentice-Hall, Inc.
A Paramount Communications Company
Englewood Cliffs, New Jersey 07632

Printed in the United States of America
10 9 8 7 6 5 4 3 2 1

ISBN 0-13-091324-3

Prentice-Hall International (UK) Limited, *London*
Prentice-Hall of Australia Pty. Limited, *Sydney*
Prentice-Hall Canada Inc., *Toronto*
Prentice-Hall Hispanoamericana, S.A., *Mexico*
Prentice-Hall of India Private Limited, *New Delhi*
Prentice-Hall of Japan, Inc., *Tokyo*
Simon & Schuster Asia Pte. Ltd., *Singapore*
Editora Prentice-Hall do Brasil, Ltda., *Rio de Janeiro*

This volume is dedicated to my wife,
Joy Lynn Fulton Baird

A capable wife is far more precious than jewels.
Strength and dignity are her clothing.
    and she laughs at the time to come.
She opens her mouth with wisdom,
    and the teaching of kindness is on her tongue.

(Proverbs 31:10, 25–26)

Contents

Preface

The Middle Ages have been depicted as a time of intellectual sterility obsessed with trivial and tiresome questions; as a valley between two great mountain ranges—Greek philosophy on one side, which medievalism distorted, and modern philosophy on the other, which happily rejected medieval precedents entirely. As late as the 1960s, medieval philosophers were described by many as being incapable of independent thought, saddled with a "sacramental" view of a God-pointing world. For example, W.T. Jones wrote in *The Medieval Mind* (New York: Harcourt, Brace & World, 1969),

> It can hardly be denied that this sacramental point of view was a block to progress . . . [and to] many it seems equally obvious, now that this viewpoint has disappeared, that men have rid themselves of much that was a liability—ignorance, superstition, intolerance.

This position led many to skip almost two millennia of human thought—from the Hellenistic philosophers to Bacon or Descartes—with only a passing nod to Augustine and Thomas Aquinas.

Much has changed. Most scholars no longer see Bacon and Descartes as the saviors of philosophy from a long medieval night. Following the lead of Étienne Gilson and others, philosphers now recognize that modern philosophy cannot be understood apart from its roots in medieval thought, that medieval philosophy was much richer than previously believed, and that medieval philosophers were as intelligent and thoughtful as the philosophers of any age. While it is true that most debates during the medieval period were framed in a "sacramental" way and that the medievals considered some answers unacceptable for religious reasons, nevertheless Christian, Jewish, and Muslim thinkers in this period did original philosophical work. Furthermore, while medieval topics may often appear only theological, they are, in fact, related to virtually every area of philosophy.

So it is appropriate that this series of the late Professor Kaufmann's *Philosophic Classics* includes a new volume devoted entierely to medieval philosophy. I am pleased by this addition and trust that it will contribute to the recovery of rich medieval philosophic thought.

*   *   *

The readings included in this volume represent the towering thinkers—Augustine, Thomas Aquinas, and William of Ockham—discussing a variety of topics and give representative texts to the other figures. The readings consider ethics and politics, but the focus is on metaphysics and epistemology—questions on the nature of universals, the nature and essence of God, the relationship of God to time and creation, and the ability of humans to know God and creation.

To make the works more accessible to students, most footnotes on textual matters (variant readings, etc.) have been omitted and all Greek words have been transliterated and put in angle brackets. Introductions for each philosopher include material that is (1) biographical (a glimpse of the life), (2) philosophical (a résumé of the philosopher's thought), and (3) bibliographical (suggestions for further reading). In addition, five period introductions provide historical context.

A note about the chapter opening sketches: With some exceptions, realistic portraits were not produced in the medieval period. The reasons for this are complex. Popular piety encouraged an emphasis on representations of religious subjects and on the activity of God rather than of individuals. Medieval European culture focused on corporate identity more than on individuality. As a result, we have few portraits, even of the most influential people, from about 500 through 1200. The drawings included here are one contemporary artist's interpretation and are included to give a feel for the period and some sense of the person behind the text.

Those who use this volume for a one-term course in medieval philosophy, philosophy of religion, or metaphysics will find more material here than can easily fit a normal semester. But this embarrassment of riches offers teachers some choice and, for those who teach the same course year after year, an opportunity to change the menu.

*   *   *

I would like to thank the many people who assisted me in this volume including the library staff of Whitworth College, especially Hans Bynagle, Gail Fielding, Jeanette Langston, and Joan Spanne; my colleagues, F. Dale Bruner, who made helpful suggestions on all the introductions and provided suggestions for material on the early Christian documents, Barbara Filo, who helped make selections for the artwork, Roger Mohrlang, who made suggestions on the early introductions, and Corliss Slack, who provided historical context; Timothy A. Robinson, The College of St. Benedict, who read some of the introductions and gave helpful advice; Suzanne Noffke, Sisters of St. Dominic, who gave advice on selections for the medieval mystics; my student assistant, Meredith TeGrotenhuis; my secretary, Lorrie Nelson; my production editor, Linda Pawelchak, and Ted Bolen of Prentice Hall. I would also like to acknowledge the following reviewers: James W. Allard, Montana State University; Robert C. Bennett, El

Centro College; Herbert L. Carson, Ferris State University; Mary T. Clark, Manhattanville College; Sandra S. Edwards, Univesity of Arkansas; Helen S. Lang, Trinity College; Scott MacDonald, University of Iowa; Angel Medina, Georgia State University; Katherin Rogers, University of Delaware; Stephen Scott, Eastern Washington University; Walter G. Scott, Oklahoma State University; and Donald Phillip Verene, Emory University.

I am especially thankful to my wife, Joy Lynn Fulton Baird, and to our children, Whitney Jaye, Sydney Tev, and Soren David, who have supported me in this arduous enterprise. To use Anselm's famous words, they have been to me a family "than-which-none-greater-can-be-thought."

Forrest E. Baird
Professor of Philosophy
Whitworth College
Spokane, WA 99251

Philosophers in This Volume

Socrates
Plato
Aristotle
Epicurus
Epictetus
Plotinus
Augustine
Boethius

Other Important Figures

Pyrrho
Alexander the Great
Zeno of Citium
Cleanthes
Julius Caesar
Lucretius
Philo of Alexandria
Jesus
Paul
Justin Martyr
Marcus Aurelius
Ptolemy (astronomer)
Clement of Alexandria
Tertullian
Origen

Sextus Empiricus
Porphyry

Pseudo-Dionysius Areopagite
Mohammed
Charlemagne

A Sampling of Major Events

Death of Socrates
Punic Wars and rise of Rome
Wall of China
Jerusalem Temple destroyed
Furthest extent of the Roman Empire
Council of Nicea
Roman Empire divided
Fall of Rome
School of Philosophy
in Athens closed
by Justinian
Buddhism introduced
in Japan
Muslim conquest
of Northern Africa
and Spain
Peak of
Mayan
civilization in
Central
America

400 B.C.   200 B.C.   0   A.D. 200   A.D. 400   A.D. 600   A.D. 800

John Scotus Eriugena
    Anselm
       Moses Maimonides
         Thomas Aquinas
          Duns Scotus
           William of Ockham
            Nicholas Cusanas
              René Descartes
               Thomas Hobbes
                Baruch
                Spinoza

John Locke
George Berkeley
George Berkeley
David Hume
Immanuel Kant
G.W.F. Hegell
John Stuart Mill
Søren Kierkegaard
Karl Marx
Friedrich
Nietzsche

Avicenna
  Peter Abelard
   Hildegard of Bingen
    Averroës
     Genghis Khan
      Francis of Assisi
       Roger Bacon
        Bonaventure
         Marco Polo
          Meister Eckhart
          Dante Alighieri

Catherine of Siena Louis XIV
  da Vinci   Isaac Newton
  Copernicus   Giovanni Battista Vico
  Martin Luther J.S. Bach
  John Calvin Voltaire
  Giordano Bruno Thomas Reid
    Francis Bacon J.W. Goethe
    Galileo   Mozart
    Shakespeare Mary Wollstonecraft
      Rembrandt Napolean Bonaparte
      Pascal Beethoven
        Simón Bolívar
        Queen Victoria

First Crusade
Construction of Romanesque Cathedrals
  Construction of Gothic Cathedrals
   Paris University founded
    Magna Carta
     Bubonic Plague
      Ming Dynasty in China
       Gutenberg invents moveable-type printing
       Columbus sails to America
       Luther begins Protestant Reformation
       English defeat Spanish Armada
       Manchu Dynasty in China
       Charles I of England executed
       English "Glorious Revolution"
       Declaration of Independence
       French Revolution
       Chaka founds
       Zulu empire
        Brazil, Colombia,
        and Ecuador
        achieve
        independence
        American
        Civil War

A.D. 1000   A.D. 1200   A.D. 1400   A.D. 1600   A.D. 1800   A.D. 2000

Prologue: Early Christian Documents

With only a few exceptions, medieval thought was deeply imbued with Christian faith. As a result, it is not possible to understand medieval philosophy without at least a rudimentary understanding of the Christian documents from which that thought draws. Whether or not today's reader accepts the veracity of the claims put forth in these writings, most medievals did believe them, and that belief formed the foundation of their thought.

Beginning as a Jewish sect, Christianity continued to hold a number of beliefs in common with Judaism, including the following bedrock convictions: that the Old Testament is the revealed Word of God; that God is superior to and distinct from the created world; that the world was created by God at a specific point in time and that the world will come to an end; that God is personal and desires a special relationship with the human race; that humans have sinned against God's Law and are in need of God's forgiveness; that God requires righteousness as a means of a right relationship with God and others; and that God would send the Anointed One ("Messiah" in Hebrew, "Christ" in Greek) to set the people of God free. The following readings from the Hebrew scriptures include these beliefs and were extremely influential on medieval thinkers:

GENESIS 1–3:   The Creation and the Fall
GENESIS 12:1–8:   The Call of Abraham and the beginning of Israel

EXODUS 20:1–20:   The Ten Commandments
ISAIAH 52:13–15; 53:1–13:   The Suffering Servant Song, Hope of Israel
AMOS 5:18–24:   The Social Justice of Yahweh

But while Christians accepted the foundational beliefs of their Jewish ancestors, they differed on one key point: the identity of the Messiah. While the Jews anticipated a spiritual-political figure to save them from the oppression of their enemies, Christians believed the Christ saved his people mainly from the spiritual oppressors of sin and death. While the Jews believed the Messiah would scrupulously follow the Law, favoring and associating only with those who did likewise, the Christians' Christ seemed to enjoy a remarkable freedom in relation to several of Israel's most venerable institutions—for example, Sabbath observances, the Temple, and ritual purity—while associating with the "lowlifes" of society. In short, while the Jewish people were (and still are) awaiting the Messiah, Christians believed Jesus of Nazareth *was* the Messiah.

Christians held that after his death by crucifixion, Jesus rose from the dead (the Resurrection) and taught his followers for forty days before ascending into heaven. As a part of that teaching, Jesus promised that he would return again (the Second Coming ⟨*parousia*⟩) and that in the meantime his followers should spread the Christian faith to all the world.

The basic Christian belief was (and still is) that Jesus is the Son of God who became a human (the Incarnation) to atone for human sin (Redemption). The severed relationship between the Holy God and sinful humanity could only be restored through the sacrifice of one who was consummate righteousness. As the Word ⟨*logos*⟩ of God made flesh, Jesus was that righteousness, made that sacrifice, and offered that restoration. Through faith, Christians accept this work done on their behalf (Justification) and receive the power of God's spirit to overcome sin and to serve others (Sanctification).

As Christians spread this message throughout the Roman Empire, they encountered resistance and persecution from both Jewish and Roman authorities. The first Christian martyr, Stephen, was stoned to death by orthodox Jews for the blasphemy of claiming Jesus as God's Son (Acts 7). Among those who participated in the stoning was an eager Christian-hunter, Saul of Tarsus. This man subsequently underwent a dramatic conversion on the road to Damascus and became the Apostle Paul.

While many Jewish leaders objected to the Christian identification of Jesus with God, Roman authorities objected to the Christians' unwillingness to participate in emperor worship. Jews, too, had refused to participate in state religion and had often been persecuted. But Christians posed a unique threat to the Romans because, unlike the Jews, Christians proclaimed a supranational, supraracial, universal Lord—one very much in competition with Caesar. And Christians indefatigably sought converts to their universal Savior. Accordingly, they were persecuted on and off for three centuries.

Despite persecution, Christianity grew steadily in the centuries after Christ. There have been many explanations for that growth. The eighteenth-century historian Edward Gibbon* listed five causes: (1) Christianity's inheritance of the zeal of the Jews; (2) its connection to the philosophical doctrine of the immortal-

---

The Decline and Fall of the Roman Empire, Chapter XV.

ity of the soul; (3) its claim of miracles; (4) the virtue of the early Christians; and (5) the organization of the church. Recent historians have pointed to the moral exclusivity of Christians, who demanded deep commitment; the definite and absolute character of Christian belief in an age of uncertainty; and the social dimensions of Christianity, which made it attractive to women, the poor, and the oppressed.*

As Christianity grew, doctrinal disputes inevitably arose. What is true Christianity? The answers tended to reflect deep convictions about two essential issues: the nature of the person and work of Jesus Christ and the relationship between faith and reason. What was the relationship between Jesus and God? Did Jesus have two distinct natures: one divine and one human? Or were they merged into a single unique nature? Moreover, if there is only one God, how could God also be three (Father, Son, and Holy Spirit)? And how could reason resolve issues of faith?

The first issue, the nature of Christ, was resolved at the Council of Nicea, convened and presided over by the first Christian emperor, Constantine, in A.D. 325. The Council determined that the Son was exactly the same substance, "consubstantial" *(homoousios)*, and not just "of like substance" *(homoiousios)*, with God the Father. By the middle of the first millenium the "Nicene Creed" was confessed by virtually all Christendom as the orthodox answer to the nature-of-Christ question. (The Nicene Creed is still authoritative in Orthodox, Catholic, and Protestant churches.)

But while the Christological question was answered at Nicea, the question of the right relation between faith and reason continued to be argued throughout the medieval period. The early Christians had a simple faith in Jesus as Messiah (if they were Jewish Christians) and as Lord (if they were Gentile Christians) and believed Jesus had lived, taught, died, and risen for them and all others. But almost immediately that simple faith encountered sophisticated Hellenistic thought throughout the Roman Empire. How much should Christian faith concede to the competence of philosophic reason? What was the relation between sacred writings (i.e., the Bible) and secular writings (i.e., philosophy)? In Acts 17, reprinted here (pages 21–22), Paul used reason and quoted pagan poets to help him preach the gospel to Epicurean and Stoic philosophers in Athens. Yet later, in Colossians 2:8, he warned, "See to it that no one takes you captive through philosophy and empty deceit. . . ." Some early Church Fathers, such as Justin Martyr, Clement of Alexandria, and Origen, used philosophy to help interpret Christian faith. Other Church Fathers, such as Tertullian, argued that reason could be inimical to faith: "What has Jerusalem to do with Athens?," he asked.

Some in the early church even claimed to have special esoteric knowledge not available to the rabble either in sacred Scriptures or secular reason. They were known as "Gnostics," from the Greek word for knowledge *(gnosis)*. These Gnostics emphasized the Platonic belief in the soul as good and the body as evil and sought to free the soul from the body by extreme ascetic practices. Some of the Gnostics taught that Jesus was not *really* a physical person (since the body is evil) and that the Old Testament God, Yahweh, who had created bodies and matter, was really the devil. Manicheaism, which rivalled Christianity in the third and

---

*Of course, Christians have always claimed that none of these reasons is entirely adequate and that the most acceptable explanation for the rise of Christianity is a supernatural one.

fourth centuries, and for a time claimed Augustine, was based on Gnostic thought.*

As Christians sought wisdom in all these complex issues, they were sustained by a peculiar faith, inherited from Judaism and deepened by their founders. As Anne Fremantle put it,

> The Christian believes that not only does he search for wisdom, but wisdom also searches for him, and with more immediate success. God is not only that than which nothing greater can be imagined, but a person who, while declaring Himself to be wholly unimaginable, has yet revealed Himself and given Himself to man . . . Christian philosophy is an intellectual inquiry into the nature of being, which accepts as a premise the possible existence of a Power outside man that is both the object and the instigator of man's search; or, as Christ put it, that He is Himself "the Way, the Truth and the Life."**

* * *

For extrabiblical source material on Christianity, see C.K. Barrett, *The New Testament Background: Selected Documents* (New York: Harper Torchbooks, 1961) and Howard Clark Kee, *The New Testament in Context: Sources and Documents* (Englewood Cliffs, NJ: Prentice Hall, 1984). For discussions of the interaction between Christianity and its surrounding culture, see A.H. Armstrong and R.A. Markus, *Christian Faith and Greek Philosophy* (New York: Sheed and Ward, 1960); E.R. Dodds, *Pagan and Christian in an Age of Anxiety* (Cambridge: Cambridge University Press, 1965); Jaroslav Pelikan, *The Christian Tradition: A History of the Development of Doctrine,* 5 vols. (Chicago: University of Chicago Press, 1971–1989); and R.A. Markus, *Christianity in the Roman World* (London: Thames & Hudson, 1974). Relevant histories of Christianity include Kenneth Scott Latourette, *A History of Christianity* (New York: Harper & Row, 1953); Martin E. Marty, *A Short History of Christianity* (New York: Meridian, 1959); Henry Chadwick, *The Early Church* (Harmondsworth, England: Penguin, 1967); W.H.C. Frend, *The Rise of Christianity* (Philadelphia: Fortress Press, 1984); and Williston Walker et al., *A History of the Christian Church,* 4th ed. (New York: Scribner's, 1985). For a discussion of Christian beliefs in their historical context, see J.N.D. Kelly, *Early Christian Doctrines,* 5th ed. (London: Black, 1978). For basic introductions to traditional Christian beliefs, see John R.W. Stott, *Basic Christianity* (Downers Grove, IL: InterVarsity Press, 1971), and Hans Küng, *On Being a Christian,* translated by Edward Quinn (Garden City, NY: Doubleday, 1976).

---

*Similar contests between faith, reason, and extrarational experience would play out later in Islam when Muslims sought to reconcile their sacred writings (the *Qur'an*) with philosophy. Some thinkers, such as Avicenna (Ibn-Sina), argued for a special interpretation of the *Qur'an* available only to the philosophically enlightened; and other thinkers, such as Algazali, protested that Islam should avoid philosophy and that Mecca, too, should have nothing to do with Athens.

**Anne Fremantle, *The Age of Belief: The Medieval Philosophers* (New York: New American Library, 1954), pp. 15–16.

Jesus
ca. 6 B.C.–ca. A.D. *30*

Jesus was born in Bethlehem in Judea sometime around 6 B.C. (the currently accepted date of Jesus' birth corrects the error of a sixth-century monk who established the Western calendar). Virtually all data about the life of Jesus come from the first four books of the New Testament, called the "Gospels" (*gospel* means "good news"). The accuracy of the gospel accounts is a matter of debate, but most medieval philosophers believed that the gospel records were not only essentially trustworthy but also actually inspired. Therefore, to understand medieval thought it is especially necessary to understand something of the life of Jesus as presented in the Bible.

According to two of the Gospels (Matthew and Luke), Jesus was conceived by the Holy Spirit and born of the Virgin Mary—a young woman engaged to a carpenter by the name of Joseph. According to Matthew, Mary and Joseph took Jesus to Egypt while he was still a small child to avoid Jesus' death at the hands of King Herod of Judea. Following Herod's death, the family settled in the northern Palestinian town of Nazareth in the province of Galilee. Apart from one temple visit in Jerusalem when Jesus was twelve (recorded in Luke), nothing further is found in the New Testament about Jesus' life until he began his adult ministry.

When Jesus was about thirty years old, John the Baptist began preaching that the "kingdom of heaven" was near. John lived an ascetic life in the wilderness and called on Israel to repent from its evil ways, return to God in good faith, and be baptized in order to express and begin a new life of repentance. Jesus left Nazareth and came to be baptized by John in the Jordan River. As Jesus was coming out of the water, the Spirit of God descended upon him; and a voice from heaven said, "This is my Son, the Beloved, with whom I am well pleased." Following a period of intense personal struggle with the Devil, Jesus began his public ministry in Galilee. For the next one to three years Jesus healed the sick, cast out demons, and preached the kingdom of heaven. A number of people followed Jesus as he travelled, including twelve specially chosen by him to be his disciples.

Jesus' preaching focused on the reality of God and the importance of other people, summarized in the "two greatest commandments": to love God deeply and to love one's neighbor heartily. In loving God, Jesus advocated moving beyond mere formal or ritual observance and being open to a divinely given "rebirth" that would change the person completely. As Jesus told the Pharisee Nicodemus, this rebirth could be received by believing in Jesus. As for love of neighbor, in the Parable (or Story) of the Good Samaritan, Jesus urged an expansion of the concept of neighbor beyond race, nation, or religion to include anyone in need. Perhaps the most impressive collection of Jesus' teachings is found in the Sermon on the Mount in Matthew's Gospel.

After one to three years of teaching in Galilee, Jesus and his followers moved south to Jerusalem where he was soon arrested and put to death by crucifixion. The religious leaders in Jerusalem objected to Jesus' claims to a special relationship to God. With the help of one of Jesus' own disciples, Judas Iscariot, they arrested Jesus, charging him with blasphemy. Following conviction by a religious court, Jesus was handed over to the Roman governor, Pontius Pilate, who condemned him to death by crucifixion. Three days after his death, Christians believed, Jesus rose bodily from the grave and appeared first to Peter and to some of his women followers, then to his eleven remaining disciples, and finally to a large group of followers. After forty days of further teaching, Jesus ascended into heaven, from which he will one day come again to judge all human beings, determining their eternal destiny. This is a bare outline of essential Christian faith—the *Credo* (literally "I believe") or creed of the medieval Western and now worldwide church.

Our first reading, from the Gospel of John, identifies Jesus as the Word ⟨*logos*⟩ of God made flesh. This Greek philosophical term (⟨*logos*⟩ was a key concept in Heraclitus' thought and in Stoic writings) in a Gospel book presaged the interaction that was to follow between Greek philosophy and the Christian church. The other readings should provide a rudimentary introduction to the fundamental deeds and teachings of Jesus of Nazareth. They are all taken from Christendom's main book, a collection of writings called the New Testament. While many today might take exception to at least the supernatural elements in New Testament texts, every one of the medieval philosophers represented in this volume, with the exception of the Jewish and Islamic thinkers, believed the Gospels to be, as we say, the gospel truth.

*   *   *

There is no such thing as an objective account of the life of Jesus. Perhaps the best starting point for further reading, after the New Testament itself in a modern translation, is C.H. Dodd's short book, *The Founder of Christianity* (New York:

Macmillan, 1970), or from a more liberal position, Adolf Harnack's still useful and classic *What Is Christianity?* (New York: G.P. Putnam's Sons, 1901). Albert Schweitzer's *The Quest of the Historical Jesus: A Critical Study of Its Progress from Reimarus to Wrede,* translated by W. Montgomery (New York: Macmillan, 1910) is, after Harnack, the classic work on the historical Jesus, while Harvey K. McArthur, ed., *In Search of the Historical Jesus* (New York: Charles Scribner's Sons, 1969), continues the quest. More recent works representing a variety of Christian interpretations of Jesus' life and teachings include Oscar Cullmann, *The Christology of the New Testament,* translated by Shirley C. Guthrie and Charles A.M. Hall (Philadelphia: Westminster, 1963); Wolfhart Pannenberg, *Jesus, God and Man,* translated by Lewis L. Wilkins and Duane A. Priebe (Philadelphia: Westminster Press, 1968); A.M. Hunter, *The Work and Words of Jesus,* rev. ed. (London: SCM Press, 1973); Günther Bornkamm, *Jesus of Nazareth,* translated by I. McCluskey and F. McCluskey (New York: Harper & Row, 1975); Gerard S. Sloyan, *Jesus in Focus: A Life in Its Setting* (Mystic, CT: Twenty-Third, 1984); and Graham N. Stanton, *The Gospel and Jesus* (Oxford: Oxford University Press, 1989).

NEW TESTAMENT: GOSPELS (in part)

PROLOGUE TO THE GOSPEL OF JOHN (JOHN 1:1–18)

1 [1]In the beginning was the Word ⟨*logos*⟩ and the Word was with God, and the Word was God. [2]He was in the beginning with God. [3]All things came into being through him, and without him not one thing came into being. What has come into being [4]in him was life and the life was the light of all people. [5]The light shines in the darkness, and the darkness did not overcome it.

[6]There was a man sent from God, whose name was John. [7]He came as a witness to testify to the light, so that all might believe through him. [8]He himself was not the light, but he came to testify to the light. [9]The true light, which enlightens everyone, was coming into the world.

[10]He was in the world, and the world came into being through him yet the world did not know him. [11]He came to what was his own, and his own people did not accept him. [12]But to all who received him, who believed in his name, he gave power to become children of God, [13]who were born, not of blood or of the will of the flesh or of the will of man, but of God.

[14]And the Word became flesh and lived among us, and we have seen his glory, the glory as of a father's only son full of grace and truth. [15]John testified to him and cried out, "This was he of whom I said, 'He who comes after me ranks ahead of me because he was before me.'" [16]From his fullness we have all received, grace upon grace. [17]The law indeed was given through Moses, grace and truth came through Jesus Christ. [18]No one has ever seen God. It is God the only Son, who is close to the Father's heart, who has made him known.

* * *

THE BAPTISM OF JESUS (MATTHEW 3:13–17)

3 13Then Jesus came from Galilee to John at the Jordan, to be baptized by him. 14John would have prevented him, saying, "I need to be baptized by you, and do you come to me?" 15But Jesus answered him, "Let it be so now for it is proper for us in this way to fulfill all righteousness." Then he consented. 16And when Jesus had been baptized, just as he came up from the water, suddenly the heavens were opened to him and he saw the Spirit of God descending like a dove and alighting on him. 17And a voice from heaven said, "This is my Son, the Beloved, with whom I am well pleased."

* * *

St. Matthew, from the Lindisfarne Gospels, before A.D. 698. *(The British Library/Superstock)*

THE TEMPTATION OF JESUS (MATTHEW 4:1–11)

4 [1]Then Jesus was led up by the Spirit into the wilderness to be tempted by the devil. [2]He fasted forty days and forty nights, and afterwards he was famished. [3]The tempter came and said to him, "If you are the Son of God, command these stones to become loaves of bread." [4]But he answered, "It is written

> 'One does not live by bread alone,
> but by every word that comes from the mouth of God.'"

[5]Then the devil took him to the holy city and placed him on the pinnacle of the temple, [6]saying to him, "If you are the Son of God, throw yourself down; for it is written,

> 'He will command his angels concerning you,'
> and 'On their hands they will bear you up
> so that you will not dash your foot against a stone.'"

[7]Jesus said to him, "Again it is written,

> 'Do not put the Lord your God to the test.'"

[8]Again, the devil took him to a very high mountain and showed him all the kingdoms of the world and their splendor; [9]and he said to him, "All these I will give you, if you will fall down and worship me." [10]Jesus said to him "Away with you, Satan! for it is written

> 'Worship the Lord your God,
> and serve only him.'"

[11]Then the devil left him, and suddenly angels came and waited on him.

* * *

THE SERMON ON THE MOUNT (MATTHEW 5–7)

5 [1]When Jesus saw the crowds, he went up the mountain; and after he sat down, his disciples came to him. [2]Then he began to speak, and taught them, saying:

[3]"Blessed are the poor in spirit, for theirs is the kingdom of heaven.

[4]"Blessed are those who mourn, for they will be comforted.

[5]"Blessed are the meek, for they will inherit the earth.

[6]"Blessed are those who hunger and thirst for righteousness, for they will be filled.

[7]"Blessed are the merciful, for they will receive mercy.

[8]"Blessed are the pure in heart, for they will see God.

[9]"Blessed are the peacemakers, for they will be called children of God.

[10]"Blessed are those who are persecuted for righteousness' sake, for theirs is the kingdom of heaven.

[11]"Blessed are you when people revile you and persecute you and utter all kinds of evil against you falsely on my account. [12]Rejoice and be glad, for your reward is great in heaven, for in the same way they persecuted the prophets who were before you.

¹³"You are the salt of the earth, but if salt has lost its taste, how can its saltiness be restored? It is no longer good for anything, but is thrown out and trampled under foot.

¹⁴"You are the light of the world. A city built on a hill cannot be hid. ¹⁵No one after lighting a lamp puts it under the bushel basket, but on the lampstand, and it gives light to all in the house. ¹⁶In the same way, let your light shine before others, so that they may see your good works and give glory to your Father in heaven.

¹⁷"Do not think that I have come to abolish the law or the prophets I have come not to abolish but to fulfill. ¹⁸For truly I tell you, until heaven and earth pass away, not one letter, not one stroke of a letter, will pass from the law until all is accomplished. ¹⁹Therefore, whoever breaks one of the least of these commandments, and teaches others to do the same, will be called least in the kingdom of heaven, but whoever does them and teaches them will be called great in the kingdom of heaven. ²⁰For I tell you, unless your righteousness exceeds that of the scribes and Pharisees, you will never enter the kingdom of heaven.

²¹"You have heard that it was said to those of ancient times, 'You shall not murder'; and 'whoever murders shall be liable to judgment.' ²²But I say to you that if you are angry with a brother or sister you will be liable to judgment, and if you insult a brother or sister, you will be liable to the council, and if you say, 'You fool,' you will be liable to the hell of fire. ²³So when you are offering your gift at the altar, if you remember that your brother or sister has something against you ²⁴leave your gift there before the altar and go, first be reconciled to your brother or sister, and then come and offer your gift. ²⁵Come to terms quickly with your accuser while you are on the way to court with him, or your accuser may hand you over to the judge, and the judge to the guard, and you will be thrown into prison. ²⁶Truly I tell you, you will never get out until you have paid the last penny.

²⁷"You have heard that it was said 'You shall not commit adultery.' ²⁸But I say to you that everyone who looks at a woman with lust has already committed adultery with her in his heart. ²⁹If your right eye causes you to sin tear it out and throw it away; it is better for you to lose one of your members than for your whole body to be thrown into hell. ³⁰And if your right hand causes you to sin, cut it off and throw it away, it is better for you to lose one of your members than for your whole body to go into hell.

³¹"It was also said, 'Whoever divorces his wife, let him give her a certificate of divorce.' ³²But I say to you that anyone who divorces his wife, except on the ground of unchastity, causes her to commit adultery; and whoever marries a divorced woman commits adultery.

³³"Again, you have heard that it was said to those of ancient times, 'You shall not swear falsely, but carry out the vows you have made to the Lord.' ³⁴But I say to you, Do not swear at all, either by heaven, for it is the throne of God, ³⁵Or by the earth, for it is his footstool, or by Jerusalem, for it is the city of the great King. ³⁶And do not swear by your head, for you cannot make one hair white or black. ³⁷Let your word be 'Yes, Yes' or 'No, No' anything more than this comes from the evil one.

³⁸"You have heard that it was said 'An eye for an eye and a tooth for a tooth.' ³⁹But I say to you, Do not resist an evildoer. But if anyone strikes you on the right cheek, turn the other also; ⁴⁰and if anyone wants to sue you and take your coat, give your cloak as well; ⁴¹and if anyone forces you to go one mile, go also the second mile. ⁴²Give to everyone who begs from you, and do not refuse anyone who wants to borrow from you.

⁴³"You have heard that it was said, 'You shall love your neighbor and hate your enemy.' ⁴⁴But I say to you, Love your enemies and pray for those who persecute you,

⁴⁵so that you may be children of your Father in heaven, for he makes his sun rise on the evil and on the good, and sends rain on the righteous and on the unrighteous. ⁴⁶For if you love those who love you what reward do you have? Do not even the tax collectors do the same? ⁴⁷And if you greet only your brothers and sisters, what more are you doing than others? Do not even the Gentiles do the same? ⁴⁸Be perfect, therefore, as your heavenly Father is perfect.

6 ¹"Beware of practicing your piety before others in order to be seen by them, for then you have no reward from your Father in heaven.

²"So whenever you give alms, do not sound a trumpet before you, as the hypocrites do in the synagogues and in the streets, so that they may be praised by others. Truly I tell you, they have received their reward. ³But when you give alms, do not let your left hand know what your right hand is doing, ⁴so that your alms may be done in secret, and your Father who sees in secret will reward you.

⁵"And whenever you pray, do not be like the hypocrites; for they love to stand and pray in the synagogues and at the street corners, so that they may be seen by others. Truly I tell you, they have received their reward. ⁶But whenever you pray, go into your room and shut the door and pray to your Father who is in secret; and your Father who sees in secret will reward you.

⁷"When you are praying, do not heap up empty phrases as the Gentiles do; for they think that they will be heard because of their many words. ⁸Do not be like them, for your Father knows what you need before you ask him.

⁹"Pray then in this way:

Our Father in heaven,
   hallowed be your name.
¹⁰Your kingdom come.
Your will be done,
   on earth as it is in heaven.
¹¹Give us this day our daily bread.
¹²And forgive us our debts,
   as we also have forgiven our debtors.
¹³And do not bring us to the time of trial,
   but rescue us from the evil one.

¹⁴For if you forgive others their trespasses, your heavenly Father will also forgive you; ¹⁵but if you do not forgive others, neither will your Father forgive your trespasses.

¹⁶"And whenever you fast, do not look dismal, like the hypocrites, for they disfigure their faces so as to show others that they are fasting. Truly I tell you, they have received their reward. ¹⁷But when you fast, put oil on your head and wash your face, ¹⁸so that your fasting may be seen not by others but by your Father who is in secret and your Father who sees in secret will reward you.

¹⁹"Do not store up for yourselves treasures on earth where moth and rust consume and where thieves break in and steal; ²⁰but store up for yourselves treasures in heaven, where neither moth nor rust consumes and where thieves do not break in and steal. ²¹For where your treasure is there your heart will be also.

²²"The eye is the lamp of the body. So, if your eye is healthy, your whole body will be full of light; ²³but if your eye is unhealthy, your whole body will be full of darkness. If then the light in you is darkness, how great is the darkness!

²⁴"No one can serve two masters for a slave will either hate the one and love the other, or be devoted to the one and despise the other. You cannot serve God and wealth.

[25]"Therefore I tell you, do not worry about your life, what you will eat or what you will drink, nor about your body, what you will wear. Is not life more than food, and the body more than clothing? [26]Look at the birds of the air; they neither sow nor reap nor gather into barns, and yet your heavenly Father feeds them. Are you not of more value than they? [27]And can any of you by worrying add a single hour to your span of life? [28]And why do you worry about clothing? Consider the lilies of the field, how they grow they neither toil nor spin, [29]yet I tell you, even Solomon in all his glory was not clothed like one of these. [30]But if God so clothes the grass of the field which is alive today and tomorrow is thrown into the oven, will he not much more clothe you—you of little faith? [31]Therefore do not worry, saying, 'What will we eat?' or 'What will we drink?' or 'What will we wear?' [32]For it is the Gentiles who strive for all these things; and indeed your heavenly Father knows that you need all these things. [33]But strive first for the kingdom of God and his righteousness, and all these things will be given to you as well.

[34]"So do not worry about tomorrow, for tomorrow will bring worries of its own. Today's trouble is enough for today.

7 [1]"Do not judge, so that you may not be judged. [2]For with the judgment you make you will be judged, and the measure you give will be the measure you get. [3]Why do you see the speck in your neighbor's eye, but do not notice the log in your own eye? [4]Or how can you say to your neighbor, 'Let me take the speck out of your eye,' while the log is in your own eye? [5]You hypocrite, first take the log out of your own eye, and then you will see clearly to take the speck out of your neighbor's eye.

[6]"Do not give what is holy to dogs and do not throw your pearls before swine, or they will trample them under foot and turn and maul you.

[7]"Ask, and it will be given you; search, and you will find; knock, and the door will be opened for you. [8]For everyone who asks receives, and everyone who searches finds, and for everyone who knocks, the door will be opened. [9]Is there anyone among you who, if your child asks for bread, will give a stone? [10]Or if the child asks for a fish, will give a snake? [11]If you then who are evil, know how to give good gifts to your children, how much more will your Father in heaven give good things to those who ask him!

[12]"In everything do to others as you would have them do to you; for this is the law and the prophets.

[13]"Enter through the narrow gate; for the gate is wide and the road is easy that leads to destruction, and there are many who take it. [14]For the gate is narrow and the road is hard that leads to life, and there are few who find it.

[15]"Beware of false prophets, who come to you in sheep's clothing but inwardly are ravenous wolves. [16]You will know them by their fruits. Are grapes gathered from thorns, or figs from thistles? [17]In the same way, every good tree bears good fruit, but the bad tree bears bad fruit. [18]A good tree cannot bear bad fruit, nor can a bad tree bear good fruit. [19]Every tree that does not bear good fruit is cut down and thrown into the fire. [20]Thus you will know them by their fruits.

[21]"Not everyone who says to me 'Lord, Lord,' will enter the kingdom of heaven, but only the one who does the will of my Father in heaven. [22]On that day many will say to me, 'Lord, Lord did we not prophesy in your name, and cast out demons in your name, and do many deeds of power in your name?' [23]Then I will declare to them, 'I never knew you; go away from me, you evildoers.'

[24]"Everyone then who hears these words of mine and acts on them will be like a wise man who built his house on rock. [25]The rain fell, the floods came, and the winds

blew and beat on that house, but it did not fall, because it had been founded on rock. 26And everyone who hears these words of mine and does not act on them will be like a foolish man who built his house on sand. 27The rain fell, and the floods came and the winds blew and beat against that house, and it fell—and great was its fall!"

28Now when Jesus had finished saying these things, the crowds were astounded at his teaching 29for he taught them as one having authority, and not as their scribes.

* * *

THE PARABLE OF THE GOOD SAMARITAN
(LUKE 10:25–37)

10 25Just then a lawyer stood up to test Jesus. "Teacher," he said, "what must I do to inherit eternal life?" 26He said to him, "What is written in the law? What do you read there?" 27He answered, "You shall love the Lord your God with all your heart, and with all your soul, and with all your strength, and with all your mind; and your neighbor as yourself." 28And he said to him, "You have given the right answer; do this, and you will live."

29But wanting to justify himself, he asked Jesus, "And who is my neighbor?" 30Jesus replied, "A man was going down from Jerusalem to Jericho, and fell into the hands of robbers, who stripped him, beat him, and went away, leaving him half dead. 31Now by chance a priest was going down that road, and when he saw him, he passed by on the other side. 32So likewise a Levite, when he came to the place and saw him, passed by on the other side. 33But a Samaritan while traveling came near him; and when he saw him, he was moved with pity. 34He went to him and bandaged his wounds, having poured oil and wine on them. Then he put him on his own animal, brought him to an inn, and took care of him. 35The next day he took out two denarii, gave them to the innkeeper and said, 'Take care of him, and when I come back, I will repay you whatever more you spend.' 36Which of these three, do you think, was a neighbor to the man who fell into the hands of the robbers?" 37He said, "The one who showed him mercy." Jesus said to him "Go and do likewise."

* * *

NICODEMUS VISITS JESUS (JOHN 3:1–21)

3 1Now there was a Pharisee named Nicodemus, a leader of the Jews. 2He came to Jesus by night and said to him, "Rabbi, we know that you are a teacher who has come from God, for no one can do these signs that you do apart from the presence of God." 3Jesus answered him, "Very truly, I tell you, no one can see the kingdom of God without being born from above." 4Nicodemus said to him, "How can anyone be born after having grown old? Can one enter a second time into the mother's womb and be born?" 5Jesus answered, "Very truly, I tell you, no one can enter the kingdom of God without being born of water and Spirit. 6What is born of the flesh is flesh, and what is born of the Spirit is spirit. 7Do not be astonished that I said to you, 'You must be born from above.' 8The wind blows where it chooses, and you hear the sound of it, but you do not know where it comes from or where it goes. So it is with everyone who is born of the Spirit." [9]Nicodemus said to him, "How can these things be?" [10]Jesus answered him, "Are you a teacher of Israel, and yet you do not understand these things?

[11]"Very truly, I tell you, we speak of what we know and testify to what we have seen; yet you do not receive our testimony. [12]If I have told you about earthly things and you do not believe, how can you believe if I tell you about heavenly things? [13]No one has ascended into heaven except the one who descended from heaven, the Son of Man. [14]And just as Moses lifted up the serpent in the wilderness so must the Son of Man be lifted up [15]that whoever believes in him may have eternal life.

[16]"For God so loved the world that he gave his only Son, so that everyone who believes in him may not perish but may have eternal life.

[17]"Indeed, God did not send the Son into the world to condemn the world, but in order that the world might be saved through him. [18]Those who believe in him are not condemned, but those who do not believe are condemned already, because they have not believed in the name of the only Son of God. [19]And this is the judgment, that the light has come into the world, and people loved darkness rather than light because their deeds were evil. [20]For all who do evil hate the light and do not come to the light, so that their deeds may not be exposed. [21]But those who do what is true come to the light, so that it may be clearly seen that their deeds have been done in God."

*   *   *

THE CRUCIFIXION AND RESURRECTION OF JESUS (MATTHEW 27:27–28:20)

27 [27]Then the soldiers of the governor took Jesus into the governor's headquarters, and they gathered the whole cohort around him. [28]They stripped him and put a scarlet robe on him, [29]and after twisting some thorns into a crown, they put it on his head. They put a reed in his right hand and knelt before him and mocked him, saying, "Hail, King of the Jews!" [30]They spat on him, and took the reed and struck him on the head. [31]After mocking him, they stripped him of the robe and put his own clothes on him. Then they led him away to crucify him.

[32]As they went out, they came upon a man from Cyrene named Simon; they compelled this man to carry his cross. [33]And when they came to a place called Golgotha (which means Place of a Skull), [34]they offered him wine to drink, mixed with gall, but when he tasted it, he would not drink it. [35]And when they had crucified him, they divided his clothes among themselves by casting lots; [36]then they sat down there and kept watch over him. [37]Over his head they put the charge against him, which read, "This is Jesus, the King of the Jews."

[38]Then two bandits were crucified with him, one on his right and one on his left. [39]Those who passed by derided him, shaking their heads [40]and saying, "You who would destroy the temple and build it in three days, save yourself! If you are the Son of God, come down from the cross." [41]In the same way the chief priests also, along with the scribes and elders, were mocking him, saying, [42]"He saved others; he cannot save himself. He is the King of Israel, let him come down from the cross now, and we will believe in him. [43]He trusts in God; let God deliver him now, if he wants to; for he said, 'I

am God's Son.'" [44]The bandits who were crucified with him also taunted him in the same way.

[45]From noon on, darkness came over the whole land until three in the afternoon. [46]And about three o'clock Jesus cried with a loud voice, "Eli, Eli, lema sabachthani?" that is, "My God, my God, why have you forsaken me?" [47]When some of the by-standers heard it, they said, "This man is calling for Elijah." [48]At once one of them ran and got a sponge, filled it with sour wine, put it on a stick, and gave it to him to drink. [49]But the others said "Wait, let us see whether Elijah will come to save him." [50]Then Jesus cried again with a loud voice and breathed his last. [51]At that moment the curtain of the temple was torn in two, from top to bottom. The earth shook, and the rocks were split. [52]The tombs also were opened, and many bodies of the saints who had fallen asleep were raised. [53]After his resurrection they came out of the tombs and entered the holy city and appeared to many. [54]Now when the centurion and those with him, who were keeping watch over Jesus saw the earthquake and what took place, they were terrified and said, "Truly this man was God's Son!"

[55]Many women were also there, looking on from a distance, they had followed Jesus from Galilee and had provided for him. [56]Among them were Mary Magdalene, and Mary the mother of James and Joseph, and the mother of the sons of Zebedee.

[57]When it was evening, there came a rich man from Arimathea, named Joseph, who was also a disciple of Jesus. [58]He went to Pilate and asked for the body of Jesus, then Pilate ordered it to be given to him. [59]So Joseph took the body and wrapped it in a clean linen cloth [60]and laid it in his own new tomb, which he had hewn in the rock. He then rolled a great stone to the door of the tomb and went away. [61]Mary Magdalene and the other Mary were there, sitting opposite the tomb.

[62]The next day, that is after the day of Preparation, the chief priests and the Pharisees gathered before Pilate [63]and said, "Sir, we remember what that impostor said while he was still alive, 'After three days I will rise again.' [64]Therefore command the tomb to be made secure until the third day; otherwise his disciples may go and steal him away, and tell the people, 'He has been raised from the dead,' and the last deception would be worse than the first." [65]Pilate said to them, "You have a guard of soldiers go, make it as secure as you can." [66]So they went with the guard and made the tomb secure by sealing the stone.

28 [1]After the sabbath, as the first day of the week was dawning Mary Magdalene and the other Mary went to see the tomb. [2]And suddenly there was a great earthquake; for an angel of the Lord, descending from heaven, came and rolled back the stone and sat on it. [3]His appearance was like lightning, and his clothing white as snow. [4]For fear of him the guards shook and became like dead men. [5]But the angel said to the women "Do not be afraid; I know that you are looking for Jesus who was crucified. [6]He is not here; for he has been raised, as he said. Come, see the place where he lay. [7]Then go quickly and tell his disciples, 'He has been raised from the dead, and indeed he is going ahead of you to Galilee; there you will see him.' This is my message for you." [8]So they left the tomb quickly with fear and great joy, and ran to tell his disciples. [9]Suddenly Jesus met them and said "Greetings!" And they came to him took hold of his feet, and worshiped him. [10]Then Jesus said to them, "Do not be afraid; go and tell my brothers to go to Galilee; there they will see me."

[11]While they were going, some of the guard went into the city and told the chief priests everything that had happened. [12]After the priests had assembled with the elders, they devised a plan to give a large sum of money to the soldiers [13]telling them, "You

must say, 'His disciples came by night and stole him away while we were asleep.' [14]If this comes to the governor's ears, we will satisfy him and keep you out of trouble." [15]So they took the money and did as they were directed. And this story is still told among the Jews to this day.

[16]Now the eleven disciples went to Galilee, to the mountain to which Jesus had directed them. [17]When they saw him, they worshiped him but some doubted. [18]And Jesus came and said to them, "All authority in heaven and on earth has been given to me. [19]Go therefore and make disciples of all nations, baptizing them in the name of the Father and of the Son and of the Holy Spirit, [20]and teaching them to obey everything that I have commmanded you. And remember, I am with you always, to the end of the age."

Paul and the Early Church
ca. A.D. 10–ca. 67

The Apostle Paul, originally named Saul, was raised in Tarsus, a small city in southeastern Asia Minor (near the south coast of present-day Turkey). He was both a Jew and a Roman citizen—a status that afforded him special privileges. He studied Hebrew Law under Rabbi Gamaliel and gave evidence in his writings of a respectable knowledge of Hellenistic thought. As a young man, Saul was a zealous observant Jew and a persecutor of Christians. According to the New Testament Book of Acts, he was present at the death of Stephen, the first Christian martyr. While on his way to Damascus to attack a group of Christians, Saul underwent a dramatic conversion. He went on to become the outstanding missionary and theologian of the early Church.

One of the questions facing the early Church was whether or not Christianity should remain a Jewish sect. Should converts to Christianity also undertake the ritual steps needed to become Jewish? Sometime around A.D. 48 a council met in Jerusalem to discuss the issue. This council determined that gentile converts did not have to undergo circumcision, but they should observe the dietary and sexual prescriptions of the Law. In so doing the council effectively endorsed Paul's work among the gentiles.

By the time of the Jerusalem council, Paul had already completed one missionary journey. Over the next ten years he travelled extensively throughout the Mediterranean world, preaching in Jewish synagogues and planting Christian communities. The Book of Acts chronicles many of these journeys. Despite his success in missionary work, Paul was not a very good public speaker. He admitted his lack of rhetorical skills and Acts records that on one occasion Paul talked so long into the night that an exhausted young man fell asleep and plunged three stories from his perch in the gallery, almost killing himself (Acts 20:7–12). But what Paul lacked in oratorical skills, he more than made up for in his writings. He dictated powerful letters, many of which are still extant and form almost a third of the New Testament. Selections from three of these letters are reprinted here along with the account from Acts of the foundation of the early Church, Paul's recounting of his conversion, his exchange with the philosophers in Athens, and the influential end-times description of the new heaven and new earth from the Revelation to St. John.

Sometime around A.D. 58, Paul was arrested and imprisoned in Jerusalem. Using the privilege of Roman citizenship, Paul requested that his case be tried by the highest Roman authority. After a long and eventful journey, Paul arrived in Rome about A.D. 60 and spent the next two years under house arrest. The outcome of his trial and the date of his death are not known, but according to tradition at some later point he was found guilty and beheaded. (Execution by beheading rather than crucifixion was another privilege of Roman citizenship.)

Despite his own Jewish ancestry, Paul taught a universal Christianity that went well beyond ethnic Judaism. The Jesus Paul preached was the God-Man, the Lord Christ whose death was an atonement for the sins of *all* humanity. Paul argued that human good works done in obedience to even the best and highest Law, the Law of Israel, were worthless in acquiring righteousness before God. While the Law could indeed point out the inadequacy of one's "flesh" (or human power) in the presence of God, the Law could not transform human nature into the consummate righteousness required for association with the holy God. Only through faith in Jesus as the Christ, a faith that was itself a gift of God, could one be restored to a right relationship with God and given the gift of God's Spirit. Such a restored relationship would be characterized by a humble acceptance of God's gift and by an answering love for others.

Besides his teachings on justification and sanctification, the passages reprinted here include such significant Pauline doctrines as the universal knowledge of God's nature and power (similar to the Stoic concept of Natural Law), the incontinent nature of the unconverted will, the divine ordination of governmental authority, the acknowledgment of the seeming "foolishness" of the Gospel to human reason, and the bodily resurrection of human beings before a judgment at the end of history. All of these tenets were accepted and developed by the Christians of the Middle Ages.

*   *   *

The classic work by Adolf Deissmann, *Paul: A Study in Social and Religious History,* 2nd ed., translated by W.E. Wilson (Garden City, NY: Doubleday, 1927), is a good beginning in the study of Paul. Günther Bornkamm, *Paul,* translated by D.M.G. Stalker (New York: Harper & Row, 1971); Michael Grant, *Saint Paul* (New York: Charles Scribner's Sons, 1976); John Ziesler, *Pauline Christianity* (Oxford: Oxford University Press, 1983); Joseph A. Fitzmyer, *Paul and His Theology: A Brief Sketch* (Englewood Cliffs, NJ: Prentice Hall, 1989); and E.P. Sanders, *Paul* (Oxford: Oxford University Press, 1991), are also helpful. E.P.

Sanders, *Paul and Palestinian Judaism* (London: SCM Press, 1977), and W.D. Davies, *Paul and Rabbinic Judaism: Some Rabbinic Elements in Pauline Theology,* 4th ed. (Philadelphia: Fortress Press, 1980) stress Paul's roots in Jewish thought, while Abraham J. Malherbe's books, *Paul and the Theologians: The Philosophic Tradition of Pastoral Care* (Philadelphia: Fortress Press, 1987), and *Paul and the Popular Philosophers* (Philadelphia: Fortress Press, 1989), focus on the connections between Paul and Hellenistic philosophy. For discussions of Paul's social environment, see Wayne Meeks, *The First Urban Christians: The Social World of the Apostle Paul* (New Haven, CT: Yale University Press, 1983). For a general study on the relationship between Jesus and Paul, see F.F. Bruce, *Paul & Jesus* (Grand Rapids, MI: Baker Book House, 1974). For a study specifically comparing their ethics, see Roger Mohrlang, *Matthew and Paul: A Comparison of Ethical Perspectives* (Cambridge: Cambridge University Press, 1984).

NEW TESTAMENT: ACTS, PAULINE LETTERS, AND REVELATION
(in part)

THE BIRTH OF THE CHRISTIAN CHURCH
(ACTS 2:1–21, 37–47)

2 [1]When the day of Pentecost had come, they were all together in one place. [2]And suddenly from heaven there came a sound like the rush of a violent wind, and it filled the entire house where they were sitting. [3]Divided tongues, as of fire, appeared among them, and a tongue rested on each of them. [4]All of them were filled with the Holy Spirit and began to speak in other languages, as the Spirit gave them ability.

[5]Now there were devout Jews from every nation under heaven living in Jerusalem. [6]And at this sound the crowd gathered and was bewildered, because each one heard them speaking in the native language of each. [7]Amazed and astonished, they asked, "Are not all these who are speaking Galileans? [8]And how is it that we hear, each of us, in our own native language? [9]Parthians, Medes, Elamites, and residents of Mesopotamia, Judea and Cappadocia, Pontus and Asia [10]Phrygia and Pamphylia, Egypt and the parts of Libya belonging to Cyrene, and visitors from Rome, both Jews and proselytes, [11]Cretans and Arabs—in our own languages we hear them speaking about God's deeds of power." [12]All were amazed and perplexed, saying to one another, "What does this mean?" [13]But others sneered and said, "They are filled with new wine."

[14]But Peter, standing with the eleven, raised his voice and addressed them, "Men of Judea and all who live in Jerusalem, let this be known to you and listen to what I say. [15]Indeed these are not drunk, as you suppose for it is only nine o'clock in the morning. [16]No, this is what was spoken through the prophet Joel:

17'In the last days it will be, God declares,
that I will pour out my Spirit upon all flesh,
and your sons and your daughters shall prophesy,
and your young men shall see visions,
and your old men shall dream dreams.
18Even upon my slaves, both men and women,
in those days I will pour out my Spirit;
and they shall prophesy.
19And I will show portents in the heaven above
and signs on the earth below,
blood, and fire, and smoky mist.
20The sun shall be turned to darkness
and the moon to blood,
before the coming of the Lord's great and glorious day.
21Then everyone who calls on the name of the Lord shall be
saved.'

*   *   *

37Now when they heard this, they were cut to the heart and said to Peter and to the other apostles, "Brothers, what should we do?" 38Peter said to them, "Repent, and be baptized every one of you in the name of Jesus Christ so that your sins may be forgiven and you will receive the gift of the holy Spirit. 39For the promise is for you, for your children, and for all who are far away, everyone whom the Lord our God calls to him." 40And he testified with many other arguments and exhorted them, saying, "Save yourselves from this corrupt generation." 41So those who welcomed his message were baptized, and that day about three thousand persons were added. 42They devoted themselves to the apostles' teaching and fellowship, to the breaking of bread and the prayers.

43Awe came upon everyone, because many wonders and signs were being done by the apostles. 44All who believed were together and had all things in common, 45they would sell their possessions and goods and distribute the proceeds to all, as any had need. 46Day by day, as they spent much time together in the temple, they broke bread at home and ate their food with glad and generous hearts 47praising God and having the goodwill of all the people. And day by day the Lord added to their number those who were being saved.

THE CONVERSION OF SAUL (ACTS 9:1–22)

9 1Meanwhile Saul, still breathing threats and murder against the disciples of the Lord, went to the high priest 2and asked him for letters to the synagogues at Damascus, so that if he found any who belonged to the Way men or women, he might bring them bound to Jerusalem. 3Now as he was going along and approaching Damascus, suddenly a light from heaven flashed around him. 4He fell to the ground and heard a voice saying to him, "Saul, Saul, why do you persecute me?" 5He asked, "Who are you, Lord?" The reply came, "I am Jesus, whom you are persecuting. 6But get up and enter the city, and you will be told what you are to do." 7The men who were traveling with him stood speechless because they heard the voice but saw no one. 8Saul got up from the ground, and though his eyes were open, he could see nothing; so they led him by the hand and brought him into Damascus. 9For three days he was without sight, and neither ate nor drank.

[10]Now there was a disciple in Damascus named Ananias. The Lord said to him in a vision, "Ananias." He answered, "Here I am, Lord." [11]The Lord said to him, "Get up and go to the street called Straight, and at the house of Judas look for a man of Tarsus named Saul. At this moment he is praying, [12]and he has seen in a vision a man named Ananias come in and lay his hands on him so that he might regain his sight." [13]But Ananias answered, "Lord, I have heard from many about this man, how much evil he has done to your saints in Jerusalem; [14]and here he has authority from the chief priests to bind all who invoke your name." [15]But the Lord said to him, "Go, for he is an instrument whom I have chosen to bring my name before Gentiles and kings and before the people of Israel; [16]I myself will show him how much he must suffer for the sake of my name." [17]So Ananias went and entered the house. He laid his hands on Saul and said, "Brother Saul, the Lord Jesus, who appeared to you on your way here, has sent me so that you may regain your sight and be filled with the Holy Spirit." [18]And immediately something like scales fell from his eyes, and his sight was restored. Then he got up and was baptized [19]and after taking some food, he regained his strength.

For several days he was with the disciples in Damascus, [20]and immediately he began to proclaim Jesus in the synagogues, saying, "He is the Son of God." [21]All who heard him were amazed and said, "Is not this the man who made havoc in Jerusalem among those who invoked this name? And has he not come here for the purpose of bringing them bound before the chief priests?" [22]Saul became increasingly more powerful and confounded the Jews who lived in Damascus by proving that Jesus was the Messiah.

*   *   *

PAUL WITH THE PHILOSOPHERS IN ATHENS (ACTS 17:16–34)

17 [16]While Paul was waiting for them in Athens, he was deeply distressed to see that the city was full of idols. [17]So he argued in the synagogue with the Jews and the devout persons, and also in the marketplace every day with those who happened to be there. [18]Also some Epicurean and Stoic philosophers debated with him. Some said, "What does this babbler want to say?" Others said, "He seems to be a proclaimer of foreign divinities." (This was because he was telling the good news about Jesus and the resurrection.) [19]So they took him and brought him to the Areopagus and asked him, "May we know what this new teaching is that you are presenting? [20]It sounds rather strange to us, so we would like to know what it means." [21]Now all the Athenians and the foreigners living there would spend their time in nothing but telling or hearing something new.

[22]Then Paul stood in front of the Areopagus and said, "Athenians, I see how extremely religious you are in every way. [23]For as I went through the city and looked carefully at the objects of your worship, I found among them an altar with the inscription, 'To an unknown god.' What therefore you worship as unknown, this I proclaim to you. [24]The God who made the world and everything in it, he who is Lord of heaven and earth, does not live in shrines made by human hands, [25]nor is he served by human hands, as though he needed anything, since he himself gives to all mortals life and breath and all things. [26]From one ancestor he made all nations to inhabit the whole

earth, and he allotted the times of their existence and the boundaries of the places where they would live, 27so that they would search for Gods and perhaps grope for him and find him—though indeed he is not far from each one of us. 28For 'In him we live and move and have our being,' as even some of your own poets have said,

'For we too are his offspring.'

29Since we are God's offspring, we ought not to think that the deity is like gold, or silver, or stone, an image formed by the art and imagination of mortals. 30While God has overlooked the times of human ignorance, now he commands all people everywhere to repent, 31because he has fixed a day on which he will have the world judged in righteousness by a man whom he has appointed, and of this he has given assurance to all by raising him from the dead."

32When they heard of the resurrection of the dead, some scoffed; but others said, "We will hear you again about this." 33At that point Paul left them. 34But some of them joined him and became believers, including Dionysius the Areopagite and a woman named Damaris, and others with them.

*   *   *

PAUL'S NATURAL THEOLOGY (ROMANS 1:16–32)

1 16For I am not ashamed of the gospel, it is the power of God for salvation to everyone who has faith, to the Jew first and also to the Greek. 17For in it the righteousness of God is revealed through faith for faith; as it is written, "The one who is righteous will live by faith."

18For the wrath of God is revealed from heaven against all ungodliness and wickedness of those who by their wickedness suppress the truth. 19For what can be known about God is plain to them, because God has shown it to them. 20Ever since the creation of the world his eternal power and divine nature, invisible though they are, have been understood and seen through the things he has made. So they are without excuse, 21for though they knew God, they did not honor him as God or give thanks to him, but they became futile in their thinking, and their senseless minds were darkened. 22Claiming to be wise, they became fools, 23and they exchanged the glory of the immortal God for images resembling a mortal human being or birds or four-footed animals or reptiles.

24Therefore God gave them up in the lusts of their hearts to impurity, to the degrading of their bodies among themselves 25because they exchanged the truth about God for a lie and worshiped and served the creature rather than the Creator, who is blessed forever! Amen.

26For this reason God gave them up to degrading passions. Their women exchanged natural intercourse for unnatural 27and in the same way also the men, giving up natural intercourse with women, were consumed with passion for one another. Men committed shameless acts with men and received in their own persons the due penalty for their error.

28And since they did not see fit to acknowledge God, God gave them up to a debased mind and to things that should not be done. 29They were filled with every kind of wickedness, evil covetousness, malice. Full of envy, murder, strife, deceit, craftiness, they are gossips, [30]slanderers, God-haters, insolent, haughty, boastful, inventors of evil, rebellious toward parents, [31]foolish, faithless, heartless, ruthless. [32]They know God's decree that those who practice such things deserve to die—yet they not only do them but even applaud others who practice them.

* * *

RIGHTEOUSNESS THROUGH FAITH (ROMANS 3:21–31)

3 [21]But now, apart from law, the righteousness of God has been disclosed, and is attested by the law and the prophets [22]the righteousness of God through faith in Jesus Christ for all who believe. For there is no distinction, [23]since all have sinned and fall short of the glory of God, [24]they are now justified by his grace as a gift through the redemption that is in Christ Jesus, [25]whom God put forward as a sacrifice of atonement by his blood, effective through faith. He did this to show his righteousness, because in his divine forbearance he had passed over the sins previously committed [26]it was to prove at the present time that he himself is righteous and that he justifies the one who has faith in Jesus.

[27]Then what becomes of boasting? It is excluded. By what law? By that of works? No, but by the law of faith. [28]For we hold that a person is justified by faith apart from works prescribed by the law. [29]Or is God the God of Jews only? Is he not the God of Gentiles also? Yes, of Gentiles also, [30]since God is one, and he will justify the circumcised on the ground of faith and the uncircumcised through that same faith. [31]Do we then overthrow the law by this faith? By no means! On the contrary, we uphold the law.

* * *

RESULTS OF JUSTIFICATION (ROMANS 5:1–11)

5 [1]Therefore, since we are justified by faith, we have peace with God through our Lord Jesus Christ, [2]through whom we have obtained access to this grace in which we stand; and we boast in our hope of sharing the glory of God. [3]And not only that but we also boast in our sufferings knowing that suffering produces endurance, [4]and endurance produces character, and character produces hope, and hope does not disappoint us, because God's love has been poured into our hearts through the Holy Spirit that has been given to us. [6]For while we were still weak, at the right time Christ died for the ungodly. [7]Indeed, rarely will anyone die for a righteous person—though perhaps for a good person someone might actually dare to die. [8]But God proves his love for us in that while we still were sinners Christ died for us. [9]Much more surely then, now that we have been justified by his blood, will we be saved through him from the wrath of God. [10]For if while we were enemies, we were reconciled to God through the death of his Son, much more surely having been reconciled, will we be saved by his life. [11]But more than that, we even boast in God through our Lord Jesus Christ, through whom we have now received reconciliation.

* * *

THE STRUGGLE BETWEEN THE FLESH
AND THE SPIRIT (ROMANS 7:14–8:39)

7 14For we know that the law is spiritual, but I am of the flesh, sold into slavery under sin. 15I do not understand my own actions. For I do not do what I want, but I do the very thing I hate. 16Now if I do what I do not want I agree that the law is good. 17But in fact it is no longer I that do it, but sin that dwells within me. 18For I know that nothing good dwells within me that is, in my flesh. I can will what is right, but I cannot do it. 19For I do not do the good I want, but the evil I do not want is what I do. 20Now if I do what I do not want, it is no longer I that do it, but sin that dwells within me.

21So I find it to be a law that when I want to do what is good, evil lies close at hand. 22For I delight in the law of God in my inmost self 23but I see in my members another law at war with the law of my mind, making me captive to the law of sin that dwells in my members. 24Wretched man that I am! Who will rescue me from this body of death? 25Thanks be to God through Jesus Christ our Lord!

So then, with my mind I am a slave to the law of God, but with my flesh I am a slave to the law of sin.

8 1There is therefore now no condemnation for those who are in Christ Jesus. 2For the law of the Spirit of life in Christ Jesus has set you free from the law of sin and of death. 3For God has done what the law, weakened by the flesh, could not do: by sending his own Son in the likeness of sinful flesh, and to deal with sin, he condemned sin in the flesh, 4so that the just requirement of the law might be fulfilled in us, who walk not according to the flesh but according to the Spirit. 5For those who live according to the flesh set their minds on the things of the flesh, but those who live according to the Spirit set their minds on the things of the Spirit. 6To set the mind on the flesh is death, but to set the mind on the Spirit is life and peace. 7For this reason the mind that is set on the flesh is hostile to God, it does not submit to God's law—indeed it cannot 8and those who are in the flesh cannot please God.

9But you are not in the flesh; you are in the Spirit, since the Spirit of God dwells in you. Anyone who does not have the Spirit of Christ does not belong to him. 10But if Christ is in you though the body is dead because of sin the Spirit is life because of righteousness. 11If the Spirit of him who raised Jesus from the dead dwells in you, he who raised Christ from the dead will give life to your mortal bodies also through his Spirit that dwells in you. 12So then, brothers and sisters, we are debtors, not to the flesh, to live according to the flesh—13for if you live according to the flesh, you will die; but if by the Spirit you put to death the deeds of the body, you will live. 14For all who are led by the Spirit of God are children of God. 15For you did not receive a spirit of slavery to fall back into fear, but you have received a spirit of adoption. When we cry, "Abba! Father!" 16it is that very Spirit bearing witness with our spirit that we are children of God 17and if children, then heirs, heirs of God and joint heirs with Christ—if, in fact, we suffer with him so that we may also be glorified with him.

18I consider that the sufferings of this present time are not worth comparing with the glory about to be revealed to us. 19For the creation waits with eager longing for the revealing of the children of God 20for the creation was subjected to futility, not of its own will but by the will of the one who subjected it, in hope 21that the creation itself will be set free from its bondage to decay and will obtain the freedom of the glory of the children of God. 22We know that the whole creation has been groaning in labor pains until now 23and not only the creation, but we ourselves, who have the first fruits of the

Spirit, groan inwardly while we wait for adoption, the redemption of our bodies. 24For in hope we were saved. Now hope that is seen is not hope. For who hopes for what is seen? 25But if we hope for what we do not see, we wait for it with patience.

26Likewise the Spirit helps us in our weakness; for we do not know how to pray as we ought, but that very Spirit intercedes with sighs too deep for words. 27And God, who searches the heart, knows what is the mind of the Spirit, because the Spirit intercedes for the saints according to the will of God.

28We know that all things work together for good for those who love God, who are called according to his purpose. 29For those whom he foreknew he also predestined to be conformed to the image of his Son, in order that he might be the firstborn within a large family. 30And those whom he predestined he also called; and those whom he called he also justified, and those whom he justified he also glorified.

31What then are we to say about these things? If God is for us, who is against us? 32He who did not withhold his own Son, but gave him up for all of us, will he not with him also give us everything else? 33Who will bring any charge against God's elect? It is God who justifies. 34Who is to condemn? It is Christ Jesus, who died, yes, who was raised, who is at the right hand of God, who indeed intercedes for us. 35Who will separate us from the love of Christ? Will hardship, or distress, or persecution, or famine, or nakedness, or peril, or sword? 36As it is written,

"For your sake we are being killed all day long;
we are accounted as sheep to be slaughtered."

37No, in all these things we are more than conquerors through him who loved us. 38For I am convinced that neither death, nor life, nor angels, nor rulers, nor things present, nor things to come, nor powers, 39nor height, nor depth, nor anything else in all creation, will be able to separate us from the love of God in Christ Jesus our Lord.

*　*　*

THE CHRISTIAN ETHIC OF PAUL (ROMANS 12–13)

12 1I appeal to you therefore, brothers and sisters, by the mercies of God, to present your bodies as a living sacrifice, holy and acceptable to God, which is your spiritual worship. 2Do not be conformed to this world, but be transformed by the renewing of your minds, so that you may discern what is the will of God—what is good and acceptable and perfect.

3For by the grace given to me I say to everyone among you not to think of yourself more highly than you ought to think, but to think with sober judgment, each according to the measure of faith that God has assigned. 4For as in one body we have many members and not all the members have the same function, 5so we, who are many, are one body in Christ, and individually we are members one of another. 6We have gifts that differ according to the grace given to us: prophecy, in proportion to faith; 7ministry, in ministering; the teacher, in teaching; 8the exhorter, in exhortation; the giver, in generosity; the leader, in diligence; the compassionate, in cheerfulness.

9Let love be genuine, hate what is evil, hold fast to what is good; 10love one another with mutual affection; outdo one another in showing honor. 11Do not lag in zeal, be ardent in spirit, serve the Lord. 12Rejoice in hope, be patient in suffering, persevere in prayer. 13Contribute to the needs of the saints; extend hospitality to strangers.

[14]Bless those who persecute you; bless and do not curse them. [15]Rejoice with those who rejoice, weep with those who weep. [16]Live in harmony with one another; do not be haughty but associate with the lowly; do not claim to be wiser than you are. [17]Do not repay anyone evil for evil, but take thought for what is noble in the sight of all. [18]If it is possible, so far as it depends on you, live peaceably with all. [19]Beloved, never avenge yourselves but leave room for the wrath of God; for it is written, "Vengeance is mine, I will repay, says the Lord." [20]No, "if your enemies are hungry, feed them; if they are thirsty, give them something to drink, for by doing this you will heap burning coals on their heads." [21]Do not be overcome by evil, but overcome evil with good.

13 [1]Let every person be subject to the governing authorities, for there is no authority except from God, and those authorities that exist have been instituted by God. [2]Therefore whoever resists authority resists what God has appointed, and those who resist will incur judgment. [3]For rulers are not a terror to good conduct, but to bad. Do you wish to have no fear of the authority? Then do what is good, and you will receive its approval; [4]for it is God's servant for your good. But if you do what is wrong, you should be afraid, for the authority does not bear the sword in vain! It is the servant of God to execute wrath on the wrongdoer. [5]Therefore one must be subject not only because of wrath but also because of conscience. [6]For the same reason you also pay taxes, for the authorities are God's servants, busy with this very thing. [7]Pay to all what is due them—taxes to whom taxes are due, revenue to whom revenue is due, respect to whom respect is due, honor to whom honor is due.

[8]Owe no one anything, except to love one another; for the one who loves another has fulfilled the law. [9]The commandments, "You shall not commit adultery, You shall not murder, You shall not steal, You shall not covet," and any other commandment are summed up in this word, "Love your neighbor as yourself." [10]Love does no wrong to a neighbor; therefore, love is the fulfilling of the law.

[11]Besides this, you know what time it is, how it is now the moment for you to wake from sleep. For salvation is nearer to us now than when we became believers; [12]the night is far gone the day is near. Let us then lay aside the works of darkness and put on the armor of light; [13]let us live honorably as in the day, not in reveling and drunkenness, not in debauchery and licentiousness, not in quarreling and jealousy. [14]Instead, put on the Lord Jesus Christ, and make no provision for the flesh, to gratify its desires.

*   *   *

THE FOOLISHNESS OF THE GOSPEL
(I CORINTHIANS 1:18–31)

1 [18]For the message about the cross is foolishness to those who are perishing, but to us who are being saved it is the power of God. [19]For it is written,

> "I will destroy the wisdom of the wise,
> and the discernment of the discerning I will thwart."

[20]Where is the one who is wise? Where is the scribe? Where is the debater of this age? Has not God made foolish the wisdom of the world? [21]For since, in the wisdom of God, the world did not know God through wisdom, God decided, through the foolishness of

our proclamation, to save those who believe. ²²For Jews demand signs and Greeks desire wisdom ²³but we proclaim Christ crucified, a stumbling block to Jews and foolishness to Gentiles, ²⁴but to those who are the called, both Jews and Greeks, Christ the power of God and the wisdom of God. ²⁵For God's foolishness is wiser than human wisdom, and God's weakness is stronger than human strength.

²⁶Consider your own call, brothers and sisters: not many of you were wise by human standards, not many were powerful, not many were of noble birth. ²⁷But God chose what is foolish in the world to shame the wise, God chose what is weak in the world to shame the strong; ²⁸God chose what is low and despised in the world, things that are not, to reduce to nothing things that are ²⁹so that no one might boast in the presence of God. ³⁰He is the source of your life in Christ Jesus, who became for us wisdom from God, and righteousness and sanctification and redemption, ³¹in order that, as it is written, "Let the one who boasts, boast in the Lord."

*   *   *

THE GIFT OF LOVE (I CORINTHIANS 13)

13 ¹If I speak in the tongues of mortals and of angels, but do not have love, I am a noisy gong or a clanging cymbal. ²And if I have prophetic powers, and understand all mysteries and all knowledge, and if I have all faith, so as to remove mountains, but do not have love, I am nothing. ³If I give away all my possessions, and if I hand over my body so that I may boast, but do not have love, I gain nothing.

⁴Love is patient, love is kind, love is not envious or boastful or arrogant ⁵or rude. It does not insist on its own way; it is not irritable or resentful; ⁶it does not rejoice in wrongdoing, but rejoices in the truth. ⁷It bears all things, believes all things, hopes all things, endures all things.

⁸Love never ends. But as for prophecies, they will come to an end; as for tongues, they will cease; as for knowledge, it will come to an end. ⁹For we know only in part, and we prophesy only in part; ¹⁰but when the complete comes, the partial will come to an end. ¹¹When I was a child, I spoke like a child, I thought like a child, I reasoned like a child; when I became an adult, I put an end to childish ways. ¹²For now we see in a mirror, dimly but then we will see face to face. Now I know only in part; then I will know fully, even as I have been fully known. ¹³And now faith, hope, and love abide, these three; and the greatest of these is love.

*   *   *

THE RESURRECTION OF THE BODY
(I CORINTHIANS 15:16–26; 51–58)

15 ¹⁶For if the dead are not raised then Christ has not been raised. ¹⁷If Christ has not been raised, your faith is futile and you are still in your sins. ¹⁸Then those also who have died in Christ have perished. ¹⁹If for this life only we have hoped in Christ, we are of all people most to be pitied.

²⁰But in fact Christ has been raised from the dead, the first fruits of those who have died. ²¹For since death came through a human being, the resurrection of the dead

has also come through a human being ²²for as all die in Adam, so all will be made alive in Christ. ²³But each in his own order: Christ the first fruits, then at his coming those who belong to Christ. ²⁴Then comes the end, when he hands over the kingdom to God the Father, after he has destroyed every ruler and every authority and power. ²⁵For he must reign until he has put all his enemies under his feet. ²⁶The last enemy to be destroyed is death.

* * *

⁵¹Listen I will tell you a mystery! We will not all die, but we will all be changed, ⁵²in a moment, in the twinkling of an eye, at the last trumpet. For the trumpet will sound, and the dead will be raised imperishable, and we will be changed. ⁵³For this perishable body must put on imperishability, and this mortal body must put on immortality. ⁵⁴When this perishable body puts on imperishability, and this mortal body puts on immortality, then the saying that is written will be fulfilled:

> "Death has been swallowed up in victory."
> ⁵⁵"Where, O death, is your victory?
> Where, O death, is your sting?"

⁵⁶The sting of death is sin, and the power of sin is the law. ⁵⁷But thanks be to God, who gives us the victory through our Lord Jesus Christ.

⁵⁸Therefore, my beloved, be steadfast, immovable, always excellling in the work of the Lord, because you know that in the Lord your labor is not in vain.

* * *

HYMM TO CHRIST (PHILIPPIANS 2:5–11)

2 ⁵Let the same mind be in you that was in Christ Jesus

> ⁶who, though he was in the form of God,
>   did not regard equality with God
>   as something to be exploited,
> ⁷but emptied himself,
>   taking the form of a slave,
>   being born in human likeness.
> And being found in human form
> ⁸he humbled himself
>   and became obedient to the point of death—
>   even death on a cross.
> ⁹Therefore God also highly
>   exalted him
>   and gave him the name
>   that is above every name,
> ¹⁰so that at the name of Jesus
>   every knee should bend,
>   in heaven and on earth and under the earth,
> ¹¹and every tongue should confess
>   that Jesus Christ is Lord,
>   to the glory of God the Father.

* * *

THE NEW HEAVEN AND THE NEW EARTH
(REVELATION 21:1–8; 22:1–5)

21 ¹Then I saw a new heaven and a new earth; for the first heaven and the first earth had passed away, and the sea was no more. ²And I saw the holy city, the new Jerusalem, coming down out of heaven from God, prepared as a bride adorned for her husband. ³And I heard a loud voice from the throne saying,

> "See, the home of God is among mortals.
> He will dwell with them as their God;
> they will be his peoples,
> and God himself will be with them;
> ⁴he will wipe every tear from their eyes.
> Death will be no more;
> mourning and crying and pain will be no more,
> for the first things have passed away."

Christ as Ruler of the Universe, Byzantine Mosaic, twelfth century. Byzantine domes often included an image or icon of Christ as ruler. Notice that the text on the left-hand page of the Bible is in Greek (the language of Byzantium), while the right-hand page is in Latin (the language of Western Europe). *(Art Resource)*

⁵And the one who was seated on the throne said, "See, I am making all things new." Also he said, "Write this for these words are trustworthy and true." ⁶Then he said to me, "It is done! I am the Alpha and the Omega, the beginning and the end. To the thirsty I will give water as a gift from the spring of the water of life. ⁷Those who conquer will inherit these things, and I will be their God and they will be my children. ⁸But as for the cowardly, the faithless, the polluted, the murderers, the fornicators, the sorcerers, the idolaters, and all liars, their place will be in the lake that burns with fire and sulfur, which is the second death."

* * *

22 ¹Then the angel showed me the river of the water of life, bright as crystal, flowing from the throne of God and of the Lamb ²through the middle of the street of the city. On either side of the river, is the tree of life with its twelve kinds of fruit, producing its fruit each month, and the leaves of the tree are for the healing of the nations. ³Nothing accursed will be found there any more. But the throne of God and of the Lamb will be in it, and his servants will worship him; ⁴they will see his face, and his name will be on their foreheads. ⁵And there will be no more night, they need no light of lamp or sun, for the Lord God will be their light, and they will reign forever and ever.

The Church Fathers

One of the earliest questions facing the growing church was the proper relationship between Christianity and Greek philosophy. On the one hand some of the early Christian writers, known as the "Church Fathers," pointed to Paul's use of pagan concepts in preaching (Acts 17) and to his appeal to universal knowledge of God's power and nature (e.g., Romans 1:20). They took this as proof that Greek philosophy might *supplement* revelation. Yet others claimed that Paul's warnings against philosophy (in Colossians 2:8, for example) and his claim that the Gospel was "foolishness" to the Greeks (e.g., I Cor. 1:18–31) indicated that Greek thought had been *superseded* by divine revelation.* Justin Martyr, Clement of Alexandria, and Origen are among the Church Fathers who advocated a rapprochement between divine revelation and secular reason, while Tertullian is the most prominent Church Father to urge a strong distinction between the two.

Justin Martyr (ca. 110–ca. 165), the first of the major Church Fathers, claimed that Christianity represented the completion of all true philosophy. Following studies in philosophy at Ephesus, Justin Martyr was converted to Christianity in his thirties. As he explained in his *Dialogue with Trypho,* he tried various philosophies but found peace only when he encountered the Christian Scriptures.

*I am indebted to James N. Jordan, *Western Philosophy: From Antiquity to the Middle Ages* (New York: Macmillan, 1987), p. 277, for this distinction.

31

Rather than seeing all his previous learning as false, he claimed that each of the pagan philosophers had spoken the truth "in proportion to the share he had of the spermatic [revealed] Word ⟨logos⟩."

Clement of Alexandria (ca. 150–ca. 215) went even further than Justin Martyr in his estimation of philosophy. As the head of a Christian school in Alexandria, Clement claimed in his *Stromata* (or *Miscellanies*) that philosophy was "a preparation, paving the way for him who is perfected in Christ." Borrowing an idea from his Jewish predecessor, Philo of Alexandria (ca. 20 B.C.–ca. A.D. 50), Clement claimed that Plato was able to come so close to the truth because Plato had directly studied the writings of Moses and had personally met the prophet Isaiah. Clement believed that parts of God's truth could be found in all philosophies—even in such apparently secular philosophies as Epicurianism.

Clement also borrowed from Philo the allegorical interpretation of scripture. But it was Origen (ca. 185–ca. 254), Clement's successor at the school in Alexandria, who took this approach to the Bible to its limits. According to Origen, every story, every teaching in the Bible can be seen as an allegory containing some deeper spiritual meaning. Using this approach to scripture, Origen combined Neoplatonic teachings with Christianity. For example, Origen accepted the biblical position that God freely created the world at a certain point in time, yet he also agreed with the Neoplatonic doctrine that God eternally and necessarily emanated creative power. Origen reconciled these apparently incompatible teachings by claiming that all souls preexisted from eternity, that all but one soul fell and became united with bodies in "the world" (Jesus being the exception), and that the biblical story of creation refers only to this particular world, not to the many others that God has created and will create. Although Origen's teachings were later rejected by the church, the question of God's relation to creation continued to be a controversial topic and echoes of Origen can be heard in Augustine.

The fourth major Church Father, Tertullian (ca. 155–ca. 220), took a position very different from that of Justin Martyr, Clement, and Origen. A successful lawyer from the northern African city of Carthage, Tertullian argued passionately against the use of philosophy to support Christianity. According to Tertullian, philosophy had already discredited itself by its patent inability to come to any unanimity about truth. And while philosophers, such as Socrates, may have occasionally said something true, it was only by chance or by the influence of biblical writings that they managed to intuit even partial truth. But even in the best cases, whatever partial truth might have been found in philosophy has been more than superseded by God's revelation. Tertullian went so far as to write, "The Son of God died; it must be believed because it is absurd. He was buried and rose again; it is certain because it is impossible." Tertullian's eloquent denial of the power of reason was to have great influence on the church. When the Council of Nicea rejected human wisdom in declaring Jesus to be both fully God and yet fully human, it was following the instincts and teachings of Paul and Tertullian.

*   *   *

The selections given here are from the classic translations of Dods and Reith (Justin Martyr), Wilson (Clement of Alexandria), Peter Holmes (Tertullian), and Frederick Crombie (Origen).

For further readings in the Church Fathers, see J.B. Lightfoot and J.R. Harmer, eds., *The Apostolic Fathers* (Grand Rapids, MI: Baker Book House, 1956); Henry

Scowcroft Bettenson, ed., *Documents of the Christian Church,* 2nd ed. (Oxford: Oxford University Press, 1967); and Eberhard Arnold, *The Early Christians After the Death of the Apostles,* translated and edited by the Society of Brothers at Rifton (Rifton, NY: Plough Publishing House, 1970). For comparative studies of the Church Fathers, see Henry Chadwick, *Early Christian Thought and the Classical Tradition: Studies in Justin, Clement, and Origen* (Oxford: Oxford University Press, 1966), and Hamilton Baird Timothy, *The Early Christian Apologists and Greek Philosophy Exemplified by Irenaeus, Tertullian and Clement of Alexandria* (Assen: Van Gorcum, 1973). For the relations between Christian doctrine and the surrounding culture, the best introduction is Jaroslav Pelikan, *The Emergence of the Catholic Tradition (100–600)* (Chicago: University of Chicago Press, 1971).

For specific Church Fathers see the following:

JUSTIN MARTYR: Leslie W. Barnard, *Justin Martyr: His Life and Thought* (Cambridge: Cambridge University Press, 1967).

CLEMENT OF ALEXANDRIA: R.B. Tollinton, *Clement of Alexandria: A Study in Christian Liberalism* (London: Williams and Norgate, 1914); Eric Francis Osborn, *The Philosophy of Clement of Alexandria* (Cambridge: Cambridge University Press, 1957).

TERTULLIAN: John B. Delaunay, *Tertullian and His Apologetics: A Study of Early Christian Thought* (Notre Dame, IN: Notre Dame University Press, 1914); Timothy David Barnes, *Tertullian: A Historical and Literary Study* (Oxford: Clarendon Press, 1971).

ORIGEN: Jean Danielou, *Origen,* translated by Walter Mitchell (New York: Sheed and Ward, 1955); Joseph Wilson Trigg, *Origen: The Bible and Philosophy in the Third-Century Church* (Atlanta, GA: John Knox, 1983); Henri Crouzel, *Origen,* translated by A.S. Worrall (San Francisco: Harper & Row, 1989).

JUSTIN MARTYR

DIALOGUE WITH TRYPHO (in part)

Chapter 2: Justin Describes His Studies in Philosophy

"I will tell you," said I, "what seems to me for philosophy is, in fact, the greatest possession, and most honorable before God, to whom it leads us and alone commends us; and these are truly holy men who have bestowed attention on philosophy. What philosophy is, however, and the reason why it has been sent down to men have escaped the observation of most; for there would be neither Platonists, nor Stoics, nor Peripatetics, nor Theoretics, nor Pythagoreans, this knowledge being *one.* I wish to tell you why it has become many-headed. It has happened that those who first handled it [i.e., philosophy], and who were therefore esteemed illustrious men were succeeded by those who made no investigations concerning truth, but only admired the perseverance and self-discipline of the former, as well as the novelty of the doctrines; and each thought that to be true which he learned from his teacher: then, moreover, those latter persons handed down to *their* successors such things, and others similar to them; and this system was called by the name of him who was styled the father of the doctrine. Being at first desirous of personally conversing with one of these men, I surrendered myself to a certain Stoic; and having spent a considerable time with him, when I had not acquired any further knowledge of God (for he did not know himself, and said such instruction was unnecessary), I left him and betook myself to another, who was called a Peripatetic, and as *he* fancied, shrewd. And this man, after having entertained me for the first few days, requested me to settle the fee, in order that our intercourse might not be unprofitable for him, too. For this reason I abandoned him, believing him to be no philosopher at all. But when my soul was eagerly desirous to hear the peculiar and choice philosophy, I came to a Pythagorean, very celebrated—a man who thought much of his own wisdom. And then, when I had an interview with him, willing to become his hearer and disciple, he said, "What then? Are you acquainted with music, astronomy, and geometry? Do you expect to perceive any of those things which conduce to a happy life, if you have not been first informed on those points which wean the soul from sensible objects, and render it fitted for objects which appertain to the mind, so that it can contemplate that which is honorable in its essence and that which is good in its essence?" Having commended many of these branches of learning, and telling me that they were necessary, he dismissed me when I confessed to him my ignorance. Accordingly I took it rather impatiently, as was to be expected when I failed in my hope, the more so because I deemed the man had some knowledge; but reflecting again on the space of time during which I would have to linger over those branches of learning, I was not able to endure longer procrastination. In my helpless condition it occurred to me to have a meeting with the Platonists, for their fame was great. I thereupon spent as much of my time as possible with one who had lately settled in our city,—a sagacious man, holding a high position among the Platonists,—and I progressed, and made the greatest improvements daily. And the perception of immaterial things quite overpowered me, and the contemplation of ideas furnished my mind with wings, so that in a little while I supposed that I had become wise; and such was my stupidity, I expected forthwith to look upon God, for this is the end of Plato's philosophy.

*   *   *

APOLOGY (in part)

Part II, Chapter 13: How the Word Has Been in All Men

For I myself, when I discovered the wicked disguise which the evil spirits had thrown around the divine doctrines of the Christians, to turn aside others from joining them, laughed both at those who framed these falsehoods, and at the disguise itself, and at popular opinion; and I confess that I both boast and with all my strength strive to be found a Christian; not because the teachings of Plato are different from those of Christ, but because they are not in all respects similar, as neither are those of the others, Stoics, and poets, and historians. For each man spoke well in proportion to the share he had of the spermatic word, seeing what was related to it. But they who contradict themselves on the more important points appear not to have possessed the heavenly wisdom, and the knowledge which cannot be spoken against. Whatever things were rightly said among all men, are the property of us Christians. For next to God, we worship and love the Word who is from the unbegotten and ineffable God, since also He became man for our sakes, that, becoming a partaker of our sufferings, He might also bring us healing. For all the writers were able to see realities darkly through the sowing of the implanted word that was in them. For the seed and imitation imparted according to capacity is one thing, and quite another is the thing itself, of which there is the participation and imitation according to the grace which is from Him.

*   *   *

HORTATORY ADDRESS TO THE GREEKS (in part)

Chapter 36: True Knowledge Not Held by the Philosophers

And if "the discovery of the truth" be given among them as one definition of philosophy, how are they who are not in possession of the true knowledge worthy of the name of philosophy? For if Socrates, the wisest of your wise men, to whom even your oracle, as you yourselves say, bears witness, saying, "Of all men, Socrates is the wisest"—if he confesses that he knows nothing, how did those who came after him profess to know even things heavenly? For Socrates said that he was on this account called wise, because, while other men pretended to know what they were ignorant of, he himself did not shrink from confessing that he knew nothing. For he said, "I seem to myself to be wisest by this little particular, that what I do not know, I do not suppose I know." Let no one fancy that Socrates ironically feigned ignorance, because he often used to do so in his dialogues. For the last expression of his apology which he uttered as he was being led away to the prison, proves that in seriousness and truth he was confessing his ignorance: "But now it is time to go away, I indeed to die, but you to live. And which of us goes to the better state, is hidden to all but God." Socrates, indeed, having uttered this last sentence in the Areopagus, departed to the prison, ascribing to God alone the knowledge of those things which are hidden from us; but those who came after him, though they are unable to comprehend even earthly things, profess to understand things heavenly as if they had seen them. Aristotle at least—as if he had seen things heavenly with greater accuracy than Plato—declared that God did not exist, as Plato said, in the fiery substance (for this was Plato's doctrine) but in the fifth element, air. And while he demanded that concerning these matters he should be believed on account of the excellence of his language, he yet departed this life because he was overwhelmed with the infamy and disgrace of being unable to discover even the nature of the Euripus in Chalcis. Let not any one, therefore, of sound judgment prefer the elegant diction of these men to his own salvation, but let him, according to that old story, stop his ears with wax, and flee the sweet hurt which these sirens would inflict upon him. For the above-mentioned men presenting their elegant language as a kind of bait, have sought to seduce many from the right religion, in imitation of him who dared to teach the first men polytheism. Be not persuaded by these persons, I entreat you, but read the prophecies of the sacred writers. And if any slothfulness or old hereditary superstition prevents you from reading the prophecies of the holy men through which you can be instructed regarding the one only God, which is the first article of the true religion, yet believe him who, though at first he taught you polytheism, yet afterwards preferred to sing a useful and necessary recantation—I mean Orpheus, who said what I quoted a little before; and believe the others who wrote the same things concerning one God. For it was the work of Divine Providence on your behalf, that they, though unwillingly, bore testimony that what the prophets said regarding one God was true, in order that, the doctrine of a plurality of gods being rejected by all, occasion might be afforded you of knowing the truth.

CLEMENT OF ALEXANDRIA

THE STROMATA (in part)

Book I, Chapter 5: Philosophy the Handmaid of Theology

Accordingly, before the advent of the Lord, philosophy was necessary to the Greeks for righteousness. And now it becomes conducive to piety; being a kind of preparatory training to those who attain to faith through demonstration. "For thy foot," it is said, "will not stumble, if thou refer what is good, whether belonging to the Greeks or to us, to Providence." For God is the cause of all good things; but of some primarily as of the Old and the New Testament; and of others by consequence, as philosophy. Perchance, too, philosophy was given to the Greeks directly and primarily, till the Lord should call the Greeks. For this was a schoolmaster to bring "the Hellenic mind," as the law, the Hebrews, "to Christ." Philosophy, therefore, was a preparation, paving the way for him who is perfected in Christ. . . . Philosophy . . . exercises the mind, rouses the intelligence, and begets an inquiring shrewdness, by means of the true philosophy, which the initiated possess, having found it, or rather received it, from the truth itself.

* * *

Book I, Chapter 7: What True Philosophy Is, and Whence So Called

. . . Now those are called philosophers, among us, who love Wisdom, the Creator and Teacher of all things, that is, the knowledge of the Son of God; and among the Greeks, those who undertake arguments on virtue. Philosophy, then, consists of such dogmas found in each sect (I mean those of philosophy) as cannot be impugned, with a corresponding life, collected into one selection; and these, stolen from the Barbarian God-given grace, have been adorned by Greek speech. For some they have borrowed, and others they have misunderstood. And in the case of others, what they have spoken, in consequence of being moved, they have not yet perfectly worked out; and others by human conjecture and reasoning, in which also they stumble. And they think that they have hit the truth perfectly; but as we understand them, only partially. They know, then, nothing more than this world. And it is just like geometry, which treats of measures and magnitudes and forms, by delineation on plane-surfaces; and just as painting appears to take in the whole field of view in the scenes represented. But it gives a false description of the view, according to the rules of the art, employing the signs that result from the incidents of the lines of vision. By this means, the higher and lower points in the view, and those between, are preserved; and some objects seem to appear in the foreground, and others in the background, and others to appear in some other way, on the smooth and level surface. So also the philosophers copy the truth, after the manner of painting. And always in the case of each one of them, their self-love is the cause of all their mistakes. Wherefore one ought not, in the desire for the glory that terminates in men, to be animated by self-love; but loving God, to become really holy with wisdom. If, then, one treats what is particular as universal, and regards that, which serves, as the Lord, he misses the truth, not understanding what was spoken by David by way of confession: "I have eaten earth [ashes] like bread." Now, self-love and self-conceit are, in his view, earth and error. But if so, science and knowledge are derived from instruction. And if there is instruction, you must seek for the master. Cleanthes claims Zeno, and Metrodorus, Epicurus, and Theophrastus Aristotle, and Plato Socrates. But if I come to Pythagoras, and Pherecydes, and Thales, and the first wise men, I come to a stand in my search for their teacher. Should you say the Egyptians, the Indians, the Babylonians, and the Magi themselves, I will not stop from asking their teacher. And I lead you up to the first generation of men; and from that point I begin to investigate Who is their teacher. No one of men: for they had not yet learned. Nor yet any of the angels: for in the way that angels, in virtue of being angels, speak, men do not hear; nor, as we have ears, have they a tongue to correspond; nor would any one attribute to the angels organs of speech, lips I mean, and the parts contiguous, throat, and windpipe, and chest, breath and air to vibrate. And God is far from calling aloud in the unapproachable sanctity, separated as He is from even the archangels.

And we also have already heard that angels learned the truth, and their rulers over them; for they had a beginning. It remains, then, for us, ascending to seek their teacher. And since the unoriginated Being is one, the Omnipotent God; one, too, is the First-begotten, "by whom all things were made, and without whom not one thing ever was made." "For one, in truth, is God, who formed the beginning of all things"; pointing out "the first-begotten Son," Peter writes, accurately comprehending the statement, "In the beginning God made the heaven and the earth." And He is called Wisdom by all the prophets. This is He who is the Teacher of all created beings, the Fellow-counsellor of God, who foreknew all things; and He from above, from the first foundation of the world, "in many ways and many times," trains and perfects; whence it is rightly said, "Call no man your teacher on earth."

You see whence the true philosophy has its handles; though the Law be the image and shadow of the truth: for the Law is the shadow of the truth. But the self-love of the Greeks proclaims certain men as their teachers. As, then, the whole family runs back to God the Creator; so also all the teaching of good things, which justifies, does to the Lord, and leads and contributes to this.

But if from any creature they received in any way whatever the seeds of the Truth, they did not nourish them; but committing them to a barren and rainless soil, they choked them with weeds, as the Pharisees revolted from the Law, by introducing human teachings,—the cause of these being not the Teacher, but those who choose to disobey. But those of them who believed the Lord's advent and the plain teaching of the Scriptures, attain to the knowledge of the law; as also those addicted to philosophy, by the teaching of the Lord, are introduced into the knowledge of the true philosophy: "For the oracles of the Lord are pure oracles melted in the fire, tried in the earth, purified seven times." Just as silver often purified, so is the just man brought to the test, becoming the Lord's coin and receiving the royal image. Or, since Solomon also calls the "tongue of the righteous man gold that has been subjected to fire," intimating that the doctrine which has been proved, and is wise, is to be praised and received, whenever it is amply tried by the earth: that is, when the gnostic soul is in manifold ways sanctified, through withdrawal from earthy fires. And the body in which it dwells is purified, being appropriated to the pureness of a holy temple. But the first purification which takes place in the body, the soul being first, is abstinence from evil things, which some consider perfection, and is, in truth, the perfection of the common believer—Jew and Greek. But in the case of the Gnostic, after that which is reckoned perfection in others, his righteousness advances to activity in well-doing. And in whomsoever the increased force of righteousness advances to the doing of good, in his case perfection abides in the fixed habit of well doing after the likeness of God. For those who are the seed of Abraham, and besides servants of God, are "the called"; and the sons of Jacob are the elect—they who have tripped up the energy of wickedness.

If, then, we assert that Christ Himself is Wisdom, and that it was His working which showed itself in the prophets, by which the gnostic tradition may be learned, as He Himself taught the apostles during His presence; then it follows that the *gnosis,* which is the knowledge and apprehension of things present, future, and past, which is sure and reliable, as being imparted and revealed by the Son of God, is wisdom.

And if, too, the end of the wise man is contemplation, that of those who are still philosophers aims at it, but never attains it, unless by the process of learning it receives the prophetic utterance which has been made known, by which it grasps both the present, the future, and the past—how they are, were, and shall be.

And the *gnosis* itself is that which has descended by transmission to a few, having been imparted unwritten by the apostles. Hence then, knowledge or wisdom ought to be exercised up to the eternal and unchangeable habit of contemplation.

TERTULLIAN

A TREATISE ON THE SOUL (in part)

Chapter 1: It Is Not to the Philosophers That We Resort for Information About the Soul but to God.

Having discussed with Hermogenes the single point of the origin of the soul, so far as his assumption led me, that the soul consisted rather in an adaptation of matter than of the inspiration of God, I now turn to the other questions incidental to the subject, and (in my treatment of these) I shall evidently have mostly to contend with the philosophers.

In the very prison of Socrates they skirmished about the state of the soul. I have my doubts at once whether the time was an opportune one for their (great) master—(to say nothing of the place), although *that* perhaps does not much matter. For what could the soul of Socrates then contemplate with clearness and serenity? The sacred ship had returned (from Delos), the hemlock draft to which he had been condemned had been drunk, death was now present before him: (his mind) was, as one may suppose, naturally excited at every emotion; or if nature had lost her influence, it must have been deprived of all power of thought. Or let it have been as placid and tranquil so you please, inflexible, in spite of the claims of natural duty, at the tears of her who was so soon to be his widow, and at the sight of his thenceforward orphan children, yet his soul must have been moved even by its very efforts to suppress emotion; and his constancy itself must have been shaken, as he struggled against the disturbance of the excitement around him. Besides, what other thoughts could any man entertain who had been unjustly condemned to die, but such as should solace him for the injury done to him? Especially would this be the case with that glorious creature, the philosopher, to whom injurious treatment would not suggest a craving for consolation, but rather the feeling of resentment and indignation. Accordingly, after his sentence, when his wife came to him with her effeminate cry, "O Socrates, you are unjustly condemned!" he seemed already to find joy in answering, "Would you then wish me justly condemned?"

It is therefore not to be wondered at, if even in his prison, from a desire to break the foul hands of Anytus and Melitus, he, in the face of death itself, asserts the immortality of the soul by a strong assumption such as was wanted to frustrate the wrong (they had inflicted upon him). So that all the wisdom of Socrates, at that moment, proceeded from the affectation of an assumed composure, rather than the firm conviction of ascertained truth. For by whom has truth ever been discovered without God? By whom has God ever been found without Christ? By whom has Christ ever been explored without the Holy Spirit? By whom has the Holy Spirit ever been attained without the mysterious gift of faith? Socrates, as none can doubt, was actuated by a different spirit. For they say that a demon clung to him from his boyhood—the very worst teacher certainly, notwithstanding the high place assigned to it by poets and philosophers—even next to, (nay, along with) the gods themselves. The teachings of the power of Christ had not yet been given—(that power) which alone can confute this most pernicious influence of evil that has nothing good in it, but is rather the author of all error, and the seducer from all truth.

Now if Socrates was pronounced the wisest of men by the oracle of the Pythian demon, which, you may be sure, neatly managed the business for his friend, of how much greater dignity and constancy is the assertion of the Christian wisdom, before the very breath of which the whole host of demons is scattered! This wisdom of the school of heaven frankly and without reserve denies the gods of this world, and shows no such inconsistency as to order a "cock to be sacrificed to Asclepius": no new gods and demons does it introduce, but expels the old ones; it corrupts not youth, but instructs them in all goodness and moderation; and so it bears the unjust condemnation not of one city only, but of all the world, in the cause of that truth which incurs indeed the greater hatred in proportion to its fullness: so that it tastes death not out of a (poisoned) cup almost in the way of jollity; but it exhausts it in every kind of bitter cruelty, on gibbets and in holocausts.

Meanwhile, in the still gloomier prison of the world amongst your Cebeses and Phaedos, in every investigation concerning (man's) soul, it directs its inquiry according to the rules of God. At all events, you can show us no more powerful expounder of the soul than the Author thereof. From God you may learn about that which you hold of God; but from none else will you get this knowledge, if you get it not from God. For who is to reveal that which God has hidden? To that quarter

must we resort in our inquiries whence we are most safe even in deriving our ignorance. For it is really better for us not to know a thing, because He has not revealed
it to us, than to know it according to man's wisdom, because *he* has been bold
enough to assume it.

* * *

PRESCRIPTIONS AGAINST THE HERETICS (in part)

Chapter 7: Pagan Philosophy the Parent of Heresies. The Connection Between Defections from Christian Faith and the Old System of Pagan Philosophy.

These are "the doctrines" of men and "of demons" produced for itching ears of the spirit
of this world's wisdom: this the Lord called "foolishness," and "chose the foolish things
of the world" to confound even philosophy itself. For (philosophy) it is which is the material of the world's wisdom, the rash interpreter of the nature and the dispensation of
God. Indeed heresies are themselves instigated by philosophy. From this source came
the Aeons, and I known not what infinite forms, and the trinity of man in the system of
Valentinus, who was of Plato's school. From the same source came Marcion's better
god, with all his tranquillity; he came of the Stoics. Then, again, the opinion that the
soul dies is held by the Epicureans; while the denial of the restoration of the body is
taken from the aggregate school of all the philosophers; also, when matter is made equal
to God, then you have the teaching of Zeno; and when any doctrine is alleged touching
a god of fire, then Heraclitus comes in. The same subject-matter is discussed over and
over again by the heretics and the philosophers; the same arguments are involved.
Whence comes evil? Why is it permitted? What is the origin of man? And in what way
does he come? Besides the question which Valentinus has very lately proposed—
Whence comes God? Which he settles with the answer: From *enthymesis* and *ectroma*.
Unhappy Aristotle! who invented for these men dialectics, the art of building up and
pulling down; an art so evasive in its propositions, so farfetched in its conjectures, so
harsh, in its arguments, so productive of contentions—embarrassing even to itself, re-
tracting everything, and really treating of nothing! Whence spring those "fables and
endless genealogies," and "unprofitable questions," and "words which spread like a
cancer?"

From all these, when the apostle would restrain us, he expressly names *philosophy* as that which he would have us be on our guard against. Writing to the Colossians
[2:8], he says, "See that no one beguile you through philosophy and vain deceit, after
the tradition of men, and contrary to the wisdom of the Holy Ghost." He had been at
Athens, and had in his interviews (with its philosophers) become acquainted with that
human wisdom which pretends to know the truth, whilst it only corrupts it, and is itself
divided into its own manifold heresies, by the variety of its mutually repugnant sects.
What indeed has Athens to do with Jerusalem? What concord is there between the
Academy and the Church? What between heretics and Christians? Our instruction
comes from "the porch of Solomon," who had himself taught that "the Lord should be
sought in simplicity of heart." Away with all attempts to produce a mottled Christianity
of Stoic, Platonic, and dialectic composition! We want no curious disputation after pos-

sessing Christ Jesus, no inquisition after enjoying the gospel! With our faith, we desire no further belief. For this is our victorious faith, that there is nothing which we ought to believe besides.

ORIGEN

ON FIRST PRINCIPLES (in part)

Book III, Chapter 5: That the World Took Its Beginning in Time

1. And now, since there is one of the article of the Church which is held principally in consequence of our belief in the truth of our sacred history, viz., that this world was created and took its beginning at a certain time, and, in conformity to the cycle of time decreed to all things, is to be destroyed on account of its corruption, there seems no absurdity in re-discussing a few points connected with this subject. And so far, indeed, as the credibility of Scripture is concerned, the declarations on such a matter seem easy of proof. Even the heretics, although widely opposed on many other things, yet on this appear to be at one, yielding to the authority of Scripture.

   Concerning, then, the creation of the world, what portion of Scripture can give us more information regarding it, than the account which Moses has transmitted respecting its origin? And although it comprehends matters of profounder significance than the mere historical narrative appears to indicate, and contains very many things that are to be spiritually understood, and employs the letter, as a kind of veil, in treating of profound and mystical subjects; nevertheless the language of the narrator shows that all visible things were created at a certain time. But with regard to the consummation of the world, Jacob is the first who gives any information, in addressing his children in the words: "Gather yourselves together unto me, ye sons of Jacob, that I may tell you what shall be in the last days," or "after the last days." If, then, there be "last days," or a period "succeeding the last days," the days which had a beginning must necessarily come to an end. David, too, declares: "The heavens shall perish, but Thou shalt endure; yea, all of them shall wax old as doth a garment: as a vesture shalt Thou change them, and they shall be changed: but Thou art the same, and Thy years shall have no end." Our Lord and Savior, indeed, in the words, "He who made them at the beginning, made them male and female," Himself bears witness that the world was created; and again, when He says, "Heaven and earth shall pass away, but My word shall not pass away," He points out that they are perishable, and must come to an end. The apostle, moreover, in declaring that "the creature was made subject to vanity, not willingly, but by reason of Him who hath subjected the same in hope, because the creature itself also shall be delivered from the bondage of corruption into the glorious liberty of the children of God," manifestly announces the end of the world; as he does also when he again says, "The fashion of this world passeth away." Now, by the expression which he employs, "that the creature was made subject to vanity," he shows that there was a beginning to this world: for if the creature were made subject to vanity on account of some hope, it was certainly made subject from a cause; and seeing it was from a cause, it must necessarily have had a beginning: for, without some beginning, the creature could not be subject to vanity, nor could that (creature) hope to be freed from the bondage of corruption, which had not begun to serve. But any one who chooses to search at his leisure, will find numerous other passages in holy Scripture in which the world is both said to have a beginning and to hope for an end.

2. Now, if there be any one who would here oppose either the authority or credibility of our Scriptures, we would ask of him whether he asserts that God can, or cannot, comprehend all things? To assert that He cannot, would manifestly be an act of impiety. If then he answer, as he must, that God comprehends all things, it follows from the very fact of their being capable of comprehension, that they are understood to have a beginning and an end, seeing that which is altogether without any beginning cannot be at all comprehended. For however far understanding may extend, so far is the faculty of comprehending illimitably withdrawn and removed when there is held to be no beginning.

3. But this is the objection which they generally raise: they say, "If the world had its beginning in time, what was God doing before the world began? For it is at once impious and absurd to say that the nature of God is inactive and immoveable, or to suppose that goodness at one time did not do good, and omnipotence at one time did not exercise its power." Such is the objection which they are accustomed to make to our statement that this world had its beginning at a certain time, and that, agreeably to our belief in Scripture, we can calculate the years of its past duration. To these propositions I consider that none of the heretics can easily return an answer that will be in conformity with the nature of their opinions. But we can give a logical answer in accordance with the standard of religion, when we say that not then for the first time did God begin to work when He made this visible world; but as, after its destruction, there will be another world, so also we believe that others existed before the present came into being. And both of these positions will be confirmed by the authority of holy Scripture. For that there will be another world after this, is taught by Isaiah, who says, "There will be new heavens, and a new earth, which I shall make to abide in my sight, saith the LORD"; and that before this world others also existed is shown by Ecclesiastes, in the words: "What is that which hath been? Even that which shall be. And what is that which has been created? Even this which is to be created: and there is nothing altogether new under the sun. Who shall speak and declare, 'Lo, this is new'? It hath already been in the ages which have been before us." By these testimonies it is established both that there were ages before our own, and that there will be others after it. It is not, however, to be supposed that several worlds existed at once, but that, after the end of this present world, others will take their beginning; respecting which it is unnecessary to repeat each particular statement, seeing we have already done so in the preceding pages.

Plotinus

A.D. 204–270

While Christianity was clearly the dominant influence throughout the Middle Ages in Europe, Neoplatonism also exerted considerable sway—especially in the early medieval period. The most famous representative of Neoplatonism was Plotinus, born in Lykopolis, Egypt, in A.D. 204. In his late twenties Plotinus began to study in Alexandria with Ammonius Saccas, a shadowy figure who was also the teacher of Origen. After eleven years with Ammonius, Plotinus joined an expedition to Persia to gain knowledge of Persian and Indian wisdom. The trek proved unsuccessful and Plotinus moved on to Rome. There he established a school of philosophy and became friends with the emperor Gallenius. At one point he sought permission to found a city based on Plato's *Republic,* but the plan came to naught. He stayed in Rome, teaching and writing, until the death of the emperor in 268. He then moved to the home of a friend where he died in 270, apparently from leprosy.

Developing Plato's dualistic understanding of reality, Plotinus taught that true reality lies "beyond" the physical world. This "reality beyond reality" has no limits and so cannot be described by words since words invariably have limits. Plotinus, again borrowing from Plato, calls it the "Good" or the "One." The One/Good has no limits and is so supremely rich that it overflows or "emanates" to produce "Intellectual-Principle" or "Divine Mind" ⟨*Nous*⟩. This Intellectual-Principle, in turn, overflows and "Divine-Soul" emanates from it. This

43

process continues as Divine-Soul generates the material world. The lowest level of emanation, at the furthest extreme from the One/Good, is the utter formlessness and unreality of matter.

The goal of philosophy is to awaken individuals to the recognition of reality beyond the material world. But philosophy alone cannot take a person to the highest reality of the One/Good. Only in a mystical experience can an individual unite with the One/Good. Plotinus himself claimed to have achieved such a union, a "flight of the Alone to the Alone" to cite his famous words, four times during his life. His experiences of nonmaterial reality were so powerful that he said he was ashamed to have a body.

Plotinus' writings were edited by one of his pupils, Porphyry, in the form of six groups of nine "Tractates" (treatises), published as the so-called *Enneads* (from the Greek word for "nine"). The selection given here, in the A.H. Armstrong translation, is Plotinus' "Treatise on Beauty." This tractate explains how the ascent of the soul to the One/Good is dependent on beauty of soul, a godlike disposition. Plotinus' description parallels the ascending dialectic in Plato's *Symposium* (210a).

Neoplatonism, with its emphasis on the otherworldly and the need for escape from the physical world, was the perfect philosophy for the chaotic final days of the Roman Empire. St. Augustine, in particular, was strongly influenced by Neoplatonic thought. Indeed, if St. Thomas is considered an Aristotelian, St. Augustine may be called a Neoplatonist. Many later thinkers, such as Eckhart, Nicholas Cusanas, Comenius, Jacob Boehme, Hegel, and Schelling, also had their philosophy molded by Neoplatonist doctrines.

*   *   *

Joseph Katz, *Plotinus' Search for the Good* (New York: King's Crown Press, 1950), and Émile Bréhier, *The Philosophy of Plotinus,* translated by Joseph Thomas (Chicago: University of Chicago Press, 1958), are good beginning points for further study of Plotinus. E.R. Dodds, *Select Passages Illustrating Neoplatonism,* translated by E.R. Dodds (New York: Macmillan, 1923), provides a topical guide to the key ideas in the *Enneads;* while Dominic J. O'Meara, *Plotinus: An Introduction to the Enneads* (Oxford: Oxford University Press, 1993), discusses specific important passages. For discussions of Neoplatonism as a school, see Thomas Whittaker, *The Neo-Platonists* (Cambridge: Cambridge University Press, 1918); Arthur O. Lovejoy, *The Great Chain of Being* (Cambridge, MA: Harvard University Press, 1936); R.T. Wallis, *Neoplatonism* (London: Duckworth, 1972); and the collection of essays, R. Baine Harris, ed., *The Structure of Being: A Neoplatonic Approach* (Norfolk, VA: International Society for Neoplatonic Studies, 1982).

ENNEADS (in part)

FIRST ENNEAD, SIXTH TRACTATE: BEAUTY

1. Beauty is mostly in sight, but it is to be found too in things we hear, in combinations of words and also in music, and in all music [not only in songs]; for tunes and rhythms are certainly beautiful: and for those who are advancing upwards from sense-perception ways of life and actions and characters and intellectual activities are beautiful, and there is the beauty of virtue. If there is any beauty prior to these, this discussion will reveal it.

Very well then, what is it which makes us imagine that bodies are beautiful and attracts our hearing to sounds because of their beauty? And how are all the things which depend on soul beautiful? Are they all made beautiful by one and the same beauty or is there one beautifulness in bodies and a different one in other things? And what are they, or what is it? Some things, bodies for instance, are not beautiful from the nature of the objects themselves, but by participation, others are beauties themselves, like the nature of virtue. The same bodies appear sometimes beautiful, sometimes not beautiful, so that their being bodies is one thing, their being beautiful another. What is this principle, then, which is present in bodies? We ought to consider this first. What is it that attracts the gaze of those who look at something, and turns and draws them to it and makes them enjoy the sight? If we find this perhaps we can use it as a stepping-stone and get a sight of the rest. Nearly everyone says that it is good proportion of the parts to each other and to the whole, with the addition of good colour, which produces visible beauty, and that with the objects of sight and generally with everything else, being beautiful is being well-proportioned and measured. On this theory nothing single and simple but only a composite thing will have any beauty. It will be the whole which is beautiful, and the parts will not have the property of beauty by themselves, but will contribute to the beauty of the whole. But if the whole is beautiful the parts must be beautiful too; a beautiful whole can certainly not be composed of ugly parts; all the parts must have beauty. For these people, too, beautiful colours, and the light of the sun as well, since they are simple and do not derive their beautifulness from good proportion, will be excluded from beauty. And how do they think gold manages to be beautiful? And what makes lightning in the night and stars beautiful to see? And in sounds in the same way the simple will be banished, though often in a composition which is beautiful as a whole each separate sound is beautiful. And when, though the same good proportion is there all the time, the same face sometimes appears beautiful and sometimes does not, surely we must say that being beautiful is something else over and above good proportion, and good proportion is beautiful because of something else? But if when these people pass on to ways of life and beautiful expressions of thought they allege good proportion as the cause of beauty in these too, what can be meant by good proportion in beautiful ways of life or laws or studies or branches of knowledge? How can speculations be well-proportioned in relation to each other? If it is because they agree, there can be concord and agreement between bad ideas. The statement that "righteousness is a fine sort of silliness" agrees with and is in tune with the saying that "morality is stupidity"; the two fit perfectly. Again, every sort of virtue is a beauty of the soul, a truer beauty than those mentioned before; but how is virtue well-proportioned? Not like magnitudes or a number. We grant that the soul has several parts, but what is the formula for the composition or mixture in the soul of parts or speculations? And what [on this theory], will the beauty of the intellect alone by itself be?

2. So let us go back to the beginning and state what the primary beauty in bodies really is. It is something which we become aware of even at the first glance; the soul speaks of it as if it understood it, recognises and welcomes it and as it were adapts itself to it. But when it encounters the ugly it shrinks back and rejects it and turns away from it and is out of tune and alienated from it. Our explanation of this is that the soul, since it is by nature what it is and is related to the higher kind of reality in the realm of being, when it sees something akin to it or a trace of its kindred reality, is delighted and thrilled and returns to itself and remembers itself and its own possessions. What likeness, then, is there between beautiful things here and There? If there is a likeness, let us agree that they are alike. But how are both the things in that world and the things in this beautiful? We maintain that the things in this world are beautiful by participating in form; for every shapeless thing which is naturally capable of receiving shape and form is ugly and outside the divine formative power as long as it has no share in formative power and form. This is absolute ugliness. But a thing is also ugly when it is not completely dominated by shape and formative power, since its matter has not submitted to be completely shaped according to the form. The form, then, approaches and composes that which is to come into being from many parts into a single ordered whole; it brings it into a completed unity and makes it one by agreement of its parts; for since it is one itself, that which is shaped by it must also be one as far as a thing can be which is composed of many parts. So beauty rests upon the material thing when it has been brought into unity, and gives itself to parts and wholes alike. When it comes upon something that is one and composed of like parts it gives the same gift to the whole; as sometimes art gives beauty to a whole house with its parts, and sometimes nature gives beauty to a single stone. So then the beautiful body comes into being by sharing in a formative power which comes from the divine forms.

3. The power ordained for the purpose recognises this, and there is nothing more effective for judging its own subject-matter, when the rest of the soul judges along with it; or perhaps the rest of the soul too pronounces the judgement by fitting the beautiful body to the form in itself and using this for judging beauty as we use a ruler for judging straightness. But how does the bodily agree with that which is before body? How does the architect declare the house outside beautiful by fitting it to the form of house within him? The reason is that the house outside, apart from the stones, is the inner form divided by the external mass of matter, without parts but appearing in many parts. When sense-perception, then, sees the form in bodies binding and mastering the nature opposed to it, which is shapeless, and shape riding gloriously upon other shapes, it gathers into one that which appears dispersed and brings it back and takes it in, now without parts, to the soul's interior and presents it to that which is within as something in tune with it and fitting it and dear to it; just as when a good man sees a trace of virtue in the young, which is in tune with his own inner truth, the sight delights him. And the simple beauty of colour comes about by shape and the mastery of the darkness in matter by the presence of light which is incorporeal and formative power and form. This is why fire itself is more beautiful than all other bodies, because it has the rank of form in relation to the other elements; it is above them in place and is the finest and subtlest of all bodies, being close to the incorporeal. It alone does not admit the others; but the others admit it for it warms them but is not cooled itself; it has colour primarily and all other

things take the form of colour from it. So it shines and glitters as if it was a form. The inferior thing which becomes faint and dull by the fire's light, is not beautiful any more, as not participating in the whole form of colour. The melodies in sounds, too, the imperceptible ones which make the perceptible ones, make the soul conscious of beauty in the same way, showing the same thing in another medium. It is proper to sensible melodies to be measured by numbers, not according to any and every sort of formula but one which serves for the production of form so that it may dominate. So much, then, for the beauties in the realm of sense, images and shadows which, so to speak, sally out and come into matter and adorn it and excite us when they appear.

4. But about the beauties beyond, which it is no more the part of sense to see, but the soul sees them and speaks of them without instruments—we must go up to them and contemplate them and leave sense to stay down below. Just as in the case of the beauties of sense it is impossible for those who have not seen them or grasped their beauty—those born blind, for instance,—to speak about them, in the same way only those can speak about the beauty of ways of life who have accepted the beauty of ways of life and kinds of knowledge and everything else of the sort; and people cannot speak about the splendour of virtue who have never even imagined how fair is the face of justice and moral order; "neither the evening nor the morning star are as fair." But there must be those who see this beauty by that with which the soul sees things of this sort, and when they see it they must be delighted and overwhelmed and excited much more than by those beauties we spoke of before, since now it is true beauty they are grasping. These experiences must occur whenever there is contact with any sort of beautiful thing, wonder and a shock of delight and longing and passion and a happy excitement. One can have these experiences by contact with invisible beauties, and souls do have them, practically all, but particularly those who are more passionately in love with the invisible, just as with bodies all see them, but all are not stung as sharply, but some, who are called lovers, are most of all.

5. Then we must ask the lovers of that which is outside sense "What do you feel about beautiful ways of life, as we call them, and beautiful habits and well-ordered characters and in general about virtuous activities and dispositions and the beauty of souls? What do you feel when you see your own inward beauty? How are you stirred to wild exultation, and long to be with yourselves, gathering your selves together away from your bodies?" For this is what true lovers feel. But what is it which makes them feel like this? Not shape or colour or any size, but soul, without colour itself and possessing a moral order without colour and possessing all the other light of the virtues; you feel like this when you see, in yourself or in someone else, greatness of soul, a righteous life, a pure morality, courage with its noble look, and dignity and modesty advancing in a fearless, calm and unperturbed disposition, and the godlike light of intellect shining upon all this. We love and delight in these qualities, but why do we call them beautiful? They exist and appear to us and he who sees them cannot possibly say anything else except that they are what really exists. What does "really exists" mean? That they exist as beauties. But the argument still requires us to explain why real beings make the soul lovable. What is this kind of glorifying light on all the virtues? Would you like to take the opposites, the uglinesses in soul, and contrast them with the beauties? Perhaps a consideration of what ugliness is and why it appears so will help us to find what we are looking for. Suppose, then, an ugly soul, dissolute and unjust, full of all lusts, and all disturbance, sunk in fears by its cowardice and jealousies by its pettiness, thinking mean and mortal thoughts as far as it thinks at all, altogether distorted, loving impure pleasures, living a life which consists of bodily sensations and finding delight in its ugliness. Shall we not say that its ugliness came to it as a "beauty" brought

in from outside, injuring it and making it impure and "mixed with a great deal of evil," with its life and perceptions no longer pure, but by the admixture of evil living a dim life and diluted with a great deal of death, no longer seeing what a soul ought to see, no longer left in peace in itself because it keeps on being dragged out, and down, and to the dark? Impure, I think, and dragged in every direction towards the objects of sense, with a great deal of bodily stuff mixed into it, consorting much with matter and receiving a form other than its own it has changed by a mixture which makes it worse; just as if anyone gets into mud or filth he does not show any more the beauty which he had; what is seen is what he wiped off on himself from the mud and filth; his ugliness has come from an addition of alien matter, and his business, if he is to be beautiful again, is to wash and clean himself and so be again what he was before. So we shall be right in saying that the soul becomes ugly by mixture and dilution and inclination towards the body and matter. This is the soul's ugliness, not being pure and unmixed, like gold, but full of earthiness; if anyone takes the earthy stuff away the gold is left, and is beautiful, when it is singled out from other things and is alone by itself. In the same way the soul too, when it is separated from the lusts which it has through the body with which it consorted too much, and freed from its other affections, purged of what it gets from being embodied, when it abides alone has put away all the ugliness which came from the other nature.

6. For, as was said in old times, self-control, and courage and every virtue, is a purification, and so is even wisdom itself. This is why the mysteries are right when they say riddlingly that the man who has not been purified will lie in mud when he goes to Hades, because the impure is fond of mud by reason of its badness; just as pigs, with their unclean bodies, like that sort of thing. For what can true self-control be except not keeping company with bodily pleasures, but avoiding them as impure and belonging to something impure? Courage, too, is not being afraid of death. And death is the separation of body and soul; and a man does not fear this if he welcomes the prospect of being alone. Again, greatness of soul is despising the things here and wisdom is an intellectual activity which turns away from the things below and leads the soul to those above. So the soul when it is purified becomes form and formative power, altogether bodiless and intellectual and entirely belonging to the divine, whence beauty springs and all that is akin to it. Soul, then, when it is raised to the level of intellect increases in beauty. Intellect and the things of intellect are its beauty, its own beauty and not another's, since only then [when it is perfectly conformed to intellect] is it truly soul. For this reason it is right to say that the soul's becoming something good and beautiful is its being made like to God, because from Him come beauty and all else which falls to the lot of real beings. Or rather, beautifulness is reality, and the other kind of thing is the ugly, and this same is the primary evil; so for God the qualities of goodness and beauty are the same, or the realities, the good and beauty. So we must follow the same line of enquiry to discover beauty and goodness, and ugliness and evil. And first we must posit beauty which is also the good; from this immediately comes intellect, which is beauty; and soul is given beauty by intellect. Everything else is beautiful by the shaping of soul, the beauties in actions and in ways of life. And soul makes beautiful the bodies which are spoken of as beautiful; for since it is a divine thing and a kind of part of beauty, it makes everything it grasps and masters beautiful, as far as they are capable of participation.

7. So we must ascend again to the good, which every soul desires. Anyone who has seen it knows what I mean when I say that it is beautiful. It is desired as good, and the desire for it is directed to good, and the attainment of it is for those who go up to the higher world and are converted and strip off what we put on in our descent; (just as for those who go up to the celebrations of sacred rites there are purifications, and strippings

off of the clothes they wore before, and going up naked) until, passing in the ascent all that is alien to the God, one sees with one's self alone That alone, simple, single and pure, from which all depends and to which all look and are and live and think for it is cause of life and mind and being. If anyone sees it, what passion will he feel, what longing in his desire to be united with it, what a shock of delight! The man who has not seen it may desire it as good, but he who has seen it glories in its beauty and is full of wonder and delight, enduring a shock which causes no hurt, loving with true passion and piercing longing; he laughs at all other loves and despises what he thought beautiful before; it is like the experience of those who have met appearances of gods or spirits and do not any more appreciate as they did the beauty of other bodies. "What then are we to think, if anyone contemplates the absolute beauty which exists pure by itself, uncontaminated by flesh or body, not in earth or heaven, that it may keep its purity?" All these other things are external additions and mixtures and not primary, but derived from it. If then one sees That which provides for all and remains by itself and gives to all but receives nothing into itself, if he abides in the contemplation of this kind of beauty and rejoices in being made like it, how can he need any other beauty? For this, since it is beauty most of all, and primary beauty, makes its lovers beautiful and lovable. Here the greatest, the ultimate contest is set before our souls; all our toil and trouble is for this, not to be left without a share in the best of visions. The man who attains this is blessed in seeing that "blessed sight," and he who fails to attain it has failed utterly. A man has not failed if he fails to win beauty of colours or bodies, or power or office or kingship even, but if he fails to win this and only this. For this he should give up the attainment of kingship and of rule over all earth and sea and sky, if only by leaving and overlooking them he can turn to That and see.

8. But how shall we find the way? What method can we devise? How can one see the "inconceivable beauty" which stays within in the holy sanctuary and does not come out where the profane may see it? Let him who can, follow and come within, and leave outside the sight of his eyes and not turn back to the bodily splendours which he saw before. When he sees the beauty in bodies he must not run after them; we must know that they are images, traces, shadows, and hurry away to that which they image. For if a man runs to the image and wants to seize it as if it was the reality (like a beautiful reflection playing on the water, which some story somewhere, I think, said riddlingly a man wanted to catch and sank down into the stream and disappeared) then this man who clings to beautiful bodies and will not let them go, will, like the man in the story, but in soul, not in body, sink down into the dark depths where intellect has no delight, and stay blind in Hades, consorting with shadows there and here. This would be truer advice "Let us fly to our dear country." What then is our way of escape, and how are we to find it? We shall put out to sea, as Odysseus did, from the witch Circe or Calypso—as the poet says (I think with a hidden meaning)—and was not content to stay though he had delights of the eyes and lived among much beauty of sense. Our country from which we came is there, our Father is there. How shall we travel to it, where is our way of escape? We cannot get there on foot; for our feet only carry us everywhere in this world, from one country to another. You must not get ready a carriage, either, or a boat. Let all these things go, and do not look. Shut your eyes, and change to and wake another way of seeing, which everyone has but few use.

9. And what does this inner sight see? When it is just awakened it is not at all able to look at the brilliance before it. So that the soul must be trained, first of all to look at beautiful ways of life then at beautiful works, not those which the arts produce, but the works of men who have a name for goodness: then look at the souls of the people who produce the beautiful works. How then can you see the sort of beauty a good soul

has? Go back into yourself and look; and if you do not yet see yourself beautiful, then, just as someone making a statue which has to be beautiful cuts away here and polishes there and makes one part smooth and clears another till he has given his statue a beautiful face, so you too must cut away excess and straighten the crooked and clear the dark and make it bright, and never stop "working on your statue" till the divine glory of virtue shines out on you, till you see "self-mastery enthroned upon its holy seat." If you have become this, and see it, and are at home with yourself in purity, with nothing hindering you from becoming in this way one, with no inward mixture of anything else, but wholly yourself, nothing but true light, not measured by dimensions, or bounded by shape into littleness, or expanded to size by unboundedness, but everywhere unmeasured, because greater than all measure and superior to all quantity; when you see that you have become this, then you have become sight; you can trust yourself then; you have already ascended and need no one to show you; concentrate your gaze and see. This alone is the eye that sees the great beauty. But if anyone comes to the sight blear-eyed with wickedness, and unpurified, or weak and by his cowardice unable to look at what is very bright, he sees nothing, even if someone shows him what is there and possible to see. For one must come to the sight with a seeing power made akin and like to what is seen. No eye ever saw the sun without becoming sun-like, nor can a soul see beauty without becoming beautiful. You must become first all godlike and all beautiful if you intend to see God and beauty. First the soul will come in its ascent to intellect and there will know the Forms, all beautiful, and will affirm that these, the Ideas, are beauty; for all things are beautiful by these, by the products and essence of intellect. That which is beyond this we call the nature of the Good, which holds beauty as a screen before it. So in a loose and general way of speaking the Good is the primary beauty; but if one distinguishes the intelligibles [from the Good] one will say that the place of the Forms is the intelligible beauty, but the Good is That which is beyond, the "spring and origin" of beauty; or one will place the Good and the primal beauty on the same level in any case, however, beauty is in the intelligible world.

Augustine
354–430

Aurelius Augustinus, Saint Augustine, was born of a Christian mother and a pagan father in Thagaste, a small town in what is now Algeria, North Africa. In many ways his family's mixed religious background represented the crumbling Roman Empire. While the influence of Christianity had grown since Emperor Constantine's edict of religious toleration in 313, there were still many rivals to his mother's faith.

As a boy, Augustine showed intellectual promise, and so at seventeen he was sent to Carthage to study rhetoric. While there, Augustine found philosophy, rejected Christianity, took a mistress (who bore him a son), and began to investigate some of the religions of the time. He turned first to the followers of the prophet Mani—the Manichaeans. Mani was a third-century prophet who called himself "the apostle of God." He developed the ancient Persian teaching of Zoroaster (or Zarathustra) that said there are two great forces in the world, one good and one evil, and that neither can overcome the other. Living a life of sensual indulgence, Augustine took comfort from the idea that God could no more overcome evil in the universe than Augustine could in his own life.

In 375 Augustine returned to Thagaste to begin teaching rhetoric. When his mother, Monica (later sainted for her perseverance in prayer for her son), discovered that he had become a Manichaean, she expelled him from her house. Finding Thagaste boring, and his mother difficult,

51

Augustine returned to Carthage. Over the next seven years he grew disenchanted with Manichaeism. In 384 he left Carthage for teaching positions in Rome and finally Milan. In Milan Augustine encountered the writings of Plotinus and was converted to Neoplatonism. At the same time he came into contact with a group of Christians led by the Bishop of Milan, Ambrose. Under the influence of this group, Augustine was forced to reconsider his earlier rejection of Christianity. In 386, while sitting in a friend's garden, he heard what he thought was a child's voice saying, "Pick it up and read it; pick it up and read it." Augustine later recounted what happened:

> So I quickly returned to the bench . . . for there I had put down the apostle's book when I had left there. I snatched it up, opened it, and in silence read the paragraph on which my eyes first fell: "Not in rioting and drunkenness, not in chambering and wantonness, not in strife and envying, but put on the Lord Jesus Christ, and make no provision for the flesh to fulfill the lusts thereof." I wanted to read no further, nor did I need to. For instantly, as the sentence ended, there was infused in my heart something like the light of full certainty and all my gloom of doubt vanished away.

The following year Augustine was baptized and returned to Africa to found a monastic community. Within two years he left the cloister, answering the church's call to priesthood. He served as a priest, and later as bishop, in the African town of Hippo for the rest of his life.

*   *   *

While at Hippo, Augustine wrote voluminously on a variety of theological and philosophical topics. Many of his works sought to define exactly what was and was not "Christian." His doctrinal works, such as *The Trinity,* established Christian essentials, while his polemical works directed against "heresies" (positions unacceptable to the church) outlined what was not admissable. Augustine fought two major heresies: the Pelagian and the Donatist. The Pelagians held that sin had affected only Adam, that the will is free from sin, and that God's grace is given on the basis of human merit. The Donatists maintained that the sacraments were only effective when administered by a priest in a state of grace. Augustine argued passionately that both heresies put too much emphasis on human ability and not enough on God's grace.

Augustine's most famous work, the *Confessions,* invented the genre of introspective autobiography. The *Confessions* are full of both psychological and spiritual insight and so can be read as either devotional tract or philosophical essay. Books I through IX are Augustine's life story from the perspective of Christian conversion (detailed in Book VIII). As Augustine reflects on his life, he sees both his sinfulness and his intellectual aimlessness apart from God's grace. He also gives early glimpses of his mature epistemological position that God must illumine the mind in order for an individual to gain wisdom. Following his conversion, Augustine continues to seek understanding—though now firmly founded on faith. Books X–XII illustrate this "faith seeking understanding," as Augustine examines the questions of memory, time, and creation. Book XI, reprinted here complete, examines the nature of time and God's relation to it. Showing it is difficult to explain what God was doing before creation, Augustine argues that God must be "outside" time in an eternal present. This view of God as timelessly eternal was developed by Boethius and is still influential today (see suggested readings that follow). I am pleased to offer this selection in the outstanding new translation by Henry Chadwick.

Among Augustine's early writings, *On the Free Choice of the Will* is one of the most interesting and provocative. Written against the Manichaeans, the book was later used by the Pelagians to support their view of radical free will. Augustine was forced to point out in his *Retractions* that while he had argued that humans can fall into sin of their own free will, he had held that they cannot rise up to relationship with God on the same basis. Book II, given here complete in the Robert P. Russell translation, includes Augustine's early theory of the will, his theory of knowledge, and his proof of God's existence on the basis of truth.

Of Augustine's many other works, *The City of God* is by far the most famous. During the fourth century, Christianity had become the state religion of the Roman Empire; in 410 Rome fell to the Visigoths, and the eternal city was sacked for the first time. Naturally, many considered the sack of Rome a punishment for the betrayal of old Roman religion. Augustine wrote *The City of God* to answer this charge and in so doing he developed yet another first: the first philosophy of history. Rather than a cycle of repeated events, Augustine described history as being linear—from creation to consummation and final judgment. As history moves from beginning to end, we can observe two cities: the City of God, consisting of those who love God, and the City of Man, those who love self rather than God. The first selection, from Book VIII of this work, gives Augustine's history of philosophy and includes his favorable appraisal of Plato.

The second selection given here, from Book XII, explains the origin of evil and of the City of Man. Augustine begins by insisting, against the Manichaeans, that there is no being capable of opposing God: God is all-powerful. But, despite the presence of evil, God is also all-good and everything God created is good. Evil arises when a moral agent (angel or human) wills to love a lesser good (self) rather than the highest good (God). There is no evil "thing" to choose—there is only evil choosing. This leads to the question of what caused the will to choose evilly—a question Augustine says cannot be answered.

The final selection, from Book XIX, presents Augustine's treatise on peace: both earthly peace and the heavenly peace of the City of God. These three selections have been ably translated by Gerald G. Walsh, Daniel J. Honan, and Grace Monahan.

Augustine's impact has been enormous. Medieval Catholic philosophers, such as Anselm and Thomas Aquinas, as well as Protestant reformers, such as Luther and Calvin, wanted to be Augustine's heirs. Many contemporary Christian thinkers still appeal to Augustine's ideas, such as his defense of grace and his explanation of evil. But Augustine's influence has not been limited to theologians and philosophers of religion. Ludwig Wittgenstein began his *Philosophical Investigations* by examining Augustine's theory of language, and Bertrand Russell claimed Augustine's theory of time superior even to that of Kant. Echoes of Augustine's understanding of history as the unfolding of divine purpose can be heard in the writings of Hegel, while Augustine's idea that some kind of faith must precede fruitful understanding has been adapted by thinkers in such fields as the sociology of knowledge and philosophy of science.

* * *

The best general account of Augustine's philosophy remains Étienne Gilson, *The Christian Philosophy of Saint Augustine,* translated by L.E.M. Lynch (New York: Random House, 1960); while Peter Brown, *Augustine of Hippo: A Biography* (Berkeley: University of California Press, 1967), provides an excellent biography. For brief introductions to Augustine's life and thought, see R.A. Markus, "Augustine," in D.J. O'Connor, *A Critical History of Western Philosophy* (New York: Free Press, 1964); and Henry Chadwick, *Augustine* (Oxford: Oxford University Press, 1986). For more extensive discussions of Augustine's thought, see Robert E. Meagher, *An Introduction to Augustine* (New York: New York University Press, 1978); and Christopher Kirwan, *Augustine* (London: Routledge, 1989). J.N. Figgis, *The Political Aspects of St. Augustine's City of God* (London: Longmans, Green, 1921); Ronald H. Nash, *The Light of the Mind: St. Augustine's Theory of Knowledge* (Lexington: University Press of Kentucky, 1969); and R.A. Markus, *Saeculum: History and Society in the Theology of St. Augustine* (Cambridge: Cambridge University Press, 1970), deal with the specialized topics indicated by their respective titles. For collections of essays, see M.C. D'Arcy et al., *Saint Augustine* (New York: Meridian, 1957), and R.A. Markus, ed., *Augustine: A Collection of Critical Essays* (Garden City, NY: Anchor, Doubleday, 1972).

CONFESSIONS (in part)

BOOK XI—TIME AND ETERNITY

i (1) Lord, eternity is yours, so you cannot be ignorant of what I tell you. Your vision of occurrences in time is not temporally conditioned. Why then do I set before you an ordered account of so many things? It is certainly not through me that you know them. But I am stirring up love for you in myself and in those who read this, so that we may all say "Great is the Lord and highly worthy to be praised" (Ps. 47:1). I have already affirmed this and will say it again: I tell my story for love of your love. We pray, and yet the truth says "Your Father knows what you need before you ask him" (Matt. 6:8). Therefore I lay bare my feelings towards you, by confessing to you my miseries and your mercies to us (Ps. 32:22), so that the deliverance you have begun may be complete. So I may cease to be wretched in myself and may find happiness in you. For you have called us to be "poor in spirit," meek, mournful, hungering and thirsting for righteousness, merciful, pure in heart, and peacemakers (Matt. 5:3–9).

See, the long story I have told to the best of my ability and will responds to your prior will that I should make confession to you, my Lord God. For "you are good, for your mercy is for ever" (Ps. 117:1).

ii (2) But when shall I be capable of proclaiming by "the tongue of my pen" (Ps. 44:2) all your exhortations and all your terrors and consolations and directives, by which you brought me to preach your word and dispense your sacrament to your people? And if I have the capacity to proclaim this in an ordered narrative, yet the drops of

Saint Augustine, *Confessions,* Book XI, translated by Henry Chadwick (Oxford: Oxford University Press, 1991). Reprinted by permission of Oxford University Press.

time are too precious to me. For a long time past I have been burning to meditate in your law (Ps. 38:4) and confess to you what I know of it and what lies beyond my powers—the first elements granted by your illumination and the remaining areas of darkness in my understanding—until weakness is swallowed up by strength. I am reluctant to expend on any other subject those hours which I find free of the necessities for restoring the body, of intellectual work, and of the service which we owe to people or that which we render to them when under no obligation.

(3) Lord my God, "hear my prayer" (Ps. 60:2), may your mercy attend to my longing which burns not for my personal advantage but desires to be of use in love to the brethren. You see in my heart that this is the case. Let me offer you in sacrifice the service of my thinking and my tongue, and grant that which I am to offer, "for I am poor and needy" (Ps. 65:15; 85:1). You are "rich to all who call upon you" (Rom. 10:12). You have no cares but take care of us. Circumcise my lips (cf. Exod. 6:12), inwardly and outwardly, from all rashness and falsehood. May your scriptures be my pure delight, so that I am not deceived in them and do not lead others astray in interpreting them. "Lord, listen and have mercy" (Ps. 26:7; 85:3), Lord my God, light of the blind and strength of the weak—and constantly also light of those who can see and strength of the mighty: Listen to my soul and hear it crying from the depth. For if your ears are not present also in the depth, where shall we go? To whom shall we cry? "The day is yours and the night is yours" (Ps. 73:16). At your nod the moments fly by. From them grant us space for our meditations on the secret recesses of your law, and do not close the gate to us as we knock. It is not for nothing that by your will so many pages of scripture are opaque and obscure. These forests are not without deer which recover their strength in them and restore themselves by walking and feeding, by resting and ruminating (Ps. 28:9). O Lord, bring me to perfection (Ps. 16:5) and reveal to me the meaning of these pages. See, your voice is my joy, your voice is better than a wealth of pleasures (Ps. 118:22). Grant what I love; for I love it, and that love was your gift. Do not desert your gifts, and do not despise your plant as it thirsts. Let me confess to you what I find in your books. "Let me hear the voice of praise" (Ps. 25:7) and drink you, and let me consider "wonderful things out of your law" (Ps. 118:18)—from the beginning in which you made heaven and earth until the perpetual reign with you in your heavenly city (Rev. 5:10; 21:2).

(4) "Lord have mercy upon me and listen to my desire" (Ps. 26:7). For I do not think my longing is concerned with earthly things, with gold and silver and precious stones, or with fine clothes or honours and positions of power or fleshly pleasures or even with the body's necessities in this life of our pilgrimage. They are all things added to us as we seek your kingdom and your righteousness (Matt. 6:33). My God, look upon the object of my desire (cf. Ps. 9:14). "The wicked have told me of delights, but they are not allowed by your law, Lord" (Ps. 118:85). See Father: look and see and give your approval. May it please you that in the sight of your mercy (Ps. 18:15) I may find grace before you, so that to me as I knock (Matt. 7:7) may be opened the hidden meaning of your words. I make my prayer through our Lord Jesus Christ your Son, "the man of your right hand, the Son of man whom you have strengthened" (Ps. 79:18) to be mediator between yourself and us. By him you sought us when we were not seeking you (Rom. 10:20). But you sought us that we should seek you, your Word by whom you made all things including myself, your only Son by whom you have called to adoption the people who believe (Gal. 4:5), myself among them. I make my prayer to you through him "who sits at your right hand and intercedes to you for us" (Rom. 8:34). "In him are hidden all the treasures of wisdom and knowledge" (Col. 2:3). For those treasures I search in your books.

Moses wrote of him (John 5:46). He himself said this; this is the declaration of the Truth.

iii (5) May I hear and understand how in the beginning you made heaven and earth (Gen. 1:1). Moses wrote this. He wrote this and went his way, passing out of this world from you to you. He is not now before me, but if he were, I would clasp him and ask him and through you beg him to explain to me the creation. I would concentrate my bodily ears to hear the sounds breaking forth from his mouth. If he spoke Hebrew, he would in vain make an impact on my sense of hearing, for the sounds would not touch my mind at all. If he spoke Latin, I would know what he meant. Yet how would I know whether or not he was telling me the truth? If I did know this, I could not be sure of it from him. Within me, within the lodging of my thinking, there would speak a truth which is neither Hebrew nor Greek nor Latin nor any barbarian tongue and which uses neither mouth nor tongue as instruments and utters no audible syllables. It would say: "What he is saying is true." And I being forthwith assured would say with confidence to the man possessed by you: "What you say is true." But since I cannot question him, I ask you who filled him when he declared what is true; you my God I ask. "Spare my sins" (Job 14:16). You have granted to your servant to utter these things; grant also to me the power to understand them.

iv (6) See, heaven and earth exist, they cry aloud that they are made, for they suffer change and variation. But in anything which is not made and yet is, there is nothing which previously was not present. To be what once was not the case is to be subject to change and variation. They also cry aloud that they have not made themselves: "The manner of our existence shows that we are made. For before we came to be, we did not exist to be able to make ourselves." And the voice with which they speak is self-evidence. You, Lord, who are beautiful, made them for they are beautiful. You are good, for they are good. You are, for they are. Yet they are not beautiful or good or possessed of being in the sense that you their Maker are. In comparison with you they are deficient in beauty and goodness and being. Thanks to you, we know this; and yet our knowledge is ignorance in comparison with yours.

v (7) How did you make heaven and earth, and what machine did you use for so vast an operation? You were not like a craftsman who makes one physical object out of another by an act of personal choice in his mind, which has the power to impose the form which by an inner eye it can see within itself. This capacity it has only because you have so made it. He imposes form on what already exists and possesses being, such as earth or stone or wood or gold or any material of that sort. And these materials exist only because you had first made them. By your creation the craftsman has a body, a mind by which he commands its members, material out of which he makes something, a skill by which he masters his art and sees inwardly what he is making outwardly. From your creation come the bodily senses which he uses to translate his mental concept into the material objects he is making, and to report back to the mind what has been made, so that the mind within may deliberate with the truth presiding over it to consider whether the work has been well done. All these praise you, the creator of everything. But how do you make them? The way, God, in which you made heaven and earth was not that you made them either in heaven or on earth. Nor was it in air or in water, for these belong to heaven and earth. Nor did you make the universe within the framework of the universe. There was nowhere for it to be made before it was brought into existence. Nor did you have any tool in your hand to make heaven and earth. How could you obtain anything you had not made as a tool for making something? What is it for something to be unless it is because you are? Therefore you spoke and they were made, and by your word you made them (Ps. 32:9,6).

God in Act of Creation, from a thirteenth-century French Bible. In the
Confessions, Augustine argues that God created the world *ex nihilo* (out
of nothing) and that God is outside of time. *(The Bettmann Archive)*

vi (8) But how did you speak? Surely not in the way a voice came out of the cloud saying, "This is my beloved Son" (Matt. 17:5). That voice is past and done with; it began and is ended. The syllables sounded and have passed away, the second after the first, the third after the second, and so on in order until, after all the others, the last one came, and after the last silence followed. Therefore it is clear and evident that the utterance came through the movement of some created thing, serving your eternal will but itself temporal. And these your words, made for temporal succession, were reported by the external ear to the judicious mind whose internal ear is disposed lo hear your eternal word. But that mind would compare these words, sounding in time, with your eternal word in silence, and say: "It is very different, the difference is enormous. The sounds are far inferior to me, and have no being, because they are fleeting and transient. But the word of my God is superior to me and abides for ever" (Isa. 40:8). If therefore it was with words which sound and pass away that you said that heaven and earth should be made, and if this was how you made heaven and earth, then a created entity belonging to the physical realm existed prior to heaven and earth; and that utterance took time to deliver, and involved temporal changes. However, no physical entity existed before heaven and earth; at least if any such existed, you had made it without using a transient utterance, which could then be used as a basis for another transient utterance, declaring that heaven and earth be made. Whatever it might have been which became the basis for such an utterance, unless it was created by you, it could not exist. Therefore for the creation of a physical entity to become the basis for those words, what kind of word would you have used?

vii (9) You call us, therefore, to understand the Word, God who is with you God (John 1:1). That word is spoken eternally, and by it all things are uttered eternally. It is not the case that what was being said comes to an end, and something else is then said, so that everything is uttered in a succession with a conclusion, but everything is said in the simultaneity of eternity. Otherwise time and change would already exist, and there would not be a true eternity and true immortality. This I know, my God, and give thanks. I know and confess it to you, Lord, and everyone who is not ungrateful for assured truth knows it with me and blesses you. We know this, Lord, we know. A thing dies and comes into being inasmuch as it is not what it was and becomes what it was not. No element of your word yields place or succeeds to something else, since it is truly immortal and eternal. And so by the Word coeternal with yourself, you say all that you say in simultaneity and eternity, and whatever you say will come about does come about. You do not cause it to exist other than by speaking. Yet not all that you cause to exist by speaking is made in simultaneity and eternity.

viii (10) Why, I ask, Lord my God? In some degree I see it, but how to express it I do not know, unless to say that everything which begins to be and ceases to be begins and ends its existence at that moment when, in the eternal reason where nothing begins or ends, it is known that it is right for it to begin and end. This reason is your Word, which is also the Beginning in that it also speaks to us. Thus in the gospel the Word speaks through the flesh, and this sounded externally in human ears, so that it should be believed and sought inwardly, found in the eternal truth where the Master who alone is good (Matt. 19:16) teaches all his disciples. There, Lord, I hear your voice speaking to me, for one who teaches us speaks to us, but one who does not teach us, even though he may speak, does not speak to us. Who is our teacher except the reliable truth? Even when we are instructed through some mutable creature, we are led to reliable truth when we are learning truly by standing still and listening to him. We then "rejoice with joy because of the voice of the bridegroom" (John 3:29), and give ourselves to the source whence we have our being. And in this way he is the Beginning because, unless he were constant, there would be no fixed point to which we could return. But when we return from error, it is by knowing that we return. He teaches us so that we may know; for he is the Beginning, and he speaks to us.

ix (11) In this Beginning, God, you made heaven and earth, in your Word, in your Son, in your power, in your wisdom, in your truth speaking in a wonderful way and making in a wonderful way. Who can comprehend it? Who will give an account of it in words? What is the light which shines right through me and strikes my heart without hurting? It fills me with terror and burning love: with terror inasmuch as I am utterly other than it, with burning love in that I am akin to it. Wisdom, wisdom it is which shines right through me, cutting a path through the cloudiness which returns to cover me as I fall away under the darkness and the load of my punishments. For "my strength is weakened by poverty" (Ps. 30:11), so that I cannot maintain my goodness until you, Lord, who "have become merciful to all my iniquities, also heal all my sicknesses." You will redeem my life from corruption and crown me with mercy and compassion, and satisfy my longing with good things, in that my youth will be renewed like an eagle's (Ps. 102:3–5). For "by hope we are saved," and we await your promises in patience (Rom. 8:24–5). Let the person who can hear you speaking within listen. Confident on the ground of your inspired utterance, I will cry out: "How magnificent are your works, Lord, you have made all things in wisdom" (Ps. 103:24). Wisdom is the beginning, and in that beginning you made heaven and earth.

x (12) See how full of old errors are those who say to us: "What was God doing before he made heaven and earth? If he was unoccupied," they say, "and doing nothing, why does he not always remain the same for ever, just as before creation he abstained from work? For if in God any new development took place and any new intention, so as to make a creation which he had never made before, how then can there be a true eternity in which a will, not there previously, comes into existence? For God's will is not a creature, but is prior to the created order, since nothing would be created unless the Creator's will preceded it. Therefore God's will belongs to his very substance. If in the substance of God anything has come into being which was not present before, that substance cannot truthfully be called eternal. But if it was God's everlasting will that the created order exist, why is not the creation also everlasting?"

xi (13) People who say this do not yet understand you, O wisdom of God, light of minds. They do not yet understand how things were made which came to be through you and in you. They attempt to taste eternity when their heart is still flitting about in the realm where things change and have a past and future; it is still "vain" (Ps. 5:10). Who can lay hold on the heart and give it fixity, so that for some little moment it may be stable, and for a fraction of time may grasp the splendour of a constant eternity? Then it may compare eternity with temporal successiveness which never has any constancy, and will see there is no comparison possible. It will see that a long time is long only because constituted of many successive movements which cannot be simultaneously extended. In the eternal, nothing is transient, but the whole is present. But no time is wholly present. It will see that all past time is driven backwards by the future, and all future time is the consequent of the past, and all past and future are created and set on their course by that which is always present. Who will lay hold on the human heart to make it still, so that it can see how eternity, in which there is neither future nor past, stands still and dictates future and past times? Can my hand have the strength for this? (Gen. 31:29). Can the hand of my mouth by mere speech achieve so great a thing?

xii (14) This is my reply to anyone who asks: "What was God doing before he made heaven and earth?" My reply is not that which someone is said to have given as a joke to evade the force of the question. He said: "He was preparing hells for people who inquire into profundities." It is one thing to laugh, another to see the point at issue, and this reply I reject. I would have preferred him to answer "I am ignorant of what I do not know" rather than reply so as to ridicule someone who has asked a deep question and to win approval for an answer which is a mistake.

No, I say that you, our God, are the Creator of every created being, and assuming that by "heaven and earth" is meant every created thing I boldly declare: Before God made heaven and earth, he was not making anything. If he was making anything, it could only be something created. I only wish that other useful matters which I long to be sure about I could know with an assurance equal to that with which I know that no created being was made before any creature came into being.

xiii (15) If, however, someone's mind is flitting and wandering over images of past times, and is astonished that you, all powerful, all creating, and all sustaining God, artificer of heaven and earth, abstained for unnumbered ages from this work before you actually made it, he should wake up and take note that his surprise rests on a mistake. How would innumerable ages pass, which you yourself had not made? You are the originator and creator of all ages. What times existed which were not brought into being by you? Or how could they pass if they never had existence? Since, therefore, you are the cause of all times, if any time existed before you made heaven and earth, how can anyone say that you abstained from working? You have made time itself. Time could not elapse before you made time. But if time did not exist before heaven and earth, why do people ask what you were then doing? There was no "then" when there was no time.

(16) It is not in time that you precede times. Otherwise you would not precede all times. In the sublimity of an eternity which is always in the present, you are before all things past and transcend all things future, because they are still to come, and when they have come they are past. "But you are the same and your years do not fail" (Ps. 101:28). Your "years" neither go nor come. Ours come and go so that all may come in succession. All your "years" subsist in simultaneity, because they do not change; those going away are not thrust out by those coming in. But the years which are ours will not all be until all years have ceased to be. Your "years" are "one day" (Ps. 89:4; 2 Pet. 3:8), and your "day" is not any and every day but Today, because your Today does not yield to a tomorrow, nor did it follow on a yesterday. Your Today is eternity. So you begat one coeternal with you, to whom you said: "Today I have begotten you" (Ps. 2:7; Heb. 5:5). You created all times and you exist before all times. Nor was there any time when time did not exist.

xiv (17) There was therefore no time when you had not made something, because you made time itself. No times are coeternal with you since you are permanent. If they were permanent, they would not be times.

What is time? Who can explain this easily and briefly? Who can comprehend this even in thought so as to articulate the answer in words? Yet what do we speak of, in our familiar everyday conversation, more than of time? We surely know what we mean when we speak of it. We also know what is meant when we hear someone else talking about it. What then is time? Provided that no one asks me, I know. If I want to explain it to an inquirer, I do not know. But I confidently affirm myself to know that if nothing passes away, there is no past time, and if nothing arrives, there is no future time, and if nothing existed there would be no present time. Take the two tenses, past and future. How can they "be" when the past is not now present and the future is not yet present? Yet if the present were always present, it would not pass into the past: it would not be time but eternity. If then, in order to be time at all, the present is so made that it passes into the past, how can we say that this present also "is"? The cause of its being is that it will cease to be. So indeed we cannot truly say that time exists except in the sense that it tends towards non-existence.

xv (18) Nevertheless we speak of "a long time" and "a short time," and it is only of the past or the future that we say this. Of the past we speak of "a long time," when, for example, it is more than a hundred years ago. "A long time" in the future may mean a hundred years ahead. By "a short time ago" we would mean, say, ten days back, and "a short time ahead" might mean "in ten days' time." But how can something be long or short which does not exist? For the past now has no existence and the future is not yet. So we ought not to say of the past "It is long," but "it was long," and of the future "it will be long." My Lord, my light, does not your truth mock humanity at this point? This time past which was long, was it long when it was past or when it was still present? It could be long only when it existed to be long. Once past, it no longer was. Therefore it could not be long if it had entirely ceased to exist.

Therefore let us not say "The time past was long." For we cannot discover anything to be long when, after it has become past, it has ceased to be. But let us say "That time once present was long" because it was long at the time when it was present. For it had not yet passed away into non-existence. It existed so as to be able to be long. But after it had passed away, it simultaneously ceased to be long because it ceased to be.

(19) Human soul, let us see whether present time can be long. To you the power is granted to be aware of intervals of time, and to measure them. What answer will you give me? Are a hundred years in the present a long time? Consider first whether a hundred years can be present. For if the first year of the series is current, it is present, but ninety-nine are future, and so do not yet exist. If the second year is current, one is already past, the second is present, the remainder lie in the future. And so between the extremes, whatever year of this century we assume to be present, there will be some years before it which lie in the past, some in the future to come after it. It follows that a century could never be present.

Consider then whether if a single year is current, that can be present. If in this year the first month is current, the others lie in the future; if the second, then the first lies in the past and the rest do not yet exist. Therefore even a current year is not entirely present; and if it is not entirely present, it is not a year which is present. A year is twelve months, of which any month which is current is present; the others are either past or future. Moreover, not even a month which is current is present, but one day. If the first day, the others are future; if the last day, the others are past; any intermediary day falls between past and future.

(20) See—present time, which alone we find capable of being called long, is contracted to the space of hardly a single day. But let us examine that also; for not even one day is entirely present. All the hours of night and day add up to twenty-four. The first of them has the others in the future, the last has them in the past. Any hour between these has past hours before it, future hours after it. One hour is itself constituted of fugitive moments. Whatever part of it has flown away is past. What remains to it is future. If we can think of some bit of time which cannot be divided into even the smallest instantaneous moments, that alone is what we can call "present." And this time flies so quickly from future into past that it is an interval with no duration. If it has duration, it is divisible into past and future. But the present occupies no space.

Where then is the time which we call long? Is it future? We do not really mean "It is long," since it does not yet exist to be long, but we mean it will be long. When will it be long? If it will then still lie in the future, it will not be long, since it will not yet exist to be long. But if it will be long at the time when, out of the future which does not yet exist, it begins to have being and will become present fact, so that it has the potentiality to be long, the present cries out in words already used that it cannot be long.

xvi (21) Nevertheless, Lord, we are conscious of intervals of time, and compare them with each other, and call some longer, others shorter. We also measure how much longer or shorter one period is than another, and answer that the one is twice or three times as much as the other, or that the two periods are equal. Moreover, we are measuring times which are past when our perception is the basis of measurement. But who can measure the past which does not now exist or the future which does not yet exist, unless perhaps someone dares to assert that he can measure what has no existence? At the moment when time is passing, it can be perceived and measured. But when it has passed and is not present, it cannot be.

xvii (22) I am investigating, Father, not making assertions. My God, protect me and rule me (Ps. 22:1; 27:9). Who will tell me that there are not three times, past, present, and future, as we learnt when children and as we have taught children, but only the present, because the other two have no existence? Or do they exist in the sense that, when the present emerges from the future, time comes out of some secret store, and then recedes into some secret place when the past comes out of the present? Where did those who sang prophecies see these events if they do not yet exist? To see what has no existence is impossible. And those who narrate past history would surely not be telling a true story if they did not discern events by their soul's insight. If the past were non-existent, it could not be discerned at all. Therefore both future and past events exist.

xviii (23) Allow me, Lord, to take my investigation further. My hope, let not my attention be distracted. If future and past events exist, I want to know where they are. If I have not the strength to discover the answer, at least I know that wherever they are, they are not there as future or past, but as present. For if there also they are future, they will not yet be there. If there also they are past, they are no longer there. Therefore, wherever they are, whatever they are, they do not exist except in the present. When a true narrative of the past is related, the memory produces not the actual events which have passed away but words conceived from images of them, which they fixed in the mind like imprints as they passed through the senses. Thus my boyhood, which is no longer, lies in past time which is no longer. But when I am recollecting and telling my story, I am looking on its image in present time, since it is still in my memory. Whether a similar cause is operative in predictions of the future, in the sense that images of realities which do not yet exist are presented as already in existence, I confess, my God, I do not know. At least I know this much: we frequently think out in advance our future actions, and that premeditation is in the present; but the action which we premeditate is not yet in being because it lies in the future. But when we have embarked on the action and what we were premeditating begins to be put into effect, then that action will have existence, since then it will be not future but present.

(24) Whatever may be the way in which the hidden presentiment of the future is known, nothing can be seen if it does not exist. Now that which already exists is not future but present. When therefore people speak of knowing the future, what is seen is not events which do not yet exist (that is, they really are future), but perhaps their causes or signs which already exist. In this way, to those who see them they are not future but present, and that is the basis on which the future can be conceived in the mind and made the subject of prediction.

Again, these concepts already exist, and those who predict the future see these concepts as if already present to their minds.

Among a great mass of examples, let me mention one instance. I look at the dawn. I forecast that the sun will rise. What I am looking at is present, what I am forecasting is future. It is not the sun which lies in the future (it already exists) but its rise, which has not yet arrived. Yet unless I were mentally imagining its rise, as now when I am speaking about it, I could not predict it. But the dawn glow which I see in the sky is not sunrise, which it precedes, nor is the imagining of sunrise in my mind the actuality. These are both discerned as present so that the coming sunrise may be foretold.

So future events do not yet exist, and if they are not yet present, they do not exist; and if they have no being, they cannot be seen at all. But they can be predicted from present events which are already present and can be seen.

xix (25) Governor of your creation, what is the way by which you inform souls what lies in the future? For you instructed your prophets. By what method then do you give information about the future—you to whom nothing is future? Is it rather that you inform how to read the future in the light of the present? What does not exist, certainly cannot be the subject of information. This method is far beyond my power of vision. "It is too mighty for me, I cannot attain it" (Ps. 138:6). But it would be in my power with your help if you granted it, sweet light of my uncomprehending eyes.

xx (26) What is by now evident and clear is that neither future nor past exists, and it is inexact language to speak of three times—past, present, and future. Perhaps it would be exact to say: there are three times, a present of things past, a present of things present, a present of things to come. In the soul there are these three aspects of time, and I do not see them anywhere else. The present considering the past is the memory, the present considering the present is immediate awareness, the present considering the future is expectation. If we are allowed to use such language, I see three times, and I admit they are three. Moreover, we may say, There are three times, past, present, and future. This customary way of speaking is incorrect, but it is common usage. Let us accept the usage. I do not object and offer no opposition or criticism, as long as what is said is being understood, namely that neither the future nor the past is now present. There are few usages of everyday speech which are exact, and most of our language is inexact. Yet what we mean is communicated.

xxi (27) A little earlier I observed that we measure past periods of time so that we can say that one period is twice as long as another or equal to it, and likewise of other periods of time which we are capable of measuring and reporting. Therefore, as I was saying, we measure periods of time as they are passing, and if anyone says to me "How do you know?" I reply: I know it because we do measure time and cannot measure what has no being; and past and future have none. But how do we measure present time when it has no extension? It is measured when it passes, but not when it has passed, because then there will be nothing there to measure.

When time is measured, where does it come from, by what route does it pass, and where does it go? It must come out of the future, pass by the present, and go into the past; so it comes from what as yet does not exist, passes through that which lacks extension, and goes into that which is now non-existent. Yet what do we measure but time over some extension? When we speak of lengths of time as single, duple, triple, and equal, or any other temporal relation of this kind, we must be speaking of periods of time possessing extension. In what extension then do we measure time as it is passing? Is it in the future out of which it comes to pass by? No, for we do not measure what does not yet exist. Is it in the present through which it passes? No, for we cannot measure that which has no extension. Is it in the past into which it is moving? No, for we cannot measure what now does not exist.

xxii (28) My mind is on fire to solve this very intricate enigma. Do not shut the door, Lord my God. Good Father, through Christ I beg you, do not shut the door on my longing to understand these things which are both familiar and obscure. Do not prevent me, Lord, from penetrating them and seeing them illuminated by the light of your mercy. Whom shall I ask about them? And to whom but you shall I more profitably confess my incompetence? You are not irritated by the burning zeal with which I study your scriptures. Grant what I love. For I love, and this love was your gift. Grant it, Father. You truly know how to give good gifts to your children (Matt. 7:11). Grant it, since I have undertaken to acquire understanding and "the labour is too much for me" (Ps. 72:16) until you open the way. Through Christ I beg you, in the name of him who is the holy of holy ones, let no one obstruct my inquiry. "I also have believed, and therefore speak" (Ps. 115:1; 2 Cor. 4:13). This is my hope. For this I live "that I may contemplate the delight of the Lord" (Ps. 26:4). "Behold you have made my days subject to ageing" (Ps. 38:6). They pass away, and how I do not know. And we repeatedly speak of time and time, of times and times: "How long ago did he say this?" "How long ago did he do this?" "For how long a time did I fail to see that?" And "These syllables take twice the time of that single, short syllable." We speak in this way, and hear people saying this, and we are understood and we understand. These usages are utterly commonplace and everyday. Yet they are deeply obscure and the discovery of the solution is new.

xxiii (29) I have heard a learned person say that the movements of sun, moon, and stars in themselves constitute time. But I could not agree. Why should not time consist rather of the movement of all physical objects? If the heavenly bodies were to cease and a potter's wheel were revolving, would there be no time by which we could measure its gyrations, and say that its revolutions were equal; or if at one time it moved more slowly and at another time faster, that some rotations took longer, others less? And when we utter these words do not we also speak in time? In our words some syllables are long, others short, in that the sounding of the former requires a longer time, whereas the latter are shorter.

God grant to human minds to discern in a small thing universal truths valid for both small and great matters. There are stars and heavenly luminaries to be "for signs and for times, and for days and for years" (Gen. 1:14). But I would not say that a revolution of that wooden wheel is a day; and that learned friend could not assert that its rotation was not a period of time.

(30) I desire to understand the power and the nature of time, which enables us to measure the motions of bodies and to say that, for instance, this movement requires twice as long as that. I have this question to raise: the word "day" is used not only of the interval of time when the sun is up over the earth, so that day is one thing, night another, but also of the sun's entire circuit from east to west, as when we say "so many days have passed" where "so many days" includes the nights, and the periods of night-time are not counted separately. So a complete day is marked by the movement and circuit of the sun from east to west. My question then is whether the sun's movement itself constitutes the day? or the actual interval of time during which it is accomplished? or both?

In the first instance, it would still be a day even if the sun completed its course in the space of a single hour. In the second case, it would not be a day if from one sunrise to the next so short an interval as one hour passed, but only if the sun completed a day of twenty-four hours. In the third case—a day being both the circuit and the time taken—it could not be called a day if the sun completed its entire circuit in an hour, nor if the sun ceased to move and the length of time passed were the twenty-four hours normally taken by the sun in completing its entire course from sunrise to sunrise. I will not, therefore, now investigate what it is which we call a day, but the nature of time by which we can measure the sun's circuit and by which we might say that, if all was accomplished in twelve hours, the sun had completed its course in half the usual time. I ask what time is when we make a comparison and say that one interval is single and another double, even if the sun were to make its transit from east to west sometimes in single time, sometimes in twice the time.

Let no one tell me then that time is the movements of heavenly bodies. At a man's prayer the sun stood still, so that a battle could be carried through to victory (Josh. 10:12 ff.): the sun stopped but time went on. That battle was fought and completed in its own space of time such as was sufficient for it. I therefore see that time is some kind of extension. But do I really see that? Or do I imagine that I see? You, light and truth, will show me.

xxiv (31) Do you command me to concur if someone says time is the movement of a physical entity? You do not. For I learn that no body can be moved except in time. You tell me so, but I do not learn that the actual movement of a body constitutes time. That is not what you tell me. For when a body is moved, it is by time that I measure the duration of the movement, from the moment it begins until it ends. Unless I have observed the point when it begins, and if its movement is continuous so that I cannot observe when it ceases, I am unable to measure except for the period from the beginning to the end of my observation. If my observing lasts for a considerable time, I can only report that a long time passed, but not precisely how much. When we say how much, we are making a comparison—as, for example, "This period was of the same length as that," or "This period was twice as long as that," or some such relationship.

If, however, we have been able to note the points in space from which and to which a moving body passes, or the parts of a body when it is spinning on its axis, then we can say how much time the movement of the body or its parts required to move from one point to another. It follows that a body's movement is one thing, the period by which we measure is another. It is self-evident which of these is to be described as time. Moreover, a body may at one point be moving, at another point at rest. We measure by time and say "It was standing still for the same time that it was in movement," or "It was still for two or three times as long as it was in movement," or any other measurement we may make, either by precise observation or by a rough estimate (we customarily say "more or less"). Therefore time is not the movement of a body.

xxv (32) I confess to you, Lord, that I still do not know what time is, and I further confess to you, Lord, that as I say this I know myself to be conditioned by time. For a long period already I have been speaking about time, and that long period can only be an interval of time. So how do I know this, when I do not know what time is? Perhaps what I do not know is how to articulate what I do know. My condition is not good if I do not even know what it is I do not know. See, my God, "before you I do not lie" (Gal. 1:21). As I speak, so is my heart. You, Lord, "will light my lamp." Lord, my God, "you will lighten my darknesses" (Ps. 17:29).

xxvi (33) My confession to you is surely truthful when my soul declares that times are measured by me. So my God, I measure, and do not know what I am measuring. I measure the motion of a body by time. Then am I not measuring time itself? I could not measure the movement of a body, its period of transit and how long it takes to go from A to B, unless I were measuring the time in which this movement occurs. How then do I measure time itself? Or do we use a shorter time to measure a longer time, as when, for example, we measure a transom by using a cubit length? So we can be seen to use the length of a short syllable as a measure when we say that a long syllable is twice its length. By this method we measure poems by the number of lines, lines by the number of feet, feet by the number of syllables, and long vowels by short, not by the number of pages (for that would give us a measure of space, not of time). The criterion is the time words occupy in recitation, so that we say "That is a long poem, for it consists of so many lines. The lines are long, for they consist of so many feet. The feet are long for they extend over so many syllables. The syllable is long, for it is double the length of a short one."

Nevertheless, even so we have not reached a reliable measure of time. It may happen that a short line, if pronounced slowly, takes longer to read aloud than a longer line taken faster. The same principle applies to a poem or a foot or a syllable. That is why I have come to think that time is simply a distension. But of what is it a distension? I do not know, but it would be surprising if it is not that of the mind itself. What do I measure, I beg you, my God, when I say without precision "This period is longer than that," or with precision "This is twice as long as that"? That I am measuring time I know. But I am not measuring the future which does not yet exist, nor the present which has no extension, nor the past which is no longer in being. What then am I measuring? Time as it passes but not time past? That is what I affirmed earlier.

xxvii (34) Stand firm, my mind, concentrate with resolution. "God is our help, he has made us and not we ourselves" (Ps. 61:9; 99:3). Concentrate on the point where truth is beginning to dawn. For example, a physical voice begins to sound. It sounds. It continues to sound, and then ceases. Silence has now come, and the voice is past. There is now no sound. Before it sounded it lay in the future. It could not be measured because it did not exist; and now it cannot be measured because it has ceased to be. At the time when it was sounding, it was possible because at that time it existed to be measured. Yet even then it had no permanence. It came and went. Did this make it more possible to measure? In process of passing away it was extended through a certain space of time by which it could be measured, since the present occupies no length of time. Therefore during that transient process it could be measured. But take, for example, another voice. It begins to sound and continues to do so unflaggingly without any interruption. Let us measure it while it is sounding; when it has ceased to sound, it will be past and will not exist to be measurable. Evidently we may at that stage measure it by saying how long it lasted. But if it is still sounding, it cannot be measured except from the starting moment when it began to sound to the finish when it ceased. What we measure is the actual interval from the beginning to the end. That is why a sound which has not yet ended cannot be measured: one cannot say how long or how short it is, nor that it is equal to some other length of time or that in relation to another it is single or double or any such proportion. But when it has come to an end, then it will already have ceased to be. By what method then can it be measured?

Nevertheless we do measure periods of time. And yet the times we measure are not those which do not yet exist, nor those which already have no existence, nor those which extend over no interval of time, nor those which reach no conclusions. So the times we measure are not future nor past nor present nor those in process of passing away. Yet we measure periods of time.

(35) "God, Creator of all things"—*Deus Creator omnium*—the line consists of eight syllables, in which short and long syllables alternate. So the four which are short (the first, third, fifth, and seventh) are single in relation to the four long syllables (the second, fourth, sixth and eighth). Each of the long syllables has twice the time of the short. As I recite the words, I also observe that this is so, for it is evident to sense-perception. To the degree that the sense-perception is unambiguous, I measure the long syllable by the short one, and perceive it to be twice the length. But when one syllable sounds after another, the short first, the long after it, how shall I keep my hold on the short, and how use it to apply a measure to the long, so as to verify that the long is twice as much? The long does not begin to sound unless the short has ceased to sound. I can

hardly measure the long during the presence of its sound, as measuring becomes possible only after it has ended. When it is finished, it has gone into the past. What then is it which I measure? Where is the short syllable with which I am making my measurement? Where is the long which I am measuring? Both have sounded; they have flown away; they belong to the past. They now do not exist. And I offer my measurement and declare as confidently as a practised sense-perception will allow, that the short is single, the long double—I mean in the time they occupy. I can do this only because they are past and gone. Therefore it is not the syllables which I am measuring, but something in my memory which stays fixed there.

(36) So it is in you, my mind, that I measure periods of time. Do not distract me; that is, do not allow yourself to be distracted by the hubbub of the impressions being made upon you. In you, I affirm, I measure periods of time. The impression which passing events make upon you abides when they are gone. That present consciousness is what I am measuring, not the stream of past events which have caused it. When I measure periods of time, that is what I am actually measuring. Therefore, either this is what time is, or time is not what I am measuring.

What happens when we measure silences and say that a given period of silence lasted as long as a given sound? Do we direct our attention to measuring it as if a sound occurred, so that we are enabled to judge the intervals of the silences within the space of time concerned? For without any sound or utterance we mentally recite poems and lines and speeches, and we assess the lengths of their movements and the relative amounts of time they occupy, no differently from the way we would speak if we were actually making sounds. Suppose someone wished to utter a sound lasting a long time, and decided in advance how long that was going to be. He would have planned that space of time in silence. Entrusting that to his memory he would begin to utter the sound which continues until it has reached the intended end. It would be more accurate to say the utterance has sounded and will sound. For the part of it which is complete has sounded, but what remains will sound, and so the action is being accomplished as present attention transfers the future into the past. The future diminishes as the past grows, until the future has completely gone and everything is in the past.

xxviii (37) But how does this future, which does not yet exist, diminish or become consumed? Or how does the past, which now has no being, grow, unless there are three processes in the mind which in this is the active agent? For the mind expects and attends and remembers, so that what it expects passes through what has its attention to what it remembers. Who therefore can deny that the future does not yet exist? Yet already in the mind there is an expectation of the future. Who can deny that the past does not now exist? Yet there is still in the mind a memory of the past. None can deny that present time lacks any extension because it passes in a flash. Yet attention is continuous, and it is through this that what will be present progresses towards being absent. So the future, which does not exist, is not a long period of time. A long future is a long expectation of the future. And the past, which has no existence, is not a long period of time. A long past is a long memory of the past.

(38) Suppose I am about to recite a psalm which I know. Before I begin, my expectation is directed towards the whole. But when I have begun, the verses from it which I take into the past become the object of my memory. The life of this act of mine is stretched two ways, into my memory because of the words I have already said and into my expectation because of those which I am about to say. But my attention is on what is present: by that the future is transferred to become the past. As the action advances further and further, the shorter the expectation and the longer the memory, until all expectation is consumed, the entire action is finished, and it has passed into the

memory. What occurs in the psalm as a whole occurs in its particular pieces and its individual syllables. The same is true of a longer action in which perhaps that psalm is a
part. It is also valid of the entire life of an individual person, where all actions are parts
of a whole, and of the total history of "the sons of men" (Ps. 30:20) where all human
lives are but parts.

xxix (39) "Because your mercy is more than lives" (Ps. 62:4), see how my life is
a distension in several directions. "Your right hand upheld me" (Ps. 17:36; 62:9) in my
Lord, the Son of man who is mediator between you the One and us the many, who live
in a multiplicity of distractions by many things; so "I might apprehend him in whom
also I am apprehended" (Phil. 3:12–14), and leaving behind the old days I might be
gathered to follow the One, "forgetting the past" and moving not towards those future
things which are transitory but to "the things which are before" me, not stretched out in
distraction but extended in reach, not by being pulled apart but by concentration. So I
"pursue the prize of the high calling" where I "may hear the voice of praise" and "contemplate your delight" (Ps. 25:7; 26:4) which neither comes nor goes. But now "my
years pass in groans" (Ps. 30:11) and you, Lord, are my consolation. You are my eternal
Father, but I am scattered in times whose order I do not understand. The storms of inco-
herent events tear to pieces my thoughts, the inmost entrails of my soul, until that day
when, purified and molten by the fire of your love, I flow together to merge into you.

xxx (40) Then shall I find stability and solidity in you, in your truth which imparts
form to me. I shall not have to endure the questions of people who suffer from a disease
which brings its own punishment and want to drink more than they have the capacity to
hold. They say "What was God doing before he made heaven and earth?," or "Why did
he ever conceive the thought of making something when he had never made anything
before?" Grant them, Lord, to consider carefully what they are saying and to make the
discovery that where there is no time, one cannot use the word "never." To say that God
has never done something is to say that there is no time when he did it. Let them therefore see that without the creation no time can exist, and let them cease to speak that vanity (Ps. 143:8). Let them also be "extended" towards "those things which are before"
(Phil. 3:13), and understand that before all times you are eternal Creator of all time. Nor
are any times or created thing coeternal with you, even if there is an order of creation
which transcends time.

xxxi (41) Lord my God, how deep is your profound mystery, and how far away
from it have I been thrust by the consequences of my sins. Heal my eyes and let me rejoice with your light. Certainly if there were a mind endowed with such great knowledge and prescience that all things past and future could be known in the way I know a
very familiar psalm, this mind would be utterly miraculous and amazing to the point of
inducing awe. From such a mind nothing of the past would be hidden, nor anything of
what remaining ages have in store, just as I have full knowledge of that psalm I sing. I
know by heart what and how much of it has passed since the beginning, and what and
how much remains until the end. But far be it from you, Creator of the universe, creator
of souls and bodies, far be it from you to know all future and past events in this kind of
sense. You know them in a much more wonderful and much more mysterious way. A
person singing or listening to a song he knows well suffers a distension or stretching in
feeling and in sense-perception from the expectation of future sounds and the memory
of past sound. With you it is otherwise. You are unchangeably eternal, that is the truly
eternal Creator of minds. Just as you knew heaven and earth in the beginning without
that bringing any variation into your knowing, so you made heaven and earth in the beginning without that meaning a tension between past and future in your activity. Let the
person who understands this make confession to you. Let him who fails to understand it

make confession to you. How exalted you are, and the humble in heart are your house (Ps. 137:6; 145:8). You lift up those who are cast down (Ps. 144:14; 145:8), and those whom you raise to that summit which is yourself do not fall.

ON THE FREE CHOICE OF THE WILL (in part)

BOOK II

Chapter 1

1. EVODIUS: Now explain to me, if that is possible, why God gave man free choice of the will since, if he had not received it, man would certainly be unable to sin.

AUGUSTINE: Do you know for sure that God has given man something which you think should not have been given him?

EVODIUS: From what I seem to gather from the previous book, we do have free choice of the will and this alone enables us to sin.

AUGUSTINE: I also recall that this point was made clear. But I have asked you just now whether you know that it was God who gave us that very thing which we obviously possess and which enables us to sin.

EVODIUS: I think it is none other, for it is from Him that we have our being and from Him that we merit reward or punishment, according as we live good or sinful lives.

AUGUSTINE: I am also eager to know whether you see this clearly or whether you are willing to believe it on authority, even though you do not understand it.

EVODIUS: I assure you that I first accepted this on authority; yet what could be truer than that everything good comes from God, that everything just is good, and that it is just that there should be punishment for sinners and rewards for the righteous? Hence the conclusion that God makes sinners unhappy and the righteous happy.

2. AUGUSTINE: I agree, but I would raise this other question as to how you know that we have our being from God. For you did not now explain this, but only that it is from Him that we merit either punishment or reward.

EVODIUS: I see that the only evidence for this point stems from our earlier conclusion that God punishes sins, since, in fact, all justice comes from Him. For while it is a mark of goodness to bestow benefits upon strangers, it is not in keeping with justice to inflict punishments upon them. Clearly, therefore, we belong to God, not only because He is most generous to us with His gifts, but also because He is most just in meting out punishment. Again, from the fact that every good comes from God, and here you agreed with my contention, we can understand that man too comes from God. For man himself, insofar as he is man, is something good because he can live an upright life whenever he so wishes.

St. Augustine, *On the Free Choice of the Will*, Book II, from *Fathers of the Church; Writings of Saint Augustine; Saint Augustine: The Free Choice of the Will,* translated by Robert R. Russell, O.S.A. (Washington, DC: The Catholic University of America Press, 1953). Reprinted by permission.

3. AUGUSTINE: Obviously, if this is so, the question you raised is already answered. If, indeed, man is something good and cannot do what is right unless he wills to, then he must have free will, without which he cannot do what is right. For we must not suppose that because a man can also sin by his free will that God gave it to him for this purpose. The fact that man cannot lead an upright life without it is sufficient reason why God should have given it. That it was given for this purpose can be seen from this, that when he has used it to commit sin, he is subject to divine punishment, which would be unjust if free will had been given him not only to live uprightly but also to commit sin. How could punishment be justly visited upon a man who used his will for the very purpose for which it was given him? But when God punishes a sinner, what does He seem to say but: "Why did you not use your free will for the purpose for which I gave it to you, namely, to do what is right?" Besides, if man were without free choice of the will, what would become of the good called justice whereby sins are punished and good deeds are honored? For, unless something is done by the will, it can be neither a sin nor a good deed. Consequently, punishments and rewards would be unjust if man did not possess free will. Moreover, there must be a place for justice both in punishments and rewards because it is one of those goods that come from God. It follows, therefore, that God should have given man free will.

Chapter 2

4. EVODIUS: I admit now that God gave it. But let me ask you this: if it was given to do good, do you not think it should have been impossible to turn it to a sinful purpose? As with justice itself, which is given man to lead a good life, how could anyone lead a bad life by reason of his being just? So, too, if the will were given to do good, no one would be able to sin by his will.

AUGUSTINE: I hope God will enable me to answer your question, or better, that He will enable you to answer it yourself, when you are enlightened by that truth within you, which is the greatest teacher of all. I wish you would tell me shortly—provided you know for sure that God gave us free will, which was what I asked you—whether we should say that something should not have been given when we acknowledge that it was God who gave it. For, if it is not certain that He gave it, it is right for us to ask whether it was a good gift, so that if we find that it was, we will also have found that it was given by Him who has given all good things to man. Now if we find that it was not a good gift, we will realize that God did not give it, since it is blasphemous to charge Him with wrongdoing. But if it is certain that He Himself gave it, then, no matter how it was given, we must acknowledge that there is no reason why it either should not have been given or been given differently than it was given. For He gave it, who may never be rightly blamed for what He has done.

5. EVODIUS: While I accept all this with a firm faith, yet, since I have no intellectual grasp of it, let us so conduct our inquiry as if it were all uncertain. As I see it, our uncertainty as to whether free will was given us to do good, since we can also sin by it, gives rise to the further uncertainty as to whether it should have been given at all. If it is uncertain that free will was given to do good, it is also uncertain whether it should have been given, and, consequently, also uncertain that God gave it to us. For, if it is uncertain whether it should have been given, it is uncertain that it was given by God since it would be impious to suppose that He has given anything which he should not have given.

AUGUSTINE: You are certain, at least, that God exists.

EVODIUS: This too I hold firmly, not from direct knowledge, but by faith.

AUGUSTINE: Suppose, then, that one of these fools of whom it is related in the Scripture, "the fool has said in his heart, there is no God" (Ps. 13:1), should say this to you, and should be unwilling to go along with what you believe, but want to know whether what you believe is true. Would you abandon this man or would you think that he should somehow be convinced of what is a matter of firm belief for you, especially if he was not stubborn in his opposition but was eager in his desire to know?

EVODIUS: What you just said clearly suggests how I should answer him. Even though he were utterly unreasonable, he would at least admit that no one should enter into a discussion on any subject at all with a man who is insincere and obstinate, and, most of all, on a subject of such importance. Once this was admitted, he would first prevail upon me to believe that he is making this inquiry in good faith and that as far as the present problem is concerned, he harbors no hidden guile or obstinacy. I would then point out (and I think this would be a simple matter for anyone) that since he wishes another to believe the hidden thoughts of his own mind, thoughts known to him but unknown to the one who believes them, it is much more reasonable for him to believe in God's existence on the authority of the books of those great men who have left a written record testifying that they lived with the Son of God. They have also recorded certain things they witnessed which could not possibly have happened if there were no God. And it would be very foolish of him to reproach me for believing these men since he wished me to believe him. Now certainly he could find no good reason for not wanting to imitate what he is unable to reproach.

AUGUSTINE: Now if you think it is enough to accept God's existence on the word of such great men without being rash, then what of those other questions which we undertook to explore, as if they were uncertain and completely unknown? Why, I ask, do you not likewise think that we should also believe these things on the authority of these men to the extent that we need expend no further effort in investigating them?

EVODIUS: But we are eager to know and understand what we believe.

6. AUGUSTINE: Your memory serves you well, and there is no denying that this was the position we took at the opening of our earlier discussion. For, unless believing and understanding were different, and unless we were first to believe those important and heavenly truths which we are eager to understand, there would be no point in the prophet's saying: "Unless you believe, you shall not understand" (Isa. 7:9). Our Lord, too, both by word and deed, exhorted those whom He called to be saved that they should first believe. Later, when He referred to the gift He would bestow upon those who believed, He did not say, "This is eternal life that they may *believe*," but, "This is eternal life that they may *know* Thee, the one true God, and Him whom Thou hast sent, Jesus Christ" (John 17:3). Then, to those who already believed, He said: "Seek and you shall find" (Matt. 7:7). Now we cannot say that we have "found" something which is believed but not known, nor can anyone become fit to find God unless he has first believed what he will afterwards come to understand. Let us, therefore, in obedience to the Lord's command, carry on our inquiry earnestly. For what we are seeking at His behest, that we shall find upon His manifesting it to us Himself, so far as these things can be found in this life and by men like ourselves. We must believe that they are perceived and grasped more clearly and perfectly by more virtuous men, even while they dwell on this earth, and certainly by all good and religious men after their present life. We must make this our hope too, and, despising all that is worldly and human, we must desire and love the higher things in every way possible.

Chapter 3

7. AUGUSTINE: Let us pursue our inquiry, if you will, according to this order: first, what evidence is there that God exists; next, do all things, insofar as they are good, come from God; lastly, should free will be numbered among things good. Once these questions have been answered, I think it will become clear enough whether it was right to give free will to man.

Hence, to begin with what is most evident, I will ask you whether you yourself exist. Possibly, you are afraid of being mistaken by this kind of a question when, actually, you could not be mistaken at all if you did not exist?

EVODIUS: Go on instead to the other questions.

AUGUSTINE: Then, since it is evident that you exist, and that this could not be so unless you were living, then the fact that you are living is also evident. Do you understand that these two points are absolutely true?

EVODIUS: I understand that perfectly well.

AUGUSTINE: Then this third point is also evident, namely, that you understand.

EVODIUS: It is evident.

AUGUSTINE: Which of these three, in your opinion, is the most excellent?

EVODIUS: Understanding.

AUGUSTINE: Why do you think so?

EVODIUS: Because, while these are three in number, existence, life, and understanding, and though the stone exists and the animal lives, yet I do not think that the stone lives or that the animal understands, whereas it is absolutely certain that whoever understands also exists and is living. That is why I have no hesitation in concluding that the one which contains all three is more excellent than that which is lacking in one or both of these. Now whatever is living is certainly also existing, but it does not follow that it also understands. This kind of life, I think, is proper to animals. But it certainly does not follow that what exists must also live and understand, for I can admit that a corpse exists, but no one would say it lives. And still less can something understand if it is not living.

AUGUSTINE: We maintain, then, that two of these three are lacking in a corpse, one in the animal, and none in man.

EVODIUS: That is true.

AUGUSTINE: We likewise maintain that the most excellent among the three is what man possesses together with the other two, namely, understanding, and that having this, he must also exist and live.

EVODIUS: We do, indeed.

8. AUGUSTINE: Now tell me whether you know you have these well-known senses of the body, sight, hearing, smell, taste, and touch.

EVODIUS: I do.

AUGUSTINE: What do you think is the function of sight, that is, what do we perceive when we see?

EVODIUS: Anything corporeal.

AUGUSTINE: When we see, we do not likewise perceive what is hard and soft, do we?

EVODIUS: No.

AUGUSTINE: What then is the proper function of the eyes, that is, what do we perceive with them?

EVODIUS: Color.

AUGUSTINE: Of the ears?

EVODIUS: Sound.

AUGUSTINE: Of smell?

EVODIUS: Odors.

AUGUSTINE: Of taste?

EVODIUS: Flavor.

AUGUSTINE: Of touch?

EVODIUS: Soft or hard, smooth or rough, and many such qualities.

AUGUSTINE: And what of the shapes of bodies? Do we not perceive that they are large, small, square, round, and so on, both by touch and sight? Consequently, these qualities are not proper either to sight or vision alone, but belong to both.

EVODIUS: I understand.

AUGUSTINE: Then you further understand that each sense has its own proper object to report while some senses have certain objects in common.

EVODIUS: I understand that also.

AUGUSTINE: Can we, therefore, determine by any of these senses what is the proper object of each sense or what those objects are which some or all of them have in common?

EVODIUS: Not at all. This is discerned by some power within.

AUGUSTINE: Might not this be the reason itself, which is wanting in beasts? For, in my opinion, reason enables us to grasp these and to know just what they are.

EVODIUS: I think it is rather reason that enables us to know that there is a kind of internal sense to which everything is referred by those well-known five senses. Now the power enabling the animal to see is one thing, that by which it shuns or seeks what it perceives by seeing is something else. The former is located in the eye, the latter within, in the soul itself. The inner sense enables the animal to seek and acquire things that delight and to repel and avoid things that are obnoxious, not only those that are perceived by sight and hearing, but all those which are grasped by the other bodily senses. But this power cannot be called either sight or hearing or smell or taste or touch, but is some other kind of power that presides over all of them together. Although, as I mentioned, we do grasp this power by our reason, yet we may not call it reason, since it is obviously present in beasts.

9. AUGUSTINE: I acknowledge that this power, whatever it is, does exist, and I do not hesitate to call it the inner sense. But unless the impressions brought to us by the bodily senses pass beyond even this inner sense, they cannot result in knowledge. For it is by reason that we grasp whatever we know. To mention but a few instances, we know that color cannot be perceived by hearing nor sound by sight. And this is something that we do not know by sight or hearing or by that inner sense which is not lacking in beasts. We are not to suppose that beasts know that light is not perceived by the ear or sound by the eye, since we discern this only by rational reflection and thought.

EVODIUS: I could not say that I have grasped this point. Suppose that beasts do discern that color cannot be perceived by hearing or sound by sight by means of that inner sense which you admit they do possess.

AUGUSTINE: You do not suppose, do you, that animals can distinguish one from another the color they perceive, the power of sense in the eye, the inner sense within the soul, and reason by which all these are enumerated and defined, one by one?

EVODIUS: Not at all.

AUGUSTINE: But could reason distinguish these four things one from another and assign their limits by definition unless color was referred to it by the sense of sight, and this sense, in turn, by that inner sense which presides over it, and this inner sense, in turn, by its direct action upon reason, provided, however, that there is no other power interposed?

EVODIUS: I fail to see how it could be otherwise.

AUGUSTINE: Are you aware of this, that color is perceived by the sense of sight, whereas this sense of sight is not perceived by sight itself? For you do not see the act of seeing itself by the same sense by which you see color.

EVODIUS: Absolutely not.

AUGUSTINE: Try now to make these further distinctions. You will not deny, I think, that color and seeing color are different, and also that the power is different by which color can be perceived in its absence as if it were present.

EVODIUS: I draw a distinction between these two, and admit that they are distinct from one another.

AUGUSTINE: Except for color, you do not see any of these three with the eyes, do you?

EVODIUS: Nothing else but color.

AUGUSTINE: Tell me then what it is that enables you to see the other two, for you could not distinguish them if they were not seen.

EVODIUS: I do not know the nature of that other power. I know it exists but nothing more.

AUGUSTINE: Then you do not know whether it is reason itself or that vital power, called the inner sense, which presides over the bodily senses, or something else?

EVODIUS: I do not know.

AUGUSTINE: But this much you do know, that reason alone can define these powers and that it can only do so with what is presented for its scrutiny.

EVODIUS: That is certain.

AUGUSTINE: It follows that this other power, whatever it is, which enables us to perceive all that we know, is the servant of reason. It presents and reports to reason whatever has come within its reach so that the objects of sense perception can be assigned their proper limits and be grasped not only by sensation but also by knowledge.

EVODIUS: That is right.

AUGUSTINE: Reason itself distinguishes between its servants and the impressions they convey to it, and likewise recognizes what a difference there is between these and itself and asserts its primacy over them. Now does reason know reason in any other way than by reason itself? Or how would you otherwise know that you had reason unless you perceived it by reason?

EVODIUS: That is very true.

AUGUSTINE: Consequently, in perceiving color, we do not perceive by the same sense our act of seeing; in hearing we do not hear our act of hearing; in smelling a rose, the act itself of smelling imparts no fragrance to us; in tasting a flavor, the act itself has no taste in our mouth, and in touching something, we cannot touch the act itself of touching. It is evident that those five senses cannot be perceived by any one of them, though all corporeal qualities can be perceived by them.

EVODIUS: It is evident.

Chapter 4

10. AUGUSTINE: I think it is likewise clear that the inner sense perceives not only what it receives from the five bodily senses but also the senses themselves. For if the beast were not aware of its act of perception, it could not otherwise direct its movements to-

ward something, or away from it. This awareness is not ordered towards knowledge, which is the function of reason, but towards movement which it does not perceive by any of the five senses.

If this is still obscure, it may become clear if you note the single example of what occurs in any one of the senses, such as sight. The beast could not open its eyes at all or turn its gaze towards the thing it wants to see were it not for the fact that while its eyes were closed or not fixed upon the object, it perceived that it was not seeing. But if it is conscious of its not seeing when in fact it does not see, it must also be aware of its seeing when it does see. The fact that, while seeing, the beast does not alter its gaze by that desire which moves it to turn its gaze when it does not see something, shows that it is aware of both states.

But whether this vital power, which is aware of its perceiving corporeal things, also perceives itself, is not so clear, except for the fact that when a person raises the question in his own mind, he comes to see that all living things shun death. Since death is the contrary of life, we must infer that the vital power is aware of itself since it shuns what is contrary to it. But if this point is still not clear, then disregard it, so that our effort to reach the desired conclusion will be based solely on clear and evident proofs.

These points are clear: corporeal qualities are perceived by the bodily senses; one and the same sense cannot perceive itself; the inner sense perceives that corporeal qualities are perceived by the bodily sense and also the bodily sense itself; all these things of sense, as well as reason itself, are known by reason and come under the heading of knowledge. Do you not think so?

EVODIUS: I do indeed.

AUGUSTINE: Come, tell me how this question arose, for we have been pursuing this avenue of inquiry a long time in our desire to reach a solution.

Chapter 5

11. EVODIUS: So far as I recall, we are now dealing with the first of those three questions which we proposed a while ago when we arranged a plan for this discussion, namely, how the existence of God can be made evident, though we must believe it with a strong and persevering faith.

AUGUSTINE: You have recalled this very well. But I want you also to keep carefully in mind that when I asked whether you were existing, it was made clear that you knew not only this but also two other things.

EVODIUS: I remember that too.

AUGUSTINE: Now see which one of these three you think is that one to which pertains everything perceived by the bodily senses, that is, in what class of things you think we should locate whatever is perceived by our senses, by the eyes or by any other organ of the body. Should it be with things that merely exist, with those that also live, or with those that also understand?

EVODIUS: With those that merely exist.

AUGUSTINE: In which of the three classes do you think the sense power itself should be placed?

EVODIUS: In the class of things living.

AUGUSTINE: Which of these two do you think is better, the sense itself or its object?

EVODIUS: The sense, of course.

AUGUSTINE: Why is that?

EVODIUS: Because whatever also has life is better than something which merely exists.

12. AUGUSTINE: And what of that inner sense which we found was inferior to reason and which we still share in common with beasts? Would you hesitate to rank this sense above that by which we perceive a body, which you said should be ranked above the body itself?

EVODIUS: I would have no hesitation whatever.

AUGUSTINE: I should like you to tell me why you have no hesitation on this point. For you cannot say that this inner sense should be placed in that one of the three classes which also includes understanding, but rather in the class of things which exist and live, although they lack understanding. This inner sense is found also in beasts which are without understanding. If this is so, I would like to know why you rank the inner sense above that which perceives corporeal qualities, since both are found in the class of things that live. You ranked the sense which perceives bodies above bodies because the latter are in the class of things which only exist, while the former are in the class of things that also live. Since the inner sense is also found in this class, tell me why you think it is better.

If you say it is because the inner sense perceives the bodily sense, I do not believe you will find any rule that we could rely upon for holding that the subject perceiving is better than what it perceives. Otherwise, we might also be forced to conclude that the person understanding is better than what he understands. This, of course, is untrue because man understands wisdom but he is not better than wisdom itself. Consider, then, why you thought that the inner sense should be ranked above the sense by which we perceive things corporeal.

EVODIUS: It is because I look upon the inner sense as a ruler and kind of judge of the latter. For if there is any shortcoming in the discharge of their function, the inner sense demands this service from the bodily senses as a kind of debt owed by its servant, as was pointed out a short time ago. The sense of sight does not see that it is seeing or not seeing and, failing to do so, it cannot judge what is missing or what is sufficient. This is done by the inner sense which directs the soul of the beast to open its eyes when they are closed and to supply what it perceives is missing. There can be no doubt in anyone's mind that what judges is better than what is judged.

AUGUSTINE: Do you understand then that even the bodily senses pass a kind of judgment on bodies? Pleasure and pain are theirs to experience whenever they come in contact gently or roughly with a body. Just as the inner sense judges as to what is missing or what is sufficient in visual perception, so the eyes themselves judge as to what is deficient or sufficient in the matter of color. So too in the case of hearing, just as the inner sense judges whether or not it is attentive enough, so the auditory sense judges concerning sounds, discerning those which either flow gently into the ear or which produce a harsh dissonance.

There is no need to continue with the rest of the bodily senses. I think you know already what I am trying to say, namely, that just as the inner sense judges the bodily senses, approving what is complete in them and requiring what is deficient, so too the bodily senses themselves judge bodies, admitting pleasurable sensations of touch found in them, while rejecting the opposite.

EVODIUS: I see these points clearly and agree that they are perfectly true.

Chapter 6

13. AUGUSTINE: See now whether reason also judges the inner sense. I am not asking whether you have any doubt that reason is better than the inner sense because I am sure that this is your judgment. Yet I feel that now we should not even have to ask whether reason passes judgment on the inner sense. For in the case of things inferior to it, namely, bodies, the bodily senses, and the inner sense, is it not, after all, reason itself that tells us how one is better than the other and how far superior reason itself is to all of them? This would not be possible at all unless reason were to judge them.

EVODIUS: Obviously.

AUGUSTINE: Consequently, that nature which not only exists but also lives, though it does not understand, such as the soul of beasts, is superior to one that merely exists and neither lives nor understands, such as the inanimate body. Again, that nature which at once exists and lives and understands, such as the rational mind in man, is superior to the animal nature. Do you think that anything can be found in us, namely, something among those elements which complete our nature and make us men, that is more excellent than that very thing which we made the third in those three classes of things? It is clear that we have a body and a kind of living principle which quickens the body itself and makes it grow, and we recognize that these two are also found in beasts. And it is also clear that there is a third something, the apex, so to speak, or eye of the soul, or whatever more appropriate term may be employed to designate reason and understanding, which the animal nature does not possess. So I ask you to consider whether there is anything in man's nature more excellent than reason.

EVODIUS: I see nothing at all that is better.

14. AUGUSTINE: But suppose we could find something which you are certain not only exists but is also superior to our reason, would you hesitate to call this reality, whatever it is, God?

EVODIUS: If I were able to find something which is better than what is best in my nature, I would not immediately call it God. I do not like to call something God because my reason is inferior to it, but rather to call that reality God which has nothing superior to it.

AUGUSTINE: That is perfectly true. For God Himself has given this reason of yours the power to think of Him with such reverence and truth. But I will ask you this: if you should find that there is nothing above our reason but an eternal and changeless reality, would you hesitate to say that this is God? You notice how bodies are subject to change, and it is clear that the living principle animating the body is not free from change but passes through various states. And reason itself is clearly shown to be changeable, seeing that at one time it endeavors to reach the truth, and at another time it does not, sometimes it arrives at the truth, sometimes it does not. If reason sees something eternal and changeless not by any bodily organ, neither by touch nor taste nor smell nor hearing nor sight, nor by any sense inferior to it, but sees this of itself, and sees at the same time its own inferiority, it will have to acknowledge that this being is its God.

EVODIUS: I will openly acknowledge that to be God, if, as all agree, there is nothing higher existing.

AUGUSTINE: Good! It will be enough for me to show that something of this kind exists. Either you will admit that this is God or, if there is something higher, you will admit that it is God. Accordingly, whether there exists something higher or not, it will become clear that God exists, when, with His assistance, I shall prove, as I promised, that there exists something above reason.

EVODIUS: Prove then what you are promising.

Chapter 7

15. AUGUSTINE: I shall do so. But first I shall ask you whether my bodily senses are the same as yours, or whether mine are mine alone and yours are yours alone. If this latter were not so, I would be unable to see anything with my eyes which you would not see.

EVODIUS: I fully agree that though the senses are of the same nature, yet each one of us has his own sense of sight or hearing, and so forth. One man cannot only see but also hear something that another man does not hear, and one man can perceive by any one of the senses something different from what another perceives. So it is obvious that your senses are yours alone and mine are mine alone.

AUGUSTINE: Would you give the same or a different answer concerning the inner sense?

EVODIUS: Not a different answer, certainly. My inner sense perceives my bodily sensations and your inner sense perceives yours. I am often asked by a man who sees something whether I also see it, simply because I am conscious of seeing or not seeing it, while he is not.

AUGUSTINE: What of reason itself? Does not each one of us have his own since, actually, it can happen that I understand something while you do not, and you may be unable to know whether I do understand, although I do know.

EVODIUS: It is also clear that each one of us has his own rational mind.

16. AUGUSTINE: You could not possibly say, could you, that we possess individually our own sun or moon, or morning star, or other such things that we see, though each one of us sees these things with his own sense?

EVODIUS: I could never say such a thing.

AUGUSTINE: So it is possible for many of us to see some one thing at one and the same time, though each of us has his own individual senses with which he perceives the same thing which we all see at the same time. Consequently, though my senses are distinct from yours, it may happen that what we see is not something different for both, but the one thing which is present to each of us and which is seen by both of us at the same time.

EVODIUS: That is perfectly clear.

AUGUSTINE: We can also hear the same voice at the same time so that, while my hearing is distinct from yours, yet it is not a different voice that we are hearing at the same time. Neither is one part of the voice heard by me and another part by you, but whatever sound is made is within the hearing of both of us, perceived as one sound in its entirety.

EVODIUS: That too is clear.

17. AUGUSTINE: With regard to the other senses, you must now take note that what we have to say in this connection holds for them in a way neither entirely the same nor entirely different from what was said about the two senses of sight and hearing. You and I can inhale the same air and perceive the quality of the air by its odor. Again, we can both taste the same honey, or any other kind of food and drink, and perceive its quality from the taste. Although the taste is the same, yet our senses are individual to us, yours belong to you, and mine to me. So when both perceive the one odor or taste, you do not perceive it with my sense nor do I perceive it with yours. Neither do I perceive it by a single sense which we can share in common, but my sense is mine entirely and so is yours, though it is the one odor or taste that is perceived by both of us.

Accordingly, these two senses of smell and taste are found to have something similar to the two senses of sight and hearing. But they differ in a way which has a bearing on the subject we are presently considering. For, though we both inhale the same air with our nostrils or taste the same food that we take, I do not breathe in that part of the air which you do, or eat the same portion of food that you eat, but I take one part, and you, another. Therefore, when I breathe, I inhale as much of all the air as I need, and you do the same. And though the same food is all eaten by both of us, yet it cannot be taken wholly by both of us in the way that we both hear a whole word at the same time and both see the same sight equally well. But in the case of food and drink, different portions have to pass into each of us. Do you have some faint understanding of all this?

EVODIUS: On the contrary, I agree that it is perfectly clear and certain.

18. AUGUSTINE: You would not say, would you, that we should compare the sense of touch with those of sight and hearing with reference to the point now under discussion? We can both perceive by the sense of touch not only the same body, but also the same part of the body. It is different with food, for each one of us cannot take all the food placed before us when we are both eating it. But you and I can touch the same body in its entirety, not just different parts of it, but the whole body.

EVODIUS: I admit that in this respect the sense of touch is very much like the two previous senses. But I see it differs in this, that both of us can see and hear all of the same thing together, that is, at the same time. Now both of us can touch a whole body at one time, but only in different parts, and only the same part at different times. I cannot apply my sense of touch to the part you are touching unless you remove yours.

19. AUGUSTINE: A very astute answer! But you should note this point too, that though some objects perceived by us are perceived together and others separately, yet each of us has an individual awareness of his own sense perceptions of the objects he perceives through the bodily sense. I am neither aware of your sensations nor are you aware of mine. In other words, with regard to things corporeal, what we can perceive individually but not together is that alone which so becomes part of us that we can change and transform it into ourselves. So it is with food and drink where both of us cannot taste the same portion. Although nurses actually serve food already masticated to infants, yet the portion which is taken to be tasted and is assimilated into the body of the nurse chewing it cannot be returned and given back as food for the infant. When the palate tastes something pleasant, no matter how small a portion it is, it claims this for itself once and for all, and makes it become part of the body's nature. If this were not the case, no taste could remain in the mouth after masticated food was rejected from the mouth. We may say the same of the parts of the air we breathe. Though you can inhale some of the air which I exhale, you cannot do so with that part which has become nourishment for me because it cannot be returned. Physicians point out that we take in nourishment even with our nostrils. When I breathe, I am the only one who can perceive this nourishment and I cannot return it by exhaling it for you to inhale it again and perceive it with your nostrils.

Although we perceive other sense objects, our perception of them does not destroy their nature and change them into our bodily substance. We can both perceive them either together or at different times, so that what I perceive, either in whole or in part, can also be perceived by you. Light, sound, and bodily objects are examples of things with which we can come in contact, but without altering their nature.

EVODIUS: I understand.

AUGUSTINE: It is clear, therefore, that those things which are not changed by us, though we perceive them with our bodily senses, are not the property of our senses and hence are all the more common to us, seeing that they are not changed or converted into our own individual or, so to speak, private property.

EVODIUS: I am in full agreement.

AUGUSTINE: We are to understand by individual and, so to speak, private property, that which is identified with each one of us and which each one alone can perceive within himself as belonging properly to his own nature. By common and, so to speak, public, we understand that which is experienced by all who perceive something, without any deterioration or change in the thing itself.

EVODIUS: That is correct.

Chapter 8

20. AUGUSTINE: Come now, and let me have your attention. Tell me whether anything can be found which all thinking men perceive in common, each one making use of his own mind and reason. Something which is seen is present to everybody and is not changed into something else useful for those to whom it is present, like food and drink, but remains whole and entire, whether it is seen or not. Or do you think that perhaps no such thing exists?

EVODIUS: On the contrary, I see there are many, but it is sufficient to single out one of them, the nature and truth of number which are present to all who make use of reason. Everyone engaged in computing them strives to grasp their nature with his own reason and intelligence. Some do this rather easily, others with more difficulty, while others cannot do it at all, though the truth makes itself equally available to all who can grasp it. And whenever someone experiences this, it is not altered or changed into a kind of nourishment for the one who perceives it. When anyone errs in judgment about it, the reality itself, which remains true and intact, is not at fault; rather, his own error is measured by his failure to behold the reality itself.

21. AUGUSTINE: That is certainly true. I see you were quick to find an answer as becomes a man not unfamiliar with such matters. But suppose I were to tell you that these numbers have not been impressed upon our mind by any nature of their own but come from things which we grasp with the bodily senses and are a kind of sense-image of things visible, how would you reply? Or would you also be of the same opinion?

EVODIUS: I could never think of such a thing. Even if I could perceive numbers by the bodily senses, I could not on this account also perceive the nature of numerical division and addition by the bodily sense. It is by the light of the mind that I show a man to be wrong whose computation indicates an incorrect total either in addition or subtraction. Besides, I cannot tell how long anything will endure which comes in contact with my bodily senses, such as the heavens and the earth, and all the other bodies which I see are contained in them. But seven and three are ten, not only now, but forever. And there has never been, nor will there ever be a time when seven and three were not ten. This is why I have said that the indestructible truth of number is common to me and to anyone at all who uses his reason.

22. AUGUSTINE: I cannot gainsay the absolute truth and certainty of your answer. But you will readily see that even the numbers themselves have not been brought in through the bodily senses if you realize that all numbers are designated as multiples of the number one. For example, twice one is two, one tripled is three, and ten times one is ten. No matter what the number, it is so designated according to the number of times it contains the number one. But anyone with a true notion of "one" will doubtless discover that it cannot be perceived by the bodily senses. Whatever comes in contact with the bodily senses can be shown to be many, and not one, since, being a body, it also has numberless parts. To say nothing of the minute and barely discernible particles, no mat-

ter how small the tiny body, it has one part on the right, another on the left, one above and another below, one to the far side and another on the near side, parts at the extremes and parts in between. We have to admit that such parts are found in any body, no matter how small it is. Accordingly, we acknowledge that no bodily reality is one, truly and simply, and yet it would be impossible to enumerate so many parts within the body unless these were differentiated by the concept of one.

Whenever I look for this "one" in a body, though I am sure I will not find it, I certainly know what I am looking for and what it is that I do not find there. I know it cannot be found, or better, that it is not present there at all. Consequently, when I recognize that a bodily reality is not one, I know the meaning of one; otherwise, I could not number the many parts in the body. Wherever it is that I come to know one, I certainly do not know it by the bodily senses, for by these I know only bodies, which, as we have shown, are not one, truly and simply. Furthermore, if we have not perceived one by the bodily sense, then neither have we perceived any number by them, none at least of those numbers which we can discern with the understanding. For there is not one of them that does not get its name from its being a given multiple of one, which is not perceived by the bodily senses. The half of any small body has itself its own half, although the whole body is made up of two halves. Hence those two parts of the body are such that even they are not simply two. But the number we call two, because it is twice that which is simply one, has one for its half, namely, that which is simply one, and this in turn cannot have a half or a third, or any other fraction, because it lacks parts and is truly one.

23. Since we are following numerical order, we see next that two follows one and that it is related to one as its double. The double of two does not follow at once, but three, and then four, which is the double of two. And this ordered sequence extends to all the remaining numbers according to a fixed and changeless law. Thus, after one, the first of all numbers, the first number, apart from one, which follows next is two, the double of one. After this second number, namely, two, the second number, apart from the number two, is the double of two, since the first number after two is three, while the second after two is four, the double of two. After the third number, apart from three, is the double of three, since after three, the first number is four, the second is five, and the third is six, which is the double of three. So too, after number four, the fourth number, apart from four, is the double of four, since following the fourth number, namely, after four, the first number is five, the second is six, the third is seven, and the fourth is eight, which is the double of four. You will also find that the same thing holds for all the other numbers, which we discovered when we combined the first two, that is, numbers one and two, namely, that the double of any number is as many times removed from that number as the number doubled is removed from the beginning of the number.

How, then, do we discern that this numerical relationship, which we observe to prevail throughout the whole range of numbers, is changeless, fixed, and indestructible? No one perceives all numbers by any bodily sense, for they are innumerable. I say, then, how do we know that this holds true for all numbers? What idea or image enables us to see with such assurance that this fixed law governing number holds throughout innumerable instances, unless it be that inner light of which the senses have no knowledge?

24. Men endowed with the God-given ability to reason and not blinded by stubbornness are constrained by these and many other such proofs to acknowledge that the law and truth of numbers do not pertain to the bodily sense, that they remain changeless and incorruptible, and belong to all who use their reason to perceive them. Many other things possibly come to mind which, as the common and, as it were, public possession of all who use reason, are there to be seen by the mind and reason of each one who perceives them, though the realities themselves remain intact and unchanging. However, I

was delighted to hear that the law and truth of numbers came especially to your mind when you wanted to give an answer to my question. It is not without some intent that number and wisdom are brought together in the Sacred Scriptures, where it is said: "I have gone round—I and my heart—to know and to consider, and to search out wisdom and number" (Eccles. 7:26).

Chapter 9

25. But let me ask you this: What, in your opinion, should be our view of wisdom itself? Do you think that each man has his own individual wisdom, or that there is one wisdom present to all alike, and that a man becomes wiser the more he shares in it?

EVODIUS: I do not yet know to what wisdom you refer, for I notice that wise actions and words are looked at differently by men. Those who wage war think they are acting wisely, while those who spurn war to devote care and effort to tilling the soil, prefer to extol this activity and to regard it as wisdom. Those shrewd enough to devise schemes for acquiring money are wise in their own eyes. Those uninterested in such things and who renounce them and all such temporal goods, to direct all their effort to the search for truth so as to know themselves and God, judge that this is the one great task of wisdom. Those who are unwilling to allow themselves such leisure for the quest and contemplation of truth, preferring to work for the welfare of men amidst burdensome cares and duties and are occupied with the task of providing just rule and government for human affairs, think that they are wise. And those who combine both of these, living part of their life in the contemplation of truth and part in the discharge of official duties, which they feel are owing to human society, think they have won the prize for wisdom. I make no mention of the countless sects where each one sets its own followers above the rest and would have it that they alone are wise.

Consequently, since the answer to our present problem must not be what we believe but what we grasp with a clear understanding, I cannot possibly reply to your question about the nature of wisdom unless I know by reflection and rational discernment what I already hold on faith.

26. AUGUSTINE: Do you think there can be any wisdom but the truth wherein the highest good is seen and possessed? Now those men whom you mentioned as pursuing different goals, all seek good and shun evil, but they pursue different goals because they have different ideas about the good. Any man, then, who seeks what should not be sought is still in error, even though he would not be seeking it unless he thought it was good. A man who seeks nothing, or who seeks what ought to be sought, is not in error.

Insofar, therefore, as all men seek the happy life, they are not in error. But to the extent that a man fails to hold to that way of life which leads to happiness, by so much is he in error, though he avows and professes that he is seeking only happiness. For there is error whenever we follow something which does not lead us where we want to go. And the more one errs in his way of life, the less wise he is, for he is all the farther from the truth wherein the highest good is seen and possessed. It is by attaining to the possession of the highest good that a man becomes happy, which is unquestionably what all of us desire.

Just as we agree that we want to be happy, so do we agree that we want to be wise since, without wisdom, no one is happy. For no one is happy except by the highest good which is found in the contemplation and possession of that truth which we call wisdom. So, just as the notion of happiness is impressed on our minds even before we are happy—this enables us to have the assurance and to state unhesitatingly that we want to be happy—so too, even before we are wise, we have the notion of wisdom impressed on our minds. And if any one of us is asked whether he wants to be happy, it is this notion that enables him to reply that he does, beyond any shadow of doubt.

27. We agree then about the nature of wisdom, though you were not able to put it in words. For if you did not perceive it at all in your mind, you simply could not know that you want to be wise or that this was your duty, which I do not think you will deny. If, then, we are in agreement about wisdom, I want you to tell me whether, as in the case of the law and truth of numbers, you think that wisdom too is present to all alike who use their reason, or whether you feel there are as many wisdoms as there are men capable of becoming wise. For there are as many minds as there are men, so that we do not perceive anything with one another's mind.

EVODIUS: If the highest good is one for all men, then that truth wherein we can contemplate and possess it, namely, wisdom, must also be common to all.

AUGUSTINE: Do you doubt that the highest good, whatever it is, is the same for all men?

EVODIUS: I really do, because I notice that different men take delight in different things as their highest good.

AUGUSTINE: I only wish that no one had any doubt about the highest good, just as no one doubts that it is only by the possession of this good, whatever it is, that man can become happy. But as this is an important question and may require a lengthy discussion, let us go all the way and suppose that there are just as many highest goods as there are different classes of things which different men seek as their highest good. It does not follow, does it, that wisdom itself is not something one and common to all alike, simply because those goods which they see and choose in the light of this wisdom are many and varied? If you think it does, you could also doubt that the sunlight is something one, since the objects we see in it are many and varied. From among these objects each one freely chooses something to enjoy through his sense of sight. One man likes to look at a mountain height and finds delight in such a view; another, at the level expanse of a meadow; another, at the slope of a valley; another, at the green forest; another, at the undulating surface of the sea; another gathers in all or several of these at once for the sheer delight of looking at them.

The things which men see in the light of the sun and which they choose for their enjoyment are many and varied, yet there is the one sunlight in which each viewer sees and takes hold of an object for his enjoyment. Similarly, the goods are many and varied from which each one chooses what he wants, and it is by contemplating and taking hold of this object of his choice that each one really and truly makes this the highest good wherein to find his enjoyment. It is still possible that the light of wisdom itself, in which these things are seen and grasped, may be one and shared by all alike who are wise.

EVODIUS: I acknowledge that this is possible and that there is nothing to prevent the one wisdom from being common to all, even though the highest goods are many and varied. But I would like to know whether this is the case, since, by granting that it is possible, it does not necessarily follow that it is so.

AUGUSTINE: We know for now that wisdom does exist. But whether there is one wisdom common to all, or whether each wise man has his own wisdom in the way that he has his own soul or mind, is something that we do not yet comprehend.

EVODIUS: That is true.

Chapter 10

28. AUGUSTINE: Well then, where do we see the truth of what we now know, namely, that wisdom or wise men exist, and that all men want to be happy? I certainly have no doubt whatever that you do see this and that it is true. Do you see then that this is true just as you see your own thoughts which are completely unknown to me unless you disclose them to me? Or do you see it in such a way as to understand that it can also be seen as true by me, though you did not tell it to me?

EVODIUS: I have no doubt indeed that you could also see it, even against my will.

AUGUSTINE: Is not this one truth, then, which we both see with our individual minds, common to both of US.

EVODIUS: Quite evidently.

AUGUSTINE: I also believe you will not deny that we should have a zeal for wisdom and will agree that this in fact is true.

EVODIUS: I do not deny this at all.

AUGUSTINE: Can we possibly deny that this truth is likewise one and that it is something to be seen by all alike who know it? Yet each one sees it with his own mind, not with mine or yours, or with anyone else's mind, since what is seen is present to all alike who behold it.

EVODIUS: We could never deny that.

AUGUSTINE: Will you not also admit that these statements have an absolute truth which is present and common to you as well as to me, and to all who see it, namely: we ought to live justly, the less perfect should be subordinated to the more perfect, like things should be equally esteemed, each one should be given his due?

EVODIUS: I agree.

AUGUSTINE: Can you deny that something incorrupt is better than the corrupt, the eternal better than the temporal, the inviolable better than what is subject to injury?

EVODIUS: Who could possibly deny it?

AUGUSTINE: Can anyone say, therefore, that this truth belongs to him alone when its changeless character is there to be seen by all who have the power to behold it?

EVODIUS: No one could truly say that this truth belongs to him alone, since it is just as much one and common to all as it is true.

AUGUSTINE: Who, again, is there to deny that the soul should turn from what is corrupt to the incorrupt, and should love, not the corrupt, but the incorrupt? Or how can anyone, once he acknowledges that something is true, fail to understand its changeless character or to see that it is present to all alike who are able to behold it?

EVODIUS: That is perfectly true.

AUGUSTINE: Well then, will anyone doubt that a life which does not turn away from its firm and moral convictions by any adversity is better than one which is easily broken and overcome by temporal misfortune?

EVODIUS: Who could doubt it?

29. AUGUSTINE: I will look for no further examples of this kind. It is enough that together we see and admit as an absolute certainty that those truths are so many rules and beacons of virtue, that they are true and changeless, and, whether taken singly or collectively, that they are present in common for all to see who can do so, each one viewing them with his own mind and reason. But what I am really asking is whether you think that these truths pertain to wisdom. I believe that in your opinion a man is wise who has acquired wisdom.

EVODIUS: I certainly think so.

AUGUSTINE: Could a man who lives justly live this way unless he knew which are the lower things that he subordinates to the higher, which the things of equal rank that he brings together, and what things he assigns as appropriate to each class?

EVODIUS: He could not.

AUGUSTINE: Then you will not deny, will you, that a man who sees these things does so wisely?

EVODIUS: I do not deny it.

AUGUSTINE: Does not the man who lives prudently choose the incorrupt and judge that it should be preferred to the corrupt?

EVODIUS: Quite clearly.

AUGUSTINE: Then when a man chooses to turn his soul to what everybody admits should be chosen, can we deny that he is making a wise choice?

EVODIUS: I could never deny that.

AUGUSTINE: Therefore, when he turns his soul to what was a wise choice, he does so wisely.

EVODIUS: Most certainly.

AUGUSTINE: And the man who is undeterred by fear or punishment from what he has wisely chosen, and to which it was wise of him to turn, is undoubtedly acting wisely.

EVODIUS: Beyond any doubt.

AUGUSTINE: It is perfectly clear then that all those truths which we call rules and beacons pertain to wisdom. The more a man uses them in the conduct of his life and lives in conformity with them, the more wisely does he live and act. And we cannot really say that what is done wisely is found apart from wisdom.

EVODIUS: That is absolutely true.

AUGUSTINE: Accordingly, just as there are true and changeless rules governing numbers whose law and truth are, as you said, unalterably present and common to all who see them, so, too, are the rules of wisdom likewise true and changeless. When you were asked just now about a few of them, one by one, you replied that they were true and evident and admitted that they are common for all to see who are capable of beholding them.

Chapter 11

30. EVODIUS: I cannot doubt it. But I would very much like to know whether these two, namely, wisdom and number, fall under some one class since you mentioned that they are placed together even in the Sacred Scriptures. Is one derived from the other, or is it contained in the other; does number, for example, derive from wisdom, or is it contained in wisdom? For I would not dare assert that wisdom derives from number or is contained in it. I do not see how I could do so because I am acquainted with many mathematicians or accountants, or whatever else they may be called, who work out perfectly accurate and remarkable calculations. But of wise men, I either know very few, or possibly none at all. Wisdom, it strikes me, is far nobler than number.

AUGUSTINE: You mention a subject at which I am also wont to marvel. For whenever I go over in my mind the unchanging truth of number, and consider, so to speak, its abode or sanctuary or sphere, or however else we may suitably indicate somehow the seat and dwelling-place of number, I am far removed from the body. And when I chance to find something that I can think of, but not something that I can adequately express in words, I return wearily to the familiar things about us in order to be able to speak, and I speak in the usual way of things that confront our gaze. This happens to me even when I do all I can to think carefully and intently about wisdom. That is why I marvel exceedingly at the fact that, while wisdom and number occupy a hidden and certain abode in Truth, and while there is also the additional scriptural testimony which I cited, linking them together—I marvel exceedingly, as I said, why number is of little value for most men, while wisdom is dear to them.

But it doubtless comes down to this, that they are one and the same thing. Yet, since the Sacred Scripture has this to say of wisdom that "it reaches from end to end strongly and orders all things gently" (Wisd. 8:1), then, possibly, the power whereby "it reaches from end to end strongly" is called number, while that whereby "it orders all things gently" is here called wisdom, though both belong to one and the same wisdom.

31. Wisdom has endowed all things with number, even the least and those at the lowest confines of the universe. Though they hold the lowest place in existence, bodies all possess these numbers. But the capacity for wisdom has not been given to bodily things or to every kind of soul, but only to rational souls. It is there that wisdom has, so to speak, taken up its abode and from where it orders all things it has endowed with number, even the lowest. Since it is easy for us to judge about bodily things, occupying, as they do, a place beneath us, and to see that they have numbers impressed on them which we also judge to be below us, we therefore set a lower value upon numbers.

But once we begin to change our course, as it were, to an upward direction, we discover that number transcends even our minds and abides unchangingly in truth itself. But since few men are capable of wisdom, whereas the ability to count has been given even to fools, men admire wisdom and have little regard for number. There are, on the other hand, men learned and devoted to study, and the more these withdraw from the taint of earthly things, the more clearly they behold in the truth itself both number and wisdom and hold both in high esteem. And when they compare truth with gold and silver and the other things for which men struggle, then not only these, but even they themselves, appear vile in their sight.

32. It should not surprise you that men have belittled number and set a high value on wisdom simply because it is easier for them to count than to acquire wisdom, when you stop to consider how much more they value gold than the light of a lamp, compared to which gold is something trivial. But greater honor is given something far inferior simply because even a beggar can light himself a candle, whereas only a few can possess gold. This is far from implying that, in comparison with number, wisdom is found inferior, since it is the same; but it must find an eye capable of discerning this identity.

Light and heat are perceived coexistent, so to speak, in the one fire and cannot be separated from each other. Yet, the heat reaches objects placed near it, while the light is spread even over a larger area. In like manner, the power of understanding, present in wisdom, warms what is near it, such as rational souls, whereas, for things farther removed, such as bodies, it does not reach them with the warmth of its wisdom, but permeates them with the light of number. Perhaps you find this obscure, for no analogy drawn from visible things to illustrate an invisible reality can be made to fit perfectly.

Only take note of this point which is enough for our problem at hand and is clear even to more lowly minds, such as ours. Though we are unable to see clearly whether number is contained in wisdom, or is derived from it, or whether wisdom itself derives from number, and is contained in it, or whether it can be shown that both are names of the same thing, this much at least is clear, that both are true and are unchangeably true.

Chapter 12

33. You would in no way deny, then, that there exists unchangeable truth that embraces all things that are immutably true. You cannot call this truth mine or yours, or anyone else's. Rather, it is there to manifest itself as something common to all who behold immutable truths, as a light that in wondrous ways is both hidden and public. But how could anyone say that anything which is present in common to all endowed with reason and understanding is something that belongs to the nature of any one of these in particular? You recall, I believe, the result of our discussion a short time ago concerning the bodily senses, namely, that the objects perceived by us in common by sight and hearing, such as color and sound, which you and I see and hear together, are not identified with the nature of our eyes or ears, but are common objects of our perception. So too, you would never say that the things each one of us perceives in common with his own mind belong to the nature of either of our minds. You cannot say that what two people perceive at the same time with their eyes is identified with the eyes of either one; it is a third something toward which the view of both is directed.

EVODIUS: That is perfectly clear and true.

34. AUGUSTINE: This truth, therefore, which we have discussed at length and in which, though it is one, we perceive so many things—do you think that compared to our minds it is more excellent, equally excellent, or inferior? Now if it were inferior, we would not be making judgments according to it, but about it. We do make judgments, for example, about bodies because they are lower, and we often state not only that they exist or do not exist this way, but also that they ought or ought not so to exist. So too with our souls; we not only know that our soul is in a certain state, but often know besides that this is the way it ought to be. We also make similar judgments about bodies, as when we say that a body is not so bright or so square as it ought to be, and so on, and also of souls, when we say the soul is not so well disposed as it ought to be, or that it is not so gentle or not so forceful, according to the dictates of our moral norms.

We make these judgments according to those rules of truth within us which we see in common, but no one ever passes judgment on the rules themselves. For whenever anyone affirms that the eternal ought to be valued above the things of time, or that seven and three are ten, no one judges that it ought to be so, but merely recognizes that it is so. He is not an examiner making corrections, but merely a discoverer, rejoicing over his discovery.

But if this truth were of equal standing with our minds, it would itself also be changeable. At times our minds see more of it, at other times less, thereby acknowledging that they are subject to change. But the truth which abides in itself, does not increase or decrease by our seeing more or less of it, but, remaining whole or inviolable, its light brings delight to those who have turned to it, and punishes with blindness those who have turned from it.

And what of the fact that we judge about our own minds in the light of this truth, though we are unable to judge at all about the truth itself? We say that our mind does not understand as well as it ought, or that it understands as much as it ought. But the mind's understanding should be in proportion to its ability to be drawn more closely and to cling to the unchangeable truth. Consequently, if truth is neither inferior nor equal to our minds, it has to be higher and more excellent.

Chapter 13

35. I had promised to show you, if you recall, that there is something higher than our mind and reason. There you have it—truth itself! Embrace it, if you can, and enjoy it; "find delight in the Lord and He will grant you the petitions of your heart" (Ps. 36:4). For what more do you desire than to be happy? And who is happier than the man who finds the firm, changeless, and most excellent truth?

Men proclaim they are happy when they embrace the beautiful bodies of their wives and even of harlots, which they desire so passionately, and shall we doubt that we are happy in the embrace of truth? Men proclaim they are happy when, suffering from parched throats, they come to a copious spring of healthful waters, or, when hungry, they come upon a big dinner or supper sumptuously prepared. Shall we deny we are happy when we are refreshed and nourished by truth? We often hear men proclaim they are happy if they recline amid roses and other flowers, or delight in the fragrance of ointments. But what is more fragrant, what more delightful, than the breath of truth? And shall we hesitate to say we are happy when we are filled with the breath of truth? Many decide that for them the happy life is found in vocal music and in the sounds of string instruments and flutes. Whenever these are absent, they account themselves unhappy, whereas when they are at hand, they are thrilled with joy. When truth steals into our minds with a kind of eloquent silence without, as it were, the noisy intrusion of words, shall we look for another happy life and not enjoy that which is so sure and intimately present to us? Men delight in the glitter of gold and silver, in the lustre of gems, and are delighted by the charm and splendor of light, whether it be the light in our own eyes, or that of fires on earth, or the light in the stars, the moon, or the sun. And they think themselves happy when they are not withdrawn from these enjoyments by some kind of trouble or penury, and they would like to go on living forever for the sake of those delights. And shall we be afraid to find our happiness in the light of truth?

36. Quite the contrary. Since it is in truth that we know and possess the highest good, and since that truth is wisdom, let us see in wisdom our highest good. Let us make it our aim to enjoy fully, for happy indeed is the man whose delight is in the highest good.

It is this truth which throws light on all things that are truly good and which men choose according to their mental capacity, either singly or severally, for their enjoyment. By the light of the sun men choose what they like to look at and find delight in it. If some of them are perchance endowed with a sound, healthy, and powerful vision, they will like nothing better than to gaze at the sun itself which also sheds its light on other things in which weaker eyes find delight. Similarly, when the sharp and strong vision of the mind beholds a number of immutable truths known with certainty, it directs its gaze to truth itself, which illumines all that is true. As if unmindful of all else, it clings to this truth and, in enjoying it, enjoys everything else at the same time. For whatever is delightful in other truths is made delightful by the truth itself.

37. Our freedom is found in submission to this truth. And it is our God Himself who frees us from death, namely, from our sinful condition. It is the Truth Himself, speaking also as a man with men, who says to those believing in him: "If you remain in

my word, you are indeed my disciples, and you shall know the truth and the truth shall make you free" (John 8:31–32). But the soul is not free in the enjoyment of anything unless it is secure in that enjoyment.

Chapter 14

Now no one is secure in the possession of goods which can be lost against his will. But no one loses truth or wisdom against his will, for he cannot be separated from them by spatial distances. What we call separation from truth and wisdom is a perverse will which makes inferior things the object of its love. But no one wills anything unwillingly.

In possessing truth, therefore, we have something which all of us can equally enjoy in common, for there is nothing wanting or defective in it. It welcomes all its lovers without any envy on their part; it is available to all, yet chaste with each. No one of them says to another: step back so I too may come close; take your hands away so I may also embrace it. All cling to it; all touch the selfsame thing. It is a food never divided into portions; you drink nothing from it that I cannot drink. By sharing in it, you make no part of it your personal possession. I do not have to wait for you to exhale its fragrance so that I too may draw it in. No part of it ever becomes the exclusive possession of any one man, or of a few, but is common to all at the same time in its entirety.

38. Consequently, the objects we touch or taste or smell bear less resemblance to such truth than those which we perceive by hearing and sight. Every word is fully heard by all who hear it and by each one at the same time; every visible object before our eyes is seen at the same time as much by one as by another.

But these analogies are quite remote. No spoken word, for instance, emits all its sound at the same time, since its sound is prolonged over intervals of time, one part coming before another. And every visible object protrudes, so to speak, through space and is not wholly present everywhere. In any case, these things can all be taken from us against our will, and there are obstacles which stand in the way of our being able to enjoy them.

And even if the beautiful singing of a vocalist were to last forever, his admirers would vie with one another to come to hear him; they would press about each other, and, as the crowd became larger, would fight over seats so that each might be closer to the singer. And as they listened, they could not take any of the sound to keep for themselves but could only be caressed by all the fleeting sounds. And if I should wish to gaze at the sun, and were able to do so uninterruptedly, it would leave me at sunset and could be covered over by a cloud, and I could be forced to give up the pleasure of seeing it because of many other hindrances. Finally, even if the delights attached to seeing light and hearing sound were to be ever present, what great advantage would be mine since I share this in common with brute animals?

But the beauty of truth and wisdom does not turn away any who come because the audience is already overcrowded, provided only that there is a steadfast will to enjoy them. This beauty does not pass with time or move from place to place; it is not interrupted by nightfall or concealed by shadows, and is not at the mercy of the bodily senses. It is near to all throughout the world who have made it the object of their love, and belongs to them forever. It occupies no one place and is nowhere absent; outwardly, it admonishes us, inwardly, it teaches us. All who behold it are changed for the better, and no one can change it for the worse. No one passes judgment on it, and without it no one can judge aright. Hence it is clear, beyond doubt, that truth is superior to our minds, each one of which is made wise by it alone, and is made a judge, not of truth itself, but of all other things in the light of truth.

Chapter 15

39. You granted that if I could prove that there was something above our minds, you would admit it was God, provided that there was still nothing higher. I agreed and stated that it would be enough for me to prove this point. For if there is anything more excellent, then this is God; if not, then truth itself is God. In either case, you cannot deny that God exists, which was the question we proposed to examine in our discussion. If you are uneasy because of what we have received on faith through the hallowed teaching of Christ, namely, that there is a Father of Wisdom, then remember that we have accepted this also on faith, namely, that the Wisdom begotten of the eternal Father is equal to Him. We are not to inquire further about this just now, but only to accept it with an unshaken faith.

God exists indeed, and He exists truly and most perfectly. As I see it, we not only hold this as certain by our faith, but we also arrive at it by a sure, though, as yet, very inadequate form of knowledge. But this is sufficient for the matter at hand and will enable us to explain the other points that have a bearing on the subject, unless, of course, you have some objections to raise.

EVODIUS: I accept all this, overwhelmed as I am with an incredible joy which I am unable to express to you in words. I declare that it is absolutely certain. I do so, prompted by that inner voice which makes me want to hear the truth itself and to cling to it. I not only grant that this is good, but also that it is the highest good and the source of happiness.

40. AUGUSTINE: You are certainly right. I too rejoice exceedingly. But I will ask you whether we are already wise and happy, or whether we are still striving to make this our goal.

EVODIUS: I think rather we are striving toward it.

AUGUSTINE: How then do you grasp those things which you rejoice in as being true and certain? You do grant that an understanding of them pertains to wisdom. Can a foolish man know wisdom?

EVODIUS: Not while he remains foolish.

AUGUSTINE: Then you must now be wise, or else you do not yet know wisdom.

EVODIUS: I am, to be sure, not yet wise, but, insofar as I do know wisdom, I would say that I am not foolish. For I cannot deny that the things I know are certain, and that this is wisdom.

AUGUSTINE: Please answer me this question: will you not grant that a man who is not just is unjust, and the man who is not prudent is imprudent, and the man who is not temperate is intemperate? Can there be any doubt about it?

EVODIUS: I grant that when a man is not just, he is unjust, and I would give the same answer regarding the prudent and temperate man.

AUGUSTINE: Why, then, is a man not foolish when he is not wise?

EVODIUS: This I will also admit, that when a man is not wise, he is foolish.

AUGUSTINE: Now which one of the two are you?

EVODIUS: Whichever one you want to call me, for I dare not say that I am wise. Yet, I see how it follows from what I have admitted that I should not hesitate to say I am foolish.

AUGUSTINE: Then the foolish man knows wisdom. For, as we have stated, he would not be sure he wanted to be wise, and that he ought to be so, unless the notion of wisdom were fixed in his mind; fixed in his mind, as are those things pertaining to wisdom itself about which, when questioned one by one, you replied, and in the knowledge of which you found delight.

EVODIUS: It is just as you say.

Chapter 16

41. AUGUSTINE: In our effort to be wise as quickly as possible, what else do we do but concentrate our soul wholly upon what the mind has discovered, and make this its permanent abode? As a result, the soul will no longer take delight in any individual good of its own that entangles it in things of a transitory nature but, once stripped of its attachment for the things of time and place, it will take hold of that which is forever one and the same. Just as the soul is the total source of life for the body, so is God the source of happiness for the soul. While we are engaged in this task, and until we have finished it, we are wayfarers. And if it is now granted us to enjoy those true and certain goods which cast their light along our darksome journey, take note whether this be not the very thing which Scripture says about the way Wisdom acts towards its lovers when they come in search of it: "She shows herself to them cheerfully in the ways, and meets them with all providence" (Wisd. 6:13).

Turn where you will, wisdom speaks to you by the imprint it has left on its works, and, when you are slipping back into what is outward, it entices you to return within by the beauty of those very forms found in things external. This is done so you may recognize that whatever delights you in a body and attracts you by the bodily senses is imbued with number. Thus, you must search for its source and return within yourself and come to see that it is not possible to pass judgment, favorable or unfavorable, on things known by the bodily senses unless you have at your disposal a knowledge of certain laws governing beauty to which you refer whatever objects you perceive outwardly.

42. Look at the heavens and the earth and the sea, and at all the things they contain. Whether these shine from above or crawl on the earth below, or fly or swim, they all have forms because they possess number. Take away number from them, and they are nothing. What then, is the source of their existence but that same source where number derives, since, in fact, they enjoy existence only insofar as they are possessed of number?

Even men who create beauty in working with bodily materials make use of numbers in their art and fashion their products in accordance with them. While producing their work, they manipulate their hands and tools until what is being formed externally is made as perfectly as possible to conform with the inward light of number. Then, through the senses as intermediaries, it wins the approval of the mind which judges within, as it contemplates the higher realm of numbers. Ask me next what it is that moves the bodily members of the artisan and it will be found to be number, for even they move in a measured rhythm. If you take from his hand what he is making, and from his mind the intention to make something, then that bodily movement is calculated to give delight, and is called pantomime. Ask what there is in pantomime to cause delight, and number will answer that it is present there.

Now examine the beauty of a graceful body, and number will be found at work in space. Examine beauty in bodily movement, and you will see how number plays a role in the proper timing. Enter into the realm of art where number has its origin, and try to find time and place there. You will find there neither place nor time, and yet it is there that number has its abode. This realm of number is devoid of spaces, nor is its duration measured in terms of days. Yet, when men desirous of becoming artists set about the task of learning this art, they are moving their bodies in space and time, but their soul they move only in time; and with the passing of time they become more proficient in their art.

Now go beyond even the soul of the artist to get a view of the eternal realm of number. Wisdom will now shine upon you from its inner abode and from the very sanctuary of truth. If your gaze, as yet weak, recoils from this light, turn the mind's eye back along the way where "wisdom showed herself cheerfully." Only remember that you have put off for a time a vision which you will seek again when you are stronger and sounder.

43. O Wisdom, O Light most pleasing to a mind made pure! Woe to those who forsake your guidance and grope about among your shadowy imitations and, more enamored of your signs than of you, are forgetful of what you wish to intimate. For you never cease to intimate your nature and excellence to us, and the entire beauty of created things consists in these signs. The artist, too, through the beauty of his work, intimates in a way to the viewer of it that he should not fasten his attention there completely but should so scan the beauty of the artistic work that he will turn his thoughts back fondly upon him who made it. Those who love the things you make instead of yourself are like men who listen to the eloquence of a wise man. In their overeagerness to hear his beautiful voice and the skillful cadence of his words, they neglect the primary importance of his thoughts for which the spoken words were to serve as signs.

Woe to those who turn away from your light and are delighted to cling to their own darkness. Turning their back, so to speak, upon you, they are enchained by works of the flesh as by their own shadow, and yet, even such delight as they experience there, comes to them from the encompassing rays of your light. But while love of the shadow continues, it makes the mind's eye weaker and less able to endure the sight of your presence. Hence, so long as a man prefers to pursue whatever is easier for his weakened condition to endure, the more is he encompassed in darkness. This is the beginning of his inability to see that which exists most perfectly, and he begins to judge as evil whatever deceives him through want of foresight, or appeals to his impoverished condition, or torments him in his state of captivity. Yet he is justly suffering these penalties for having turned from wisdom; and what is just cannot be evil.

44. Hence, if you take a look at any changeable reality, you will be unable to grasp it either by the bodily senses or by mental reflection unless it is held together by some numerical determinant, without which it will fall back into nothing. Have no doubt that there exists an eternal and changeless form which keeps such changeable things from losing their existence and enables them to pass, as it were, through the phases of their temporal duration by the regularity of their movements and their separate and varied forms. Such a form is neither circumscribed by place nor spread, as it were, through space; nor is it extended or changed in the course of time. In virtue of this form, all changeable realities are able to receive their forms, each according to its nature, and to realize fully their numerical perfection in place and time.

Chapter 17

45. Every changeable reality must also be capable of receiving form. Just as we call something changeable which is capable of undergoing change, so I would call "formable," whatever is capable of receiving form. But nothing can impart form to itself, because nothing can give itself what it does not have, and, surely, a thing is given form so that it may have form. So if anything possesses form, there is no need for it to receive what it has. But if it does not have form, it cannot receive from itself what it does not have. Nothing, therefore, as we have said, can give itself form. Now what more can we say about the changing nature of body and soul, since enough has been said previously? We may conclude, then, that body and soul both receive forms from an immutable and everlasting form, with reference to which it was said: "Thou shalt change them and they shall be changed, but Thou art forever the same and thy years fail not" (Ps. 51:27). The Prophet spoke of years that do not fail to indicate eternity. Of the same form it is likewise said that "abiding in itself, it renews all things" (Wisd. 7:27).

By this we may also understand that all things are ruled by providence. If everything in existence would become nothing, once form was entirely taken away, then this unchangeable form is itself their providence. Through it all changing realities subsist so as to achieve their perfection and movements by the numerical principles belonging to their forms. If this form did not exist, these would have no being. Accordingly, the man who is making his way toward wisdom will see, as he gazes thoughtfully upon the whole of creation, how wisdom reveals itself cheerfully to him along the way and comes to meet him with all providential care. And he will yearn all the more eagerly to complete this journey as the path itself is made more beautiful by that wisdom which he so ardently desires to reach.

46. If you are able to find some other class of creature besides that which exists without life, and that which exists with life but without understanding, and that which exists with life and understanding, then you might venture to affirm that there is something good which does not come from God. These three classes may even be expressed by two words, if we call them body and life. For that which has only life and no understanding, as animals, and that which has understanding, as man, are rightly said to have life. Now these two, namely, body and life, are reckoned among things created, since we also speak of life of the Creator Himself, and this is the highest form of life. Since these two, namely, body and life, are capable of receiving form, as our earlier remarks have shown, and since they would fall back into nothingness were all form to be taken away, they give sufficient indication that they owe their existence to that form which is always the same.

Consequently, all good things, however great or small, can only come from God. What can be greater among creatures than life endowed with understanding, or what can be less than body? No matter how far these deteriorate and tend towards nothingness, something of form remains in them to give them such existence as they have. Whatever form is left in anything undergoing such deterioration, comes to it from that form which knows no deterioration and which does not permit even the movements of things, whether towards progress or deterioration, to go beyond the limits imposed by their numbers. Consequently, whatever we find praiseworthy in nature, whether it be deemed worthy of great or of slight praise, must be referred to the highest and unspeakable praise of the Creator. But you may have something further to add.

Chapter 18

47. EVODIUS: I am, I admit, sufficiently convinced that God exists and that all goods come from God, so far as such evidence is possible in the present life and for men like ourselves. All existing things come from God, whether they have understanding and life and existence, or have only life and existence, or have only existence. Now let us examine the third question to see whether it can be shown that free will should be reckoned among things that are good. Once this is proven, I will have no hesitation in granting that God gave it to us and that it is something that should have been given.

AUGUSTINE: You recall very well the questions proposed, and you were quick to notice that the second question has already been cleared up. But you should have seen that the third was also settled. You gave it as your opinion that free will should not have been given because people commit sin by it. In opposition to your view, I retorted that moral conduct is only possible by free will and went on to assert that God had given it for this purpose. You replied that free will should have been given us in the same way as justice, which one can only use rightly. This reply of yours compelled us to embark upon these roundabout discussions to prove that good things, great and small, come from God alone. This point could only be clarified after we had refuted the wicked folly expressed by the fool who said in his heart, "there is no God." Some kind of reasoning, suited to our feeble mentality, was undertaken on this important matter in order to give us something certain by way of conclusion, while God Himself was helping us along so perilous a course. Although these two truths, namely, that God exists, and that all good things come from Him, were at first held firmly by faith, they have now been examined in such a way that this third truth is manifestly evident, namely, that free will must be numbered among things that are good.

48. In an earlier discussion it was proven and agreed upon by us that a corporeal nature occupies a lower place in existence than does the nature of the soul, and that the soul is therefore a greater good than the body. If, then, among goods of the body we find some which man can misuse, we do not say that they should not therefore have been given, since we do acknowledge that these are good. We should not be surprised then if we also find in the soul some goods which we can also misuse. But because they are good, they could only be given by Him from whom all good things come.

You can see how a great good is wanting in a body having no hands; yet a man who perpetrates cruel and shameful deeds with them makes bad use of his hands. If you were to see someone with no feet, you would admit that an important good is wanting to the body's integrity, and yet you could not deny that a man who uses his feet to injure someone or to disgrace himself is making bad use of his feet.

With our eyes we can perceive light and distinguish bodily forms one from another. This power of sight is the noblest endowment of our body and for this reason these organs have been given a kind of exalted place of honor in our body. Our eyes also serve to protect health and furnish many other benefits to life. Yet, many men do much that is shameful with their eyes and enlist them to serve the cause of lust. You can see what a great good is wanting to a face having no eyes, but when we possess them, who else has given them but God, the Giver of all goods?

Just as you look favorably upon these goods in the body and praise Him who gave them, without regard to those who misuse them, so you should also grant that free will, without which no one can live right, is good and is given by God. You should further acknowledge that those who misuse this good should be condemned rather than admit that He who gave free will should not have given it.

49. EVODIUS: I would like you to prove for me first that free will is a good, and then I would grant that God gave it to us, because I acknowledge that all things good come from God.

AUGUSTINE: Have I failed then to prove this to you after so much effort in our earlier discussion? You granted at the time that the beauty and form of a body are wholly derived from the supreme form of all things, namely, the truth, and that these are good. Truth itself says in the Gospel that even the hairs of our head are numbered. Have you forgotten what we said about the supremacy of number and how its power extends from end to end? What perversity to count the hairs of our head, small and lowly as they are, among things good, and fail to discover their cause and to see that God alone is the Creator of everything good, since all good things, great and small, derive from Him, from whom comes every good. Again, what perversity to doubt about free will, without which it is impossible to lead an upright life, as even they acknowledge who live wickedly.

In any case, please tell me now which you think is the higher good in us. Is it that without which we can live rightly, or that without which we cannot live rightly?

EVODIUS: Please go easy on me, for I am ashamed that I could not see this. How could anyone doubt that that without which there can be no right living is the more excellent good by far?

AUGUSTINE: Would you deny then that a man with one eye can live rightly?

EVODIUS: May I never be guilty of such colossal folly!

AUGUSTINE: Since you grant, then, that the eye is something good in the body, even though its loss is no hindrance to leading a good life, will you take the view that free will is not a good, when no one can live rightly without it?

50. Think of justice, which no one can put to bad use. It is reckoned among the greatest goods found in man and among all the virtues of the soul which make for a good and upright life. Nor does anyone put to bad use the virtues of prudence or courage or temperance. In all these virtues, as well as in justice itself, which you mentioned, it is right reason that prevails, and without it the virtues cannot exist. But no one can put right reason to a bad use.

Chapter 19

These virtues are, therefore, great goods. But you must remember that not only the great but even the least goods exist through Him alone from whom all good things come, namely, from God. Our earlier discussion led to this conclusion, to which you gladly gave assent time after time.

As I was saying, these virtues which enable us to live rightly are great goods, whereas all forms of bodily beauty are the least goods, since we can live rightly without them. But the powers of the soul, without which there can be no right living, are intermediate goods. No one puts virtues to a bad use, but anyone can put the other goods, namely, the intermediate and least, not only to good, but also to bad use. So no one puts virtues to bad use, since the function of virtue is the good use of those things which we can also put to bad use. No one makes bad use of what he puts to good use. Accordingly, the vast liberality of God's goodness has brought into existence not only the great, but also the intermediate and least goods. His goodness is more to be praised for the great than for the intermediate goods, and more for the intermediate than for the least goods, but still to be praised more for all of them than if He had not give existence to them all.

51. EVODIUS: I agree. But, since in our discussion of free will we see that it can make either good or bad use of other things, I am perplexed as to how free will is to be numbered among the things which we use.

AUGUSTINE: In the same way that our reason gives us certain knowledge of all that we know, though reason itself is numbered among the things we know by reason. Have you forgotten that when we were inquiring as to what reason could know, you admitted that reason too is known by reason? If we make use of other things by our free will, you must not therefore think it strange that we can also make use of free will by free will itself. As in using other things, the will is making use of itself, so in knowing other things, reason also knows itself. Memory, too, embraces not only all the other things we remember, but, by our not forgetting that we have a memory, it also remains somehow within us. It remembers not only other things but also itself; or better yet, it is by memory that we remember ourselves, other things, and memory itself.

52. Consequently, a man possesses the happy life when his will, an intermediate good, clings to the changeless good. This is not his own good exclusively but is common to all, like truth, which we discussed at length without doing it justice. And this happy life, namely, the state of the soul in union with the changeless good, is man's proper and principal good. In this good, too, are found all the virtues which no one can put to bad use. And while these are important and principal goods in man, we understand well enough that they belong to each man and are not the common possession of all.

Men become wise and happy by clinging to truth and wisdom, which are common to all. But one man does not become happy by the happiness of another. Even when he emulates the happy man in order to be happy himself, he seeks happiness from the same source which he knows made the first man happy, namely, the truth, which is changeless and common to all. Nor does one man become prudent or courageous or temperate or just by the presence of these virtues in another. But he acquires these by conforming his soul to the changeless norms and beacons of the virtues, which abide indestructibly in truth itself and in wisdom, which are common to all. The man whose soul is conformed and fixed to these principles is endowed with such virtues and is set up as an example for one's imitation.

53. By adhering to the changeless good, which is common to all, the will acquires the principal and important goods, though the will is itself an intermediate good. But when it turns away from the changeless good, common to all, and turns towards a good of its own, or to an external or lower good, then the will sins. It turns towards a good of its own whenever it wants to be its own master; to an external good, when it is eager to know the personal affairs of others, or whatever is none of its own business; to a lower good, when it loves the pleasures of the body. Thus, a man who becomes proud, curious, and sensuous is delivered over to another kind of life which, in comparison with the higher life, is a death. And yet, this life is subject to the rule of Divine Providence, which assigns everything to its proper place and gives to each one his due.

As a consequence, neither those goods sought after by sinners are in any way evil, nor free will itself, which we found was to be counted among the intermediate goods. Evil consists rather in the will's turning away from the changeless good and in its turning to goods that are changeable. Since this turning from one thing to another is not done from necessity, but freely, the unhappiness which results is justly deserved.

Chapter 20

54. Since the will undergoes movement when it turns from the unchangeable to the changeable good, you may perhaps ask how this movement originates. It is really evil, though free will must be reckoned as a good, since it is impossible to live rightly without it. For if this movement, namely, the turning away of the will from the Lord, is unquestionably sinful, we could not say, could we, that God is the cause of sin? If this movement, therefore, does not come from God, then where does it come from?

If I reply to your question by saying that I do not know, you may be distressed all the more. Yet, I would be answering you correctly, because what is nothing, cannot be known. Only make sure to hold firm to your religious conviction that you know of no good, either by the senses, or by the intellect, or in any other way, that does not come from God. Hence, no kind of nature will be found that does not come from God. Wherever you find things possessed of measure, number, and order, have no hesitation in ascribing them all to God their Maker. Remove these three from things entirely, and nothing at all will be left. Even were some vestige of an inchoative form to remain where you see no measure or number or order (since wherever these exist, form is complete), you would have to disallow even this inchoative form, since this seems to serve as material which the maker must bring to perfection. For, if the full perfection of form is a good, the beginning of form is something good. Hence, if all good is taken away entirely, there will remain not something, but nothing at all. All good is from God and, consequently, there is no nature that is not from God. Hence, that movement of the soul's turning away, which we admitted was sinful, is a defective movement, and every defect arises from non-being. Look for the source of this movement and be sure that it does not come from God.

Yet, since it is voluntary, this defect lies within our power. If you are fearful of it, then your will is against it, and unless you will it, it will not exist. What could be more secure than to live a life where nothing can happen to you which you do not will? But, since man cannot rise of his own will as he fell of his own will, the right hand of God, namely, our Lord Jesus Christ, is outstretched to us from above. Let us embrace Him with a strong faith, await Him with a sure hope, and love Him with an ardent charity.

If you think there is something further that we should investigate more carefully on the origin of sin—I see no need for it at all—but if you think there is, it will have to be put off for another discussion.

EVODIUS: I will certainly comply with your wish to put off for another time the problems arising from our discussion. For I cannot agree with your view that this matter has already been sufficiently investigated.

CITY OF GOD (in part)

BOOK VIII

Chapter 1

I must now turn to a matter which calls for much deeper thought than was needed to resolve the issues raised in the previous Books. I mean natural theology. Unlike the poetical theology of the stage which flaunts the crimes of the gods and the political theology of the city which publicizes their evil desires, and both of which reveal them as dangerous demons rather than deities, natural theology cannot be discussed with men in the street but only with philosophers, that is, as the name implies, with lovers of wisdom.

I may add that, since divine truth and scripture clearly teach us that God, the Creator of all things, is Wisdom, a true philosopher will be a lover of God. That does not mean that all who answer to the name are really in love with genuine wisdom, for it is one thing to be and another to be called a philosopher. And, therefore, from all the philosophers whose teachings I have learned from books I shall select only those with whom it would not be improper to discuss this subject.

I shall not bother in this work to refute all the errors of all the philosophers, but only such as pertain to theology—which term from its Greek derivation I take to mean a study of the divine nature. My only purpose is to challenge the opinions of those philosophers who, while admitting that there is a God who concerns himself with human affairs, claim that, since the worship of this one unchangeable God is not sufficient to attain happiness even after death, lesser gods, admittedly created and directed by this supreme God, should also be reverenced.

I must say that such philosophers were nearer to the truth than Varro was. His idea of natural theology embraced at most the universe and the world-soul. They, on the contrary, acknowledged a God who transcends the nature of every kind of soul, a God who created the visible cosmos of heaven and earth, and the spirit of every living creature, and who, by the communication of His own immutable and immaterial light, makes blessed the kind of rational and intellectual soul which man possesses.

Even the most superficial student will recognize in these men the Platonic philosophers, so named after their master, Plato. I shall speak briefly about Plato's ideas, in so far as they are relevant to the matter in hand, but first I must review the opinions of his predecessors in the field of philosophy.

Chapter 2

The legacy of literature written in the universally admired Greek language records two schools of philosophy. They are, first, the Italian, established in that part of Italy formerly known as Magna Graecia; and second, the Ionian, in that country which is now

St. Augustine, *City of God,* Book VIII, 1–12; XII, 1–9; XIX, 11–17 from *Fathers of the Church; Writings of Saint Augustine; Saint Augustine: City of God,* translated by Gerald G. Walsh, Daniel J. Honan, and Grace Monahan (Washington, DC: The Catholic University of America Press, 1952, 1954). Reprinted by permission.

called Greece. Pythagoras of Samos is said to be the founder of the Italian school and also the originator of the word philosophy. Before his time, any person of outstanding achievement was called a sage. But when Pythagoras, who considered it arrogance to call one's self wise, was asked his profession, he replied that he was a philosopher, that is to say, a man in pursuit of, or in love with, wisdom.

Thales of Miletus, who initiated the Ionian School, was one of the celebrated Seven Wise Men. While the remaining six were distinguished by balanced lives and moral teachings, Thales took up the study of nature and committed the results of his researches to writing. He won particular applause by his mastery of astronomical calculations and by his predictions of solar and lunar eclipses. His deliberate purpose in this was to found a school that would survive him. His main theory was that the primary stuff of all things is water, and that from this principle originated the elements, the cosmos and everything which the world produced. As far as he was concerned, nothing of all this universe, so marvelous to gaze upon, was directed by divine intelligence.

His disciple and successor, Anaximander, proposed a new cosmological theory. For him, there could be no one ultimate element of all things such as water; rather, each thing is derived from principles of its own. Hence, he held, the number of principles is infinite, and from these arise uncounted worlds and all that they produce. And, in an endless succession of dissolution and becoming, no one world endures longer than its period permits. Like Thales, he found no place for any divine direction in the processes of nature.

Anaximander's disciple, Anaximenes, believed that all cosmic energy is derived from air, which he considered infinite. He neither denied nor ignored the gods; nevertheless, he taught that they were creatures of the air and not its creators. His pupil, Anaxagoras, realizing that divine spirit was the cause of all visible things, held that the divine mind, using infinite matter, consisting of unlike particles, made each particular thing out of its own kind of like particles.

Diogenes, another follower of Anaximenes, held that air was the ultimate element of all things, but that nothing could be produced from it without the agency of the divine reason, which permeated it. Anaxagoras was followed by his pupil Archelaus. He, too, asserted that everything in the universe was composed of like particles, which, however, were informed by intelligence. This mind, by causing the conjunction and dissolution of the eternal bodies or particles, was the source of all movements. Archelaus is said to have taught Socrates, the master of Plato. This brief review has been but a preparation for the discussion of Plato's philosophy.

Chapter 3

To Socrates goes the credit of being the first one to channel the whole of philosophy into an ethical system for the reformation and regulation of morals. His predecessors without exception had applied themselves particularly to physics or natural science. I do not think that it can be definitely decided just why Socrates chose to follow this course. It has been suggested that he did so because he had become wearied of obscure and uncertain investigations, and preferred to turn his mind to a clean-cut objective, to that secret of human happiness which seems to have been the sole purpose of all philosophical research. Others have claimed, more kindly, that he did not think it right for minds darkened with earthly desires to reach out beyond their limits to the realm of the divine.

Socrates realized that his predecessors had been seeking the origin of all things, but he believed that these first and highest causes could be found only in the will of the single and supreme Divinity and, therefore, could be comprehended only by a mind purified from passion. Hence his conclusion, that he must apply himself to the acquisition of virtue, so that his mind, freed from the weight of earthly desires, might, by its own natural vigor, lift itself up to eternal realities and, with purified intelligence, contemplate the very nature of that immaterial and immutable light in which the causes of all created natures abidingly dwell. Nevertheless, with his marvelous combination of wit and words, pungency and politeness, and with his trick of confessing ignorance and concealing knowledge he used to tease and poke fun at the folly of ignoramuses who talked as though they knew the answers to those moral problems in which he seemed wholly absorbed.

The result was that he incurred their enmity. He was falsely accused and condemned to death. However, the very city of Athens that had publicly condemned him began publicly to mourn his loss, and the wrath of the people was so turned against his two accusers that one of them was killed by an angry mob and the other escaped a similar death only by voluntary and perpetual exile.

Socrates was thus so highly distinguished both in life and in death that he left behind him numerous disciples. They rivaled one another in zealous discussions of those ethical problems where there is question of the supreme good and, hence, of human happiness.

In his discussions, Socrates had a way of proposing and defending his theories and then demolishing them. No one could make out exactly what he believed. Consequently, each of his followers picked what he preferred and sought the supreme good in his heart's desire.

Now the truth is that the supreme good is that which, when attained, makes all men happy. Yet, so varied in regard to this good were the views of the Socratics that is seems hardly credible that all of them were followers of one and the same master. Some, like Aristippus, claimed that pleasure was the highest good; others, like Antisthenes, virtue. The men and their views are so numerous and varied that is would be irksome to mention them all.

Chapter 4

Of the pupils of Socrates, Plato was so remarkable for his brilliance that he has deservedly outshone all the rest. He was born in Athens of a good family and by his marvelous ability easily surpassed all his fellow disciples. Realizing, however, that neither his own genius nor Socratic training was adequate to evolve a perfect system of philosophy, he traveled far and wide to wherever there was any hope of gaining some valuable addition to knowledge. Thus, in Egypt he mastered the lore which was there esteemed. From there he went to lower Italy, famous for the Pythagorean School, and there successfully imbibed from eminent teachers all that was then in vogue in Italian philosophy.

However, Plato's special affection was for his old master—so much so that in practically all the Dialogues he makes Socrates, with all his charm, the mouthpiece not only of his own moral arguments but of all that Plato learned from others or managed to discover himself.

Now, the pursuit of wisdom follows two avenues—action and contemplation. Thus, one division of philosophy may be called active; the other part, contemplative.

The former deals with the conduct of life; that is to say, with the cultivation of morals. Contemplative philosophy considers natural causality and truth as such. Socrates excelled in practical wisdom; Pythagoras favored contemplation, and to this he applied his whole intelligence.

It is to Plato's praise that he combined both in a more perfect philosophy, and then divided the whole into three parts: first, moral philosophy which pertains to action; second, natural philosophy whose purpose is contemplation; third, rational philosophy which discriminates between truth and error. Although this last is necessary for both action and contemplation, it is contemplation especially which claims to reach a vision of the truth. Hence, this threefold division in no way invalidates the distinction whereby action and contemplation are considered the constituent elements of the whole of philosophy. Just what Plato's position was in each of these three divisions—that is to say, just what he knew or believed to be the end of all action, the cause of all nature, the light of all reason—I think it would be rash to affirm and would take too long to discuss at length.

Plato was so fond of following the well-known habit of his master of dissimulating his knowledge or opinions that in Plato's own works (where Socrates appears as a speaker) it is difficult to determine just what views he held even on important questions. However, of the views which are set forth in his writings, whether his own or those of others which seemed to have pleased him, a few must be recalled and included here. In some places, Plato is on the side of the true religion which our faith accepts and defends. At other times he seems opposed; for example, on the respective merits of monotheism and polytheism in relation to genuine beatitude after death.

Perhaps this may be said of the best disciples of Plato—of those who followed most closely and understood most clearly the teachings of a master rightly esteemed above all other pagan philosophers—that they have perceived, at least, these truths about God: that in Him is to be found the cause of all being, the reason of all thinking, the rule of all living. The first of these truths belongs to natural, the second to rational, the third to moral philosophy.

Now, if man was created so that by his highest faculty he might attain to the highest of all realities, that is, to the one, true and supreme God, apart from whom no nature exists, no teaching is true, no conduct is good, then let us seek Him in whom all we find is real, know Him in whom all we contemplate is true, love Him in whom all things for us are good.

Chapter 5

If, then, Plato defined a philosopher as one who knows, loves and imitates the God in whom he finds his happiness, there is little need to examine further. For, none of the other philosophers has come so close to us as the Platonists have, and, therefore, we may neglect the others. Take for example, the theology of the stage. It beguiles the minds of the pagans with the crimes of the gods. Or, take political theology, according to which impure demons under the name of gods seduce the populace who are slaves of earthly pleasures, and demand human errors as divine honors for themselves. They excite in their worshipers an impure passion to watch the demons sinning on the stage as though this were an act of worship, and they are even more satisfied than the spectators with the plays that exhibit their human passions. Proper as such rites may seem in places of worship, they are debased by connection with the obscenity of the theatres;

while the filth of the stage loses its foulness by comparison with the rites that take place in the temples.

Nor is the theology of Varro any better in its interpretation of these rites as symbolic of heaven and earth and the origins and movements of mortal affairs. The fact is, they do not denote what he tries to insinuate. His fancy gets the better of the truth. And, even were he right, it would still be wrong for a rational soul to worship as a god something which, in the order of nature, is in a lower category or to submit as to gods to those very things over which the true God has put men in charge.

Finally, the Platonic theology is superior to those revealing writings about the sacred rites which Numa Pompilius had buried with himself in order to hide them and which, when turned up by a plough, the Senate ordered to be burned. And to do justice to Numa, we should include in this class the letter that Alexander of Macedon wrote to his mother, telling her what had been revealed to him by Leo, an Egyptian high priest, to the effect that all the gods, major as well as minor, were nothing more than mortal men—not only Picus and Faunus, Aeneas and Romulus, Hercules and Aesculapius, Bacchus, son of Semele, the twin sons of Tyndareus, and such like mortals who are reckoned as gods, but even the greater gods whom Cicero in his *Tusculan Disputations* alludes to without mentioning their names; that is, Jupiter, Juno, Saturn, Vulcan, Vesta, and many others whom Varro attempts to identify with the parts or elements of the world. Fearful that he had revealed a great mystery, Leo begged Alexander to have his mother burn the message conveyed to her.

Certainly, all such fancies of both the mythical and civil theologies should yield to the Platonists who acknowledged the true God as the author of being, the light of truth and the giver of blessedness. So, too, those philosophers, the materialists who believe that the ultimate principles of nature are corporeal, should yield to those great men who had knowledge of so great a God. Such were Thales, who found the cause and principle of things in water, Anaximenes in air, the Stoics in fire, Epicurus in atoms, that is, minute indivisible and imperceptible corpuscles. And so of the rest, whose names it is needless to mention, who maintained that bodies, simple or compound, animate or inanimate, but nevertheless material, were the root of all reality.

The Epicureans, for example, believed that life could be produced from lifeless matter. Others taught that both animate and inanimate things derive from a living principle but that this principle must be as material as the things themselves. The Stoics claimed that fire, one of the four material elements of this visible world, had life and intelligence, that it was the creator of the universe and all within it; in fact, that it was God.

Now, philosophers of this type could think only about such matters as their sense-bound minds suggested to them. Yet they have within themselves something they have never seen and they can see in their imagination, without looking at it, an external object which they have previously seen. Now, whatever can be so imagined in the mind's eye is certainly not a body but only the likeness of a body, and that power of the mind which can perceive this likeness is itself neither a body nor an image of a body. Moreover, that faculty which perceives and judges whether this likeness is beautiful or ugly is certainly superior to the object judged.

Now, this faculty is a man's reason, the essence of his rational soul, which is certainly not material, since the likeness of a body which is seen and judged in the mind of a thinking person is not material. The soul, then, cannot be one of the four elements out of which the visible, material cosmos is composed—earth, water, air, and fire. And if our mind is not material, how can God the Creator of the soul be material?

As I said before, let all such philosophers give place to the Platonists. That goes for those, too, who were ashamed to acknowledge a material god, yet thought that men's souls were of the same nature as His—so little were they moved by the fact of a mutability in the soul that it would be unthinkable to attribute to the nature of God. Their answer to this difficulty was that the soul is unalterable in itself but is affected by the body. They might as well have said that the flesh is wounded because of the body, but in itself is invulnerable. The fact is that what is immutable can be changed by nothing. But, if a thing can be changed by a body, it can be changed by something and, therefore, cannot rightly be called immutable.

Chapter 6

The Platonic philosophers, then, so deservedly considered superior to all the others in reputation and achievement, well understood that no body could be God and, therefore, in order to find Him, they rose beyond all material things. Convinced that no mutable reality could be the Most High, they transcended every soul and spirit subject to change in their search for God. They perceived that no determining form by which any mutable being is what it is—whatever be the reality, mode or nature of that form—could have any existence apart from Him who truly exists because His existence is immutable.

From this it follows that neither the whole universe, with its frame, figures, qualities and ordered movement, all the elements and bodies arranged in the heavens and on earth, nor any life—whether merely nourishing and preserving as in trees, or both vegetative and sensitive as in animals, or which is also intellectual as in man, or which needs no nourishment but merely preserves, feels and knows as in angels can have existence apart from Him whose existence is simple and indivisible. For, in God, being is not one thing and living another—as though He could be and not be living. Nor in God is it one thing to live and another to understand—as though He could live without understanding. Nor in Him is it one thing to know and another to be blessed—as though He could know and not be blessed. For, in God, to live, to know, to be blessed is one and the same as to be.

The Platonists have understood that God, by reason of His immutability and simplicity, could not have been produced from any existing thing, but that He Himself made all those things that are. They argued that whatever exists is either matter or life; that life is superior to matter; that the appearance of a body is sensible, whereas the form of life is intelligible. Hence, they preferred intelligible form to sensible appearance. We call things sensible which can be perceived by sight and bodily touch.

If there is any loveliness discerned in the lineaments of the body, or beauty in the movement of music and song, it is the mind that makes this judgment. This means that there must be within the mind a superior form, one that is immaterial and independent of sound and space and time. However, the mind itself is not immutable, for, if it were, all minds would judge alike concerning sensible forms. Actually, a clever mind judges more aptly than the stupid one; a skilled one better than one unskilled; an experienced one better than one inexperienced. Even the same mind, once it improves, judges better than it did before.

Undoubtedly, anything susceptible of degrees is mutable, and for this reason, the most able, learned and experienced philosophers readily concluded that the first form of all could not be in any of these things in which the form was clearly mutable. Once they perceived various degrees of beauty in both body and mind, they realized that, if all form were lacking, their very existence would end. Thus, they argued that there must be some reality in which the form was ultimate, immutable and, therefore, not susceptible of degrees. They rightly concluded that only a reality unmade from which all other realities originate could be the ultimate principle of things.

So that what is known about God, God Himself manifested to them, since "his invisible attributes are clearly seen by them—his everlasting power also and divinity—being understood through the things that are made" (Rom. 1:19–20). By Him, also all visible and temporal things were created. Enough has been said, I think, concerning what the Platonists call physical or natural philosophy.

Chapter 7

As for the second part of philosophy, logic or rational philosophy, the Platonists are beyond all comparison with those who taught that the criterion of truth is in the bodily senses, and who would have us believe that all knowledge is to be measured and ruled by such doubtful and deceitful testimony. I mean the Epicureans and even the Stoics. For all their passion for adroitness in disputation or, as they would say, dialectics, even this was reckoned a matter of sense perception. They maintained that it was by sensation that the mind conceived those notions (or *ennoíai* as they would say) which are needed for clear definitions and, hence, for the unification and communication of the whole system of learning and teaching.

When these philosophers quote their famous dictum that only the wise are beautiful, I often wonder by just what bodily senses they have perceived that beauty, by what kind of fleshy eyes they could have possibly beheld the form and fairness of wisdom.

Certainly, the Platonists, whom we rightly prefer to all others, were able to distinguish what is apprehended by the mind from what is experienced by the senses, without either denying or exaggerating the faculties of sense. As for that light of our minds by which all can be learned, that, they declared, was the very God by whom all things were made.

Chapter 8

The final division is moral philosophy or, to use the Greek name, ethics. It deals with the supreme good, by reference to which all our actions are directed. It is the good we seek for itself and not because of something else and, once it is attained, we seek nothing further to make us happy. This, in fact, is why we call it our end, because other things are desired on account of this *summum bonum,* while it is desired purely for itself.

Now, some philosophers maintained that this happiness-giving good for man arises from the body; others claimed that it has its source in the soul; while a third group held that it derives from both.

All philosophers have realized that man is made up of body and soul and, therefore, that the possibility of his well-being must proceed either from one of these constituents or from both together, the final good, whereby man would be happy, being the one to which all human actions would be referred and beyond which they would seek nothing to which it might be referred.

Hence, those who are said to have added to the list of goods the "extrinsic" good—such as honor, glory, wealth and so on—did not mean this as though it were a supreme good to be sought for its own sake, but merely as a relative good and one that was good for good men but bad for the wicked.

Thus, those who sought for human good either in man's body or in his mind or in both did not think they had to search outside of man himself to find it. Only those who looked to the body sought it in man's lower nature; those who looked to the soul, in man's higher nature; and the others, in man as a whole; but in every case they sought it only in man himself.

This threefold division of opinion concerning the *summum bonum* resulted, not in three, but in a multitude of philosophical sects and dissensions because of the varying views as to what constituted the good of the body, the good of the soul and the good of the whole man.

The definers of all these defective conclusions should yield to those philosophers who taught that man is never fully blessed, in the enjoyment of either corporal or spiritual good, but only by a fruition in God. This joy in God is not like any pleasure found in physical or intellectual satisfaction. Nor is it such as a friend experiences in the presence of a friend. But, if we are to use any such analogy, it is more like the eye rejoicing in light. Elsewhere, with God's help I shall try to explain the nature of this analogy. For the moment, let it suffice to recall the doctrine of Plato that a virtuous life is the ultimate end of man and that only those attain to it who know and imitate God and find their blessedness wholly in this. Consequently, Plato did not hesitate to say that to philosophize is to love that God whose nature is incorporeal.

From this we infer that the pursuer of wisdom, that is, the philosopher, will only be truly happy when he begins to rejoice in God. Certainly, not every one who delights in what he loves is always blessed, for many are unhappy in loving things they should not love and still more wretched once they begin to enjoy them. On the other hand, no one is really happy until his love ends in fruition. For, even those who love what they should not love do not consider loving but only fruition as the source of their satisfaction.

Who, then, but the very sorriest of persons would deny that a man is really happy who finds fruition in what he loves when what he loves is his true and highest good? Now, for Plato, this true and highest good was God, and, therefore, he calls a philosopher a lover of God, implying that philosophy is a hunt for happiness which ends only when a lover of God reaches fruition in God.

Chapter 9

Philosophers, therefore, of whatever sort who have believed that the true and supreme God is the cause of created things, and the light by which they are known and the good toward which our actions are directed, and that He is the source from which our nature has its origin, our learning truth, our life its happiness—all these we prefer to others and recognize them as our neighbors. It does not matter whether they call themselves—as, perhaps, they should—Platonists, or whether they give their school some other name. Nor need we enquire whether it was only the leaders of the Ionian School—like Plato and his best disciples—who were teachers of these truths, or whether we should include the Italians on account of Pythagoras and the Pythagoreans and, perhaps, others of similar views. For all I know, there may have been men reckoned as wise men or philosophers in other parts of the world who shared these views and doctrines—Atlantic Libyans, Egyptians, Indians, Persians, Chaldeans, Scythians, Gauls, and Spaniards.

Chapter 10

Doubtless, it could happen that a Christian, well versed in ecclesiastical literature, might not be familiar with the name of Platonists nor even know that among Greek-speaking people two distinct schools of philosophy have flourished: the Ionian and the Italian. Nevertheless, he is not so naive as not to know that philosophers look upon themselves as the lovers, if not the possessors, of wisdom; and he is on his guard against materialistic philosophers, who give no thought to the Creator of the world.

The Christian heeds carefully the apostolic admonition which says: "See to it that no one deceives you by philosophy and vain deceit . . . according to the elements of the world" (Col. 2:8). But the same Apostle tells him not to decry all as materialistic philosophers, for of some he says: "What may be known about God is manifest to them. For God has manifested it to them. For since the creation of the world his invisible attributes are clearly seen—his everlasting power also and divinity—being understood through the things that are made" (Rom. 1:19–20). And again, speaking to the Athenians, after the magnificent remark about God which so few can appreciate, namely, that "in Him we live and move and have our being," he went on to add: "as indeed some of your own (poets) have said" (Acts 17:28).

The Christian knows, of course, how to distrust the doctrines of even these latter where they are wrong. Thus, the very Scripture which says that God manifested His invisible attributes to be seen and understood also says that they failed to worship the true God rightly because they rendered to creatures divine honors that were due to Him alone. "Although they knew God, they did not glorify him as God or give thanks, but became vain in their reasonings, and their senseless minds have been darkened. For while professing to be wise, they have become fools, and they have changed the glory of the incorruptible God for an image made like to corruptible man and to birds and four-footed beasts and creeping things" (Rom. 1:21–23). Here the Apostle has in mind the Romans, Greeks and Egyptians, all boastful of their renown for wisdom.

This is a matter that I intend to debate with these philosophers later on. Yet we prefer them to all others inasmuch as they agree with us concerning one God, the Creator of the universe, who is not only incorporeal, transcending all corporeal beings, but also incorruptible, surpassing every kind of soul—our source, our light, our goal.

Now, it may happen that the Christian has not studied the works of these philosophers, nor learned to use their terms in disputation. He may not designate that part of philosophy which treats of the investigation of nature as natural (if he speaks Latin) or as physical (if Greek); nor that part which seeks the ways by which truth may be perceived as rational or logical; nor that part which treats of conduct, with the highest good which is to be sought and the supreme evil to be avoided, as moral or ethics. Nevertheless, he knows that from the one, true and infinitely good God we have a nature by which we were made in His image, faith by which we know God and ourselves, and grace whereby we reach beatitude in union with God.

This, then, is the reason for preferring the Platonists to all other philosophers. While the others consumed time and talent in seeking the causes of things, and the right ways of learning and living, the Platonists, once they knew God, discovered where to find the cause by which the universe was made, the light by which all truth is seen, the fountain from which true happiness flows.

If philosophers, then, whether Platonists or wise men of any nation whatsoever, hold these truths concerning God, they agree with us. However, I have preferred to plead this cause with the Platonists because I know their writings better. The Greeks, whose language is universally esteemed, have eloquently eulogized these writings. The Latins, captivated either by their fascination or their fame, have gladly studied them, and, by translating them into our own language, have added to them new light and luster.

Chapter 11

Some of our fellow Christians are astonished to learn that Plato had such ideas about God and to realize how close they are to the truths of our faith. Some even have been led to suppose that he was influenced by the Prophet Jeremias during his travels in Egypt or, at least, that he had access to the scriptural prophecies; and this opinion I followed in some of my writings.

However, a careful calculation of dates according to historical chronology shows that Plato was born almost one hundred years after Jeremias prophesied, and that nearly sixty years intervened between Plato's death at the age of eighty-one and the time when the Septuagint translation was begun. Ptolemy, King of Egypt, it will be remembered, asked that the Hebraic prophecies be sent to him from Judea and he arranged to have them translated and safeguarded by seventy Hebrew scholars who were also experts in Greek.

Therefore, it follows that, while journeying in Egypt, Plato could not have seen Jeremias who was long since dead, nor could he have read the Scriptures which had not yet been rendered into Greek, his native tongue. Of course, it is just possible that Plato, who was an indefatigable student and who used an interpreter to delve into Egyptian literature, may have done the same with the Scriptures. I do not mean to suggest that he undertook a translation of them. That was a feat which Ptolemy alone could accomplish by virtue of his liberality and of others' respect for his kingly power. But Plato could have learned from conversation the content of the Scriptures, without fully understanding their meaning.

Certain evidence favors this belief. For example, the first book of Genesis begins: "In the beginning God created the heavens and the earth; the earth was waste and void; darkness covered the abyss, and the spirit of God was stirring above the waters" (Gen. 1:1–2). Plato in the *Timaeus* (31b), which deals with the origin of the world, says that in this work God first united earth and fire. Now it is clear that Plato locates fire in the heavens. His statement, therefore, bears a certain resemblance to the words: "In the beginning God created the heavens and the earth."

Plato also mentions two intermediary elements, water and air, by means of which the extremes, earth and fire, were united. This idea, perhaps, originated from his interpretation of the verse: "the spirit of God was stirring above the waters." Paying little attention to the meaning which Scripture habitually ascribes to spirit and remembering that air is often called breath or spirit, Plato could easily have assumed that all four elements were mentioned in this text.

Then, too, Plato's definition of a philosopher—one who loves God—contains an idea which shines forth everywhere in Scripture. But the most palpable proof to my mind that he was conversant with the sacred books is this, that when Moses, informed by an angel that God wished him to deliver the Hebrews from Egypt, questioned the angel concerning the name of the one who had sent him, the answer received was this: "I AM WHO AM. Thus shalt thou say to the children of Israel: He who is, hath sent me to you" (Exod. 3:14), as though, in comparison with Him who, being immutable, truly is, all mutable things are as if they were not. Now, Plato had a passionate perception of this truth and was never tired of teaching it. Yet, I doubt whether this idea can be found in any of the works of Plato's predecessors except in the text: "I AM WHO AM, and you shall say to them: He who is hath sent me to you."

Chapter 12

Whether, then, Plato got his ideas from the works of earlier writers or, as seems more likely, in the way described in the words of the Apostle: "Because that which is known of God is manifest in them. For God hath manifested it unto them. For the invisible things of him, from the creation of the world, are clearly seen, being understood by the things that are made: His eternal power also and divinity" (Rom. 1:19–20), it seems to me that I have sufficiently justified my choice of the Platonic philosophers for the purpose of discussing this present problem in natural theology. The question is this: In order to secure happiness after death, should man worship a single God or many?

The main reason for selecting the Platonists is the superiority of their conceptions concerning one God, Creator of heaven and earth, and, hence, their greater reputation in the judgment of posterity. It is true that Aristotle, a disciple of Plato, was a man of extraordinary genius and wide reputation (though in literary style inferior to Plato) who easily surpassed many others, and no less true that the Peripatetic school (so called from Aristotle's custom of teaching while walking) attracted many disciples even while his teacher, Plato, was alive. So, too, after the death of Plato, a son of his sister, Speusippus, and Xenocrates, Plato's favorite pupil, succeeded him in his Academy and, for this reason, they and their successors are called Academics. Nevertheless, the very best of the Platonists are those relatively recent philosophers who, refusing to be styled either Peripatetics or Academics, have called themselves Platonists. Among these last are those highly distinguished Greek scholars, Plotinus, Iamblichus and Porphyry. A hardly less notable Platonist was the African Apuleius, who was a master of both Greek and Latin. All of these and many others of the same school, not to mention Plato himself, believed in polytheistic worship.

* * *

BOOK XII

Chapter 1

In the previous book we saw something of the beginning of the two cities, so far as angels are concerned. In the same way, we must now proceed to the creation of men and see the beginning of the cities so far as it concerns the kind of rational creatures who are mortal. First, however, a few remarks about the angels must be made in order to make it as clear as I can how there is no real difficulty or impropriety in speaking of a single society composed of both men and angels; and why, therefore, it is right to say that there are not four cities or societies, namely, two of angels and two of men, but only two, one of them made up of the good—both angels and men—and the other of those who are evil.

There is no reason to doubt that the contrary dispositions which have developed among these good and bad angels are due, not to different natures and origins, for God the Author and Creator of all substances has created them both, but to the dissimilar choices and desires of these angels themselves. Some, remaining faithful to God, the common good of all, have lived in the enjoyment of His eternity, truth, and love, while others, preferring the enjoyment of their own power, as though they were their own good, departed from the higher good and common blessedness for all and turned to goods of their own choosing.

Preferring the pomp of pride to this sublimity of eternity, the craftiness of vanity to the certainty of truth, and the turmoil of dissension to the union of love, they became proud, deceitful, and envious.

Since the happiness of all angels consists in union with God, it follows that their unhappiness must be found in the very contrary, that is, in not adhering to God. To the question: "Why are the good angels happy?" the right answer is: "Because they adhere to God." To the question: "Why are the others unhappy?" the answer is: "Because they do not adhere to God." In fact, there is no other good which can make any rational or intellectual creature happy except God. Not every creature has the potentialities for happiness. Beasts, trees, stones, and such things neither acquire nor have the capacity for this gift. However, every creature which has this capacity receives it, not from itself, since it has been created out of nothing, but from its Creator. To possess Him is to be happy; to lose Him is to be in misery. And, of course, that One whose beatitude depends upon Himself as His own good and not on any other good can never be unhappy since He can never lose Himself.

Thus, there can be no unchangeable good except our one, true, and blessed God. All things which He has made are good because made by Him, but they are subject to change because they were made, not out of Him, but out of nothing. Although they are not supremely good, since God is a greater good than they, these mutable things are, none the less, highly good by reason of their capacity for union with and, therefore, beatitude in the Immutable Good which is so completely their good that, without this good, misery is inevitable.

But it does not follow that other creatures in the universe are better off merely because they are incapable of misery. That would be like saying that other members of the body are better than the eyes because they can never become blind. A sentient nature even in pain is better than a stone that cannot suffer. In the same way, a rational nature even in misery is higher than one which, because it lacks reason or sensation, cannot suffer misery.

This being the case, it is nothing less than a perversion of the nature of the angels if they do not adhere to God. For, remember, their nature is so high in the order of creation that, mutable as it is, it can attain beatitude by adhering to the immutable and supreme Good, which is God, and that, unless it achieves beatitude, this nature fails to satisfy its inmost exigencies, and, finally, that nothing but God can satisfy these needs of the angelic nature.

Now, this perversion, like every imperfection in a nature, harms nature and, therefore, is contrary to the nature. It follows, therefore, that what makes the wicked angels differ from the good ones is not their nature but a perversion or imperfection; and this very blemish is a proof of how highly to be esteemed is the nature itself. Certainly, no blemish in a thing ought to be blamed unless we are praising the thing as a whole, for the whole point of blaming the blemish is that it mars the perfection of something we would like to see praised.

For example, when we say that blindness is a defect of the eyes, we imply that it is the very nature of the eyes to see, and when we say that deafness is a malady of the ears, we are supposing that it is their nature to hear. So, too, when we say that it is a failure in an angel not to attain union with God, we openly proclaim that they were meant by nature to be one with God.

Of course, no one can fully comprehend or properly express the ineffable union of being one with God in His life, in His wisdom, in His joy, and all this without a shadow of death or darkness or disturbance. One thing is certain. The very failure of the bad angels to cling to God—a desertion that damaged their nature like a disease—is itself proof enough that the nature God gave them was good—so good that not to be one with God was for them a disaster.

Chapter 2

This explanation just given seemed to me necessary to forestall the objection that the apostate spirits might have received from some principle other than God a nature different from that of the other angels. The malice of this mistake can be more easily and speedily removed the more clearly one grasps what God meant by the words, "I AM WHO AM" (Exod. 3:14), spoken through the medium of an angel at the time when Moses was being sent to the children of Israel.

Since God is supreme being, that is, since He supremely is and, therefore, is immutable, it follows that He gave "being" to all that He created out of nothing; not, however, absolute being. To some things He gave more of being and to others less and, in this way, arranged an order of natures in a hierarchy of being. (This noun, "being," is derived from the verb "to be" just as "wisdom" from the verb "to be wise." In Latin, *essentia,* being, is a new word, not used by the ancient writers, recently adopted in order to find an equivalent of the Greek, *ousía,* of which *essentia* is the exact translation.)

Consequently, no nature—except a non-existent one—can be contrary to the nature which is supreme and which created whatever other natures have being. In other words, nonentity stands in opposition to that which is. Therefore, there is no being opposed to God who is the Supreme Being and Source of all beings without exception.

Chapter 3

In Scripture, those who oppose God's rule, not by nature but by sin, are called His enemies. They can do no damage to Him, but only to themselves; their enmity is not a power to harm, but merely an inclination to oppose Him. In any case, God is immutable and completely invulnerable. Hence, the malice by which His so-called enemies oppose God is not a menace to Him, but merely bad for themselves—an evil because what is good in their nature is wounded. It is not their nature, but the wound in their nature, that is opposed to God—as evil is opposed to good.

No one will deny that God is supremely good. Thus, any lack of goodness is opposed to God as evil is opposed to good. At the same time, the nature itself is not less

good because the lack of goodness is evil and, therefore, the evil of lacking some goodness is opposed to this good, which is the goodness of the nature. Note that in respect to
God the contrast is merely that of evil to good, but in respect to the nature which suffers
a lack of something good, the lack is not only evil but also harmful. No evils, of course,
can be harmful to God, but only to mutable and corruptible natures—and, even then, the
harm done bears witness to the goodness of the natures which suffer, for, unless they
were good, they could not suffer the wounds of a lack of goodness.

Just consider the harm done by these wounds—the loss of integrity, of beauty, of
health, of virtue, or of any other natural good which can be lost or lessened by sin or
sickness. If a nature has nothing of goodness to lose, then there is no harm done by lacking this nothing and, consequently, there is nothing wrong. For, there is no such thing as
something wrong that does no harm.

The conclusion is that, although no defect can damage an unchangeable good,
no nature can be damaged by a defect unless that nature itself is good—for the simple reason that a defect exists only where harm is done. To put the matter in another
way: a defect can never be found in the highest good, nor ever apart from some kind
of good.

Thus, good things without defects can sometimes be found; absolutely bad things,
never—for even those natures that were vitiated at the outset by an evil will are only
evil in so far as they are defective, while they are good in so far as they are natural. And
when a vitiated nature is being punished, in addition to the good of being what it is, it is
a good for it not to go unpunished, since this is just and whatever is just is certainly
good. No one is punished for natural defects, but only for deliberate faults. And even for
a vice to develop, by force of habit and overindulgence, into a strong natural defect, the
vice must have begun in the will. But here, of course, I am speaking of the vices of that
nature which has a mind illumined by an immaterial light in virtue of which it can distinguish what is just from what is unjust.

Chapter 4

Of course, in the case of beasts, trees, and other mutable and mortal creatures which
lack not merely an intellect, but even sensation or life itself, it would be ridiculous to
condemn in them the defects which destroy their corruptible nature. For, it was by the
will of the Creator that they received that measure of being whereby their comings and
goings and fleeting existences should contribute to that special, if lowly, loveliness of
our earthly seasons which chimes with the harmony of the universe. For, there was
never any need for the things of earth either to rival those of heaven or to remain uncreated merely because the latter are better.

It is, in fact, the very law of transitory things that, here on earth where such things
are at home, some should be born while others die, the weak should give way to the
strong and the victims should nourish the life of the victors. If the beauty of this order
fails to delight us, it is because we ourselves, by reason of our mortality, are so en-
meshed in this corner of the cosmos that we fail to perceive the beauty of a total pattern
in which the particular parts, which seem ugly to us, blend in so harmonious and beautiful a way. That is why, in those situations where it is beyond our power to understand
the providence of God, we are rightly commanded to make an act of faith rather than allow the rashness of human vanity to criticize even a minute detail in the masterpiece of
our Creator.

Although these defects in the things of earth are involuntary and unpunishable, yet, like voluntary ones, when properly contemplated, they reveal the excellence in the natures themselves, all of which have God for their Author and Creator. For, in both cases, what we dislike is the lack by defect of something which we like in the nature as a whole. Sometimes, of course, natures themselves are displeasing to men because they happen to be harmful. It is a case of regarding only their utility, not the things themselves, as with the plague of frogs and flies which scourged the pride of the Egyptians. But, with such reasoning, fault could be found even with the sun, since criminals and debtors have sometimes been judicially condemned to solar exposure. It is not by our comfort or inconvenience, but by the nature considered in itself, that glory is given to its Creator. So, even the nature of unquenchable fire is, without doubt, worthy of praise, although it is to serve as a punishment for the damned. Is there anything, in fact, more beautiful than a leaping, luminous flame of fire? Or anything more useful, when it warms us, heals us, cooks our food? Yet, nothing is more painful when it burns us. Thus, the same thing applied in one way is harmful, but when properly used is extremely beneficial. It is all but impossible to enumerate all the good uses to which fire is put throughout the world.

We should pay no attention to those who praise fire for its light but condemn its heat—on the principle that a thing should be judged not by its nature, but by our comfort or inconvenience. They like to see it, but hate to be burnt. What they forget is that the same light which they like is injurious and unsuitable for weak eyes, and that the heat which they hate is, for some animals, the proper condition for a healthy life.

Chapter 5

All natures, then, are good simply because they exist and, therefore, have each its own measure of being, its own beauty, even, in a way, its own peace. And when each is in the place assigned by the order of nature, it best preserves the full measure of being that was given to it. Beings not made for eternal life, changing for better or for worse according as they promote the good and improvement of things to which, by the law of the Creator, they serve as means, follow the direction of Divine Providence and tend toward the particular end which forms a part of the general plan for governing the universe. This means that the dissolution which brings mutable and mortal things to their death is not so much a process of annihilation as a progress toward something they were designed to become.

The conclusion from all this is that God is never to be blamed for any defects that offend us, but should ever be praised for all the perfection we see in the natures He has made. For God is Absolute Being and, therefore, all other being that is relative was made by Him. No being that was made from nothing could be on a par with God, nor could it even be at all, were it not made by Him.

Chapter 6

It follows that the true cause of the good angels' beatitude lies in their union with Absolute Being. And if we seek the cause of the bad angels' misery, we are right in finding it in this, that they abandoned Him whose Being is absolute and turned to themselves whose being is relative—a sin that can have no better name than pride. "For pride is the beginning of all sin" (Eccli. 10:15). They refused to reserve their strength for Him. They might have had more of being if they had adhered to Him whose Being is supreme, but, by preferring themselves to Him, they preferred what was less in the order of being.

Such was the first defect, the first lack, the first perversion of that nature which, being created, could not be absolute, and yet, being created for beatitude, might have rejoiced in Him who is Absolute Being; but which, having turned from Him, was doomed, not to be nothing but to have so much less of being that it was bound to be wretched.

If one seeks for the efficient cause of their evil will, none is to be found. For, what can make the will bad when it is the will itself which makes an action bad? Thus, an evil will is the efficient cause of a bad action, but there is no efficient cause of an evil will. If there is such a cause, it either has or has not a will. If it has, then that will is either good or bad. If good, one would have to be foolish enough to conclude that a good will makes a bad will. In that case, a good will becomes the cause of sin—which is utterly absurd. On the other hand, if the hypothetical cause of a bad will has itself a bad will, I would have to ask what made this will bad, and, to put an end to the inquiry: What made the first bad will bad? Now, the fact is that there was no first bad will that was made bad by any other bad will—it was made bad by itself. For, if it were preceded by a cause that made it evil, that cause came first. But, if I am told that nothing made the will evil but that it always was so, then I ask whether or not it existed in some nature.

If this evil will existed in no nature, then it did not exist at all. If it existed in some nature, then it vitiated, corrupted, injured that nature and, therefore, deprived it of some good. An evil will could not exist in an evil nature but only in a good one, mutable enough to suffer harm from this deprivation. For, if no harm were done, then there was no deprivation and, consequently, no right to call the will evil. But, if harm was done, it was done by destroying or diminishing what was good. Thus, an evil will could not have existed from all eternity in a nature in which a previously existing good had to be eliminated before the evil will could harm the nature. But, if it did not exist from all eternity, who, then, caused this evil will?

The only remaining suggestion is that the cause of the evil will was something which had no will. My next question is whether this "something" was superior, inferior, or equal to the will. If superior, then it was better. So, then, how can it have had no will and not rather a good will? If equal, the case is the same: for, as long as two wills are equally good, one cannot produce an evil will in the other. The supposition remains, then, that it was an inferior thing without a will which produced the evil will of the angelic nature which first sinned.

But that thing itself, whatever it was, even though it was low to the lowest point of earthliness, was, without doubt good since it was a nature and a being having its own character and species in its own genus and order. How, then, can a good thing be the efficient cause of an evil will? How, I ask, can good be the cause of evil? For, when the will, abandoning what is above it, turns itself to something lower, it becomes evil because the very turning itself and not the thing to which it turns is evil. Therefore, an inferior being does not make the will evil but the will itself, because it is a created will, wickedly and inordinately seeks the inferior being.

Take the case of two men whose physical and mental make-up is exactly the same. They are both attracted by the exterior beauty of the same person. While gazing at this loveliness, the will of one man is moved with an illicit desire; the will of the other remains firm in its purity. Why did the will become evil in one case and not in the other? What produced the evil will in the man in whom it began to be evil? The physical beauty of the person could not have been the cause, since that was seen by both in exactly the same way and yet both wills did not become evil. Was the cause the flesh of one of those who looked? Then why not the flesh of the other, also? Or was the cause the mind of one of them? Again, why not the mind of both? For the supposition is that both are equally constituted in mind and body. Must we say, then, that one was tempted by a secret suggestion of the Devil, as if it were not rather by his own will that he consented to this suggestion or enticement or whatever it was?

If so, then what was it in him that was the cause of his consent, of the evil will to follow the evil suggestion? To settle this difficulty, let us suppose that the two men are tempted equally, that one yields and consents to the temptation, that the other remains as he was before. The obvious conclusion is that one was unwilling, the other willing, to fail in chastity. And what else could be the cause of their attitudes but their own wills, since both men have the same constitution and temperament? The beauty which attracted the eyes of both was the same; the secret suggestion by which both were tempted was the same. However carefully they examine the situation, eager to learn what is was that made one of the two evil, no cause is apparent.

For, suppose we say that the man himself made his will evil. Very well, but what was the man himself before he made his will evil? He was a good nature, created by God, the immutable God.

Take a person who says that the one who consents to the temptation and enticement made his own will evil although previously he had been entirely good. Recall the facts. The one consents, while the other does not, to a sinful desire concerning a beautiful person; the beauty was seen by both equally, and before the temptation both men were absolutely alike in mind and body. Now, the person who talks of a man making his own will evil must ask why the man made his will evil, whether because he is a nature or because he is nature made out of nothing? He will learn that the evil arises not from the fact that the man is a nature, but from the fact that the nature was made out of nothing.

For, if a nature is the cause of an evil will, then we are compelled to say that evil springs from good and that good is the cause of evil—since a bad will comes from a good nature. But how can it come about that a good, though mutable, nature, even before its will is evil, can produce something evil, namely, this evil will itself?

Chapter 7

No one, therefore, need seek for an efficient cause of an evil will. Since the "effect" is, in fact, a deficiency, the cause should be called "deficient." The fault of an evil will begins when one falls from Supreme Being to some being which is less than absolute. Trying to discover causes of such deficiencies—causes which, as I have said, are not efficient but deficient—is like trying to see darkness or hear silence. True, we have some knowledge of both darkness and silence: of the former only by the eyes; of the latter only by the ears. Nevertheless, we have no sensation but only the privation of sensation.

So there is no point in anyone trying to learn from me what I know I do not know—unless, perhaps, he wants to know how not to know what, as he ought to know, no one can know. For, things we know, not by sensation, but by the absence of sensation, are known—if the word says or means anything—by some kind of "unknowing," so that they are both known and not known at the same time. For example, when the vision of the eye passes from sensation to sensation, it sees darkness only when it begins not to see. So, too, no other sense but the ear can perceive silence, yet silence can only be heard by not being heard.

So, too, it is only the vision of the mind that discerns the *species intellegibilis* when it understands intelligible realities. But, when the realities are no longer intelligible, the mind, too, knows by "unknowing." For "who can understand sins?" (Ps. 18:13).

Chapter 8

This I know, that the nature of God can never and nowhere be deficient in anything, while things made out of nothing can be deficient. In regard to these latter, the more they have of being and the more good things they do or make—for then they are doing or making something positive—the more their causes are efficient; but in so far as they fail or are defective and, in that sense, "do evil"—if a "defect" can be "done"—then their causes are "deficient." I know, further, that when a will "is made" evil, what happens would not have happened if the will had not wanted it to happen. That is why the punishment which follows is just, since the defection was not necessary but voluntary. The will does not fall "into sin"; it falls "sinfully." Defects are not mere relations to natures that are evil; they are evil in themselves because, contrary to the order of natures, there is a defection from Being that is supreme to some lesser being.

Thus, greed is not a defect in the gold that is desired but in the man who loves it perversely by falling from justice which he ought to esteem as incomparably superior to gold; nor is lust a defect in bodies which are beautiful and pleasing: it is a sin in the soul of the one who loves corporal pleasures perversely, that is, by abandoning that temperance which joins us in spiritual and unblemishable union with realities far more beautiful and pleasing; nor is boastfulness a blemish in words of praise: it is a failing in the soul of one who is so perversely in love with other peoples' applause that he despises the voice of his own conscience; nor is pride a vice in the one who delegates power, still less a flaw in the power itself: it is a passion in the soul of the one who loves his own power so perversely as to condemn the authority of one who is still more powerful.

In a word, anyone who loves perversely the good of any nature whatsoever and even, perhaps, acquires this good makes himself bad by gaining something good and sad by losing something better.

Chapter 9

There is, then, no natural efficient cause of an evil will or, if I may use the word, no essential cause. The reason for this is that it is the evil will itself that starts that evil in mutable spirits, which is nothing but a weakening and worsening of the good in their nature. What "makes" the will evil is, in reality, an "unmaking," a desertion from God. The very defection is deficient—in the sense of having no cause. However, in saying that there is no efficient cause even of a good will, we must beware of believing that the good will of the good angels was uncreated and co-eternal with God. But, if good angels were created, how can we say that their good will was not created? The fact is, it was created; the only question is whether it was created simultaneously with the creation of the angels or whether they first existed without a good will. If simultaneously, then, undoubtedly, it was created by Him who created the angels, so that, as soon as they were created, they adhered to Him who created them by means of that love with which they were created. Thus, the reason why the bad were separated from the society of good angels was that the good persevered in the same good will, whereas the others changed themselves into bad angels by defection from good will. The only thing that "made" their will bad was that they fell away from a will which was good. Nor would they have fallen away, had they not chosen to fall away.

In the hypothesis, however, that the good angels, existing at first without a good will, produced it in themselves without the help of God, they must have made themselves better than what they were when God created them. This is nonsense. For, without a good will, what could they be but evil? Or, if we may not say evil, since their will was not yet evil—for they could hardly fall away from what they had not yet begun to have—at least, they certainly were not good angels—not as good as they were to become when they came to possess a good will.

So much for the hypothesis. Since they could not make themselves better than God made them—for no one can make anything better than God can—then it follows that, without the co-operation of their Creator, they could never have come into possession of that good will which made them better.

Now, it is true that their good will was not only the cause of their turning and adhering to Him, who is Perfect Being, rather than to themselves, whose being was less than perfect, but also the reason why they had more of being than before and could live wisely and happily in union with God. Nevertheless, this merely shows that any will, however good, would have been destitute and destined to remain in hopeless desire, did not He who had created their good nature out of nothing, and had given it a capacity for union with Himself, first awaken in the will a greater longing for this union and then fill the will with some of His very Being in order to make it better.

This raises another issue. For, if the good angels did something themselves to bring about their good will, did they do this with or without a will? If without, then, of course, they were not the agents. If with a will, was it an evil or a good one? If evil, how could it produce a good will? If good, well, then, they had a good will already. And who made this but God Himself who created them with a good will (that is, with the unblemished love by which they could adhere to Him) and who at the same time created their nature and enriched it with grace?

Thus, we are compelled to believe that the holy angels never existed without a good will, that is, without the love of God. But what of those angels who were created good and became evil by their own bad will for which their good nature is not responsible except in so far as there was a deliberate defection from good—for it is never good, but a defection from good, that is the cause of evil? These angels either received less grace of divine love than those who persevered in grace, or, if both were created equally good, then, while the former were falling by bad will, the latter were increasingly aided to reach that plenitude of beatitude which made them certain that they would never fall—a matter which I discussed in the preceding Book.

Thus with our praise to our Creator, we should all proclaim that, not only of holy men, but also of holy angels, it may be said that "the charity of God is poured forth" in them "by the Holy Spirit who has been given" to them (Rom. 5:5). Nor is it the good only of men, but first and foremost that of angels, which is referred to in the words: "It is good for me to adhere to my God" (Ps. 72:28).

And they who share this common good are in a holy communion both with Him to whom they adhere and one with another, and they form a single community, one City of God, which is also His living sacrifice and His living temple.

This ends the discussion of the origin of this City in so far as it concerns the angels. I must now turn to the rise of that part of the City which is made up of mortal men, created by the same God, who will one day be united to the immortal angels and who, at present, are either sojourning on earth or, if dead, are resting in the hidden sanctuaries where the souls of the departed have their abode.

It was from one man, the first whom God created, that the whole human race took its start. This is the faith revealed in Holy Scripture, a faith that has gained marvelous and merited authority throughout the world and among all peoples—as, along with other truths, Scripture itself divinely predicted would be the case.

*   *   *

BOOK XIX

*   *   *

Chapter 11

Thus, we may say of peace what we have said of eternal life—that it is our highest good; more particularly because the holy Psalmist was addressing the City of God (the nature of which I am trying, with so much difficulty, to make clear) when he said: "Praise the Lord, O Jerusalem; praise thy God, O Zion. Because he hath strengthened the bolts of thy gates, he hath blessed thy children within thee. He hath placed peace in thy borders" (Ps. 146:12–14). For, when the bolts of that city's gates will have been strengthened, none will enter in and none will issue forth. Hence, its borders (fines) must be taken to mean that peace which I am trying to show is our final good. Note, too, that Jerusalem, the mystical name which symbolizes this City, means, as I have already mentioned, "the vision of peace."

However, the word "peace" is so often applied to conditions here on earth, where life is not eternal, that it is better, I think, to speak of "eternal life" rather than of "peace" as the end or supreme good of the City of God. It is in this sense that St. Paul says: "But now being made free from sin, and become servants of God, you have your fruit unto sanctification, and the end life everlasting" (Rom. 6:22).

It would be simplest for all concerned if we spoke of "peace in eternal life," or of "eternal" or of "eternal life in peace," as the end or supreme good of this City. The trouble with the expression "eternal life" is that those unfamiliar with the Scriptures might take this phrase to apply also to the eternal loss of the wicked, either because, as philosophers, they accept the immortality of the soul, or even because, as Christians, they know by faith that the punishment of the wicked has no end and, therefore, that they could not be punished forever unless their life were eternal.

The trouble with "peace" is that, even on the level of earthly and temporal values, nothing that we can talk about, long for, or finally get, is so desirable, so welcome, so good as peace. At any rate, I feel sure that if I linger a little longer on this topic of peace I shall tire very few of my readers. After all, peace is the end of this City which is the theme of this work; besides, peace is so universally loved that its very name falls sweetly on the ear.

Chapter 12

Any man who has examined history and human nature will agree with me that there is no such thing as a human heart that does not crave for joy and peace. One has only to think of men who are bent on war. What they want is to win, that is to say, their battles are but bridges to glory and to peace. The whole point of victory is to bring opponents to their knees—this done, peace ensues. Peace, then, is the purpose of waging war; and this is true even of men who have a passion for the exercise of military prowess as rulers and commanders.

What, then, men want in war is that it should end in peace. Even while waging a war every man wants peace, whereas no one wants war while he is making peace. And even when men are plotting to disturb the peace, it is merely to fashion a new peace nearer to the heart's desire; it is not because they dislike peace as such. It is not that they love peace less, but that they love their kind of peace more. And even when a secession is successful, its purpose is not achieved unless some sort of peace remains among those who plotted and planned the rebellion. Take even a band of highwaymen. The more violence and impunity they want in disturbing the peace of other men, the more they demand peace among themselves. Take even the case of a robber so powerful that he dispenses with partnership, plans alone, and single-handed robs and kills his victims. Even he maintains some kind of peace, however shadowy, with those he cannot kill and whom he wants to keep in the dark with respect to his crimes. Certainly in his own home he wants to be at peace with his wife and children and any other members of his household. Of course, he is delighted when his every nod is obeyed; if it is not obeyed, he rages, and scolds, and demands peace in his own home and, if need be, gets it by sheer brutality. He knows that the price of peace in domestic society is to have everyone subject in the home to some head—in this instance, to himself.

Suppose, now, a man of this type were offered the allegiance of a larger society, say of a city or of a nation, with the pledge that he would be obeyed as he looks to be obeyed under his own roof. In this case, he would no longer hide himself away in a darksome robber's den; he would show himself off as a high and mighty king—the same man, however, with all of his old greed and criminality. Thus it is that all men want peace in their own society, and all want it in their own way. When they go to war what they want is to make, if they can, their enemies their own, and then to impose on them the victor's will and call it peace.

Now let us imagine a man like the one that poetry and mythology tell us about, a being so wild and anti-social that it was better to call him half-human than fully a man. He was called Cacus, which is Greek for "bad." His kingdom was the solitude of a dreadful cave and it was his extraordinary wickedness that gave him his name. He had no wife to exchange soft words with him; no tiny children to play with; no bigger ones to keep in order; no friend whose company he could enjoy, not even his father, Vulcan—than whom he was at least this much luckier that he had never begotten a monster like himself! There was no one to whom he would give anything, but whenever and from whomsoever he could he would take whatever he wanted and whenever he wanted it.

Nevertheless, all alone as he was in a cave that was always "warm with the blood of some recent victim," his sole longing was for peace in which no force would do him harm and no fear disturb his rest. Even with his own body he wanted to be at peace, and he was at ease only when peace was there. Even when he was bidding his members to obey him and was seizing, killing, and devouring his victims, his purpose was peace—the speediest possible peace with his mortal nature, driven by its needs to rebellion, and with his hunger, in sedition, clamoring for the breakup of the union of body and soul. Brutal and wild as he was and brutal and wild as were his ways, what he wanted was to have his life and limbs in peace. So much so that, had he been as willing to be at peace with his neighbors as he was active in procuring peace within himself and in his cave, no one would have called him wicked, nor a monster, nor even sub-human; or, at least, despite the shape of his body and the smoke and fire that issued from his mouth and kept all neighbors at a distance, people would have said that what looked like injustice, greed, and savagery were merely means to self-preservation. The truth is, of course, that there never existed any such being, or at least, none just like the foil the poets' fancy invented to glorify Hercules at the expense of Cacus. As is the case with most poetic inventions, we need not believe that any such creature, human or subhuman, ever lived.

I turn now to real wild beasts (from which category the animal part of the so-called half-beast, Cacus, was borrowed). They, too, keep their own particular genus in a kind of peace. Their males and females meet and mate, foster and feed their young, even though many of them by nature are more solitary than gregarious, like lions, foxes, eagles, and owls—as contrasted with deer, pigeons, starlings, and bees. Even a tigress purrs over her cubs and curbs all her fierceness when she fondles them. Even a falcon which seems so lonely when hovering above its prey mates and builds a nest, helps to hatch the eggs and feed the young, and makes every effort to maintain with the mother falcon a peaceful domestic society.

It is even more so with man. By the very laws of his nature, he seems, so to speak, forced into fellowship and, as far as in him lies, into peace with every man. At any rate, even when wicked men go to war they want peace for their own society and would like, if possible, to make all men members of that society, so that every one and every thing might be at the service of one head. Of course, the only means such a conqueror knows is to have all men so fear or love him that they will accept the peace which he imposes. For, so does pride perversely copy God. Sinful man hates the equality of all men under God and, as though he were God, loves to impose his sovereignty on his fellow men. He hates the peace of God which is just and prefers his own peace which is unjust. However, he is powerless not to love peace of some sort. For, no man's sin is so unnatural as to wipe out all traces whatsoever of human nature. Anyone, then, who is rational enough to prefer right to wrong and order to disorder can see that the kind of peace that is based on injustice, as compared with that which is based on justice, does not deserve the name of peace.

Of course, even disorder, in whole or in part, must come to some kind of terms either with the situation in which it finds itself or with the elements out of which it takes its being—otherwise it would have no being at all.

Take a man hanging upside down. Certainly his members are in disorder and the posture of the body as a whole is unnatural. The parts which nature demands should be above and below have become topsy-turvy. Such a position disturbs the peace of the body and is therefore painful. Nevertheless, the soul remains at peace with the body and continues to work for its welfare. Otherwise, the man would not live to feel the agony. And even if the soul is driven from the body by excess of pain, nevertheless, so long as the limbs hold together, some kind of peace among these parts remains. Otherwise, there would be no corpse to go on dangling there. Further, the fact that by gravity the corpse, made out of earth, tends to fall to the ground and pulls at the noose that holds it up proves that there is some order in which it seeks peace, and that its weight is, as it were, crying out for a place where it can rest. Lifeless and insensible though the body now is, it does not renounce that appropriate peace in the order of nature which it either has or seeks to have.

So, too, when a corpse is treated to embalming, to prevent dissolution and decay, there is a kind of peace which holds the parts together while the whole is committed to the earth, its proper resting place, and, therefore, a place with which the body is at peace. If, on the other hand, embalming is omitted and nature is allowed to take its course, the corpse remains a battleground of warring exhalations (that attack our senses with the stench we smell) only until such time as they finally fall in with the elements of this world and, slowly, bit by bit, become indistinguishable in a common peace.

Even afterward, however, the law and ordering of the Creator who is supreme in the whole cosmos and the regulator of its peace are still in control. Even when tiny bacteria spring from the corpse of a larger animal, it is by the same law of the Creator that all these minute bodies serve in peace the organic wholes of which they are parts. Even when the flesh of dead animals is eaten by other animals, there is no change in the universal laws which are meant for the common good of every kind of life, the common good that is effected by bringing like into peace with like. It makes no difference what disintegrating forces are at work, or what new combinations are made, or even what changes or transformations are effected.

Chapter 13

The peace, then, of the body lies in the ordered equilibrium of all its parts; the peace of the irrational soul, in the balanced adjustment of its appetites; the peace of the reasoning soul, in the harmonious correspondence of conduct and conviction; the peace of body and soul taken together, in the well-ordered life and health of the living whole. Peace between a mortal man and his Maker consists in ordered obedience, guided by faith, under God's eternal law; peace between man and man consists in regulated fellowship. The peace of a home lies in the ordered harmony of authority and obedience between the members of a family living together. The peace of the political community is an ordered harmony of authority and obedience between citizens. The peace of the heavenly City lies in a perfectly ordered and harmonious communion of those who find their joy in God and in one another in God. Peace, in its final sense, is the calm that comes of order. Order is an arrangement of like and unlike things whereby each of them is disposed in its proper place.

This being so, those who are unhappy, in so far as they are unhappy, are not in peace, since they lack the calm of that Order which is beyond every storm; nevertheless, even in their misery they cannot escape from order, since their very misery is related to responsibility and to justice. They do not share with the blessed in their tranquility, but this very separation is the result of the law of order. Moreover, even the miserable can be momentarily free from anxiety and can reach some measure of adjustment to their surroundings and, hence, some tranquility of order and, therefore, some slender peace. However, the reason why they remain unhappy is that, although they *may* be momentarily free from worry and from pain, they are not in a condition where they *must* be free both from worry and pain. Their condition of misery is worse when such peace as they have is not in harmony with that law which governs the order of nature. Their peace can also be disturbed by pain and in proportion to their pain; yet, some peace will remain, so long as the pain is not too acute and their organism as a whole does not disintegrate.

Notice that there can be life without pain, but no pain without some kind of life. In the same way, there can be peace without any kind of war, but no war that does not suppose some kind of peace. This does not mean that war as war involves peace; but war, in so far as those who wage it or have it waged upon them are beings with organic natures, involves peace—for the simple reason that to be organic means to be ordered and, therefore, to be, in some sense, at peace.

Similarly, there can be a nature without any defect and, even, a nature in which there can be no kind of evil whatever, but there can be no nature completely devoid of good. Even the nature of the Devil, in so far as it is a nature, is not evil; it was perversity—not being true to itself—that made it bad. The Devil did not "stand in the truth" (John 8:44) and, therefore, did not escape the judgment of truth. He did not stand fast in the tranquility of order—nor did he, for all that, elude the power of the Ordainer. The goodness which God gave to his nature does not withdraw him from the justice of God by which that nature is subject to punishment. Yet, even in that punishment, God does not hound the good which He created, but only the evil which the Devil committed. So it is that God does not take back the whole of His original gift. He takes a part and leaves a part; He leaves a nature that can regret what God has taken back. Indeed, the very pain inflicted is evidence of both the good that is lost and the good that is left. For, if there were no good left, there would be no one to lament the good that has been lost.

A man who sins is just that much worse if he rejoices in the loss of holiness; but one who suffers pain, and does not benefit by it, laments, at least, the loss of his health. Holiness and health are both good things and, because the loss of any good is more a cause for grief than for gladness (unless there be some higher compensation—the soul's holiness, to be sure, is preferable to the body's health), it is more in accordance with nature that a sinner grieve over his punishment than that he rejoice over his offense. Consequently, just as a man's happiness in abandoning the good of wrong-doing betrays his bad will, so his sorrowing for the good he has lost when in pain bears witness to the good of his nature. For, anyone who grieves over the loss of peace to his nature does so out of some remnant of that peace wherewith his nature loves itself. This is what happens—deservedly, too—in eternal punishment. In the midst of their agonies the evil and the godless weep for the loss of their nature's goods, knowing, meanwhile, that God whose great generosity they condemned was perfectly just when He took these goods away.

God, the wise Creator and just Ordainer of all natures, has made the mortal race of man the loveliest of all lovely things on earth. He has given to men good gifts suited to their existence here below. Among these is temporal peace, according to the poor limits of mortal life, in health, security, and human fellowship; and other gifts, too, needed to preserve this peace or regain it, once lost—for instance, the blessings that lie all around us, so perfectly adapted to our senses: daylight, speech, air to breathe, water to drink, everything that goes to feed, clothe, cure, and beautify the body. These good gifts are granted, however, with the perfectly just understanding that whoever uses the goods which are meant for the mortal peace of mortal men, as these goods should be used, will receive more abundant and better goods— nothing less than immortal peace and all that goes with it, namely, the glory and honor of enjoying God and one's neighbor in God everlastingly; but that whoever misuses his gifts on earth will both lose what he has and never receive the better gifts of heaven.

Chapter 14

In the earthly city, then, temporal goods are to be used with a view to the enjoyment of earthly peace, whereas, in the heavenly City, they are used with a view to the enjoyment of eternal peace. Hence, if we were merely unthinking brutes, we would pursue nothing beyond the orderly interrelationship of our bodily part and the appeasing of our appetites, nothing, that is, beyond the comfort of the flesh and plenty of pleasures, so that the peace of body might contribute to peace of the soul. For, if order in the body be lacking, the peace of an irrational soul is checked, since it cannot attain the satisfaction of its appetites. Both of these forms of peace meanwhile subserve that other form of peace which the body and soul enjoy between them, the peace of life and health in good order.

For, just as brutes show that they love the peace or comfort of their bodies by shunning pain, and the peace of their souls by pursuing pleasure to satisfy their appetites, so, too, by running from death, they make clear enough how much they love the peace which keeps body and soul together.

Because, however, man has a rational soul, he makes everything he shares with brutes subserve the peace of his rational soul, so that he first measures things with his mind before he acts, in order to achieve that harmonious correspondence of conduct and conviction which I called the peace of the rational soul. His purpose in desiring not to be vexed with pain, nor disturbed with desire, nor disintegrated by death is that he may learn something profitable and so order his habits and way of life. However, if the infirmity of his human mind is not to bring him in his pursuit of knowledge to some deadly error, he needs divine authority to give secure guidance, and divine help so that he may be unhampered in following the guidance given.

And because, so long as man lives in his mortal body and is a pilgrim far from the Lord, he walks, not by vision, but by faith. Consequently, he refers all peace of body or soul, or their combination, to that higher peace which unites a mortal man with the immortal God and which I defined as "ordered obedience guided by faith, under God's eternal law."

Meanwhile, God teaches him two chief commandments, the love of God and the love of neighbor. In these precepts man finds three beings to love, namely, God, himself, and his fellow man, and knows that he is not wrong in loving himself so long as he loves God. As a result, he must help his neighbor (whom he is obliged to love as himself) to love God. Thus, he must help his wife, children, servants, and all others whom he can influence. He must wish, moreover, to be similarly helped by his fellow man, in case he himself needs such assistance. Out of all this love he will arrive at peace, as much as in him lies, with every man—at that human peace which is regulated fellowship. Right order here means, first, that he harm no one, and, second, that he help whomever he can. His fundamental duty is to look out for his own home, for both by natural and human law he has easier and readier access to their requirements.

St. Paul says: "But if any does not take care of his own, and especially of his household, he has denied the faith and is worse than an unbeliever" (I Tim. 5:8). From this care arises that peace of the home which lies in the harmonious interplay of authority and obedience among those who live there. For, those who have the care of the others give the orders—a man to his wife, parents to their children, masters to their servants. And those who are cared for must obey—wives their husband, children their parents, servants their masters. In the home of a religious man, however, of a man living by faith and as yet a wayfarer from the heavenly City, those who command serve those whom they appear to rule—because, of course, they do not command out of lust to domineer, but out of a sense of duty—not out of pride like princes but out of solicitude like parents.

Chapter 15

This family arrangement is what nature prescribes, and what God intended in creating man: "let them have dominion over the fish of the sea, the birds of the air, the cattle, over all the wild animals and every creature that crawls on the earth" (Gen. 1:26). God wanted rational man, made to His image, to have no dominion except over irrational nature. He meant no man, therefore, to have dominion over man, but only man over beast. So it fell out that those who were holy in primitive times became shepherds over sheep rather than monarchs over men, because God wishes in this way to teach us that the normal hierarchy of creatures is different from that which punishment for sin has made imperative. For, when subjection came, it was merely a condition deservedly imposed on sinful man. So, in Scripture, there is no mention of the word "servant" until holy Noah used it in connection with the curse on his son's wrong-doing. It is a designation that is not natural, but one that was deserved because of sin.

The Latin word for "slave" is *servus* and it is said that this word is derived from the fact that those who, by right of conquest, could have been killed were sometimes kept and guarded, *servabantur,* by their captors and so became slaves and were called *servi.* Now, such a condition of servitude could only have arisen as a result of sin, since whenever a just war is waged the opposing side must be in the wrong, and every victory, even when won by wicked men, is a divine judgment to humble the conquered and to reform or punish their sin. To this truth Daniel, the great man of God, bore witness. When he was languishing in the Babylonian captivity he confessed to God his sins and those of his people and avowed, with pious repentance, that these sins were the cause of the captivity. It is clear, then, that sin is the primary cause of servitude, in the sense of a social status in which one man is compelled to be subjected to another man. Nor does this befall a man, save by the decree of God, who is never unjust and who knows how to impose appropriate punishments on different sinners.

Our heavenly Master says: "everyone who commits sin is a slave of sin" (John 8:34). So it happens that holy people are sometimes enslaved to wicked masters who are, in turn, themselves slaves. For, "by whatever a man is overcome, of this also he is a slave" (II Pet. 2:19). Surely it is better to be the slave of a man than the slave of passion as when, to take but one example, the lust for lordship raises such havoc in the hearts of men. Such, then, as men now are, is the order of peace. Some are in subjection to others, and, while humility helps those who serve, pride harms those in power. But, as men once were, when their nature was as God created it, no man was a slave either to man or to sin. However, slavery is now penal in character and planned by that law which commands the preservation of the natural order and forbids its disturbance. If no crime had ever been perpetrated against this law, there would be no crime to repress with the penalty of enslavement.

It is with this in mind that St. Paul goes so far as to admonish slaves to obey their masters and to serve them so sincerely and with such good will that, if there is no chance of manumission, they may make their slavery a kind of freedom by serving with love and loyalty, free from fear and feigning, until injustice becomes a thing of the past and every human sovereignty and power is done away with, so that God may be all in all.

Chapter 16

Our holy Fathers in the faith, to be sure, had slaves, but in the regulation of domestic peace it was only in matters of temporal importance that they distinguished the position of their children from the status of their servants. So far as concerns the worship of God—from whom all must hope for eternal blessings—they had like loving care for all the household without exception. This was what nature demanded, and it was from this kind of behavior that there grew the designation "father of the family," which is so widely accepted that even wicked and domineering men love to be so called.

Those who are true fathers are as solicitous for every one in their households as for their own children to worship and to be worthy of God. They hope and yearn for all to arrive in that heavenly home where there will be no further need of giving orders to other human beings, because there will be no longer any duty to help those who are happy in immortal life. In the meantime, fathers ought to look upon their duty to command as harder than the duty of slaves to obey.

Meanwhile, in case anyone in the home behaves contrary to its peace, he is disciplined by words or whipping or other kind of punishment lawful and licit in human society, and for his own good, to readjust him to the peace he has abandoned. For, there is no more benevolence and helpfulness in bringing about the loss of a greater good than there is innocence and compassion in allowing a culprit to go from bad to worse. It is the duty of a blameless person not just to do no wrong, but to keep others from wrongdoing and to punish it when done, so that the one punished may be improved by the experience and others be warned by the example.

Now, since every home should be a beginning or fragmentary constituent of a civil community, and every beginning related to some specific end, and every part to the whole of which it is a part, it ought to follow that domestic peace has a relation to political peace. In other words, the ordered harmony of authority and obedience between those who live together has a relation to the ordered harmony of authority and obedience between those who live in a city. This explains why a father must apply certain regulations of civil law to the governance of his home, so as to make it accord with the peace of the whole community.

Chapter 17

While the homes of unbelieving men are intent upon acquiring temporal peace out of the possessions and comforts of this temporal life, the families which live according to faith look ahead to the good things of heaven promised as imperishable, and use material and temporal goods in the spirit of pilgrims, not as snares or obstructions to block their way to God, but simply as helps to ease and never to increase the burdens of this corruptible body which weighs down the soul. Both types of homes and their masters have this in common, that they must use things essential to this mortal life. But the respective purposes to which they put them are characteristic and very different.

So, too, the earthly city which does not live by faith seeks only an earthly peace, and limits the goal of its peace, of its harmony of authority and obedience among its citizens, to the voluntary and collective attainment of objectives necessary to mortal existence. The heavenly City, meanwhile—or, rather, that part that is on pilgrimage in mortal life and lives by faith—must use this earthly peace until such time as our mortality which needs such peace has passed away. As a consequence, so long as her life in the earthly city is that of a captive and an alien (although she has the promise of ultimate delivery and the gift of the Spirit as a pledge), she has no hesitation about keeping in step with the civil law which governs matters pertaining to our existence here below. For, as mortal life is the same for all, there ought to be common cause between the two cities in what concerns our purely human living.

Now comes the difficulty. The city of this world, to begin with, has had certain "wise men" of its own mold, whom true religion must reject, because either out of their own daydreaming or out of demonic deception these wise men came to believe that a multiplicity of divinities was allied with human life, with different duties, in some strange arrangement, and different assignments: this one over the body, that one over the mind; in the body itself, one over the head, another over the neck, still others, one for each bodily part; in the mind, one over the intelligence, another over learning, another over temper, another over desire; in the realities, related to life, that lie about us, one over flocks and one over wheat, one over wine, one over oil, and another over forests, one over currency, another over navigation, and still another over warfare and victory, one over marriage, a different one over fecundity and childbirth, so on and so on.

The heavenly City, on the contrary, knows and, by religious faith, believes that it must adore one God alone and serve Him with that complete dedication which the Greeks call *latreía* and which belongs to Him alone. As a result, she has been unable to share with the earthly city a common religious legislation, and has had no choice but to dissent on this score and so to become a nuisance to those who think otherwise. Hence, she has had to feel the weight of their anger, hatred, and violence, save in those instances when, by sheer numbers and God's help, which never fails, she has been able to scare off her opponents.

So long, then, as the heavenly City is wayfaring on earth, she invites citizens from all nations and all tongues, and unites them into a single pilgrim band. She takes no issue with that diversity of customs, laws, and traditions whereby human peace is sought and maintained. Instead of nullifying or tearing down, she preserves and appropriates whatever in the diversities of diverse races is aimed at one and the same objective of human peace, provided only that they do not stand in the way of the faith and worship of the one supreme and true God.

Thus, the heavenly City, so long as it is wayfaring on earth, not only makes use of earthly peace but fosters and actively pursues along with other human beings a common platform in regard to all that concerns our purely human life and does not interfere with faith and worship. Of course, though, the City of God subordinates this earthly peace to that of heaven. For this is not merely true peace, but, strictly speaking, for any rational creature, the only real peace, since it is, as I said, "the perfectly ordered and harmonious communion of those who find their joy in God and in one another in God."

When this peace is reached, man will be no longer haunted by death, but plainly and perpetually endowed with life, nor will his body, which now wastes away and weighs down the soul, be any longer animal, but spiritual, in need of nothing, and completely under the control of our will.

This peace the pilgrim City already possesses by faith and it lives holily and according to this faith so long as, to attain its heavenly completion, it refers every good act done for God or for his fellow man. I say "fellow man" because, of course, any community life must emphasize social relationships.

Early Medieval Philosophy

The philosophical questions of the early Middle Ages tended to focus on what is real and how it is known. Such questions by Christians, of course, included queries about the nature of God, about God's relation to the created order (including the problem of evil), and about the status of universals. Questions about knowledge probed the relation between faith and reason, especially the limits of reason in knowing the divine. Late medieval thinkers added questions about the nature of humankind and the role of society, and they went about philosophizing in quite different ways. But the issues of early medieval thought and the categories established to deal with those issues were critical for centuries.

For the most part the early medieval philosophers worked within the broad framework of Platonic thought, while later medieval thinkers tended to adopt Aristotelian categories. Augustine (as either the last classical thinker or the first medieval one), Pseudo-Dionysius, Boethius, John Scotus Eriugena, and Anselm all used Neoplatonic concepts. It was only later that such thinkers as John of Salisbury, Abelard, and, especially, Thomas Aquinas adapted the works of Aristotle. On the other hand, most medieval mystics, whether from the early or later Middle Ages, used Neoplatonic categories.

* * *

Étienne Gilson is most responsible for the reappraisal of medieval philosophy. His major work is *History of Christian Philosophy in the Middle Ages* (New York: Random House, 1955), while several of his other works, including *Reason and Revelation in the Middle Ages* (New York: Scribners, 1936), and *The Spirit of Mediæval Philosophy,* translated by A.H.C. Downes (New York: Scribners, 1936), are worth noting. Maurice De Wulf's work, particularly *History of Mediaeval Philosophy* (New York: Dover, 1952), has also been influential. Anne Fremantle, *The Age of Belief: The Medieval Philosophers* (New York: New American Library, 1954), provides a helpful short guide with brief passages from medieval philosophers, while Armand A. Maurer, *Medieval Philosophy* (New York: Random House, 1962); A.H. Armstrong, ed., *The Cambridge History of Later Greek and Early Medieval Philosophy* (Cambridge: Cambridge University Press, 1967); and Michael Haren, *Medieval Thought: The Western Intellectual Tradition from Antiquity to the Thirteenth Century* (New York: St. Martin's Press, 1985), provide more extensive works.

For books specifically on the early medieval period, see Frederick Copleston, *A History of Philosophy, Volume II: Medieval Philosophy, Part I: Augustine to Bonaventure* (1950; reprinted Garden City, NY: Image Doubleday, 1962), and John Marenbon, *Early Medieval Philosophy (480–1150): An Introduction* (London: Routledge & Kegan Paul, 1983).

For a general discussion of mysticism, see Evelyn Underhill's classic work, *Mysticism: A Study in the Nature and Development of Man's Spiritual Consciousness* (London: Methuen, 1930). Andrew Louth, *The Origins of the Christian Mystical Tradition from Plato to Denys* (Oxford: Clarendon Press, 1981), explains the background of medieval mysticism, while Paul E. Szarmach, ed., *An Introduction to the Medieval Mystics of Europe* (Albany: State University of New York Press, 1984), includes brief summaries of specific mystics. For a topical collection of mystical writings (primarily from the Middle Ages), see Patrick Grant, *Literature of Mysticism in Western Tradition* (New York: St. Martin's Press, 1983).

Pseudo-Dionysius Areopagite
Late Fifth-Early Sixth Century?

Sometime around the beginning of the sixth century there appeared a group of Neoplatonic writings that attracted special attention. It was widely believed that the writings were the work of Dionysius the Areopagite, a man converted in the first century by the Apostle Paul's preaching in Athens (Acts 17:34). Because of his supposed connection with the Apostle, "Dionysius'" writings were held to be uniquely authoritative. However, scholars trace the writings of the Pseudo [or "false"]-Dionysius to about A.D. 500.*

The writings emphasize the Neoplatonic doctrines of the unity of God and the unity of the world. Every apparent diversity participates in the unity of the being "above" it, from which it emanates. God is at the top of this hierarchy. But emphasis on the unity of God posed problems for traditional explanations of the Christian doctrine of God's Tri-Unity (Trinity). Apparently the Pseudo-Dionysius considered the three realities of the Trinity to be eternal manifestations from within the oneness of God. This teaching was often held to be unorthodox. Orthodox Christians, who considered the Pseudo-Dionysius' writings authoritative, were in considerable consternation. The attempted synthesis of Christianity and Dionysian Neoplatonic notions of unity and emanation informed John Scotus Eri-

*It was once supposed by others that the works were written by Denis (or Denys), the patron saint of France. This is also impossible.

ugena's thought and eventually led to his condemnation by the Catholic Church.

But two other themes of the Pseudo-Dionysius had greater influence on medieval thought. The first was the Neoplatonic concept of evil as the absence of good. According to the Pseudo-Dionysius, what we experience as evil is, quite literally, nothing. Evil, as such, "is not be-ing nor in beings." This Neoplatonic idea had already been given a Christian interpretation by Augustine, but it was the Pseudo-Dionysius' formulation of it that was influential in subsequent thinkers. The first selection given here from *The Divine Names,* translated by John D. Jones, summarizes the Pseudo-Dionysius' position.

The second important theme from the Pseudo-Dionysius was the knowledge of God. There are two ways of knowing God: the affirmative and the negative. The affirmative way predicates characteristics of God that are consistent with God's infinite being, such as goodness. The negative way denies predicating of God characteristics that apply to creatures, such as mutability. Our second selection from *The Divine Names* expresses these two ways of knowing God when the Pseudo-Dionysius says, "God is known through knowledge, and through unknowing." In presenting this negative way of knowing God through "unknowing," the Pseudo-Dionysius often used hymnlike poetry and mystical utterances. Both the content and style of his writings were influential on medieval mystics.

*   *   *

The introductory essay in the Pseudo-Dionysius Areopagite, *The Divine Names and Mystical Theology,* translated by John D. Jones (Milwaukee, WI: Marquette University Press, 1980), pp. 1–105, is a good place to begin learning about our author. A.H. Armstrong, ed., *The Cambridge History of Later Greek and Early Medieval Philosophy* (Cambridge: Cambridge University Press, 1959); Frederick Copleston, *A History of Philosophy, Volume II: Medieval Philosophy, Part I: Augustine to Bonaventure* (1950; reprinted Garden City, NY: Image Doubleday, 1962); E.R. Dodds, *The Greeks and the Irrational* (Oxford: Oxford University Press, 1968); and Andrew Louth, *The Origins of the Christian Mystical Tradition from Plato to Denys* (Oxford: Clarendon Press, 1981), also include discussions of the Pseudo-Dionysius. For a book-length thesis, see Caroline Canfield Putnam, *Beauty in the Pseudo-Denis* (Washington, DC: Catholic University of America Press, 1960).

THE DIVINE NAMES (in part)

CHAPTER 4: CONCERNING THE GOOD, LIGHT, BEAUTY, LOVE, ECSTASIS, AND ZEAL, THAT EVIL IS NEITHER BE-ING, NOR FROM BE-ING, NOR IN BEINGS

*   *   *

18

*   *   *

In general, what is evil? From what source does it subsist? In which beings is it? How did the good will to produce it? How was such a will possible? If evil is from another cause than the good, what cause is there for beings beside the good? How is there evil if there is providence? How does evil come to be at all? Why is it not destroyed? Finally, how does any being desire it instead of the good?

19

Such questions as these will perhaps be raised in a perplexed discourse. But we demand that one look away from such a discourse into the truth of the matter. Thus we shall at first say this freely and boldly. Evil is not from the good; if something is from the good, it is not evil. As what is cold does not bring forth fire, what is not good does not bring forth what is good. Now it is the nature of the good to produce and to conserve while that of evil is to destroy and to ruin. Thus if all beings are from the good, no be-ing is from evil. Indeed, evil itself will not be, for it would be evil to itself.

If this is not so, evil will not be wholly evil but will have some aspect of the good according to which it is able to be at all. Further, if all beings desire the good and beautiful, if all these produce whatever they produce through producing what appears good, and if the intention of beings has the good as its source and end—for no being focuses on the nature of evil to produce what it produces—how will evil be in beings or be produced from such a good desire? Now if all beings are from the good and the good is beyond all beings, then that which is not is in the good. Thus, evil is neither be-ing (if not, [evil is] not wholly evil) nor not be-ing (for, nothing will be wholly non be-ing unless it is said to be in the good according to what is beyond being). The good lies beyond and is much prior to what simply is and what is not. Evil is neither in what is nor in what is not. Rather, it has a greater absence and estrangement from the good than what is not; it is more greatly without being than what is not.

"But when, then, is evil?" someone will say. "For if there is no evil, both virtue and vice will be the same in whole and, by analogy, in part and what wars against virtue will not be evil. Nonetheless, temperance and intemperance are opposed and justice and injustice are opposed. I speak not only of just or unjust persons or temperate or intemperate persons. For even before the outward manifestation of their differ-

Pseudo-Dionysius Areopagite, *The Divine Names and Mystical Theology,* Chap. 4, 18–21, 30; Chap. 7, 3, translated by John D. Jones (Milwaukee, WI: Marquette University Press, 1980). Reprinted by permission of Marquette University Press.

ence there is the much earlier opposition in the soul itself, in which the vices have already warred against the virtues, and the passions have already revolted against the logos. From these considerations some evil necessarily shows itself to be opposed to the good. For the good is not opposed to itself, but since it is from one source and has come to be from one cause, it rejoices in communion, unity and friendship. Further, the lesser good is not opposed to the greater good, just as lower heat or less cold are not opposed to greater heat or cold. Thus, evil is in beings and is be-ing; it is placed against and is opposed to the good. If evil is a destruction of beings this does not remove evil from *being* but it will itself be be-ing and generative of beings. For does not the destruction of one being frequently come to be the genesis of this other being? Thus evil contributes to the completion of all that is and provides through itself non-imperfection to the whole.

20

About these charges the true logos responds that evil as evil in no way produces being or genesis but only makes bad and destroys the subsistence of beings as far as it is able. But if someone says that evil is generative of beings and that by the destruction of one being genesis is given to another, one must respond truly that, as destructive, evil does not give genesis or being but that destruction and evil only destroys and makes bad. For genesis and being come to be through the good. Thus evil is destructive through itself but generative through the good. Evil as evil is neither be-ing nor productive of beings; through the good it is good, be-ing, and productive of what is good. Or, to put the matter another way, the same thing is not both good and evil in the same respect; the same power—whether itself a power or a destruction—will not be both productive and generative of the same thing in the same respect. Evil itself is neither be-ing, good, nor generative or productive of beings or what is good.

Now in those beings in which it comes to be complete, the good produces complete, unmixed, and whole goods. However, those which participate in less of it are non-complete and mixed goods through their lack of the good. Evil is neither good nor productive of good, but those which draw more or less near to the good will be analogically good. Further, the all-complete goodness wanders through all beings; it does not extend merely to the completely good beings about it but it stretches itself down to the last of beings. It is wholly present to some, present in a diminished fashion to others, and in the extreme it is present to others as each is able to partake of it. Thus some beings partake wholly of the good, some are more or less deprived of it, some have a share of the good in a more inferior manner, and to others, which are the last among beings, the good is present as an echo. For if the good were not analogically present to each, then the most divine and eldest beings would have the order of the least among beings. But how would it be possible for all to uniformly partake in the good since not all are enabled to partake in the whole of it in the same way?

Now this is the exceeding greatness of the power of the good: it empowers both those which are deprived of it and the privation of itself toward the whole participation of itself. And if it is necessary to speak the truth freely and clearly, those which war against it do and are able to do battle against it by its power. Hence to speak in a comprehensive fashion: all beings, in whatever way they are, are and are good and are from the good. Insofar as they are deprived of the good they are neither good nor being. For with respect to other conditions such as heat or cold, there are those which are heated and those losing heat; further, many beings are without life and intellect. Even God is apart from being and "is" beyond every manner of being. And simply, with respect to everything else, there are many beings which are able to subsist, yet which have abandoned or have not achieved their own condition. But that which is deprived from the good in every respect was, is, will be, or is able to be in no manner whatsoever.

Thus the intemperate person who lacks the good by his irrational desires neither is nor desires what is; yet he shares the good according to the obscure echo of his unity and friendship. Even anger partakes of the good, for through its movement and desire it directs and returns what seems to be evil to what seems to be good. Moreover, even those who desire the worst life still desire life and what seems best to them; thus, they partake in the good by their very desire, their desire for life, and their search for [what seems to them to be] the best life.

If the good were wholly annihilated there would be neither being, life, desire, motion, or anything else. Hence the genesis which emerges from destruction is not a power of evil but is the presence of a lesser good. In this respect, disease is a lack of order, but not of every order. For if this were so the disease itself would not subsist; yet the disease is and it abides by having being with the least possible order. Nevertheless, it subsists along with the order.

That which is wholly apart from the good, is neither be-ing nor in beings. But that which is a mixed good is in beings on account of the good; thus it is be-ing and is in beings by partaking of the good. Hence all beings will be more or less insofar as they partake of the good. For even with respect to being itself, that which is in no manner whatever will not be. But that which somehow is, somehow is not. Insofar as it has fallen away from what always is, it is not. Insofar as it partakes in be-ing, it is and its whole being and non be-ing are protected and preserved.

Evil, that which has entirely fallen from the good, will not be in those which are more or less good. But that which is somehow good—thus, somehow not good—wars against some beings that are good but not against the whole good. It is protected by its participation in the good, for the good gives being to the privation of itself [with a view] towards the whole participation of itself. Given the complete absence of the good, nothing will be good, mixed or even evil itself. For if evil is non-complete good and the complete absence of the good would involve the absence of both mixed and complete goods, then evil will be and be seen only in respect to those to which it is opposed, and will be removed from others as good. For it is impossible for the same things in the same respect to war against one another in every respect.

21

Evil is not be-ing nor in beings. For if all beings are from the good and the good is in all beings and encompasses all, then evil will not be in beings; it will not be in the good; nor will it be destructive through the good. (For, clearly, evil will no more be in the good than cold is in fire.) Yet if this were so, how would evil be in the good? It is impossible and absurd that evil be from the good. For as the writings say, "a good tree does not bring forth evil fruit"; clearly, the opposite is not so. But if evil is not from the good, it is evident that it is from another source and cause. For either evil will be from the good or the good will be from evil. If this is not possible, then evil and the good will be from some other source and cause. However, no dyad is a source; for the source of every dyad is one. Nevertheless, it is absurd that before *being* "are" two which are completely opposed and that these are from one and the same; for this source would not be simple and one but opposed to itself, so that it would become other than itself.

Also it is clearly not possible for there to be two opposed sources of beings warring against one another and all beings. If this were so, God would be neither at rest nor separated from dispute, for something would be an adversary to him. Further, everything would be without order and always at war. Yet the good gives a share of friendship and peace itself to all beings; these gifts of peace are celebrated by the sacred writings. Wherefore, everything that is good is friendly, and harmonious, a descendant of one life, ordered together toward one life, and are like and gentle and agreeable with one another.

Evil is not in God nor is evil divine. Evil is not from God; for either God is not good or he is good-producing and productive of good things. Now God does not sometimes produce what is good and at other times not produce what is good, nor does God not produce all that is good. For this would bring change and otherness in God in regard to causality which is the most divine of all. But if the good constitution is in God then when he changes from the good he will sometimes be and at other times not be. Further if God participates in the good and derives this participation from another, he will sometimes have it and at other times not have it. Thus evil is not from God nor in God, neither simply nor temporally.

[Sections 22-29 argue that evil is not in angels, in irrational animals, in the whole of nature, in bodies, nor in matter as matter and that even demons are not evil by nature.]

*   *   *

30

To speak in a summary fashion: the good is from one whole cause; evil is from many partial defects. God knows evil as good and with God the causes of evils are good-producing powers. But if evil is everlasting, creates, has power, is, and acts, whence does it obtain these? For either they are from the good or the good is from evil or they are both from other causes.

All that is in conformity with nature comes to be from defined causes. But if nature is without cause and undefined, it is not by nature. For that contrary to nature [does not come to be] by nature any more than what is contrary to art [comes to be] by art. But is not the soul the cause of evils, just as fire is the cause of what is hot, so that whatever comes in contact with it is full of evils? Is the nature of the soul good but does it not sometimes act in one manner and sometimes in another? But if the being and nature of the soul are evil, whence does it obtain these except from the good creative cause of the totality of what is? But if the soul is from this how is it evil in being? For all that is good is descended from the good creative cause. But if it is evil in its activities, this is not unchangeable. For if not, from whence does it obtain its virtues unless it itself has come to be good formed? Thus it remains that evil is a weakness and lack of the good.

*   *   *

CHAPTER 7: CONCERNING WISDOM, INTELLECT, LOGOS, TRUTH, AND FAITH

*   *   *

3

*   *   *

According to our power,
   we attain to that beyond all
   by a path and order
   in the denial and preeminence of all, and
   in the cause of all.

God is known
   in all, and
   apart from all.

God is known
   through knowledge, and
   through unknowing.

Of God there is
   intellect, reason, knowledge,
   contact, sensation, opinion, imagination, name, and
   everything else.

God is
   not known, not spoken, not named,
   not something among beings, and
   not known in something among beings.

God is
   all in all,
   nothing in none,
   known to all in reference to all,
   known to no one in reference to nothing.
     For we say all of this correctly about God
     who is celebrated according
     to the analogy of all,
     of which it is the cause.

The most divine knowledge of God is
   one which knows through unknowing
     in the unity beyond intellect
   when the intellect stands away from beings
     and then stands away from itself,
     it is united to the more than resplendent rays,
     and is then and there illumined
     by the inscrutable depths of wisdom.

Nevertheless, as we have said,
   it is known from all;

(for according to the writings)
it is
    productive of all,
    always harmonizing the all,
    cause of the indissoluable
        concordance and harmony of all,
    always joining together
        the end of those which are prior to
        the beginnings of secondaries, and
    beautifying the agreement and harmony of all.

Boethius

ca. 480–ca. 524

Anicius Manlius Severinus Boethius was the son of a high Roman government official. Possibly educated in Athens or Alexandria, Boethius had a special interest in the writings of Plato and Aristotle. It was his intention to translate all their works into Latin and provide full commentary. He hoped to show the essential unity between Plato and Aristotle, but he translated only Aristotle's logical works. In 510 Boethius became consul and first minister to King Theodoric, the Ostrogothic ruler of Italy, and served the next twelve years in government, wrote commentaries on Porphyry and Cicero, and began his work on Plato and Aristotle. In 522 Boethius' sons were named consuls, and Boethius was made the important "master of the offices." But within a year tragedy struck. Boethius was accused of treason, imprisoned, and executed sometime around 524. The specific charges are not known but probably involved religious differences between the Catholic Boethius and the Arian Theodoric.

Boethius wrote on a variety of philosophical and theological topics. The treatise *From the Same to the Same: How Substances Are Good in Virtue of Their Existence without Being Substantial Goods,* reprinted here (complete) in the Loeb Classics translation of Stewart, Rand, and Tester, is a good example of his theological writing. In this treatise, Boethius makes a distinction between "being" *(esse)* and "the thing that is" *(id quod est),* a distinction that Thomas Aquinas develops into the distinction between "essence" and "existence."

Our second selection, translated by Richard McKeon, is from the second edition of Boethius' commentary on Porphyry's introduction to Aristotle's *Categories.* (Such commentary on a commentary was quite common in the early Middle Ages as philosophers grappled with the few classical texts that were available.) In the piece excerpted here, Boethius raises the question of the ontological status of universals, an issue that would vex philosophers for the next thousand years. Do universals, such as genera and species, subsist in themselves apart from the mind? If so, what kind of existence do they have? After summarizing the issues, Boethius presents a review of Plato's and Aristotle's answers—though he does not give an answer of his own.

While in prison Boethius wrote his most famous work, *The Consolation of Philosophy.* Written as a dialogue between Boethius and Lady Philosophy, it begins with Boethius protesting innocence and complaining of God's injustice and fortune's caprice. Using arguments rooted in both Stoic and Platonic thought, Philosophy replies that fortune is indeed fickle, but that the highest Good is found not in circumstances but in God. The selection given here, also in the Loeb Classics translation, is from the final book of the *Consolation* and examines how God's foreknowledge is compatible with free will. Boethius asks how one could be free to perform an action if God knew *beforehand* what one would do. Using a conception of time similar to Augustine's in Book XI of the *Confessions,* Lady Philosophy explains that God is completely outside time. This means that God's knowledge "views in its own direct comprehension everything as though it were taking place in the present." Just as I know what my son is doing now even though his action is free, so God can know what I will do tomorrow though I act freely—because for God tomorrow *is* now.

It may seem odd that a devout Catholic presented his final thoughts in Neoplatonic and Stoic terms, without any specifically Christian references. Yet Boethius' *magnum opus* was a source of great comfort to Christians in the Middle Ages for, as Étienne Gilson points out, "even when he is speaking only as a philosopher Boethius thinks as a Christian."

*   *   *

For background work on Boethius, see Howard Rollin Patch, *The Tradition of Boethius: A Study of His Importance in Medieval Culture* (New York: Oxford University Press, 1935), and Helen Marjorie Barrett, *Boethius: Some Aspects of His Times and Work* (Cambridge: Cambridge University Press, 1940). Henry Chadwick, *Boethius: The Consolations of Music, Logic, Theology, and Philosophy* (Oxford: Clarendon Press, 1981), and Edmund Reiss, *Boethius* (Boston: Twayne, 1982), study Boethius' writings, while Ralph M. McInerny, *Boethius and Aquinas* (Washington, DC: Catholic University of America Press, 1990), shows his influence on Thomas Aquinas. For collections of essays see Michael Masi, ed., *Boethius and the Liberal Arts: A Collection of Essays* (Las Vegas, NV: Peter Lang, 1981), and Margaret Gibson, ed., *Boethius, His Life, Thought, and Influence* (Oxford: Blackwell, 1981).

In recent years there has been renewed interest in the problems posed by Boethius' conception of God's timelessness and foreknowledge. Paul Helm,

Eternal God: A Study of God Without Time (Oxford: Clarendon Press, 1988), for example, argues in favor of Boethius' position, while Richard Swinburne, *The Coherence of Theism* (Oxford: Clarendon Press, 1977), and Stephen T. Davis, *Logic and the Nature of God* (Grand Rapids, MI: Eerdmans, 1983), oppose it. Much of the most interesting work in this area is found only in journals such as the *Journal of Philosophy* and *Faith and Philosophy.*

FROM THE SAME TO THE SAME: HOW SUBSTANCES ARE GOOD IN VIRTUE OF THEIR EXISTENCE WITHOUT BEING SUBSTANTIAL GOODS

You ask me to state and explain somewhat more clearly that obscure question in my *Hebdomands* concerning the manner in which substances are good in virtue of existence without being substantial goods. You urge that this demonstration is necessary because the method of this kind of treatise is not clear to all. I can bear witness with what eagerness you have already attacked the subject. But I think over my *Hebdomands* with myself, and I keep my speculations in my own memory rather than share them with any of those pert and frivolous persons who will not tolerate an argument unless it is made amusing. Wherefore do not you take objection to obscurities consequent on brevity, which are the sure treasure-house of secret doctrine and have the advantage that they speak only with those who are worthy. I have therefore followed the example of the mathematical and cognate sciences and laid down bounds and rules according to which I shall develop all that follows.

I. A common conception of the mind is a statement which anyone accepts as soon as he hears it. Of these there are two kinds. I or one is common in that all men possess it; as, for instance, if you say, "If you take equals from two equals, the remainders are equal." Nobody who grasps that would deny it. But the other kind is intelligible only to the learned, though it is derived from the same class of common conceptions; as "Things which are incorporeal are not in space," and the like; these conceptions are approved as obvious to the learned but not to the common herd.

II. Being *(esse)* and the thing that is *(id quod est)* are different. For simple being awaits manifestation, but the thing that is is and exists as soon as it has received the form which gives it being.

III. What is, can participate in something, but simple being does not participate in any way in anything. For participation is effected when something already is; but something is, when it has acquired being.

IV. That which is can possess something besides what it is itself. But simple being has no admixture of aught besides itself.

V. Merely to be something and to be something in virtue of existence are different; the former signifies an accident, the latter a substance.

VI. Everything that is participates in absolute being in order to exist; but it participates in something else in order to be something. Hence that which is participates in absolute being in order to exist, but it exists in order to participate in something else.

VII. Every simple thing possesses as a unity its existence and its particular being.

VIII. In every composite thing existence is one thing, its particular being is another.

IX. All diversity repels, likeness must be attracted. That which seeks something else is demonstrably of the same nature as that which it seeks.

These preliminaries are enough then for our purpose. The intelligent interpreter of the discussion will supply the arguments appropriate to each point.

Now the problem is this. Things which are, are good. I or the common opinion of the learned holds that everything that is tends to good and everything tends to its like. Therefore things which tend to good are themselves good. We must, however, inquire how they are good—by participation or by substance. If by participation, they are in no wise good in themselves; for a thing which is white by participation is not white in itself by virtue of its own being. So with all other qualities. If then they are good by participation, they are in no way good in themselves; therefore they do not tend to good. But we have agreed that they do. Therefore they are good not by participation but by substance. But of those things whose substance is good the particular being is good. But they owe their particular being to absolute being. Their existence therefore is good; therefore mere existence of all things is good. But if their existence is good, things which exist are good in virtue of their existence, and their existence is the same as the existence of the good. Therefore they are substantial goods, since they do not participate in goodness. But if the particular being in them is good, there is no doubt but that since they are substantial goods, they are like the first good, and thereby they will be that good itself; for nothing is like it save itself. Hence all things that are, are God—an impious assertion. Wherefore they are not substantial goods, and so there is not in them good existence; therefore they are not good in virtue of their existence. But neither do they participate in goodness; for they would in no wise tend to good. Therefore they are in no wise good.

This problem will admit of the following solution. There are many things which are separated by a mental process, though they cannot be separated in fact. No one, for instance, actually separates a triangle or other mathematical figure from the underlying matter; but separating it mentally one considers the triangle itself and its properties apart from matter. Let us therefore remove from the mind for a moment the presence of the first good, which it is certainly agreed exists, as can be known from the opinion of all men, learned and unlearned, and from the religious beliefs of savage races. This having been thus for a moment removed, let us postulate that all things that are good exist, and let us consider how they could possibly be good if they did not derive from the first good. This leads me to perceive that their goodness and their existence are two different things. For let us suppose that one and the same good substance is white, heavy and round. Then its particular substance, its roundness, colour and goodness would all be different things. For if each of these qualities were the same as its particular substance, weight would be the same thing as colour, colour as goodness, and goodness as weight—which is contrary to nature. Then in that case existence in them would be one thing, their particular being another, and then they would be good, but they would not have their particular being good. Therefore if they existed in any way, they would not be from the good and so good, and they would not be the same because good, but for them existence would be one thing, being good another. But if they were nothing else at all except good, and were neither heavy nor coloured nor extended in a spatial dimension, and there were in them no quality save only that they were good, then they (or rather it) would seem to be not things but the principle of things; for there is one thing alone of this kind, that is only good and nothing else. But since they are not simple, they could not even exist at all unless that which is the one sole good had willed them to exist. They are called good simply because their existence has derived from the will of the good. For the first good, since it exists, is good in virtue of its existence; but the secondary good, since it has derived from that whose existence is itself good, is itself also good. But the particular being of all things has derived from that which is the first good and which is such a good that it is rightly said to be good in virtue of its existence. Therefore their particular being is good; for then it is in the first good.

Thereby the problem is solved. For though they are good in virtue of their existence, they are not therefore like the first good, since their particular being is not good under all circumstances, but because the particular being of things cannot exist unless it has derived from the first being, that is, the good; therefore their particular being is good, but it is not like that from which it derives. For that is good in any conditions in virtue of its existence; for it is nothing else than good. But if the former were not derived from that good, it could perhaps be good, but it could not be good in virtue of its existence. For in that case it might perhaps participate in the good; but their par-

Theodoric exiles Boethius from Rome to Padua, 1521, woodcut.
Boethius was consul and first minister to King Theodoric, the
Ostrogothic ruler of Italy. But in 522 Boethius was accused of treason,
imprisoned, and executed sometime around 524. The specific charges
are not known, but probably involved religious differences between the
Catholic Boethius and the Arian Theodoric. *(Library of
Congress/Instructional Resources Corp.)*

ticular being, which such things would not have from the good, they could not have as good. Therefore, the first good being removed from these things by a mental process, these things, though they might be good, yet could not be good in virtue of their existence, and since they could not actually have existed unless that which is truly good had produced them, therefore their existence is good and yet that which has derived from the substantial good is not like its source; and unless they had derived from it, though they were good yet they could not be good in virtue of their existence, since they would be both apart from the good and not derived from it, while that very first good is existence itself and good itself and good existence itself. But will not those things which are white also have to be white in virtue of their being white, since they have derived from the will of God that they should be white? By no means. For existence is one thing, their being white is another; and that because he who produced them so that they existed is indeed good, but certainly not white. It is therefore in accordance with the will of the good that they should be good in virtue of their existence; but that which is a property of a thing like whiteness is not in accordance with the will of him who is not white, that it should be white in virtue of its existence; for such things have not derived from the will of one who is white. And so they are white simply because one who was not white willed them to be white; but because he willed them to be good who was good, they are good in virtue of their existence. Ought, then, according to this reasoning, all things to be just, since he himself is just who willed them to exist? That is not so either. For being good refers to essence, being just, to action. But in him being and acting are the same; and therefore being good is the same as being just. But for us being is not the same as acting; for we are not simple. Therefore being good is not the same for us as being just, but being is the same for all of us in virtue of our existence. Therefore all things are good, but not also just. Moreover, good is a genus, but just is a species, and this species does not apply to all. Therefore some things are just, others are something else, but all things are good.

THE SECOND EDITION
OF THE COMMENTARIES
ON THE ISAGOGE OF PORPHYRY (in part)

BOOK I

10. . . . The mind, whatever it understands, either conceives by understanding and describes to itself by reason that which is established in the nature of things, or else depicts to itself in vacant imagination that which is not. It is inquired therefore of which sort the understanding of genus and of the rest is: whether we understand species and genera as we understand things which are and from which we derive a true understanding, or whether we deceive ourselves, since we form for ourselves, by the empty cogitation of the mind, things which are not. But even if it should be established that they are, and if we should say that the understanding of them is conceived from things which are, then another greater, and more difficult question would occasion doubt, since the most grave difficulty is revealed in distinguishing and understanding the nature of genus itself. For since it is necessary that everything which is, be either corporeal or incorporeal, genus and species will have to be in one of these. Of what sort then will that which is called genus be, corporeal or incorporeal? Nor in fact can attention be turned seriously to what it is, unless it is known in which of these classes it must be placed. But even when this question has been solved, all ambiguity will not be avoided. For there remains something which, should genus and species be called incorporeal, besets the understanding and detains it, demanding that it be resolved, to wit, whether they subsist in bodies themselves, or whether they seem to be incorporeal subsistences beyond bodies. Of course, there are two forms of the incorporeal, so that some things can be outside bodies and perdure [persist] in their incorporeality separated from bodies, as God, mind, soul; but others, although they are incorporeal, nevertheless can not be apart from bodies, as line, or surface, or number, or particular qualities, which, although we pronounce them to be incorporeal because they are not at all extended in three dimensions, nevertheless are in bodies in such fashion that they can not be torn from them or separated. Or if they have been separated from bodies, they in no manner continue to be. These questions although they are difficult, to the point that even Porphyry for the time refused to solve them, I shall nevertheless take up, that I may neither leave the mind of the reader uneasy, nor myself consume time and energy in these things which are outside the sequence of the task I have undertaken. First of all I shall state a few things concerning the ambiguity of the question, and then I shall attempt to remove and untie that knot of doubt.

Genera and species either are and subsist or are formed by the understanding and thought alone. But genera and species can not be. This moreover is understood from the following considerations. For anything that is common at one time to many can not be one; indeed, that which is common is of many, particularly when one and the same thing is completely in many things at one time. Howsoever many species indeed there are, there is one genus in them all, not that the individual species share, as it were, some part of it, but each of them has at one time the whole genus. It follows, from this that the whole genus, placed at one time in many individuals, can not be one; nor in fact can it happen that, since it is, wholly in many at one time, it be one in number in itself. But if this is so, no genus can possibly be one, from which it follows that it is absolutely nothing; for everything which is, is because it is one. And the same thing may properly be said of species. Yet if there are genus and species, but they are multiplex and not one in number, there will be no last genus, but it will have some other genus superposed on it, which would include that multiplicity in the word of its single name. For as the genera of many animals are sought for the following reason, that they have something similar, yet are not the same, so too, since the genus, which is in many and is therefore multiplex, has the likeness of itself, which is the genus, but is not one, because it is in many, another genus of this genus must likewise be looked for, and when that has been found, for the reason which has been mentioned above, still a third genus is to be sought out. And so reason must proceed *in infinitum,* since no end of the process occurs. But if any genus is one in number, it can not possibly be common to many. For a single thing, if it is common, is common by parts, and then it is not common as a whole, but the parts of it are proper to individual things, or else it passes at different times into the use of those having it, so that it is common as a servant or a horse is; or else it is made common to all at one time, not however that it constitute the substance of those to which it is common, but like some theatre or spectacle, which is common to all who look on. But genus can be common to the species according to none of these modes; for it must be common in such fashion that it is in the individuals wholly and at one time, and that it is able to constitute and form the substance of those things to which it is common. For this reason, if it is neither one, because it is common, nor many, because still another genus must be sought for that multitude, it will be seen that genus absolutely is not, and the same conclusion must be applied to the others. But if genera and species and the others are grasped only by understandings, since every idea is made either from the subject thing as the thing is constituted itself or as the thing is not constituted—for an idea can not be made from no subject—if the idea of genus and species and the others comes from the subject thing as the thing itself is constituted which is understood, then they are not only placed in the understanding but are placed also in the truth of things. And again it must be sought out what their nature is which the previous question investigated. But if the idea of genus and the rest is taken from the thing not as the thing is constituted which is subject to the idea, the idea must necessarily be vain, which is taken from the thing but not as the thing is constituted; for that is false which is understood otherwise than the thing is. Thus, therefore, since genus and species neither are nor, when they are understood, is the idea of them true, it is not uncertain that all this must be set forth relative to the care which is needed for investigating concerning the five predicables aforementioned, seeing that the inquiry is neither concerning the thing which is, nor concerning that of which something true can be understood or adduced.

11. This for the present is the question with regard to the aforementioned predicables, which we solve, in accord with Alexander, by the following reasoning. We say that it is not necessary that every idea which is formed from a subject but not as the subject itself is constituted, seem false and empty. For false opinion, but not understanding, is in only those ideas which are made by composition. For if any one composes and joins by the understanding that which nature does not suffer to be joined, no one is unaware that that is false, as would be the case should one join by the imagination horse and man and construct a centaur. But if it be done by division and by abstraction, the thing would not be constituted as the idea is, yet for all that, the idea is still not in the least false; for there are many things which have their being in others, from which either they can not at all be separated, or if they should be separated they subsist by no reason. And in order that this be shown to us in a well known example, the line is something in a body, and it owes to the body that which it is, namely, it retains its being through body. Which is shown thus: if it should be separated from body, it does not subsist; for who ever perceived with any sense a line separated from body? But when the mind receives from the senses things confused and intermingled with each other, it distinguishes them by its own power and thought. For sense transmits to us, besides bodies themselves, all incorporeal things of this sort which have their being in bodies, but the mind which has the power to compound that which is disjoined and to resolve that which is composite, so distinguishes the things which are transmitted by the senses, confused with and joined to bodies, that it may contemplate and see the incorporeal nature in itself and without the bodies in which it is concrete. For the characteristics of incorporeal things mixed with bodies are diverse even when they are separated from body. Genera therefore and species and the others are found either in incorporeal things or in those which are corporeal. And if the mind finds them in incorporeal things, it has in that instance an incorporeal understanding of a genus, but if it has perceived the genera and species of corporeal things, it bears off, as is its wont, the nature of incorporeals from bodies, and beholds it alone and pure as the form itself is in itself. So when the mind receives these incorporeals intermixed with bodies, separating them, it looks upon them and contemplates them. No one, therefore, may say that we think about the line falsely because we seize it by the mind as if it were outside bodies, since it can not be outside bodies. For not every idea which is taken from subject things otherwise than the things are themselves constituted, must be considered to be false but, as has been said above, that only is false which does this by composition, as when one thinks, joining man and horse, that there is a centaur; but that which accomplishes it by divisions, and abstractions, and assumptions from the things in which they are, not only is not false, but it alone can discover that which is true with respect to the characteristic of the thing. Things of this sort therefore are in corporeal and sensible things, but they are understood without sensible things, in order that their nature can be perceived and their characteristic comprehended. Since genera and species are thought, therefore their likeness is gathered from the individuals in which they are, as the likeness of humanity is gathered from individual men unlike each other, which likeness conceived by the mind and perceived truly is made the species; again when the likeness of these diverse species is considered, which can not be except in the species themselves or in the individuals of the species, it forms the genus. Consequently, genera and species are in individuals, but they are thought universals; and species must be considered to be nothing other than the thought collected from the substantial likeness of individuals unlike in number, and genus the thought collected from the likeness of species. But this likeness when it is in individual things is made sensible, when it is in universals it is made intelligible; and in the same way when it is sensible, it remains in individuals, when it is understood, it is made universal. Therefore, they subsist in sensibles, but they are understood without bodies. For there is nothing to prevent two things which are in the same subject from being different in reason, like a concave and a convex line, which things, although they are defined by diverse definitions and although the understanding of them is diverse, are nevertheless always found in the same subject; for it is the same line which is convex and concave. So too for genera and species, that is, for singularity and universality, there is only one subject, but it is universal in one manner when it is thought, and singular in another when it is perceived in those things in which it has its being.

Once these distinctions are made, therefore, the whole question, I believe, is solved. For genera and species subsist in one manner, but are understood in another; and they are incorporeal, but they subsist in sensible things joined to sensible things. They are understood, to be sure, as subsisting through themselves and not as having their being in others. Plato, however, thinks that genera, and species, and the rest not only are understood as universals, but also are and subsist without bodies; whereas Aristotle thinks that they are understood as incorporeal and universal, but subsist in sensibles; we have not considered it proper to determine between their opinions, for that is of more lofty philosophy. But we have followed out the opinion of Aristotle very diligently for this reason, not in the least because we approved of it, but because this book has been written for the *Categories,* of which Aristotle is the author.

THE CONSOLATION OF PHILOSOPHY
(in part)

BOOK V

Chapter 2

. . . In [a] close-linked series of causes, is there any freedom of our will, or does [a] chain of fate also bind even the motions of men's minds?"

"Freedom there is," she said, "for there could not be any nature rational, did not that same nature possess freedom of the will. For that which can by its nature use reason, has the faculty of judgement, by which it determines everything; of itself, therefore, it distinguishes those things which are to be avoided, and those things that are to be desired. Now what a man judges is to be desired, that he seeks; but he runs away from what he thinks is to be avoided. And therefore those who have in themselves reason have also in them freedom to will or not to will, but this freedom is not, I am sure, equal in all of them. For heavenly, divine substances possess penetrating judgement, an uncorrupted will, and the ability to achieve what they desire. But human souls must indeed be more free when they preserve themselves in the contemplation of the divine mind; less free, however, when they slip down to the corporeal, and still less free when they are bound into earthly limbs. But their ultimate servitude is when, given over to vice, they have lapsed from the possession of the reason proper to them. For when from the light of the highest truth they have lowered their eyes to inferior, darkling things, at once they are befogged by the cloud of unknowing, they are disturbed by destructive affections, by giving in and by consenting to which they strengthen that servitude which they have brought upon themselves, and are in a way made captive by their freedom. Yet that regard of providence which looks forth on all things from eternity, sees this and disposes all that is predestined to each according to his deserts."

> That Phoebus shining with pure light
> "Sees all and all things hears,"
> So Homer sings, he of the honeyed voice;
> Yet even he, with the light of his rays, too weak,
> Cannot burst through
> To the inmost depths of earth or ocean.
> Not thus the Maker of this great universe:
> Him, viewing all things from his height,
> No mass of earth obstructs,
> No night with black clouds thwarts.
> What is, what has been, and what is to come,
> In one swift mental stab he sees;
> Him, since he only all things sees,
> The true sun could you call.

Reprinted by permission of the publishers and the Loeb Classical Library from Boethius: *The Theological Tracts,* translated by H.F. Stewart, E.K. Rand, and S.J. Tester. Cambridge, MA: Harvard University Press, 1973. Copyright © 1973 by Harvard University Press.

Chapter 3

Then I said: "See, I am again confused, with a still more difficult doubt."

"What is that?" she asked. "Tell me, for I already guess what troubles you."

"It seems," I said, "much too conflicting and contradictory that God foreknows all things and that there is any free will. For if God foresees all and cannot in any way be mistaken, then that must necessarily happen which in his providence he foresees will be. And therefore if he foreknows from all eternity not only the deeds of men but even their plans and desires, there will be no free will; for it will be impossible for there to be any deed at all or any desire whatever except that which divine providence, which cannot be mistaken, perceives beforehand. For if they can be turned aside into a different way from that foreseen, then there will no longer be firm foreknowledge of the future, but rather uncertain opinion, which I judge impious to believe of God.

For neither do I agree with that argument according to which some believe that they can solve this knotty question. For they say that a thing is not going to happen because providence has foreseen that it will be, but rather to the contrary, that since something is going to be, it cannot be hidden from divine providence, and in this way the necessity slips over to the opposite side. For, they say, it is not necessary that those things happen which are foreseen, but it is necessary that those things that will happen are foreseen; as if indeed our work were to discover which is the cause of which, foreknowledge of future things' necessity, or future things' necessity of providence, and as if we were not striving to show this, that whatever the state of the ordering of causes, the outcome of things foreknown is necessary, even if that foreknowledge were not to seem to confer on future things the necessity of occurring.

For indeed, if anyone sit, then the opinion that thinks that he sits must be true; and conversely also, if the opinion about any man be true, that he sits, then he must be sitting. There is thus a necessity in both cases: in the latter, he must be sitting, but in the former, the opinion must be true. But a man does not sit because the opinion about him is true, but rather that opinion is true because that someone is sitting happened first. So that although the cause of truth proceeds from the one part, yet there is in both a common necessity.

Obviously the same reasoning holds with regard to providence and future events: for even if the reason they are foreseen is that they are future events, yet they do not happen simply because they are foreseen; and yet nevertheless things either must be foreseen by God because they are coming or happen because they are foreseen, and that alone is enough to destroy the freedom of the will. But now how upside-down it is that it should be said that the cause of eternal foreknowledge is the occurrence of temporal things! But what else is it, to think that God foresees future things because they are going to happen, than to think that those things, once they have happened, are the cause of his highest providence? Furthermore, just as when I know that something is, then that necessarily is so, so when I know something will be, then that necessarily will be so; and so it happens that the occurrence of a thing foreknown cannot be avoided. Lastly, if a man think a thing to be otherwise than it is, that is not only not knowledge, but it is a mistaken opinion very different indeed from the truth of knowledge. And therefore if something is future in such a way that its occurrence is not certain or necessary, how will it be possible for it to be foreknown that it will occur? For just as real knowledge is unmixed with falsity, so that which is grasped by knowledge cannot be otherwise than as it is grasped. For the real reason why knowledge lacks any falsehood is that every single thing must necessarily be just as knowledge comprehends it to be.

Well then, how does God foreknow that these uncertain things shall be? For if he thinks those things will inevitably occur which it is yet possible may not occur, he is mistaken, which it is not only impious to think but still more impious to say aloud. But if he sees that those future things are just as indeed they are, so that he knows that they can equally either happen or not happen, what sort of foreknowledge is this, that grasps nothing certain, nothing stable? Or how does it compare with that ridiculous prophecy of Tiresias?—"Whatever I say will either happen or not?" And in what will divine providence be better than the opinions of men, if it judges in the way men do those things to be uncertain the occurrence of which is uncertain? But if in him, the most certain fount of all things, there can be nothing uncertain, then the occurrence is certain of those things which he firmly foreknows will be.

And therefore there is no freedom in human intentions or actions, which the divine mind, foreseeing all without mistaken error, binds and constrains to one actual occurrence. This once accepted, it is clear what a great collapse of human affairs follows! For it is vain to propose for good and evil men rewards or punishments which no free and voluntary act of their minds has deserved. And that very thing will seem most unjust of all which now is judged most just, that either the wicked are punished or the good rewarded, since they have not been brought by their own wills but driven by the certain necessity of what shall be to one or other end. And therefore there would be no vices nor virtues, but rather a mixed-up and indistinguishable confusion of all deserts, and—than which nothing more wicked can be conceived!—since the whole ordering of things proceeds from providence and nothing is really possible to human intentions, it follows that even our vices are to be referred to the author of all things good. And therefore there is no sense in hoping for anything or in praying that anything may be averted; for what even should any man hope for or pray to be averted when an inflexible course links all that can be desired?

And so that sole intercourse between men and God will be removed, that is, hope and prayer for aversion (if indeed at the price of a proper humility we deserve the inestimable return of God's grace), and that is the only way in which men seem able to converse with God and to be joined by the very manner of their supplication to that inaccessible light, even before they receive what they seek. Now if these things, once the necessity of what shall be is admitted, be thought to have no power, how should we be able to be joined and cleave to him, the highest principle of all things? So it will necessarily follow, as you sang a little while ago, that human kind would, torn apart and disjoined, in pieces fall from their origin.

What cause discordant breaks the world's compact?
What god sets strife so great
Between two truths,
That those same things which stand, alone and separate,
Together mixed, refuse to be so yoked?
Or is there no such discord between truths,
And do they ever each to other firmly cleave,
But is it the mind, eclipsed by the body's unseeing parts,
That cannot recognize, by its suppressed light's fire,
The world's fine fastenings?
But why does it blaze with so great love
To find the hidden characters of truth?
Does it know what it anxiously seeks to know?
But who is there labours to know known things?
Yet if it does not know, why then in blindness seek?

For who would long for anything he knows not of,
Or who could follow after things unknown,
Or how discover them? Who could in ignorance recognize
The form of what he found?
Or, when it perceived the highest mind,
Did it know at once the whole and the separate parts?
Now, clouded and hidden by the body's parts,
It is not totally forgetful of itself,
And the whole it keeps, losing the separate parts.
Therefore whoever seeks the truth
Is of neither class: for he neither knows
Nor is altogether ignorant of all,
But the whole he keeps, remembers and reflects on,
All from that height perceived goes over once again,
That he might to those things he has preserved
Add the forgotten parts."

*   *   *

Chapter 6

"Since, then, as was shown a little while ago, everything which is known is known not according to its own nature but according to the nature of those comprehending it, let us now examine, so far as is allowable, what is the nature of the divine substance, so that we may be able to recognize what kind of knowledge his is. Now that God is eternal is the common judgement of all who live by reason. Therefore let us consider, what is eternity; for this makes plain to us both the divine nature and the divine knowledge. Eternity, then, is the whole, simultaneous and perfect possession of boundless life, which becomes clearer by comparison with temporal things. For whatever lives in time proceeds in the present from the past into the future, and there is nothing established in time which can embrace the whole space of its life equally, but tomorrow surely it does not yet grasp, while yesterday it has already lost. And in this day to day life you live no more than in that moving and transitory moment. Therefore whatever endures the condition of time, although, as Aristotle thought concerning the world, it neither began ever to be nor ceases to be, and although its life is drawn out with the infinity of time, yet it is not yet such that it may rightly be believed to be eternal. For it does not simultaneously comprehend and embrace the whole space of its life, though it be infinite, but it possesses the future not yet, the past no longer. Whatever therefore comprehends and possesses at once the whole fullness of boundless life, and is such that neither is anything future lacking from it, nor has anything past flowed away, that is rightly held to be eternal, and that must necessarily both always be present to itself, possessing itself in the present, and hold as present the infinity of moving time.

And therefore those are not right who, when they hear that Plato thought this world neither had a beginning in time nor would have an end, think that in this way the created world is made co-eternal with the Creator. For it is one thing to be drawn out through a life without bounds, which is what Plato attributes to the world, but it is a different thing to have embraced at once the whole presence of boundless life, which it is clear is the property of the divine mind. Nor should God seem to be more ancient than created things by some amount of time, but rather by his own simplicity of nature. For this present nature of unmoving life that infinite movement of temporal things imitates, and since it cannot fully represent and equal it, it fails from immobility into motion, it shrinks from the simplicity of that present into the infinite quantity of the future and the past and, since it cannot possess at once the whole fullness of its life, in this very respect, that it in some way never ceases to be, it seems to emulate to some degree which it cannot fully express, by binding itself to the sort of present of this brief and fleeting moment, a present which since it wears a kind of likeness of that permanent present, grants to whatsoever things it touches that they should seem to be. But since it could not be permanent, it seized on the infinite journeying of time, and in that way became such that it should continue by going on a life the fullness of which it could not embrace by being permanent. And so if we should wish to give things names befitting them, then following Plato we should say that God indeed is eternal, but that the world is perpetual.

Since then every judgment comprehends those things subject to it according to its own nature, and God has an always eternal and present nature, then his knowledge too, surpassing all movement of time, is permanent in the simplicity of his present, and embracing all the infinite spaces of the future and the past, considers them in his simple act of knowledge as though they were now going on. So if you should wish to consider his foreknowledge, by which he discerns all things, you will more rightly judge it to be not foreknowledge as it were of the future but knowledge of a never-passing instant. And therefore it is called not prevision (*praevidentia*) but providence (*providentia*), because set far from the lowest of things it looks forward on all things as though from the highest peak of the world. Why then do you require those things to be made necessary which are scanned by the light of God's sight, when not even men make necessary those things they see? After all, your looking at them does not confer any necessity on those things you presently see, does it?"

"Not at all."

"But if the comparison of the divine and the human present is a proper one, just as you see certain things in this your temporal present, so he perceives all things in his eternal one. And therefore this divine foreknowledge does not alter the proper nature of things, but sees them present to him just such as in time they will at some future point come to be. Nor does he confuse the ways things are to be judged, but with one glance of his mind distinguishes both those things necessarily coming to be and those not necessarily coming to be, just as you, when you see at one and the same time that a man is walking on the ground and that the sun is rising in the sky, although the two things are seen simultaneously, yet you distinguish them, and judge the first to be voluntary, the second necessary. So then the divine perception looking down on all things does not disturb at all the quality of things that are present indeed to him but future with reference to imposed conditions of time. So it is that it is not opinion but a knowledge grounded rather upon truth, when he knows that something is going to happen, something which he is also aware lacks all necessity of happening.

If at this point you were to say that what God sees is going to occur cannot not occur, and that what cannot not occur happens from necessity, and so bind me to this word 'necessity,' I will admit that this is a matter indeed of the firmest truth, but one which scarcely anyone except a theologian could tackle. For I shall say in answer that the same future event, when it is related to divine knowledge, is necessary, but when it is considered in its own nature it seems to be utterly and absolutely free. For there are really two necessities, the one simple, as that it is necessary that all men are mortal; the other conditional, as for example, if you know that someone is walking, it is necessary that he is walking. Whatever anyone knows cannot be otherwise than as it is known, but this conditional necessity by no means carries with it that other simple kind. For this sort of necessity is not caused by a thing's proper nature but by the addition of the condition; for no necessity forces him to go who walks of his own will, even though it is necessary that he is going at the time when he is walking. Now in the same way, if providence sees anything as present, that must necessarily be, even if it possesses no necessity of its nature. But God beholds those future events which happen because of the freedom of the will, as present; they therefore, related to the divine perception, become necessary through the condition of the divine knowledge, but considered in themselves do not lose the absolute freedom of their nature. Therefore all those things which God foreknows will come to be, will without doubt come to be, but certain of them proceed from free will, and although they do come to be, yet in happening they do not lose their proper nature, according to which, before they happened, they might also not have happened. What then does it matter that they are not necessary, since on account of the condition of the divine knowledge it will turn out in all respects like necessity? Surely as much as those things I put before you a moment ago, the rising sun and the walking man: while these things are happening, they cannot not happen, but of the two one, even before it happened, was bound to happen, while the other was not. So also, those things God possesses as present, beyond doubt will happen, but of them the one kind is consequent upon the necessity of things, the other upon the power of those doing them. So therefore we were not wrong in saying that these, if related to the divine knowledge, are necessary, if considered in themselves, are free from the bonds of necessity, just as everything which lies open to the senses, if you relate it to the reason, is universal, if you look at it by itself, is singular.

But if, you will say, it lies in my power to change my intention, I shall make nonsense of providence, since what providence foreknows, I shall perhaps have changed. I shall reply that you can indeed alter your intention, but since the truth of providence sees in its present both that you can do so, and whether you will do so and in what direction you will change, you cannot avoid the divine prescience, just as you could not escape the sight of an eye that was present, even though of your own free will you changed to different courses of action. What then will you say? Will the divine knowledge be changed by my disposition, so that, since I want to do this at one time and that at another, it too alternates from this kind of knowledge to that? Not at all. For the divine perception runs ahead over every future event and turns it back and recalls it to the present of its own knowledge, and does not alternate, as you suggest, foreknowing now this, now that, but itself remaining still anticipates and embraces your changes at one stroke. And God possesses this present instant of comprehension and sight of all things not from the issuing of future events but from his own simplicity. In this way that too is resolved which you suggested a little while ago, that it is not right that our future actions should be said to provide the cause of the knowledge of God. For the nature of his knowledge as we have described it, embracing all things in a present act of knowing, establishes a measure for everything, but owes nothing to later events. These things being so, the freedom of the will remains to mortals, inviolate, nor are laws proposing rewards and punishments for wills free from all necessity unjust. There remains also as an observer from on high foreknowing all things, God, and the always present eternity of his sight runs along with the future quality of our actions dispensing rewards for the good and punishments for the wicked. Nor vainly are our hopes placed in God, nor our prayers, which when they are right cannot be ineffectual. Turn away then from vices, cultivate virtues, lift up your mind to righteous hopes, offer up humble prayers to heaven. A great necessity is solemnly ordained for you if you do not want to deceive yourselves, to do good, when you act before the eyes of a judge who sees all things."

John Scotus Eriugena
ca. 810–ca. 877

The collapse of the Western Roman Empire led to a period of economic and social anarchy. Living conditions from the end of the sixth to the middle of the eleventh centuries were so primitive that, according to historians, "one can almost speak of five centuries of camping out."* Government was largely tribal in nature, led by warriors who considered loyalty to one's liege lord the primary virtue. What little social stability there was tended to depend upon exceptional individuals, such as Charlemagne and Alfred the Great. One of the few remaining places for intellectual endeavor was the monastery; and monasteries were often far from population centers, many on the very edges of Europe. It should not be surprising, then, that the one philosopher of note to emerge from this period was a monk from Ireland: John Scotus Eriugena.

John Scotus Eriugena's two last names both mean "from Ireland" (at that time the Irish were called "Scoti," and "Eriugena" means "of the people of Erin [Ireland]"). Eriugena, as he is commonly called, studied Greek in an Irish monastery and eventually became a teacher in the court of the king of the Franks, Charles the Bald. While there he was embroiled in a controversy on the nature of the Eucharist, and one of his books was burned. Apart from these slim data, we know little about Eriugena's life and can-

*Robert E. Lerner et al., *Western Civilizations,* 11th ed., (New York: Norton, 1988), p. 278.

not even say for certain when or how he died (though 877 is the frequently given date).

In the selection from *The Division of Nature* given here, in the I.P. Sheldon-Williams translation revised by John O'Meara, Eriugena shows his Neoplatonic roots in giving two ways of dividing "nature" (meaning all of reality). In the first method, based on the concepts of creating and being created, Eriugena divides nature into four parts. First is "that which creates and is not created" (i.e., God), then "that which is created and also creates" (i.e., Platonic Forms), then "that which is created and does not create" (i.e., the material world), and finally "that which neither creates nor is created" (God again). The first and fourth divisions turn out to be the Creator, while the second and third are the creation (immaterial and material, respectively).

The second, and more basic, division of nature is into "things that are" and "things that are not." It might seem that "things that are not" would be sheer nothingness and so not really a part of "nature" at all. But, Eriugena explains, there are several "things" that do not exist in one mode or another. These include (1) anything beyond our faculties of apprehension, (2) the negation of the superior, (3) potential beings, (4) changing particulars, and (5) the sinful nature of humans (who have lost their essential nature). The first of these modes of nonbeing has the dubious distinction of making God one of the "things that are not." Eriugena asserted that indeed "God is not," but, borrowing terminology from the Pseudo-Dionysius, Eriugena pointed out that this way of thinking and talking is simply the *via negativa*—the negative way of confessing God. There is also a *via affirmativa,* which allows the affirmation of God's essential properties. So, for example, it is correct (using the *via negativa*) to say that "God is not good," while it is also correct (using the *via affirmativa*) to say that "God *is* good." Eriugena resolved this seeming contradiction by claiming that while God is not (literally) good, God is (metaphorically) good—in short, God is "*super*-good."

Eriugena's fourfold division of reality looks a good deal like Plotinus' emanations and seems to put God and God's creation in the same category ("Nature"). Not surprisingly, Eriugena was accused by the Catholic Church of Neoplatonic pantheism, and his work was eventually condemned as heretical in 1225.

*   *   *

In addition to the appropriate chapters in the surveys of medieval philosophy previously listed (page 128), the following studies of Eriugena should be consulted for further reading: Henry Bett, *Johannes Scotus Erigena: A Study in Mediaeval Philosophy* (1925; reprinted New York: Russell & Russell, 1964); John O'Meara, *Eriugena* (Oxford: Clarendon Press, 1988); and Dermot Moran, *The Philosophy of John Scotus Eriugena: A Study of Idealism in the Middle Ages* (Cambridge: Cambridge University Press, 1989). For a collection of essays, see F.X. Martin and J.A. Richmond, eds., *From Augustine to Eriugena: Essays on Neoplatonism and Christianity* (Washington, DC: Catholic University of America Press, 1991).

THE DIVISION OF NATURE
(PERIPHYSEON) (in part)

CHAPTER 1

NUTRITOR:*   As I frequently ponder and, so far as my talents allow, ever more care-fully investigate the fact that the first and fundamental division of all things which ei-ther can be grasped by the mind or lie beyond its grasp is into those that are and those that are not, there comes to mind as a general term for them all what in Greek is called *Physis* and in Latin *Natura.* Or do you think otherwise?

ALUMNUS: No, I agree. For I too, when I enter upon the path of reasoning, find that this is so.

NUTRITOR: Nature, then, is the general name, as we said, for all things, for those that are and those that are not.

ALUMNUS: It is. For nothing at all can come into our thought that would not fall under this term.

NUTRITOR: Then since we agree to use this term for the genus, I should like you to suggest a method for its division by differentiations into species; or, if you wish, I shall first attempt a division, and your part will be to offer sound criticism.

ALUMNUS: Pray begin. For I am impatient to hear from you a true account of this matter.

NUTRITOR: It is my opinion that the division of Nature by means of four dif-ferences results in four species, (being divided) first into that which creates and is not created, secondly into that which is created and also creates, thirdly into that which is created and does not create, while the fourth neither creates nor is created. But within these four there are two pairs of opposites. For the third is the opposite of the first, the fourth of the second; but the fourth is classed among the impossibles, for it is of its essence that it cannot be. Does such a division seem right to you or not?

ALUMNUS: Right, certainly. But please go over it again so as to elucidate more fully the opposition(s) within these four forms.

NUTRITOR: I am sure you see the opposition of the third species to the first—for the first creates and is not created; it therefore has as its contrary that [which is created and does not create—and of the second to the fourth, for the second both is created and creates; it therefore has as its contrary in all respects the fourth,] which neither creates nor is created.

ALUMNUS: I see (that) clearly. But I am much perplexed by the fourth species which you have introduced. For about the other three I should not presume to raise any question at all, because, as I think, the first is understood to be the Cause of all things that are and that are not, Who is God; the second to be the primordial causes; and the third those things that become manifest through coming into being in times and places. For this reason a more detailed discussion which shall take each species individually is required, as I think.

*["Nutritor" is the master; "Alumnus" is the disciple.]

John Scotus Eriugena, *Periphyseon (The Division of Nature)*, Chap. 1, 1–7; 11–12, 13–14 translated by I.P. Sheldon-Williams, revised by John O'Meara (Washington, DC, and Montréal: Dumbarton Oaks and Éditions Bellarmin, 1987). Reprinted by permission.

NUTRITOR: You are right to think so. But in what order we should pursue our path of reasoning, that is to say, which of the species of Nature we should take first, I leave it to you to decide.

ALUMNUS: It seems to me beyond question that before the others we should say of the first species whatever the light of minds has granted us to utter.

NUTRITOR: Let it be so. But first I think a few words should be said about the first and fundamental [division]—as we called it—of all things into the things that are and the things that are not.

ALUMNUS: It would be correct and wise to do so. For I see no other beginning from which reasoning ought to start, and this not only because this difference is the first of all, but because both in appearance and in fact it is more obscure than the others.

NUTRITOR: This basic difference, then, which separates all things requires for itself five modes of interpretation:

I. Of these modes the first seems to be that by means of which reason convinces us that all things which fall within the perception of bodily sense or (within the grasp of) intelligence are truly and reasonably said to be, but that those which because of the excellence of their nature elude not only all sense but also all intellect and reason rightly seem not to be—which are correctly understood only of God and matter and of the reasons and essences of all the things that are created by Him. And rightly so: for as Dionysius the Areopagite says, He is the Essence of all things Who alone truly is. "For," says he, "the being of all things is the Divinity Who is above Being." Gregory the Theologian too proves by many arguments that no substance or essence of any creature, whether visible or invisible, can be comprehended by the intellect or by reason as to what it is. For just as God as He is in Himself beyond every creature is comprehended by no intellect, so is He equally incomprehensible when considered in the innermost depths of the creature which was made by Him and which exists in Him; while whatsoever in every creature is either perceived by the bodily sense or contemplated by the intellect is merely some accident to each creature's essence which, as has been said, by itself is incomprehensible, but which, either by quality or by quantity or by form or by matter or by some difference or by place or by time, is known not as to what it is but as to that it is.

That, then, is the first and fundamental mode [of division] of those things of which it is said that they are and those (of which it is said) that they are not. For what somehow appears to be (a mode of division) based upon privations of substances and accidents should certainly not be admitted, in my opinion. For how can that which absolutely is not, and cannot be, and which does not surpass the intellect because of the pre-eminence of its existence, be included in the division of things? [—unless perhaps someone should say that the absences and privations of things that exist are themselves not altogether nothing, but are implied by some strange natural virtue of those things of which they are the privations and absences and oppositions, so as to have some kind of existence.]

II. Let then the second mode of being and not being be that which is seen in the orders and *differences* of created natures, which, beginning from the intellectual power, which is the highest and is constituted nearest to God, descends to the furthermost (degree) of the rational [and irrational] creature, or, to speak more plainly, from the most exalted angel to the furthermost element of the rational [and irrational] soul [—I mean the nutritive and growth-giving life-principle, which is the least part of the soul in the general acceptance of the term because it nourishes the body and makes it grow]. Here, by a wonderful mode of understanding, each order, including the last at the lower end [which is that of bodies and in which the whole division comes to an end], can be said to be and not to be. For an affirmation concerning the lower (order) is a negation concerning the higher, and so too a negation concerning the lower (order) is an affirmation concerning the higher [and similarly an affirmation concerning the higher (order) is a negation concerning the lower, while a negation concerning the higher (order) will be an affirmation concerning the lower]. Thus, the affirmation of "man" (I mean, man while still in his mortal state) is the negation of "angel," while the negation of "man" is the affirmation of "angel" [and vice versa]. For if man is a rational, mortal, risible animal, then an angel is certainly neither a rational animal nor mortal nor risible: likewise, if an angel is an essential intellectual motion about God and the causes of things, then man is certainly not an essential intellectual motion about God and the causes of things. And the same rule is found to apply in all the celestial essences until one reaches the highest order of all. This, however, terminates [in] the highest negation [upward]; for its negation confirms the existence of no higher creature. Now, there are three orders which they call "of equal rank": the first of these are the Cherubim, Seraphim, and Thrones; the second, the Virtues, Powers, and Dominations; the third, the Principalities, Archangels, and Angels. Downwards, on the other hand, the last (order) merely [denies or confirms the one above it, because it has nothing below it which it might either take away or establish] since it is preceded by all the orders higher than itself but precedes none that is lower than itself.

It is also on these grounds that every order of rational or intellectual creatures is said to be and not to be: it is in so far as it is known by the orders above it and by itself; but it is not in so far as it does not permit itself to be comprehended by the orders that are below it.

III. The third mode can suitably be seen in those things of which the visible plenitude of this world is made up, and in their causes in the most secret folds of nature, which precede them. For whatsoever of these causes through generation is known as to matter and form, as to times and places, is by a certain human convention said to be, while whatsoever is still held in those folds of nature and is not manifest as to form or matter, place or time, and the other accidents, by the same convention referred to is said not to be. Clear examples of this mode are provided over a wide range (of experience), and especially in human nature. Thus, since God in that first and one man whom He made in His image established all men at the same time, yet did not bring them all at the same time into this visible world, but brings the nature which He considers all at one time into visible essence at certain times and places according to a certain sequence which He Himself knows: those who already [are becoming, or] have become visibly manifest in the world are said to be, while those who are as yet hidden, though destined to be, are said not to be. Between the first and third (mode) there is this difference: the first (is found) generically in all things which at the same time and once for all have been made in (their) causes and effects; the *third* specifically in those which partly are still hidden in their causes, partly are manifest in (their) effects, of which in particular the fabric of this world is woven. To this mode belongs the reasoning which considers the potentiality of seeds, whether in animals or in trees or in plants. For during the time when the potentiality of the seeds is latent in the recesses of nature, because it is not yet manifest it is said not to be; but when it has become manifest in the birth and growth of animals or of flowers or of the fruits of trees and plants it is said to be.

IV. The fourth mode is that which, not improbably according to the philosophers, declares that only those things which are contemplated by the intellect alone truly are, while those things which in generation, through the expansions or contractions of matter, and the intervals of places and motions of times are changed, brought together, or dissolved, are said not to be truly, as is the case with all bodies which can come into being and pass away.

V. The fifth mode is that which reason observes only in human nature, which, when through sin it renounced the honour of the divine image in which it was properly substantiated, deservedly lost its being and therefore is said not to be; but when, restored by the grace of the only-begotten Son of God, it is brought back to the former condition of its substance in which it was made after the image of God, it begins to be, and in him who has been made in the image of God begins to live. It is to this mode, it seems, that the Apostle's saying refers: "and He calls the things that are not as the things that are"; that is to say, those who in the first man were lost and had fallen into a kind of non-subsistence God the Father calls through faith [in His Son] to be as those who are already reborn in Christ. But this too may also be understood of those whom God daily calls forth from the secret folds of nature, in which they are considered not to be, to become visibly manifest in form and matter and in the other (conditions) in which hidden things are able to become manifest.

Although keener reasoning can discover some modes besides these, yet I think at the present (stage) enough has been said about these things, unless you disagree.

ALUMNUS: Quite plainly so . . .

* * *

NUTRITOR: . . . And now, I think, we must return to the task we have set ourselves, namely to the division of Nature.

ALUMNUS: Certainly we must return to it: for in what is going to be said some sort of moderation must be observed if it is ever to come to a conclusion.

NUTRITOR: Well, then: of the aforesaid divisions of Nature the first difference, as has seemed to us, is that which creates and is not created. And rightly so: for such a species of Nature is correctly predicated only of God, Who, since He alone creates all things, is understood to be ⟨*anarxos*⟩, that is, without beginning, because He alone is the principal Cause of all things which are made from Him and through Him, and therefore He is also the End of all things that are from Him, for it is He towards Whom all things strive. Therefore He is the Beginning, the Middle and the End: the Beginning because from Him are all things that participate in essence; the Middle, because in Him and through Him they subsist and move; the End, because it is towards Him that they move in seeking rest from their movement and the stability of their perfection.

ALUMNUS: I most firmly believe and, as far as I may, understand that only of the Divine Cause of all things is this rightly predicated; for it alone creates all things that are from it, and is not itself created by any cause which is superior (to itself) or precedes it. For it is the supreme and unique Cause of all things which take their existence from it and exist in it. But I would like [to know] your opinion about this. For I am not a little perplexed when I so often find in the books of the Holy Fathers who have attempted to treat of the Divine Nature that not only does it create all things that are, but itself also is created. *For,* according to them, it makes and is made, [and] creates and is created. If, then, this is the case, I do not find it easy to see how our reasoning may stand. For we say that it creates only, but is not created by anything.

NUTRITOR: You have every reason for being perplexed. For I too am greatly puzzled by this, and I should like [to be able] to learn [by] your guidance how it can be that these (statements), which seem to contradict one another, are prevented from conflicting [with one another]; and how to approach this question according to right reason.

ALUMNUS: Please speak first yourself: for in such matters I look to you rather than to myself for an opinion, and for a lead in reasoning.

NUTRITOR: First, then, I think we must consider that name which is so commonly used in Holy Scripture, that is, (the Name of) God. For although there are many names by which the Divine Nature is called, such as Goodness, Essence, Truth, and others of this kind, yet that is the name which most frequently occurs in Scripture.

ALUMNUS: It is certainly seen to be so.

NUTRITOR: Of this name [then] an etymology has been taken over from the Greeks: for either it is derived from the verb ⟨*theoro*⟩, that is, "I see"; or from the verb ⟨*theo*⟩, that is, "I run"; or—which is more likely [since] the meaning of both *is* [one and] the same—it is correctly *held* to be derived from both. For when it is *derived* from the verb ⟨*theoro*⟩, ⟨*theos*⟩ is interpreted to mean "He Who sees," for He sees in Himself all things that are [while] He looks upon nothing that is outside Himself because outside Him there is nothing. But when ⟨*theos*⟩ is derived from the verb ⟨*theo*⟩ it is correctly interpreted "He Who runs," for He runs *throughout all things* and never stays but by His running fills out all things, as it is written: "His Word runneth swiftly."

[And yet He is not moved at all. For of God] it is most truly said that He is motion at rest and rest in motion. For He is at rest unchangingly in Himself, never departing from the stability of His Nature; yet He sets Himself in motion through all things in order that those things which essentially subsist by Him may be. For by His motion all things are made. And thus there is one and the same meaning in the two interpretations of the same name, which is God. For in God to run through all things is not something other than to see all things, but as by His seeing so too by His running all things are made.

ALUMNUS: What has been said of the etymology of the name is sufficient and convincing. But I do not satisfactorily see whether He may move Who is everywhere, without Whom nothing can be, and beyond Whom nothing extends. For He is the place and the circumference of all things.

NUTRITOR: I did not say that God moves beyond Himself, but from Himself in Himself towards Himself. For it ought not to be believed that there is any motion in Him except that of His Will, by which He wills all things to be made; just as His rest [is understood] not as though He *comes to rest* after motion but as the immoveable determination of His same Will, by which He limits all things so that they remain in the immutable stability of their reasons. *For* properly speaking there is in Him neither rest nor motion. For these two are seen to be opposites one of the other. But right reason forbids us to suppose or understand that there are opposites in Him—especially as rest is, properly speaking, the end of motion, whereas God does not begin to move in order that He may attain to some end. Therefore these names, like many similar ones also, are transferred from the creature by a kind of divine metaphor to the Creator. Not without reason; for of all things that are at rest or in motion He is the Cause. For from Him they begin to run in order that they may be, since He is the Principle of them all; and [through Him] they are carried towards Him by their natural motion so that in Him they may rest immutably and eternally since He is the End and Rest of them all. For beyond Him there is nothing that they strive for since in Him they find the beginning and end of their motion. God, therefore, is called "He Who runs" not because He runs beyond Himself, Who is always immutably at rest in Himself, Who fills out all things; but because He makes all things run from a state of non-existence into one of existence.

ALUMNUS: Return to the subject. For these things seem to be not unreasonably spoken.

NUTRITOR: Please tell me which subject you mean. For in trying to say something about intervening questions we commonly forget the main one.

ALUMNUS: Was not this the task we set ourselves: to try our best to find out on what grounds those who treat of the Divine Nature say that *the same* (Nature) creates and is created? For that it creates all things no one of sound intellect is in doubt; but how it is said to be created is not, we thought, a question to be cursorily passed over.

NUTRITOR: Just so. But, as I think, in what has already been said considerable headway has been made towards the solution of this question. For we agreed that the motion of the Divine Nature is to be understood as nothing else but the purpose of the Divine Will to establish the things that are to be made. Therefore it is said that in all things the Divine Nature is being made, which is nothing else than the Divine Will. For in that Nature being is not different from willing, but willing and being are one and the same in the establishment of all things that are to be made. For example, one might say: this is the end to which the motion of the Divine Will is directed: that the things that are may be. Therefore it creates all things which it leads forth out of nothing so that they may be, from not-being into being; but it is (also) created because nothing except itself exists as an essence since itself is the essence of all things. For as there is nothing that is good by its nature, except (the divine nature) itself, but everything which is said to be good is so by participation in the One Supreme Good, so everything which is said to exist exists not in itself but by participation in the Nature which truly exists. Not only, therefore, as was mentioned earlier in our discussion, is the Divine Nature said to be made when in those who are reformed by faith and hope and charity and the other virtues the Word of God in a miraculous and ineffable manner is born—as the Apostle says, speaking of Christ, "Who from God is made in us wisdom and justification and sanctification and redemption"; but also, because that which is invisible in itself becomes manifest in all things that are, it is not inappropriately said to be made. For our intellect also, before it enters upon thought and memory, is not unreasonably said [not] to be. For in itself it is invisible and known only to God and ourselves; but when it enters upon thoughts and takes shape in certain phantasies it is not inappropriately said to come into being. For it does so in the memory when it receives certain forms [of things and sounds and colours and [other] sensibles]—for it had no form before it entered into the memory—; then it receives, as it were, a second formation when it takes the form of certain signs of [forms and] sounds—I mean the letters which are the signs of sounds, and the figures which are the signs of mathematical forms—or other perceptible indicators by which it can be communicated to the senses of *sentient beings.* By this analogy, far removed as it is from the Divine Nature, I think it can be shown all the same how that Nature, although it creates all things and cannot be created by anything, is in an admirable manner created in all things which take their being from it; so that, as the intelligence of the mind or its purpose or its intention or however this first and innermost motion of ours may be called, having, as we said, entered upon thought and received the forms of certain phantasies, and having then proceeded into the symbols of sounds or the signs of sensible motions, is not inappropriately said to become—for, being in itself without any sensible form, it becomes formed in fantasies—, so the Divine Essence which when it subsists by itself surpasses every intellect is correctly said to be created in those things which are made by itself and through itself and in itself [and for itself], so that in them either by the intellect, if they are only intelligible, or by the sense, if they are sensible, it comes to be known by those who investigate it in the right spirit.

ALUMNUS: Enough has been said about this, I think.

*   *   *

NUTRITOR: You observe well. Here too is something which I see should not be passed over without consideration, and therefore I should like you to tell me whether you understand that anything opposed to God or conceived alongside of Him exists. By "opposed" I mean either deprived of Him or contrary to Him or related to Him or absent from Him; while by "conceived alongside of Him" I mean something that is understood to exist eternally with Him without being of the same essence with him.

ALUMNUS: I see clearly what you mean. And therefore I should not dare to say that there is either anything that is opposed to Him or anything understood in association with Him which is ⟨heterousion⟩, that is, which is of another essence than what He is. For opposites by relation are always so opposed to one another that they both begin to be at the same time and cease to be at the same time, whether they are of the same nature, like single to double or 2/3 to 3/2, or of different natures, like light and darkness, or in respect of privation, like death and life, sound and silence. For these are correctly thought to belong to the things which are subject to coming into being and passing away. For those things which are in discord with one another cannot be eternal. For if they were eternal they would not be in discord with one another, since eternity is always like what it is and ever eternally subsists in itself as a single and indivisible unity. For it is the one beginning of all things, and their one end, in no way at discord with itself. For the same reason I do not know of anyone who would be so bold as to affirm that anything is co-eternal with God which is not co-essential with Him. For if such a thing can be conceived or discovered it necessarily follows that there is not one Principle of all things, but two [or more], widely differing from each other—which right reason invariably rejects without any hesitation: for from the One all things take their being; from two [or more], nothing.

NUTRITOR: You judge correctly, as I think. If therefore the aforesaid Divine Names are confronted by other names directly opposed to them, the things which are properly signified by them must also of necessity be understood to have contraries opposite to them; and therefore they cannot properly be predicated of God, to Whom nothing is opposed, and with Whom nothing is found to be co-eternal which differs from Him by nature. For right reason cannot find a single one of the names already mentioned or others like them to which *another* name, disagreeing *with it,* being opposed or differing from it within the same genus, is not found; and what we know to be the case with the names we must necessarily know to be so with the [things] which are signified by them. But since the expressions of divine significance which are predicated of God in Holy Scripture by transference from the creature to the Creator—if, indeed, it is right to say that anything can be predicated of Him, which must be considered in another place—are innumerable and cannot be found or gathered together within the small compass of our reasoning, only a few of the Divine Names can be set forth for the sake of example. Thus, [God] is called Essence, but strictly speaking He is not essence: for to being is opposed not-being. Therefore He is ⟨hyperousios⟩, that is, superessential. Again, He is called Goodness, but strictly speaking He is not goodness: for to goodness wickedness is opposed. Therefore (He is) ⟨hyperagathos⟩ that is, more-than-good, and ⟨hyperagathotas⟩, that is, more-than-goodness. He is called God, but He is not strictly speaking God: for to vision is opposed blindness, and to him who sees he who does not see. Therefore He is ⟨hypertheos⟩ that is, more-than-God—for ⟨theos⟩ is interpreted "He Who sees." But if you have recourse to the alternative origin of this name, so that you understand ⟨theos⟩, that is, God, to be derived not from the verb ⟨theoro⟩, that is, "I see," but from the verb ⟨theo⟩, that is, "I run," the same reason *confronts* you. For to him who runs he who does not run is opposed, as slowness to speed. Therefore He will be ⟨hypertheos⟩, that is, more-than-running, as it is written: "His Word runneth swiftly": for we understand this to refer to God the Word, Who in an ineffable way runs through all things that are, in order that they may be. We ought to think in the same way concerning Truth: for to truth is opposed falsehood, and therefore strictly speaking He is not truth. Therefore He is ⟨*hyperalathas*⟩ and ⟨*hyperalatheia*⟩, that is, more-than-true and (more than-)truth. The same reason must be observed in all the Divine Names. For He is not called Eternity properly, since to eternity is opposed temporality. Therefore He is ⟨*hyperaionios*⟩, and ⟨*hyperaionia*⟩, that is, more-than-eternal and (more-than-)eternity. Concerning Wisdom also no other reason applies, and therefore it must not be thought that it is predicated of God properly, since against wisdom and the wise are set the fool and folly. Hence rightly and truly He is called ⟨*hypersophos*⟩, that is, more-than-wise, and ⟨*hypersophia*⟩, that is, more-than-wisdom. Similarly, He is more-than-life because to life is opposed death. Concerning Light it must be understood in the same way: for against light is set darkness. For the present, as I think, enough has been said [concerning these (matters)].

Anselm (and Gaunilo)
1033–1109

Saint Anselm was born to a noble family in Aosta, in what is now Italy. Following a youth of travel and learning, Anselm joined the Benedictine monastery in the town of Bec, Normandy (in modern France). He remained in this monastery for the next thirty-three years, the last fifteen as abbot. During this time he wrote a number of books on theological and philosophical topics. In 1093 Anselm was coerced into leaving the monastery to become Archbishop of Canterbury. Most of his sixteen years in Canterbury were spent skirmishing with the king of England for control of the church (a pattern that continued for five centuries until Henry VIII severed the English church from Rome entirely in 1534). Anselm died in 1109 and was canonized in 1494.

Anselm's thought can be summed up in the Augustinian phrase, "faith seeking understanding." Anselm was a deeply devoted Christian who began his thinking with the assumption that the doctrines of Christianity are true. And this faith drove him to seek understanding, to find rational explanations for the Christian teachings he already believed. His writings reflected this yearning to understand rationally particular problems in faith; he wrote a number of short treatises on such subjects as the Incarnation and the Trinity. He believed that he could demonstrate the truth of these revealed doctrines.

Anselm's most famous work is his attempt to prove the existence of God in Chapters II–IV of the *Proslogion* (or *Discourse*) known now as the "ontological argument" (from Immanuel Kant's description). The ontological argument attempts to show that if one can conceive of a "being than which nothing greater can be conceived," one must also acknowledge that this being exists in reality as well as in the understanding. That is, if God is thought of, then God must exist. Recent scholars have pointed out that there are actually two arguments here: one, in Chapter II, that proves that God exists in reality; and another, in Chapters III–IV, that proves that God's existence is necessary.

Anselm's argument was immediately attacked by a fellow monk named Gaunilo. Anselm's exchange with Gaunilo has been preserved and the key sections are reprinted here, along with *Proslogion* II–IV, in the M.J. Charlesworth translation.

Despite the fact that this argument has fascinated thinkers for over nine hundred years, a student's first response to this passage is often one of confusion or simple denial: "He can't do that!" The student is not alone in being confused; the history of the argument is full of misrepresentations and misinterpretations. To be sure, careful thinkers such as Hume and Kant have attacked this argument. But it is notoriously difficult to say exactly what is wrong with Anselm's logic, and many purported refutations have actually been refutations of arguments quite different from Anselm's.

In recent years there has been renewed interest in the argument, with Charles Hartshorne, Norman Malcom, and Alvin Plantinga claiming that it is successful. There has also been a tradition, beginning with the medieval thinker Bonaventure and continuing through Karl Barth in this century, that claims *Proslogion* II–IV is not a philosophical argument at all. These theologians are convinced that Anselm is not "proving" anything, that he is simply showing the implications of God's self-revelation.

While the debate continues to rage, one fact is clear: Anselm raised some of the most basic questions in the history of philosophy. Questions about modes of existence, possible beings, necessity and contingency, as well as a range of issues in logic, all emerge in discussions of this provocative passage.

*   *   *

For a study of the complete *Proslogion,* see, M.J. Charlesworth, *St. Anselm's Proslogion* (Oxford: Clarendon Press, 1965). For the rest of Anselm's major works see, Anselm, *Basic Writings,* translated by S.N. Deane (1902; reprinted LaSalle, IL: Open Court, 1962). For a study of Anselm's life and times, see R.W. Southern, *Saint Anselm and His Biographer* (Cambridge: Cambridge University Press, 1963). Jasper Hopkins, *A Companion to the Study of St. Anselm* (Minneapolis: University of Minnesota Press, 1972), provides a comprehensive discussion of Anselm and his work.

For further reading on the ontological argument, the best source is John Hick and Arthur C. McGill, eds., *The Many-Faced Argument* (New York: Macmillan Co., 1967). Charles Hartshorne, *Anselm's Discovery: A Re-Examination of the Ontological Argument for God's Existence* (LaSalle, IL: Open Court, 1965); Alvin Plantinga, *The Nature of Necessity* (Oxford: Clarendon Press, 1974)— and his "simplified" version of this difficult work, Alvin Plantinga, *God, Freedom, and Evil* (Grand Rapids, MI: Eerdmans, 1977); and Richard Campbell, *From Belief to Understanding* (Canberra: Australian National University Press, 1976), all defend the argument. For theological interpretations see Karl Barth,

Anselm: Fides Quaren Intellectum, translated by Ian W. Robinson (London: SCM Press Ltd., 1960) (key chapters from this work are included in *The Many-Faced Argument*).

PROSLOGION (in part)

CHAPTER 2

That God truly exists

Well then, Lord, You who give understanding to faith, grant me that I may understand, as much as You see fit, that You exist as we believe You to exist, and that You are what we believe You to be. Now we believe that You are something than which nothing greater can be thought. Or can it be that a thing of such a nature does not exist, since "the Fool has said in his heart, there is no God" (Ps. xiii. 1, lii. 1)? But surely, when this same Fool hears what I am speaking about, namely, "something-than-which-nothing-greater-can-be-thought," he understands what he hears, and what he understands is in his mind, even if he does not understand that it actually exists. For it is one thing for an object to exist in the mind, and another thing to understand that an object actually exists. Thus, when a painter plans beforehand what he is going to execute, he has [the picture] in his mind, but he does not yet think that it actually exists because he has not yet executed it. However, when he has actually painted it, then he both has it in his mind and understands that it exists because he has now made it. Even the Fool, then, is forced to agree that something-than-which-nothing-greater-can-be-thought exists in the mind, since he understands this when he hears it, and whatever is understood is in the mind. And surely that-than-which-a-greater-cannot-be-thought cannot exist in the mind alone. For if it exists solely in the mind even, it can be thought to exist in reality also, which is greater. If then that-than-which-a-greater-cannot-be-thought exists in the mind alone, this same that-than-which-a-greater-*cannot*-be-thought is that-than-which-a-greater-*can*-be-thought. But this is obviously impossible. Therefore there is absolutely no doubt that something-than-which-a-greater-cannot-be-thought exists both in the mind and in reality.

CHAPTER 3

That God cannot be thought not to exist

And certainly this being so truly exists that it cannot be even thought not to exist. For something can be thought to exist that cannot be thought not to exist, and this is greater than that which can be thought not to exist. Hence, if that-than-which-a-

From M.J. Charlesworth, *St. Anselm's Proslogion* (Oxford: Oxford University Press, 1965). Reprinted by permission of Oxford University Press.

greater-cannot-be-thought can be thought not to exist, then that-than-which-a-greater-cannot-be-thought is not the same as that-than-which-a-greater-cannot-be-thought, which is absurd. Something-than-which-a-greater-cannot-be-thought exists so truly then, that it cannot be even thought not to exist. And You, Lord our God, are this being. You exist so truly, Lord my God, that You cannot even be thought not to exist. And this is as it should be, for if some intelligence could think of something better than You, the creature would be above its creator and would judge its creator—and that is completely absurd. In fact, everything else there is, except You alone, can be thought of as not existing. You alone, then, of all things most truly exist and therefore of all things possess existence to the highest degree; for anything else does not exist as truly, and so possesses existence to a lesser degree. Why then did "the Fool say in his heart, there is no God" (Ps. xiii. 1, lii. 1) when it is so evident to any rational mind that You of all things exist to the highest degree? Why indeed, unless because he was stupid and a fool?

CHAPTER 4

*How "the Fool said in his heart" what cannot
be thought*

How indeed has he "said in his heart" what he could not think; or how could he not think what he "said in his heart," since to "say in one's heart" and to "think" are the same? But if he really (indeed, since he really) both thought because he "said in his heart" and did not "say in his heart" because he could not think, there is not only one sense in which something is "said in one's heart" or thought. For in one sense a thing is thought when the word signifying it is thought; in another sense when the very object which the thing is is understood. In the first sense, then, God can be thought not to exist, but not at all in the second sense. No one, indeed, understanding what God is can think that God does not exist, even though he may say these words in his heart either without any [objective] signification or with some peculiar signification. For God is that-than-which-nothing-greater-can-be-thought. Whoever really understands this understands clearly that this same being so exists that not even in thought can it not exist. Thus whoever understands that God exists in such a way cannot think of Him as not existing.

I give thanks, good Lord, I give thanks to You, since what I believed before through Your free gift I now so understand through Your illumination, that if I did not want to *believe* that You existed, I should nevertheless be unable not to *understand* it.

GAUNILO AND ANSELM: DEBATE*

Gaunilo

[5.] That, however, [this nature] necessarily exists in reality is demonstrated to me from the fact that, unless it existed, whatever exists in reality would be greater than it and consequently it would not be that which is greater than everything that undoubtedly had already been proved to exist in the mind. To this I reply as follows: if something that cannot even be thought in the true and real sense must be said to exist in the mind, then I do not deny that this also exists in my mind in the same way. But since from this one cannot in any way conclude that it exists also in reality, I certainly do not yet concede that it actually exists, until this is proved to me by an indubitable argument. For he who claims that it actually exists because otherwise it would not be that which is greater than everything does not consider carefully enough whom he is addressing. For I certainly do not yet admit this greater [than everything] to be any truly existing thing; indeed I doubt or even deny it. And I do not concede that it exists in a different way from that— if one ought to speak of "existence" here—when the mind tries to imagine a completely unknown thing on the basis of the spoken words alone. How then can it be proved to me on that basis that that which is greater than everything truly exists in reality (because it is evident that it is greater than all others) if I keep on denying and also doubting that this is evident and do not admit that this greater [than everything] is either in my mind or thought, not even in the sense in which many doubtfully real and unreal things are? It must first of all be proved to me then that this same greater than everything truly exists in reality somewhere, and then only will the fact that it is greater than everything make it clear that it also subsists in itself.

Anselm

[II.] I said further that if a thing exists even in the mind alone, it can be thought to exist also in reality, which is greater. If, then, it (namely, "that-than-which-a-greater-cannot-be-thought") exists in the mind alone, it is something than which a greater can be thought. What, I ask you, could be more logical? For if it exists even in the mind alone, cannot it be thought to exist also in reality? And if it can [be so thought], is it not the case that he who thinks this thinks of something greater than it, if it exists in the mind alone? What, then, could follow more logically than that, if "that-than-which-a-greater-*cannot*-be-thought" exists in the mind alone, it is the same as that-than-which-a-greater-*can*-be-thought? But surely "that-than-which-a-greater-*can*-be-thought" is not for any mind [the same as] "that-than-which-a-greater-*cannot*-be-thought." Does it not follow, then, that "that-than-which-a-greater-*cannot*-be-thought," if it exists in anyone's mind, does not exist in the mind alone? For if it exists in the mind alone, it is that-than-which-a-greater-*can*-be-thought, which is absurd.

*[I have followed the procedure of John Hick, *Classical and Contemporary Readings in the Philosophy of Religion* (Englewood Cliffs, NJ: Prentice Hall, 1964) and put the main points of Gaunilo's critique together with Anselm's replies. The numbers before each section refer to the paragraph numbers of Gaunilo's *A Reply to the Foregoing by a Certain Writer on Behalf of the Fool* (in Arabic numbers) and Anselm's *Reply to the Foregoing by the Author of the Book in Question* (in Roman numerals).]

*   *   *

[IX.] It is evident, moreover, that in the same way one can think of and understand that which cannot not exist. And one who thinks of this thinks of something greater than one who thinks of what can not exist. When, therefore, one thinks of that-than-which-a-greater-cannot-be-thought, if one thinks of what can not exist, one does not think of that-than-which-a-greater-cannot-be-thought. Now the same thing cannot at the same time be thought of and not thought of. For this reason he who thinks of that-than-which-a-greater-cannot-be-thought does not think of something that can not exist but something that cannot not exist. Therefore what he thinks of exists necessarily, since whatever can not exist is not what he thinks of.

Gaunilo

[6.] They say that there is in the ocean somewhere an island which, because of the difficulty (or rather the impossibility) of finding that which does not exist, some have called the "Lost Island." And the story goes that it is blessed with all manner of priceless riches and delights in abundance, much more even than the Happy Isles, and, having no owner or inhabitant, it is superior everywhere in abundance of riches to all those other lands that men inhabit. Now, if anyone tells me that it is like this, I shall easily understand what is said, since nothing is difficult about it. But if he should then go on to say, as though it were a logical consequence of this: You cannot any more doubt that this island that is more excellent than all other lands truly exists somewhere in reality than you can doubt that it is in your mind; and since it is more excellent to exist not only in the mind alone but also in reality, therefore it must needs be that it exists. For if it did not exist, any other land existing in reality would be more excellent than it, and so this island, already conceived by you to be more excellent than others, will not be more excellent. If, I say, someone wishes thus to persuade me that this island really exists beyond all doubt, I should either think that he was joking, or I should find it hard to decide which of us I ought to judge the bigger fool—I, if I agreed with him, or he, if he thought that he had proved the existence of this island with any certainty, unless he had first convinced me that its very excellence exists in my mind precisely as a thing existing truly and indubitably and not just as something unreal or doubtfully real.

Anselm

[III.] You claim, however, that this is as though someone asserted that it cannot be doubted that a certain island in the ocean (which is more fertile than all other lands and which, because of the difficulty or even the impossibility of discovering what does not exist, is called the "Lost Island") truly exists in reality since anyone easily understands it when it is described in words. Now, I truly promise that if anyone should discover for me something existing either in reality or in the mind alone—except "that-than-which-a-greater-cannot-be-thought"—to which the logic of my argument would apply, then I shall find that Lost Island and give it, never more to be lost, to that person.

Gaunilo

[7.] If then someone should assert [to the Fool in *Proslogium* III] that this greater [than everything] is such that it cannot be thought not to exist (again without any other proof than that otherwise it would not be greater than everything), then he could make this same reply and say: When have I said that there truly existed some being that is "greater than everything," such that from this it could be proved to me that this same being really existed to such a degree that it could not be thought not to exist? That is why it must first be conclusively proved by argument that there is some higher nature, namely that which is greater and better than all the things that are, so that from this we can also infer everything else which necessarily cannot be wanting to what is greater and better than everything.

Anselm

[III.] It has already been clearly seen, however, that "that-than-which-a-greater-cannot-be-thought" cannot be thought not to exist, because it exists as a matter of such certain truth. Otherwise it would not exist at all. In short, if anyone says that he thinks that this being does not exist, I reply that, when he thinks of this, either he thinks of something than which a greater cannot be thought, or he does not think of it. If he does not think of it, then he does not think that what he does not think of does not exist. If, however, he does think of it, then indeed he thinks of something which cannot be even thought not to exist. For if it could be thought not to exist, it could be thought to have a beginning and an end—but this cannot be. Thus, he who thinks of it thinks of something that cannot be thought not to exist; indeed, he who thinks of this does not think of it as not existing, otherwise he would think what cannot be thought. Therefore "that-than-which-a-greater-cannot-be-thought" cannot be thought not to exist.

Gaunilo

[7.] When, however, it is said that this supreme being cannot be *thought* not to exist, it would perhaps be better to say that it cannot be *understood* not to exist nor even to be able not to exist. For, strictly speaking, unreal things cannot be *understood,* though certainly they can be *thought* of in the same way as the Fool *thought* that God does not exist. I know with complete certainty that I exist, but I also know at the same time nevertheless that I can not-exist. And I *understand* without any doubt that that which exists to the highest degree, namely God, both exists and cannot not exist. I do not know, however, whether I can *think* of myself as not existing while I know with absolute certainty that I do exist; but if I can, why cannot [I do the same] with regard to anything else I know with the same certainty? If however I cannot, this will not be the distinguishing characteristic of God [namely, to be such that He cannot be thought not to exist].

Anselm

[IV.] You say, moreover, that when it is said that this supreme reality cannot be *thought* not to exist, it would perhaps be better to say that it cannot be *understood* not to exist or even to be able not to exist. However, it must rather be said that it cannot be *thought.*

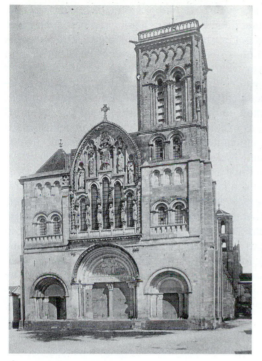

a.   *b.*

The Romanesque Cathedral

a. *Exterior view of the Abbey Church of the Madeleine, Vezelay,
France,* built in the twelfth century. This church typifies the Romanesque
style that flourished from about 1000 to 1200. The rounded arches
above the portals are reminiscent of the arches of Roman construction.
The thickness of the stone walls, together with the relatively simple
facade, gives the structure the impression of solidity and solemnity.
(Italian Tourist Office)

b. *Central portal looking into the nave.* The rounded interior arches
distribute the weight of the roof outward as well as downward,
necessitating thick stone walls. As a result, only a few small windows
are possible in a Romanesque church—adding to the fortress-like feel
of the architecture. *(Scala/Art Resource)*

For if I had said that the thing in question could not be *understood* not to exist, perhaps
you yourself (who claim that we cannot understand—if this word is to be taken
strictly—things that are unreal) would object that nothing that exists can be understood
not to exist. For it is false [to say that] what exists does not exist, so that it is not the distinguishing characteristic of God not to be able to be understood not to exist. But, if any
of those things which exist with absolute certainty can be understood not to exist, in the
same way other things that certainly exist can be understood not to exist. But, if the matter is carefully considered, this objection cannot be made apropos [the term] "thought."
For even if none of those things that exist can be *understood* not to exist, all however
can be *thought* as not existing, save that which exists to a supreme degree. For in fact all

those things (and they alone) that have a beginning or end or are made up of parts and, as I have already said, all those things that do not exist as a whole in a particular place or at a particular time can be thought as not existing. Only that being in which there is neither beginning nor end nor conjunction of parts, and that thought does not discern save as a whole in every place and at every time, cannot be thought as not existing.

Know then that you can think of yourself as not existing while yet you are absolutely sure that you exist. I am astonished that you have said that you do not know this. For we think of many things that we know to exist, as not existing; and [we think of] many things that we know not to exist, as existing—not judging that it is really as we think but imagining it to be so. We *can,* in fact, think of something as not existing while knowing that it does exist, since we can [think of] the one and know the other at the same time. And we *cannot* think of something as not existing if yet we know that it does exist, since we cannot think of it as existing and not existing at the same time. He, therefore, who distinguishes these two senses of this assertion will understand that [in one sense] nothing can be thought as not existing while yet it is known to exist, and that [in another sense] whatever exists, save that-than-which-a-greater-cannot-be-thought, can be thought of as not existing even when we know that it does exist. Thus it is that, on the one hand, it is the distinguishing characteristic of God that He cannot be thought of as not existing [in the one sense], and that, on the other hand, many things, the while they do exist, cannot be thought of as not existing [in the other sense]. In what sense, however, one can say that God can be thought of as not existing I think I have adequately explained in my tract.

Peter Abelard
ca. 1079–ca. 1142

Peter Abelard (or Pierre Abailard) was born into a noble family of warriors in Le Palais (or Pallet), near Nantes, France. Though he chose to "follow Minerva [the goddess of learning] instead of Mars [the god of war]," this warrior's son was every bit as combative as his ancestors. As he himself put it, "To the prizes of victory in war I preferred the battle of minds in disputation."

Abelard's skill in logical debate, and his lack of prudence in using it, was legendary. While studying dialectics (or logic) with the eminent Parisian teacher William of Champeaux, Abelard humiliated his master in public debate. He forced William to acknowledge that his (William's) position on the question of universals was incorrect. Abelard then compounded the insult by setting up his own school of dialectics and stealing most of William's students. Over the next forty years Abelard's *curriculum vitae* included dismissal from the theology school of Anselm of Laon, two flights from monasteries where he had enraged the monks (once for proving that the founder of the monastery could not possibly have been Dionysius the Areopagite), and two church condemnations of his writings. Abelard's primary antagonist in later life was Bernard of Clairvaux, a man of deep faith—and of deep suspicions regarding Abelard's intellectualism.

But Abelard's most disastrous adventure took place while he was teaching in Paris in his early thirties. Next door to Abelard's school lived a cathedral official by the name of Fulbert, who had under his care a beautiful and intelligent teenage niece, Heloise. Abelard used his fame to arrange a position tutoring Heloise and, as Abelard later described it, "under the pretext of study we spent our hours in the happiness of love . . . our kisses far outnumbering our reasoned words." When Heloise became pregnant, Abelard agreed to marry her on the condition that the marriage be kept secret to preserve his career. He was, after all, in holy orders and supposedly celibate. When Fulbert proceeded to publicize the wedding, both Abelard and Heloise vehemently denied their marriage. Fulbert was so enraged by this denial that he hired thugs who castrated Abelard. Abelard retired to a monastery and Heloise joined a convent. While apart, Abelard and Heloise wrote poignant love letters, which are still considered classics. Though they were separated in life, they were eventually buried side by side.

Apart from this ill-starred affair, Abelard is best known for his work on the problem of universals. Boethius had formulated the question, "Do universals, such as genera and species, subsist in themselves?" Those who said "yes" were called "realists" because they believed universals to be *real* things.* Some, such as William of Champeaux, even went so far as to say that each member of a species has the same essence and that all apparent differences are only accidental. So, for example, the race horse Secretariat and the old nag in the barn share the same essential nature of "horse." The characteristics that differentiate them— size, color, speed, and so on—are merely accidental properties. On the other hand, the "nominalists" went in the opposite direction and denied that universals were anything other than names (*nomina* in Latin). Another of Abelard's former teachers, Roscelin, apparently held that a universal was nothing more than a word or "vocal wind."

Abelard rejected both positions. Abelard argued in public debate that William's extreme realism would mean that the same substance could have contrary accidental properties. For example, the exact same substance, "horse," would have the property of being fast (in the case of Secretariat) and slow (in the case of the old nag). Against the nominalism of Roscelin, Abelard claimed that if a universal is only a word, then it is a "thing" (namely the vocal wind being blown), and a thing cannot be predicated of a thing. But more importantly, a universal is not just a word, it is a *meaningful* word. The question left unanswered by the extreme nominalist is what that word, or vocal wind, *means.*

In the selection on universals given here, from A.B. Wolter's translation of *Logica "Ingredientibus,"* Abelard articulates a position similar to that of Aristotle. Abelard argues that universals name real similarities between individuals, though these similarities do not exist as separate things in themselves. The similarities consist not in shared essences but in shared predicates. Secretariat, the old nag, and all other individual horses are not similar "in horse" as if "horse" were a separate thing. Instead they are similar "in *being* a horse"—that is, in sharing the predicate of "horse." While his student John of Salisbury would later classify him as a nominalist, Abelard's position has usually been classified as "conceptualism" or moderate realism.

---

*The word "realist" has a quite different meaning today, and we would now probably describe medieval realists as "idealists."

In his *Ethics,* Abelard argues that morality is concerned with intention. In the passages reprinted here, in J. Ramsay McCallum's translation, Abelard argues that no action is good or bad in itself. Instead he argues, in anticipation of Immanuel Kant, that an action is good if "it issues from a good intention."

*   *   *

For studies on the problem of universals, see Meyrick Heath Carré, *Realists and Nominalists* (Oxford: Oxford University Press, 1946); Nicholas Wolterstorff, *On Universals: An Essay in Ontology* (Chicago: Chicago University Press, 1970); and Martin M. Tweedale, *Abailard on Universals* (Amsterdam: North Holland Publishing Co., 1976).

For general introductions to Abelard's life and thought, see Joseph McCabe, *Peter Abelard* (1901, reprinted Freeport, NY: Books for Libraries Press, 1971); Ailbe John Luddy, *The Case of Peter Abelard* (Westminster, MD: Newman Bookshop, 1947); Roger B. Lloyd, *Peter Abelard: The Orthodox Rebel* (London: Latimer House, 1947); A. Victor Murray, *Abelard and St. Bernard: A Study in Twelfth Century "Modernism"* (Manchester, England: Manchester University Press, 1967); and Jeffery Garrett Sikes, *Peter Abailard* (1932, reprinted New York: Russell & Russell, 1965). Abelard's troubled life has inspired both a novel, Helen Waddell, *Peter Abelard* (New York: Literary Guild, 1933), and an epic poem, Cedric Hubbell Whitman, *Abelard* (Cambridge, MA: Harvard University Press, 1965). For Abelard's description of his misfortunes, see Peter Abelard, *The Letters of Abelard and Heloise,* translated by Betty Radice (Harmondsworth, England: Penguin Classics, 1974). Étienne Gilson, *Heloise and Abelard,* translated by L.K. Shook (Chicago: Regnery, 1951), provides an essay on this interesting topic.

ON UNIVERSALS (selections)

Porphyry, as Boethius points out [in his Commentary on the *Isagoge*], raises three profitable questions whose answers are shrouded in mystery and though not a few philosophers have attempted to solve them, few have succeeded in doing so. The first is: Do genera and species really exist or are they simply something in the mind? It is as if [Porphyry] were asking whether their existence is a fact or merely a matter of opinion. The second is: Granting they do exist, are they corporeal or incorporeal? The third is: Do they exist apart from sensible things or only in them? For there are two types of incorporeal things. Some, like God or the soul, can subsist in their incorporeality apart from anything sensible. Others are unable to exist apart from the sensible objects in which they are found. A line, for example, is unable to exist apart from some bodily subject.

Porphyry sidesteps answering them with the remark: "For the present I refuse to be drawn into a discussion as to whether genus and species exist in reality or solely and simply in thought; or if they do exist whether they are corporeal or incorporeal, or whether, on the admission they are incorporeal, they are separated from sensibles or exist only in and dependent upon sensible things, and other things of this sort."

"Other things of this sort" can be interpreted in various ways. We could take him to mean: "I refuse to discuss these three questions and other related matters." For other relevant questions could be raised that pose similar problems. For instance, what is the common basis or reason for applying universal names to things; which boils down to explaining to what extent different things agree; or how should one understand those universal names wherein one seems to conceive of nothing, where the universal term in a word seems to have no referent? And there are many other difficult points. By understanding "other things of this sort" in this way, we can add a fourth question: Do genera and species, as long as they remain such, require that the subject they name have some reality or, if all the things they designate were destroyed, could the universal consist simply in its significance for the mind, as would be the case with the name "rose" when no roses are in bloom which it could designate in general? . . .

Since genera and species are obviously instances of universals and in mentioning them Porphyry touches on the nature of universals in general, we may distinguish the properties common to universals by studying them in these samples. Let us inquire then whether they apply only to *words* or to *things* as well.

Aristotle defines the universal as "that which is of such a nature as to be predicated of many." Porphyry, on the other hand, goes on to define the singular or individual as "that which is predicated of a single individual."

Authorities then seem to apply "universal" to things as much as they do to words. Aristotle himself does this, declaring by way of preface to his definition of the universal, that "some things are universal, others individual. Now by 'universal' I mean that which is of such a nature as to be predicated of many, whereas 'individual' is not something of this kind." Porphyry too, having stated that the species is composed of a genus and difference, proceeds to locate it in the nature of things. From this it is clear that things themselves fall under a universal noun.

Nouns too are called universals. That is why Aristotle says: "The genus specifies the quality with reference to substance, for it signifies what sort of thing it is."

"It seems then that things as well as words are called universals." . . .

However, things taken either singly or collectively cannot be called universals, because they are not predicable of many. Consequently it remains to ascribe this form of universality to words alone. Just as grammarians call certain nouns proper and others appellative, so dialecticians call certain simple words particulars, that is, individuals, and others universals. A universal word is one which is able to be predicated of many by reason of its intention, such as the noun "man," which can be joined with the names of particular men by reason of the nature of the subject on which they are imposed. A particular word, however, is one which is predicable only of a single subject, as *Socrates* when it is taken as the name of but one individual. For if you take it equivocally, you give it the signification not of one word but of many. For according to Priscian, many nouns can obviously be brought together in a single word. When a universal then is described as "that which is predicable of many," *that which* indicates not only the simplicity of the word as a discrete expression, but also the unity of signification lacking in an equivocal term. . . .

Now that we have defined "universal" and "particular" in regard to words, let us investigate in particular the properties of those which are universal. For questions have been raised about universals, since serious doubts existed as to their meaning because there seemed to be no subject to which they referred. Neither did they express the sense of any one thing. These universal terms then appeared to be imposed on nothing, since it is clear that all things subsisting in themselves are individuals and, as has been shown, they do not share in some one thing by virtue of which a universal name could be given to them. Since it is certain then that (a) universals are not imposed on things by reason of their individual differences, for then they would not be common but singular, (b) nor can they designate things which share in some identical entity, for it is not a thing in which they agree, there seems to be nothing from which universals might derive their meaning, particularly since their sense is not restricted to any one thing. . . . Since "man" is imposed on individuals for an identical reason, viz. because each is a rational, mortal animal, the very generality of the designation prevents one from understanding the term of just one man in the way, for example, that one understands by Socrates just one unique person, which is why it is called a particular. But the common term "man" does not mean just Socrates, or any other man. Neither does it designate a collection, nor does it, as some think, mean just Socrates insofar as he is man. For even if Socrates alone were sitting in this house and because of that the proposition "A man sits in this house" is true, still by the name "man," there is no way of getting to Socrates except insofar as he too is a man. Otherwise, from the proposition itself, "sitting" would be understood to inhere in Socrates, so that from "A man sits in this house," one could infer "Socrates sits in this house." And the same applies to any other individual man. Neither can "A man sits in this house" be understood of a collection, since the proposition can be true if only one man is there. Consequently, there is not a single thing that "man" or any other universal term seems to signify, since there is not a single thing whose sense the term seems to express. Neither does it seem there could be any sense if no subject is thought of. Universals then appear to be totally devoid of meaning.

And yet this is not the case. For universals do signify distinct individuals to the extent of giving names to them, but this significative function does not require that one grasps a sense which arises out of them and which belongs to each of them. "Man," for example, does name individual things, but for the common reason that they are all men. That is why it is called a universal. Also there is a certain sense—common, not proper—that is applicable to those individuals which one conceives to be alike.

But let us look carefully now into some matters we have touched on only briefly, viz. (a) what is the common reason for imposing a universal name on things, (b) what is this intellectual conception of a common likeness, and (c) is a word said to be common because of some common cause by virtue of which all the things it designates are alike, or is it merely because we have a common concept for all of them, or is it for both of these reasons?

Let us consider first the question of the common cause. As we noted earlier, each individual man is a discrete subject since he has as proper to himself not only an essence but also whatever forms [or qualifications] that essence may have. Nevertheless, they agree in this that they are all men. Since there is no man who is not a discrete or distinct individual thing, I do not say they agree "in man," but "in being a man." Now if you consider the matter carefully, man or any other thing is not the same as "to be a man," even as "not to be in a subject" is not a thing, nor is there anything which is "not to undergo contrariety" or "not to be subject to greater or lesser degrees," and still Aristotle says these are points in which all substances agree. Since there is no *thing* in which things could possibly agree, if there is any agreement among certain things, this must not be taken to be some *thing*. Just as Socrates and Plato are alike in being men, so a horse and donkey are alike in not being men. It is for this reason that they are called "nonmen." Different individuals then agree either in being the same or in not being the same, e.g. in being men or white, or in not being men or being white.

Still this agreement among things (which itself is not a thing) must not be regarded as a case of bringing together things which are real on the basis of nothing. In point of fact we do speak of this agreeing with that to the extent of their having the same status, that of man, i.e. the two agree in that they are men. But what we perceive is merely that they are men, and there is not the slightest difference between them, I say, in their being men, even though we may not call this an essence. But "being a man" (which is not a thing) we do call "the status of man" and we have also called it "the common cause for imposing on individuals a universal name." For we frequently give the name "cause" to some characteristic that is not itself a thing as when one says "He was beaten because he did not wish to appear in court." His not wishing to appear in court, cited here as a cause is not a [constitutive] essence [of his being beaten].

We can also designate as "the status of man" those things themselves in a man's nature which the one who imposed the word conceives according to a common likeness.

Having shown how universals signify, namely by functioning as names of things, and having presented what the reason for imposing such general names is, let us indicate just what these universal meanings consist of.

To begin with, let us point out the distinguishing features of all intellectual conception or understanding. Though sense perception as well as intellectual conception are both functions of the soul, there is a difference between the two. Bodies and what inhere in them are objects of sensory knowledge, e.g. a tower or its sensory qualities. In the exercise of this function, however, the soul makes use of corporeal instruments. In understanding or conceiving something intellectually, the soul needs no corporeal organ and consequently no bodily subject in which the thought object inheres is required. It is enough that the mind constructs for itself a likeness of these things and the action called intellection is concerned with this [cognitive content]. Hence, if the tower is removed or destroyed, the sense perception that dealt with it perishes, but the intellectual conception of the tower remains in the likeness preserved in the mind. As the act of sense perception is not the sensed thing itself, so the act of the intellect is not itself the form understood or conceived intellectually. Understanding is an activity of the soul by virtue of which it is said to understand, but the form toward which understanding is directed is a kind of image or construct which the mind fashions for itself at will, like those imaginary cities seen in dreams or the form of a projected building which the architect conceives after the manner of a blueprint. This construct is not something one can call either substance or accident.

Nevertheless, there are those who simply identify it with the act itself through which it is understood or conceived. Thus they speak of the tower building itself, which I think of when the tower is not there and which I conceive to be lofty, square, and situated in a spacious plain, as being the same as thinking of a tower. But we prefer to call the [conceptual] image as such the likeness of the thing.

There is of course nothing to prevent the act of understanding itself from being called in some sense a "likeness" because it obviously conceives what is, properly speaking, a likeness of the thing. Still, as we have said—and rightly so—the two are not the same. For, I ask: "Does the squareness or loftiness represent the actual form or quality possessed by the act of understanding itself when one thinks of the height and the way the tower is put together?" Surely the actual squareness and height are present only in bodies and from an imagined quality no act of understanding or any other real essence can be constructed. What remains then but that the substance, like the quality of which it is the subject, is also fictive? Perhaps one could also say that a mirror or reflected image is not itself a true "thing," since there often appears on the whitish surface of the mirror a color of contrary quality. . . .

Having treated in general the nature of understanding, let us consider how a universal and a particular conception differ. The conception associated with a universal name is an image that is general and indiscriminate, whereas the image associated with a singular word represents the proper and characteristic form, as it were, of a single thing, i.e. it applies to one and only one person. When I hear the word "man," for instance, a certain likeness arises in my mind which is so related to individual men that it is proper to none but common to all. But when I hear "Socrates," a certain form arises in my mind which is the likeness of a particular person. . . . Hence it is correct to say "man" does not rightly signify Socrates or any other man, since by virtue of this name no one in particular is identified; yet it is a name of particular things. "Socrates," on the other hand, must not only name a particular thing, but it must also determine just what thing is its subject. . . . To show what pertains to the nature of all lions, a picture can be constructed which represents nothing that is the peculiar property of only one of them. On the other hand, a picture suited to distinguish any one of them can be drawn by depicting something proper to the one in question, for example, by painting it as limping, maimed, or wounded by the spear of Hercules. Just as one can paint one figure that is general and another that is particular, so too can one form one conception of things that is common and another conception that is proper.

There is some question, however, and not without reason, whether or not this [universal] name also signifies this conceptual form to which the understanding is directed. Both authority and reason, however, seem to be unanimous in affirming that it does.

For Priscian, after first showing how universals were applied commonly to individuals, seemed to introduce another meaning they had, namely the common form. He states that "the general and special forms of things which were given intelligibility in the divine mind before being produced in bodies could be used to reveal what the natural genera and species of things are." In this passage he views God after the fashion of an artist who first conceives in his mind a [model or] exemplar form of what he is to fashion and who works according to the likeness of this form, which form is said to be embodied when a real thing is constructed in its likeness.

It may be all right to ascribe such a common conception to God, but not to man. For those works of God like a man, a soul, or a stone represent general or special states of nature, whereas those of a human artisan like a house or a sword do not. For "house" and "sword" do not pertain to nature as the other terms do. They are the names not of a substance but of something accidental and therefore they are neither genera not ultimate species. Conceptions by abstraction [of the true nature of things] may well be ascribed to the divine mind but may not be ascribed to that of man, because men, who know things only through the medium of their senses, scarcely ever arrive at such an ideal understanding and never conceive the [underlying] natures of things in their purity. But God knew all things he created for what they were and this even before they actually existed. He can discriminate between these individual states as they are in themselves; senses are no hindrance to him who alone has true understanding of things. Of those things which men have not experienced through the senses, they happen to have opinions rather than understanding, as we learn from experience. For having thought of some city before seeing it, we find on arriving there that it is quite different than we had thought.

And so I believe we have only an opinion about those forms like rationality, mortality, paternity, or what is within. Names for what we experience, however, produce understanding to the extent they can do so, for the one who coined the terms intended that they be imposed in accord with the [true] nature or properties of things, even though he himself was unable to do justice in thought to the nature or property of the thing. It is these common concepts, however, which Priscian calls general and special [i.e. generic and specific], that these general names or the names of species bring to the mind. He says that the universals function as proper names with regard to such conceptions, and although these names refer to the essences named only in an indiscriminate fashion, they direct the mind of the hearer immediately to that common conception in the same way that proper names direct attention to the one thing that they signify.

Porphyry too, in distinguishing between things constituted only in the likeness of matter and form and those actually composed of matter and form, seems to understand this common conception by the former. Boethius also, when he calls the conception gathered from a likeness of many things a genus or a species, seems to have in mind this same common conception. Some think that Plato subscribed to this view, i.e. to these common ideas—which he located in the *nous*—he gave the names of genus and species. On this point, perhaps, Boethius indicates some disagreement between Plato and Aristotle, where he speaks of Plato claiming not only that genera, species, and the rest should be understood to be universals, but also that they also have true existence and subsistence apart from bodies, as if to say that Plato understood these common concepts, which he assumed to exist in a bodiless form in the nous, to be universals. He means here by universal "a common likeness of many things" perhaps, rather than "predicable of many" as Aristotle understood the term. For this conception [itself] does not seem to be predicated of many in the way that a name is able to be applied to each of many things.

But his [i.e. Boethius'] statement that Plato thinks universals subsist apart from sensibles can be interpreted in another way, so that there is no disagreement between the philosophers. For Aristotle's statements about universals always subsisting in sensibles is to be understood of the way they actually do exist, because the animal nature (which the universal name "animal" designates and which is called a kind of universal in a transferred sense of the term) is never found to exist in anything which is not sensible. Plato, however, thinks this nature has such a natural subsistence in itself that it would retain its existence if it were not subject to sense [i.e. if it were not clothed with sensible accidents]. Hence what Aristotle denies to be actually the case, Plato, the investigator of the nature, ascribes to a natural capacity. Consequently there is no real disagreement between them.

Reason too seems to agree with these authorities in their apparent claim that the universal names designate these common concepts or forms. For what else does to conceive of them by name mean but that names signify them? But since we hold that these forms conceived are not simply the same as the acts of knowing them, there is in addition to the real thing and the act of understanding a third factor, viz. the signification or meaning of the name. Now while there is no authority for holding this, still it is not contrary to reason.

At this point, let us give an answer to the question we promised earlier to settle, namely whether the ability of universal words to refer to things in general is due to the fact that there is in them a common cause for imposing the words on them, or whether it is due to the fact that a common concept of them exists, or whether it is for both of these reasons. Now there seems to be no ground why it should not be for both of these reasons, but if we understand "common cause" as involving something of the nature of the things, then this seems to be the stronger of the two reasons.

Another point we must clarify is the one noted earlier, namely that these universal conceptions are formed by abstraction, and we must show how one can speak of them as isolated, naked, and pure without their being empty. But first about abstraction. Here we must remember that while matter and form are always fused together, the rational power of the mind is such that it can consider matter alone or form alone or both together. The first two are considerations by way of abstraction, since in order to study its precise nature, they abstract one thing from what does not exist alone. The third type of consideration is by way of synthesis. The substance of man, for instance, is a body, an animal, a man; it is invested with no end of forms. But when I turn my attention exclusively to the material essence of a substance, disregarding all its additional forms or qualifications, my understanding takes the form of a concept by abstraction. If I direct my attention, however, to nothing more than the corporeity of this substance, the resulting concept, though it represents a synthesis when compared with the previous concept (that of substance alone), is still formed by abstraction from the forms other than corporeity, such as animation, sensitivity, rationality, or whiteness, none of which I consider.

Such conceptions by abstraction might appear to be false or empty, perhaps, since they look to the thing in a way other than that in which it exists. For since they consider matter or form exclusively, and neither of these subsists separately, they clearly represent a conception of the thing otherwise than the way it is. Consequently, they seem to be vacuous, yet this is not really the case. For it is only when a thing is considered to have some property or nature which it does not actually possess that the conception which represents the thing otherwise than it is, is indeed empty. But this is not what happens in abstraction. For when I consider this man only in his nature as a substance or a body, but not as an animal, a man, or a grammarian, certainly I do not think of anything that is not in that nature, and still I do not attend to all that it has. And when I say that I attend only to what is in it, "only" refers to my attention and not to the way this characteristic exists, for otherwise my conception would be empty. For the thing does not only have this, but I only consider it as having this. And while I do consider it in some sense to be otherwise than it actually is, I do not consider it to be in a state or condition other than that in which it is, as was pointed out earlier. "Otherwise" means merely that the mode of thought is other than the mode of existing. For the thing in question is thought of not as separated, but separately from the other, even though it does not exist separately. Matter is perceived purely, form simply, even though the former does not exist purely nor the latter simply. Purity and simplicity, in a word, are features of our understanding, not of existence; they are characteristic of the way we think, not of the way things exist. Even the senses often function discriminatively where composite objects are concerned. If a statue is half gold, half silver, I can look separately at the gold and silver combined there, studying first the gold, then the silver exclusively, thus viewing piecemeal what is actually joined together, and yet I do not perceive to be divided what is not divided. In much the same way "understanding by way of abstraction" means "considering separately" but not "considering [it] as separated." Otherwise such understanding would be vacuous. . . .

But let us return to our *universal* conceptions, which must always be produced by way of abstraction. For when I hear "man" or "whiteness" or "white," I do not recall in virtue of the name all the natures or properties in those subjects to which the name refers. "Man" gives rise to the conception, indiscriminate, not discrete, of animal, rational and mortal only, but not of the additional accidents as well. Conceptions of individuals also can be formed by abstraction, as happens for example when one speaks of "this substance," "this body," "this animal," "this white," or "this whiteness." For by "this man," though I consider just man's nature, I do so as related to a certain subject, whereas by "man" I regard this nature simply in itself and not in relation to some one man. That is why a universal concept is correctly described as being *isolated, bare,* and *pure:* i.e "isolated from sense," because it is not a perception of the thing as sensory;

"bare," because it is abstracted from some or from all forms; "pure," because it is unadulterated by any reference to any single individual, since there is not just one thing, be it the matter or the form, to which it points, as we explained earlier when we described such a conception as indiscriminate.

Now that we have considered these matters, let us proceed to answer the questions posed by Porphyry about genera and species. This we can easily do now that we have clarified the nature of universals in general. The point of the first question was whether genera and species exist. More precisely, are they signs of something which really exists or of something that merely exists in thought, i.e. are they simply vacuous, devoid of any real reference, as is the case with words like "chimera" or "goat-stag," which fail to produce any coherent meaning? To this one has to reply that as a matter of fact they do serve to name things that actually exist and therefore are not the subjects of purely empty thoughts. But what they name are the selfsame things named by singular names. And still, there is a sense in which they exist as isolated, bare, and pure only in the mind, as we have just explained. . . .

The second question, viz. "Are they corporeal or incorporeal?" can be taken in the same way, that is, "Granting that they are signs of existing things, are these things corporeal or incorporeal?" For surely everything that exists, as Boethius puts it, is either corporeal or incorporeal, regardless of whether these words mean respectively: (1) a bodily or a bodiless substance, (2) something perceptible to the senses like man, wood, and whiteness, or something imperceptible in this way like justice or the soul. (3) "Corporeal" can also have the meaning of something discrete or individual, so that the question boils down to asking whether genera and species signify discrete individuals or not. A thoroughgoing investigator of truth considers not only what can be factually stated but also such possible opinions as might be proposed. Consequently, even though one is quite certain that only individuals are real, in view of the fact that someone might be of the opinion that there are other things that exist, it is justifiable to inquire about them. Now this third meaning of "corporeal" makes better sense of our question, reducing it to an inquiry as to whether it is discrete individuals or not that are signified. On the other hand, since nothing existing is incorporeal, i.e. nonindividual, "incorporeal" would seem to be superfluous in Boethius' statement that everything existing is either corporeal or incorporeal. Here the order of the questions, it seems, suggests nothing that would be of help except perhaps that corporeal and incorporeal, taken in another sense, do represent divisions of whatever exists and that this might also be the case here. The inquirer in this case would seem to be asking, in effect: "Since I see that some existing things are called corporeal and others incorporeal, I would like to know which of these names we should use for what universals signify?" The answer to this would be: "To some extent, 'corporeal' would be appropriate, since the *significata* are in essence discrete individuals. 'Incorporeal' would be a better description, however, of the way a universal term names things, for it does not point to them in an individual and specific fashion but points only in an indiscriminate way, as we have adequately explained above." Hence universal names are described both as corporeal (because of the nature of the things they point to) and as incorporeal (because of the way these things are signified, for although they name discrete individuals, universals do not name them individually or properly).

The third question ("Do they exist apart from or only in sensible things?") arises from the admission that they are incorporeal, since, as we noted [in the opening paragraph], there is a certain sense in which "existing in the sensible" and "not existing in the sensible" represent a division of the incorporeal. Now universals are said to exist in sensible things to the extent that they signify the inner substance of something which is sensible by reason of its external forms. While they signify this same substance actually existing in sensible garb, they point to what is by its nature something distinct from the sensible thing [i.e. as substance it is other than its accidental garb], as we said above in our reinterpretation of Plato. That is why Boethius does not claim that genera and species exist apart from sensible things, but only that they are understood apart from them, to the extent namely that the things conceived generically or specifically are viewed with reference to their nature in a rational fashion rather than in a sensory way, and they could indeed subsist in themselves [i.e. as individual substances] even if stripped of the exterior or [accidental] forms by which they come to the attention of the senses. For we admit that all genera and species exist in things perceptible to the senses. Since our understanding of them has always been described as something apart from the senses, however, they appeared not to be in sensible things in any way. There was every reason, then, to ask whether they could be in sensibles. And to this question, the answer is that some of them are, but only to the extent, as was explained, that they represent the enduring substrate that lies beneath the sensible.

We can take corporeal and incorporeal in this second question as equivalent to sensible and insensible, so that the sequence of questions becomes more orderly. And since our understanding of universals is derived solely from sense perceptions, as has been said, one could appropriately ask whether universals were sensible or insensible. Now the answer is that some of them are sensible (we refer here to the nature of those things classed as sensible) and the same time not sensible (we refer here to the way they are signified). For while it is sensible things that these universals name, they do not designate these things in the way they are perceived by the senses, i.e. as distinct individuals, and when things are designated only in universal terms the senses cannot pick them out. Hence the question arose: "Do universals designate only sensible things, or is there something else they signify?" And the answer to this is that they signify both the sensible things themselves and also that common concept which Priscian ascribes above all to the divine mind.

As for the fourth question we added to the others, our solution is this. We do not want to speak of there being universal *names* when the things they name have perished and they can no longer be predicated of many and are not common names of anything, as would be the case when all the roses were gone. Nevertheless, "rose" would still have meaning for the mind even though it names nothing. Otherwise, "There is no rose" would not be a proposition.

ETHICS (in part)

PROLOGUE

In the study of morals we deal with the defects or qualities of the mind which dispose us to bad or good actions. Defects and qualities are not only mental, but also physical. There is bodily weakness; there is also the endurance which we call strength. There is

Abailard's Ethics, Prologue, 1–3, 10–12, translated by J. Ramsay McCallum (Oxford: Basil Blackwell, 1935). Reprinted by permission.

sluggishness or speed; blindness or sight. When we now speak of defects, therefore, we pre-suppose defects of the mind, so as to distinguish them from the physical ones. The defects of the mind are opposed to the qualities; injustice to justice; cowardice to constancy; intemperance to temperance.

CHAPTER 1: THE DEFECT OF MIND BEARING UPON CONDUCT

Certain defects or merits of mind have no connection with morals. They do not make human life a matter of praise or blame. Such are dull wits or quick insight; a good or a bad memory; ignorance or knowledge. Each of these features is found in good and bad alike. They have nothing to do with the system of morals, nor with making life base or honourable. To exclude these we safeguarded above the phrase "defects of mind" by adding "which dispose to bad actions," that is, those defects which incline the will to what least of all either should be done or should be left undone.

CHAPTER 2: HOW DOES SIN DIFFER FROM A DISPOSITION TO EVIL?

Defect of this mental kind is not the same thing as sin. Sin, too, is not the same as a bad action. For example, to be irascible, that is, prone or easily roused to the agitation of anger is a defect and moves the mind to unpleasantly impetuous and irrational action. This defect, however, is in the mind so that the mind is liable to wrath, even when it is not actually roused to it. Similarly, lameness, by reason of which a man is said to be lame, is in the man himself even when he does not walk and reveal his lameness. For the defect is there though action be lacking. So, also, nature or constitution renders many liable to luxury. Yet they do not sin because they are like this, but from this very fact they have the material of a struggle whereby they may, in the virtue of temperance, triumph over themselves and win the crown. As Solomon says: "Better a patient than a strong man; and the Lord of his soul than he that taketh a city." (Prov. xvi, 32.) For religion does not think it degrading to be beaten by man; but it is degrading to be beaten by one's lower self. The former defeat has been the fate of good men. But, in the latter, we fall below ourselves. The Apostle commends victory of this sort; "No one shall be crowned who has not truly striven." (2 Tim. ii, 5.) This striving, I repeat, means standing less against men than against myself, so that defects may not lure me into base consent. Though men cease to oppose us, our defects do not cease. The fight with them is the more dangerous because of its repetition. And as it is the more difficult, so victory is the more glorious. Men, however much they prevail over us, do not force baseness upon us, unless by their practice of vice they turn us also to it and overcome us through our own wretched consent. They may dominate our body; but while our mind is free, there is no danger to true freedom. We run no risk of base servitude. Subservience to vice, not to man, is degradation. It is the overlordship of defects and not physical serfdom which debases the soul.

CHAPTER 3: DEFINITION OF "DEFECT" AND OF SIN

Defect, then, is that whereby we are disposed to sin. We are, that is, inclined to consent to what we ought not to do, or to leave undone what we ought to do. Consent of this kind we rightly call sin. Here is the reproach of the soul meriting damnation or being declared guilty by God. What is that consent but to despise God and to violate his laws? God cannot be set at enmity by injury, but by contempt. He is the highest power, and is not diminished by any injury, but He avenges contempt of Himself. Our sin, therefore, is contempt of the Creator. To sin is to despise the Creator; that is, not to do for Him what we believe we should do for Him, or, not to renounce what we think should be renounced on His behalf. We have defined sin negatively by saying that it means not doing or not renouncing what we ought to do or renounce. Clearly, then, we have shown that sin has no reality. It exists rather in *not being* than in *being*. Similarly we could define shadows by saying: The absence of light where light usually is.

Perhaps you object that sin is the desire or will to do an evil deed, and that this will or desire condemns us before God in the same way as the will to do a good deed justifies us. There is as much quality, you suggest, in the good will as there is sin in the evil will; and it is no less "in being" in the latter than in the former. By willing to do what we believe to be pleasing to God we please Him. Equally, by willing to do what we believe to be displeasing to God, we displease Him and seem either to violate or despise His nature.

But diligent attention will show that we must think far otherwise of this point. We frequently err; and from no evil will at all. Indeed, the evil will itself, when restrained, though it may not be quenched, procures the palm-wreath for those who resist it. It provides, not merely the materials for combat, but also the crown of glory. It should be spoken of rather as a certain inevitable weakness than as sin. Take, for example, the case of an innocent servant whose harsh master is moved with fury against him. He pursues the servant, drawing his sword with intent to kill him. For a while the servant flies and avoids death as best he can. At last, forced all unwillingly to it, he kills his master so as not to be killed by him. Let anyone say what sort of evil will there was in this deed. His will was only to flee from death and preserve his own life. Was this an evil will? You reply: "I do not think this was an evil will. But the will that he had to kill the master who was pursuing him was evil." Your answer would be admirable and acute if you could show that the servant really willed what you say that he did. But, as I insisted, he was unwillingly forced to his deed. He protracted his master's life as long as he could, knowing that danger also threatened his own life from such a crime. How, then was a deed done voluntarily by which he incurred danger to his own life?

Your reply may be that the action was voluntary because the man's will was to escape death even though it may not have been to kill his master. This charge might easily be preferred against him. I do not rebut it. Nevertheless, as has been said, that will be which he sought to evade death, as you urge, and not to kill his master, cannot at all be condemned as bad. He did, however, fail by consenting, though driven to it through fear of death, to an unjust murder which he ought rather to have endured than committed. Of his own will, I mean, he took the sword. It was not handed to him by authority. The Truth saith: "Everyone that taketh the sword shall perish by the sword." (Matt. xxvi, 52.) By his rashness he risked the death and damnation of his soul. The servant's wish, then, was not to kill has master, but to avoid death. Because he *consented,* however, as he should not have done, to murder, this wrongful consent preceding the crime was sin.

Someone may interpose: "But you cannot conclude that he wished to kill his master because, in order to escape death, he was willing to kill his master. I might say to a man: I am willing for you to have my cape so that you may give me five shillings. Or, I am glad for you to have it at this price. But I do not hand it over because I desire you to have possession of it." No, and if a man in prison desired under duress, to put his son there in his place that he might secure his own ransom, should we therefore admit that he wished to send his son to prison?

It was only with many a tear and groan that he consented to such a course.

The fact is that this kind of will, existing with much internal regret, is not, if I may so say, *will,* but a passive submission of mind. It is so because the man wills one thing on account of another. He puts up with *this* because he really desires *that.* A patient is said to submit to cautery or lancet that he may obtain health. Martyrs endured that they might come to Christ; and Christ, too, that we may be saved by his passion.

Yet we are not bound to admit simply that these people therefore wish for this mental unease. Such unease can only be where something occurs contrary to wish. No man suffers so long as he fulfills his wish and does what he likes to experience. The Apostle says: "I desire to depart and to be with Christ" (Phil. i, 23), that is, to die so that I may attain to him. Elsewhere this apostle says: "We desire not to be despoiled of our garments, but to be clothed from above, that our mortal part may be swallowed up in life." This notion, Blessed Augustine reminds us, was contained in the Lord's address to Peter: "Thou shalt extend thy hands and another shall gird thee, and lead thee whither thou willest not." (John xxi, 18.) The Lord also spoke to the Father out of the weakness of the human nature which he had taken upon himself: "If it be possible, let this cup pass from me; nevertheless not as I will, but as thou willest." (Matt. xxvi, 39.) His spirit naturally trembled before the great terror of death: and he could not speak of what he knew to be punishment as a matter of his own will. When elsewhere it is written of Him: "He was offered because He himself willed it" (Isaiah liii, 7), it must be understood either of His divine nature, in whose will it was that he should suffer as a man, or "He himself willed it" must be taken according to the Psalmist's phrase: "Whatsoever he willed, that he did." (Ps. cxiii, 3.)

Sin, therefore, is sometimes committed without an evil will. Thus sin cannot be defined as "will." True, you will say, when we sin under constraint, but not when we sin willingly, for instance, when we will to do something which we know ought not to be done by us. There the evil will and sin seem to be the same thing. For example a man sees a woman; his concupiscence is aroused; his mind is enticed by fleshly lust and stirred to base desire. This wish, this lascivious longing, what else can it be, you say, than sin?

I reply: What if that wish may be bridled by the power of temperance? What if its nature is never to be entirely extinguished but to persist in struggle and not fully fail even in defeat? For where is the battle if the antagonist is away? Whence the great reward without grave endurance? When the fight is over nothing remains but to reap the reward. Here we strive in contest in order elsewhere to obtain as victors a crown. Now, for a contest, an opponent is needed who will resist, not one who simply submits. This opponent is our evil will over which we triumph when we subjugate it to the divine will. But we do not entirely destroy it. For we needs must ever expect to encounter our enemy. What achievement before God is it if we undergo nothing contrary to our own will, but merely practice what we please? Who will be grateful to us if in what we say we do for him we merely satisfy our own fancy?

You will say, what merit have we with God in acting willingly or unwillingly? Certainly none: I reply. He weighs the intention rather than the deed in his recompense.

Nor does the deed, whether it proceed from a good or an evil will, add anything to the merit, as we shall show shortly. But when we set His will before our own so as to follow His and not ours, our merit with God is magnified, in accordance with that perfect word of Truth: "I came not to do mine own will, but the will of Him that sent me." (John vi, 38.) To this end He exhorts us: "If anyone comes to me, and does not hate father, and mother . . . yea his own soul also, he is not worthy of me." (Luke xiv, 26.) That is to say, "unless a man renounces his parents' influence and his own will and submits himself to my teaching, he is not worthy of me." Thus we are bidden to hate our father, not to destroy him. Similarly with our own will. We must not be led by it; at the same time, we are not asked to root it out altogether.

When the Scripture says: "Go not after your own desires" (Eccles. xviii, 30) and: "Turn from your own will" (ibid.), it instructs us not to fulfil our desires. Yet it does not say that we are to be wholly without them. It is vicious to give in to our desires; but not to have any desires at all is impossible for our weak nature.

The sin, then, consists not in desiring a woman, but in consent to the desire, and not the wish for whoredom, but the consent to the wish is damnation.

Let us see how our conclusions about sexual intemperance apply to theft. A man crosses another's garden. At the sign of the delectable fruit his desire is aroused. He does not, however, give way to desire so as to take anything by theft or rapine, although his mind was moved to strong inclination by the thought of the delight of eating. Where there is desire, there, without doubt, will exists. The man desires the eating of that fruit wherein he doubts not that there will be delight. The weakness of nature in this man is compelled to desire the fruit which, without the master's permission, he has no right to take. He conquers the desire, but does not extinguish it. Since, however, he is not enticed into consent, he does not descend to sin.

What, then, of your objection? It should be clear from such instances, that the wish or desire itself of doing what is not seemly is never to be called sin, but rather, as we said, the consent is sin. We consent to what is not seemly when we do not draw ourselves back from such a deed, and are prepared, should opportunity offer, to perform it completely. Whoever is discovered in this intention, though his guilt has yet to be completed in deed, is already guilty before God in so far as he strives with all his might to sin, and accomplishes within himself, as the blessed Augustine reminds us, as much as if he were actually taken in the act.

But while wish is not sin, and, as we have said, we sometimes commit sin unwillingly, there are nevertheless those who assert that every sin is voluntary. In this respect they discover a certain difference between sin and will. Will is one thing, they say, but a voluntary act is another. They mean that there is a distinction between will and what is done willingly. If, however, we call sin what we have already decided that it essentially is, namely, contempt of God or consent to that which we believe should not, for God's sake, be done how can we say that sin is voluntary? I mean, how can we say that we wish to despise God? What is sin but sinking below a standard, or becoming liable to damnation? For although we desire to do what we know deserves punishment, yet we do not desire to be punished. Thus plainly we are reprobate. We are willing to do wrong; but we are unwilling to bear the just punishment of wrongdoing. The punishment which is just displeases: the deed which is unjust pleases. Often we woo a married woman because of her charm. Our wish is not so much to commit adultery as a longing that she were unmarried. On the other hand, many covet the wives of influential men for the sake of their own fame, and not for the natural attractiveness of these ladies. Their wish is for adultery rather than sexual relationship, the major in preference to the minor excess. Some, too, are ashamed altogether of being betrayed into any consent to concupiscence or evil will; and thus from the weakness of the flesh are compelled to wish what they least of all wish to wish.

How, then, a wish which we do not wish to have can be called voluntary, as it is according to those thinkers I have mentioned, so that all sin becomes a matter of voluntary action, I assuredly do not understand, unless by voluntary is meant that no action is determined, since a sin is never a predestined event. Or perhaps we are to take "voluntary" to be that which proceeds from some kind of will. For although the man who slew his master had no will to perform the actual murder, nevertheless he did it from some sort of will, because he certainly wished to escape or defer death.

Some are intensely indignant when they hear us assert that the act of sinning adds nothing to guilt or damnation before God. Their contention is that in this act of sinning a certain delight supervenes, which increases the sin, as in sexual intercourse or indulgence in food which we referred to above. Their statement is absurd unless they can prove that physical delight of this kind is itself sin, and that such pleasure cannot be taken without a sin being thereby committed. If it be as they suppose, then no one is permitted to enjoy physical pleasure. The married do not escape sin when they employ their physical privilege; nor yet the man who eats with relish his own fruits.

Invalids, too, who are treated to more delicate dishes to aid their recovery of strength would likewise be guilty, since they are not able to eat without a sense of delight and should this be lacking, the food does them no good. Finally, God, the Creator of nourishment and of the bodies which receive it, would not be without guilt for having instilled savours which necessarily involve in sin those who ignorantly use them. Yet how should He supply such things for our consumption, or permit them to be consumed, if it were impossible for us to eat them without sin? How, again, can it be said that there is sin in doing what is allowed? In regard to those matters which once were unlawful and forbidden, if they are later allowed and made lawful, they can be done entirely without sin. For instance, the eating of pork and many other things once out of bounds to the Jew are now free to us Christians. When, therefore, we see Jews turned Christian gladly eating food of this sort which the law had prohibited, how can we defend their rectitude except by affirming that this latitude has now been conceded to them by God?

Well, in what was formerly a food restriction and is now food freedom, the concession of freedom excludes sin and eliminates contempt of God. Who then shall say that a man sins in respect of a matter which the divine permission has made lawful for him? If the marriage-bed or the eating of even delicate food was permitted from the first day of our creation, when we lived in Paradise without sin, who can prove that we transgress in these enjoyments, so long as we do not pass the limits of the permission? Another objection is that matrimonial intercourse and the eating of tasty food are only allowed on condition of being taken without pleasure. But, if this is so, then they are allowed to be done in a way in which they never can be done. That concession is not reasonable which concedes that a thing shall be so done as it is certain that it cannot be done. By what reasoning did the law aforetime enforce matrimony so that each might leave his seed to Israel? Or, how did the Apostle oblige wives to fulfil the mutual debt if these acts could not be done without sinning? How can he refer to this debt when already it is of necessity sin? Or how should a man be compelled to do what he will grieve God by doing? Hence, I think that it is plain that no natural physical delight can be set down as sin, nor can it be called guilt for men to delight in what, when it is done, must involve the feeling of delight.

For example, if anyone obliged a monk, bound in chains, to lie among women, and the monk by the softness of the couch and by contact with his fair flatterers is allured into delight, though not into consent, who shall presume to designate guilt the delight which is naturally awakened?

You may urge, with some thinkers, that the carnal pleasure, even in lawful intercourse, involves sin. Thus David says: "Behold in sin was I conceived." (Ps. 1, 7.) And the Apostle, when he had said: "Ye return to it again" (1 Cor. vii, 5), adds, nevertheless, "This I say by way of concession, not of command." (ibid., v, 6.) Yet authority rather than reason, seems to dictate the view that we should allow simple physical delight to be sin. For, assuredly, David was conceived not in fornication, but in matrimony: and concession, that is forgiveness, does not, as this standpoint avers, condone when there is no guilt to forgive. As for what David meant when he says that he had been conceived "in iniquity" or "in sin" and does not say "whose" sin, he referred to the general curse of original sin, wherein from the guilt of our first parents each is subject to damnation, as it is elsewhere stated: "None are pure of stain, not the infant a day old, if he has life on this earth." As the blessed Jerome reminds us and as manifest reason teaches, the soul of a young child is without sin. If, then, it is pure of sin, how is it also impure by sinful corruption? We must understand the infant's purity from sin in reference to its personal guilt. But its contact with sinful corruption, its "stain," is in reference to penalty owed by mankind because of Adam's sin. He who has not yet perceived by reason what he ought to do cannot be guilty of contempt of God. Yet he is not free from the contamination of the sin of his first parents, from which he contracts the penalty, though not the guilt, and bears in penalty what they committed in guilt. When, therefore, David says that he was conceived in iniquity or sin, he sees himself subject to the general sentence of damnation from the guilt of his racial parents, and he assigns these sins, not to his father and mother but to his first parents.

When the Apostle speaks of indulgence, he must not be understood as some would wish to understand him, to mean permission to be equivalent to pardon for sin. His statement is: "By way of indulgence not of command." He might equally have said: "By permission, not by force." If husband and wife wish and decide upon mutual agreement they can abstain altogether from intercourse, and may not be compelled to it by command. But should they not so decide they have indulgence, that is, permission to substitute a less perfect for a more perfect rule of life. The Apostle, in this passage, did not therefore refer to pardon for sin, but to the permission of a less strict life for the avoidance of fornication. He meant that this lower level might elude the peaks of sin, and by its inferior standing escape the greater guilt.

We come, then, to this conclusion, that no one who sets out to assert that all fleshly desire is sin may say that the sin itself is increased by the doing of it. For this would mean extending the consent of the soul into the exercise of the action. In short, one would be stained not only by consent to baseness, but also by the mire of the deed, as if what happens externally in the body could possibly soil the soul. Sin is not, therefore, increased by the doing of an action: and nothing mars the soul except what is of its own nature, namely consent. This we affirmed was alone sin, preceding action in will, or subsequent to the performance of action. Although we wish for, or do, what is unseemly, we do not therefore sin. For such deeds not uncommonly occur without there being any sin. On the other hand, there may be consent without the external effects, as we have indicated. There was wish without consent in the case of the man who was attracted by a woman whom he caught sight of, or who was tempted by his neighbour's fruit, but who was not enticed into consent. There was evil consent without evil desire in the servant who unwillingly killed his master.

Certain acts which ought not to be done often are done, and without any sin, when, for instance, they are committed under force or ignorance. No one, I think, ignores this fact. A woman under constraint of violence, lies with another's husband. A man, taken by some trick, sleeps with one whom he supposed to be his wife, or kills a man, in the belief that he himself has the right to be both judge and executioner. Thus to desire the wife of another or actually to lie with her is not sin. But to consent to that desire or to that action is sin. This consent to covetousness the law calls covetousness in saying: "Thou shalt not covet." (Deut. v, 21.) Yet that which we cannot avoid ought not to be forbidden, nor that wherein, as we said, we do not sin. But we should be cautioned about the consent to covetousness. So, too, the saying of the Lord must be understood: "Whosoever shall look upon a woman to desire her." (Matt. v, 28.) That is, whosoever shall so look upon her as to slip into consent to covetousness, "has already committed adultery with her in his heart" (Matt. v, 28), even though he may not have committed adultery in deed. He is guilty of sin, though there be no sequel to his intention.

Careful account will reveal that wherever actions are restricted by some precept or prohibition, these refer rather to will and consent than to the deeds themselves. Otherwise nothing relative to a person's moral merit could be included under a precept. Indeed, actions are so much the less worth prescribing as they are less in our power to do. At the same time, many things we are forbidden to do for which there exists in our will both the inclination and the consent.

The Lord God says: "Thou shalt not kill. Thou shalt not bear false witness." (Deut. v, 17, 20.) If we accept these cautions as being only about actions, as the words suggest, then guilt is not forbidden, but simply the activity of guilt. For we have seen that actions may be carried out without sin, as that it is not sin to kill a man or to lie with another's wife. And even the man who desires to bear false testimony, and is willing to utter it, so long as he is silent for some reason and does not speak, is innocent before the law, that is, if the prohibition in this matter be accepted literally of the action. It is not said that we should not *wish* to give false witness, or that we should not *consent* in bearing it, but simply that we should not bear false witness.

Similarly, when the law forbids us to marry or have intercourse with our sisters, if this prohibition relates to deed rather than to intention, no one can keep the commandment, for a sister unless we recognize her, is just a woman. If a man, then, marries his sister in error, is he a transgressor for doing what the law forbade? He is not, you will reply, because, in acting ignorantly in what he did, he did not consent to a transgression. Thus a transgressor is not one who *does* what is prohibited. He is one who *consents* to what is prohibited. The prohibition is, therefore, not about action, but about consent. It is as though in saying: "Do not do this or that," we meant: "Do not consent to do this or that," or "Do not wittingly do this."

Blessed Augustine, in his careful view of this question, reduces every sin or command to terms of charity and covetousness, and not to works. "The law," he says, "inculcates nothing but charity, and forbids nothing but covetousness." The Apostle, also, asserts: "All the law is contained in one word: thou shalt love thy neighbour as thyself," (Rom. xiii, 8, 10), and again, "Love is the fulfilling of the law." (ibid.)

Whether you actually give alms to a needy person, or charity makes you ready to give, makes no difference to the merit of the deed. The will may be there when the opportunity is not. Nor does it rest entirely with you to deal with every case of need which you encounter. Actions which are right and actions which are far from right are done by good and bad men alike. The intention alone separates the two classes of men.

Augustine reminds us that in the self-same action we find God the Father, the Lord Jesus Christ, and also Judas the betrayer. The betrayal of the Son was accomplished by God the Father, and by the Son, and by the betrayer. For "the Father delivered up the Son, and the Son Himself" (Rom. viii, 32; Gal. ii, 22), as the Apostle says, and Judas delivered up his Master. The traitor, therefore, did the same thing as God Himself. But did Judas do anything well? No. Good certainly came of his act; but his act was not well done, nor was it destined to benefit him.

God considers not the action, but the spirit of the action. It is the intention, not the deed wherein the merit or praise of the doer consists. Often, indeed, the same action is done from different motives: for justice sake by one man, for an evil reason by another. Two men, for instance, hang a guilty person. The one does it out of zeal for justice; the other in resentment for an earlier enmity. The action of hanging is the same. Both men do what is good and what justice demands. Yet the diversity of their intentions causes the same deed to be done from different motives, in the one case good, in the other bad.

Everyone knows that the devil himself does nothing without God's permission, when he either punishes a wicked man according to his deserts, or is allowed to afflict a just man for moral cleansing or for an example of endurance. Since, however, in doing what God permits the devil moves at the spur of his own malice, the power which he has may be called good, or even just, while his will is for ever unjust. He receives, that is, the power from God, but his will is of himself.

Who, among the elect, can ever emulate the deeds of hypocrites? Who, for the love of God, ever endures or undertakes so much as they do from thirst for human praise? Who does not agree that sometimes what God forbids may rightly be done, while, contrarily, He may counsel certain things which of all things are least convenient? We note how He forbade certain miracles, whereby He had healed infirmities, to be made public. He set an example of humility lest any man should claim glory for the grace bestowed on him. Nevertheless, the recipients of those benefits did not cease to broadcast them, to the praise of Him who had done such things, and yet had forbidden them to be revealed. Thus we read: "As much as He bade them not to speak, so much the more did they publish abroad, etc." Will you judge these men guilty of a fault who acted contrary to the command which they had received, and did so wittingly? Who can acquit them of wrong-doing, unless by finding that they did not act out of contempt for the One who commanded, but decided to do what was to His honour? How, then, did the matter stand? Did Christ command what ought not to have been commanded? Or, did the newly-healed men disobey when they should have obeyed? The command was a good thing; yet it was not good for it to be obeyed.

In the case of Abraham, also, you will accuse God for first enjoining the sacrifice of Abraham's son, and then revoking the command. Has, then, God never *wisely commanded* anything which, *if it had come about,* would not have been good? If good, you will object, why was it afterwards forbidden? But conceive that it was good for the same thing to be prescribed and also to be prohibited. God, we know, permits nothing, and does not himself consent to achieve anything apart from rational cause. Thus it is the pure intention of the command, not the execution of the action which justifies God in wisely commanding what would not in actual fact be good. God did not intend Abraham to sacrifice his son, or command this sacrifice to be put into effect. His aim was to test Abraham's obedience, constancy of faith, and love towards Him, so that these qualities should be left to us as an example. This intention the Lord God plainly asserts afterwards in saying: "Now know I that thou fearest the Lord." (Gen. xxii, 12.) It is as if he frankly said: "I commanded you: you showed yourself ready to obey Me. Both these things were done so that others might know what I had Myself known of you from the beginning." There was a right intention on God's part; but it was not right for it to be put in practice. The prohibition, too, in the case of the miracles of healing was right. The object of this prohibition was not for it to be obeyed, but for an example to be given to our weak spirit in avoiding empty applause. God, in the one case enjoined an action which, if obeyed, would not have been good. In the other case, He forbade what was worth putting into fact, namely, a knowledge of Christ's miracles. The intention excuses Him in the first matter, just as the intention excuses the men who, in the second instance, were healed and did not carry out his injunction. They knew that the precept was not given to be practised, but in order that the aforenamed example of moderation in a successful miracle might be set. In keeping, then, the spirit of the command they showed, by actually disobeying no contempt for Him with whose intention they knew that they were acting.

A scrutiny of the deed rather than of the intention will reveal, then, cases where men frequently not only wish to go against God's bidding, but carry their wish knowingly into effect, and do so without any guilt of sin. An action or a wish must not be called bad because it does not in actual fact fall in with God's command. It may well be that the doer's intention does not at all differ from the will of his divine superior. The intention exonerates Him who gave a practically unseemly command: the intention excuses the man who, out of kindness, disobeyed the command to conceal the miracle.

Briefly to summarize the above argument: Four things were postulated which must be carefully distinguished from one another.

1. Imperfection of soul, making us liable to sin.
2. Sin itself, which we decided is consent to evil or contempt of God.
3. The will or desire of evil.
4. The evil deed.

To wish is not the same thing as to fulfil a wish. Equally, to sin is not the same as to carry out a sin. In the first case, we sin by consent of the soul: the second is a matter of the external effect of an action, namely, when we fulfil in deed that whereunto we have previously consented. When, therefore, temptation is said to proceed through three stages, suggestion, delight, consent, it must be understood that, like our first parents, we are frequently led along these three paths to the commission of sin. The devil's persuasion comes *first* promising from the taste of the forbidden fruit immortality. Delight follows. When the woman sees the beautiful tree, and perceives that the fruit is good, her appetite is whetted by the anticipated pleasure of tasting. This desire she ought to have repressed, so as to obey God's command. But in consenting to it, she was drawn *secondly* into sin. By penitence she should have put right this fault, and obtained pardon. Instead, she *thirdly* consummated the sin by the deed. Eve thus passed through the three stages to the commission of sin.

By the same avenues we also arrive not at sin, but at the action of sin, namely, the doing of an unseemly deed through the suggestion or prompting of something within us. If we already know that such a deed will be pleasant, our imagination is held by anticipatory delight and we are tempted thereby in thought. So long as we give consent to such delight, we sin. Lastly, we pass to the third stage, and actually commit the sin.

It is agreed by some thinkers that carnal suggestion, even though the person causing the suggestion be not present, should be included under sinful suggestion. For example, a man having seen a woman falls into a sensual desire of her. But it seems that this kind of suggestion should simply be called delight. This delight, and other delights of the like kind, arise naturally and, as we said above, they are not sinful. The Apostle calls them "human temptations." "No temptation has taken you yet which was not common to men. God is faithful, and will not suffer you to be tempted above what you are able; but will, with the temptation make a way of escape, that you may be able to bear it." By temptation is meant, in general, any movement of the soul to do something unseemly, whether in wish or consent. We speak of human temptation without which it is hardly or never possible for human weakness to exist. Such are sexual desire, or the pleasures of the table. From these the Psalmist asks to be delivered when he says: "Deliver me from my wants, O Lord" (Ps. xxiv, 17); that is, from the temptations of natural and necessary appetites that they may not influence him into sinful consent. Or, he may mean: "When this life is over, grant me to be without those temptations of which life has been full."

When the Apostle says: "No temptation has taken you but what is human," his statement amounts to this: Even if the soul be stirred by that delight which is, as we said, human temptation, yet God would not lead the soul into that consent wherein sin consists. Someone may object: But by what power of our own are we able to resist those desires? We may reply: "God is faithful, who will not allow you to be tempted," as the Scripture says. In other words: We should rather trust him than rely upon ourselves. He promises help, and is true to his promises. He is faithful, so that we should have complete faith in him. Out of pity God diminishes the degree of human temptation, "does not suffer us to be tempted above what we are able," in order that it may not drive us to sin at a pace we cannot endure, when, that is, we strive to resist it. Then, too, God turns the temptation to our advantage: for He trains us thereby so that the recurrence of temptation causes us less care, and we fear less the onset of a foe over whom we have already triumphed, and whom we know how to meet.

Every encounter, not as yet undertaken, is for that reason, to us, a matter of more anxiety and dismay. But when such an encounter comes to those accustomed to victory, its force and terror alike vanish.

*　　*　　*

CHAPTER 10: A NUMBER OF GOOD THINGS IS NOT BETTER THAN ONE OF THESE GOOD THINGS

The number of actions is of no importance for their intention. For to speak of good intention and good action, that is action proceeding from good intention, is to refer merely to the goodness of the intention. We cannot retain the term good in this same sense and talk of many "goods."

When we say that a man is simple, and speech simple, we do not therefore allow that there exist many "simples" just because this word "simple" is employed in the first instance of a man, and in the second instance of speech. No one can then compel us to concede that when the good act is added to the good intention, good is added to good, as though there could be many goods in proportion to whose number recompense ought to be increased. As we have said, we cannot call those actions "additional goods," for the word "good" does not properly apply to them.

CHAPTER 11: THE GOOD ACTION SPRINGS FROM THE GOOD INTENTION

We call the intention good which is right in itself, but the action is good, not because it contains within it some good, but because it issues from a good intention. The same act may be done by the same man at different times. According to the diversity of his intention, however, this act may be at one time good, at another bad. So goodness and badness vary. Compare the proposition: "Socrates sits." One conceives this statement either truly or falsely according as Socrates actually does sit, or stands. This alternation in truth and falsity, Aristotle affirms, comes about not from any change in the circumstances which compose the true or false situation, but because the subject-matter of the statement (that is, Socrates) moves in itself, I mean changes from sitting to standing or vice versa.*

CHAPTER 12: WHAT ARE THE GROUNDS OF GOOD INTENTIONS?

Good or right intention is held by some to be when anyone believes that he acts well, and that what he does pleases God. An example is supplied by those who persecuted the martyrs. About them the Gospel Truth says: "The hour comes when everyone who kills you will think that he is obedient to God." (John xvi, 2.) In sympathy with the ignorance of such the Apostle exclaims: "I bear this testimony on their behalf, that they are zealous for God but not according to knowledge." That is to say, they are fervently eager to do what they believe pleases God. Since, however, in this desire or keenness of mind they are deceived, their intention is a mistake. The eye of the heart is not so simple as to be capable of seeing clearly and to guard itself from error. For this reason the Lord, when he distinguished works according to right and wrong intention, spoke of the eye of the mind, that is the intention, as either *single,* pure, as it were, from spot, so that it could see clearly, or, on the contrary, as *clouded.* "If thine eye be single, thy whole body shall be full of light." This means that, provided the intention was right, all the acts proceeding from the intention which can possibly be foreseen in the manner of mortal affairs, will be worthy of the light, that is to say, good. And, contrarily, from wrong intention arise dark deeds.

The intention, therefore, must not be called good, merely because it seems good, but over and above this, because it is such as it is estimated to be. I mean that, if it thinks to please God in what it aims as its aim therein should not be mistaken. Otherwise the heathen, just like us, could count their good works, since they no less than we believe themselves either to be saved or to please God by their deeds.

---

*We may do the same action twice, just as we may say "Socrates sits" twice. But just as the same statement will be true when Socrates sits and false when he stands, so the same action will be good when the intention is good, and bad when the intention is bad.

Hildegard of Bingen
1098–1179

The monasteries and convents were as important to the intellectual life of twelfth-century Europe as were the developing universities. In those religious houses could be found both scholars seeking the reconciliation of faith and reason and contemplatives who emphasized the nonrational and mystical elements of Christianity. For example, both the academic Peter Abelard and the mystic St. Bernard of Clairvaux, his adversary, were monks. The cloister was also one of the few places where women could get an education, write, and assume positions of intellectual leadership. Among the leading nuns who wrote during this period was the mystic, Hildegard of Bingen.

Hildegard was born in Bermersheim, near Mainz, Germany. As the tenth and last child, her parents gave her as a "tithe" (literally a "tenth") to the church when she was eight years old. At about fifteen she took the vows of the Order of St. Benedict and spent her next two decades as a devoted Benedictine nun at Disibodenberg. In 1137 Hildegard became the abbess of her convent and soon thereafter began her writing career. Over the next forty-two years Hildegard not only wrote, she also founded two new convents, worked for social and church reform, and preached throughout the Rhine River basin. Sought out for advice by kings and popes as well as by common people, she wrote numerous letters of counsel and warning. In these letters Hildegard was fearlessly direct, as the opening lines of her letter to Pope Anastasius IV indicate:

So it is, O man, that you who sit in the chief seat of the Lord, hold him in contempt when you embrace evil, since you do not reject [evil] but kiss it, by silently tolerating it in depraved men. . . . Beware, therefore, of wanting to associate yourself with the ways of the pagans, lest you fall.*

In addition to letters, Hildegard's works include an explication of the Rule of St. Benedict (a list of rules used to govern monastic life), commentaries on the Gospels, scientific and medical treatises, poetry, songs, and the earliest known morality play. But Hildegard is best known for her visionary trilogy, *Scivias.*

Perhaps from as early as age three, Hildegard had visions, and she continued to have them throughout her life. As she explained in her preface to the *Scivias,* these visions did not come to her while sleeping or in a trance, "but by God's will [I] beheld them wide awake and clearly, with the mind, eyes, and ears of the inner person." In the passage from this work, reprinted here as translated by Mother Columba Hart and Jane Bishop, Hildegard relates a vision of a fetus receiving a soul. She goes on to discuss the relation between the body and the soul, as well as the interrelations among the various parts of the soul: senses, intellect, will, reason. She ends this interesting discussion with a pictorial analogy that illustrates her visual style.

*   *   *

For an overview of mysticism, begin with the classic by Evelyn Underhill, *Mysticism: A Study in the Nature and Development of Man's Spiritual Consciousness,* 12th ed. (London: Methuen, 1930). W.T. Stace, *Mysticism and Philosophy* (London: Macmillan, 1960); M.D. Knowles, *The Nature of Mysticism* (New York: Hawthorn Books, 1966); Georgia Harkness, *Mysticism: Its Meaning and Message* (Nashville: Abingdon Press, 1973); and S.T. Katz, *Mysticism and Philosophical Analysis* (New York: Oxford University Press, 1978), also give good general introductions. Paul E. Szarmach, *An Introduction to the Medieval Mystics of Europe* (Albany: State University of New York Press, 1984), provides sketches of virtually every major medieval mystic.

For a recent study of Hildegard of Bingen's life and thought, see Sabina Flanagan, *Hildegard of Bingen, 1098–1179: A Visionary Life* (London: Routledge, 1989). Surveys with sections on Hildegaard include Lina Eckenstein, *Women under Monasticism* (New York: Russell and Russell, 1963); Peter Dronke, *Women Writers of the Middle Ages* (Cambridge: Cambridge University Press, 1984); Margaret Alic, *Hypatia's Heritage: A History of Women in Science from Antiquity through the Nineteenth Century* (Boston: Beacon Press, 1986); and Elisabeth Gössmann, "Hildegard of Bingen" in Mary Ellen Waithe, *A History of Women Philosophers, Volume II: Medieval, Renaissance and Enlightenment Women Philosophers, 500–1600* (Dordrecht, The Netherlands: Kluwer Academic Publishers, 1989).

---

*Hildegard of Bingen, *Mystical Writings,* edited by Fiona Bowie and Oliver Davies, translated by Robert Carver (New York: Crossroads, 1990), p. 134. Portentously, Pope Athanasius died soon after this letter was sent.

SCIVIAS (in part)

BOOK I, VISION FOUR

16: An Infant Is Vivified in the Womb and Confirmed by a Soul on Leaving It

And you see the image of a woman who has a perfect human form in her womb. This means that after a woman has conceived by human semen, an infant with all its members whole is formed in the secret chamber of her womb. And behold! *By the secret design of the Supernal Creator that form moves with vital motion;* for, by God's secret and hidden command and will, fitly and rightly at the divinely appointed time the infant in the maternal womb receives a spirit, and shows by the movements of its body that it lives, just as the earth opens and brings forth the flowers of its use when the dew falls on it. *So that a fiery globe which has no human lineaments possesses the heart of that form;* that is, the soul, burning with a fire of profound knowledge, which discerns whatever is within the circle of its understanding, and, without the form of human members, since it is not corporeal or transitory like a human body, gives strength to the heart and rules the whole body as its foundation, as the firmament of Heaven contains the lower regions and touches the higher. *And it also touches the person's brain;* for in its powers it knows not only earthly but also heavenly things, since it wisely knows God; *and it spreads itself through all the person's members;* for it gives vitality to the marrow and veins and members of the whole body, as the tree from its root gives sap and greenness to all the branches. *But then this human form, in this way vivified, comes forth from the woman's womb, and changes its color according to the movement the globe makes in that form;* which is to say that after the person has received the vital spirit in the maternal womb and is born and begins his actions, his merits will be according to the works his soul does with the body, for he will put on brightness from the good ones and darkness from the evil ones.

17: How the Soul Shows Its Powers According to the Powers of the Body

The soul now shows its powers according to the powers of the body, so that in a person's infancy it produces simplicity, in his youth strength, and in adulthood, when all the person's veins are full, it shows its strongest powers in wisdom; as the tree in its first shoots is tender and then shows that it can bear fruit, and finally, in its full utility, bears it. But then in human old age, when the marrow and veins start to incline to weakness, the soul's powers are gentler, as if from a weariness at human knowledge; as when winter approaches the sap of the tree diminishes in the branches and the leaves, and the tree in its old age begins to bend.

Hildegard of Bingen, *Scivias,* Bk. I, 4, 16–26, translated by Mother Columba Hart and Jane Bishop (New York: Paulist Press, 1990). Copyright © Abbey of Regina Laudis: Benedictine Congregation Regina Laudis of the Strict Observance, Inc. Reprinted by permission.

Body and Soul, from an early edition of *Scivias.* One of the souls in heaven (represented by the eyes) is entering the fetus in the womb. As Hildegard writes, ". . . at the divinely appointed time the infant in the maternal womb receives a spirit, and shows by the movements of its body that it lives." *(From "Hildegard of Bingen," Paulist Press, New York: page 107. Illustration by Mother Placid Dempsey.)*

18: A Person Has Three Paths Within Himself

But a person has within himself three paths. What are they? The soul, the body and the senses; and all human life is led in these. How? The soul vivifies the body and conveys the breath of life to the senses; the body draws the soul to itself and opens the senses; and the senses touch the soul and draw the body. For the soul gives life to the body as fire gives light to darkness, with two principal powers like two arms, intellect and will; the soul has arms not so as to move itself, but so as to show itself in these powers as the sun shows itself by its brilliance. Therefore, O human, who are not just a bundle of marrow, pay attention to scriptural knowledge!

19: On the Intellect

The intellect is joined to the soul like an arm to the body. For as the arm, joined to the hand with its fingers, branches out from the body, so the intellect, working with the other powers of the soul, by which it understands human actions, most certainly proceeds from the soul. For before all the other powers of the soul it understands whatever is in human works, whether good or evil, so that through it, as through a teacher, everything is understood; for it sifts things as wheat is purified of any foreign matter, inquiring whether they are useful or useless, lovable or hateful, pertinent to life or death. Thus, as food without salt is tasteless, the other powers of the soul without intellect are insipid and undiscerning. But the intellect is also to the soul as the shoulder is to the body, the very core of the other powers of the soul; as the bodily shoulder is strong, so it understands the divinity and the humanity in God, which is the joint of the arm, and it has true faith in its work, which is the joint of the hand, with which it chooses among the various works wisely as if with fingers. But it does not work in the same way as the other powers of the soul. What does this mean?

20: On the Will

The will activates the work, and the mind receives it, and the reason produces it. But the intellect understands the work, knowing good and evil, just as the angels, who have intellect, love good and despise evil. And where the heart is in the body, there the intellect is in the soul, exercising its power in that part of the soul as the will does in another part. How? Because the will has great power in the soul. How? The soul stands in a corner of the house, that is, by the prop of the heart, like a man who stands in a corner of his house, so that looking through the whole house he may command all its contents, lifting his right arm to point out what is useful in the house and turning to the East. Thus the soul should do, looking along the streets of the body toward the rising sun. Thus it puts its will, like a right arm, as the support of the veins and marrow and the movement of the whole body; for the will does every work, whether it be good or bad.

21: Analogy of Fire and Bread

For the will is like a fire, baking each deed as if in a furnace. Bread is baked so that people may be nourished by it and be able to live. So too the will is the strength of the whole work, for it starts by kneading it and when it is firm adds the yeast and pounds it severely; and, thus preparing the work in contemplation as if it were bread, it bakes it in perfection by the full action of its ardor, and so makes a greater food for humans in the work they do than in the bread they eat. A person stops eating from time to time, but the work of his will goes on in him till his soul leaves his body. And in whatever differing circumstances the work is performed, whether in infancy, youth, adulthood or bent old age, it always progresses in the will and in the will comes to perfection.

22: How in the Will's Tabernacle All Powers Are Activated and Come Together

But the will has in the human breast a tabernacle, the mind, upon which the intellect and that same will and a sort of force of the soul all breathe in strength. And all these are activated and come together in the same tabernacle. How? If anger arises, gall is produced and brings the anger to its height by filling the tabernacle with smoke. If wicked delight rises up, the flame of lust touches its structure, and so the wantonness that pertains to that sin is elevated and in that tabernacle united with it. But there is another, lovely kind of joy, which is kindled in that tabernacle by the Holy Spirit, and the rejoicing soul receives it faithfully and perfects good works in the desire of Heaven. And there is a kind of sadness that engenders in the tabernacle, out of those humors that surround the gall, the sloth which produces disdain, obduracy and stubbornness in people and depresses the soul, unless the grace of God comes quickly to rescue it.

But since in that tabernacle there occur contrary conditions, it is often disturbed by hatred and other deadly emotions, which kill the soul and try to lay it waste in perdition. But when the will wills, it can move the implements in the tabernacle and in its burning ardor dispose of them, whether they are good or evil. But if these implements please the will, it bakes its food there and offers it to people to enjoy. So in that tabernacle a great throng of good and evil things arises, like an army gathered in some place of assembly; when the commander of an army arrives, if the army pleases him he accepts it, but if it displeases him he orders it to disband. The will does the same. How? If good or evil arises in the breast, the will either carries it out or ignores it.

23: On the Reason

But both in the intellect and in the will reason stands forth as the loud sound of the soul, which makes known every work of God or Man. For sound carries words on high, as the wind lifts the eagle so that it can fly. Thus the soul utters the sound of reason in the hearing and the understanding of humanity, that its powers may be understood and its every work brought to perfection. But the body is the tabernacle and support of all the powers of the soul, since the soul resides in the body and works with the body, and the body with it, whether for good or for evil.

24: On the Senses

It is the senses on which the interior powers of the soul depend, so that these powers are known through them by the fruits of each work. The senses are subject to these powers, since they guide them to the work, but the senses do not impose work on the powers, for they are their shadow and do what pleases them. The exterior human being awakens with senses in the womb of his mother before he is born, but the other powers of the soul still remain in hiding. What is this? The dawn announces the daylight; just so the human senses manifest the reason and all the powers of the soul. And as on the two commandments of God hang all the Law and the prophets, so also on the soul and its powers depend the human senses. What does this mean?

The Law is ordained for human salvation, and the prophets show forth the hidden things of God; so also human senses protect a person from harmful things and lay bare the soul's interior. For the soul emanates the senses. How? It vivifies a person's face and glorifies him with sight, hearing, taste, smell and touch, so that by this touch he becomes watchful in all things. For the senses are the sign of all the powers of the soul, as the body is the vessel of the soul. What does this mean? A person is recognized by his face, sees with his eyes, hears with his ears, opens his mouth to speak, feels with his hands, walks with his feet; and so the senses are to a person as precious stones and as a rich treasure sealed in a vase. But as the treasure within is known when the vase is seen, so also the powers of the soul are inferred by the senses.

25: That the Soul Is the Mistress and the Flesh the Handmaid

The soul is the mistress, the flesh the handmaid. How? The soul rules the body by vivifying it, and the body is ruled by this vivification, for if the soul did not vivify the body it would fall apart and decay. But when a person does an evil deed and the soul knows it, it is as bitter for the soul as poison is for the body when it knowingly takes it. But the soul rejoices in a sweet deed as the body delights in sweet food. And the soul flows through the body like sap through a tree. What does this mean? By the sap, the tree grows green and produces flowers and then fruit. And how is this fruit matured? By the air's tempering. How? The sun warms it, the rain waters it, and thus by the tempering of the air it is perfected. What does this mean? The mercy of God's grace, like the sun, will illumine the person, the breath of the Holy Spirit, like the rain, will water him, and so discernment, like the tempering of the air, will lead him to the perfection of good fruits.

26: Analogy of a Tree to the Soul

The soul in the body is like sap in a tree, and the soul's powers are like the form of the tree. How? The intellect in the soul is like the greenery of the tree's branches and leaves, the will like its flowers, the mind like its bursting firstfruits, the reason like the perfected mature fruit, and the senses like its size and shape. And so a person's body is strengthened and sustained by the soul. Hence, O human, understand what you are in your soul, you who lay aside your good intellect and try to liken yourself to the brutes.

John of Salisbury
ca. 1120–1180

Born into a family of humble means in Old Sarum (Salisbury), England, John of Salisbury first studied with a rural priest. In 1136 John went to Paris where he spent the next twelve years studying with such renown teachers as Peter Abelard. After his training, John was ordained to the priesthood. He served first in the papal court in Rome for five or six years before being sent home to England in 1154 to become the secretary of and trusted advisor to Theobald, Archbishop of Canterbury. For the next seven years he assisted in Theobald's struggle for the independence of the church from the government of King Henry II.

When Thomas Becket, the king's former chancellor, was made archbishop in 1161, after Theobald's death, John continued his service as secretary and advisor. Many scholars believe that John may have shared responsibility for the transformation of Becket from king's counselor to church defender. As the conflict between King Henry and the church intensified, it was John who was attacked first. Accused by the king of going over his head by encouraging appeals to Rome, John was forced into exile in 1163. For the next seven years John worked for Becket's interests with King Louis VII of France and other leaders. When Becket himself was banished from England, he joined John in exile. When Henry allowed Becket to return to Canterbury, John joined him again. John was at Canterbury Cathedral on the night of December 29, 1170, when Henry's knights murdered Becket. Returning again to France, John was made Bishop of Chartres by King Louis in 1176 and served in that position until his death four years later.

While John of Salisbury wrote on a number of topics, he is best known for the *Metalogicon* and the *Policratus,* two works addressed in 1159 to then Chancellor Thomas Becket. The *Metalogicon* is a treatise on education, which argues against technical logic in favor of the civilizing effects of what we would call the liberal arts. In this work John criticizes the obsession of his age with the problem of universals. His criticism includes a brief and interesting summary of the various positions taken on this important question. This treatise is reprinted here in the Daniel D. McGarry translation.

John's other major work, the *Policratus* or "Statesman," is typical of twelfth-century political theory. John clearly asserts the superiority of the church over the state, claiming that the role of the state is to carry out duties beneath the dignity of the church. In the selection given here, translated by Eugene Fairweather, John holds that, unlike the tyrant, the prince rules by law and recognizes that he is a servant of law. Furthermore, the true prince is also the servant of the church and of her priesthood. Given this emphasis on the power of the church over the state—and given that the *Policratus* ends with a section condoning the assassination of a political tyrant—it is not difficult to see why John was exiled by King Henry II.

*   *   *

For studies of John of Salisbury, see Clement C.J. Webb, *John of Salisbury* (London: Methuen, 1932), and Hans Liebeschutz, *Mediaeval Humanism in the Life and Writings of John of Salisbury* (London: Warburg Institute, University of London, 1950). Roger Lloyd, *The Golden Middle Age* (1939, reprinted Freeport, NY: Books for Libraries Press, 1969), discusses John of Salisbury in the context of twelfth-century education.

For works on the problem of universals, see the suggested readings in the introduction to Peter Abelard (p. 173). For primary source readings in medieval political thought, see Ralph Lerner and Muhsin Mahdi, eds., *Medieval Political Philosophy: A Sourcebook* (New York: Free Press, 1963); and for secondary works consult R.W. Carlyle, *A History of Mediaeval Political Theory in the West,* 6 vols. (New York: Barnes & Noble, 1927–1936); Otto Friedrich von Gierke, *Political Theories of the Middle Age,* translated by Frederic William Maitland (Boston: Beacon Press, 1958); John B. Morrall, *Political Thought in Medieval Times* (London: Hutchinson, 1958); Walter Ullmann, *A History of Political Thought: The Middle Ages* (Harmondsworth, England: Penguin Books, 1965); and J.H. Burns, ed., *The Cambridge History of Medieval Political Thought ca. 350–ca. 1450* (Cambridge: Cambridge University Press, 1988).

METALOGICON (in part)

BOOK II

Chapter 17: In What a Pernicious Manner Logic Is Sometimes Taught; and the Ideas of Moderns About [the Nature of] Genera and Species

To show off their knowledge, our contemporaries dispense their instruction in such a way that their listeners are at a loss to understand them. They seem to have the impression that every letter of the alphabet is pregnant with the secrets of Minerva. They analyze and press upon tender ears everything that anyone has ever said or done. Falling into the error condemned by Cicero, they frequently come to be unintelligible to their hearers more because of the multiplicity than the profundity of their statements. "It is indeed useful and advantageous for disputants," as Aristotle observes, "to take cognizance of several opinions on a topic." From the mutual disagreement thus brought into relief, what is seen to be poorly stated may be disproved or modified. Instruction in elementary logic does not, however, constitute the proper occasion for such procedure. Simplicity, brevity, and easy subject matter are, so far as is possible, appropriate in introductory studies. This is so true that it is permissible to expound many difficult points in a simpler way than their nature strictly requires. Thus, much that we have learned in our youth must later be amended in more advanced philosophical studies. Nevertheless, at present, all are here [in introductory logical studies] declaiming on the nature of universals, and attempting to explain, contrary to the intention of the author, what is really a most profound question, and a matter [that should be reserved] for more advanced studies. One holds that universals are merely word sounds, although this opinion, along with its author Roscelin, has already almost completely passed into oblivion. Another maintains that universals are word concepts, and twists to support his thesis everything that he can remember to have ever been written on the subject. Our Peripatetic of Pallet, Abelard, was ensnared in this opinion. He left many, and still has, to this day, some followers and proponents of his doctrine. They are friends of mine, although they often so torture the helpless letter that even the hardest heart is filled with compassion for the latter. They hold that it is preposterous to predicate a thing concerning a thing, although Aristotle is author of this monstrosity. For Aristotle frequently asserts that a thing is predicated concerning a thing, as is evident to anyone who is really familiar with his teaching. Another is wrapped up in a consideration of acts of the [intuitive] understanding, and says that genera and species are nothing more than the latter. Proponents of this view take their cue from Cicero and Boethius, who cite Aristotle as saying that universals should be regarded as and called "notions." "A notion," they tell us, "is the cognition of something, derived from its previously perceived form, and in need of unravelment." Or again [they say]: "A notion is an act of the [intuitive] understanding, a simple mental

John of Salisbury, *The Metalogicon of John Salisbury: A Twelfth-Century Defense of the Verbal and Logical Arts of the Trivium,* translated by Daniel D. McGarry (Berkeley: Univesity of California Press, 1955).

comprehension." They accordingly distort everything written, with an eye to making acts of [intuitive] understanding or "notions" include the universality of universals. Those who adhere to the view that universals are things, have various and sundry opinions. One, reasoning from the fact that everything which exists is singular in number, concludes that either the universal is numerically one, or it is non-existent. But since it is impossible for things that are substantial to be non-existent, if those things for which they are substantial exist, they further conclude that universals must be essentially one with particular things. Accordingly, following Walter of Mortagne, they distinguish [various] states [of existence], and say that Plato is an individual in so far as he is Plato; a species in so far as he is a man; a genus of a subaltern [subordinate] kind in so far as he is an animal; and a most general genus in so far as he is a substance. Although this opinion formerly had some proponents, it has been a long time since anyone has asserted it. Walter now upholds [the doctrine of] ideas, emulating Plato and imitating Bernard of Chartres, and maintains that genus and species are nothing more nor less than these, namely, ideas. "An idea," according to Seneca's definition, "is an eternal exemplar of those things which come to be as a result of nature." And since universals are not subject to corruption, and are not altered by the changes that transform particular things and cause them to come and go, succeeding one another almost momentarily, ideas are properly and correctly called "universals." Indeed, particular things are deemed incapable of supporting the substantive verb, [i.e., of being said "to be"], since they are not at all stable, and disappear without even waiting to receive names. For they vary so much in their qualities, time, location, and numerous different properties, that their whole existence seems to be more a mutual transition than a stable status. In contrast, Boethius declares: "We say that things 'are' when they may neither be increased nor diminished, but always continue as they are, firmly sustained by the foundations of their own nature." These [foundations] include their quantities, qualities, relations, places, times, conditions, and whatever is found in a way united with bodies. Although these adjuncts of bodies may seem to be changed, they remain immutable in their own nature. In like manner, although individuals [of species] may change, species remain the same. The waves of a stream wash on, yet the same flow of water continues, and we refer to the stream as the same river. Whence the statement of Seneca, which, in fact, he has borrowed from another: "In one sense it is true that we may descend twice into the same river, although in another sense this is not so." These "ideas," or "exemplary forms," are the original plans of all things. They may neither be decreased nor augmented; and they are so permanent and perpetual, that even if the whole world were to come to an end, they could not perish. They include all things, and, as Augustine seems to maintain in his book *On Free Will,* their number neither increases nor diminishes, because the ideas always continue on, even when it happens that [particular] temporal things cease to exist. What these men promise is wonderful, and familiar to philosophers who rise to the contemplation of higher things. But, as Boethius and numerous other authors testify, it is utterly foreign to the mind of Aristotle. For Aristotle very frequently opposes this view, as is clear from his books. Bernard of Chartres and his followers labored strenuously to compose the differences between Aristotle and Plato. But I opine that they arrived on the scene too late, so that their efforts to reconcile two dead men, who disagree as long as they were alive and could do so, were in vain. Still another, in his endeavor to explain Aristotle, places universality in "native forms," as does Gilbert, Bishop of Poitiers, who labors to prove that "native forms" and universals are identical. A "native form" is an example of an original [exemplar]. It [the native form, unlike the original] inheres in created things, instead of subsisting in the divine mind. In Greek it is called the *idos,* since it stands in relation to the idea as the example does to its exemplar. The native form is sensible in things that are perceptible by the senses; but insensible as conceived in the mind. It is singular in individuals, but universal in all [of a kind]. Another, with Joscelin, Bishop of Soissons, attributes universality to collections of things, while denying it to things as individuals. When Joscelin tries to explain the authorities, he has his troubles and is hard put, for in many places he cannot bear the gaping astonishment of the indignant letter. Still another takes refuge in a new tongue, since he does not have sufficient command of Latin. When he hears the words "genus" and "species," at one time he says they should be understood as universals, and at another that they refer to the *maneries** of things. I know not in which of the authors he has found this term or this distinction, unless perhaps he has dug it out of lists of abstruse and obsolete words, or it is an item of jargon [in the baggage] of present-day doctors. I am further at a loss to see what it can mean here, unless it refers to collections of things, which would be the same as Joscelin's view, or to a universal thing, which, however, could hardly be called a *maneries.* For a *maneries* may be interpreted as referring to both [collections and universals], since a number of things, or the status in which a thing of such and such a type continues to exist may be called a *maneries.* Finally, there are some who fix their attention on the status of things, and say that genera and species consist in the latter.

STATESMAN *(POLICRATUS)* (in part)

CHAPTER 1: THE DIFFERENCE BETWEEN A PRINCE AND A TYRANT, AND WHAT A PRINCE IS

This, then, is the sole (or at least the greatest) difference between a tyrant and a prince, that the latter conforms to the law, and rules the people, whose servant he believes himself to be, by its judgment. Also, when he performs the duties of the commonwealth and undergoes its burdens, he claims for himself the first place by privilege of law, and is set before others in so far as universal burdens hang over the prince, while individuals are bound to individual concerns. On this account, the power over all his subjects is rightly conferred on him, so that, in seeking and accomplishing the welfare of each and all, he may be self-sufficient and the state of the human commonwealth may be best disposed, while one is the member of another. In this, indeed, we follow nature, the best guide for living, which arranged all the senses of its microcosm—that is, its little world, man—in the head, and subjected all the members to the latter so that they all are rightly moved, as long as they follow the decision of a sound head. Therefore, the princely crown is exalted and shines with priv-

---

*[Ways, modes, or manners.]

From *A Scholastic Miscellany: Anselm to Ockham,* edited and translated by Eugene R. Fairweather (Volume X: The Library of Christian Classics). First published in MCMLV by SCM Press Ltd., London and The Westminster Press, Philadelphia. Used by permission of Westminster/John Knox Press.

ileges as many and as great as it has believed to be necessary for itself. And this is done rightly, because nothing is more beneficial for the people than for the prince's necessity to be met—when his will is not opposed to justice, to be sure. Therefore (as many define him) the prince is the public ruler and a kind of image of the divine Majesty on earth. Beyond doubt, it is shown that something great in the way of divine power indwells princes, when men submit their necks to their nods and very often fearlessly yield their necks to be smitten, and each for whom he is a matter of dread fears him by divine instigation. I do not think that this could happen, save by the act of the divine pleasure. For all power is from the Lord God, and it has been with him always, and is with him eternally. Therefore, what the prince can do comes from God in such a way that the power does not depart from the Lord, but he exercises it by a hand that is subject to him, and that follows in all things the instruction of his clemency or justice. Thus "he that resisteth the power resisteth the ordinance of God," with whom rests the authority to confer it and (when he wills) to take it away or lessen it. For when a mighty one decides to rage against his subjects, this involves not just himself but also the divine dispensation, by which those who are subject to it are punished or vexed for God's good pleasure. So, for instance, during the depredations of the Huns, Attila was asked, by the devout bishop of a certain city, who he was, and replied, "I am Attila, the scourge of God." It is written that, when the bishop had reverenced the divine Majesty in him, he said, "Welcome to the servant of God," and, repeating, "Blessed is he that cometh in the name of the Lord," opened the doors of the church and admitted the persecutor, and through him attained to the palm of martyrdom. For he did not dare to shut out the scourge of God, knowing as he did that it is the beloved son that is scourged, and that the very power of the scourge comes from the Lord alone. If, then, the power is to be reverenced in this way by the good, even when it brings misfortune to the elect, who will not reverence it? After all, it was instituted by the Lord "for the punishment of evildoers, and for the praise of the good," and it serves the laws with the readiest devotion. For, as the emperor says, it is a statement worthy of the majesty of the ruler that the prince should acknowledge that he is bound by laws, because the authority of the prince depends on the authority of the law, and it is certainly a greater thing for the realm when sovereignty is set under the laws, so that the prince understands that nothing is permitted to him if it is at variance with justice and equity.

CHAPTER 2: WHAT LAW IS, AND THAT THE PRINCE, ALTHOUGH HE IS RELEASED FROM THE OBLIGATIONS OF LAW, IS STILL THE BONDSERVANT OF LAW AND EQUITY, AND BEARS A PUBLIC CHARACTER, AND SHEDS BLOOD BLAMELESSLY

Princes should not think that anything is taken away from them in all this, unless they believe that the statutes of their own justice are to be preferred to the justice of God, whose justice is justice forever, and his law equity. Besides, as legal experts affirm, equity is the fitness of things, which makes everything equal by reason and desires equal laws for unequal things; it is equitable toward all and assigns to each what belongs to him. But law is its interpreter, in so far as the will of equity and justice has been made known to it. Therefore, Chrysippus claimed that law has power over all things human and divine, and on that account is superior to all goods and evils and is the chief and guide of things and men alike. Papinian, a really great expert in the law, and Demosthenes, the powerful orator, seem to uphold the law and to subject the obedience of all men to it, inasmuch as in truth all law is the device and gift of God, the doctrine of wise men, the corrector of inclinations to excess, the settlement of the state, and the banishment of all crime, so that all who are engaged in the whole world of political affairs must live according to it. Thus all are closely bound by the necessity of maintaining the law, unless there may perhaps be someone to whom license seems to have been conceded for wickedness. Nevertheless, the prince is said to be released from legal obligations, not because evil actions are allowed him, but because he should be one who cherishes equity, not from fear of punishment but from love of justice, and in everything puts others' advantage before his personal desires. But who will speak of the desires of the prince in connection with public business, since in this area he is permitted to desire nothing for himself save what law or equity suggests or the nature of the common welfare determines? For in these things his will ought to have the effect of a judgment, and it is quite right that what pleases him in such matters should have the force of law, in so far as his sentence is not in disagreement with the intention of equity. "Let my judgment," the psalmist says, "come forth from thy countenance; let thine eyes behold the thing that is equitable," for an uncorrupt judge is he whose sentence is the image of equity, because of assiduous contemplation. The prince, then, is the servant of the public welfare and the bondservant of equity, and in that sense plays a public role, because he both avenges the injuries and losses of all and punishes all crimes with impartial justice. Moreover, his rod and staff, applied with wise moderation, bring the agreements and the errors of all into the way of equity, so that the spirit rightly gives thanks to the princely power, when it says, "Thy rod and thy staff, they have comforted me." It is true also that his shield is strong, but it is the shield of the weak and it effectively intercepts the darts aimed at the innocent by the malicious. His function also is of the utmost benefit to those who have the least power, and is most strongly opposed to those who desire to do harm. Therefore, "he beareth not the sword in vain," when he sheds blood by it, but blamelessly, so that he is not a man of blood, but often kills men without thereby incurring the name or the guilt of a homicide. For if the great Augustine is to be believed, David was called a "man of blood," not because of his wars but on account of Uriah. And it is nowhere written that Samuel was a man of blood or a homicide, even though he slew Agag, the very rich king of Amalek. In fact, the princely sword is the "sword of the dove," which strives without animosity, smites without fury, and, when it goes into combat, conceives no bitterness whatsoever. For, just as the law proceeds against crimes without any hatred of persons, so the prince also punishes offenders most rightly, not by any impulse of anger but by the decision of a mild law. For though the prince may seem to have his own "lictors,"* we should believe that in fact he is his only (or his foremost) lictor, but that it is lawful for him to smite by the hand of a substitute. For if we consult the Stoics, who diligently search out the origins of names, we shall learn that he is called a "lictor"—as it were, a "striker of the law"—inasmuch as it pertains to his office to smite him who, in the law's judgment, is to be smitten. On this account also, when the guilty were threatened with the sword, it used to be said in ancient days to the officials by whose hand the judge punished evildoers, "Comply with the decision of the law," or "Fulfill the law," so that the mildness of the words might in fact modify the sadness of the event.

*[Attendants who carried the symbols of power.]

CHAPTER 3: THAT THE PRINCE IS THE SERVANT OF PRIESTS AND BENEATH THEM, AND WHAT IT MEANS TO CARRY OUT THE PRINCELY OFFICE FAITHFULLY

The prince, therefore, receives this sword from the hand of the Church, even though, to be sure, the latter does not possess the sword of blood. Nevertheless, she does possess it as well, but makes use of it by the hand of the prince, to whom she has conceded the power of keeping bodies under restraint, although she has retained authority in spiritual matters for her pontiffs. Thus the prince is in fact the servant of the priesthood, and exercises that part of the sacred duties which seems unworthy of the hands of the priesthood. For while every duty imposed by the sacred laws is a matter of religion and piety, the function of punishing crimes, which seems to constitute a kind of image of the hangman's office, is lower than others. It was on account of this inferiority that Constantine, the most faithful emperor of the Romans, when he had convoked the council of priests at Nicaea, did not dare to take the first place or mingle with the assemblies of the presbyters, but occupied the lowest seat. Indeed, he reverenced the conclusions which he heard approved by them as if he supposed that they proceeded from the judgment of the divine Majesty. As for the written accusations, stating the offenses of the priests, which they had drawn up against one another and presented to the emperor, he received them and put them away, still unopened, in his bosom. Moreover, when he had recalled the council to charity and concord, he said that it was unlawful for him (as a man, and as one who was subject to the judgment of priests) to consider the cases of the gods, who can be judged by God alone. And he committed the books which he had received to the fire, without looking at them, because he was afraid to disclose the crimes or vices of the Fathers, lest he bring on himself the curse of Ham, the rejected son, who failed to cover what he should have respected in his father. For the same reason, he is said (in the writings of Nicholas, the Roman Pontiff) to have stated: "Truly, if with my own eyes I had seen a priest of God, or anyone who had been clothed in the monastic habit, committing sin, I should have spread out my cloak and covered him, lest he be seen by anyone." Theodosius also, the great emperor, when he was suspended from the use of the regalia and the badges of sovereignty by the bishop of Milan, because of a crime that was real enough, but not quite that serious, patiently and solemnly did the penance imposed on him for homicide. Certainly, to appeal to the testimony of the doctor of the Gentiles, he who blesses is greater than he who is blessed, and he who possesses the authority to confer a dignity surpasses in the privilege of honor him on whom the dignity itself is conferred. Besides, according to the very nature of law, it pertains to the same person to will and not to will, and it is he who has the right to confer who also has the right to take away. Did not Samuel bring sentence of deposition against Saul on account of his disobedience, and substitute the lowly son of Jesse for him in the highest place in the kingdom? But if he who is set up as prince has faithfully performed the function he received, he is to be shown great honor and great reverence, in proportion to the superiority of the head over all the members of the body. Now he performs his task faithfully when, mindful of his rank, he remembers that he bears in himself the totality of his subjects, and knows that he owes his own life not to himself but to others, and as it were distributes it among them with due charity. He owes his entire self then, to God, most of himself to his fatherland, much to his kinsfolk and neighbors, and least (but still something) to strangers. He is debtor, then, to the wise and the unwise, to the small and the great. In fact, this concern is common to all who are set over others, both to those who

Murder of Thomas Becket, from an English Psalter, ca. 1200. Infuriated by his former chancellor's defiance of the crown in favor of the church, King Henry II made remarks that led some of his knights to kill Becket. The priest shown in the background may well have been John of Salisbury who, as Becket's secretary and advisor, was at Canterbury Cathedral when Becket was murdered. *(Walters Art Gallery)*

bear the care of spiritual things and to those who exercise worldly jurisdiction. On this account we read of Melchizedek, who is the first king and priest referred to in Scripture—not to mention, for the present, the mystery by which he prefigures Christ, who was born in heaven without a mother and on earth without a father—we read, I say, that he had neither father nor mother. It is not that he lacked either, but that flesh and blood do not by their nature bring forth kingship and priesthood, since in the creation of either respect of parents should not carry weight without regard for meritorious virtue, but the wholesome desires of faithful subjects should have priority. Thus, when anyone reaches the pinnacle of either kingship or priesthood, he should forget the affection of the flesh and do only what the welfare of his subjects demands. Let him be, therefore, the father and husband of his subjects, or, if he knows a more tender affection, let him practice it; let him strive to be loved more than he is feared, and let him show himself to them in such a light that out of sheer devotion they may put his life before their own and reckon his safety to be a kind of public life. Then everything will go well with him, and if need be a few guards will prevail by their obedience against countless enemies. For "love is strong as death," and a wedge which the cords of love hold together is not easily broken.

Islamic and Jewish Philosophy in the Middle Ages

When Emperor Justinian closed the schools in Athens in 529, many of the teachers moved east to Syria, taking their books with them. There the works of Aristotle and many of the Neoplatonists were translated into Syriac and, later, into Arabic. These works were to return to Western Europe centuries later in the hands of Islamic and Jewish philosophers.

The religion of Islam began with Muhammad (571–632), an Arab from the town of Mecca. Repelled by the polytheism of his day and believing himself to be called as a prophet, Muhammad taught that there is no God but Allah. According to Islam, over a period of twenty-three years Muhammad received messages from Allah, which he wrote down in the *Qur'ān (or Koran)*. These sacred writings taught an uncomplicated message of submission (which is what the word "Islam" means), submission to the will of Allah, expressed in a life of obedience and in deeds such as prayer, almsgiving, periods of fasting, and a once-in-a-lifetime Hajj or pilgrimage to Mecca. Through the work of Muhammad and his immediate successors, Islam spread quickly throughout the Arabian peninsula. Within a century Islam was the dominant religion in the Middle East, Northern Africa, and even European Spain. Throughout this expansion, Islam was relatively tolerant of Christianity and Judaism, holding that the adherents of these monotheistic religions were also "people of the Book."

The Islamic culture of this period was

very sophisticated and cosmopolitan—especially when compared to that of Western Europe. When Western Europe was largely illiterate, the Muslims (adherents of Islam) were making advances in astronomy, mathematics, and medicine. There was also a group of Muslim thinkers known as *falyasufs* ("philosophers") who studied and applied the manuscripts of Aristotle and the Neoplatonists that had come through Syria. As Islamic thinkers worked with these texts, they encountered the problems their colleagues in the West knew well: how to reconcile philosophy with sacred texts; how to combine reason and faith. The *falyasufs* were centered in two different regions and times. An early group, around Baghdad, included al-Kindî (ca. 800–870), al-Fārābī (870–950), al-Ghazālī (1058–1111) and, most prominently, Ibn-Sīnā (or Avicenna, his Latin name, 980–1037). A later group in Spain included Ibn Bājjah (d. 1138), Ibn Tufayl (ca. 1100–1185), and, most prominently, Ibn Rushd (or Averroës, 1126–1198).

During the early years of Islam, Jewish philosophy coexisted and interacted freely with Islamic thought. Jewish thinkers such as Saadia ben Joseph al-Fayyumi (882–942) and Isaac Israeli (ca. 855–955) in the East and later Solomon Ibn-Gabirol (ca. 1021–1070) and Judah Halevi (ca. 1075–1141) in Spain worked with the same categories and used many of the same texts as their Islamic neighbors. Jews mixed socially with Muslims, often even serving as advisors to Muslim rulers. Moses Maimonides of Spain (1135–1204), the greatest of the medieval Jewish thinkers, even served the powerful sultan Saladin.

It was through Islamic and Jewish philosophers that Aristotle was reintroduced to the West, an event that radically changed the course of medieval philosophy.

The previous sentence, typical in Western descriptions of medieval Islamic and Jewish philosophies, represents a certain cultural bias. Clearly Islamic and Jewish thinkers did not live and work solely for the purpose of transmitting Aristotle, nor is our small collection of texts representative of the range of Jewish or Islamic thought. There is another story to tell, and a student wanting to move beyond the confines of Western philosophy would do well to consult some of the books listed here.

*   *   *

For general surveys, see De Lacy Evans O'Leary, *Arabic Thought and Its Place in History* (London: K. Paul, Trench, Trubner, 1939); T.J. de Boer, *The History of Philosophy in Islam,* translated by Edward R. Jones (New York: Dover, 1967); Majid Fakhry, *A History of Islamic Philosophy* (New York: Columbia University Press, 1970); Isaac Husik, *A History of Mediaeval Jewish Philosophy* (1916; reprinted New York: Atheneum, 1976); and Colette Sirat, *A History of Jewish Philosophy in the Middle Ages* (Cambridge: Cambridge University Press, 1985). A.J. Arberry, *Revelation and Reason in Islam* (London: George Allen & Unwin, 1957); F.E. Peters, *Aristotle and the Arabs: The Aristotelian Tradition in Islam* (New York: New York University Press, 1968); I.R. Netton, *Muslim Neoplatonists* (London: George Allen & Unwin, 1982); Herbert Davidson, *Proofs for Eternity, Creation, and the Existence of God in Medieval Islamic and Jewish Philosophy* (New York: Oxford University Press, 1987); and Mehdi

Ha'iri Yazdi, *The Principles of Epistemology in Islamic Philosophy* (Albany: State University of New York Press, 1992), provide studies of particular areas. For collections of essays, see Parviz Morewedge, ed., *Neoplatonism and Islamic Thought* (Albany: State University of New York Press, 1992), and Lenn E. Goodman, ed., *Neoplatonism and Jewish Thought* (Albany: State University of New York Press, 1992).

Avicenna
980–1037

Abū 'Alī al-Husayn Ibn 'Abd-Allāh Ibn Sīnā, better known as Avicenna, was a Persian born near the capital of the Samānid dynasty, Bukhara (today part of Uzbekistan). As a boy Avicenna showed exceptional intellectual abilities. By the age of ten he had learned Arabic and studied the *Qur'ān;* by age sixteen he had finished his study of medicine; and by age eighteen he had read and mastered all the philosophy available. Only with Aristotle's *Metaphysics* did he meet his match. He claimed he read it forty times without comprehension before finding al-Fārābī's clarifying commentary. Beginning at age eighteen Avicenna became a physician and aide to a series of princes and ministers. His associations often proved short-lived, and his fortunes waxed and waned with those of his patrons. During this time he wrote extensively on varied topics, including a medical book, *The Canon of Medicine,* which served as a reference work in Western Europe clear into the seventeenth century. He died at the age of fifty-eight, reportedly from a profligate life.

Using Aristotelian categories, Avicenna held that the study of "Being" is the proper study of metaphysics, and that this study applies in its fullest sense only to Allah. Only God has existence as a part of His nature. We could, for example, describe the characteristics of a given species without knowing whether such creatures actually exist; their existence is only possible, not necessary. But God's

213

essence includes *necessary* existence. This means that whatever is a part of God's essence is also necessary, and so all of God's attributes are necessary. By implication, then, God did not freely choose to create the world, since a necessary attribute of being God is being Creator. And if being Creator is a necessary attribute of the eternal God, then the world must have existed eternally and everything in the world must be exactly as it is, by necessity.

Using Neoplatonic categories, Avicenna explained that God did not create the world directly but through a series of intermediate Intelligences. The last of these Intelligences, "Active Intelligence" (associated with the moon), "created" the physical world by putting form onto matter. Our individual souls are also emanations from Active Intelligence, and Active Intelligence "imprints" forms into our souls, giving us the rational principles that are the basis of our knowledge.

While Avicenna used Aristotle's division of the soul into vegetative, animal, and rational parts, he held that the individual soul is separate from the body and that it is immortal—a view never explicitly stated by Aristotle. Because the soul can conceive of itself apart from a body, the soul must not be a material thing (thus anticipating Descartes' "I think, therefore I am" by six hundred years).

These three beliefs—that God acts out of necessity, that God emanates through intermediate Intelligences, and that the soul is immortal apart from the body—are all contrary to the teachings of the *Qur'ān*. Avicenna dealt with this problem by explaining that the *Qur'ān* uses symbolic or metaphorical language and that only the multitude took it literally.

The selection from *Concerning the Soul* given here explains how Active Intelligence imparts knowledge of the "middle terms" (universals) through intuition. The translation is that of Fazlur Rahman.

*　*　*

For translations and commentary on two of Avicenna's major works, see Avicenna, *Avicenna on Theology,* translated by Arthur J. Arberry (London: Murray, 1951), and Parviz Morewedge, *The "Metaphysica" of Avicenna* (London: Routledge & Kegan Paul, 1973).

For general information on Avicenna, see Soheil Muhsin Afnan, *Avicenna, His Life and Works* (London: George Allen & Unwin, 1958), or his autobiography, Avicenna, *The Life of Ibn Sina,* translated by William E. Gohlman (Albany: State University of New York Press, 1974). E.G. Brown, *Arabian Medicine* (Cambridge: Cambridge University Press, 1921), and Henri Corbin, *Avicenna and the Visionary Recital,* translated by W.R. Trask (New York: Pantheon, 1960), provide specialized studies, while Seyyed Hossein Nasr, *Three Muslim Sages: Avicenna, Suhrawardi, Ibn Arabi* (Cambridge, MA: Harvard University Press, 1964); David B. Burrell, *Knowing the Unknowable God: Ibn-Sina, Maimonides, Aquinas* (Notre Dame, IN: University of Notre Dame Press, 1986); and Herbert A. Davidson, *Alfarabi, Avicenna, and Averroes: Their Cosmologies, Theories of Active Intellect and Theories of the Human Intellect* (Oxford: Oxford University Press, 1992), offer comparisons to other thinkers.

CONCERNING THE SOUL (in part)

CHAPTER 1

The Vegetative Soul

When the elements are mixed together in a more harmonious way, i.e. in a more balanced proportion than in the cases previously mentioned, other beings also come into existence out of them due to the powers of the heavenly bodies. The first of these are plants. Now some plants are grown from seed and set aside a part of the body bearing the reproductive faculty, while others grow from spontaneous generation without seeds.

Since plants nourish themselves they have the faculty of nutrition. And because it is of the nature of plants to grow, it follows that they have the faculty of growth. Again, since it is the nature of certain plants to reproduce their like and to be reproduced by their like, they have a reproductive faculty. The reproductive faculty is different from the faculty of nutrition, for unripe fruits possess the nutritive but not the reproductive faculty; just as they possess the faculty of growth, but not that of reproduction. Similarly, the faculty of nutrition differs from that of growth. Do you not see that decrepit animals have the nutritive faculty but lack that of growth?

The nutritive faculty transmits food and replaces what has been dissolved with it; the faculty of growth increases the substance of the main structural organs in length, breadth, and depth, not haphazard but in such a way that they can reach the utmost perfection of growth. The reproductive faculty gives the matter the form of the thing; it separates from the parent body a part in which a faculty derived from its origin inheres and which, when the matter and the place which are prepared to receive its activity are present, performs its functions.

It will be evident from the foregoing that all vegetable, animal, and human functions are due to faculties over and above bodily functions, and even over and above the nature of the mixture itself.

After the plant comes the animal, which emerges from a compound of elements whose organic nature is much nearer to the mean than the previous two and is therefore prepared to receive the animal soul, having passed through the stage of the vegetable soul. And so the nearer it approaches the mean the greater is its capacity for receiving yet another psychical faculty more refined than the previous one.

The soul is like a single genus divisible in some way into three parts. The first is the vegetable soul, which is the first entelechy of a natural body possessing organs in so far as it is reproduced, grows, and assimilates nourishment. Food is a body whose function it is to become similar to the nature of the body whose food it is said to be, and adds to that body either in exact proportion or more or less what is dissolved.

The second is the animal soul, which is the first entelechy of a natural body possessing organs in so far as it perceives individuals and moves by volition.

The third is the human soul, which is the first entelechy of a natural body possessing organs in so far as it acts by rational choice and rational deduction, and in so far as it perceives universals.

Avicenna, *Concerning the Soul* from *Avicenna's Psychology,* translated by Fazlur Rahman (London: Geoffrey Cumberlege, Oxford University Press, 1952). Reprinted by permission of Oxford University Press.

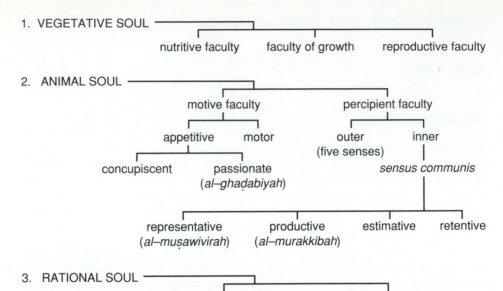

The vegetable soul has three faculties. First, the nutritive faculty which transforms another body into a body similar to that in which it is itself present, and replaces what has been dissolved. Secondly, the faculty of growth which increases every aspect of the body in which it resides, by length, breadth, and depth in proportion to the quantity necessary to make it attain its perfection in growth. Thirdly, the reproductive faculty which takes from the body in which it resides a part which is potentially similar to it and acts upon it with the help of other similar bodies, generating and mixing them so as to render that part actually similar to the body (to which it had been only potentially similar).

CHAPTER 2

The Animal Soul

The animal soul, according to the primary division, has two faculties—the motive and the perceptive. The motive faculty again is of two kinds: either it is motive in so far as it gives an impulse, or in so far as it is active. Now the motive faculty, in so far as it provides the impulse, is the faculty of appetence. When a desirable or repugnant image is imprinted on the imagination of which we shall speak before long, it rouses this faculty to movement. It has two subdivisions: one is called the faculty of desire which provokes a movement (of the organs) that brings one near to things imagined to be necessary or useful in the search for pleasure. The second is called the faculty of anger, which impels the subject to a movement of the limbs in order to repulse things imagined to be harmful or destructive, and thus to overcome them. As for the motive faculty in its active capacity, it is a power which is distributed through the nerves and muscles, and its function is to contract the muscles and to pull the tendons and ligaments towards the starting-point of the movement, or to relax them or stretch them so that they move away from the starting-point.

The perceptive faculty can be divided into two parts, the external sense and the internal sense. The external senses are the five or eight senses. One of them is sight, which is a faculty located in the concave nerve; it perceives the image of the forms of coloured bodies imprinted on the vitreous humour. These forms are transmitted through actually transparent media to polished surfaces. The second is the sense of hearing, which is a faculty located in the nerves distributed over the surface of the ear-hole; it perceives the form of what is transmitted to it by the vibration of the air which is compressed between two objects, one striking and the other being struck, the latter offering it resistance so as to set up vibrations in the air which produce the sound. This vibration of the air outside reaches the air which lies motionless and compressed in the cavity of the ear, moving it in a way similar to that in which it is itself moved. Its waves touch that nerve, and so it is heard.

The third sense is that of smell, a faculty located in the two protuberances of the front part of the brain which resemble the two nipples of the breasts. It perceives the odour conveyed to it by inhaled air, which is either mixed with the vapour in the air or is imprinted on it through qualitative change in the air produced by an odorous body.

The fourth sense is that of taste, a faculty located in the nerves distributed over the tongue, which perceives the taste dissolved from bodies touching it and mingling with the saliva it contains, thus producing a qualitative change in the tongue itself.

The fifth sense is that of touch, which is a faculty distributed over the entire skin and flesh of the body. The nerves perceive what touches them and are affected when it is opposed to them in quality, and changes are then wrought in their constitution or structure.

Probably this faculty is not one species but a genus including four faculties which are all distributed throughout the skin. The first of them judges the opposition between hot and cold; the second that between dry and moist; the third that between hard and soft; and the fourth that between rough and smooth. But their coexistence in the same organ gives the false impression that they are essentially one.

The forms of all the sensibles reach the organs of sense and are imprinted on them, and then the faculty of sensation perceives them. This is almost evident in touch, taste, smell, and hearing. But concerning sight, a different view has been maintained, for some people have thought that something issues from the eye, meets the object of sight, takes its form from without—and that this constitutes the act of seeing. They often call the thing which according to them issues from the eye, light.

But true philosophers hold the view that when an actually transparent body, i.e. a body which has no colour, intervenes between the eye and the object of sight, the exterior form of the coloured body on which light is falling is transmitted to the pupil of the eye and so the eye perceives it.

This transmission is similar to the transmission of colours by means of light being refracted from a coloured thing and giving its colour to another body. The resemblance is not complete, however, for the former is more like an image in a mirror.

The absurdity of the view that light issues from the eye is shown by the following consideration. What emanates is either a body or a non-body. If it is not a body it is absurd to attribute motion and change of place to it, except figuratively in that there may be a power in the eye which transforms the air and other things it encounters into some sort of quality, so that it may be said that this quality "came out of the eye." Likewise, it is absurd to hold the view that it is a body, because if so then either—

(1) it will remain intact, issuing from the eye and reaching to the sphere of the fixed stars. In this case there will have emerged from the eye, despite its smallness, a conical body of immense size, which will have compressed the air and repulsed all the heavenly bodies, or it will have traversed an empty space. Both these views are manifestly absurd. Or—

(2) it will be dispersed, diffused and split up. In that case the percipient animal will of necessity feel something being detached from him and then dispersed and diffused; also, he will perceive the spots where that ray falls to the exclusion of the spots where it does not fall, so that he will only partially perceive the body, sensing some points here and there but missing the major part. Or—

(3) this emanating body is united with the air and the heavens and becomes one with them, so that the uniform whole is like one organ of the animal. In this case the uniform whole in its entirety will possess sensation. This is a most peculiar change indeed! It follows necessarily that if many eyes co-operate, it will be more powerful. Thus a man when in the company of others would have keener sight than when alone, for many people can effect a more powerful change than a single person. Again, this emanating body will necessarily be either simple or composite, and its composite nature will also be of a particular kind. Its motion then must be either voluntary or natural. But we know that this movement is not voluntary and by choice, although the opening and closing of the eyelids are voluntary. The only remaining alternative is that the movement is natural. But the simple natural movement will be only in one direction, not in many; and so the composite movement will also be, according to the dominant element, only in one direction, not in many. But it is not so with this movement according to those who support the theory of the "issuing body."

Again, if the sensed object is seen through the base of the conical emanating body which touches it, and not through the angle, it will necessarily follow that the shape and magnitude of the object perceived at a distance will also be perceptible as well as its colour. This is because the percipient subject comes in contact with it and encompasses it. But if it is perceived through the angle, I mean the section between the vitrium and the hypothetical cone, then the remoter the object the smaller will be the angle and also the common section, and consequently the form imprinted on it will also be smaller and will be so perceived. Sometimes the angle will be so small that the object will fail to be perceived and so the form will not be seen at all.

As for the second part, namely that the emanating something is not a body but an accident or a quality, this "changing" or "being changed" will inevitably be more powerful with the increase of the percipient subjects. In that case the same absurdity which we mentioned before will arise. Again, the air will either be merely a medium of transmission or percipient in itself. If it is only a medium of transmission and not percipient, then, as we maintain, perception takes place in the pupil of the eye and not outside it. But if the percipient is the air, then the same absurdity which we have already mentioned will be repeated; and it will necessarily follow that whenever there is commotion or disturbance in the air, sight will be distorted with the renewal of "change" and the renewed action of the percipient in perceiving one thing after another, just as when a man runs in calm air his perception of minute things is confused. All this shows that sight is not due to something issuing from us towards the sensed object. It must therefore be due to something coming towards us from the sensed object; since this is not the body of the object, it must be its form. If this view were not correct, the creation of the eye with all its strata and humours and their respective shape and structure would be useless.

*   *   *

CHAPTER 4

The Rational Soul

The human rational soul is also divisible into a practical and a theoretical faculty, both of which are equivocally called intelligence. The practical faculty is the principle of movement of the human body, which urges it to individual actions characterized by deliberation and in accordance with purposive considerations. This faculty has a certain correspondence with the animal faculties of appetence, imagination, and estimation, and a certain dual character in itself. Its relationship to the animal faculty of appetence is that certain states arise in it peculiar to man by which it is disposed to quick actions and passions such as shame, laughter, weeping, etc. Its relationship to the animal faculty of imagination and estimation is that it uses that faculty to deduce plans concerning transitory things and to deduce human arts. Finally, its own dual character is that with the help of the theoretical intelligence it forms the ordinary and commonly accepted opinions concerning actions, as, for instance, that lies and tyranny are evil and other similar premises which, in books of logic, have been clearly distinguished from the purely rational ones. This faculty must govern all the other faculties of the body in accordance with the laws of another faculty which we shall mention, so that it should not submit to them but that they should be subordinated to it, lest passive dispositions arising from the body and derived from material things should develop in it. These passive dispositions are called bad morals. But far from being passive and submissive this faculty must govern the other bodily faculties so that it may have excellent morals.

It is also possible to attribute morals to the bodily faculties. But if the latter predominate they are in an active state, while the practical intelligence is in a passive one. Thus the same thing produces morals in both. But if the practical intelligence predominates, it is in an active state while the bodily faculties are in a passive one, and this is morals in the strict sense (even so there would be two dispositions or moral characters); or character is only one with two different relationships. If we examine them more closely the reason why morals are attributed to this faculty is that the human soul, as will be shown later, is a single substance which is related to two planes—the one higher and the other lower than itself. It has special faculties which establish the relationship between itself and each plane: the practical faculty which the human soul possesses in relation to the lower plane, which is the body, and its control and management; and the theoretical faculty in relation to the higher plane, from which it passively receives and acquires intelligibles. It is as if our soul has two faces: one turned towards the body and it must not be influenced by any requirements of the bodily nature; and the other turned towards the higher principles, and it must always be ready to receive from what is There in the Higher Plane and to be influenced by it. So much for the practical faculty.

* * *

CHAPTER 6

How the Rational Soul Acquires Knowledge

The acquisition of knowledge, whether from someone else or from within oneself, is of various degrees. Some people who acquire knowledge come very near to immediate perception, since their potential intellect which precedes the capacity we have mentioned is the most powerful. If a person can acquire knowledge from within himself, this strong capacity is called "intuition." It is so strong in certain people that they do not need great effort, or instruction and actualization, in order to make contact with the active intelligence. But the primary capacity of such a person for this is so powerful that he might also be said to possess the second capacity; indeed, it seems as though he knows everything from within himself. This is the highest degree of this capacity. In this state the material intelligence must be called "Divine Spirit." It belongs to the genus of *intellectus in habitu,* but is so lofty that not all people share it. It is not unlikely, indeed, that some of these actions attributed to the "Divine Intelligence" because of their powerful and lofty nature overflow into the imagination which symbolizes them in sense-imagery and words in the way which we have previously indicated.

What proves this is the evident fact that the intelligible truths are acquired only when the middle term of a syllogism is obtained. This may be done in two ways: sometimes through intuition, which is an act of mind by which the mind itself immediately perceives the middle term. This power of intuition is quickness of apprehension. But sometimes the middle term is acquired through instruction, although even the first principles of instruction are obtained through intuition, since all knowledge can be reduced ultimately to certain intuitive principles handed down by those who first accepted them to their students.

It is possible that a man may find the truth within himself, and that the syllogism may be effected in his mind without any teacher. This varies both quantitatively and qualitatively; quantitatively, because some people possess a greater number of middle terms which they have discovered themselves; and qualitatively, because some people find the term more quickly than others. Now since these differences are unlimited and always vary in degrees of intensity, and since their lowest point is reached in men who are wholly without intuition, so their highest point must be reached in people who possess intuition regarding all or most problems, or in people who have intuition in the shortest possible time. Thus there might be a man whose soul has such an intense purity and is so firmly linked to the rational principles that he blazes with intuition, i.e. with the receptivity of inspiration coming from the active intelligence concerning everything. So the forms of all things contained in the active intelligence are imprinted on his soul either all at once or nearly so, not that he accepts them merely on authority but on account of their logical order which encompasses all the middle terms. For beliefs accepted on authority concerning those things which are known only through their causes possess no rational certainty. This is a kind of prophetic inspiration, indeed its highest form and the one most fitted to be called Divine Power; and it is the highest human faculty.

The Hierarchy of Faculties

It should be seen how some of these faculties govern others. You will find the acquired intellect to be the governor whom all the rest serve. It is the ultimate goal. The *intellectus in habitu* serves the *intellectus in actu,* and is in turn served by the material intellect with all its capacities. The practical intellect serves them all, for attachment to the body, as will shortly become clear, exists for the sake of the perfection and purification of the theoretical intellect, and the practical intellect governs this relationship. It is served by the faculty of estimation which, in its turn, is served by two faculties: an anterior and a posterior. The posterior conserves what is brought to it by estimation, while the anterior is the totality of animal faculties. The faculty of representation is served by two faculties of different origins: the appetitive faculty serves it by obeying it, for the representative faculty impels the appetitive to movement, and the faculty of imagination serves it by accepting the combination and separation of its images. In their turn those two are the governors of two groups. The faculty of imagination is served by *fantasia* or *sensus communis,* which is itself served by the five senses, while the appetitive faculty is served by desire and anger. These last two are served by the motive faculty distributed through the muscles. Here the animal faculties come to an end.

The animal faculties in their entirety are served by the vegetable faculties, of which the reproductive is the first in rank and the highest one. The faculty of growth serves the reproductive, and the nutritive faculty serves them both. The four "natural" faculties—of digestion, retention, assimilation, and excretion—are subservient to all these. The digestive faculty is served on the one hand by the retentive and the assimilative, and on the other by the excretive. The four physical qualities serve these, with cold subservient to heat, while dryness and moisture serve them both. This is the last degree of the faculties.

*   *   *

CHAPTER 12

Concerning the Temporal Origin of the Soul

We say that human souls are of the same species and concept. If they existed before the body, they would either be multiple entities or one single entity. But it is impossible for them to be either the one or the other, as will be shown later, therefore it is impossible for them to exist before the body. We now begin with the explanation of the impossibility of its numerical multiplicity and say that the mutual difference of the souls before [their attachment to] bodies is either due to their quiddity and form; or to the element and matter which is multiple in space, a particular part of which each matter occupies; or to the various times peculiar to every soul when it becomes existent in its matter; or to the causes which divide their matter. But their difference is not due to their quiddity or form, since their form is one, therefore their difference is due to the recipient of the quiddity or to the body to which the quiddity is specifically related. Before its attachment to the body the soul is quiddity pure and simple; thus it is impossible for one soul to be numerically different from another, or for the quiddity to admit of essential differentiation. This holds absolutely true in all cases; for the multiplicity of the species of those things whose essences are pure concepts is only due to the substrata which receive them and to what is affected by them, or due only to their times. But when they are absolutely separate, i.e. when the categories we have enumerated are not applicable to them, they cannot be diverse. It is therefore impossible for them to have any kind of diversity or multiplicity among them. Thus it is untrue that before they enter bodies souls have numerically different essences.

I say that it is also impossible for souls to have numerically one essence, for when two bodies come into existence two souls also come into existence in them. Then either—

1. these two souls are two parts of the same single soul, in which case one single thing which does not possess any magnitude and bulk would be potentially divisible. This is manifestly absurd according to the principles established in physics. Or—
2. a soul which is numerically one would be in two bodies. This also does not require much effort to refute.

It is thus proved that the soul comes into existence when ever a body does so fit to be used by it. The body which thus comes into being is the kingdom and instrument of the soul. In the very disposition of the substance of the soul which comes into existence together with a certain body—a body, that is to say, with the appropriate qualities to make it suitable to receive the soul which takes its origin from the first principles— there is a natural yearning to occupy itself with that body, to use it, control it, and be attracted by it. This yearning binds the soul specially to this body, and turns it away from other bodies different from it in nature so that the soul does not contact them except through it. Thus when the principle of its individualization, namely, its peculiar dispositions, occurs to it, it becomes an individual. These dispositions determine its attachment to that particular body and form the relationship of their mutual suitability, although this relationship and its condition may be obscure to us. The soul achieves its first entelechy through the body; its subsequent development, however, does not depend on the body but on its own nature.

But after their separation from their bodies the souls remain individual owing to the different matters in which they had been, and owing to the times of their birth and their different dispositions due to their bodies which necessarily differ because of their peculiar conditions.

*   *   *

CHAPTER 13

The Soul Does Not Die with the Death of the Body; It Is Incorruptible

We say that the soul does not die with the death of the body and is absolutely incorruptible. As for the former proposition, this is because everything which is corrupted with the corruption of something else is in some way attached to it. And anything which in some way is attached to something else is either coexistent with it or posterior to it in existence or prior to it, this priority being essential and not temporal. If, then, the soul is so attached to the body that it is coexistent with it, and this is not accidental but pertains to its essence, then they are essentially interdependent. Then neither the soul nor the body would be a substance; but in fact they are substances. And if this is an accidental and not an essential attachment, then, with the corruption of the one term only the accidental relationship of the other term will be annulled, but its being will not be corrupted with its corruption. If the soul is so attached to the body that it is posterior to it in existence, then, in that case, the body will be the cause of the soul's existence. Now the causes are four; so either the body is the efficient cause of the soul and gives it existence, or it is its receptive and material cause—maybe by way of composition as the elements are for the body or by way of simplicity as bronze is for the statue—or the body is the soul's formal or final cause. But the body cannot be the soul's efficient cause, for body, as such, does not act; it acts only through its faculties. If it were to act through its essence, not through its faculties, every body would act in the same way. Again, the bodily faculties are all of them either accidents or material forms, and it is impossible that either accidents or forms subsisting in matter should produce the being of a self-subsisting entity independent of matter or that of an absolute substance. Nor is it possible that the body should be the receptive and material cause of the soul, for we have clearly shown and proved that the soul is in no way imprinted in the body. The body, then, is not "informed" with the form of the soul, either by way of simplicity or composition so that certain parts of the body are composed and mixed together in a certain way and then the soul is imprinted in them. It is also impossible that the body should be the formal or the final cause of the soul, for the reverse is the more plausible case.

Thus the attachment of the soul to the body is not the attachment of an effect to a necessary cause. The truth is that the body and the temperament are an accidental cause of the soul, for when the matter of a body suitable to become the instrument of the soul and its proper subject comes into existence, the separate causes bring into being the individual soul, and that is how the soul originates from them. This is because it is impossible to bring arbitrarily into being different souls without any specific cause. Besides, the soul does not admit of numerical multiplicity, as we have shown. Again, whenever a new thing comes into being, it must be preceded by a matter which is prepared to receive it or to have a relationship with it, as has been shown in the other sciences. Again, if an individual soul were to come into being without an instrument through which it acts and attains perfection, its being would be purposeless; but there is nothing purposeless in nature. In truth, when the suitability and preparation for such a relationship exist in the instrument, it becomes necessary that such a thing as a soul should originate from the separate causes.

But if the existence of one thing necessitates the existence of another, the corruption of the former does not necessarily entail that of the latter. This happens only where its very being subsists through or in that thing. Many things originating from other things survive the latter's corruption; when their being does not subsist in them, and especially when they owe their existence to something other than what was merely preparatory for the emanation of their being. And the being of the soul does in fact emanate from something different from the body and bodily functions, as we have shown; its source of emanation must be something different from the body. Thus when the soul owes its being to that other thing and only the time of its realization to the body, its being would be independent of the body which is only its accidental cause; it cannot then be said that they have a mutual relationship which would necessitate the body preceding the soul as its necessary cause.

Let us turn to the third division which we mentioned in the beginning, namely, that the attachment of the soul to the body might be in the sense that the soul is prior to the body in existence. Now in that case the priority will be either temporal as well as essential, and so the soul's being could not possibly be attached to the body since it precedes the body in time, or the priority will be only essential and not temporal, for in time the soul will not be separate from the body. This sort of priority means that when the prior entity comes into existence, the being of the posterior entity must follow from it. Then the prior entity cannot exist, if the posterior is supposed to be non-existent. I do not say that the supposition of the non-existence of the posterior necessitates the non-existence of the prior, but that the posterior cannot be non-existent except when first something has naturally happened to the prior which has made it nonexistent, too. Thus it is not the supposition of the non-existence of the posterior entity which necessitates the nonexistence of the prior, but the supposition of the non-existence of the prior itself, for the posterior can be supposed to be non-existent only after the prior itself has ceased to exist. This being so, it follows that the cause of non-existence must occur in the substance of the soul necessitating the body's corruption along with it, and that the body cannot be corrupted through a cause special to itself. But in fact the corruption of the body does take place through a cause special to itself, namely, through changes in its composition and its temperament. Thus it is false to hold that the soul is attached to the body as essentially prior to it, and that at the same time the body is indeed corrupted through a cause in itself; so no such relationship subsists between the two.

This being so, all the forms of attachment between the body and the soul have proved to be false and it only remains that the soul, in its being, has no relationship with the body but is related with other principles which are not subject to change or corruption.

As for the proposition that the soul does not admit of corruption at all, I say that there is another conclusive reason for the immortality of the soul. Everything which might be corrupted through some cause has in itself the potentiality of corruption and, before corruption, has the actuality of persistence. But it is absurd that a single thing in the same sense should possess both, the potentiality of corruption and the actuality of persistence; its potentiality of corruption cannot be due to its actual persistence, for the concept of potentiality is contrary to that of actuality. Also, the relation of this potentiality is opposed to the relation of this actuality, for the one is related with corruption, the other with persistence. These two concepts, then, are attributable to two different factors in the concrete thing. Hence we say that the actuality of persistence and the potentiality of corruption may be combined in composite things and in such simple things as subsist in composite ones. But these two concepts cannot come together in simple things whose essence is separate. I say in another absolute sense that these two concepts cannot exist together in a simple thing whose essence is unitary. This is because everything which persists and has the potentiality of corruption also has the potentiality of persistence, since its persistence is not necessary. When it is not necessary, it is possible; and possibility is of the nature of potentiality. Thus the potentiality of persistence is in its very substance. But, of course, it is clear that the actuality of persistence of a thing is not the same as its potentiality of persistence. Thus its actuality of persistence is a fact which happens to the body which has the potentiality of persistence. Therefore that potentiality does not belong to something actual but to something of which actual existence is only an accident and does not constitute its real essence. From this it necessarily follows that its being is composed of a factor the possession of which gives actual existence to it (this factor is the form in every concrete existent), and another factor which attains this actual existence but which in itself has only the potentiality of existence (and this factor is the matter in the concrete existent).

So if the soul is absolutely simple and is not divisible into matter and form, it will not admit of corruption. But if it is composite, let us leave the composite and consider only the substance which is its matter. We say: either that matter will continue to be divisible and so the same analysis will go on being applied to it and we shall then have a regress *ad infinitum,* which is absurd; or this substance and base will never cease to exist. But if so, then our present discourse is devoted to this factor which is the base and origin (i.e. the substance) and not to the composite thing which is composed of this factor and some other. So it is clear that everything which is simple and not composite, or which is the origin and base (i.e. the substance) of the composite thing, cannot in itself possess both the actuality of persistence and the potentiality of corruption. If it has the potentiality of corruption, it cannot possibly have the actuality of persistence, and if it has the actuality of persistence and existence, it cannot have the potentiality of corruption. Obviously, then, the substance of the soul does not have the potentiality of corruption. Of those things which come to be and are corrupted, the corruptible is only the concrete composite. The potentiality of corruption and of persistence at the same time does not belong to something which gives unity to the composite, but to the matter which potentially admits of both contraries. So the corruptible composite as such possesses neither the potentiality of persistence nor that of corruption, let alone both. As to the matter itself, it either has persistence not due to any potentiality, which gives it the capacity for persistence—as some people think—or it has persistence through a potentiality which gives it persistence, but does not have the potentiality of corruption; this latter being something which it acquires. The potentiality of corruption of simple entities which subsist in matter is due to matter and is not in their own substance. The argument which proves that everything which comes to exist passes away on account of the finitude of the potentialities of persistence and corruption is relevant only to those things whose being is composed of matter and form. Matter has the potentiality that this form may persist in it, and at the same time the potentiality that this form may cease to exist in it. It is then obvious that the soul is absolutely incorruptible. This is the point which we wanted to make, and this is what we wanted to prove.

Averroës
1126–1198

Abū al-Walīd Muhammad Ibn Ahmed Ibn Rushd, better known as Averroës, was born into a prominent family of jurists in Córdoba, Spain. Moving in high society, Averroës made the acquaintance of the sultan of Marrakesh and, through the sultan's favor, became a *qādī*, or judge, serving first in Seville and later in Córdoba. The sultan also expressed an interest in philosophy and commissioned Averroës to write three sets of commentaries (short, intermediate, and long) on each of Aristotle's writings. These commentaries were to become so influential in Western Europe that Averroës became known simply as "The Commentator." In addition to the thirty-eight commentaries he produced on Aristotle, Averroës also wrote books on politics, religion, logic, astronomy, and medicine. His expertise in medicine led to his being called to Marrakesh to serve as the sultan's personal physician in 1182. He remained in that post until 1195 when he was forced to leave for religious reasons (apparently because of his glorification of Aristotle). He regained his standing and returned to Marrakesh shortly before his death in 1198. Soon after his death Islamic culture in Spain virtually disappeared; and while his thought continued to influence Latin Europe, Averroës had surprisingly little impact on the Muslim world.

Through his writings Averroës sought to counter two misconceptions. First, he wrote his commentaries to rid Aristotle of the misinterpretations of Avicenna and others. For example, Averroës rejected Avicenna's doctrine of the immortality of the soul. Instead he agreed with Aristotle that individual souls cannot exist apart from a body. But in agreement with the teachings of the *Qur'ān,* Averroës also taught that there is a bodily resurrection. According to Averroës, after death we receive new bodies which "emanate from the heavenly bodies." In this way he denied Avicenna's immortality of the soul and managed to agree with both Aristotle and the *Qur'ān.*

While Averroës was opposed to several of Avicenna's teachings, he was even more opposed to Avicenna's chief critic, al-Ghazālī. Al-Ghazālī (1058–1111) had opposed Avicenna's three controversial positions (see the previous introduction to Avicenna), claiming that Avicenna had put philosophy above the *Qur'ān.* In his major work, *The Incoherence of Philosophy,* al-Ghazālī had argued that philosophy led to disbelief in Allah. In his rejoinder, *The Incoherence of the Incoherence,* Averroës sought to refute al-Ghazālī by dividing people into three classes. The majority of people can understand truth only in imaginative form. For them philosophy would, indeed, be dangerous and they must take the *Qur'ān* literally. A smaller group of people, the theologians, can understand dialectical arguments and draw probable inferences from the *Qur'ān.* But the elite, the philosophers, are capable of understanding truth in its pure, rational form. For them, the *Qur'ān* can be read for its "deeper" allegorical meanings.

As Averroës' teachings reached Christendom, this last (allegorical) conviction was taken to mean he advocated a "double truth": Truth in philosophy might be entirely different—even opposite—from truth in religion. Averroës himself denied this in his *Decisive Treatise Determining the Nature of the Connection Between Religion and Philosophy,* given here, complete, in the George F. Hourani translation. In the *Decisive Treatise* Averroës claims that there is only one truth, but that there are many ways to access this truth. Unfortunately for Averroës' reputation, this work was lost to the West until the Renaissance.

*   *   *

For Averroës' major work, see Averroës, *Tahafut al-Tahafut (The Incoherence of the Incoherence),* translated by Simon van den Bergh (London: Luzac, 1954). For the work he was opposing, see al-Ghazālī, *Tahafut al-Falsifah (The Incoherence of the Philosophers),* translated by Sabih Ahmad Kamali (Lahore, Pakistan: Pakistan Philosophical Congress, 1963); and for a medieval response see Thomas Aquinas, *On The Unity of the Intellect Against the Averroists,* translated by Beatrice H. Zedler (Milwaukee, WI: Marquette University Press, 1968).

For a general overview of Averroës' thought, see Oliver Leaman, *Averroës and His Philosophy* (Oxford: Oxford University Press, 1988). For more specialized studies see Barry S. Kogan, *Averroës and the Metaphysics of Causation* (Albany: State University of New York Press, 1985), and Herbert A. Davidson, *Alfarabi, Avicenna, and Averroës: Their Cosmologies, Theories of Active Intellect and Theories of the Human Intellect* (Oxford: Oxford University Press, 1992).

THE DECISIVE TREATISE, DETERMINING THE NATURE OF THE CONNECTION BETWEEN RELIGION AND PHILOSOPHY

What is the attitude of the Law to philosophy?

Thus spoke the lawyer, *imām,* judge, and unique scholar, Abul Walīd Muḥammad Ibn Aḥmad Ibn Rushd:

Praise be to God with all due praise, and a prayer for Muhammad His chosen servant and apostle. The purpose of this treatise is to examine, from the standpoint of the study of the Law, whether the study of philosophy and logic is allowed by the Law, or prohibited, or commanded—either by way of recommendation or as obligatory.

CHAPTER 1

The Law Makes Philosophic Studies Obligatory

If teleological study of the world is philosophy, and if the Law commands such a study, then the Law commands philosophy.

We say: If the activity of "philosophy" is nothing more than study of existing beings and reflection on them as indications of the Artisan, i.e. inasmuch as they are products of art (for beings only indicate the Artisan through our knowledge of the art in them, and the more perfect this knowledge is, the more perfect the knowledge of the Artisan becomes), and if the Law has encouraged and urged reflection on beings, then it is clear that what this name signifies is either obligatory or recommended by the Law.

The Law commands such a study.

That the Law summons to reflection on beings, and the pursuit of knowledge about them, by the intellect is clear from several verses of the Book of God, Blessed and Exalted, such as the saying of the Exalted, "Reflect, you have vision:" (lix, 2)* this is textual authority for the obligation to use intellectual reasoning, or a combination of intellectual and legal reasoning. Another example is His saying, "Have they not studied the kingdom of the heavens and the earth, and whatever things God has created?" (viii, 185): this is a text urging the study of the totality of beings. Again, God the Exalted has taught that one of those whom He singularly honoured by this knowledge was Abraham, peace on him, for the Exalted said, "So we made Abraham see the kingdom of the heavens and the earth, that he might be" [and so on to the end

*[References from the *Qur'ān* are noted in parentheses in the text.]

From *Averroes on the Harmony of Religion and Philosophy,* translated by George F. Hourani (London: Luzac & Co., 1961).

of the verse] (vi, 75). The Exalted also said, "Do they not observe the camels, how they have been created, and the sky, how it has been raised up?" (lxxxviii, 17–18), and He said, "and they give thought to the creation of the heavens and the earth" (iii, 191), and so on in countless other verses.

This study must be conducted in the best manner, by demonstrative reasoning.
Since it has now been established that the Law has rendered obligatory the study of beings by the intellect, and reflection on them, and since reflection is nothing more than inference and drawing out of the unknown from the known, and since this is reasoning or at any rate done by reasoning, therefore we are under an obligation to carry on our study of beings by intellectual reasoning. It is further evident that this manner of study, to which the Law summons and urges, is the most perfect kind of study using the most perfect kind of reasoning; and this is the kind called "demonstration."

To master this instrument the religious thinker must make a preliminary study of logic, just as the lawyer must study legal reasoning. This is no more heretical in the one case than in the other. And logic must be learned from the ancient masters, regardless of the fact that they were not Muslims.
The Law, then, has urged us to have demonstrative knowledge of God the Exalted and all the beings of His creation. But it is preferable and even necessary for anyone, who wants to understand God the Exalted and the other beings demonstratively, to have first understood the kinds of demonstration and their conditions [of validity], and in what respects demonstrative reasoning differs from dialectical, rhetorical and fallacious reasoning. But this is not possible unless he has previously learned what reasoning as such is, and how many kinds it has, and which of them are valid and which invalid. This in turn is not possible unless he has previously learned the parts of reasoning, of which it is composed, i.e. the premises and their kinds. Therefore he who believes in the Law, and obeys its command to study beings, ought prior to his study to gain a knowledge of these things, which have the same place in theoretical studies as instruments have in practical activities.

For just as the lawyer infers from the Divine command to him to acquire knowledge of the legal categories that he is under obligation to know the various kinds of legal syllogisms, and which are valid and which invalid, in the same way he who would know [God] ought to infer from the command to study beings that he is under obligation to acquire a knowledge of intellectual reasoning and its kinds. Indeed it is more fitting for him to do so, for if the lawyer infers from the saying of the Exalted, "Reflect, you who have vision," the obligation to acquire a knowledge of legal reasoning, how much more fitting and proper that he who would know God should infer from it the obligation to acquire a knowledge of intellectual reasoning!

It cannot be objected: "This kind of study of intellectual reasoning is a heretical innovation since it did not exist among the first believers." For the study of legal reasoning and its kinds is also something which has been discovered since the first believers, yet it is not considered to be a heretical innovation. So the objector should believe the same about the study of intellectual reasoning. (For this there is a reason, which it is not the place to mention here.) But most [masters] of this religion support intellectual reasoning, except a small group of gross literalists, who can be refuted by [sacred] texts.

Since it has now been established that there is an obligation of the Law to study intellectual reasoning and its kinds, just as there is an obligation to study legal reasoning, it is clear that, if none of our predecessors had formerly examined intellectual reasoning and its kinds, we should be obliged to undertake such an examination from the beginning, and that each succeeding scholar would have to seek help in that task from his predecessor in order that knowledge of the subject might be completed. For it is difficult or impossible for one man to find out by himself and from the beginning all that he needs of that subject, as it is difficult for one man to discover all the knowledge that he needs of the kinds of legal reasoning; indeed this is even truer of knowledge of intellectual reasoning.

But if someone other than ourselves has already examined that subject, it is clear that we ought to seek help towards our goal from what has been said by such a predecessor on the subject, regardless of whether this other one shares our religion or not. For when a valid sacrifice is performed with a certain instrument, no account is taken, in judging the validity of the sacrifice, of whether the instrument belongs to one who shares our religion or to one who does not, so long as it fulfils the conditions for validity. By "those who do not share our religion" I refer to those ancients who studied these matters before Islam. So if such is the case, and everything that is required in the study of the subject of intellectual syllogisms has already been examined in the most perfect manner by the ancients, presumably we ought to lay hands on their books in order to study what they said about that subject; and if it is all correct we should accept it from them, while if there is anything incorrect in it, we should draw attention to that.

After logic we must proceed to philosophy proper. Here too we have to learn from our predecessors, just as in mathematics and law. Thus it is wrong to forbid the study of ancient philosophy. Harm from it is accidental, like harm from taking medicine, drinking water, or studying law.

When we have finished with this sort of study and acquired the instruments by whose aid we are able to reflect on beings and the indications of art in them (for he who does not understand the art does not understand the product of art, and he who does not understand the product of art does not understand the Artisan), then we ought to begin the examination of beings in the order and manner we have learned from the art of demonstrative syllogisms.

And again it is clear that in the study of beings this aim can be fulfilled by us perfectly only through successive examinations of them by one man after another, the later ones seeking the help of the earlier in that task, on the model of what has happened in the mathematical sciences. For if we suppose that the art of geometry did not exist in this age of ours, and likewise the art of astronomy, and a single person wanted to ascertain by himself the sizes of the heavenly bodies, their shapes, and their distances from each other, that would not be possible for him—e.g. to know the proportion of the sun to the earth or other facts about the sizes of the stars—even though he were the most intelligent of men by nature, unless by a revelation or something resembling revelation. Indeed if he were told that the sun is about 150 or 160 times as great as the earth, he would think this statement madness on the part of the speaker, although this is a fact which has been demonstrated in astronomy so surely that no one who has mastered that science doubts it.

But what calls even more strongly for comparison with the art of mathematics in this respect is the art of the principles of law; and the study of law itself was completed only over a long period of time. And if someone today wanted to find out by himself all the arguments which have been discovered by the theorists of the legal schools on controversial questions, about which debate has taken place between them in most countries of Islam (except the West), he would deserve to be ridiculed, because such a task is impossible for him, apart from the fact that the work has been done already. Moreover, this is a situation that is self-evident not in the scientific arts alone but also in the practical arts; for there is not one of them which a single man can construct by himself. Then how can he do it with the art of arts, philosophy? If this is so, then whenever we find in the works of our predecessors of former nations a theory about beings and a reflection on them conforming to what the conditions of demonstration require, we ought to study what they said about the matter and what they affirmed in their books. And we should accept from them gladly and gratefully whatever in these books accords with the truth, and draw attention to and warn against what does not accord with the truth, at the same time excusing them.

From this it is evident that the study of the books of the ancients is obligatory by Law, since their aim and purpose in their books is just the purpose to which the Law has urged us, and that whoever forbids the study of them to anyone who is fit to study them, i.e. anyone who unites two qualities, (1) natural intelligence and (2) religious integrity and moral virtue, is blocking people from the door by which the Law summons them to knowledge of God, the door of theoretical study which leads to the truest knowledge of Him; and such an act is the extreme of ignorance and estrangement from God the Exalted.

And if someone errs or stumbles in the study of these books owing to a deficiency in his natural capacity, or bad organization of his study of them, or being dominated by his passions, or not finding a teacher to guide him to an understanding of their contents, or a combination of all or more than one of these causes, it does not follow that one should forbid them to anyone who is qualified to study them. For this manner of harm which arises owing to them is something that is attached to them by accident, not by essence; and when a thing is beneficial by its nature and essence, it ought not to be shunned because of something harmful contained in it by accident. This was the thought of the Prophet, peace on him, on the occasion when he ordered a man to give his brother honey to drink for his diarrhoea, and the diarrhoea increased after he had given him the honey: when the man complained to him about it, he said, "God spoke the truth; it was your brother's stomach that lied." We can even say that a man who prevents a qualified person from studying books of philosophy, because some of the most vicious people may be thought to have gone astray through their study of them, is like a man who prevents a thirsty person from drinking cool, fresh water until he dies of thirst, because some people have choked to death on it. For death from water by choking is an accidental matter, but death by thirst is essential and necessary.

Moreover, this accidental effect of this art is a thing which may also occur accidentally from the other arts. To how many lawyers has law been a cause of lack of piety and immersion in this world! Indeed we find most lawyers in this state, although their art by its essence calls for nothing but practical virtue. Thus it is not strange if the same thing that occurs accidentally in the art which calls for practical virtue should occur accidentally in the art which calls for intellectual virtue.

For every Muslim the Law has provided a way to truth suitable to his nature, through demonstrative, dialectical or rhetorical methods.

Since all this is now established, and since we, the Muslim community, hold that this divine religion of ours is true, and that it is this religion which incites and summons us to the happiness that consists in the knowledge of God, Mighty and Majestic, and of His creation, that [end] is appointed for every Muslim by the method of assent which his temperament and nature require. For the natures of men are on different levels with respect to [their paths to] assent. One of them comes to assent through demonstration; another comes to assent through dialectical arguments, just as firmly as the demonstrative man through demonstration, since his nature does not contain any greater capacity;

while another comes to assent through rhetorical arguments, again just as firmly as the demonstrative man through demonstrative arguments.

Thus since this divine religion of ours has summoned people by these three methods, assent to it has extended to everyone, except him who stubbornly denies it with his tongue or him for whom no method of summons to God the Exalted has been appointed in religion owing to his own neglect of such matters. It was for this purpose that the Prophet, peace on him, was sent with a special mission to "the white man and the black man" alike; I mean because his religion embraces all the methods of summons to God the Exalted. This is clearly expressed in the saying of God the Exalted, "Summon to the way of your Lord by wisdom and by good preaching, and debate with them in the most effective manner" (xvi, 125).

CHAPTER 2

Philosophy Contains Nothing Opposed to Islam

Demonstrative truth and scriptural truth cannot conflict.

Now since this religion is true and summons to the study which leads to knowledge of the Truth, we the Muslim community know definitely that demonstrative study does not lead to [conclusions] conflicting with what Scripture has given us; for truth does not oppose truth but accords with it and bears witness to it.

If the apparent meaning of Scripture conflicts with demonstrative conclusions it must be interpreted allegorically, i.e. metaphorically.

This being so, whenever demonstrative study leads to any manner of knowledge about any being, that being is inevitably either unmentioned or mentioned in Scripture. If it is unmentioned there is no contradiction, and it is in the same case as an act whose category is unmentioned, so that the lawyer has to infer it by reasoning from Scripture. If Scripture speaks about it, the apparent meaning of the words inevitably either accords or conflicts with the conclusions of demonstration about it. If this [apparent meaning] accords there is no argument. If it conflicts there is a call for allegorical interpretation of it. The meaning of "allegorical interpretation" is: extension of the significance of an expression from real to metaphorical significance, without forsaking therein the standard metaphorical practices of Arabic, such as calling a thing by the name of something resembling it or a cause or consequence or accompaniment of it, or other things such as are enumerated in accounts of the kinds of metaphorical speech.

If the lawyer can do this, the religious thinker certainty can. Indeed these allegorical interpretations always receive confirmation from the apparent meaning of other passages of Scripture.

Now if the lawyer does this in many decisions of religious law, with how much more right is it done by the possessor of demonstrative knowledge! For the lawyer has at his disposition only reasoning based on opinion, while he who would know [God] [has at his disposition] reasoning based on certainty. So we affirm definitely that whenever the conclusion of a demonstration is in conflict with the apparent meaning of Scripture, that apparent meaning admits of allegorical interpretation according to the rules for such interpretation in Arabic. This proposition is questioned by no Muslim and doubted by no believer. But its certainty is immensely increased for those who have had close dealings with this idea and put it to the test, and made it their aim to reconcile the assertions of intellect and tradition. Indeed we may say that whenever a statement in Scripture conflicts in its apparent meaning with a conclusion of demonstration, if Scripture is considered carefully, and the rest of its contents searched page by page, there will invariably be found among the expressions of Scripture something which in its apparent meaning bears witness to that allegorical interpretation or comes close to bearing witness.

All Muslims accept the principle of allegorical interpretation; they only disagree about the extent of its application.

In the light of this idea the Muslims are unanimous in holding that it is not obligatory either to take all the expressions of Scripture in their apparent meaning or to extend them all from their apparent meaning by allegorical interpretation. They disagree [only] over which of them should and which should not be so interpreted: the Ash'arites for instance give an allegorical interpretation to the verse about God's directing Himself and the Tradition about His descent, while the Hanbalites take them in their apparent meaning.

The double meaning has been given to suit people's diverse intelligence. The apparent contradictions are meant to stimulate the learned to deeper study.

The reason why we have received a Scripture with both an apparent and an inner meaning lies in the diversity of people's natural capacities and the difference of their innate dispositions with regard to assent. The reason why we have received in Scripture texts whose apparent meanings contradict each other is in order to draw the attention of those who are well grounded in science to the interpretation which reconciles them. This is the idea referred to in the words received from the Exalted, "He it is who has sent down to you the Book, containing certain verses clear and definite" [and so on] down to the words "those who are well grounded in science" (iii, 7).

In interpreting texts allegorically we must never violate Islamic consensus, when it is certain. But to establish it with certainty with regard to theoretical texts is impossible, because there have always been scholars who would not divulge their interpretation of such texts.

It may be objected: "There are some things in Scripture which the Muslims have unanimously agreed to take in their apparent meaning, others [which they have agreed] to interpret allegorically, and others about which they have disagreed; is it permissible, then, that demonstration should lead to interpreting allegorically what they have agreed to take in its apparent meaning, or to taking in its apparent meaning what they have agreed to interpret allegorically?" We reply: If unanimous agreement is established by a method which is certain, such [a result] is not sound; but if [the existence of] agreement on those things is a matter of opinion, then it may be sound. This is why Abū Ḥāmid, Abul-Ma'ālī, and other leaders of thought said that no one should be definitely called an unbeliever for violating unanimity on a point of interpretation in matters like these.

That unanimity on theoretical matters is never determined with certainty, as it can be on practical matters, may be shown to you by the fact that it is not possible for unanimity to be determined on any question at any period unless that period is strictly limited by us, and all the scholars existing in that period are known to us (i.e. known as individuals and in their total number), and the doctrine of each of them on the question has been handed down to us on unassailable authority, and, in addition to all this, unless we are sure that the scholars existing at the time were in agreement that there is not both an apparent and an inner meaning in Scripture, that knowledge of any question ought not to be kept secret from anyone, and that there is only one way for people to understand Scripture. But it is recorded in Tradition that many of the first believers used to hold that Scripture has both an apparent and an inner meaning, and that the inner meaning ought not to be learned by anyone who is not a man of learning in this field and who is incapable of understanding it. Thus, for example, Bukhārī reports a saying of 'Alī Ibn Abī Tālib, may God be pleased with him, "Speak to people about what they know. Do you want God and His Prophet to be accused of lying?" Other examples of the same kind are reported about a group of early believers. So how can it possibly be conceived that a unanimous agreement can have been handed down to us about a single theoretical question, when we know definitely that not a single period has been without scholars who held that there are things in Scripture whose true meaning should not be learned by all people?

The situation is different in practical matters: everyone holds that the truth about these should be disclosed to all people alike, and to establish the occurrence of unanimity about them we consider it sufficient that the question [at issue] should have been widely discussed and that no report of controversy about it should have been handed down to us. This is enough to establish the occurrence of unanimity on matters of practice, but on matters of doctrine the case is different.

Ghazālī's charge of unbelief against Fārābī and Ibn Sīnā, for asserting the world's eternity and God's ignorance of particulars and denying bodily resurrection, is only tentative, not definite.

You may object: "If we ought not to call a man an unbeliever for violating unanimity in cases of allegorical interpretation, because no unanimity is conceivable in such cases, what do you say about the Muslim philosophers, like Abū Naṣr and Ibn Sīnā? For Abū Ḥāmid called them both definitely unbelievers in the book of his known as *The disintegration*, on three counts: their assertions of the pre-eternity of the world and that God the Exalted does not know particulars" (may He be Exalted far above that [ignorance]!), "and their allegorical interpretation of the passages concerning the resurrection of bodies and states of existence in the next life."

We answer: It is apparent from what he said on the subject that his calling them both unbelievers on these counts was not definite, since he made it clear in *The book of distinction* that calling people unbelievers for violating unanimity can only be tentative.

Such a charge cannot be definite, because there has never been a consensus against allegorical interpretation. The Qur'ān itself indicates that it has inner meanings which it is the special function of the demonstrative class to understand.

Moreover, it is evident from what we have said that a unanimous agreement cannot be established in questions of this kind, because of the reports that many of the early believers of the first generation, as well as others, have said that there are allegorical interpretations which ought not to be expressed except to those who are qualified to receive allegories. These are "those who are well grounded in science"; for we prefer to place the stop after the words of God the Exalted "and those who are well grounded in science" (iii, 7), because if the scholars did not understand allegorical interpretation, there would be no superiority in their assent which would oblige them to a belief in Him not found among the unlearned. God has described them as those who believe in Him, and this can only be taken to refer to the belief which is based on demonstration; and this [belief] only occurs together with the science of allegorical interpretation. For the unlearned believers are those whose belief in Him is not based on demonstration; and if this belief which God has attributed to the scholars is peculiar to them, it must come through demonstration, and if it comes through demonstration it only occurs together with the science of allegorical interpretation. For God the Exalted has informed us that those [verses] have an allegorical interpretation which is the truth, and demonstration can only be of the truth. That being the case, it is not possible for general unanimity to be established about allegorical interpretations, which God has made peculiar to scholars. This is self-evident to any fair-minded person.

> *Besides, Ghazālī was mistaken in ascribing to the Peripatetics the opinion that God does not know particulars. Their view is that His knowledge of both particulars and universals differs from ours, in being the cause, not an effect, of the object known. They even hold that God sends premonitions in dreams of particular events.*

In addition to all this we hold that Abū Ḥāmid was mistaken about the Peripatetic philosophers, in ascribing to them the assertion that God, Holy and Exalted, does not know particulars at all. In reality they hold that God the Exalted knows them in a way which is not of the same kind as our way of knowing them. For our knowledge of them is an effect of the object known, originated when it comes into existence and changing when it changes; whereas Glorious God's Knowledge of existence is the opposite of this: it is the cause of the object known, which is existent being. Thus to suppose the two kinds of knowledge similar to each other is to identify the essences and properties of opposite things, and that is the extreme of ignorance. And if the name of "knowledge" is predicated of both originated and eternal knowledge, it is predicated by sheer homonymy, as many names are predicated of opposite things: e.g. *jalal* of great and small, *sarīm* of light and darkness. Thus there exists no definition embracing both kinds of knowledge at once, as the theologians of our time imagine. We have devoted a separate essay to this question, impelled by one of our friends.

But how can anyone imagine that the Peripatetics say that God the Glorious does not know particulars with His eternal Knowledge, when they hold that true visions include premonitions of particular events due to occur in future time, and that this warning foreknowledge comes to people in their sleep from the eternal Knowledge which orders and rules the universe? Moreover, it is not only particulars which they say God does not know in the manner in which we know them, but universals as well; for the universals known to us are also effects of the nature of existent being, while with His Knowledge the reverse is true. Thus the conclusion to which demonstration leads is that His Knowledge transcends qualification as "universal" or "particular." Consequently there is no point in disputing about this question, i.e. whether to call them unbelievers or not.

> *On the question of the world, the ancient philosophers agree with the Ash'arites that it is originated and coeval with time. The Peripatetics only disagree with the Ash'arites and the Platonists in holding that past time is infinite. This difference is insufficient to justify a charge of unbelief.*

Concerning the question whether the world is pre-eternal or came into existence, the disagreement between the Ash'arite theologians and the ancient philosophers is in my view almost resolvable into a disagreement about naming, especially in the case of certain of the ancients. For they agree that there are three classes of beings: two extremes and one intermediate between the extremes. They agree also about naming the extremes; but they disagree about the intermediate class.

[1] One extreme is a being which is brought into existence from something other than itself and by something, i.e. by an efficient cause and from some matter; and it, i.e. its existence, is preceded by time. This is the status of bodies whose generation is apprehended by sense, e.g. the generation of water, air, earth, animals, plants, and so on. All alike, ancients and Ash'arites, agree in naming this class of beings "originated." [2] The opposite extreme to this is a being which is not made from or by anything and not preceded by time; and here too all members of both schools agree in naming it "preeternal." This being is apprehended by demonstration; it is God, Blessed and Exalted, Who is the Maker, Giver of being and Sustainer of the universe; may He be praised and His Power exalted!

[3] The class of being which is between these two extremes is that which is not made from anything and not preceded by time, but which is brought into existence by something, i.e. by an agent. This is the world as a whole. Now they all agree on the presence of these three characters in the world. For the theologians admit that time does not precede it, or rather this is a necessary consequence for them since time according to them is something which accompanies motion and bodies. They also agree with the ancients in the view that future time is infinite and likewise future being. They only disagree about past time and past being: the theologians hold that it is finite (this is the doctrine of Plato and his followers), while Aristotle and his school hold that it is infinite, as is the case with future time.

Thus it is clear that [3] this last being bears a resemblance both to [1] the being which is really generated and to [2] the pre-eternal Being. So those who are more impressed with its resemblance to the pre-eternal than its resemblance to the originated name it "pre-eternal," while those who are more impressed with its resemblance to the originated name it "originated." But in truth it is neither really originated nor really preeternal, since the really originated is necessarily perishable and the really pre-eternal has no cause. Some—Plato and his followers—name it "originated and coeval with time," because time according to them is finite in the past.

Thus the doctrines about the world are not so very far apart from each other that some of them should be called irreligious and others not. For this to happen, opinions must be divergent in the extreme, i.e. contraries such as the theologians suppose to exist on this question; i.e. [they hold] that the names "pre-eternity" and "coming into existence" as applied to the world as a whole are contraries. But it is now clear from what we have said that this is not the case.

Anyhow, the apparent meaning of Scripture is that there was a being and time before God created the present being and time. Thus the theologians' interpretation is allegorical and does not command unanimous agreement.

Over and above all this, these opinions about the world do not conform to the apparent meaning of Scripture. For if the apparent meaning of Scripture is searched, it will be evident from the verses which give us information about the bringing into existence of the world that its form really is originated, but that being itself and time extend continuously at both extremes, i.e. without interruption. Thus the words of God the Exalted, "He it is Who created the heavens and the earth in six days, and His throne was on the water" (xi, 7), taken in their apparent meaning imply that there was a being before this present being, namely the throne and the water, and a time before this time, i.e. the one which is joined to the form of this being, namely the number of the movement of the celestial sphere. And the words of the Exalted, "On the day when the earth shall be changed into other than earth, and the heavens as well" (xiv, 48), also in their apparent meaning imply that there will be a second being after this being. And the words of the Exalted, "Then He directed Himself towards the sky, and it was smoke" (xli, 11), in their apparent meaning imply that the heavens were created from something.

Thus the theologians too in their statements about the world do not conform to the apparent meaning of Scripture but interpret it allegorically. For it is not stated in Scripture that God was existing with absolutely nothing else: a text to this effect is nowhere to be found. Then how is it conceivable that the theologians' allegorical interpretation of these verses could meet with unanimous agreement, when the apparent meaning of Scripture which we have mentioned about the existence of the world has been accepted by a school of philosophers!

> *On such difficult questions, error committed by a qualified judge of his subject is excused by God, while error by an unqualified person is not excused.*

It seems that those who disagree on the interpretation of these difficult questions earn merit if they are in the right and will be excused [by God] if they are in error. For assent to a thing as a result of an indication [of it] arising in the soul is something compulsory, not voluntary: i.e. it is not for us [to choose] not to assent or to assent, as it is to stand up or not to stand up. And since free choice is a condition of obligation, a man who assents to an error as a result of a consideration that has occurred to him is excused, if he is a scholar. This is why the Prophet, peace on him, said, "If the judge after exerting his mind makes a right decision, he will have a double reward; and if he makes a wrong decision he will [still] have a single reward." And what judge is more important than he who makes judgements about being, that it is thus or not thus? These judges are the scholars, specially chosen by God for [the task of] allegorical interpretation, and this error which is forgivable according to the Law is only such error as proceeds from scholars when they study the difficult matters which the Law obliges them to study.

But error proceeding from any other class of people is sheer sin, equally whether it relates to theoretical or to practical matters. For just as the judge who is ignorant of the [Prophet's] way of life is not excused if he makes an error in judgement, so he who makes judgements about beings without having the proper qualifications for [such] judgements is not excused but is either a sinner or an unbeliever. And if he who would judge what is allowed and forbidden is required to combine in himself the qualifications for exercise of personal judgement, namely knowledge of the principles [of law] and knowledge of how to draw inferences from those principles by reasoning, how much more properly is he who would make judgements about beings required to be qualified, i.e. to know the primary intellectual principle and the way to draw inferences from them!

> *Texts of Scripture fall into three kinds with respect to the excusability of error. [1] Texts which must be taken in their apparent meaning by everyone. Since the meaning can be understood plainly by demonstrative, dialectical and rhetorical methods alike, no one is excused for the error of interpreting these texts allegorically. [2] Texts which must be taken in their apparent meaning by the lower classes and interpreted allegorically by the demonstrative class. It is inexcusable for the lower classes to interpret them allegorically or for the demonstrative class to take them in their apparent meaning. [3] Texts whose classification under the previous headings is uncertain. Error in this matter by the demonstrative class is excused.*

In general, error about Scripture is of two types: either error which is excused to one who is a qualified student of that matter in which the error occurs (as the skilful doctor is excused if he commits an error in the art of medicine and the skilful judge if he

gives an erroneous judgement), but not excused to one who is not qualified in that subject; or error which is not excused to any person whatever, and which is unbelief if it
concerns the principles of religion, or heresy if it concerns something subordinate to the
principles.

This [latter] error is that which occurs about [1] matters, knowledge of which is
provided by all the different methods of indication, so that knowledge of the matter in
question is in this way possible for everyone. Examples are acknowledgement of God,
Blessed and Exalted, of the prophetic missions, and of happiness and misery in the next
life; for these three principles are attainable by the three classes of indication, by which
everyone without exception can come to assent to what he is obliged to know: I mean
the rhetorical, dialectical and demonstrative indications. So whoever denies such a
thing, when it is one of the principles of the Law, is an unbeliever, who persists in defiance with his tongue though not with his heart, or neglects to expose himself to learning
the indication of its truth. For if he belongs to the demonstrative class of men, a way has
been provided for him to assent to it, by demonstration; if he belongs to the dialectical
class, the way is by dialectic; and if he belongs to the class [which is convinced] by
preaching, the way for him is by preaching. With this in view the Prophet, peace on
him, said, "I have been ordered to fight people until they say `There is no god but God'
and believe in me"; he means, by any of the three methods of attaining belief that suits
them.

[2] With regard to things which by reason of their recondite character are only
knowable by demonstration, God has been gracious to those of His servants who have
no access to demonstration, on account of their natures, habits or lack of facilities for
education: He has coined for them images and likenesses of these things, and summoned them to assent to those images, since it is possible for assent to those images to
come about through the indications common to all men, i.e. the dialectical and rhetorical indications. This is the reason why Scripture is divided into apparent and inner
meanings: the apparent meaning consists of those images which are coined to stand for
those ideas, while the inner meaning is those ideas [themselves], which are clear only to
the demonstrative class. These are the four or five classes of beings mentioned by Abū
Ḥāmid in *The book of the distinction.*

[1] But when it happens, as we said, that we know the thing itself by the three
methods, we do not need to coin images of it, and it remains true in its apparent meaning, not admitting allegorical interpretation. If an apparent text of this kind refers to
principles, anyone who interprets it allegorically is an unbeliever, e.g. anyone who
thinks that there is no happiness or misery in the next life, and that the only purpose of
this teaching is that men should be safeguarded from each other in their bodily and sensible lives, that it is but a practical device, and that man has no other goal than his sensible existence.

If this is established, it will have become clear to you from what we have said that
there are [1] apparent texts of Scripture which it is not permitted to interpret allegorically; to do so on fundamentals is unbelief, on subordinate matters, heresy. There are
also [2] apparent texts which have to be interpreted allegorically by men of the demonstrative class; for such men to take them in their apparent meaning is unbelief, while for
those who are not of the demonstrative class to interpret them allegorically and take
them out of their apparent meaning is unbelief or heresy on their part.

Of this [latter] class are the verse about God's directing Himself and the Tradition
about His descent. That is why the Prophet, peace on him, said in the case of the black
woman, when she told him that God was in the sky, "Free her, for she is a believer."
This was because she was not of the demonstrative class; and the reason for his decision

was that the class of people to whom assent comes only through the imagination, i.e. who do not assent to a thing except in so far as they can imagine it, find it difficult to assent to the existence of a being which is unrelated to any imaginable thing. This applies as well to those who understand from the relation stated merely [that God has] a place; these are people who have advanced a little in their thought beyond the position of the first class, [by rejecting] belief in corporeality. Thus the [proper] answer to them with regard to such passages is that they belong to the ambiguous texts, and that the stop is to be placed after the words of God the Exalted, "And no one knows the interpretation thereof except God" (iii, 7). The demonstrative class, while agreeing unanimously that this class of text must be interpreted allegorically, may disagree about the interpretation, according to the level of each one's knowledge of demonstration.

There is also [3] a third class of Scriptural texts falling uncertainly between the other two classes, on which there is doubt. One group of those who devote themselves to theoretical study attach them to the apparent texts which it is not permitted to interpret allegorically, others attach them to the texts with inner meanings which scholars are not permitted to take in their apparent meanings. This [divergence of opinions] is due to the difficulty and ambiguity of this class of text. Anyone who commits an error about this class is excused, I mean any scholar.

The texts about the future life fall into [3], since demonstrative scholars do not agree whether to take them in their apparent meaning or interpret them allegorically. Either is permissible. But it is inexcusable to deny the fact of a future life altogether.

If it is asked, "Since it is clear that scriptural texts in this respect fall into three grades, to which of these three grades, according to you, do the descriptions of the future life and its states belong?," we reply: The position clearly is that this matter belongs to the class [3] about which there is disagreement. For we find a group of those who claim an affinity with demonstration saying that it is obligatory to take these passages in their apparent meaning, because there is no demonstration leading to the impossibility of the apparent meaning in them—this is the view of the Ash'arites; while another group of those who devote themselves to demonstration interpret these passages allegorically, and these people give the most diverse interpretations of them. In this class must be counted Abū Ḥāmid and many of the Sūfīs; some of them combine the two interpretations of the passages, as Abū Ḥāmid does in some of his books.

So it is likely that a scholar who commits an error in this matter is excused, while one who is correct receives thanks or a reward: that is, if he acknowledges the existence [of a future life] and merely gives a certain sort of allegorical interpretation, i.e. of the mode of the future life not of its existence, provided that the interpretation given does not lead to denial of its existence. In this matter only the negation of existence is unbelief, because it concerns one of the principles of religion and one of those points to which assent is attainable through the three methods common to "the white man and the black man."

The unlearned classes must take such texts in their apparent meaning. It is unbelief for the learned to set down allegorical interpretations in popular writings. By doing this Ghazālī caused confusion among the people. Demonstrative books should be banned to the unqualified, but not to the learned.

But anyone who is not a man of learning is obliged to take these passages in their apparent meaning, and allegorical interpretation of them is for him unbelief because it *leads* to unbelief. That is why we hold that, for anyone whose duty it is to believe in the apparent meaning, allegorical interpretation is unbelief, because it leads to unbelief. Anyone of the interpretative class who discloses such [an interpretation] to him is summoning him to unbelief, and he who summons to unbelief is an unbeliever.

Therefore allegorical interpretations ought to be set down only in demonstrative books because if they are in demonstrative books they are encountered by no one but men of the demonstrative class. But if they are set down in other than demonstrative books and one deals with them by poetical, rhetorical or dialectical methods, as Abū Ḥāmid does, then he commits an offence against the Law and against philosophy, even though the fellow intended nothing but good. For by this procedure he wanted to increase the number of learned men, but in fact he increased the number of the corrupted not of the learned! As a result, one group came to slander philosophy, another to slander religion, and another to reconcile the [first] two [groups]. It seems that this [last] was one of his objects in his books; an indication that he wanted by this [procedure] to arouse minds is that he adhered to no one doctrine in his books but was an Ash'arite with the Ash'arites, a Sūfīs with the Sūfīs and a philosopher with the philosophers, so that he was like the man in the verse:

> "One day a Yamani, if I meet a man of Yaman,
> And if I meet a Ma'addi, I'm an 'Adnani."

The *imāms* of the Muslims ought to forbid those of his books which contain learned matter to all save the learned, just as they ought to forbid demonstrative books to those who are not capable of understanding them. But the damage done to people by demonstrative books is lighter, because for the most part only persons of superior natural intelligence become acquainted with demonstrative books, and this class of persons is only misled through lack of practical virtue, unorganized reading, and tackling them without a teacher. On the other hand their total prohibition obstructs the purpose to which the Law summons, because it is a wrong to the best class of people and the best class of beings. For to do justice to the best class of beings demands that they should be known profoundly. by persons equipped to know them profoundly, and these are the best class of people; and the greater the value of the being, the greater is the injury towards it, which consists of ignorance of it. Thus the Exalted has said, "Associating [other gods] with God is indeed a great wrong" (xxxi, 12).

> *We have only discussed these questions in a popular work because they were already being publicly discussed.*

This is as much as we see fit to affirm in this field of study, i.e. the correspondence between religion and philosophy and the rules for allegorical interpretation in religion. If it were not for the publicity given to the matter and to these questions which we have discussed, we should not have permitted ourselves to write a word on the subject; and we should not have had to make excuses for doing so to the interpretative scholars, because the proper place to discuss these questions is in demonstrative books. God is the Guide and helps us to follow the right course!

CHAPTER 3

Philosophical Interpretations of Scripture Should Not Be Taught to the Majority. The Law Provides Other Methods of Instructing Them

The purpose of Scripture is to teach true theoretical and practical science and right practice and attitudes.

You ought to know that the purpose of Scripture is simply to teach true science and right practice. True science is knowledge of God, Blessed and Exalted, and the other beings as they really are, and especially of noble beings, and knowledge of happiness and misery in the next life. Right practice consists in performing the acts which bring happiness and avoiding the acts which bring misery; and it is knowledge of these acts that is called "practical science." They fall into two divisions: (1) outward bodily acts; the science of these is called "jurisprudence"; and (2) acts of the soul such as gratitude, patience and other moral attitudes which the Law enjoins or forbids; the science of these is called "asceticism" or "the sciences of the future life." To these Abū Hāmid turned his attention in his book: as people had given up this sort [of act] and become immersed in the other sort, and as this sort [2] involves the greater fear of God, which is the cause of happiness, he called his book *"The revival of the sciences of religion."* But we have digressed from our subject, so let us return to it.

Scripture teaches concepts both directly and by symbols, and uses demonstrative, dialectical and rhetorical arguments. Dialectical and rhetorical arguments are prevalent because the main aim of Scripture is to teach the majority. In these arguments concepts are indicated directly or by symbols, in various combinations in premises and conclusion.

We say: The purpose of Scripture is to teach true science and right practice; and teaching is of two classes, [of] concepts and [of] judgements, as the logicians have shown. Now the methods available to men of [arriving at] judgements are three: demonstrative, dialectical and rhetorical; and the methods of forming concepts are two: either [conceiving] the object itself or [conceiving] a symbol of it. But not everyone has the natural ability to take in demonstrations, or [even] dialectical arguments, let alone demonstrative arguments which are so hard to learn and need so much time [even] for those who are qualified to learn them. Therefore, since it is the purpose of Scriptures simply to teach everyone, Scripture has to contain every method of [bringing about] judgements of assent and every method of forming concepts.

Now some of the methods of assent comprehend the majority of people, i.e. the occurrence of assent as a result of them [is comprehensive]: these are the rhetorical and the dialectical [methods]—and the rhetorical is more comprehensive than the dialectical. Another method is peculiar to a smaller number of people: this is the demonstrative. Therefore, since the primary purpose of Scripture is to take care of the majority (without neglecting to arouse the élite), the prevailing methods of expression in religion are the common methods by which the majority comes to form concepts and judgements.

These [common] methods in religion are of four classes:

One of them occurs where the method is common, yet specialized in two respects: i.e. where it is certain in its concepts and judgements, in spite of being rhetorical or dialectical. These syllogisms are those whose premises, in spite of being based on accepted ideas or on opinions, are accidentally certain, and whose conclusions are accidentally to be taken in their direct meaning without symbolization. Scriptural texts of this class have no allegorical interpretations, and anyone who denies them or interprets them allegorically is an unbeliever.

The second class occurs where the premises, in spite of being based on accepted ideas or on opinions, are certain, and where the conclusions are symbols for the things which it was intended to conclude. [Texts of] this [class], i.e. their conclusions, admit of allegorical interpretation.

The third is the reverse of this: it occurs where the conclusions are the very things which it was intended to conclude, while the premises are based on accepted ideas or on opinions without being accidentally certain. [Texts of] this [class] also, i.e. their conclusions, do not admit of allegorical interpretation, but their premises may do so.

The fourth [class] occurs where the premises are based on accepted ideas or opinions, without being accidentally certain, and where the conclusions are symbols for what it was intended to conclude. In these cases the duty of the élite is to interpret them allegorically, while the duty of the masses is to take them in their apparent meaning.

> *Where symbols are used, each class of men, demonstrative, dialectical and rhetorical, must try to understand the inner meaning symbolized or rest content with the apparent meaning, according to their capacities.*

In general, everything in these [texts] which admits of allegorical interpretation can only be understood by demonstration. The duty of the élite here is to apply such interpretation; while the duty of the masses is to take them in their apparent meaning in both respects, i.e. in concept and judgement, since their natural capacity does not allow more than that.

But there may occur to students of Scripture allegorical interpretations due to the superiority of one of the common methods over another in [bringing about] assent, i.e. when the indication contained in the allegorical interpretation is more persuasive than the indication contained in the apparent meaning. Such interpretations are popular; and [the making of them] is possibly a duty for those powers of theoretical understanding have attained the dialectical level. To this sort belong some of the interpretations of the Ash'arites and Mu'tazilites—though the Mu'tazilites are generally sounder in their statements. The masses on the other hand, who are incapable of more than rhetorical arguments, have the duty of taking these [texts] in their apparent meaning, and they are not permitted to know such interpretations at all.

Thus people in relation to Scripture fall into three classes:

One class is these who are not people of interpretation at all: these are the rhetorical class. They are the overwhelming mass, for no man of sound intellect is exempted from this kind of assent.

Another class is the people of dialectical interpretation: these are the dialecticians, either by nature alone or by nature and habit.

Another class is the people of certain interpretation: these are the demonstrative class, by nature and training, i.e. in the art of philosophy. This interpretation ought not to be expressed to the dialectical class, let alone to the masses.

> *To explain the inner meaning to people unable to understand it is to destroy their belief in the apparent meaning without putting anything in its place. The result is unbelief in learners and teachers. It is best for the learned to profess ignorance, quoting the* Qur'ān *on the limitation of man's understanding.*

When something of these allegorical interpretations is expressed to anyone unfit to receive them—especially demonstrative interpretations because of their remoteness from common knowledge—both he who expresses it and he to whom it is expressed are

led into unbelief. The reason for that [in the case of the latter] is that allegorical interpretation comprises two things, rejection of the apparent meaning and affirmation of the
allegorical one; so that if the apparent meaning is rejected in the mind of someone who
can only grasp apparent meanings, without the allegorical meaning being affirmed in his
mind, the result is unbelief, if it [the text in question] concerns the principles of religion.

Allegorical interpretations, then, ought not to be expressed to the masses nor set
down in rhetorical or dialectical books, i.e. books containing arguments of these two
sorts, as was done by Abū Ḥāmid. They should [not] be expressed to this class; and with
regard to an apparent text, when there is a [self-evident] doubt whether it is apparent to
everyone and whether knowledge of its interpretation is impossible for them, they
should be told that it is ambiguous and [its meaning] known by no one except God; and
that the stop should be put here in the sentence of the Exalted, "And no one knows the
interpretation thereof except God" (iii, 7). The same kind of answer should also be
given to a question about abstruse matters, which there is no way for the masses to understand; just as the Exalted has answered in His saying, "And they will ask you about
the Spirit. Say, 'The Spirit is by the command of my Lord; you have been given only a
little knowledge'" (xvii, 85).

> *Certain people have injured the masses particularly, by giving them allegorical
> interpretations which are false. These people are exactly analogous to bad medi-
> cal advisers. The true doctor is related to bodily health in the same way as the
> Legislator to spiritual health, which the* Qur'ān *teaches us to pursue. The true al-
> legory is "the deposit" mentioned in the* Qur'ān.

As for the man who expresses these allegories to unqualified persons, he is an unbeliever on account of his summoning people to unbelief. This is contrary to the summons of the Legislator, especially when they are false allegories concerning the principles of religion, as has happened in the case of a group of people of our time. For we
have seen some of them thinking that they were being philosophic and that they perceived, with their remarkable wisdom, things which conflict with Scripture in every respect, i.e. [in passages] which do not admit of allegorical interpretation; and that it was
obligatory to express these things to the masses. But by expressing those false beliefs to
the masses they have been a cause of perdition to the masses and themselves, in this
world and the next.

The relation between the aim of these people and the aim of the Legislator [can be
illustrated by] a parable of a man who goes to a skilful doctor. [This doctor's] aim is to
preserve the health and cure the diseases of all the people, by prescribing for them rules
which can be commonly accepted, about the necessity of using the things which will
preserve their health and cure their diseases, and avoiding the opposite things. He is unable to make them all doctors, because a doctor is one who knows by demonstrative
methods the things which preserve health and cure disease. Now this [man whom we
have mentioned] goes out to the people and tells them, "These methods prescribed by
this doctor for you are not right"; and he sets out to discredit them, so that they are rejected by the people. Or he says, "They have allegorical interpretations"; but the people
neither understand these nor assent to them in practice. Well, do you think that people
in this condition will do any of the things which are useful for preserving health and
curing disease, or that this man who has persuaded them to reject what they formerly
believed in will now be able to use those [things] with them, I mean for preserving
health? No, he will be unable to use those [things] with them, nor will they use them,
and so they will all perish.

This [is what will happen] if he expresses to them true allegories about those matters, because of their inability to understand them; let alone if he expresses to them false

The Lion's Court, the Alhambra, Granada, Spain, begun in 1230. This palace of the rulers is the best example of the Islamic culture that dominated Spain from the early eighth century until the surrender of Granada in 1492. *(Scala/Art Resource)*

allegories, because this will lead them to think that there are no such things as health which ought to be preserved and disease which ought to be cured—let alone that there are things which preserve health and cure disease. It is the same when someone expresses allegories to the masses, and to those who are not qualified to understand them, in the sphere of Scripture; thus he makes it appear false and turns people away from it; and he who turns people away from Scripture is an unbeliever.

Indeed this comparison is certain, not poetic as one might suppose. It presents a true analogy, in that the relation of the doctor to the health of bodies is [the same as] the relation of the Legislator to the health of souls; i.e. the doctor is he who seeks to preserve the health of bodies when it exists and to restore it when it is lost, while the Legislator is he who desires this [end] for the health of souls. This health is what is called "fear of God." The precious Book has told us to seek it by acts conformable to the Law, in several verses. Thus the Exalted has said, "Fasting has been prescribed for you, as it was prescribed for those who were before you; perhaps you will fear God" (ii, 183). Again the Exalted has said, "Their flesh and their blood shall not touch God, but your fear shall touch him" (xxii, 37); "Prayer prevents immorality and transgression" (xxix, 45); and other verses to the same effect contained in the precious Book. Through knowledge of Scripture and practice according to Scripture the Legislator aims solely at this health; and it is from this health that happiness in the future life follows, just as misery in the future life follows from its opposite.

From this it will be clear to you that true allegories ought not to be set down in popular books, let alone false ones. The true allegory is the deposit which man was charged to hold and which he held, and from which all beings shied away, i.e. that which is mentioned in the words of the Exalted, "We offered the deposit to the heavens, the earth and the mountains" (xxxiii, 72), [and so on to the end of] the verse.

It was due to the wrong use of allegorical interpretation by the Mu'tazilites and Ash'arites that hostile sects arose in Islam.

It was due to allegorical interpretations—especially the false ones—and the supposition that such interpretations of Scripture ought to be expressed to everyone, that the sects of Islam arose, with the result that each one accused the others of unbelief or heresy. Thus the Mu'tazilites interpreted many verses and Traditions allegorically, and expressed their interpretations to the masses, and the Ash'arites did the same, although they used such interpretations less frequently. In consequence they threw people into hatred, mutual detestation and wars, tore the Scriptures to shreds, and completely divided people.

In addition to all this, in the methods which they followed to establish their interpretations they neither went along with the masses nor with the élite: not with the masses, because their methods were [more] obscure than the methods common to the majority, and not with the élite, because if these methods are inspected they are found deficient in the conditions [required] for demonstrations, as will be understood after the slightest inspection by anyone acquainted with the conditions of demonstration. Further, many of the principles on which the Ash'arites based their knowledge are sophistical, for they deny many necessary truths such as the permanence of accidents, the action of things on other things, the existence of necessary causes for effects, of substantial forms, and of secondary causes.

And their theorists wronged the Muslims in this sense, that a sect of Ash'arites called an unbeliever anyone who did not attain knowledge of the existence of the Glorious Creator by the methods laid down by them in their books for attaining this knowledge. But in truth it is they who are the unbelievers and in error! From this point they proceeded to disagree, one group saying "The primary obligation is theoretical study," another group saying "It is belief"; i.e. [this happened] because they did not know which are the methods common to everyone, through whose doors the Law has summoned all people [to enter]; they supposed that there was only one method. Thus they mistook the aim of the Legislator, and were both themselves in error and led others into error.

The proper methods for teaching the people are indicated in the Qur'ān, *as the early Muslims knew. The popular portions of the Book are miraculous in providing for the needs of every class of mind. We intend to make a study of its teachings at the apparent level, and thus help to remedy the grievous harm done by ignorant partisans of philosophy and religion.*

It may be asked: "If these methods followed by the Ash'arites and other theorists are not the common methods by which the Legislator has aimed to teach the masses, and by which alone it is possible to teach them, then what are those [common] methods in this religion of ours"? We reply: They are exclusively the methods set down in the precious Book. For if the precious Book is inspected, there will be found in it the three methods that are available for all the people, [namely] the common methods for the instruction of the majority of the people and the special method. And if their merits are inspected, it becomes apparent that no better common methods for the instruction of the masses can be found than the methods mentioned in it.

Thus whoever tampers with them, by making an allegorical interpretation not apparent in itself, or [at least] not more apparent to everyone than they are (and that [greater apparency] is something non-existent), is rejecting their wisdom and rejecting their intended effects in procuring human happiness. This is very apparent from [a comparison of] the condition of the first believers with the condition of those who came after them. For the first believers arrived at perfect virtue and fear of God only by using these sayings [of Scripture] without interpreting them allegorically; and anyone of them who did find out an allegorical interpretation did not think fit to express it [to others]. But when those who came after them used allegorical interpretation, their fear of God grew less, their dissensions increased, their love for one another was removed, and they became divided into sects.

So whoever wishes to remove this heresy from religion should direct his attention to the precious Book, and glean from it the indications present [in it] concerning everything in turn that it obliges us to believe, and exercise his judgement in looking at its apparent meaning as well as he is able, without interpreting any of it allegorically, except where the allegorical meaning is apparent in itself, i.e. commonly apparent to everyone. For if the sayings set down in Scripture for the instruction of the people are inspected, it seems that in mastering their meaning one arrives at a point, beyond which none but a man of the demonstrative class can extract from their apparent wording a meaning which is not apparent in them. This property is not found in any other sayings.

For those religious sayings in the precious Book which are expressed to everyone have three properties that indicate their miraculous character: (1) There exist none more completely persuasive and convincing to everyone than they. (2) Their meaning admits naturally of mastery, up to a point beyond which their allegorical interpretation (when they are of a kind to have such an interpretation) can only be found out by the demonstrative class. (3) They contain means of drawing the attention of the people of truth to the true allegorical meaning. This [character] is not found in the doctrines of the Ash'arites nor in those of the Mu'tazilites, i.e. their interpretations do not admit of mastery nor contain [means of] drawing attention to the truth, nor are they true; and this is why heresies have multiplied.

It is our desire to devote our time to this object and achieve it effectively, and if God grants us a respite of life we shall work steadily towards it in so far as this is made possible for us; and it may be that that work will serve as a starting point for our successors. For our soul is in the utmost sorrow and pain by reason of the evil fancies and perverted beliefs which have infiltrated this religion, and particularly such [afflictions] as have happened to it at the hands of people who claim an affinity with philosophy. For injuries from a friend are more severe than injuries from an enemy. I refer to the fact that philosophy is the friend and milk-sister of religion; thus injuries from people related to philosophy are the severest injuries [to religion]—apart from the enmity, hatred and quarrels which such [injuries] stir up between the two, which are companions by nature and lovers by essence and instinct. It has also been injured by a host of ignorant friends who claim an affinity with it: these are the sects which exist within it. But God directs all men aright and helps everyone to love Him; He unites their hearts in the fear of Him, and removes from them hatred and loathing by His grace and His mercy!

Indeed God has already removed many of these ills, ignorant ideas and misleading practices, by means of this triumphant rule. By it He has opened a way to many benefits, especially to the class of persons who have trodden the path of study and sought to know the truth. This [He has done] by summoning the masses to a middle way of knowing God the Glorious, [a way] which is raised above the low level of the followers of authority but is below the turbulence of the theologians; and by drawing the attention of the élite to their obligation to make a thorough study of the principles of religion. God is the Giver of success and the Guide by His Goodness.

Moses Maimonides
1135–1204

Moses ben Maimon, or Maimonides (referred to by Jewish scholars as "Rambam" for "Rabbi Moses ben Maimon"), was born at 1 P.M. on March 30, 1135, and died on December 13, 1204. The fact that we have such precise dates indicates the esteem with which he was held in his lifetime. As a boy in Córdoba, Spain, he was taught the Torah and the Talmud by his father, along with philosophy and science. At age thirteen Maimonides and his family were forced to flee Spain after a time of peaceful coexistence between Jews and Muslims came to an end. Following a period of travel, which included a stay in Palestine, Maimonides and his family settled in Cairo, Egypt. There, Maimonides and his brother David became jewel merchants. Within a few years Maimonides lost both his father and David, the latter killed in a shipwreck in the Indian Ocean during a business trip. Maimonides gave up the jewel business and turned to medicine. His expertise as a doctor eventually led to his appointment as a court physician for the ruler Saladin (the same Saladin who defeated Richard the Lionhearted in the Third Crusade). Maimonides' spiritual insights led to his being named the head of the Egyptian Jewish community. While serving both his religion and the state, he still found time to write extensively. His death in 1204 was mourned by Jews throughout the Mediterranean region, and his remains were taken from Cairo to Tiberias, on the Sea of Galilee, where his tomb is still visited today.

Maimonides' philosophical fame rests squarely on his major work, *The Guide for the Perplexed.* This work was written not for the majority of believers, but for those who knew both Jewish Law and Greek philosophy and were perplexed on how to harmonize the two. Though his religion was different, Maimonides was dealing with the same question as his neighboring Muslims and Christians: how to reconcile faith and reason. In the *Guide,* Maimonides asserts that there can be no conflict between faith and reason. Using Aristotle's philosophy (with some Neoplatonic spin), Maimonides believed he could answer a number of philosophical questions about the nature of God and of God's creation in a way that was consistent with sacred writings. Apparent disagreements between philosophy and theology were frequently the result of either taking figurative passages in Scripture literally or misunderstanding difficult philosophical arguments. Occasionally, philosophy is simply incapable of answering a given question and one must accept "the authority of Prophecy, which can teach things beyond the reach of human speculation." But even in such cases, philosophy can still provide general reasons for believing Scripture. For example, philosophy is inconclusive in determining whether or not the world is eternal. But whichever position we assume, says Maimonides, we can use that assumption to prove that God exists (when using arguments that Maimonides collected).

The selections from the *Guide* given here, in the M. Friedländer translation, present Maimonides' discussions of the nature of God, the arguments for God's existence, the temporal creation of the world, and the problem of evil. These passages greatly influenced Thomas Aquinas, and echoes of Maimonides' thought can be heard throughout Thomas's writings.

*   *   *

For selections from Maimonides' writings, see Jacob Samuel Minkin, *The World of Moses Maimonides, with Selections From His Writings* (New York: T. Yoseloff, 1957), and Moses Maimonides, *Rambam: Readings in the Philosophy of Moses Maimonides,* translated by Lenn Evan Goodman (New York: Viking Press, 1976).

Among the many general introductions to Maimonides' life and thought, recent helpful studies include Abraham Joshua Heschel, *Maimonides: A Biography,* translated by Joachim Neugroschel (New York: Farrar, Straus, Giroux, 1982), and Oliver Leaman, *Moses Maimonides* (London: Routledge, 1990). For more specialized studies, see Carol Klein, *The Credo of Maimonides: A Synthesis* (New York: Philosophical Library, 1958); Jehuda Melber, *The Universality of Maimonides* (New York: Jonathan David, 1968); and Menachem Marc Kellner, *Dogma in Medieval Jewish Thought: From Maimonides to Abravanel* (Oxford: Oxford University Press, 1986). For collections of essays, see Salo Whittmay Baron, ed., *Essays on Maimonides: An Octocennial Volume* (New York: Columbia University Press, 1941); Joseph A. Buijs, ed., *Maimonides: A Collection of Critical Essays* (Notre Dame, IN: University of Notre Dame Press, 1988); and Eric L. Ormsby, ed., *Moses Maimonides and His Time* (Washington, DC: Catholic University of America Press, 1989).

THE GUIDE FOR THE PERPLEXED
(in part)

PART I

Chapter 51

There are many things whose existence is manifest and obvious; some of these are innate notions or objects of sensation, others are nearly so; and in fact they would require no proof if man had been left in his primitive state. Such are the existence of motion, of man's free will, of phases of production and destruction, and of the natural properties perceived by the senses, e.g., the heat of fire, the coldness of water, and many other similar things. False notions, however, may be spread either by a person labouring under error, or by one who has some particular end in view, and who establishes theories contrary to the real nature of things, by denying the existence of things perceived by the senses, or by affirming the existence of what does not exist. Philosophers are thus required to establish by proof things which are self-evident, and to disprove the existence of things which only exist in man's imagination. Thus Aristotle gives a proof for the existence of motion, because it had been denied; he disproves the reality of atoms, because it had been asserted.

To the same class belongs the rejection of essential attributes in reference to God. For it is a self-evident truth that the attribute is not inherent in the object to which it is ascribed, but it is superadded to its essence, and is consequently an *accident;* if the attribute denoted the essence of the object, it would be either mere tautology, as if, e.g., one would say "man is man," or the explanation of a name, as, e.g., "man is a speaking animal"; for the words "speaking animal" include the true essence of man, and there is no third element besides life and speech in the definition of man; when he, therefore, is described by the attributes of life and speech, these are nothing but an explanation of the name "man," that is to say, that the thing which is called man, consists of life and speech. It will now be clear that the attribute must be one of two things, either the essence of the object described—in that case it is a mere explanation of a name, and on that account we might admit the attribute in reference to God, but we reject it from another cause as will be shown—or the attribute is something different from the object described, some extraneous superadded element; in that case the attribute would be an accident, and he who merely rejects the appellation "accidents" in reference to the attributes of God, does not thereby alter their character; for everything superadded to the essence of an object joins it without forming part of its essential properties, and that constitutes an accident. Add to this the logical consequence of admitting many attributes, viz., the existence of many eternal beings. There cannot be any belief in the unity of God except by admitting that He is one simple substance, without any composition or plurality of elements; one from whatever side you view it, and by whatever test you examine it; not divisible into two parts in any way and by any cause, nor capable of any form of plurality either objectively or subjectively, as will be proved in this treatise.

Some thinkers have gone so far as to say that the attributes of God are neither His essence nor anything extraneous to His essence. This is like the assertion of some theorists, that the ideals, i.e., the *universalia,* are neither existing nor non-existent, and like the views of others, that the atom does not fill a definite place, but keeps an atom of space occupied; that man has no freedom of action at all, but has acquirement. Such things are only said; they exist only in words, not in thought, much less in reality. But as you know, and as all know who do not delude themselves, these theories are preserved by a multitude of words, by misleading similes sustained by declamation and invective, and by numerous methods borrowed both from dialectics and sophistry. If after uttering them and supporting them by such words, a man were to examine for himself his own belief on this subject, he would see nothing but confusion and stupidity in an endeavour to prove the existence of things which do not exist, or to find a mean between two opposites that have no mean. Or is there a mean between existence and non-existence, or between the identity and non-identity of two things? But, as we said, to such absurdities men were forced by the great licence given to the imagination, and by the fact that every existing material thing is necessarily imagined as a certain substance possessing several attributes; for nothing has ever been found that consists of one simple substance without any attribute. Guided by such imaginations, men thought that God was also composed of many different elements, viz., of His essence and of the attributes superadded to His essence. Following up this comparison, some believed that God was corporeal, and that He possessed attributes; others, abandoning this theory, denied the corporeality, but retained the attributes. The adherence to the literal sense of the text of Holy Writ is the source of all this error, as I shall show in some of the chapters devoted to this theme.

Chapter 52

Every description of an object by an affirmative attribute, which includes the assertion that an object is of a certain kind, must be made in one of the following five ways:—

First. The object is described by its *definition,* as e.g., man is described as a being that lives and has reason; such a description, containing the true essence of the object, is, as we have already shown, nothing else but the explanation of a name. All agree that this kind of description cannot be given of God; for there are no previous causes to His existence, by which He could be defined: and on that account it is a well-known principle, received by all the philosophers, who are precise in their statements, that no definition can be given of God.

Secondly. An object is described by *part of its definition,* as when, e.g., man is described as a living being or as a rational being. This kind of description includes the necessary connection [of the two ideas]; for when we say that every man is rational we mean by it that every being which has the characteristics of man must also have reason. All agree that this kind of description is inappropriate in reference to God; for if we were to speak of a portion of His essence, we should consider His essence to be a compound. The inappropriateness of this kind of description in reference to God is the same as that of the preceding kind.

Thirdly. An object is described by something different from its true essence, by something that does not complement or establish the essence of the object. The description, therefore, relates to a *quality;* but quality, in its most general sense, is an accident. If God could be described in this way, He would be the substratum of accidents: a sufficient reason for rejecting the idea that He possesses quality, since it diverges from the true conception of His essence. It is surprising how those who admit the application of attributes to God can reject, in reference to Him, comparison and qualification. For when they say "He cannot be qualified," they can only mean that He possesses no quality; and yet every positive essential attribute of an object either constitutes its essence,—and in that case it is identical with the essence,—or it contains a quality of the object.

There are, as you know, four kinds of quality; I will give you instances of attributes of each kind, in order to show you that this class of attributes cannot possibly be applied to God. *(a)* A man is described by any of his intellectual or moral qualities, or by any of the dispositions appertaining to him as an animate being, when, e.g., we speak of a person who is a carpenter, or who shrinks from sin, or who is ill. It makes no difference whether we say, a carpenter, or a sage, or a physician; by all these we represent certain physical dispositions; nor does it make any difference whether we say "sin-fearing" or "merciful." Every trade, every profession, and every settled habit of man are certain physical dispositions. All this is clear to those who have occupied themselves with the study of Logic. *(b)* A thing is described by some physical quality it possesses, or by the absence of the same, e.g., as being soft or hard. It makes no difference whether we say "soft or hard," or "strong or weak"; in both cases we speak of physical conditions. *(c)* A man is described by his passive qualities, or by his emotions; we speak, e.g., of a person who is passionate, irritable, timid, merciful, without implying that these conditions have become permanent. The description of a thing by its color, taste, heat, cold, dryness, and moisture, belongs also to this class of attributes. *(d)* A thing is described by any of its qualities resulting from quantity as such; we speak, e.g., of a thing which is long, short, curved, straight, etc.

Consider all these and similar attributes, and you will find that they cannot be employed in reference to God. He is not a magnitude that any quality resulting from quantity as such could be possessed by Him; He is not affected by external influences, and therefore does not possess any quality resulting from emotion. He is not subject to physical conditions, and therefore does not possess strength or similar qualities; He is not an animate being, that He should have a certain disposition of the soul, or acquire certain properties, as meekness, modesty, etc., or be in a state to which animate beings as such are subject, as, e.g., in that of health or of illness. Hence it follows that no attribute coming under the head of quality in its widest sense, can be predicated of God. Consequently, these three classes of attributes, describing the essence of a thing, or part of the essence, or a quality of it, are clearly inadmissible in reference to God, for they imply composition, which, as we shall prove, is out of question as regards the Creator. We say, with regard to this latter point, that He is absolutely One.

Fourthly. A thing is described by its *relation* to another thing, e.g., to time, to space, or to a different individual; thus we say, Zaid, the father of A, or the partner of B, or who dwells at a certain place, or who lived at a stated time. This kind of attribute does not necessarily imply plurality or change in the essence of the object described; for the same Zaid, to whom reference is made, is the partner of Amru, the father of Becr, the master of Khalid, the friend of Zaid, dwells in a certain house, and was born in a certain year. Such relations are not the essence of a thing, nor are they so intimately connected with it as qualities. At first thought, it would seem that they may be employed in reference to God, but after careful and thorough consideration we are convinced of their inadmissibility. It is quite clear that there is no relation between God and time or space. For time is an accident connected with motion, in so far as the latter includes the relation of anteriority and posteriority, and is expressed by number, as is explained in books devoted to this subject; and since motion is one of the conditions to which only material bodies are subject, and God is immaterial, there can be no relation between Him and time. Similarly there is no relation between Him and space.

But what we have to investigate and to examine is this: whether some real relation exists between God and any of the substances created by Him, by which He could be described? That there is no correlation between Him and any of His creatures can easily be seen; for the characteristic of two objects correlative to each other is the equality of their reciprocal relation. Now, as God has absolute existence, while all other beings have only possible existence, as we shall show, there consequently cannot be any correlation [between God and His creatures]. That a certain kind of relation does exist between them is by some considered possible, but wrongly. It is impossible to imagine a relation between intellect and sight, although, as we believe, the same kind of existence is common to both; how, then, could a relation be imagined between any creature and God, who has nothing in common with any other being; for even the term existence is applied to Him and other things, according to our opinion, only by way of pure homonymity. Consequently there is no relation whatever between Him and any other being. For whenever we speak of a relation between two things, these belong to the same kind; but when two things belong to different kinds though of the same class, there is no relation between them. We therefore do not say, this red compared with that green, is more, or less, or equally intense, although both belong to the same class—color; when they belong to two different classes, there does not appear to exist any relation between them, not even to a man of ordinary intellect, although the two things belong to the same category; e.g., between a hundred cubits and the heat of pepper there is no relation, the one being a quality, the other a quantity; or between wisdom and sweetness, between meekness and bitterness, although all these come under the head of quality in its more general signification. How, then, could there be any relation between God and His creatures, considering the important difference between them in respect to true existence, the greatest of all differences. Besides, if any relation existed between them, God would be subject to the accident of relation; and although that would not be an accident to the essence of God, it would still be, to some extent, a kind of accident. You would, therefore, be wrong if you applied affirmative attributes in their literal sense to God, though they contained only relations; these, however, are the most appropriate of all attributes, to be employed, in a less strict sense, in reference to God, because they do not imply that a plurality of eternal things exists, or that any change takes place in the essence of God, when those things change to which God is in relation.

Fifthly. A thing is described by its *actions;* I do not mean by "its actions" the inherent capacity for a certain work, as is expressed in "carpenter," "painter," or "smith"—for these belong to the class of qualities which have been mentioned above—but I mean the action the latter has performed—we speak, e.g., of Zaid, who made this door, built that wall, wove that garment. This kind of attributes is separate from the essences of the thing described, and, therefore, appropriate to be employed in describing the Creator, especially since we know that these different actions do not imply that different elements must be contained in the substance of the agent, by which the different actions are produced, as will be explained. On the contrary, all the actions of God emanate from His essence, not from any extraneous thing superadded to His essence, as we have shown.

What we have explained in the present chapter is this: that God is one in every respect, containing no plurality or any element superadded to His essence: and that the many attributes of different significations applied in Scripture to God, originate in the multitude of His actions, not in a plurality existing in His essence, and are partly employed with the object of conveying to us some notion of His perfection, in accordance with what we consider perfection, as has been explained by us. The possibility of one simple substance excluding plurality, though accomplishing different actions, will be illustrated by examples in the next chapter.

Chapter 53

The circumstance which caused men to believe in the existence of divine attributes is similar to that which caused others to believe in the corporeality of God. The latter have not arrived at that belief by speculation, but by following the literal sense of certain passages in the Bible. The same is the case with the attributes; when in the books of the Prophets and of the Law, God is described by attributes, such passages are taken in their literal sense, and it is then believed that God possesses attributes; as if He were to be exalted above corporeality, and not above things connected with corporeality, i.e., the accidents, I mean psychical dispositions, all of which are qualities [and connected with corporeality]. Every attribute which the followers of this doctrine assume to be essential to the Creator, you will find to express, although they do not distinctly say so, a quality similar to those which they are accustomed to notice in the bodies of all living beings. We apply to all such passages the principle, "The Torah speaketh in the language of man," and say that the object of all these terms is to describe God as the most perfect being, not as possessing those qualities which are only perfections in relation to created living beings. Many of the attributes express different acts of God, but that difference does not necessitate any difference as regards Him from whom the acts proceed. This fact, viz., that from one agency different effects may result, although that agency has not free will, and much more so if it has free will, I will illustrate by an instance taken from our own sphere. Fire melts certain things and makes others hard, it boils and burns, it bleaches and blackens. If we described the fire as bleaching, blackening, burning, boiling, hardening and melting, we should be correct, and yet he who does not know the nature of fire, would think that it included six different elements, one by which it blackens, another by which it bleaches, a third by which it boils, a fourth by which it consumes, a fifth by which it melts, a sixth by which it hardens things—actions which are opposed to one another, and of which each has its peculiar property. He, however, who knows the nature of fire, will know that by virtue of one quality in action, namely, by heat, it produces all these effects. If this is the case with that which is done by nature, how much more is it the case with regard to beings that act by free will, and still more with regard to God, who is above all description. If we, therefore, perceive in God certain relations of various kinds—for wisdom in us is different from power, and power from will—it does by no means follow that different elements are really contained in Him, that He contains one element by which He knows, another by which He wills, and another by which He exercises power, as is, in fact, the signification of the attributes of God according to the Attributists. Some of them express it plainly, and enumerate the attributes as elements added to the essence. Others, however, are more reserved with regard to this matter, but indicate their opinion, though they do not express it in distinct and intelligible words. Thus, e.g., some of them say: "God is omnipotent by His essence, wise by His essence, living by His essence, and endowed with a will by His essence." (I will mention to you, as an instance, man's reason, which being one faculty and implying no plurality, enables him to know many arts and sciences; by the same faculty man is able to sow, to do carpenter's work, to weave, to build, to study, to acquire a knowledge of geometry, and to govern a state. These various acts resulting from one simple faculty, which involves no plurality, are very numerous; their number, that is, the number of the actions originating in man's reason, is almost infinite. It is therefore intelligible how in reference to God, those different actions can be caused by one simple substance, that does not include any plurality or any additional element. The attributes found in Holy Scripture are either qualifications of His actions, without any reference to His essence, or indicate absolute perfection, but do not imply that the essence of God is a compound of various elements.) For in not admitting the *term* "compound," they do not reject the *idea* of a compound when they admit a substance with attributes.

There still remains one difficulty which led them to that error, and which I am now going to mention. Those who assert the existence of the attributes do not found their opinion on the variety of God's actions; they say it is true that one substance can be the source of various effects, but His essential attributes cannot be qualifications of His actions, because it is impossible to imagine that the Creator created Himself. They vary with regard to the so-called essential attributes—I mean as regards their number—according to the text of the Scripture which each of them follows. I will enumerate those on which all agree, and the knowledge of which they believe that they have derived from reasoning, not from some words of the Prophets, namely, the following four:—life, power, wisdom, and will. They believe that these are four different things, and such perfections as cannot possibly be absent from the Creator, and that these cannot be qualifications of His actions. This is their opinion. But you must know that wisdom and life in reference to God are not different from each other; for in every being that is conscious of itself, life and wisdom are the same thing, that is to say, if by wisdom we understand the consciousness of self. Besides, the subject and the object of that consciousness are undoubtedly identical [as regards God]; for according to our opinion, He is not composed of an element that apprehends, and another that does not apprehend; He is not like man, who is a combination of a conscious soul and an unconscious body. If, therefore, by "wisdom" we mean the faculty of self-consciousness, wisdom and life are one and the same thing. They, however, do not speak of wisdom in this sense, but of His power to apprehend His creatures. There is also no doubt that power and will do not exist in God in reference to Himself; for He cannot have power or will as regards Himself; we cannot imagine such a thing. They take these attributes as different relations between God and His creatures, signifying that He has power in creating things, will in giving to things existence as He desires, and wisdom in knowing what He created. Consequently, these attributes do not refer to the essence of God, but express relations between Him and His creatures.

Therefore we, who truly believe in the Unity of God, declare, that as we do not believe that some element is included in His essence by which He created the heavens, another by which He created the [four] elements, a third by which He created the ideals, in the same way we reject the idea that His essence contains an element by which He has power, another element by which He has will, and a third by which He has a knowledge of His creatures. On the contrary, He is a simple essence, without any additional element whatever; He created the universe, and knows it, but not by any extraneous force. There is no difference whether these various attributes refer to His actions or to relations between Him and His works; in fact, these relations, as we have also shown, exist only in the thoughts of men. This is what we must believe concerning the attributes occurring in the books of the Prophets; some may also be taken as expressive of the perfection of God by way of comparison with what we consider as perfections in us. . . .

*   *   *

Chapter 58

This chapter is even more recondite than the preceding. Know that the negative attributes of God are the true attributes: they do not include any incorrect notions or any deficiency whatever in reference to God, while positive attributes imply polytheism, and are inadequate, as we have already shown. It is now necessary to explain how negative expressions can in a certain sense be employed as attributes, and how they are distinguished from positive attributes. Then I shall show that we cannot describe the Creator by any means except by negative attributes. An attribute does not exclusively belong to the one object to which it is related; while qualifying one thing, it can also be employed to qualify other things, and is in that case not peculiar to that one thing. E.g., if you see an object from a distance, and on enquiring what it is, are told that it is a living being, you have certainly learnt an attribute of the object seen, and although that attribute does not exclusively belong to the object perceived, it expresses that the object is not a plant or a mineral. Again, if a man is in a certain house, and you know that something is in the house, but not exactly what, you ask what is in that house, and you are told, not a plant nor a mineral. You have thereby obtained some special knowledge of the thing; you have learnt that it is a living being, although you do not yet know what kind of a living being it is. The negative attributes have this in common with the positive, that they necessarily circumscribe the object to some extent, although such circumscription consists only in the exclusion of what otherwise would not be excluded. In the following point, however, the negative attributes are distinguished from the positive. The positive attributes, although not peculiar to one thing, describe a portion of what we desire to know, either some part of its essence or some of its accidents; the negative attributes, on the other hand, do not, as regards the essence of the thing which we desire to know, in any way tell us what it is, except it be indirectly, as has been shown in the instance given by us.

After this introduction, I would observe that,—as has already been shown— God's existence is absolute, that it includes no composition, as will be proved, and that we comprehend only the fact that He exists, not His essence. Consequently it is a false assumption to hold that He has any positive attribute; for He does not possess existence in addition to His essence; it therefore cannot be said that the one may be described as an attribute [of the other]; much less has He [in addition to His existence] a compound essence, consisting of two constituent elements to which the attribute could refer; still less has He accidents, which could be described by an attribute. Hence it is clear that He has no positive attribute whatever. The negative attributes, however, are those which are necessary to direct the mind to the truths which we must believe concerning God; for, on the one hand, they do not imply any plurality, and, on the other, they convey to man the highest possible knowledge of God; e.g., it has been established by proof that some being must exist besides those things which can be perceived by the senses, or apprehended by the mind; when we say of this being, that it exists, we mean that its non-existence is impossible. We then perceive that such a being is not, for instance, like the four elements, which are inanimate, and we therefore say that it is living, expressing thereby that it is not dead. We call such a being incorporeal, because we notice that it is unlike the heavens, which are living, but material. Seeing that it is also different from the intellect, which, though incorporeal and living, owes its existence to some cause, we say it is the first, expressing thereby that its existence is not due to any cause. We further notice, that the existence, that is the essence, of this being is not limited to its own existence; many existences emanate from it, and its influence is not like that of the fire in producing heat, or that of the sun in sending forth light, but consists in constantly giving them stability and order by well-established rule, as we shall show: we say, on that account, it has power, wisdom, and will, i.e., it is not feeble or ignorant, or hasty, and does not abandon its creatures; when we say that it is not feeble, we mean that its existence is capable of producing the existence of many other things; by saying that it is not ignorant, we mean "it perceives" or "it lives,"—for everything that perceives is living—by saying "it is not hasty, and does not abandon its creatures," we mean that all these creatures preserve a certain order and arrangement; they are not left to themselves; they are not produced aimlessly, but whatever condition they receive from that being is given with design and intention. We thus learn that there is no other being like unto God, and we say that He is One, i.e., there are not more Gods than one.

It has thus been shown that every attribute predicated of God either denotes the quality of an action, or—when the attribute is intended to convey some idea of the Divine Being itself, and not of His actions—the negation of the opposite. Even these negative attributes must not be formed and applied to God, except in the way in which, as you know, sometimes an attribute is negatived in reference to a thing, although that attribute can naturally never be applied to it in the same sense, as, e.g., we say, "This wall does not see." Those who read the present work are aware that, notwithstanding all the efforts of the mind, we can obtain no knowledge of the essence of the heavens—a revolving substance which has been measured by us in spans and cubits, and examined even as regards the proportions of the several spheres to each other and respecting most of their motions—although we know that they must consist of matter and form; but the matter not being the same as sublunary matter, we can only describe the heavens in terms expressing negative properties, but not in terms denoting positive qualities. Thus we say that the heavens are not light, not heavy, not passive and therefore not subject to impressions, and that they do not possess the sensations of taste and smell; or we use similar negative attributes. All this we do, because we do not know their substance. What, then, can be the result of our efforts, when we try to obtain a knowledge of a Being that is free from substance, that is most simple, whose existence is absolute, and not due to any cause, to whose perfect essence nothing can be superadded, and whose perfection consists, as we have shown, in the absence of all defects. All we understand is the fact that He exists, that He is a Being to whom none of His creatures is similar, who has nothing in common with them, who does not include plurality, who is never too feeble to produce other beings, and whose relation to the universe is that of a steersman to a boat; and even this is not a real relation, a real simile, but serves only to convey to us the idea that God rules the universe; that is, that He gives it duration, and preserves its necessary arrangement. This subject will be treated more fully. Praised be He! In the contemplation of His essence, our comprehension and knowledge prove insufficient; in the examination of His works, how they necessarily result from His will, our knowledge proves to be ignorance, and in the endeavor to extol Him in words, all our efforts in speech are mere weakness and failure!

Chapter 59

The following question might perhaps be asked: Since there is no possibility of obtaining a knowledge of the true essence of God, and since it has also been proved that the only thing that man can apprehend of Him is the fact that He exists, and that all positive attributes are inadmissible, as has been shown; what is the difference among those who have obtained a knowledge of God? Must not the knowledge obtained by our teacher Moses, and by Solomon, be the same as that obtained by any one of the lowest class of philosophers, since there can be no addition to this knowledge? But, on the other hand, it is generally accepted among theologians and also among philosophers, that there can be a great difference between two persons as regards the knowledge of God obtained by them. Know that this is really the case, that those who have obtained a knowledge of God differ greatly from each other, for in the same way as by each additional attribute an object is more specified, and is brought nearer to the true apprehension of the observer, so by each additional negative attribute you advance toward the knowledge of God, and you are nearer to it than he who does not negative, in reference to God, those qualities which you are convinced by proof must be negatived. There may thus be a man who after having earnestly devoted many years to the pursuit of one science, and to the true understanding of its principles, till he is fully convinced of its truths, has obtained as the sole result of this study the conviction that a certain quality must be negatived in reference to God, and the capacity of demonstrating that it is impossible to apply it to Him. Superficial thinkers will have no proof for this, will doubtfully ask, Is that thing existing in the Creator, or not? And those who are deprived of sight will positively ascribe it to God, although it has been clearly shown that He does not possess it. E.g., while I show that God is incorporeal, another doubts and is not certain whether He is corporeal or incorporeal; others even positively declare that He is corporeal, and appear before the Lord with that belief. Now see how great the difference is between these three men; the first is undoubtedly nearest to the Almighty; the second is remote, and the third still more distant from Him. If there be a fourth person who holds himself convinced by proof that emotions are impossible in God, while the first who rejects the corporeality, is not convinced of that impossibility, that fourth person is undoubtedly nearer the knowledge of God than the first, and so on, so that a person who, convinced by proof, negatives a number of things in reference to God, which according to our belief may possibly be in Him or emanate from Him, is undoubtedly a more perfect man than we are, and would surpass us still more if we positively believed these things to be properties of God. It will now be clear to you, that every time you establish by proof the negation of a thing in reference to God, you become more perfect, while with every additional positive assertion you follow your imagination and recede from the true knowledge of God. Only by such ways must we approach the knowledge of God, and by such researches and studies as would show us the inapplicability of what is inadmissible as regards the Creator, not by such methods as would prove the necessity of ascribing to Him anything extraneous to His essence, or asserting that He has a certain perfection, when we find it to be a perfection in relation to us. The perfections are all to some extent acquired properties, and a property which must be acquired does not exist in everything capable of making such acquisition.

You must bear in mind, that by affirming anything of God, you are removed from Him in two respects; first, whatever you affirm, is only a perfection in relation to us; secondly, He does not possess anything superadded to this essence; His essence includes all His perfections, as we have shown. Since it is a well-known fact that even that knowledge of God which is accessible to man cannot be attained except by negations, and that negations do not convey a true idea of the being to which they refer, all people, both of past and present generations, declared that God cannot be the object of human comprehension, that none but Himself comprehends what He is, and that our knowledge consists in knowing that we are unable truly to comprehend Him. All philosophers say, "He has overpowered us by His grace, and is invisible to us through the intensity of His light," like the sun which cannot be perceived by eyes which are too weak to bear its rays. Much more has been said on this topic, but it is useless to repeat it here. The idea is best expressed in the book of Psalms, "Silence is praise to Thee" (lxv. 2). It is a very expressive remark on this subject; for whatever we utter with the intention of extolling and of praising Him, contains something that cannot be applied to God, and includes derogatory expressions; it is therefore more becoming to be silent, and to be content with intellectual reflection, as has been recommended by men of the highest culture, in the words "Commune with your own heart upon your bed, and be still" (Ps. iv. 4). You must surely know the following celebrated passage in the Talmud—would that all passages in the Talmud were like that!—although it is known to you, I quote it literally, as I wish to point out to you the ideas contained in it: "A certain person, reading prayers in the presence of Rabbi Haninah, said, 'God, the great, the valiant and the tremendous, the powerful, the strong and the mighty.'—The rabbi said to him, Have you finished all the praises of your Master? The three epithets, 'God, the great, the valiant and the tremendous,' we should not have applied to God, had Moses not mentioned them in the Law, and had not the men of the Great Synagogue come forward subsequently and established their use in the prayer; and you say all this! Let this be illustrated by a parable. There was once an earthly king, possessing millions of gold coin; he was praised for owning millions of silver coin; was this not really dispraise to him?" Thus for the opinion of the pious rabbi. Consider, first, how repulsive and annoying the accumulation of all these positive attributes was to him; next, how he showed that if we had only to follow our reason, we should never have composed these prayers, and we should not have uttered any of them. It has, however, become necessary to address men in words that should leave some idea in their minds, and, in accordance with the saying of our Sages, "The Torah speaks in the language of men," the Creator has been described to us in terms of our own perfections; but we should not on that account have uttered any other than the three above-mentioned attributes, and we should not have used them as names of God except when meeting with them in reading the Law. Subsequently, the men of the Great Synagogue, who were prophets, introduced these expressions also into the prayer, but we should not on that account use [in our prayers] any other attributes of God. The principal lesson to be derived from this passage is that there are two reasons for our employing those phrases in our prayers: first, they occur in the Pentateuch; secondly, the Prophets introduced them into the prayer. Were it not for the first reason, we should never have uttered them; and were it not for the second reason, we should not have copied them from the Pentateuch to recite them in our prayers; how then could we approve of the use of those numerous attributes! You also learn from this that we ought not to mention and employ in our prayers all the attributes we find applied to God in the books of the Prophets; for he does not say, "Were it not that Moses, our Teacher, said them, we should not have been able to use them"; but he adds another condition—"and had not the men of the Great Synagogue come forward and established their use in the prayer," because only for that reason are we allowed to use them in our prayers. We cannot approve of what those foolish persons do who are extravagant in praise, fluent and prolix in the prayers they compose, and in the hymns they make in the desire to approach the Creator. They describe God in attributes which would be an offence if applied to a human being; for those persons have no knowledge of these great and important principles, which are not accessible to the ordinary intelligence of man. Treating the Creator as a familiar object, they describe Him and speak of Him in any expressions they think proper; they eloquently continue to praise Him in that manner, and believe that they can thereby influence Him and produce an effect on Him. If they find some phrase suited to their object in the words of the Prophets they are still more inclined to consider that they are free to make use of such texts—which should at least be explained—to employ them in their literal sense, to derive new expressions from them, to form from them numerous variations, and to found whole compositions on them. This license is frequently met with in the compositions of the singers, preachers, and others who imagine themselves to be able to compose a poem. Such authors write things which partly are real heresy, partly contain such folly and absurdity that they naturally cause those who hear them to laugh, but also to feel grieved at the thought that such things can be uttered in reference to God. Were it not that I pitied the authors for their defects, and did not wish to injure them, I should have cited some passages to show you their mistakes; besides, the fault of their compositions is obvious to all intelligent persons. You must consider it, and think thus: If slander and libel is a great sin, how much greater is the sin of those who speak with looseness of tongue in reference to God, and describe Him by attributes which are far below Him; and I declare that they not only commit an ordinary sin, but unconsciously at least incur the guilt of profanity and blasphemy. This applies both to the multitude that listens to such prayers, and to the foolish man that recites them. Men, however, who understand the fault of such compositions, and, nevertheless, recite them, may be classed, according to my opinion, among those to whom the following words are applied: "And the children of Israel used words that were not right against the Lord their God" (2 Kings xvii. 9); and "utter error against the Lord" (Isa. xxxii. 6). If you are of those who regard the honor of their Creator, do not listen in any way to them, much less utter what they say, and still less compose such prayers, knowing how great is the offence of one who hurls aspersions against the Supreme Being. There is no necessity at all for you to use positive attributes of God with the view of magnifying Him in your thoughts, or to go beyond the limits which the men of the Great Synagogue have introduced in the prayers and in the blessings, for this is sufficient for all purposes, and even more than sufficient, as Rabbi Haninah said. Other attributes, such as occur in the books of the Prophets, may be uttered when we meet with them in reading those books; but we must bear in mind what has already been explained, that they are either attributes of God's actions, or expressions implying the negation of the opposite. This likewise should not be divulged to the multitude; but a reflection of this kind is fitted for the few only who believe that the glorification of God does not consist in *uttering* that which is not to be uttered, but in *reflecting* on that on which man should reflect.

We will now conclude our exposition of the wise words of R. Haninah. He does not employ any such simile as: "A king who possesses millions of gold denarii, and is praised as having hundreds"; for this would imply that God's perfections, although more perfect than those ascribed to man are still of the same kind; but this is not the case, as has been proved. The excellence of the simile consists in the words: "who possesses golden denarii, and is praised as having silver denarii"; this implies that these attributes, though perfections as regards ourselves, are not such as regards God; in reference to Him they would all be defects, as is distinctly suggested in the remark, "Is this not an offence to Him?"

I have already told you that all these attributes, whatever perfection they may denote according to your idea, imply defects in reference to God, if applied to Him in the same sense as they are used in reference to ourselves. Solomon has already given us sufficient instruction on this subject by saying, "For God is in heaven, and thou upon earth; therefore let thy words be few" (Eccles. v. 2).

Chapter 60

I will give you in this chapter some illustrations, in order that you may better understand the propriety of forming as many negative attributes as possible, and the impropriety of ascribing to God any positive attributes. A person may know for certain that a "ship" is in existence, but he may not know to what object that name is applied, whether to a substance or to an accident; a second person then learns that the ship is not an accident; a third, that it is not a mineral; a fourth, that it is not a plant growing in the earth; a fifth, that it is not a body whose parts are joined together by nature; a sixth, that it is not a flat object like boards or doors; a seventh, that it is not a sphere; an eighth, that it is not pointed; a ninth, that it is not round-shaped; nor equilateral; a tenth, that it is not solid. It is clear that this tenth person has almost arrived at the correct notion of a "ship" by the foregoing negative attributes, as if he had exactly the same notion as those have who imagine it to be a wooden substance which is hollow, long, and composed of many pieces of wood, that is to say, who know it by positive attributes. Of the other persons in our illustration, each one is more remote from the correct notion of a ship than the next mentioned, so that the first knows nothing about it but the name. In the same manner you will come nearer to the knowledge and comprehension of God by the negative attributes. But you must be careful, in what you negative, to negative by proof, not by mere words, for each time you ascertain by proof that a certain thing, believed to exist in the Creator, must be negatived, you have undoubtedly come one step nearer to the knowledge of God.

It is in this sense that some men come very near to God, and others remain exceedingly remote from Him, not in the sense of those who are deprived of vision, and believe that God occupies a place, which man can physically approach or from which he can recede. Examine this well, know it, and be content with it. The way which will bring you nearer to God has been clearly shown to you; walk in it, if you have the desire. On the other hand, there is a great danger in applying positive attributes to God. For it has been shown that every perfection we could imagine, even if existing in God in accordance with the opinion of those who assert the existence of attributes, would in reality not be of the same kind as that imagined by us, but would only be called by the same name, according to our explanation; it would in fact amount to a negation. Suppose, e.g., you say He has knowledge, and that knowledge, which admits of no change and of no plurality, embraces many changeable things; His knowledge remains unaltered, while new things are constantly formed, and His knowledge of a thing before it exists, while it exists, and when it has ceased to exist, is the same without the least change: you would thereby declare that His knowledge is not like ours; and similarly that His existence is not like ours. You thus necessarily arrive at some negation, without obtaining a true conception of an essential attribute; on the contrary, you are led to assume that there is a plurality in God, and to believe that He, though one essence, has several unknown attributes. For if you intend to affirm them, you cannot compare them with those attributes known by us, and they are consequently not of the same kind. You are, as it were, brought by the belief in the reality of the attributes, to say that God is one subject of which several things are predicated; though the subject is not like ordinary subjects, and the predicates are not like ordinary predicates. This belief would ultimately lead us to associate other things with God, and not to believe that He is One. For of every subject certain things can undoubtedly be predicated, and although in reality subject and predicate are combined in one thing, by the actual definition they consist of two elements, the notion contained in the subject not being the same as that contained in the predicate. In the course of this treatise it will be proved to you that God cannot be a compound, and that He is simple in the strictest sense of the word.

I do not merely declare that he who affirms attributes of God has not sufficient knowledge concerning the Creator, admits some association with God, or conceives Him to be different from what He is; but I say that he unconsciously loses his belief in God. For he whose knowledge concerning a thing is insufficient, understands one part of it while he is ignorant of the other, as, e.g., a person who knows that man possesses life, but does not know that man possesses understanding; but in reference to God, in whose real existence there is no plurality, it is impossible that one thing should be known, and another unknown. Similarly he who associates an object with [the properties of] another object, conceives a true and correct notion of the one object, and applies that notion also to the other, while those who admit the attributes of God, do not consider them as identical with His essence, but as extraneous elements. Again, he who conceives an incorrect notion of an object, must necessarily have a correct idea of the object to some extent; he, however, who says that taste belongs to the category of quantity has not, according to my opinion, an incorrect notion of taste, but is entirely ignorant of its nature, for he does not know to what object the term "taste" is to be applied.—This is a very difficult subject; consider it well.

According to this explanation you will understand, that those who do not recognize, in reference to God, the negation of things, which others negative by clear proof, are deficient in the knowledge of God, and are remote from comprehending Him. Consequently, the smaller the number of things is which a person can negative in relation to God, the less he knows of Him, as has been explained in the beginning of this chapter; but the man who affirms an attribute of God, knows nothing but the name; for the object to which, in his imagination, he applies that name, does not exist; it is a mere fiction and invention, as if he applied that name to a non-existing being, for there is, in reality, no such object. E.g., some one has heard of the elephant, and knows that it is an animal, and wishes to know its form and nature. A person, who is either misled or misleading, tells him it is an animal with one leg, three wings, lives in the depth of the sea, has a transparent body; its face is wide like that of a man, has the same form and shape, speaks like a man, flies sometimes in the air, and sometimes swims like a fish. I should not say, that he described the elephant incorrectly, or that he has an insufficient knowledge of the elephant, but I would say that the thing thus described is an invention and fiction, and that in reality there exists nothing like it; it is a non-existing being, called by the name of a really existing being, and like the griffin, the centaur, and similar imaginary combinations for which simple and compound names have been borrowed from real things. The present case is analogous; namely, God, praised be His name, exists, and His existence has been proved to be absolute and perfectly simple, as I shall explain. If such a simple, absolutely existing essence were said to have attributes, as has been contended, and were combined with extraneous elements, it would in no way be an existing thing, as has been proved by us; and when we say that that essence, which is called "God," is a substance with many properties by which it can be described, we apply that name to an object which does not at all exist. Consider, therefore, what are the consequences of affirming attributes to God! As to those attributes of God which occur in the Pentateuch, or in the books of the Prophets, we must assume that they are exclusively employed, as has been stated by us, to convey to us some notion of the perfections of the Creator, or to express qualities of actions emanating from Him.

* * *

PART II

Introduction

Twenty-five of the propositions which are employed in the proof for the existence of God, or in the arguments demonstrating that God is neither corporeal nor a force connected with a material being, or that He is One, have been fully established, and their correctness is beyond doubt. Aristotle and the Peripatetics who followed him have proved each of these propositions. There is, however, one proposition which we do not accept—namely, the proposition which affirms the Eternity of the Universe, but we will admit it for the present, because by doing so we shall be enabled clearly to demonstrate our own theory.

PROPOSITION I: The existence of an infinite magnitude is impossible.

PROPOSITION II: The co-existence of an infinite number of finite magnitudes is impossible.

PROPOSITION III: The existence of an infinite number of causes and effects is impossible, even if these were not magnitudes; if, e.g., one Intelligence were the cause of a second, the second the cause of a third, the third the cause of a fourth, and so on, the series could not be continued ad infinitum.

Proposition IV: Four categories are subject to change:—

(a.) *Substance.*—Changes which affect the substance of a thing are called genesis and destruction.

(b.) *Quantity.*—Changes in reference to quantity are increase and decrease.

(c.) *Quality.*—Changes in the qualities of things are transformations.

(d.) *Place.*—Change of place is called motion.

The term "motion" is properly applied to change of place, but is also used in a general sense of all kinds of changes.

PROPOSITION V: Motion implies change and transition from potentiality to actuality.

PROPOSITION VI: The motion of a thing is either essential or accidental; or it is due to an external force, or to the participation of the thing in the motion of another thing. This latter kind of motion is similar to the accidental one. An instance of essential motion may be found in the translation of a thing from one place to another. The accident of a thing, as, e.g., its black color, is said to move when the thing itself changes its place. The upward motion of a stone, owing to a force applied to it in that direction, is an instance of a motion due to an external force. The motion of a nail in a boat may serve to illustrate motion due to the participation of a thing in the motion of another thing; for when the boat moves, the nail is said to move likewise. The same is the case with everything composed of several parts: when the thing itself moves, every part of it is likewise said to move.

PROPOSITION VII: Things which are changeable are, at the same time, divisible. Hence everything that moves is divisible, and consequently corporeal; but that which is indivisible cannot move, and cannot therefore be corporeal.

PROPOSITION VIII: A thing that moves accidentally must come to rest, because it does not move of its own accord; hence accidental motion cannot continue for ever.

PROPOSITION IX: A corporeal thing that sets another corporeal thing in motion can only effect this by setting itself in motion at the time it causes the other thing to move.

PROPOSITION X: A thing which is said to be contained in a corporeal object must satisfy either of the two following conditions: it either exists through that object, as is the case with accidents, or it is the cause of the existence of that object; such is, e.g., its essential property. In both cases it is a force existing in a corporeal object.

PROPOSITION XI: Among the things which exist through a material object, there are some which participate in the division of that object, and are therefore accidentally divisible, as, e.g., its color, and all other qualities that spread throughout its parts. On the other hand, among the things which form the essential elements of an object, there are some which cannot be divided in any way, as, e.g., the soul and the intellect.

PROPOSITION XII: A force which occupies all parts of a corporeal object is finite, that object itself being finite.

PROPOSITION XIII: None of the several kinds of change can be continuous, except motion from place to place, provided it be circular.

PROPOSITION XIV: Locomotion is in the natural order of the several kinds of motion the first and foremost. For genesis and corruption are preceded by transformation, which, in its turn, is preceded by the approach of the transforming agent to the object which is to be transformed. Also, increase and decrease are impossible without previous genesis and corruption.

PROPOSITION XV: Time is an accident that is related and joined to motion in such a manner that the one is never found without the other. Motion is only possible in time, and the idea of time cannot be conceived otherwise than in connection with motion; things which do not move have no relation to time.

PROPOSITION XVI: Incorporeal bodies can only be numbered when they are forces situated in a body; the several forces must then be counted together with substances or objects in which they exist. Hence purely spiritual beings, which are neither corporeal nor forces situated in corporeal objects, cannot be counted, except when considered as causes and effects.

PROPOSITION XVII: When an object moves, there must be some agent that moves it, from without, as, e.g., in the case of a stone set in motion by the hand; or from within, e.g., when the body of a living being moves. Living beings include in themselves, at the same time, the moving agent and the thing moved; when, therefore, a living being dies, and the moving agent, the soul, has left the body, i.e., the thing moved, the body remains for some time in the same condition as before, and yet cannot move in the manner it has moved previously. The moving agent, when included in the thing moved, is hidden from, and imperceptible to, the senses. This circumstance gave rise to the belief that the body of an animal moves without the aid of a moving agent. When we therefore affirm, concerning a thing in motion, that it is its own moving agent, or, as is generally said, that it moves of its own accord, we mean to say that the force which really sets the body in motion exists in that body itself.

PROPOSITION XVIII: Everything that passes over from a state of potentiality to that of actuality, is caused to do so by some external agent; because if that agent existed in the thing itself, and no obstacle prevented the transition, the thing would never be in a state of potentiality, but always in that of actuality. If, on the other hand, while the thing itself contained that agent, some obstacle existed, and at a certain time that obstacle was removed, the same cause which removed the obstacle would undoubtedly be described as the cause of the transition from potentiality to actuality, [and not the force situated within the body]. Note this.

PROPOSITION XIX: A thing which owes its existence to certain causes has in itself merely the possibility of existence; for only if these causes exist, the thing likewise exists. It does not exist if the causes do not exist at all, or if they have ceased to exist, or if there has been a change in the relation which implies the existence of that thing as a necessary consequence of those causes.

PROPOSITION XX: A thing which has in itself the necessity of existence cannot have for its existence any cause whatever.

PROPOSITION XXI: A thing composed of two elements has necessarily their composition as the cause of its present existence. Its existence is therefore not necessitated by its own essence; it depends on the existence of its two component parts and their combination.

PROPOSITION XXII: Material objects are always composed of two elements [at least], and are without exception subject to accidents. The two component elements of all bodies are substance and form. The accidents attributed to material objects are quantity, geometrical form, and position.

PROPOSITION XXIII: Everything that exists potentially, and whose essence includes a certain state of possibility, may at some time be without actual existence.

PROPOSITION XXIV: That which is potentially a certain thing is necessarily material, for the state of possibility is always connected with matter.

PROPOSITION XXV: Each compound substance consists of matter and form, and requires an agent for its existence, viz., a force which sets the substance in motion, and thereby enables it to receive a certain form. The force which thus prepares the substance of a certain individual being, is called the immediate motor. Here the necessity arises of investigating into the properties of motion, the moving agent and the thing moved. But this has already been explained sufficiently; and the opinion of Aristotle may be expressed in the following proposition: Matter does not move of its own accord—an important proposition that led to the investigation of the Prime Motor (the first moving agent).

Of these foregoing twenty-five propositions some may be verified by means of a little reflection and the application of a few propositions capable of proof, or of axioms or theorems of almost the same force, such as have been explained by me. Others require many arguments and propositions, all of which, however, have been established by conclusive proofs partly in the Physics and its commentaries, and partly in the Metaphysics and its commentary. I have already stated that in this work it is not my intention to copy the books of the philosophers or to explain difficult problems, but simply to mention those propositions which are closely connected with our subject, and which we want for our purpose.

To the above propositions one must be added which enunciates that the universe is eternal, and which is held by Aristotle to be true, and even more acceptable than any other theory. For the present we admit it, as a hypothesis, only for the purpose of demonstrating our theory. It is the following proposition:—

PROPOSITION XXVI: Time and motion are eternal, constant, and in actual existence.

In accordance with this proposition, Aristotle is compelled to assume that there exists actually a body with constant motion, viz., the fifth element. He therefore says that the heavens are not subject to genesis or destruction, because motion cannot be generated nor destroyed. He also holds that every motion must necessarily be preceded by another motion, either of the same or of a different kind. The belief that the locomotion of an animal is not preceded by another motion, is not true; for the animal is caused to move, after it had been in rest, by the intention to obtain those very things which bring about that locomotion. A change in its state of health, or some image, or some new idea can produce a desire to seek that which is conducive to its welfare and to avoid that which is contrary. Each of these three causes sets the living being in motion, and each of them is produced by various kinds of motion. Aristotle likewise asserts that everything which is created must, before its actual creation, have existed *in potentiâ*. By inferences drawn from this assertion he seeks to establish his proposition, viz., The thing that moves is finite, and its path finite; but it repeats the motion in its path an infinite number of times. This can only take place when the motion is circular, as has been stated in Proposition XIII. Hence follows also the existence of an infinite number of things which do not co-exist but follow one after the other.

Aristotle frequently attempts to establish this proposition; but I believe that he did not consider his proofs to be conclusive. It appeared to him to be the most probable and acceptable proposition. His followers, however, and the commentators of his books, contend that it contains not only a probable but a demonstrative proof, and that it has, in fact, been fully established. On the other hand, the Mutakallemim try to prove that the proposition cannot be true, as, according to their opinion, it is impossible to conceive how an infinite number of things could even come into existence successively. They assume this impossibility as an axiom. I, however, think that this proposition is admissible, but neither demonstrative, as the commentators of Aristotle assert, nor, on the other hand, impossible, as the Mutakallemim say. We have no intention to explain here the proofs given by Aristotle, or to show our doubts concerning them, or to set forth our opinions on the creation of the universe. I here simply desire to mention those propositions which we shall require for the proof of the three principles stated above. Having thus quoted and admitted these propositions, I will now proceed to explain what may be inferred from them.

*   *   *

Chapter 13

Among those who believe in the existence of God, there are found three different theories as regards the question whether the Universe is eternal or not.

First Theory.—Those who follow the Law of Moses, our Teacher, hold that the whole Universe, i.e., everything except God, has been brought by Him into existence out of non-existence. In the beginning God alone existed, and nothing else; neither angels, nor spheres, nor the things that are contained within the spheres existed. He then produced from nothing all existing things such as they are, by His will and desire. Even time itself is among the things created; for time depends on motion, i.e., on an accident in things which move, and the things upon whose motion time depends are themselves created beings, which have passed from non-existence into existence. We say that God *existed* before the creation of the Universe, although the verb *existed* appears to imply the notion of time; we also believe that He existed an infinite space of time before the Universe was created; but in these cases we do not mean time in its true sense. We only use the term to signify something analogous or similar to time. For time is undoubtedly an accident, and, according to our opinion, one of the created accidents, like blackness and whiteness; it is not a quality, but an accident connected with motion. This must be clear to all who understand what Aristotle has said on time and its real existence.

The following remark does not form an essential part of our present research; it will nevertheless be found useful in the course of this discussion. Many scholars do not know what time really is, and men like Galen were so perplexed about it that they asked whether time has a real existence or not; the reason for this uncertainty is to be found in the circumstance that time is an accident of an accident. Accidents which are directly connected with material bodies, e.g., color and taste, are easily understood, and correct notions are formed of them. There are, however, accidents which are connected with other accidents, e.g., the splendor of color, or the inclination and the curvature of a line; of these it is very difficult to form a correct notion, especially when the accident which forms the substratum for the other accident is not constant but variable. Both difficulties are present in the notion of time: it is an accident of motion, which is itself an accident of a moving object; besides, it is not a fixed property; on the contrary, its true and essential condition is, not to remain in the same state for two consecutive moments. This is the source of ignorance about the nature of time.

We consider time a thing created; it comes into existence in the same manner as other accidents, and the substances which form the substratum for the accidents. For this reason, viz., because time belongs to the things created, it cannot be said that God produced the Universe *in the beginning*. Consider this well; for he who does not understand it is unable to refute forcible objection raised against the theory of *Creatio ex nihilo*. If you admit the existence of time before the Creation, you will be compelled to accept the theory of the Eternity of the Universe. For time is an accident and requires a substratum. You will therefore have to assume that something [beside God] existed before this Universe was created, an assumption which it is our duty to oppose.

This is the first theory, and it is undoubtedly a fundamental principle of the Law of our teacher Moses; it is next in importance to the principle of God's unity. Do not follow any other theory. Abraham, our father, was the first that taught it, after he had established it by philosophical research. He proclaimed, therefore, "the name of the Lord the God of the Universe" (Gen. xxi. 33); and he had previously expressed this theory in the words, "The Possessor of heaven and earth" (*ibid.* xiv. 22).

Second Theory.—The theory of all philosophers whose opinions and works are known to us is this: It is impossible to assume that God produced anything from nothing, or that He reduces anything to nothing; that is to say, it is impossible that an object consisting of matter and form should be produced when that matter is absolutely absent, or that it should be destroyed in such a manner that that matter be absolutely no longer in existence. To say of God that He can produce a thing from nothing or reduce a thing to nothing is, according to the opinion of these philosophers, the same as if we were to say that He could cause one substance to have at the same time two opposite properties, or produce another being like Himself, or change Himself into a body, or produce a square the diagonal of which be equal to its side, or similar impossibilities. The philosophers thus believe that it is no defect in the Supreme Being that He does not produce impossibilities, for the nature of that which is impossible is constant—it does not depend on the action of an agent, and for this reason it cannot be changed, Similarly there is, according to them, no defect in the greatness of God, when He is unable to produce a thing from nothing, because they consider this as one of the impossibilities. They therefore assume that a certain substance has coexisted with God from eternity in such a manner that neither God existed without that substance nor the latter without God. But they do not hold that the existence of that substance equals in rank that of God; for God is the cause of that existence, and the substance is in the same relation to God as the clay is to the potter, or the iron to the smith; God can do with it what He pleases; at one time He forms of it heaven and earth, at another time He forms some other thing. Those who hold this view also assume that the heavens are transient, that they came into existence, though not from nothing, and may cease to exist, although they cannot be reduced to nothing. They are transient in the same manner as the individuals among living beings which are produced from some existing substance, and are again reduced to some substance that remains in existence. The process of genesis and destruction is, in the case of the heavens, the same as in that of earthly beings.

The followers of this theory are divided into different schools, whose opinions and principles it is useless to discuss here; but what I have mentioned is common to all of them. Plato holds the same opinion. Aristotle says in his *Physics* that according to Plato the heavens are transient. This view is also stated in Plato's *Timeus*. His opinion, however, does not agree with our belief; only superficial and careless persons wrongly assume that Plato has the same belief as we have. For whilst we hold that the heavens have been created from absolutely nothing, Plato believes that they have been formed out of something.—This is the second theory.

Third Theory.—viz., that of Aristotle, his followers, and commentators. Aristotle maintains, like the adherents of the second theory, that a corporeal object cannot be produced without a corporeal substance. He goes, however, farther, and contends that the heavens are indestructible. For he holds that the Universe in its totality has never been different, nor will it ever change: the heavens, which form the permanent element in the Universe, and are not subject to genesis and destruction, have always been so; time and motion are eternal, permanent, and have neither beginning nor end; the sublunary world, which includes the transient elements, has always been the same, because the *materia prima* is itself eternal, and merely combines successively with different forms; when one form is removed, another is assumed. This whole arrangement, therefore, both above and here below, is never disturbed or interrupted, and nothing is produced contrary to the laws or the ordinary course of Nature. He further says—though not in the same terms—that he considers it impossible for God to change His will or conceive a new desire; that God produced this Universe in its totality by His will, but not from nothing. Aristotle finds it as impossible to assume that God changes His will or conceives a new desire, as to believe that He is nonexisting, or that His essence is changeable. Hence it follows that this Universe has always been the same in the past, and will be the same eternally.

This is a full account of the opinions of those who consider that the existence of God, the First Cause of the Universe, has been established by proof. But it would be quite useless to mention the opinions of those who do not recognize the existence of God, but believe that the existing state of things is the result of accidental combination and separation of the elements, and that the Universe has no Ruler or Governor. Such is the theory of Epicurus and his school, and similar philosophers, as stated by Alexander

[Aphrodisiensis]; it would be superfluous to repeat their views, since the existence of God has been demonstrated whilst their theory is built upon a basis proved to be untenable. It is likewise useless to prove the correctness of the followers of the second theory in asserting that the heavens are transient, because they at the same time believe in the Eternity of the Universe, and so long as this theory is adopted, it makes no difference to us whether it is believed that the heavens are transient, and that only their substance is eternal, or the heavens are held to be indestructible, in accordance with the view of Aristotle. All who follow the Law of Moses, our Teacher, and Abraham, our Father, and all who adopt similar theories, assume that nothing is eternal except God, and that the theory of *Creatio ex nihilo* includes nothing that is impossible, whilst some thinkers even regard it as an established truth.

After having described the different theories, I will now proceed to show how Aristotle proved his theory, and what induced him to adopt it.

*   *   *

Chapter 17

Everything produced comes into existence from non-existence; even when the substance of a thing has been in existence, and has only changed its form, the thing itself, which has gone through the process of genesis and development, and has arrived at its final state, has now different properties from those which it possessed at the commencement of the transition from potentiality to reality, or before that time. Take, e.g., the human ovum is contained in the female's blood when still included in its vessels; its nature is different from what it was in the moment of conception, when it is met by the semen of the male and begins to develop; the properties of the semen in that moment are different from the properties of the living being after its birth when fully developed. It is therefore quite impossible to infer from the nature which a thing possesses after having passed through all stages of its development, what the condition of the thing has been in the moment when this process commenced; nor does the condition of a thing in this moment show what its previous condition has been. If you make this mistake, and attempt to prove the nature of a thing in potential existence by its properties when actually existing, you will fall into great confusion; you will reject evident truths and admit false opinions. Let us assume, in our above instance, that a man born without defect had after his birth been nursed by his mother only a few months; the mother then died, and the father alone brought him up in a lonely island, till he grew up, became wise, and acquired knowledge. Suppose this man has never seen a woman or any female being; he asks some person how man has come into existence, and how he has developed, and receives the following answer: "Man begins his existence in the womb of an individual of his own class, namely, in the womb of a female, which has a certain form. While in the womb he is very small; yet he has life, moves, receives nourishment, and gradually grows, till he arrives at a certain stage of development. He then leaves the womb and continues to grow till he is in the condition in which you see him." The orphan will naturally ask: "Did this person, when he lived, moved, and grew in the womb, eat and drink, and breathe with his mouth and his nostrils? Did he excrete any substance?" The answer will be, "No." Undoubtedly he will then attempt to refute the statements of that person, and to prove their impossibility, by referring to the properties of a fully developed person, in the following manner: "When any one of us is deprived of breath for a short time he dies, and cannot move any longer: how then can we imagine that any one of us has been inclosed in a bag in the midst of a body for several months and remained alive, able to move? If any one of us would swallow a living bird, the bird would die immediately when it reached the stomach, much more so when it came to the lower part of the belly; if we should not take food or drink with our mouth, in a few days we should undoubtedly be dead: how then can man remain alive for months without taking food? If any person would take food and would not be able to excrete it, great pains and death would follow in a short time, and yet I am to believe that man has lived for months without that function! Suppose by accident a hole were formed in the belly of a person, it would prove fatal, and yet we are to believe that the navel of the fetus has been open! Why should the fetus not open the eyes, spread forth the hands and stretch out the legs, if, as you think, the limbs are all whole and perfect." This mode of reasoning would lead to the conclusion that man cannot come into existence and develop in the manner described.

If philosophers would consider this example well and reflect on it, they would find that it represents exactly the dispute between Aristotle and ourselves. We, the followers of Moses, our Teacher, and of Abraham, our Father, believe that the Universe has been produced and has developed in a certain manner, and that it has been created in a certain order. The Aristotelians oppose us, and found their objections on the properties which the things in the Universe possess when in actual existence and fully developed. We admit the existence of these properties, but hold that they are by no means the same as those which the things possessed in the moment of their production; and we hold that these properties themselves have come into existence from absolute non-existence. Their arguments are therefore no objection whatever to our theory; they have demonstrative force only against those who hold that the nature of things as at present in existence proves the Creation. But this is not my opinion.

I will now return to our theme, viz., to the description of the principal proofs of Aristotle, and show that they prove nothing whatever against us, since we hold that God brought the entire Universe into existence from absolute non-existence, and that He caused it to develop into the present state. Aristotle says that the *materia prima* is eternal, and by referring to the properties of transient beings he attempts to prove this statement, and to show that the *materia prima* could not possibly have been produced. He is right; we do not maintain that the *materia prima* has been produced in the same manner as man is produced from the ovum, and that it can be destroyed in the same manner as man is reduced to dust. But we believe that God created it from nothing, and that since its creation it has its own properties, viz., that all things are produced of it and again reduced to it, when they cease to exist; that it does not exist without Form; and that it is the source of all genesis and destruction. Its genesis is not like that of the things produced from it, nor its destruction like theirs; for it has been created from nothing, and if it should please the Creator, He might reduce it to absolutely nothing. The same applies to motion. Aristotle founds some of his proofs on the fact that motion is not subject to genesis or destruction. This is correct; if we consider motion as it exists at present, we cannot imagine that in its totality it should be subject, like individual motions, to genesis and destruction. In like manner Aristotle is correct in saying that circular motion is without beginning, in so far as seeing the rotating spherical body in actual existence, we cannot conceive the idea that that rotation has ever been absent. The same argument we employ as regards the law that a state of potentiality precedes all actual genesis. This law applies to the Universe as it exists at present, when everything produced originates in another thing; but nothing perceived with our senses or comprehended in our mind can prove that a thing created from nothing must have been previously in a state of potentiality. Again, as regards the theory that the heavens contain no opposites [and are therefore indestructible], we admit its correctness; but we do not maintain that the production of the heavens has taken place in the same way as that of a horse or ass, and we do not say that they are like plants and animals, which are destructible on account of the opposite elements they contain. In short, the properties of things when fully developed contain no clue as to what have been the properties of the things before their perfection. We therefore do not reject as impossible the opinion of those who say that the heavens were produced before the earth, or the reverse, or that the heavens have existed without stars, or that certain species of animals have been in existence, and others not. For the state of the whole Universe when it came into existence may be compared with that of animals when their existence begins; the heart evidently precedes the testicles, the veins are in existence before the bones; although, when the animal is fully developed, none of the parts is missing which is essential to its existence. This remark is not superfluous, if the Scriptural account of the Creation be taken literally; in reality, it cannot be taken literally, as will be shown when we shall treat of this subject.

The principle laid down in the foregoing must be well understood; it is a high rampart erected round the Law and able to resist all missiles directed against it. Aristotle, or rather his followers, may perhaps ask us how we know that the Universe has been created; and that other forces than those it has at present were acting in its Creation, since we hold that the properties of the Universe, as it exists at present, prove nothing as regards its creation? We reply, there is no necessity for this according to our plan; for we do not desire to prove the Creation, but only its possibility; and this possibility is not refuted by arguments based on the nature of the present Universe, which we do not dispute. When we have established the admissibility of our theory, we shall then show its superiority. In attempting to prove the inadmissibility of Creatio ex nihilo, the Aristotelians can therefore not derive any support from the nature of the Universe; they must resort to the notion our mind has formed of God. Their proofs include the three methods which I have mentioned above, and which are based on the notion conceived of God. In the next chapter I will expose the weak points of these arguments, and show that they really prove nothing.

*   *   *

PART III

Chapter 12

Men frequently think that the evils in the world are more numerous than the good things; many savings and songs of the nations dwell on this idea. They say that a good thing is found only exceptionally, whilst evil things are numerous and lasting. Not only common people make this mistake, but even many who believe that they are wise. Al-Razi wrote a well-known book *On Metaphysics* [or Theology]. Among other mad and foolish things, it contains also the idea, discovered by him, that there exists more evil than good. For if the happiness of man and his pleasure in the times of prosperity be compared with the mishaps that befall him,—such as grief, acute pain, defects, paralysis of the limbs, fears, anxieties, and troubles,—it would seem as if the existence of man is a punishment and a great evil for him. This author commenced to verify his opinion by counting all the evils one by one; by this means he opposed those who hold the correct view of the benefits bestowed by God and His evident kindness, viz., that God is perfect goodness, and that all that comes from Him is absolutely good. The origin of the error is to be found in the circumstance that this ignorant man, and his party among the common people, judge the whole universe by examining one single person. For an ignorant man believes that the whole universe only exists for him; as if nothing else required any consideration. If, therefore, anything happens to him contrary to his expectation, he at once concludes that the whole universe is evil. If, however, he would take into consideration the whole universe, form an idea of it, and comprehend what a small portion he is of the Universe, he will find the truth. For it is clear that persons who have fallen into this widespread error as regards the multitude of evils in the world, do not find the evils among the angels, the spheres and stars, the elements, and that which is formed of them, viz., minerals and plants, or in the various species of living beings, but only in some individual instances of mankind. They wonder that a person, who became leprous in consequence of bad food, should be afflicted with so great an illness and suffer such a misfortune; or that he who indulges so much in sensuality as to weaken his sight, should be struck with blindness and the like. What we have, in truth, to consider is this:—The whole mankind at present in existence, and *a fortiori,* every other species of animals, form an infinitesimal portion of the permanent universe. Comp. "Man is like to vanity" (Ps. cxliv. 4); "How much less man, that is a worm; and the son of man, which is a worm" (Job xxv. 6); "How much less in them who dwell in houses of clay" (*ibid.* iv. 19); "Behold, the nations are as a drop of the bucket" (Isa. xl. 15). There are many other passages in the books of the prophets expressing the same idea. It is of great advantage that man should know his station, and not erroneously imagine that the whole universe exists only for him. We hold that the universe exists because the Creator wills it so; that mankind is low in rank as compared with the uppermost portion of the universe, viz., with the spheres and the stars; but, as regards the angels, there cannot be any real comparison between man and angels, although man is the highest of all beings on earth; i.e., of all beings formed of the four elements. Man's existence is nevertheless a great boon to him, and his distinction and perfection is a divine gift. The numerous evils to which individual persons are exposed are due to the defects existing in the persons themselves. We complain and seek relief from our own faults; we suffer from the evils which we, by our own free will, inflict on ourselves and ascribe them to God, who is far from being connected with them! Comp. "Is destruction his [work]? No. Ye [who call yourselves] wrongly his sons, you who are a perverse and crooked generation" (Deut. xxxii. 5). This is explained by Solomon, who says, "The foolishness of man perverteth his way, and his heart fretteth against the Lord" (Prov. xix. 3).

I explain this theory in the following manner. The evils that befall man are of three kinds:—

(1) The first kind of evil is that which is caused to man by the circumstance that he is subject to genesis and destruction, or that he possesses a body. It is on account of the body that some persons happen to have great deformities or paralysis of some of the organs. This evil may be part of the natural constitution of these persons, or may have developed subsequently in consequence of changes in the elements, e.g., through bad air, or thunderstorms, or landslips. We have already shown that, in accordance with the divine wisdom, genesis can only take place through destruction, and without the destruction of the individual members of the species the species themselves would not exist permanently. Thus the true kindness, and beneficence, and goodness of God is clear. He who thinks that he can have flesh and bones without being subject to any external influence, or any of the accidents of matter, unconsciously wishes to reconcile two opposites, viz., to be at the same time subject and not subject to change. If man were never

subject to change there could be no generation; there would be one single being, but no individuals forming a species. Galen, in the third section of his book, *The Use of the Limbs,* says correctly that it would be in vain to expect to see living beings formed of the blood of menstruous women and the semen virile, who will not die, will never feel pain, or will move perpetually, or will shine like the sun. This dictum of Galen is part of the following more general proposition:—Whatever is formed of any matter receives the most perfect form possible in that species of matter; in each individual case the defects are in accordance with the defects of that individual matter. The best and most perfect being that can be formed of the blood and the semen is the species of man, for as far as man's nature is known, he is living, reasonable, and mortal. It is therefore impossible that man should be free from this species of evil. You will, nevertheless, find that the evils of the above kind which befall man are very few and rare; for you find countries that have not been flooded or burned for thousands of years; there are thousands of men in perfect health, deformed individuals are a strange and exceptional occurrence, or say few in number if you object to the term exceptional,—they are not one-hundredth, not even one-thousandth part of those that are perfectly normal.

(2) The second class of evils comprises such evils as people cause to each other, when, e.g., some of them use their strength against others. These evils are more numerous than those of the first kind; their causes are numerous and known; they likewise originate in ourselves, though the sufferer himself cannot avert them. This kind of evil is nevertheless not widespread in any country of the whole world. It is of rare occurrence that a man plans to kill his neighbor or to rob him of his property by night. Many persons are, however, afflicted with this kind of evil in great wars; but these are not frequent, if the whole inhabited part of the earth is taken into consideration.

(3) The third class of evils comprises those which every one causes to himself by his own action. This is the largest class, and is far more numerous than the second class. It is especially of these evils that all men complain,—only few men are found that do not sin against themselves by this kind of evil. Those that are afflicted with it are therefore justly blamed in the words of the prophet, "This hath been by your means" (Mal. i. 9); the same is expressed in the following passage, "He that doeth it destroyeth his own soul" (Prov. vi. 32). In reference to this kind of evil, Solomon says, "The foolishness of man perverteth his way" (*ibid.* xix. 3). In the following passage he explains also that this kind of evil is man's own work, "Lo, this only have I found, that God hath made man upright, but they have thought out many inventions" (Eccles. vii. 29), and these inventions bring the evils upon him. The same subject is referred to in Job (v. 6), "For affliction cometh not forth of the dust, neither doth trouble spring out of the ground." These words are immediately followed by the explanation that man himself is the author of this class of evils, "But man is born unto trouble." This class of evils originates in man's vices, such as excessive desire for eating, drinking, and love; indulgence in these things in undue measure, or in improper manner, or partaking of bad food. This course brings diseases and afflictions upon body and soul alike. The sufferings of the body in consequence of these evils are well known; those of the soul are twofold:— First, such evils of the soul as are the necessary consequence of changes in the body, in so far as the soul is a force residing in the body; it has therefore been said that the properties of the soul depend on the condition of the body. Secondly, the soul, when accustomed to superfluous things, acquires a strong habit of desiring things which are neither necessary for the preservation of the individual nor for that of the species. This desire is without a limit, whilst things which are necessary are few in number and restricted within certain limits; but what is superfluous is without end—e.g., you desire to have your vessels of silver, but golden vessels are still better: others have even vessels of sap-

phire, or perhaps they can be made of emerald or rubies, or any other substance that could be suggested. Those who are ignorant and perverse in their thought are constantly in trouble and pain, because they cannot get as much of superfluous things as a certain other person possesses. They as a rule expose themselves to great dangers, e.g., by sea-voyage, or service of kings, and all this for the purpose of obtaining that which is superfluous and not necessary. When they thus meet with the consequences of the course which they adopt, they complain of the decrees and judgments of God; they begin to blame the time, and wonder at the want of justice in its changes; that it has not enabled them to acquire great riches, with which they could buy large quantities of wine for the purpose of making themselves drunk, and numerous concubines adorned with various kind of ornaments of gold, embroidery, and jewels, for the purpose of driving themselves to voluptuousness beyond their capacities, as if the whole Universe existed exclusively for the purpose of giving pleasure to these low people. The error of the ignorant goes so far as to say that God's power is insufficient, because He has given to this Universe the properties which they imagine cause these great evils, and which do not help all evil-disposed persons to obtain the evil which they seek, and to bring their evil souls to the aim of their desires, though these, as we have shown, are really without limit. The virtuous and wise, however, see and comprehend the wisdom of God displayed in the Universe. Thus David says, "All the paths of the Lord are mercy and truth unto such as keep His covenant and His testimonies" (Ps. xxv. 10). For those who observe the nature of the Universe and the commandments of the Law, and know their purpose, see clearly God's mercy and truth in everything; they seek, therefore, that which the Creator intended to be the aim of man, viz., comprehension. Forced by the claims of the body, they seek also that which is necessary for the preservation of the body, "bread to eat and garment to clothe," and this is very little; but they seek nothing superfluous; with very slight exertion man can obtain it, so long as he is contented with that which is indispensable. All the difficulties and troubles we meet in this respect are due to the desire for superfluous things; when we seek unnecessary things, we have difficulty even in finding that which is indispensable. For the more we desire to have that which is superfluous, the more we meet with difficulties; our strength and possessions are spent in unnecessary things, and are wanting when required for that which is necessary. Observe how Nature proves the correctness of this assertion. The more necessary a thing is for living beings, the more easily it is found and the cheaper it is; the less necessary it is, the rarer and dearer it is. E.g., air, water, and food are indispensable to man: air is most necessary, for if man is without air a short time he dies; whilst he can be without water a day or two. Air is also undoubtedly found more easily and cheaper [than water]. Water is more necessary than food; for some people can be four or five days without food, provided they have water; water also exists in every country in larger quantities than food, and is also cheaper. The same proportion can be noticed in the different kinds of food; that which is more necessary in a certain place exists there in larger quantities and is cheaper than that which is less necessary. No intelligent person, I think, considers musk, amber, rubies, and emerald as very necessary for man except as medicines; and they, as well as other like substances, can be replaced for this purpose by herbs and minerals. This shows the kindness of God to His creatures, even to us weak beings. His righteousness and justice as regards all animals are well known; for in the transient world there is among the various kinds of animals no individual being distinguished from the rest of the same species by a peculiar property or an additional limb. On the contrary, all physical, psychical, and vital forces and organs that are possessed by one individual are found also in the other individuals. If any one is somehow different it is by accident, in consequence of some exception, and not by a natural property; it is also a rare occurrence. There is no difference between individuals of a species in the due course of Nature; the difference originates in the various dispositions of their substances. This is the necessary consequence of the nature of the substance of that species; the nature of the species is not more favorable to one individual than to the other. It is no wrong or injustice that one has many bags of finest myrrh and garments embroidered with gold, while another has not those things, which are not necessary for our maintenance; he who has them has not thereby obtained control over anything that could be an essential addition to his nature, but has only obtained something illusory or deceptive. The other, who does not possess that which is not wanted for his maintenance, does not miss anything indispensable: "He that gathered much had nothing over, and he that gathered little had no lack: they gathered every man according to his eating" (Exod. xvi. 18). This is the rule at all times and in all places; no notice should be taken of exceptional cases, as we have explained.

In these two ways you will see the mercy of God toward His creatures, how He has provided that which is required, in proper proportions, and treated all individual beings of the same species with perfect equality. In accordance with this correct reflection the chief of the wise men says, "All his ways are judgment" (Deut. xxxii. 4); David likewise says: "All the paths of the Lord are mercy and truth" (Ps. xxv. 10); he also says expressly, "The Lord is good to all; and his tender mercies are over all his works" (*ibid.* cxlv. 9); for it is an act of great and perfect goodness that He gave us existence; and the creation of the controlling faculty in animals is a proof of His mercy towards them, as has been shown by us.

Thirteenth-Century Philosophy

Thirteenth-century Western European philosophy was shaped by three movements: the rise of the mendicant (or begging) orders, the development of the university, and, most importantly, the rediscovery of the complete works of Aristotle.

Having survived the collapse of the Roman Empire and having helped fight back the Islamic expansion in southern Europe, the Catholic Church had gained new influence and power in society. As the church grew in temporal authority, spiritual concerns and doctrinal purity often became less important. Advocating a simple life of obedience, poverty, and chastity, the Franciscan and Dominican orders sought to reverse this secularizing trend. Founded by St. Francis of Assisi (1181–1226), the Franciscans fostered spiritual renewal and often served as dedicated teachers and missionaries. The Dominicans, founded by St. Dominic (1170–1221), sought doctrinal purity and became leading university professors throughout the West.

The thirteenth century also witnessed the rise of universities. Usually founded as schools attached to cathedrals, the universities were corporations of scholars with a measure of independence from the church. Acting as magnets for scholars, students, and collections of great works, the universities quickly became important, crowded intellectual centers. (The greatest of the early universities, in Paris, had as many as twenty thousand students.)

Among the issues discussed at the emerging universities, none was more controversial than the recently rediscovered books of Aristotle. While some of Aristotle's works had been available to Western Europeans, his most important writings had been preserved only in the Islamic world. Texts brought as loot from the Crusades' incursions into Muslim strongholds in Spain and Sicily found their way to the University of Paris. There, Aristotle's ideas provided fertile ground for many new questions.

But with Aristotle's works came the problems with which Islamic and Jewish thinkers had earlier struggled. Aristotle taught the eternity of the world and apparently denied life after death—teachings at variance with the Bible as well as with the *Qur'ān*. Fortunately for Christendom, along with Aristotle's works came the commentaries of the great Muslim teachers Avicenna and Averroës. Thirteenth-century Western thinkers were able to appeal not only to Aristotle, but also to his Muslim glosses in the attempt to harmonize Aristotle and Christianity.

In general, the Dominicans, led by St. Thomas Aquinas, were enthusiastic about Aristotelian thought, while the Franciscans, led by St. Bonaventure, preferred Augustinian Platonism. But the conflict was in fact much more complicated than such a generalization might indicate. There were numerous variations on Aristotle's thought. Some, such as Siger of Brabant, emphasized the Averroist interpretation of Aristotle. Others, such as Robert Grosseteste and Roger Bacon, used Aristotelian categories when they suited their purposes; but they were actually more Neoplatonic than Aristotelian. Even opponents of Aristotle, such as Bonaventure, used Aristotelian categories in their criticisms of Aristotle. But whether defended or attacked, the spirit of Aristotle ruled Western philosophy in the thirteenth century.

* * *

Frederick Copleston, *A History of Philosophy, Volume II: Medieval Philosophy, Part II: Albert the Great to Duns Scotus* (1950; reprinted Garden City, NY: Image Doubleday, 1962); Fernand van Steenberghen, *The Philosophical Movement in the Thirteenth Century* (Edinburgh: Thomas Nelson's Sons, 1955); and Fernand van Steenberghen, *Aristotle in the West: The Origins of Latin Aristotelianism,* translated by Leonard Johnston (Louvain, Belgium: E. Nauwelaerts, 1955), provide overviews of thirteenth-century thought. For general introductions to Scholasticism, see Maurice M.C.J. de Wulf, *An Introduction to Scholastic Philosophy, Medieval and Modern: Scholasticism Old and New,* translated by P. Coffey (New York: Dover Publications, 1956); and Josef Pieper, *Scholasticism: Personalities and Problems of Medieval Philosophy,* translated by Richard and Clara Winston (New York: Pantheon Books, 1960).

Robert Grosseteste

ca. 1168–1253

Robert Grosseteste was born to a peasant family at Stradbroke, in Suffolk, England, sometime around 1168. Despite his humble origins, he studied law, medicine, and theology at Oxford University. He may have studied in Paris as well. He served for a time under the Bishop of Hereford, perhaps as a teacher at the Hereford school, after which he returned to teaching at Oxford. King John's troubles with France and with his own nobles led to the closing of Oxford from 1209–1214, when Grosseteste presumably studied theology in Paris. He returned to England in time to be present at the signing of the *Magna Carta* in 1215. Sometime after the reopening of Oxford, Grosseteste was made the first chancellor of the university and taught at the Oxford Franciscan house. He remained in that post until 1235 when he was made bishop of Lincoln, then the largest diocese in England. For his last eighteen years he served in Lincoln and was often called "the Lincolnian" by his contemporaries.

The specifics of Grosseteste's life are sketchy, and we now know that some works attributed to him were written by others. But we also know that he did write the work *On Light*, reprinted here in the Clare C. Riedl translation. In this work Grosseteste claims that God created light (*lux* or "light at its source") as the first form along with simple unextended matter. This light immediately "multiplied itself by its very nature an infinite number of times on all sides and spread itself out uniformly in every direction." As light spread out in all directions, it drew matter "along with itself into a mass the size of the material universe" forming the perfect outer sphere of "the firmament." After the material universe had been formed in this way, the light (*lumen* or "reflected light") on the periphery was reflected back to the center where it gathered the dense mass of matter inside the firmament and spread it outward in a sphere smaller than the first. This process continued until the thirteen spheres—the nine spheres of the heavens and the four elements of fire, air, water, and earth—had been formed. This process of expansion and reflection managed to combine the cosmologies of Aristotle and Ptolemy with elements of the Neoplatonists' emanation theory.

While his treatise *On Light* may seem ethereal, Grosseteste was in fact one of the first medieval scientists. He sought to divide complex phenomena into smaller units that could then be examined separately. He attempted to limit possible causes of a given effect in an effort to remove unnecessary variables. He used both working hypotheses and experiments in his scientific investigations. Finally, since he believed that light is the cause of all motion and that light operates according to geometrical rules, he held that all motion can be explained mathematically. These scientific advances proved fruitful in succeeding centuries.

* * *

The best general introduction to Grosseteste is the recently updated Richard W. Southern, *Robert Grosseteste: The Growth of an English Mind in Medieval Europe,* 2nd ed. (Oxford: Clarendon Press, 1992). Other introductions include James McEvoy, *The Philosophy of Robert Grosseteste* (Oxford: Clarendon Press, 1982), and Steven P. Marrone, *William of Auvergne and Robert Grosseteste: New Ideas of Truth in the Early Thirteenth Century* (Princeton, NJ: Princeton University Press, 1983). S. Harrison Thomson, *The Writings of Robert Grosseteste, Bishop of Lincoln, 1235–1253* (Cambridge: Cambridge University Press, 1940), provides a commentary on Grosseteste's writings, while Lee M. Friedman, *Robert Grosseteste and the Jews* (Cambridge, MA: Harvard University Press, 1934), and Alistair Cameron Crombie, *Robert Grosseteste and the Origins of Experimental Science, 1100–1700* (Oxford: Clarendon Press, 1953), have written studies of particular topics. For critical essays, see Daniel Angelo Philip Callus, ed., *Robert Grosseteste: Scholar and Bishop: Essays in Commemoration of the Seventh Centenary of His Death* (Oxford: Clarendon Press, 1955). For general introductions to medieval science, see the suggested readings in the introduction to Roger Bacon (p. 286).

ON LIGHT

The first corporeal form which some call corporeity is in my opinion light. For light of its very nature diffuses itself in every direction in such a way that a point of light will produce instantaneously a sphere of light of any size whatsoever, unless some opaque

Robert Grosseteste, *On Light,* translated by Clare C. Riedl (Milwaukee, WI: Marquette University Press, 1942, 1978). Reprinted by permission of Marquette University Press.

object stands in the way. Now the extension of matter in three dimensions is a necessary concomitant of corporeity, and this despite the fact that both corporeity and matter are in themselves simple substances lacking all dimension. But a form that is in itself simple and without dimension could not introduce dimension in every direction into matter, which is likewise simple and without dimension, except by multiplying itself and diffusing itself instantaneously in every direction and thus extending matter in its own diffusion. For the form cannot desert matter, because it is inseparable from it, and matter itself cannot be deprived of form.—But I have proposed that it is light which possesses of its very nature the function of multiplying itself and diffusing itself instantaneously in all directions. Whatever performs this operation is either light or some other agent that acts in virtue of its participation in light to which this operation belongs essentially. Corporeity, therefore, is either light itself or the agent which performs the aforementioned operation and introduces dimensions into matter in virtue of its participation in light, and acts through the power of this same light. But the first form cannot introduce dimensions into matter through the power of a subsequent form. Therefore light is not a form subsequent to corporeity, but it is corporeity itself.

Furthermore, the first corporeal form is, in the opinion of the philosophers, more exalted and of a nobler and more excellent essence than all the forms that come after it. It bears, also, a closer resemblance to the forms that exist apart from matter. But light is more exalted and of a nobler and more excellent essence than all corporeal things. It has, moreover, greater similarity than all bodies to the forms that exist apart from matter, namely, the intelligences. Light therefore is the first corporeal form.

Thus light, which is the first form created in first matter, multiplied itself by its very nature an infinite number of times on all sides and spread itself out uniformly in every direction. In this way it proceeded in the beginning of time to extend matter which it could not leave behind, by drawing it out along with itself into a mass the size of the material universe. This extension of matter could not be brought about through a finite multiplication of light, because the multiplication of a simple being a finite number of times does not produce a quantity, as Aristotle shows in the *De Caelo et Mundo*. However, the multiplication of a simple being an infinite number of times must produce a finite quantity, because a product which is the result of an infinite multiplication exceeds infinitely that through the multiplication of which it is produced. Now one simple being cannot exceed another simple being infinitely, but only a finite quantity infinitely exceeds a simple being. For an infinite quantity exceeds a simple being by infinity times infinity. Therefore, when light, which is in itself simple, is multiplied an infinite number of times, it must extend matter, which is likewise simple, into finite dimensions.

It is possible, however, that an infinite sum of number is related to an infinite sum in every proportion, numerical and non-numerical. And some infinites are larger than other infinites, and some are smaller. Thus the sum of all numbers both even and odd is infinite. It is at the same time greater than the sum of all the even numbers although this is likewise infinite, for it exceeds it by the sum of all the odd numbers. The sum, too, of all numbers starting with one and continuing by doubling each successive number is infinite, and similarly the sum of all the halves corresponding to the doubles is infinite. The sum of these halves must be half of the sum of their doubles. In the same way the sum of all numbers starting with one and multiplying by three successively is three times the sum of all the thirds corresponding to these triples. It is likewise clear in regard to all kinds of numerical proportion that there can be a proportion of finite to infinite according to each of them.

But if we posit an infinite sum of all doubles starting with one, and an infinite sum of all the halves corresponding to these doubles, and if one, or some other finite number, be subtracted from the sum of the halves, then, as soon as this subtraction is made, there will no longer be a two to one proportion between the first sum and what is left of the second sum. Indeed there will not be any numerical proportion, because if a second numerical proportion is to be left from the first as the result of subtraction from the lesser member of the proportion, then what is subtracted must be an aliquot* part or aliquot parts of an aliquot part of that from which it is subtracted. But a finite number cannot be an aliquot part or aliquot parts of an aliquot part of an infinite number. Therefore when we subtract a number from an infinite sum of halves there will not remain a numerical proportion between the infinite sum of doubles and what is left from the infinite sum of halves.

Since this is so, it is clear that light through the infinite multiplication of itself extends matter into finite dimensions that are smaller and larger according to certain proportions that they have to one another, namely, numerical and non-numerical. For if light through the infinite multiplication of itself extends matter into a dimension of two cubits, by the doubling of this same infinite multiplication it extends it into a dimension of four cubits, and by the dividing in half of this infinite multiplication, it extends it into a dimension of one cubit. Thus it proceeds according to numerical and non-numerical proportions.

It is my opinion that this was the meaning of the theory of those philosophers who held that everything is composed of atoms, and said that bodies are composed of surfaces, and surfaces of lines, and lines of points. This opinion does not contradict the theory that a magnitude is composed only of magnitudes, because for every meaning of the word whole, there is a corresponding meaning of the word part. Thus we say that a half is part of a whole, because two halves make a whole. We say, too, that a side is part of a diameter, but in a different sense, because no matter how many times a side is taken it does not make a diameter, but is always less than the diameter. Again we say that an angle of contingence is part of a right angle because there is an infinite number of angles of contingence in a right angle, and yet when an angle of contingence is subtracted from a right angle a finite number of times the latter becomes smaller. It is in a different sense, however, that a point is said to be part of a line in which it is contained an infinite number of times, for when a point is taken away from a line a finite number of times this does not shorten the line.

To return therefore to my theme, I say that light through the infinite multiplication of itself equally in all directions extends matter on all sides equally into the form of a sphere and, as a necessary consequence of this extension, the outermost parts of matter are more extended and more rarefied than those within, which are close to the center. And since the outermost parts will be rarefied to the highest degree, the inner parts will have the possibility of further rarefaction.

In this way light, by extending first matter into the form of a sphere, and by rarefying its outermost parts to the highest degree, actualized completely in the outermost sphere the potentiality of matter, and left this matter without any potency to further impression. And thus the first body in the outermost part of the sphere, the body which is called the firmament, is perfect, because it has nothing in its composition but first matter and first form. It is therefore the simplest of all bodies with respect to the parts that constitute its essence and with respect to its quantity which is the greatest possible in extent. It differs from the genus body only in this respect, that in it the matter is completely actualized through the first form alone. But the genus body, which is in this and in other bodies and has in its essence first matter and first form, abstracts from the com-

*[The part of a number that divides the given number without a remainder.]

plete actualization of matter through the first form and from the diminution of matter through the first form.

When the first body, which is the firmament, has in this way been completely actualized, it diffuses its light *(lumen)* from every part of itself to the center of the universe. For since light *(lux)* is the perfection of the first body and naturally multiplies itself from the first body, it is necessarily diffused to the center of the universe. And since this light *(lux)* is a form entirely inseparable from matter in its diffusion from the first body, it extends along with itself the spirituality of the matter of the first body. Thus there proceeds from the first body light *(lumen),* which is a spiritual body, or if you prefer, a bodily spirit. This light *(lumen)* in its passing does not divide the body through which it passes, and thus it passes instantaneously from the body of the first heaven to the center of the universe. Furthermore, its passing is not to be understood in the sense of something numerically one passing instantaneously from that heaven to the center of the universe, for this is perhaps impossible, but its passing takes place through the multiplication of itself and the infinite generation of light *(lumen).* This light *(lumen),* expanded and brought together from the first body toward the center of the universe, gathered together the mass existing below the first body; and since the first body could no longer be lessened on account of its being completely actualized and unchangeable, and since, too, there could not be a space that was empty, it was necessary that in the very gathering together of this mass the outermost parts should be drawn out and expanded. Thus the inner parts of the aforesaid mass came to be more dense and the outer parts more rarefied; and so great was the power of this light *(lumen)* gathering together—and in the very act of gathering, separating—that the outermost parts of the mass contained below the first body were drawn out and rarefied to the highest degree. Thus in the outermost parts of the mass in question, the second sphere came into being, completely actualized and susceptible of no further impression. The completeness of actualization and the perfection of the second sphere consist in this that light *(lumen)* is begotten from the first sphere and that light *(lux)* which is simple in the first sphere is doubled in the second.

Just as the light *(lumen)* begotten from the first body completed the actualization of the second sphere and left a denser mass below the second sphere, so the light *(lumen)* begotten from the second sphere completed the actualization of the third sphere, and through its gathering left below this third sphere a mass of even greater density. This process of simultaneously gathering together and separating continued in this way until the nine heavenly spheres were completely actualized and there was gathered together below the ninth and lowest sphere the dense mass which constitutes the matter of the four elements. But the lowest sphere, the sphere of the moon, which also gives forth light *(lumen)* from itself, by its light *(lumen)* gathered together the mass contained below itself and, by gathering it together, thinned out and expanded its outermost parts. The power of this light *(lumen),* however, was not so great that by drawing together it could expand the outermost parts of this mass to the highest degree. On this account every part of the mass was left imperfect and capable of being gathered together and expanded. The highest part of this mass was expanded, although not to the greatest possible extent. Nevertheless by its expansion it became fire, although remaining still the matter of the elements. This element giving forth light from itself and drawing together the mass contained below it expanded its outermost parts, but not to as great an extent as the fire was expanded, and in this way it produced air. Air, also, in bringing forth from itself, a spiritual body or a bodily spirit, and drawing together what is contained within itself, and by drawing together, expanding its outer parts, produced water and earth. But because water retained more of the power of drawing

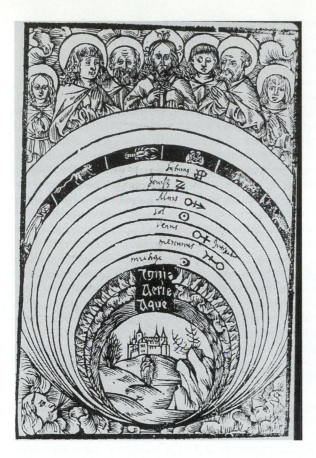

The Ptolemaic Conception of the Universe, from *Introductorium,* 1513, woodcut by Jon Glagowczyke. Grosseteste's theory of light combines Ptolemaic cosmology and the Neoplatonists' emanation theory. According to Grosseteste, through a process of multiplication and reflection, light forms thirteen spheres—the nine spheres of the heavens and the four elements of fire, air, water, and earth. *(Library of Congress/Instructional Resources Corporation)*

together than of the power of expanding, water as well as earth was left with the attribute of weight.

In this way, therefore, the thirteen spheres of this sensible world were brought into being. Nine of them, the heavenly spheres, are not subject to change, increase, generation or corruption because they are completely actualized. The other four spheres have the opposite mode of being, that is, they are subject to change, increase, generation and corruption, because they are not completely actualized. It is clear that every higher body, in virtue of the light *(lumen)* which proceeds from it, is the form *(species)* and perfection of the body that comes after it. And just as unity is potentially every number that comes after it, so the first body, through the multiplication of its light, is every body that comes after it.

Earth is all the higher bodies because all the higher lights come together in it. For this reason earth is called Pan by the poets, that is "the whole," and it is also given the name Cybele, which is almost like *cubile,* from cube *(cubus)* that is, a solid. The reason for this is that earth, that is to say, Cybele, the mother of all the gods, is the most compact of all bodies, because, although the higher lights are gathered together in it, nevertheless they do not have their source in the earth through its own operations, but the light *(lumen)* of any sphere whatever can be educed from it into act and operation. Thus every one of the gods will be begotten from it as from a kind of mother. The intermediate bodies have a twofold relationship. Towards lower bodies they have the same relation as the first heaven has to all other things, and they are related to the higher bodies as earth is related to all other things. And thus in a certain sense each thing contains all other things.

The form *(species)* and perfection of all bodies is light, but in the higher bodies it is more spiritual and simple, whereas in the lower bodies it is more corporeal and multiplied. Furthermore, all bodies are not of the same form *(species)* even though they all proceed from light, whether simple or multiplied, just as all numbers are not the same in form *(species)* despite the fact that they are all derived from unity by a greater or lesser multiplication.

This discussion may perhaps clarify the meaning of those who say that "all things are one by the perfection of one light" and also the meaning of those who say that "things which are many are many through the multiplication of light itself in different degrees."

But since lower bodies participate in the form of the higher bodies, the lower body because it participates in the same form as the higher body, receives its motion from the same incorporeal moving power by which the higher body is moved. For this reason the incorporeal power of intelligence or soul, which moves the first and highest sphere with a diurnal motion, moves all the lower heavenly spheres with this same diurnal motion. But in proportion as these spheres are lower they receive this motion in a more weakened state, because in proportion as a sphere is lower the purity and strength of the first corporeal light is lessened in it.

But although the elements participate in the form of the first heaven, nevertheless they are not moved by the mover of the first heaven with a diurnal motion. Although they participate in that first light, they are not subject to the first moving power since that light in them is impure, weak, and far removed from the purity which it has in the first body, and also because they possess the denseness of matter which is the principle of resistance and stubbornness. Nevertheless, there are some who think that the sphere of fire rotates with a diurnal motion, and they take the rotating motion of comets to be an indication of this. They say also that this motion extends even to the waters of the sea, in such a way that the tide of the seas proceeds from it. But all sound philosophers say that the earth is free from this motion.

In this same way, too, the spheres that come after the second sphere, which is usually called the eighth when we compute from the earth upward, all share in the motion of this second sphere because they participate in its form. Indeed this motion is proper to each of them in addition to the diurnal motion.

But because the heavenly spheres are completely actualized and are not receptive of rarefaction or condensation, light *(lux)* in them does not incline the parts of matter either away from the center so as to rarefy them, or toward the center to condense them. On this account the heavenly spheres are not receptive of up or down motion but only of circular motion by an intellectual moving power, which by directing its glance upon them in a corporeal way revolves the spheres themselves in a circular corporeal motion. But because the elements are incompletely actualized and subject to rarefaction and condensation, the light *(lumen)* which is in them inclines them away from the center so as to rarefy them, or toward the center so as to condense them. And on this account they are naturally capable of being moved in an upward or downward motion.

The highest body, which is the simplest of all bodies, contains four constituents, namely form, matter, composition and the composite. Now the form being the simplest holds the position of unity. But matter on account of its twofold potency, namely its susceptibility to impressions and its receptiveness of them, and also on account of its denseness which belongs fundamentally to matter but which is primarily and principally characteristic of a thing which is a duality, is rightly allotted the nature of a duality. But composition has a trinity in itself because there appears in it informed matter and materialized form and that which is distinctive of the composition, which is found in every composite as a third constituent distinct from matter and form. And that which is the composite proper, over and above these three constituents, is classed as a quaternary. There is, therefore, in the first body, in which all other bodies exist virtually, a quaternary and therefore the number of the remaining bodies is basically not more than ten. For the unity of the form, the duality of the matter, the trinity of the composition and the quaternity of the composite when they are added make a total of ten. On this account ten is the number of the bodies of the spheres of the world, because the sphere of the elements, although it is divided into four, is nevertheless one by its participation in earthly corruptible nature.

From these considerations it is clear that ten is the perfect number in the universe, because every perfect whole has something in it corresponding to form and unity, and something corresponding to matter and duality, something corresponding to composition and trinity, and something corresponding to the composite and quaternity. Nor is it possible to add a fifth to these four. For this reason every perfect whole is ten.

On this account it is manifest that only five proportions found in these four numbers, one, two, three, four, are suited to composition and to the harmony that gives stability to every composite. For this reason these five proportions are the only ones that produce harmony in musical melodies, in bodily movements, and in rhythmic measures.

This is the end of the treatise on light of the Bishop of Lincoln.

Roger Bacon
ca. 1214–ca. 1292

Born somewhere in England, Roger Bacon studied at the universities of Oxford and Paris. By 1237 he was teaching at Paris—one of the first to lecture on the newly rediscovered works of Aristotle. After ten years of studying theology and teaching Aristotle, Bacon returned to England. In Oxford he encountered the writings and perhaps even the person of Robert Grosseteste. Bacon joined the Franciscans, but he soon found himself in trouble with them. He naively accepted the work of the apocalyptic extremist Joachim of Floris, which made Bacon's own work suspect. Sometimes Bacon was also too blunt in criticizing his superiors, claiming that the first cause of human ignorance was undue reverence for authority. The Franciscan General, St. Bonaventure, ordered him not to publish. In 1266 Pope Clement IV asked to see Bacon's work. Hoping to find papal support, Bacon wrote his *Opus Majus* and sent it to Rome. Unfortunately, Clement died before he could intervene on Bacon's behalf. Without the pope's patronage, Bacon's novel teachings—and his candid assessment of fellow teachers—led to imprisonment. Continuing to write, he spent as many as fourteen of his last years in prison.

The works of Aristotle that Bacon taught, despite their empirical orientation, did not always lead to an emphasis on what we call "science." Aristotle advocated inductive reasoning from observed particulars to universals. But many thirteenth-century philosophers accepted not only Aristotle's observational method, but his observational *conclusions* as well. With Aristotle's conclusions *given,* these philosophers saw little need for more empirical data and so considered further scientific inquiry pointless. And where Aristotle had been motivated to study natural phenomena to discover their purpose or *entelechy,* medieval theologians believed they already knew the *entelechy* of all of nature—the service of God's purposes. With God's purposes known, there seemed little reason for Aristotelian exploration.

However, some theologians granted that if human sin or reason's incompetence keeps us from knowing God's purposes, empirical testing can be useful in the quest for ends. While one cannot know the *ultimate* purposes of God by reason alone, one can know *something* of God's purposes by examining God's creation. Ironically, Franciscan skepticism about human ability to know divine purposes was a factor in the rise of experimental science. Bacon, for example, argued that experiments were a way of overcoming the sinful errors of previous thinkers.

Like his later namesake, Sir Francis Bacon, Roger Bacon was more of an advocate for than a practitioner of empirical science. Roger Bacon did not actually perform many experiments, and his writings mix science with astrology and alchemy. But he did argue for experience as a major component in scientific knowledge, and he agreed with Grosseteste on the importance of mathematics for science. More importantly, he saw the practical applications of science and predicted the invention of automobiles, airplanes, and submarines.

The *Opus Majus* calls for educational reform and provides a blueprint. The selections given here, in the Robert Belle Burke translation, argue for the general importance of science, the necessity of mathematics in science, and science's need for experience as well as reason. Our selections end with Bacon's famous claim that the most important characteristic of science is that it "investigates by experiment."

*   *   *

For works on Bacon, see John Henry Bridges, *The Life & Work of Roger Bacon: An Introduction to the* Opus Majus (London: William & Norgate, 1914); William Romaine Newbold, *The Cipher of Roger Bacon* (Philadelphia: University of Pennsylvania Press, 1928); Evalyn Westacott, *Roger Bacon in Life and Legend* (New York: Philosophical Library, 1953); and the collection of essays, A.G. Little, ed., *Roger Bacon Essays* (Oxford: Clarendon Press, 1914).

For works on medieval science, see Alistair Cameron Crombie, *Augustine to Galileo: Medieval and Early Modern Science,* 2 vols., 2nd ed. (Garden City, NY: Doubleday, 1959); Charles Homer Haskins, *Studies in the History of Mediaeval Science* (New York: F. Ungar, 1960); Richard C. Dales, *The Scientific Achievement of the Middle Ages* (Philadelphia: University of Pennsylvania Press, 1973); and David C. Lindberg, *The Beginnings of Western Science: The European Scientific Tradition in Philosophical, Religious, and Institutional Context, 600 B.C.* to A.D. 1450 (Chicago: University of Chicago Press, 1992). Of special interest is P.L. Jacob, *Science and Literature in the Middle Ages and the Renaissance* (New York: F. Ungar, 1964), which includes several hundred wood engravings.

THE OPUS MAJUS (in part)

PART IV OF THIS PLEA

First Distinction, in Three Chapters:

Chapter 1: In Which Is Shown the Power of Mathematics in the Sciences and in the Affairs and Occupations of this World

After making it clear that many famous roots of knowledge depend on the mastery of the languages through which there is an entrance into knowledge on the part of the Latins, I now wish to consider the foundations of this same knowledge as regards the great sciences, in which there is a special power in respect to the other sciences and the affairs of this world. There are four great sciences, without which the other sciences cannot be known nor a knowledge of things secured. If these are known any one can make glorious progress in the power of knowledge without difficulty and labor, not only in human sciences, but in that which is divine. The virtue of each of these sciences will be touched upon not only on account of knowledge itself, but in respect to the other matters aforesaid. Of these sciences the gate and key is mathematics, which the saints discovered at the beginning of the world, as I shall show, and which has always been used by all the saints and sages more than all other sciences. Neglect of this branch now for thirty or forty years has destroyed the whole system of study of the Latins. Since he who is ignorant of this cannot know the other sciences nor the affairs of this world, as I shall prove. And what is worse men ignorant of this do not perceive their own ignorance, and therefore do not seek a remedy. And on the contrary the knowledge of this science prepares the mind and elevates it to a certain knowledge of all things, so that if one learns the roots of knowledge placed about it and rightly applies them to the knowledge of the other sciences and matters, he will then be able to know all that follows without error and doubt, easily and effectually. For without these neither what precedes nor what follows can be known; whence they perfect what precedes and regulate it, even as the end perfects those things pertaining to it, and they arrange and open the way to what follows. This I now intend to intimate through authority and reason; and in the first place I intend to do so in the human sciences and in the matters of this world, and then in divine knowledge, and lastly according as they are related to the Church and the other three purposes.

*   *   *

Chapter 3: In Which It Is Proved by Reason that Every Science Requires Mathematics

What has been shown as regards mathematics as a whole through authority, can now be shown likewise by reason. And I make this statement in the first place, because other sciences use mathematical examples, but examples are given to make clear the subjects

Roger Bacon, *The Opus Majus of Roger Bacon,* Part IV, 1, 3; VI, 1, 2, translated by Robert Belle Burke (Philadelphia: University of Pennsylvania Press, 1928).

treated by the sciences; wherefore ignorance of the examples involves an ignorance of the subjects for the understanding of which the examples are adduced. For since change in natural objects is not found without some augmentation and diminution nor do these latter take place without change, Aristotle was not able to make clear without complications the difference between augmentation and change by any natural example, because augmentation and diminution go together always with change in some way; wherefore he gave the mathematical example of the rectangle which augmented by a gnomon* increases in magnitude and is not altered in shape. This example cannot be understood before the twenty-second proposition of the sixth book of the *Elements*. For in that proposition of the sixth book it is proved that a smaller rectangle is similar in every particular to a larger one and therefore a smaller one is not altered in shape, although it becomes larger by the addition of the gnomon.

Secondly, because comprehension of mathematical truths is innate, as it were, in us. For a small boy, as Tullius states in the first book of the *Tusculan Disputations,* when questioned by Socrates on geometrical truths, replied as though he had learned geometry. And this experiment has been tried in many cases, and does not hold in other sciences, as will appear more clearly from what follows. Wherefore since this knowledge is almost innate, and as it were precedes discovery and learning, or at least is less in need of them than other sciences, it will be first among sciences and will precede others disposing us toward them; since what is innate or almost so disposes toward what is acquired.

Thirdly, because this science of all the parts of philosophy was the earliest discovered. For this was first discovered at the beginning of the human race. Since it was discovered before the flood and then later by the sons of Adam, and by Noah and his sons, as is clear from the prologue to the *Construction of the Astrolabe* according to Ptolemy, and from Albumazar in the larger introduction to astronomy, and from the first book of the *Antiquities,* and this is true as regards all its parts, geometry, arithmetic, music, astronomy. But this would not have been the case except for the fact that this science is earlier than the others and naturally precedes them. Hence it is clear that it should be studied first, that through it we may advance to all the later sciences.

Fourthly, because the natural road for us is from what is easy to that which is more difficult. But this science is the easiest. This is clearly proved by the fact that mathematics is not beyond the intellectual grasp of any one. For the people at large and those wholly illiterate know how to draw figures and compute and sing, all of which are mathematical operations. But we must begin first with what is common to the laity and to the educated; and it is not only hurtful to the clergy, but disgraceful and abominable that they are ignorant of what the laity knows well and profitably. Fifthly, we see that the clergy, even the most ignorant, are able to grasp mathematical truths, although they are unable to attain to the other sciences. Besides, a man by listening once or twice can learn more about this science with certainty and reality without error, than he can by listening ten times about the other parts of philosophy, as is clear to one making the experiment. Sixthly, since the natural road for us is to begin with things which befit the state and nature of childhood, because children begin with facts that are better known by us and that must be acquired first. But of this nature is mathematics, since children are first taught to sing, and in the same way they can learn the method of making figures and of counting, and it would be far easier and more necessary for them to know about

---

*[That which is added to three sides of a parallelogram to produce a larger parallelogram of the same shape.]

numbers before singing, because in the relations of numbers in music the whole theory of numbers is set forth by example, just as the authors on music teach, both in ecclesiastical music and in philosophy. But the theory of numbers depends on figures, since numbers relating to lines, surfaces, solids, squares, cubes, pentagons, hexagons, and other figures, are known from lines, figures, and angles. For it has been found that children learn mathematical truths better and more quickly, as is clear in singing, and we also know by experience that children learn and acquire mathematical truths better than the other parts of philosophy. For Aristotle says in the sixth book of the *Ethics* that youths are able to grasp mathematical truths quickly, not so matters pertaining to nature, metaphysics, and morals. Wherefore the mind must be trained first through the former rather than through these latter sciences. Seventhly, where the same things are not known to us and to nature, there the natural road for us is from the things better known to us to those better known to nature, or known more simply; and more easily do we grasp what is better known to ourselves, and with great difficulty we arrive at a knowledge of those things which are better known to nature. And the things known to nature are erroneously and imperfectly known by us, because our intellect bears the same relation to what is so clear to nature, as the eye of the bat to the light of the sun, as Aristotle maintains in the second book of the Metaphysics; such, for example, are especially God and the angels, and future life and heavenly things, and creatures nobler than others, because the nobler they are the less known are they to us. And these are called things known to nature and known simply. Therefore, on the contrary, where the same things are known both to us and to nature, we make much progress in regard to what is known to nature and in regard to all that is there included, and we are able to attain a perfect knowledge of them. But in mathematics only, as Averroës says in the first book of the *Physics* and in the seventh of the *Metaphysics* and in his commentary on the third book of the *Heavens and the World,* are the same things known to us and to nature or simply. Therefore as in mathematics we touch upon what is known fully to us, so also do we touch upon what is known to nature and known simply. Therefore we are able to reach directly an intimate knowledge of that science. Since, therefore, we have not this ability in other sciences, clearly mathematics is better known. Therefore the acquisition of this subject is the beginning of our knowledge.

Likewise, eighthly, because every doubt gives place to certainty and every error is cleared away by unshaken truth. But in mathematics we are able to arrive at the full truth without error, and at a certainty of all points involved without doubt; since in this subject demonstration by means of a proper and necessary cause can be given. Demonstration causes the truth to be known. And likewise in this subject it is possible to have for all things an example that may be perceived by the senses, and a test perceptible to the senses in drawing figures and in counting, so that all may be clear to the sense. For this reason there can be no doubt in this science. But in other sciences, the assistance of mathematics being excluded, there are so many doubts, so many opinions, so many errors on the part of man, that these sciences cannot be unfolded, as is clear since demonstration by means of a proper and necessary cause does not exist in them from their own nature because in natural phenomena, owing to the genesis and destruction of their proper causes as well as of the effects, there is no such thing as necessity. In metaphysics there can be no demonstration except through effect, since spiritual facts are discovered through corporeal effects and the creator through the creature, as is clear in that science. In morals there cannot be demonstrations from proper causes, as Aristotle teaches. And likewise neither in matters pertaining to logic nor in grammar, as is clear, can there be very convincing demonstrations because of the weak nature of the material concerning which those sciences treat. And therefore in mathematics alone are there demonstrations of the most convincing kind through a necessary cause. And therefore here alone can a man arrive at the truth from the nature of this science. Likewise in the other sciences there are doubts and opinions and contradictions on our part, so that we scarcely agree on the most trifling question or in a single sophism; for in these sciences there are from their nature no processes of drawing figures and of reckonings, by which all things must be proved true. And therefore in mathematics alone is there certainty without doubt.

Wherefore it is evident that if in other sciences we should arrive at certainty without doubt and truth without error, it behooves us to place the foundations of knowledge in mathematics, in so far as disposed through it we are able to reach certainty in other sciences and truth by the exclusion of error. This reasoning can be made clearer by comparison, and the principle is stated in the ninth book of Euclid. The same holds true here as in the relation of the knowledge of the conclusion to the knowledge of the premises, so that if there is error and doubt in these, the truth cannot be arrived at through these premises in regard to the conclusion, nor can there be certainty, because doubt is not verified by doubt, nor is truth proved by falsehood, although it is possible for us to reason from false premises, our reasoning in that case drawing in inference and not furnishing a proof; the same is true with respect to sciences as a whole; those in which there are strong and numerous doubts and opinions and errors, I say at least on our part, should have doubts of this kind and false statements cleared away by some science definitely known to us, and in which we have neither doubts nor errors. For since the conclusions and principles belonging to them are parts of the sciences as a whole, just as part is related to part, as conclusion to premises, so is science related to science, so that a science which is full of doubts and besprinkled with opinions and obscurities, cannot be rendered certain, nor made clear, nor verified except by some other science known and verified, certain and plain to us, as in the case of a conclusion reached through premises. But mathematics alone, as was shown above, remains fixed and verified for us with the utmost certainty and verification. Therefore by means of this science all other sciences must be known and verified.

Since we have now shown by the peculiar property of that science that mathematics is prior to other sciences, and is useful and necessary to them, we now proceed to show this by considerations taken from its subject matter. And in the first place we so conclude, because the natural road for us is from sense perception to the intellect, since if sense perception is lacking, the knowledge related to that sense perception is lacking also, according to the statement in the first book of the *Posterior Analytics,* since as sense perception proceeds so does the human intellect. But quantity is especially a matter of sense perception, because it pertains to the common sense and is perceived by the other senses, and nothing can be perceived without quantity, wherefore the intellect is especially able to make progress as respects quantity. In the second place, because the very act of intelligence in itself is not completed without continuous quantity, since Aristotle states in his book on *Memory and Recollection* that our whole intellect is associated with continuity and time. Hence we grasp quantities and bodies by a direct perception of the intellect, because their forms are present in the intellect. But the forms of incorporeal things are not so perceived by our intellect; or if such forms are produced in it, according to Avicenna's statement in the third book of the *Metaphysics,* we, however, do not perceive this fact owing to the more vigorous occupation of our intellect in respect to bodies and quantities. And therefore by means of argumentation and attention to corporeal things and quantities we investigate the idea of incorporeal things, as Aristotle does in the eleventh book of the *Metaphysics.* Wherefore the intellect will make progress especially as regards quantity itself for this reason, that quantities and bodies as far as they are such belong peculiarly to the human intellect as respects the common condition of understanding. Each and every thing exists as an antecedent for some result, and this is true in higher degree of that which has just been stated.

Moreover, for full confirmation the last reason can be drawn from the experience of men of science; for all scientists in ancient times labored in mathematics, in order that they might know all things, just as we have seen in the case of men of our own times, and have heard in the case of others who by means of mathematics, of which they had an excellent knowledge, have learned all science. For very illustrious men have been found, like Bishop Robert of Lincoln and Friar Adam de Marisco, and many others, who by the power of mathematics have learned to explain the causes of all things, and expound adequately things human and divine. Moreover, the sure proof of this matter is found in the writings of those men, as, for example, on impressions such as the rainbow, comets, generation of heat, investigation of localities on the earth and other matters, of which both theology and philosophy make use. Wherefore it is clear that mathematics is absolutely necessary and useful to other sciences.

These reasons are general ones, but in particular this point can be shown by a survey of all the parts of philosophy disclosing how all things are known by the application of mathematics. This amounts to showing that other sciences are not to be known by means of dialectical and sophistical argument as commonly introduced, but by means of mathematical demonstrations entering into the truths and activities of other sciences and regulating them, without which they cannot be understood, nor made clear, nor taught, nor learned. If any one in particular should proceed by applying the power of mathematics to the separate sciences, he would see that nothing of supreme moment can be known in them without mathematics. But this simply amounts to establishing definite methods of dealing with all sciences, and by means of mathematics verifying all things necessary to the other sciences. But this matter does not come within the limits of the present survey.

*   *   *

PART VI OF THIS PLEA

It Is Also the Sixth Part of the Opus Majus, on Experimental Science

Chapter 1

Having laid down fundamental principles of the wisdom of the Latins so far as they are found in language, mathematics, and optics, I now wish to unfold the principles of experimental science, since without experience nothing can be sufficiently known. For there are two modes of acquiring knowledge, namely, by reasoning and experience. Reasoning draws a conclusion and makes us grant the conclusion, but does not make the conclusion certain, nor does it remove doubt so that the mind may rest on the intuition of truth, unless the mind discovers it by the path of experience; since many have the arguments relating to what can be known, but because they lack experience they neglect the arguments, and neither avoid what is harmful nor follow what is good. For if a man who has never seen fire should prove by adequate reasoning that fire burns and injures things and destroys them, his mind would not be satisfied thereby, nor would he avoid fire, until he placed his hand or some combustible substance in the fire, so that he might prove by experience that which reasoning taught. But when he has had actual experience of combustion his mind is made certain and rests in the full light of truth. Therefore reasoning does not suffice, but experience does.

This is also evident in mathematics, where proof is most convincing. But the mind of one who has the most convincing proof in regard to the equilateral triangle will never cleave to the conclusion without experience, nor will he heed it, but will disregard it until experience is offered him by the intersection of two circles, from either intersection of which two lines may be drawn to the extremities of the given line; but then the man accepts the conclusion without any question. Aristotle's statement, then, that proof is reasoning that causes us to know is to be understood with the proviso that the proof is accompanied by its appropriate experience, and is not to be understood of the bare proof. His statement also in the first book of the *Metaphysics* that those who understand the reason and the cause are wiser than those who have empiric knowledge of a fact, is spoken of such as know only the bare truth without the cause. But I am here speaking of the man who knows the reason and the cause through experience. These men are perfect in their wisdom, as Aristotle maintains in the sixth book of the *Ethics,* whose simple statements must be accepted as if they offered proof, as he states in the same place.

He therefore who wishes to rejoice without doubt in regard to the truths underlying phenomena must know how to devote himself to experiment. For authors write many statements, and people believe them through reasoning which they formulate without experience. Their reasoning is wholly false. For it is generally believed that the diamond cannot be broken except by goat's blood, and philosophers and theologians misuse this idea. But fracture by means of blood of this kind has never been verified, although the effort has been made, and without that blood it can be broken easily. For I have seen this with my own eyes, and this is necessary, because gems cannot be carved except by fragments of this stone. Similarly it is generally believed that the castors employed by physicians are the testicles of the male animal. But this is not true, because the beaver has these under its breast, and both the male and female produce testicles of this kind. Besides these castors the male beaver has its testicles in their natural place; and therefore what is subjoined is a dreadful lie, namely, that when the hunters pursue the beaver, he himself knowing what they are seeking cuts out with his teeth these glands. Moreover, it is generally believed that hot water freezes more quickly than cold water in vessels, and the argument in support of this is advanced that contrary is excited by contrary, just like enemies meeting each other. But it is certain that cold water freezes quickly for any one who makes the experiment. People attribute this to Aristotle in the second book of the *Meteorologics;* but he certainly does not make this statement but he does make one like it, by which they have been deceived, namely, that if cold water and hot water are poured on a cold place, as upon ice, the hot water freezes more quickly, and this is true. But if hot water and cold are placed in two vessels, the cold will freeze more quickly. Therefore all things must be verified by experience.

But experience is of two kinds; one is gained through our external senses, and in this way we gain our experience of those things that are in the heavens by instruments made for this purpose, and of those things here below by means attested by our vision. Things that do not belong in our part of the world we know through other scientists who have had experience of them. As, for example, Aristotle on the authority of Alexander sent two thousand men through different parts of the world to gain experimental knowledge of all things that are on the surface of the earth, as Pliny bears witness in his *Natural History*. This experience is both human and philosophical, as far as man can act in accordance with the grace given him; but this experience does not suffice him, because it does not give full attestation in regard to things corporeal owing to its difficulty and does not touch at all on things spiritual. It is necessary, therefore, that the intellect of man should be otherwise aided, and for this reason the holy patriarchs and prophets, who first gave sciences to the world, received illumination within and were not dependent on sense alone. The same is true of many believers since the time of Christ. For the grace of faith illuminates greatly, as also do divine inspirations, not only in things spiritual, but in things corporeal and in the sciences of philosophy; as Ptolemy states in the *Centilogium,* namely, that there are two roads by which we arrive at the knowledge of facts, one through the experience of philosophy, the other through divine inspiration, which is far the better way, as he says.

Moreover, there are seven stages of this internal knowledge, the first of which is reached through illuminations relating purely to the sciences. The second consists in the virtues. For the evil man is ignorant, as Aristotle says in the second book of the *Ethics.* Moreover, Algazel says in his *Logic* that the soul disfigured by sins is like a rusty mirror, in which the species of objects cannot be seen clearly; but the soul adorned with virtues is like a well-polished mirror, in which the forms of objects are clearly seen. For this reason true philosophers have labored more in morals for the honor of virtue, concluding in their own case that they cannot perceive the causes of things unless they have souls free from sins. Such is the statement of Augustine in regard to Socrates in the eighth book of the *City of God,* chapter III. Wherefore the Scripture says, "in a malevolent soul, etc." For it is not possible that the soul should rest in the light of truth while it is stained with sins, but like a parrot or magpie it will repeat the words of another which it has learned by long practice. The proof of this is that the beauty of truth known in its splendor attracts men to the love of it, but the proof of love is the display of a work of love. Therefore he who acts contrary to the truth must necessarily be ignorant of it, although he may know how to compose very elegant phrases, and quote the opinions of other people, like an animal that imitates the words of human beings, and like an ape that relies on the aid of men to perform its part, although it does not understand their reason. Virtue, therefore, clarifies the mind, so that a man comprehends more easily not only moral but scientific truths. I have proved this carefully in the case of many pure young men, who because of innocency of soul have attained greater proficiency than can be stated, when they have had sane advice in regard to their study. Of this number is the bearer of this present treatise, whose fundamental knowledge very few of the Latins have acquired. For since he is quite young, about twenty years of age, and very poor, nor has he been able to have teachers, nor has he spent one year in learning his great store of knowledge, nor is he a man of great genius nor of a very retentive memory, there can be no other cause except the grace of God, which owing to the purity of his soul has granted to him those things that it has as a rule refused to show to all other students. For as a spotless virgin he has departed from me, nor have I found in him any kind of mortal sin, although I have examined him carefully, and he has, therefore, a soul so bright and clear that with very little instruction he has learned more than can be estimated. And I have striven to aid in bringing it about that these two young men should be useful vessels in God's Church, to the end that they may reform by the grace of God the whole course of study of the Latins.

The third stage consists in the seven gifts of the Holy Spirit, which Isaiah enumerates. The fourth consists in the beatitudes, which the Lord defines in the Gospels. The fifth consists in the spiritual senses. The sixth consists in fruits, of which is the peace of God which passes all understanding. The seventh consists in raptures and their states according to the different ways in which people are caught up to see many things of which it is not lawful for a man to speak. And he who has had diligent training in these experiences or in several of them is able to assure himself and others not only in regard to things spiritual, but also in regard to all human sciences. Therefore since all the divisions of speculative philosophy proceed by arguments, which are either based on a point from authority or on the other points of argumentation except this division which I am now examining, we find necessary the science that is called experimental. I wish to explain it, as it is useful not only to philosophy, but to the knowledge of God, and for the direction of the whole world; just as in the preceding divisions I showed the relationship of the languages and sciences to their end, which is the divine wisdom by which all things are disposed.

Chapter 2

Since this Experimental Science is wholly unknown to the rank and file of students, I am therefore unable to convince people of its utility unless at the same time I disclose its excellence and its proper signification. This science alone, therefore, knows how to

Master with Students, engraving after a fifteenth-century miniature. Roger Bacon objected to the Scholastic style of education depicted here, arguing that scientific experimentation is necessary for a proper education. *(The Bettmann Archive)*

test perfectly what can be done by nature, what by the effort of art, what by trickery, what the incantations, conjurations, invocations, deprecations, sacrifices, that belong to magic, mean and dream of, and what is in them, so that all falsity may be removed and the truth alone of art and nature may be retained. This science alone teaches us how to view the mad acts of magicians, that they may be not ratified but shunned, just as logic considers sophistical reasoning.

This science has three leading characteristics with respect to other sciences. The first is that it investigates by experiment the notable conclusions of all those sciences. For the other sciences know how to discover their principles by experiments, but their conclusions are reached by reasoning drawn from the principles discovered. But if they should have a particular and complete experience of their own conclusions, they must have it with the aid of this noble science. For it is true that mathematics has general experiments as regards its conclusions in its figures and calculations, which also are applied to all sciences and to this kind of experiment, because no science can be known without mathematics. But if we give our attention to particular and complete experiments and such as are attested wholly by the proper method, we must employ the principles of this science which is called experimental. I give as an example the rainbow and phenomena connected with it, of which nature are the circle around the sun and the stars, the streak *(virga)* also lying at the side of the sun or of a star, which is apparent to the eye in a straight line, and is called by Aristotle in the third book of the *Meteorologics* a perpendicular, but by Seneca a streak, and the circle is called a corona, phenomena which frequently have the colors of the rainbow. The natural philosopher discusses these phenomena, and the writer on Perspective has much to add pertaining to the mode of vision that is necessary in this case. But neither Aristotle nor Avicenna in their Natural Histories has given us a knowledge of phenomena of this kind, nor has Seneca, who composed a special book on them. But Experimental Science attests them.

Bonaventure
1221–1274

Born Giovanni Fidanza, St. Bonaventure came from Tuscany in what is now central Italy. As a boy Bonaventure was healed of a serious illness and his mother attributed the healing to St. Francis of Assisi. As a young man Bonaventure went to study at the University of Paris and there joined the Franciscan Order. Following completion of his baccalaureate studies, Bonaventure composed his *Commentary on the "Sentences" of Peter Lombard* between 1250 and 1252.* In 1255 Bonaventure became a victim of the conflict between the "seculars" (priests who did not belong to religious orders) and the "regulars" (priests who did). The growing influence of the mendicant orders at the University of Paris led to a backlash by the seculars. The seculars excluded Bonaventure and St. Thomas Aquinas, his Dominican counterpart, from the faculty. It took the direct intervention of the pope in 1257 before the regulars were allowed to return to the university staff.

By then Bonaventure was no longer teaching. Early in 1257 he had been appointed Minister General of the Franciscan Order. While he held this post, Bonaventure also found time to write a number of works, including a series of Lenten reflections on the Ten Command-

*In the twelfth century, Peter Lombard wrote the *Sentences*—a theological textbook that gathered the opinions of the great theologians and grouped them into four sections: on God, on creation, on the incarnation, and on redemption. While the work itself was not original, its carefulness and system inspired a number of important commentaries.

ments, *De Decem Praeceptis.* In 1273 Bonaventure was made Cardinal Bishop of Albano. The following year he attended the Council of Lyons. He died while in Lyons and was buried there in the presence of Pope Gregory X.

Bonaventure had grave doubts about the use of Aristotle's philosophy. He did accept a number of Aristotelian concepts, such as the necessity of experience to know the sensible world. He also used the Aristotelian categories of his time, such as substance, accident, form, and matter. But Bonaventure could not accept a number of Aristotle's teachings. In the first place, Aristotle had rejected the Platonic notion of Forms. Bonaventure held that Augustine's reworking of this Platonic concept was correct and that the Divine Exemplars (Augustine's "Forms") were the proper basis for metaphysics. Second, Aristotle taught that the universe was eternal. In the selections given here on the eternity of the world, translated by Paul M. Byrne, Bonaventure argues for the absurdity of this Aristotelian doctrine. It is important to note that Bonaventure was not content to appeal to theology alone—he sought to persuade by rational argument as well.

But beyond rejecting particular Aristotelian doctrines, Bonaventure believed it impossible that any pagan philosophy could adequately describe even the natural world. Indeed, the idea of a "natural world" itself is an abstraction, since the world is God's creation. Only when metaphysics acknowledges God's activity can truth be found. While the natural philosopher can prove God's existence and unity (and Bonaventure produced several such proofs), without a theological understanding of that unity, the philosopher will err. In *Retracing the Arts to Theology,* given here (complete) in the Emma Therese Healy translation, Bonaventure explains the dependence of knowledge on theology using the metaphor of light. The various kinds of knowledge are depicted as different kinds of light, but it is God who is the "Father of Lights." Hence all knowledge is finally knowledge of God, and all fields of knowledge (the "arts") reduce to theology.

*   *   *

The best general introduction to Bonaventure's life and teaching remains Étienne Gilson, *The Philosophy of St. Bonaventure,* translated by Dom Illtyd Trethowan and F.J. Sheed (New York: Sheed and Ward, 1938). Jacques Guy Bougerol, *Introduction to the Works of Bonaventure,* translated by Jose de Vinck (Paterson, NJ: St. Anthony Guild Press, 1964), also provides a general introduction, while Mary Bernetta Quinn, *To God Alone the Glory: A Life of St. Bonaventure* (Westminster, MD: Newman Press, 1962), gives a laudatory biography. For a comparison of Bonaventure and his more famous contemporary Thomas Aquinas, see Robert W. Shahan and Francis J. Kovach, eds., *Bonaventure & Aquinas: Enduring Philosophers* (Norman: University of Oklahoma Press, 1976).

There are a number of doctoral dissertations on Bonaventure, including Mary Rachael Dady, *The Theory of Knowledge of Saint Bonaventure* (Washington, DC: Catholic University of America Press, 1939), and Michael P. Malloy, *Civil Authority in Medieval Philosophy: Lombard, Aquinas, and Bonaventure* (Lanham, MD: University Press of America, 1985). The Franciscan Institute (of the appropriately named St. Bonaventure, New York) has produced monographs such as that of Emma Jane Marie Spargo, *The Category of the Aesthetic in the Philosophy of Saint Bonaventure* (1953). But most of these dissertations and monographs are too difficult for the beginning student (and often include long untranslated Latin passages).

RETRACING THE ARTS TO THEOLOGY

1. *Every good gift and every perfect gift is from above, coming down from the Father of Lights,* says James in the first chapter of his epistle. These words of Sacred Scripture not only indicate the source of all illumination but they likewise point out the generous flow of the manifold rays which issue from that Fount of light. Notwithstanding the fact that every illumination of knowledge is within, still we can with reason distinguish what we may call the *external* light, or the light of mechanical art; the *lower* light, or the light of sense perception; the *inner* light, or the light of philosophical knowledge; and the *higher* light, or the light of grace and of Sacred Scripture. The first light illumines in regard to structure of *artifacts;* the second, in regard to *natural forms;* the third, in regard to *intellectual truth;* the fourth and last, in regard to *saving truth.*

2. The first light, then, since it enlightens the mind in reference to structure of *artifacts,* which are, as it were, exterior to man and intended to supply the needs of the body, is called the light of *mechanical art.* Being, in a certain sense, servile and of a lower nature than philosophical knowledge, this light can rightly be termed external. It has seven divisions corresponding to the seven mechanical arts enumerated by Hugh in his *Didascalicon,* namely, weaving, armour-making, agriculture, hunting, navigation, medicine, and the dramatic art. That the above-mentioned arts *suffice* (for us) is shown in the following way. Every mechanical art is intended for man's *consolation* or for his comfort; its purpose, therefore, is to banish either *sorrow* or *want;* it either *benefits* or *delights,* according to the words of Horace:

> Either to serve or to please is the wish of the poets.

And again:

> He hath gained universal applause who hath combined the profitable with the pleasing.

If its aim is to afford *consolation* and amusement, it is *dramatic art,* or the art of exhibiting plays, which embraces every form of entertainment, be it song, music, poetry, or pantomime. If, however, it is intended for the *comfort* or betterment of the exterior man, it can accomplish its purpose by providing either *covering* or *food,* or by *serving as an aid in the acquisition of either.* In the matter of *covering,* if it provides a soft and light material, it is *weaving;* if a strong and hard material, it is *armour-making* or metal-working, an art which extends to every tool or implement fashioned either of iron or of any metal whatsoever, or of stone, or of wood.

In the matter of *food,* mechanical art may benefit us in two ways, for we derive our sustenance from *vegetables* and from *animals.* As regards *vegetables,* it is *farming;* as regards *flesh meats,* it is *hunting.* Or again, as regards *food,* mechanical art has a twofold advantage: it aids either in the *production* and multiplication of crops, in which case it is agriculture, or in the various ways of preparing food, under which aspect it is hunting, an art which extends to every conceivable way of preparing foods, drinks, and delicacies—a task with which bakers, cooks, and innkeepers are concerned. The term

St. Bonaventure, *Retracing the Arts to Theology,* translated by Sr. Emma Therese Healy, from *The Works of St. Bonaventure,* Vol. I (St. Bonaventure, NY: The Franscican Institute, 1955). Reprinted by permission.

"hunting" *(venatio),* however, is used for all these things because it has a certain excellence and courtliness.

Furthermore, as an aid in the acquisition of each (clothing and food), the mechanical arts contribute to the welfare of man in two ways: either by *supplying a want,* and in this case it is *navigation,* which includes all *commerce of articles* of covering or of food; or by *removing impediments* and ills of the body, under which aspect it is *medicine,* whether it is concerned with the preparation of drugs, potions, or ointments, with the healing of wounds, or with the amputation of members, in which latter case it is called surgery. Dramatic art, on the other hand, is the only one of its kind. Thus the sufficiency (of the mechanical arts) is evident.

3. The second light, which enables us to discern *natural forms,* is the light of *sense perception.* Rightly is it called the *lower* light because sense perception begins with a material object and takes place by the aid of corporeal light. It has five divisions corresponding to the five senses. In his *Third Book on Genesis,* Saint Augustine bases the *adequacy* of the senses on the nature of the light present in the elements in the following way. If the light or brightness which makes possible the discernment of things corporeal exists in a *high degree of its own property* and in a certain purity, it is the sense of *sight; commingled with the air,* it is *hearing; with vapor,* it is *smell; with fluid,* it is *taste; with solidity of earth,* it is *touch.* Now the sensitive life of the body partakes of the nature of light for which reason it thrives in the nerves, which are naturally unobstructed and capable of transmitting impressions, and in these five senses it possesses more or less vigor according to the greater or less soundness of the nerves. And so, since there are in the world five simple substances, namely, the four elements and the fifth essence, man has for the perception of all these corporeal forms five senses well adapted to these substances, because, on account of the well-defined nature of each sense, apprehension can take place only when there is a certain conformity and fitness between the organ and the object. There is another way of determining the adequacy of the senses, but Saint Augustine sanctions this method and it seems reasonable, since corresponding elements on the part of the organ, the medium, and the object lend joint support to the proof.

4. The third light, which enlightens man in the investigation of *intelligible truths,* is the light of *philosophical knowledge.* It is called inner because it inquires into inner and hidden causes through principles of learning and natural truth, which are inherent in man. There is a triple diffusion of this light in *rational, natural,* and *moral* philosophy, which seems adequate, since it covers the three aspects of truth—truth of *speech,* truth of *things,* and truth of *morals. Rational* philosophy considers the truth of *speech;* natural philosophy, the truth of *things;* and *moral* philosophy, the truth of *conduct.* Or we may consider it in a different light. Just as we find in the Most High God efficient, formal or exemplary, and final causality, since "He is the Cause of being, the Principle of knowledge, and the Pattern of human life," so do we find it in the illumination of philosophy, which enlightens the mind to discern the *causes of being,* in which case it is *physics;* or to grasp the *principles of understanding,* in which case it is *logic;* or to learn the *right way of living,* in which case it is *moral* or practical philosophy. We are now considering it under its third aspect. The light of philosophical knowledge illumines the intellectual faculty itself and this enlightenment may be threefold: if it governs the *motive power,* it is *moral* philosophy; if it *rules itself,* it is *natural* philosophy; if it directs *interpretation,* it is *discursive* philosophy. As a result, man is enlightened as regards the truth of life, the truth of knowledge, and the truth of doctrine.

And since one may, through the medium of *speech,* give expression to what he has in mind with a threefold purpose in view: namely, to manifest his thought, to induce someone to believe, or to arouse love or hatred, for this reason, *discursive* or rational philosophy has three sub-divisions: *grammar, logic,* and *rhetoric.* Of these sciences the first aims to express; the second, to teach; the third, to persuade. The first considers the reasoning faculty as *apprehending;* the second, as *judging;* the third, as *persuading.* Since the mind apprehends by means of *correct* speech, judges by means of *true* speech, and persuades by means of *embellished* speech, with good reason does this triple science consider these three qualities in speech.

Again, since our intellect must be guided in its judgment by formal principles, these principles, likewise, can be considered under three aspects: in relation to *matter,* they are termed *formal;* in relation to the *mind,* they are termed *intellectual;* and in relation to *Divine Wisdom,* they are called *ideal. Natural* philosophy, therefore, is subdivided into *physics* proper, *mathematics,* and *metaphysics.* Thus *physics* treats of the generation and corruption of things according to natural powers and seminal causes; *mathematics* considers forms that can be abstracted in their pure intelligibility; *metaphysics* treats of the cognition of all beings, which it leads back to one first Principle from which they proceeded according to the *ideal causes,* that is, to God, since He is the *Beginning,* the *End,* and the *Exemplar.* Concerning these ideal causes, however, there has been some controversy among metaphysicians.

Since the government of the motive power is to be considered in a threefold way, namely, as regards the *individual,* the *family,* and the *state,* so there are three corresponding divisions of *moral* philosophy: namely, *ethical, economic,* and *political,* the content of each being clearly indicated by its name.

5. Now the fourth light, which illumines the mind for the understanding of *saving truth,* is the light of *Sacred Scripture.* This light is called *higher* because it leads to things above by the manifestation of truths which are beyond reason and also because it is not acquired by human research, but comes down by inspiration from the *"Father of Lights."* Although in its *literal* sense it is *one,* still, in its spiritual and *mystical* sense, it is *threefold,* for in all the books of Sacred Scripture, in addition to the literal meaning which the words outwardly express, there is understood a threefold spiritual meaning: namely, the *allegorical,* by which we are taught what to believe concerning the Divinity and humanity; the *moral,* by which we are taught how to live; and the *anagogical,* by which we are taught how to be united to God. Hence all Sacred Scripture teaches these three truths: namely, the eternal generation and Incarnation of Christ, the pattern of human life, and the union of the soul with God. The first regards *faith;* the second, *morals;* and the third, the *ultimate end of both.* The doctors should labor at the study of the first; the preachers, at the study of the second; the contemplatives, at the study of the third. The first is taught chiefly by Augustine; the second, by Gregory; the third, by Dionysius. Anselm follows Augustine; Bernard follows Gregory; Richard (of Saint Victor) follows Dionysius. For Anselm excels in reasoning; Bernard, in preaching; Richard, in contemplating; but Hugh (of Saint Victor) in all three.

6. From the foregoing statements it can be inferred that, although according to our first classification the light coming down from above is *fourfold,* it still admits of *six* modifications: namely, the light of *Sacred Scripture,* the light of *sense perception,* the light of *mechanical art,* the light of *rational philosophy,* the light of *natural philosophy,* and the light of *moral philosophy.* And for that reason there are in this life six illuminations, and they have their twilight, for all *knowledge will be destroyed;* for that reason too there follows a seventh day of rest, a day which knows no evening, *the illumination of glory.*

7. Wherefore, very fittingly may these six illuminations be related to the six days of creation or illumination in which the world was made, the knowledge of Sacred

Scripture corresponding to the creation of the first day, that is, to the creation of light, and so on, one after the other in order. Moreover, just as all those creations had their origin in one light, so too are all these branches of knowledge ordained for the knowledge of Sacred Scripture; they are contained in it; they are perfected by it; and by means of it they are ordained for eternal illumination. Wherefore, all our knowledge should end in the knowledge of Sacred Scripture, and especially is this true of the *anagogical* knowledge through which the illumination is reflected back to God whence it came. And there the cycle ends; the number six is complete and consequently there is rest.

8. Let us see, therefore, how the other illuminations of knowledge are to be brought back to the light of Sacred Scripture. First of all, let us consider the illumination of *sense perception,* which is concerned exclusively with the cognition of sense objects, a process in which there are three phases to be considered: namely, the *medium* of perception, the *exercise* of perception, and the *delight* of perception. If we consider the *medium* of perception, we shall see therein the Word begotten from all eternity and made man in time. Indeed, a sense object can stimulate a cognitive faculty only through the medium of a similitude which proceeds from the object as an offspring from its parent, and this by generation, by reality, or by exemplarity, for every sense. This similitude, however, does not complete the act of perception unless it is brought into contact with the sense organ and the sense faculty, and once that contact is established, there results a new percept. Through this percept the mind is led back to the object by means of the similitude. And even though the object is not always present to the senses, still the fact remains that the object by itself, when in its finished state, begets a similitude. In like manner, know that from the mind of the Most High, Who is knowable by the interior senses of our mind, from all eternity there emanated a Similitude, an Image, and an Offspring; and afterwards, when "the fullness of time came," He was united to a mind and a body and assumed the form of man, which had never been before. Through Him the minds of all of us which receive that Similitude of the Father through faith in our hearts, are brought back to God.

9. If we consider the *exercise* of sense perception, we shall see therein *the pattern of human life,* for each sense applies itself to its proper object, shrinks from what may harm it, and does not usurp what does not belong to it. In like manner, the *spiritual sense* lives in an orderly way when it exercises itself for its own purpose, against *negligence;* when it refrains from what is harmful, against *concupiscence;* and when it refrains from usurping what does not belong to it, against *pride.* Of a truth, every disorder springs from negligence, from concupiscence, or from pride. Surely then, he who lives a prudent, temperate, and submissive life leads a well-ordered life, for thereby he avoids negligence in things to be done, concupiscence in things to be desired, and pride in things that are excellent.

10. Furthermore, if we consider the *delight* of sense perception, we shall see therein the union of God and the soul. Indeed every sense seeks its proper sense object with longing, finds it with delight, and never wearied, seeks it again and again, because "the eye is not filled with seeing, neither is the ear filled with hearing." In the same way, our spiritual senses must seek with longing, find with joy, and time and again experience the beautiful, the harmonious, the fragrant, the sweet, or the delightful to the touch. Behold how the Divine Wisdom lies hidden in sense perception and how wonderful is the contemplation of the five spiritual senses in the light of their conformity to the senses of the body.

11. By the same process of reasoning is Divine Wisdom to be found in the illumination of the *mechanical arts,* the sole purpose of which is the *production of artifacts.* In this illumination we can see the *eternal generation and Incarnation of the*

Word, the *pattern of human life,* and the *union of the soul with God.* And this is true if we consider the *production,* the *effect,* and the *fruit* of a work, or if we consider the *skill of the artist,* the *quality of the effect produced,* and the *utility of the product derived therefrom.*

12. If we consider the *production,* we shall see that the work of art proceeds from the artificer according to a similitude existing in his mind; this pattern or model the artificer studies carefully before he produces and then he produces as he has pre-determined. The artificer, moreover, produces an exterior work bearing the closest possible resemblance to the interior exemplar, and if it were in his power to produce an effect which would know and love him, this he would assuredly do; and if that effect could know its maker, it would be by means of the similitude according to which it came from the hands of the artificer; and if the eyes of the understanding were so darkened that it could not elevate itself to things above itself in order to bring itself to a knowledge of its maker, it would be necessary for the similitude according to which the effect was produced to lower itself even to that nature which the effect could grasp and know. In like manner, understand that no creature has proceeded from the Most High Creator except through the Eternal Word, "in Whom He ordered all things," and by which Word He produced creatures bearing not only the nature of His *vestige* but also of His *image* so that through knowledge they might become like unto Him. And since by sin the rational creature had dimmed the eye of contemplation, it was most fitting that the Eternal and Invisible should become visible and take flesh that He might lead us back to the Father. Indeed, this is what is related in the fourteenth chapter of Saint John: "No one comes to the Father but through Me," and in the eleventh chapter of Saint Matthew: "No one knows the Son except the Father; nor does anyone know the Father except the Son, and him to whom the Son chooses to reveal him." For that reason, then, it is said, "the Word was made flesh." Therefore, considering the illumination of mechanical art as regards the production of the work, we shall see therein the Word begotten and made incarnate, that is, the Divinity and the Humanity and the integrity of all faith.

13. If we consider the *effect,* we shall see therein the *pattern of human life,* for every artificer, indeed, aims to produce a work that is beautiful, useful, and enduring, and only when it possesses these three qualities is the work highly valued and acceptable. Corresponding to the above-mentioned qualities, in the pattern of life there must be found three elements: *"knowledge, will,* and *unaltering* and *persevering toil."* *Knowledge* renders the work beautiful; the *will* renders it useful; *perseverance* renders it lasting. The first resides in the rational, the second in the concupiscible, and the third in the irascible appetite.

14. If we consider the *fruit,* we shall find therein *the union of the soul with God,* for every artificer who fashions a work does so that he may derive *praise, benefit,* or *delight* therefrom—a threefold purpose which corresponds to the three formal objects of the appetites: namely, a *noble* good, a *useful* good, and an *agreeable* good. It was for this threefold reason that God made the soul rational, namely, that of its own accord, it might *praise* Him, *serve* Him, *find delight* in Him, and be at rest; and this takes place through charity. "He who abides in it, abides in God, and God in him," in such a way that there is found therein a kind of wondrous union and from that union comes a wondrous delight, for in the Book of Proverbs it is written, "My delights were to be with the children of men." Behold how the illumination of mechanical art is the path to the illumination of Sacred Scripture. There is nothing therein which does not bespeak true wisdom and for this reason Sacred Scripture quite rightly makes frequent use of such similitudes.

15. In like manner is Divine Wisdom to be found in the illumination of *rational philosophy,* the main concern of which is *speech.* Here are to be considered three elements corresponding to the three aspects of speech itself: namely, the *person speaking,* the *delivery* of the speech, and its final purpose or its effect upon the *hearer.*

16. Considering speech in the light of the *speaker,* we see that all speech signifies a *mental concept.* That inner concept is the word of the mind and its offspring which is known to the person conceiving it; but that it may become known to the hearer, it assumes the form of the voice, and clothed therein, the intelligible word becomes sensible and is heard without; it is received into the ear of the person listening and still it does not depart from the mind of the person uttering it. Practically the same procedure is seen in the begetting of the Eternal Word, because the Father conceived Him, begetting Him from all eternity, as it is written in the eighth chapter of the Book of Proverbs, "The depths were not as yet, and I was already conceived." But that He might be known by man who is endowed with senses. He assumed the nature of flesh, and "the Word was made flesh and dwelt amongst us," and yet He remained "in the bosom of the Father."

17. Considering speech in the light of its *delivery,* we shall see therein the pattern of *human life,* for three essential qualities work together for the perfection of speech: namely, *suitability, truth,* and *ornament.* Corresponding to these three qualities, every act of ours should be characterized by *measure, beauty,* and *order* so that it may be *controlled* by its proper measure in its external work, *rendered beautiful* by purity of affection, and *regulated* and adorned by uprightness of intention. For then truly does one live an upright and well-ordered life when his intention is upright, his affection pure, and his activity within its proper limit.

18. Considering speech in the light of its *purpose,* we find that it aims to *express,* to *instruct,* and to *persuade;* but it never *expresses* except by means of a likeness; it never *teaches* except by means of a clear light; it never *persuades* except by power; and it is evident that these effects are accomplished only by means of an inherent likeness, light, and power intrinsically *united to the soul.* Therefore, Saint Augustine concludes that he alone is a true teacher who can impress a likeness, shed light, and grant power to the heart of his hearer. Hence it is that "he who teaches within hearts has his Chair in heaven." Now as perfection of speech requires the union of power, light, and a likeness within the soul, so, too, for the instruction of the soul in the knowledge of God by interior conversation with Him, there is required a union with Him who is "the brightness of his glory and the image of his substance, and upholding all things by the word of his power." Hence we see how wondrous is this contemplation by which Saint Augustine in his many writings leads souls to Divine Wisdom.

19. By the same mode of reasoning is the Wisdom of God to be found in the illumination of *natural philosophy,* which is concerned chiefly with the *formal causes* in *matter,* in the *soul,* and in the *Divine Wisdom.* These formal causes it is fitting to consider under three aspects: namely, as regards the *relation of proportion,* the *effect of causality,* and their *medium of union;* and in these three can be accordingly found the three (central ideas of the three senses of Holy Scripture) mentioned above.

20. Considering the formal causes according to their *relation of proportion,* we shall see therein the *Word Eternal* and the *Word Incarnate.* The *intellectual* and abstract causes are, as it were, midway between the *seminal* and the *ideal* causes. But *seminal* causes cannot exist in *matter* without the generation and production of form; neither can *intellectual* causes exist in the *soul* without the generation of the word in the mind. Therefore, *ideal* causes cannot exist *in God* without the generation of the Word from the Father in due proportion. Truly, this is a mark of dignity, and if it becomes the creature, how much more so the Creator. It was for this reason that Saint Augustine said the Son

of God is the "art of the Father." Again, the natural tendency in matter is so ordained toward intellectual causes that the generation is in no way perfect unless the rational soul be united to the material body. By similar reasoning, therefore, we come to the conclusion that the highest and noblest perfection can exist in this world only if a nature in which there are the seminal causes, and a nature in which there are the intellectual causes, and a nature in which there are the ideal causes are simultaneously combined in the unity of one person, as was done in the Incarnation of the Son of God. Therefore all natural philosophy, by reason of the relation of proportion, predicates the Word of God begotten and become Incarnate so that He is the *Alpha* and the *Omega,* that is, He was begotten in the beginning and before all time but became Incarnate in the fullness of time.

21. Now if we think of these causes according to the *effect of causality,* we shall be considering the *pattern of human life,* since generation by seminal causes can take place in generative and corruptible matter only by the beneficent light of the heavenly bodies which are far removed from generation and corruption, that is, by the *sun,* the *moon,* and the *stars.* So too the soul can perform no living works unless it receive from the sun, that is, from Christ, the aid of His gratuitous light; unless it seek the protection of the moon, that is, of the Virgin Mary, Mother of Christ; and unless it imitate the example of the other saints. When all these concur, there is accomplished in the soul a living and perfect work; therefore the right order of living depends upon this threefold cooperation.

22. Moreover, if we consider these formal causes as regards their *medium of union,* we shall understand how *union of the soul with God* takes place, for the corporeal nature can be united to the soul only through the medium of moisture, (vital) spirit, and warmth—three conditions which dispose the body to receive life from the soul. So too we may understand that God gives life to the soul and is united to it only on the condition that it be *moistened* with tears of compunction and filial love, made *spiritual* by contempt of every earthly thing, and *be warmed* by desire for its heavenly home and its Beloved. Behold how in natural philosophy lies hidden the Wisdom of God.

23. In the same way is the light of *Sacred Scripture* to be found in the illumination of *moral philosophy.* Since moral philosophy is concerned principally with rectitude, it treats of general justice which Saint Anselm calls the "rectitude of the will." The term "right" has a threefold signification and accordingly, in the consideration of rectitude are revealed the three central ideas (of the senses of Sacred Scripture) previously mentioned. In one sense of the word, that is called "*right,* the middle of which is not out of line with its extreme points." If then God is perfect rectitude and that by His very nature since He is the Beginning and the End of all things, it follows that in God there must be an intermediary of *His own nature* so that there may be one Person who only produces, another who is only produced, but an intermediary who both produces and is produced. There is likewise need of an intermediary in the *going forth* and in the *return* of things: in the *going forth,* an intermediary which will be more on the part of the one producing; in the *return,* one which will be more on the part of the one returning. Therefore, as creatures went forth from God by the Word of God, so for a perfect return, it was necessary that the Mediator *between God and man* be not only God but also man so that He might lead men back to God.

24. In another sense, that is called "*right*" which is conformed to rule. Accordingly, in the consideration of rectitude there is seen the *rule of life.* For he indeed lives rightly who is guided by the regulations of the divine law, as is the case when the will of man accepts necessary *precepts,* salutary *warnings,* and *counsels* of perfection that he may thereby prove *the good and acceptable and perfect will of God.* And then is the rule of life right when no obliquity can be found therein.

25. In the third sense, that is called *"right"* the summit of which is raised upward, as for instance, we say that man has an upright posture. And in this sense, in the consideration of rectitude there is manifested the *union of the soul with God;* for since God is above, it necessarily follows that the apex of the mind itself must be raised aloft. And indeed this is what actually happens when man's *rational nature* assents to the First Truth for His own sake and above all things, when his *irascible nature* strives after the Highest Bounty, and when his *concupiscible nature* clings to the Greatest Good. He who thus keeps close to God *is one spirit with him.*

26. And so it is evident how the *manifold Wisdom of God,* which is clearly revealed in Sacred Scripture, lies hidden in all knowledge and in all nature. It is evident too how all divisions of knowledge are handmaids of theology, and it is for this reason that theology makes use of illustrations and terms pertaining to every branch of knowledge. It is likewise evident how wide is the illuminative way and how in everything which is perceived or known God Himself lies hidden within. And this is the fruit of all sciences, that in all, faith may be strengthened, *God may be honored,* character may be formed, and consolation may be derived from union of the Spouse with His beloved, a union which takes place through charity, to the attainment of which the whole purpose of Sacred Scripture, and consequently, every illumination descending from above, is directed—a charity without which all knowledge is vain—because no one comes to the Son except through the Holy Ghost who teaches us *all the truth, who is blessed forever. Amen.*

ON THE ETERNITY OF THE WORLD
(selections)

COMMENTARY ON THE "SENTENCES" OF PETER LOMBARD

d. 1, p. 1, a. 1, q. 2

The question is: Has the world been produced in time or from eternity. That it has not been produced in time is shown:

1. By two arguments based on motion, the first of which is demonstrative in the following way: *Before every motion and change, there is the motion of the first moveable thing (primum mobile);* but everything which begins to be begins by way of motion or change; therefore that motion (viz., of the first moveable thing) is before all that which begins to be. But that motion could not have preceded itself or its movable thing *(mobile);* therefore it could not possibly have a beginning. The first proposition is a basic one and its proof is as follows: It is a basic principle in philosophy that "in every kind the complete is prior to the incomplete of that kind"; but movement toward place

From C. Vollert, L. Kendzierski, and P.M. Byrne, editors and translators, *St. Thomas Aquinas, Siger of Brabant, St. Bonaventure: On the Eternity of the World* (Milwaukee, WI: Marquette University Press, 1964). This Question was translated by Paul M. Byrne. Reprinted by permission of Marquette University Press.

is the more perfect among all the kinds of motion inasmuch as it is the motion of a complete being, and circular motion is both the swifter and the more perfect among all the kinds of local motion; but the motion of the heaven is of this kind, therefore most perfect, therefore the first. Therefore it is evident that, etc.

2. This is likewise shown by an absurdity consequent upon the alternative. *Everything which comes to be comes to be through motion or change;* consequently, if motion comes to be it comes to be through motion or change, and with regard to this latter motion the question is similarly raised. Therefore, either there is to be an infinite regress or a positing of some motion lacking a beginning; if the motion, then also the movable thing and, consequently, also the world.

3. Similarly, a demonstrative argument based on time is as follows: *Everything which begins to be either begins to be in an instant or in time.* If, therefore, the world begins to be, it does so either in an instant or in time. But before every time there is time, and time is before every instant. Consequently there is time before all those things which have begun to be. But it could not have been before the world and motion; therefore the world has not had a beginning. The first proposition is *per se* known. The second, namely that before every time there is time, is evident from the fact that if it is flowing, it was of necessity flowing beforehand. Similarly, it is evident that there is time before every instant since time is a circular measure suited to the motion and the movable thing; but every point in a circle is a beginning even as it is an end; therefore every instant of time is a beginning of the future even as it is a terminus of the past. Accordingly, before every "now" there has been a past. It is evident, therefore, etc.

4. Again, this is shown by the absurdity consequent upon the alternative. If time is produced, it is produced either in time or in an instant; therefore in time. But in every time there is a prior and a posterior, both a past and a future. Consequently, if time has been produced in time, there has been time before every time, and this is impossible. Therefore, etc.

These are Aristotle's arguments based on the character of the world itself.

5. Besides these, there are other arguments based on the character of the producing cause. In general, these can be reduced to two, the first of which is demonstrative and the second based on the absurdity consequent upon the alternative. The first is as follows: *Given all adequate and actual cause, the effect is given;* but God from eternity has been the adequate and actual cause of this world; therefore, etc. The major premise is *per se* known. The minor, namely that God is the adequate cause, is evident. Since He needs nothing extrinsic for the creating of the world, but only the power, wisdom and goodness which have been most perfect in God from eternity, evidently He has, from eternity, been the adequate cause. That He has also been the actual cause is evident as follows: God is pure act and is His own act of willing, as Aristotle says; and our philosophers *(Sancti)* say that He is His own acting. It follows, therefore, etc.

6. Also, by the absurdity of the alternative. *Everything which begins to act or produce, when it was not producing beforehand, passes from rest into act.* If, therefore, God begins to produce the world, He passes from rest into act; but all such things are subject to rest and change or mutability. Therefore God is subject to rest and mutability. This, however, contradicts His absolute goodness and absolute simplicity, and, consequently, is impossible. It is to blaspheme God; and to say that the world has had a beginning amounts to the same thing.

These are arguments which the commentators and more recent men *(moderniores)* have added over and beyond the arguments of Aristotle; or, at least, they are reducible to these.

But there are arguments to the contrary, based on *per se* known propositions of reason and philosophy:

1. The first of these is: *It is impossible to add to the infinite.* This is *per se* evident because everything which receives an addition becomes more; "but nothing is more than infinite." If the world lacks a beginning, however, it has had an infinite duration, and consequently there can be no addition to its duration. But this is certainly false because every day a revolution is added to a revolution; therefore, etc. If you were to say that it is infinite in past time and yet is actually finite with respect to the present, which now is, and, accordingly, that it is in this respect, in which it is finite, that the "more" is to be found, it is pointed out to you that, to the contrary, it is in the past that the "more" is to be found. This is an infallible truth: If the world is eternal, then the revolutions of the sun in its orbit are infinite in number. Again, there have necessarily been twelve revolutions of the moon for every one of the sun. Therefore the moon has revolved more times than the sun, and the sun an infinite number of times. Accordingly, that which exceeds the infinite as infinite is discovered. But this is impossible; therefore, etc.

2. The second proposition is: *It is impossible for the infinite in number to be ordered.* For every order flows from a principle toward a mean. Therefore, if there is no first, there is no order; but if the duration of the world or the revolutions of the heaven are infinite, they do not have a first; therefore they do not have an order, and one is not before another. But since this is false, it follows that they have a first. If you say that it is necessary to posit a limit *(statum)* to all ordered series only in the case of things ordered in a causal relation, because among causes there is necessarily a limit, I ask why not in other cases. Moreover, you do not escape in this way. For there has never been a revolution of the heaven without there being a generation of animal from animal. But an animal is certainly related causally to the animal from which it is generated. If, therefore, according to Aristotle and reason it is necessary to posit a limit among those things ordered in a causal relation, then in the generation of animals it is necessary to posit a first animal. And the world has not existed without animals; therefore, etc.

3. The third proposition is: *It is impossible to traverse what is infinite.* But if the world had no beginning, there has been an infinite number of revolutions; therefore it was impossible for it to have traversed them; therefore impossible for it to have come down to the present. If you say that they (i.e., numerically infinite revolutions) have not been traversed because there has been no first one, or that they well could be traversed in an infinite time you do not escape in this way. For I shall ask you if any revolution has infinitely preceded today's revolution or none. If none, then all are finitely distant from this present one. Consequently, they are all together finite in number and so have a beginning. If some one is infinitely distant, then I ask whether the revolution immediately following it is infinitely distant. If not, then neither is the former (infinitely) distant since there is a finite distance between the two of them. But if it (i.e., the one immediately following) is infinitely distant, then I ask in a similar way about the third, the fourth, and so on to infinity. Therefore, one is no more distant than another from this present one, one is not before another, and so they are all simultaneous.

4. The fourth proposition is: *It is impossible for the infinite to be grasped by a finite power.* But if the world had no beginning, then the infinite is grasped by a finite power; therefore, etc. The proof of the major is *per se* evident. The minor is shown as follows. I suppose that God alone is with a power actually infinite and that all other things have limitation. Also I suppose that there has never been a motion of the heaven without there being a created spiritual substance who would either cause or, at least, know it. Further, I also suppose that a spiritual substance forgets nothing. If, therefore, there has been, at the same time as the heaven, any spiritual substance with finite power,

there has been no revolution of the heaven which he would not know and which would have been forgotten. Therefore, he is actually knowing all of them and they have been infinite in number. Accordingly, a spiritual substance with finite power is grasping simultaneously an infinite number of things. If you assert that this is not unsuitable because all the revolutions, being of the same species and in every way alike, are known by a single likeness, there is the objection that not only would he have known the rotations, but also their effects as well, and these various and diverse effects are infinite in number. It is clear, therefore, etc.

5. The fifth proposition is: *It is impossible that there be simultaneously an infinite number of things.* But if the world is eternal and without a beginning, then there has been an infinite number of men, since it would not be without there being men—for all things are in a certain way for the sake of man and a man lasts only for a limited length of time. But there have been as many rational souls as there have been men, and so an infinite number of souls. But, since they are incorruptible forms, there are as many souls as there have been; therefore an infinite number of souls exist. If this leads you to say that there has been a transmigration of souls or that there is but the one soul for all men, the first is an error in philosophy, because, as Aristotle holds, "appropriate act is in its own matter." Therefore, the soul, having been the perfection of one, cannot be the perfection of another, even according to Aristotle. The second position is even more erroneous since much less is it true that there is but the one soul for all.

6. The last argument to this effect is: *It is impossible for that which has being after non-being to have eternal being,* because this implies a contradiction. But the world has being after non-being. Therefore it is impossible that it be eternal. That it has being after non-being is proven as follows: everything whose having of being is totally from another is produced by the latter out of nothing; but the world has its being totally from God; therefore the world is out of nothing. But not out of nothing as a matter *(materialiter);* therefore out of nothing as an origin *(originaliter).* It is evident that everything which is totally produced by something differing in essence has being out of nothing. For what is totally produced is produced in its matter and form. But matter does not have that out of which it would be produced because it is not out of God *(ex Deo).* Clearly, then, it is out of nothing. The minor, viz., that the world is totally produced by God, is evident from the discussion of another question.

CONCLUSION

Whether positing that all things have been produced out of nothing would imply saying that the world is eternal or has been produced eternally.

I answer: It has to be said that to maintain that the world is eternal or eternally produced by claiming that all things have been produced out of nothing is entirely against truth and reason, as the last of the above arguments proves; and it is so against reason that I do not believe that any philosopher, however slight his understanding, has maintained this. For such a position involves an evident contradiction. But, with the eternity of matter presupposed, to maintain an eternal world seems reasonable and understandable, and this by way of two analogies which can be drawn. For the procession of earthly things from God is after the fashion of an imprint *(vestigium).* Accordingly, if a foot and the dust in which its print were formed were eternal, nothing would prevent our understanding that the footprint is coeternal with the foot and, nevertheless, it still would be an imprint from the foot. If matter, or the potential principle, were in this fashion coeternal with the maker, what would keep that imprint from being eternal? Rather, on the contrary, it would seem quite fitting that it should be.

Again, another reasonable analogy offers itself. For, from God the creature proceeds as a shadow, the Son as brightness. But as soon as there is light, there is immediately brightness, and immediately shadow if there should be an opaque object in its way. If, therefore, matter, as opaque, is coeternal with the maker, just as it is reasonable to posit the Son, the brightness of the Father, to be coeternal, so it seems reasonable that creatures or the world, shadow in relation to the Highest Light, is eternal. Moreover, this view is more reasonable than its contrary, viz., that matter has been eternally incomplete, without form or the divine influence, as certain philosophers have maintained. In fact, it is more reasonable to such an extent that even that outstanding philosopher, Aristotle, has fallen into this error, according to the charges of our philosophers *(Sancti)*, the exposition of the commentators, and the apparent meaning of his text.

On the other hand, modern scholars say that the Philosopher has never thought this nor did he intend to prove that the world had no beginning *in any way at all*, but rather that it did not begin *by way of a natural motion.*

Which of these interpretations is the truer one I do not know. This one thing I do know, that if he held that the world has not begun *according to nature*, he maintained what is true, and his arguments based on motion and time are conclusive. But if he thought that it has *in no way begun*, he has clearly erred, as has been shown above by many arguments. Moreover, in order to avoid self-contradiction, he had to maintain either that the world has not been made, or that it has not been made out of nothing. In order to avoid an actual infinity, however, he had to hold for either the corruption of the rational soul, or its unicity, or its transmigration; thus, in any case, he had to destroy its beatitude. So it is that this error has both a bad beginning and the worst of endings.

1. To the first objection, regarding motion, viz., that there is a first among all motions and changes because there is a most perfect one, it must be granted as true with respect to *natural* motions and changes and there is nothing against it. But with respect to the *supernatural* change, through which that *mobile* (i.e., the heaven) has proceeded into being, it is not true. For this latter change precedes every created thing, and so precedes the *primum mobile* and, of course, its motion.

2. To the objection, every motion passes into being through motion, it must be answered that motion does not pass into being *through itself* nor *in itself*, but *with another* and *in another*. And since God has, in the same instant, made the *mobile* and, as mover, acted upon the *mobile*, then He has cocreated the motion with the *mobile*. If, however, you were to seek further with regard to that creating, it must be said that there a limit is reached as in the very first of things. Further on, this will be made better known.

3. To the third objection, regarding the "now" of time, it must be said that just as there is a two-fold indicating of a point in a circle, either when the circle is being made or after it has been made, and just as when it is being made there is a placing and indicating of a first point but when it already is there is no locating of a first, so also with regard to time there is a twofold acceptance of the "now." In the very production of time, there has been a first "now" before which there has been no other and which was the beginning of time in which all things are said to have been produced. But with respect to time after it has been made, it is true that it is the terminus of the past and it is in the fashion of a circle. But things have not been produced in this way in a time already complete. Thus it is clear that the Philosopher's arguments do not at all establish this conclusion. With regard to the statement that before every time is time, this is true in terms of dividing time from within, but not in the sense of preceding as outside time.

4. To the objection concerning time, as to when has it begun, it must be said that it began in its own beginning *(principium)*. But the source *(principium)* of time is the instant or "now"; and so it began in an instant. Also, the argument: Time has not been in an instant and so has not begun in an instant does not stand because things which are successive are not in their own beginning. This same thing can be said in another way since there are two ways of speaking about time, either according to its essence or according to its being *(esse)*. If one speaks of it according to its essence, then the "now" is the whole essence of time, and that has begun to be with the mobile thing, not in another "now" but in its own self since it has been established in the very beginning and thus it has not had another measure. If one speaks of it according to its being, then it has begun with the motion of change, viz., it has not begun by way of creation, but rather through the change of the changeable, and especially of the *primum mobile.*

5. To the objection based on the adequacy and actuality of the cause, it must be said that the adequate cause of any effect is of two kinds, either as operative through its *nature* or as operative through *will and reason.* If operative through *nature,* then, as soon as it is, it produces its effect. On the other hand, if operative through *will,* even though it be adequate, it is not necessarily operative as soon as it is, since a cause of this sort is operative by way of wisdom and discernment and so takes suitability into account. Therefore, inasmuch as eternity did not befit the nature of the creature itself, it was not fitting that God should grant this most excellent of states to any thing. Accordingly, the divine will, which operates by way of wisdom, has produced the world not from eternity but in time, since, as He has produced, so has He disposed and so has He willed. For He has willed from eternity to produce then when He has produced, just as I will now to hear Mass tomorrow. It is thus evident that the adequacy of the cause is not pertinent to this question.

Similarly with regard to actuality, it must be said that a cause can be in act in two ways, either in itself, as if I were to say: The sun shines, or in its effect *(in effectu),* as if I were to say: The sun illumines. In the first way God has always been in act, since He is pure act unadulterated by the merely possible. In the other way He is not always in act, for He has not always been producing.

6. To the sixth objection: If from being non-producing He has become producing, He has changed from rest to act, it must be said that there is a type of agent in which action and production add something over and beyond the agent and producer. Such an agent is changed in some way when from non-acting it becomes acting, and in this case rest precedes operation and by operation completion is achieved. But there is another agent which is its own action, and nothing at all is added to such an agent when it produces nor does anything come to be in it which it was not beforehand. An agent of this sort neither receives completion in operating nor is it idle in nonoperating, nor, when from non-producing it comes to be producing, is it changed from rest to act. But such is God, even according to the philosophers, who have asserted God to be the most simple of beings. It is evident, therefore, that their argument is a foolish one. For if He had produced things from eternity in order to avoid idleness, then He would not be, *without things,* the perfect good, nor consequently would He *with things,* since that which is most perfect is perfect by its own self. Moreover, if because of His immutability it were necessary that things be from eternity, then He could produce nothing new now. And what kind of God would He be who is now essentially incapable of anything? All these consequences imply nonsense rather than philosophy or an argumentation.

If you were to ask how this is to be understood, viz., that God acts by His own self and yet does not begin to act, the answer would have to be that, even though this cannot be fully understood because of the conjoined imagination, nevertheless it can be established by argumentation necessitating assent; and anyone who withdraws from sense experience in order to consider the intelligibles will, to some extent perceive it. For if anyone were to ask whether an angel could make a pottery cup or throw a stone in spite of no hands, the answer would be that he could because he is capable, by his own power alone and without an organ, of what the soul is capable of with the body and its members. If, therefore, an angel, because of its simplicity and perfection, exceeds man to such an extent that he can do, without an organ as a means, that for which man necessarily requires an organ, can even do through one [power] what man is capable of only through many, how much more can God, Who is at the very limit of the whole of simplicity and perfection, produce all things without any means by the command of His own will which is nothing other than Himself, and thereby remain immutable in producing! In this way a man can be led to an understanding of this truth. But that man will grasp it more perfectly who can consider these two aspects of his Maker, namely that He is most perfect and most simple. Because He is most perfect, all the perfections there are are to be attributed to Him; because most simple, these introduce no diversity into Him, and accordingly no change or mutability. So it is, "remaining at rest He causes all things to be moved."

*   *   *

CONFERENCES ON THE HEXAEMERON

IV, 13

The sixth division is into cause and caused; and here there are many errors. For some say that the world has been from eternity. Wise men agree that something could not come to be from nothing and in this way be from eternity, since it is necessarily the case that, just as when a thing passes into nothing it ceases to be, so also when it comes to be from nothing it begins to be. But some seem to have posited an unoriginated matter; from this it follows that God does not make anything. For He does not make matter, since it is unoriginated. Nor does He make form since either it comes to be from something or from nothing; not from matter since the being *(essentia)* of form cannot come from the being *(essentia)* of matter; and not from nothing since, as they suppose, God can make nothing from nothing. But let perish the notion that the power of God has matter as its supporting foundation.

*   *   *

V, 29

And it is in this way that the Philosopher proceeds to prove the world eternal on the basis that circular local motion, because it is perfect, precedes every motion and change. But I answer: It must be said that the perfect is before the diminished when speaking of the simply perfect, but not when speaking of the perfect in a genus, as is the case with local motion.

*   *   *

VI, 2–5

2. Just as it has been said of the angels, *God separated the light from the darkness,* so also it may be said of the philosophers. But what was the first step that some have taken toward darkness? It was this: although all of them have seen that the first cause is the beginning of all things as well as their end, still they have differed from one another about an intermediary. For some have denied that the exemplars of things are in that first cause. The leader of this group seems to have been Aristotle who at the beginning and at the end of his *Metaphysics,* and in many other places, condemns Plato's Ideas. Accordingly, he says that God knows only Himself, He does not need knowledge of any other thing, and moves as desired and loved. On this ground these men assert that He has no knowledge of the particular. As a consequence, Aristotle especially attacks the Ideas in his *Ethics* where he says that the highest good cannot be an Idea. His arguments do not hold, and the commentator [on the *Ethics,* Eustratius] has destroyed them.

3. From this error follows a further error, namely, that God does not have fore-knowledge or providence since He does not have within Himself the intelligibilities (*rationes*) of things through which He might know them. Also they say that the only truth about the future is truth about the necessary, that truth about the contingent is not truth. And from this it follows that all things come to be either by chance or by the necessity of fate. Because it is impossible to come to be by chance, the Arabs introduce the necessity of fate, namely, that the sphere-moving substances are the necessary causes of all things. From this it follows that the truth that there is a disposition of earthly things according to penalties and glory is obscured. For if those substances unerringly move, nothing is affirmed regarding hell, nor that there is a devil. Nor, as it seems, has Aristotle ever asserted that there is a devil, and that there is a beatitude after this life. This threefold error, then, consists in hiding away within darkness, exemplareity, divine providence and the disposition of earthly things.

4. There follows upon these a threefold blindness or mental dullness. First, about the eternity of the world, as Aristotle seems to hold according to all the Greek doctors, such as Gregory of Nyssa, Gregory Nazianzenus, Damascene, Basil, as well as according to all the Arabic commentators, who say that Aristotle taught this and they seem to speak his words. You will never find him saying that the world had a source or a beginning; rather he argued against Plato who alone seems to have held that time had a beginning. And this is in direct conflict with the light of truth.

From this follows another blindness, about the unicity of the intellect. For if an eternal world is posited, some one of these consequences follows necessarily: either there is an infinite number of souls since men would have been infinite in number, or the soul is perishable, or there is a transition from body to body, or the intellect is one in all men, the error attributed to Aristotle by the Commentator.

From these two it follows that after this life there is neither happiness nor punishment.

5. These men, therefore, have fallen into errors, nor have they been "separated from the darkness"; and such errors as these are the very worst. Nor has the abysmal pit been as yet locked up. This is the darkness of Egypt; for although great light might be discerned in them in knowledges prior to this, still it is entirely extinguished through the aforementioned errors. And some men, seeing that Aristotle was so outstanding in other matters and in them spoke the truth, cannot believe that he has not said what is true in these matters.

*   *   *

VII, 1–2

1. *God saw the light, that it was good, and He divided the light from darkness,* etc. This text has been discussed in order to explain vision by the understanding naturally bestowed upon us. He causes us to see this, *that it was good,* both in the order of scientific consideration and also in that of sapiential contemplation. In the order of scientific consideration, inasmuch as He illumines as light, namely, as the truth of things, as the truth of speech, and as the truth of conduct. In the order of sapiential contemplation, inasmuch as He illumines through the influx into the soul of a ray from the eternal light, in order that the soul may see that light in its own self as in a mirror, in the separate Intelligence as in a transmitting medium as it were *(medio quodam delativo),* in the eternal light as in a subject-source *(in subjecto fontano).* Also it has been said that He divided the light from darkness, because certain ones have attacked the Ideas, and as a result a threefold understanding of truth has been hidden in darkness, namely, the truth about the eternal art, the truth about divine providence, and the truth about the angelic fall, which follows if the angel would not have his perfection except through motion. From this there follows a threefold blindness, namely, about the eternity of the world, about the unicity of the intellect, and about punishment and glory.

2. The first one Aristotle seems to posit, as well as the last one since he does not place happiness in an afterlife; with regard to the middle one, the Commentator says he thought this. On the eternity of the world, he could be excused because he understood this as a philosopher, speaking as a naturalist, saying that it could not begin to be through nature. That Intelligences would have their perfection through motion, this he could have said inasmuch as they are not useless, because there is nothing useless in the very ground work of nature. Likewise that he placed happiness in this life may be because, although he thought it eternal, about that he did not interject his own view *(se),* perhaps because it was not a part of his treatment of the question. About the unicity of the intellect it could be said that he understood the intellect to be one by reason of the inflowing light, not by reason of itself, since it is many according to subject.

* * *

BREVILOQUIM

II, 1, 1–3

1. These matters regarding the Trinity having been, in a summary fashion, grasped, some remarks now have to be made about that creature that is the world. What must be held in this matter is, briefly, as follows: The whole of the earthly contrivance has been produced in being in time *(ex tempore)* and from nothing *(de nihilo)* by one, sole, and highest first Principle whose power, though itself immeasurable, has disposed *all things in a certain weight, number, and measure.*

2. From these points, understood in a general way, about the production of things, truth is gained and error rejected. By "in time" is excluded the error of those positing an eternal world. By "from nothing" is excluded the error of those positing an eternal material principle. By "by one Principle" is excluded the error of the Manichees positing a plurality of principles. By "sole and highest" is excluded the error of those

positing that God has produced lower creatures through the ministry of the Intelligences. By adding "in a certain weight, number, and measure" it is pointed out that the creature is an effect of the creating Trinity under a threefold causality: *efficient,* by which in the creature is unity, mode, and measure; *exemplar,* by which there is in creature truth, species, and number; *final,* by which there is in the creature goodness, order, and weight. And, indeed, these are found in every creature, as a vestige of the Creator, whether they are corporeal or spiritual or composed of both.

    3. The basis for understanding the aforesaid is as follows: For there to be perfect order and repose among things, all things must be reduced to one principle which indeed is first so that it may give repose to others and most perfect so that it may give completion to all others. The first principle through which there is repose can be one and only one. This first principle, if it produces the world, since it could not produce it out of its own self, must produce it out of nothing. And because production out of nothing posits being *(esse)* after non-being *(non-esse)* on the part of the produced and immeasurability in producing power on the part of the producing principle, and since this belongs to God alone, it is necessary that the world as a creature be produced in time by that immeasurable power acting *per se* and immediately.

Siger of Brabant
ca. 1240–ca. 1284

The specifics of Siger of Brabant's life are unknown. Neither the dates nor the places of his birth and death are certain, though there is a story that he was murdered by his secretary while visiting Italy around 1284. Beyond that story, the only solid fact about Siger's life is that he was involved in controversy while teaching at the University of Paris.

The controversy centered around the application of the works of Aristotle and his commentator Averroës. As we have seen, Aristotle's philosophy included several tenets antithetical to the revealed Scriptures of Jews, Christians, and Muslims. To be sure, Averroës had advocated allegorical understandings of some sacred writings as a way to overcome "apparent" differences: The *Qur'ān,* if understood in a deeper allegorical sense, did not conflict with Aristotle. Philosophers at the University of Paris, known as the Latin Averroists, adapted this insight and developed a "double truth" theory. According to this theory, there are two truths—philosophical truths and theological truths—that can contradict each other and yet still be true. (Averroës himself denied such a theory in his *Decisive Treatise,* but that work was not available to the Latin Averroists.)

Siger's colleagues at Paris considered him the leader of the Latin Averroists and the champion of the double truth theory. There is some doubt about the fairness of this characterization. Siger claimed that there was only one truth: the truth of revelation. In presenting Aristotelian doctrines that contradicted scripture, Siger was simply *reporting* what Aristotle said. Even when he presented arguments in favor of Aristotle's antiscriptural views, he claimed he was simply following Aristotle's logic. For example, the selection given here, *Question on the Eternity of the World,* translated by Lottie H. Kendzierski, argues in an Aristotelian manner that the universe of caused being must be eternal. But since such arguments seem counter to revelation, Siger asserted that in the end they must give way to faith.

This gloss was not accepted by the Parisian authorities. In 1270 the bishop of Paris, Étienne Tempier, condemned thirteen theses—including several held by Siger. In 1272 Siger was mentioned by name in another censure against certain forms of Aristotelian philosophy. Five years later Bishop Tempier published an extended list of 219 censured propositions. The bishop was apparently trying to rein in the growth of Aristotelian thinking. Many of the censured views were Siger's (and, ironically, a number of them were also those of Thomas Aquinas). Within a year, Siger was called before the French Inquisition. But he fled Paris and, apart from the unsubstantiated story of his death by murder, nothing more is known of him.

*   *   *

There are no book-length introductions to Siger of Brabant in English. The reader can consult the general introductions to thirteenth-century philosophy given at the beginning of this section (see p. 276). In addition, the introductions to St. Thomas Aquinas, *On the Unity of the Intellect against the Averroists,* translated by Beatrice H. Zedler (Milwaukee, WI: Marquette University Press, 1968), and C. Vollert, L. Kendzierski, and P.M. Byrne, editors and translators, *St. Thomas Aquinas, Siger of Brabant, St. Bonaventure: On the Eternity of the World* (Milwaukee, WI: Marquette University Press, 1964), include brief discussions of Siger.

QUESTION ON THE ETERNITY OF THE WORLD

The first question is whether the human species and in general the species of all individuals began to exist only by way of the propagation of generable and corruptible things when it had no previous existence whatsoever; and it seems that this is so.

That species of which any individual began to exist when it had had no previous existence at all is new and began to have existence since it universally and entirely had had no previous existence. The human species is such, and in general the species of all individuals generable and corruptible, because every individual of this type of species began to exist when it had had no previous existence. And, therefore, any species of such things is also new and began, since in all cases it had not previously existed. The

From C. Vollert, L. Kendzierski, and P.M. Byrne, editors and translators, *St. Thomas Aquinas, Siger of Brabant, St. Bonaventure: On the Eternity of the World* (Milwaukee, WI: Marquette University Press, 1964). This selection was translated by L. Kendzierski. Reprinted by permission of Marquette University Press.

major is stated thus: because the species does not have being nor is caused except in singulars and in causing singulars. If, therefore, any individual of some species has been created when it had not existed before, the species of those beings will be such a kind.

Secondly, this same conclusion is also able to be reached in a different manner thus: universals, just as they do not have existence in singulars, so neither are they caused. Every being is caused by God. Therefore, if man has been caused by God, since he is some being of the world, it is necessary that he come to exist in a certain determined individual; just as the heaven and whatever else has been caused by God. Because, if man does not have an individual eternity as has the sensible heaven according to philosophers, then the human species will have been caused by God so that it began to exist when it had not existed before.

To prove this one must consider, in the first place how the human species was caused, and in general any other universals of generable and corruptible things; and in this way an answer should be made to the question and the forementioned argument.

Secondly, since the foregoing argument admits that universals exist in singulars, one must seek or consider how this may be true.

Thirdly, because some species began to exist when it had surely not existed before, and because it follows that potentiality precedes act in duration, it should be seen which of these preceded the other in duration. For, this presents a difficulty within itself.

I

Concerning the first, therefore, we should know that the human species has not been caused, according to philosophers, except through generation. Now, because in general the being of all things is in matter which is in potency to form, they are made by a generation which is either essential or accidental. From this, however, that the human species has been made by God through generation, it follows that it does not proceed directly from Him. The human species, however, and in general the species of all things which are in matter, since it is made through generation, is not generated essentially but accidentally. It is not generated essentially, because if any one were to study those things which are made universally, then every thing which is made is made from this determined and individual matter. For, although arguments and knowledge are concerned with universals, yet operations are regarding singulars. Now, however, determined matter does not pertain to the meaning of species, and therefore is not generated essentially; and this is held by Aristotle in VII *Metaphysicae.* The same reason why form is not generated is also the reason why the composite which is species is not generated. And I call the species a composite, just as Callias in his own nature is this soul in this body, so also animal is soul in body. The common nature of form and species that they are not generated essentially is because individuated matter pertains to the consideration or reasoning of neither of the things from which generation essentially comes, through the transmutation of the thing from nonbeing to being, or from privation to form. The human species, however, although not generated essentially has nevertheless been generated accidentally, because it thus happens if man, just as he has been abstracted in thought from individual matter and from the individual, so he might be abstracted in existence. Then, just as he is not generated essentially, it might be thought that he is also not generated accidentally; but, because man in his being is this man, Socrates or Plato, then Socrates is also a man, as Aristotle says in VII *Metaphysicae,* that generating a brass sphere generates a sphere because a brass sphere is a sphere. And since just as Socrates is a man, so is Plato, and so with the others. Hence it is that man is generated through the generation of any individual, and not only of one determined individual.

Now, from the explanation it is clear in what way the human species is considered by philosophers eternal and caused. For, it is not to be thought of as eternal and caused as if it existed abstracted from individuals. Nor is it eternally caused in the sense that it exists in an eternally caused individual, as the species of heaven or an intelligence; but rather because in the individuals of the human species one is generated before the other eternally, and the species has to be and to be caused through an individual's existing and being caused. Hence it is that; the human species always exists and that it did not begin to be after previous nonexistence. For, to say that it began to be after it had not existed before is to say that there began to be a certain individual before whom no other individual of that species had existed. And since the human species has not been caused otherwise than generated through the generation of individual before individual, the human species or that which is called by the name of man begins to exist because universally everything generated begins to exist; begins, nevertheless, to exist when it existed and had previously existed. For, man begins to be through the generation of Socrates who is generated, he exists, nevertheless, through the existence of Plato of the previous generation. Those things are not contradictory about the universal; just as there is nothing repugnant for a man to run and not to run. Indeed, man runs in the person of Socrates, and man does not run in the person of Plato. From the fact, nevertheless, that Socrates runs, it is not true to say that man universally and entirely does not run. So also, in the fact that Socrates is generated man begins to be, is not to say that man begins to be in such a way that he had not in any wise previously existed.

From the previous discourse the solution to the forementioned argument is clear.

And first, it must be said that this argument as just stated, namely, that that species is new and began to exist when it had not previously existed, must be denied. Any individual of this kind began to be when it did not previously exist because even though it be true that no individual man began to be after not existing, yet no individual of this kind begins to be unless another one had previously existed. Species does not have existence so much through the existence of one of its individuals as another, and so the human species does not begin to be when it had not existed before. For, to admit that the species is such is to say that not only a certain individual of it began to be when he had not been before, but any individual of it began to be when neither he nor another individual of that species had existed before.

And the given reason is similar to the reasoning by which Aristotle speculates in IV *Physicorum* whether past time is finite. All past time whether near or remote is a certain *then,* and the certain *then* has a measured distance to the present *now;* therefore all past time is finite. And each of the forementioned propositions is clear from the meaning of that *then* which Aristotle speaks of in IV *Physicorum.* The solution of this reasoning, according to Aristotle, is that although every second is finite, nevertheless since in time there is a then before the *then* to infinity, therefore not all past time is finite. For, what is composed of things finite in quantity yet infinite in number has to be infinite. So also, although there is no individual man but that he has begun to exist when he had not existed before, yet there is an individual before the individual to infinity; it is thus that man does not begin to be when he had in no wise existed before, and neither does time. And the case is similar—just as past time has to be through a certain *then,* so also species have to be through the existence of any one of its individuals.

Finally, as regards the form of the reasoning as proposed in the second way, it must be said that the universal does not have existence nor is caused except in singulars;

since it is also said that all being has been caused by God, it must be conceded that man also exists as a being of the world and caused by God. But since it is brought in the discussion and inferred that man has come into existence in some determined individual, it must be said that this conclusion is in no wise to be drawn from the premises; indeed, that reasoning is a hindrance to itself. For, it is accepted in the first place, that man does not have existence except in singulars nor is caused except in singulars; and it is clear that according to this reasoning he has existence and is created through one or through another. For this reason, therefore, it must be concluded that it is reasonable that man has come into existence in some determined individual. Indeed, the human species comes and came into being accidentally by the generation of individual before individual to infinity. This is not to say, however, that it (the human species) comes into existence only in some determined individual and when it had not existed before. Whence we should wonder about those arguing thus since they want to argue that the human species had begun through its being made; and yet that it was not made essentially but rather by the making of the individual, as they confess. To show their intention they ought to show that individual has not been generated before individual to infinity. This, however, they do not show but they propose one false theory, that the human species is not able to have been made eternal by God unless it had been created in some determined and eternal individual, just as the species of heaven was made eternal; and when they find no eternal being among the individuals of man, they think that they have demonstrated that the whole species began to exist when it had not been at all before.

II

The second question is whether universals are in particulars, and it is clear that they are not since Aristotle says in II *De Anima,* that universals in themselves exist in the mind. And Themistius in a similar book, says that concepts are similar things which are universals, which the mind collects and stores within itself. And the same Themistius, in *super principium De Anima,* says that genus is a certain concept gathered from the slight similitude of the singulars; the concepts however are in the conceiving mind, and universals, since they are concepts, are also in the mind.

But on the other hand, universals are universal things for otherwise they might not be said of particulars; and for this reason universals are not within the mind.

Moreover, the thing itself, which is the subject for universality, the man or the stone, is not in the mind. Also, the intention of universality must consist in its being called and denominated universal; and hence man and stone since they are called universals, the intention of universality is in these. Either both, the thing and the intention, or neither is in the mind. Because, if man and stone in respect to the fact that they are, are not in the mind, it seems that neither are they there in respect to the fact that they are universals.

The solution. The universal, because it is a universal, is not a substance, as Aristotle states in VII *Metaphysicae.* And so this is clear. The universal, in that it is a universal, is different from any singular. If, therefore, the universal, in that it is universal, would be a substance, then it would be differing in substance from any of the singulars, and each (singular) would be a substance in act, both singular and universal; the act however would be distinguished. Therefore universals would be distinct substances and separated from particulars; on this account with Aristotle it amounts to the same thing to say that universals are substances as to say that they are separated from particulars.

And if the universal, in that it is universal, is not a substance, then it is evident that there are two things in the universal, namely, the thing which is denominated universal, the man or stone, which is not in the mind, and the intention itself of universality, and this is in the mind; so that the universal in that it is universal does not exist except in the mind, as is evident in this way. For, nothing is called a universal because it exists of its own nature commonly and abstractly from particulars, or by the work of the intellect in the nature of things; because if in its own nature, in its very being, it were to exist abstracted from particulars, it would not be spoken of them since it would be separated from them and we would not need an active intellect. Moreover, the active intellect does not give things any abstraction in existence from individual matter or from particulars, but gives to them an abstraction according to intellection by producing an abstract intellection of those things. If, therefore, the man or stone are universals, it is not except that these things are known universally and abstractly from individual matter. These things do not exist thus in the nature of things because if understood, those things, the man and the stone, do not have existence except in the mind. Since the abstract comprehension of these things is not in things, then those things, because they are universals, are in the mind. And this can also be seen in like cases.

A certain thing is said to be known because there is a knowledge of it and it happens that it is understood. The thing itself, however, with respect to what it is, although it be outside the mind, yet in respect to its being understood, that is, in so far as there is understanding of it, exists only in the mind. Because, if universals are universals, and they are understood as such, namely, abstract and common to particulars, then the universals as universals do not exist except in the mind. And this is what Averroës says in *super Illum De Anima,* that universals as universals are entirely intelligibles; not as beings but as intelligibles. The intelligible, however, as intelligible, that is, in so far as there is an understanding of it, is entirely in the soul. Thus also Themistius says that universals are concepts.

But it must be observed that the abstract and common understanding of any nature, although it be something common, as a common understanding of particulars, yet is not common according to its being predicated of particulars in that it has to be abstracted from particulars; but that which is abstractly and commonly understood and of consequence is so signified, is spoken concerning particulars. For this reason—because that very nature which is spoken of and comprehended as a general thing is in things and is therefore spoken concerning particulars. Although those things are known and understood abstractly and commonly, they do not exist as such; therefore things of this kind are not predicated of particulars according to the ideas of genus and species.

And one must also consider that it is not necessary that the universal exist in actuality before it may be known because the universal in actuality is intelligible in actuality. Now, it is one and the same actuality whether of the intelligible in actuality or of the intellect in actuality; just as it is one motion whether of the active or of the passive, although they be different. But the intelligible in potency certainly precedes the understanding of it; however, such a thing is not universal also except in potency, and so it is not necessary that the universal have to be universal except in potency before it is understood.

Nevertheless, some have held the contrary in this discussion because the very activity of understanding precedes in the natural order the object causing that act. Now, however, the universal, in that it is universal, moves the intellect and is the object which causes the act of understanding; on this account it seems to them that the universal is not universal in that it is so understood, indeed, because the universal in the natural order is universal before it is so understood and is the cause of that understanding of it.

But the solution of this is that that nature by which is caused the act of the intelligible and of the intellect, which is the intellect in act, is the active intellect and also the phantasm which naturally precede that act. In what manner, however, those two concur to cause the act of understanding must be sought in *super Illum De Anima*. But this must be said that the universal is not a universal before the concept and the act of understanding, as at least that act is of the active intellect. For, the understanding of the thing which is in the possible intellect, since it is possible as regards the subject, belongs to the active intellect as efficient. Thus the universal does not have formally that which is universal from the nature which causes the act of understanding. Indeed, as has been mentioned before, it is the concept and the actuality from which the universal receives its universality. Therefore universals, in that they are universals, are entirely in the mind. On this account they are not generated by nature inasmuch as they are universals, neither essentially nor accidentally. For, the nature which is stated and understood universally is in particular things and is generated accidentally.

To the first objection it must be said that the fact that universals are universal things can be understood in two ways; either because they exist universally or because they are understood universally. Universals, however, are not universal things in the first manner as if they existed universally in the nature of things, for they then would not be concepts of the mind. But universals are universal things in a second manner, that is, they are understood universally and abstractly; in this way universals, in so far as they are universals and since they are concepts, cannot be spoken of particulars as such. For, the idea of genus or species is not said of them, but the very nature which is thus understood as that which is itself included, is not in the mind, and is said of particulars.

In regard to another point, it must be said that things are rightly named after something which does not exist in reality. For, a thing understood is named from the understanding of it which is not in it but in the mind; and so also the universal is named from the universal and abstract understanding of it which is not in it but in the mind.

III

Consequently we must investigate the third question. Although act precedes potency in thought, for potentiality is defined through act, as we say the builder is able to build, potency nevertheless is prior to act in substance and in perfection in a thing which proceeds from potency to act because the things which are later in generation are, in substance and perfection, prior, since generation proceeds from the imperfect to the perfect and from potentiality to act. Act is also before potentiality in substance and perfection in the respect that potentiality and act are looked at in different ways; because eternal things are prior to corruptible things in substance and perfection. But nothing eternal, in respect that it is such a thing, is in potentiality. In corruptible beings, however, there is an admixture of potency.

The question is whether act precedes potentiality in time or potentiality the act.

And it seems that the act does not precede potentiality in time because in eternal beings one is not before the other in time. But when the act of a certain species and the potentiality to that act are looked upon according to the species, they are both eternal. For, man is always in act and is always able to be man. Therefore the act thought of in relation to the species does not precede potentiality in time.

Moreover, in this matter in which one is to come from the other in a cycle to infinity, there is none which is first in time. But the seed is from the man and the man from the seed to infinity. Therefore, in those things the one does not precede the other in time. Just as in the case of the seed from which a man is generated there is another generating man previously existing, so also previous to that generating man, since he himself was generated, there must have been a seed from which he was generated.

What is first in the order of generation is first in the order of time. But potentiality is prior to act in the order of generation since generation proceeds from potentiality to act, and therefore it is prior in the order of time.

Moreover, there is no reason why act should precede potentiality in time except that by a power a being is made in act through some agent of its own kind existing in act. But, although from this it follows that the act of the agent precedes in time the act and perfection of the generated thing by that agent, nevertheless, it does not seem to happen that the act of the one generating precedes in time that which is in potentiality to the act of generation. Nor from this also does act simply precede potentiality in time, although some act precedes some potentiality to that act. For, just as being in potentiality comes into actuality through something of its own species in act, so also the thing existing in act in that species is generated from something existing in potentiality to the act of that species. For, just as that which is in potentiality, namely a man, is brought into act by a man in act, so also the man generating is generated from the previous seed and from a man in potency; and so in that reasoning the hen has preceded the egg in time and the egg the hen, as people argue.

On the other side is Aristotle in IX *Metaphysicae.* For, he holds that although what proceeds from potentiality to act is the same in number, yet potentiality precedes the act in time, nevertheless, the same being in relation to species and existing in act precedes potentiality.

Moreover, everything existing in potentiality is brought into actuality through something existing in act and at length is brought into the order of moving things by a mover existing completely in act who did not previously have in his power to be anything except in act. Therefore, according to this, act is seen simply to precede potency in time.

To prove this we must first consider that something numerically the same which has existence at some time in potentiality and some time in act is able to be prior in time than it is. But because this potency is preceded by act in another, since every being in potentiality comes into actuality by that which is in some way of its species, therefore it is not proper to say simply that potentiality precedes act in time.

Secondly, one must consider that if the whole universe of caused beings were at some time not being, as certain poets, theologians and natural philosophers claimed, Aristotle says in XII *Metaphysicae,* then potentiality would precede act simply. And also if some entire species of being, as the human species, would begin to exist when it had never existed before, just as some think they have demonstrated, the potentiality for the actuality of that species would simply precede the act. But each of these is impossible, as is evident from the first consideration.

For, if the whole universe of beings at some time had been in potentiality, so that none of the beings would be totally in act—always an agent in act and the mover—then the beings and the world would not now be except in potentiality and matter of itself would come into act, which is impossible. Thus Aristotle says in XII *Metaphysicae,* and so does his Commentator, that for things to be at rest in an infinite time and afterwards to be in motion is the same as for matter to be self-moving.

From the second question it is evident that this is impossible. For, since the prime mover and agent is always in act, and something in potency is not prior to something in act, it follows that it always moves and acts and makes anything or does anything without an intermediate movement. From this, however, that it is always moving and so acting, it follows that no species of being proceeds to actuality, but that it has proceeded before, so that the same species which were, return in a cycle; and so also opinions and laws and religions and all other things so that the lower circle around from the circling of the higher, although because of the antiquity there is no memory of the cycle of these. We say these things as the opinion of the Philosopher, although not asserting them as true. One, nevertheless, should notice that a certain species of being is able to go into act when it did not exist except in potentiality, although at another time it also was in act, as is evident. For, it happens in the heavens that a certain spectacle and constellation appear in the heavens previously not existing, the effect of which is properly another species of being here below, which is then caused and which yet previously existed.

Thirdly, it must be considered that when it is taken that the potency to an act and the act educing that potency are of the same kind in the generator and thing generated, it is not said in so taking them that act precedes potentiality simply nor potentiality act, unless the act is taken according to the species and the proper potentiality is taken according to the individual. For, a man in act, and a certain man in act, inasmuch as he is generating, precedes in time that which is being in potency, namely, man generated. But because in this order, just as being in potency proceeds into act through something existing in act, and so act precedes any given potentiality, so also everything existing in act in this species goes from potentiality to act, and so potentiality in this species precedes any given act. Therefore neither simply precedes the other in time, but one comes before the other to infinity, as was stated.

In the fourth question we must consider that in a certain order of moving and acting beings it is necessary that that thing which proceeds from potentiality to act come to some act that educes that potentiality to actuality, and this act does not have to go from potentiality to act. Therefore, since every being in potentiality goes to actuality through some being of its own species in act, not all being, however, in actuality and generating proceeds from potentiality to act. Hence it is that in any given being in potentiality to some act, the act of the species in a certain way, although not entirely for the same reason, precedes that potentiality in time; not however in any given being in act does potentiality from which it proceeds to act, precede. And, therefore, the act is simply said to precede potentiality in time, as has been explained, namely, because the first mover leading into act all being in potentiality does not precede in time the being in potentiality, since the being in potentiality is regarded in the rank of prime matter. For, just as God always exists, according to Aristotle, so also does the potential man, since he is regarded as in prime matter. Moreover, the prime mover does not precede in time the being in potentiality, since it is looked upon as in matter properly considered in relation to species, as man is in the seed. For, it is never true, according to Aristotle, to say that God existed, unless potential man existed or had existed, as in the seed. But in a third manner from what has been said, act simply precedes potentiality in time because in any being in potentiality, as given in proper matter, the act of that potentiality having to educe the potency to act, precedes in time. It is not thus with any given being in act that the potentiality to that act precedes it in time, as is evident in prime movers educing to actuality all beings in potentiality. In the aforementioned we utilize, as also does Aristotle, prime movers as species of things which are educed from potentiality to actuality by them; and unless they were the beings of a certain kind in act which do not proceed from potentiality to actuality, the act would not simply precede the potentiality in time, as Aristotle has said in IX *Metaphysicae,* saying that act precedes potentiality in time, adding the reason, because one act is always taken as before another up to the one which is always the prime mover.

From this the solution of the reasoning of those opposed is clear.

To the first problem, therefore, it must be said that being in potentiality is not eternal unless when it is regarded as in prime matter. For, when taken as in its proper matter, according to which anything is said to exist properly in potentiality, as is said in IX *Metaphysicae,* it is new, unless it were taken according to species. For, just as nothing generated is corruptible in infinite time, so also nothing generable is not generated in infinite time since the generable has been taken as in proper matter and in a position near to generation, as the Commentator says in *super Ium Caeli et Mundi.*

To the second problem it must be said, as has been mentioned, that in the order of things generating existing in act which also proceed from potentiality to act, there is no being in act before the being in potentiality, but one there is always before the other to infinity. Because every being in potentiality in the essential order of moving and acting beings at length comes to some being existing in act which does not go from potentiality to act, hence it is that on account of that order the act is said simply to precede that potency.

To the third problem it must be said that it is well established that in a being which is the same in number proceeding from potency to act, potency precedes act; but that, nevertheless, before the being in potency there is another of the same species in act, educing it from potency to act.

To the last problem we must say that it is truly spoken that the act precedes potentiality, because all being in potentiality goes into actuality through something existing in act. Nor do those two things which are contradictory hinder one another. In the first place, this is not so because the being in act educing that which is in potentiality into act precedes in time not only the act in the being generated, but also the potentiality proper to the actuality of the being generated because of the fact that not only is the act of the generated being from the one generating, but also the being in potentiality to the act of the generated being is also from the one generating, as the seed from the man. And universally, proper matters are from the prime mover educing each thing from potentiality to act. In the second place, what is opposed does not hinder, as is evident from what has been said above. Although in the order of moving beings, on the basis of which the argument is made, it is necessary to admit that before being in act, there is a being in potency from which it proceeds into act, so also before being in potency there is a being in act which educes itself from potentiality to act; nevertheless, in another order of moving things it is necessary to hold that there is a being in act which educes into act what is in potency, since the being in potency from which it is made does not precede it, as is evident.

Thomas Aquinas
1225–1274

Saint Thomas Aquinas was indisputably the greatest of the medieval philosophers. He was born in his family's castle of Roccasecca near the town of Aquino, about halfway between Rome and Naples. He was the seventh son of the Count of Aquino, Landolfo, and his wife Teodora. At the age of five he was sent to the Benedictine monastery of Monte Casino, where his uncle was the abbot. His parents hoped he would get a good education at the monastery and perhaps one day become abbot of Monte Casino. However, political struggles between the pope and the emperor made the monastery unsafe, and at age fourteen Thomas moved to the Imperial University in Naples.

At this university Thomas came under the influence of the Dominicans, a mendicant, or begging, order of friars. While the Domicans were admired by many for their religious commitment, Thomas's family was appalled when in 1244 he announced his plans to join the order. They considered the Dominicans religious fanatics, virtually a cult, with none of the sophistication, prestige, or power of the long-established Benedictines. At his parents' instigation, Thomas's brothers kidnapped him and held him captive in the family castle. For a year they tried reasoning, shouting, intimidating—even tempting him with a prostitute—but Thomas would not be swayed. He eventually managed to escape and became a Dominican friar.

Thomas went to Paris, where he studied with Albertus Magnus (Albert the Great), an advocate of the newly rediscovered Aristotelian writings, and even followed his teacher to Cologne to continue his study of Aristotle. As a student Thomas was so stolid and methodical that many of his peers thought he was dull or downright stupid. Given his deliberate manner and his portly build, his classmates dubbed him "the Dumb Ox." But Albertus saw his potential and turned this cruel epithet into a prophecy, saying, "You call him a Dumb Ox; I tell you the Dumb Ox will bellow so loud his bellowing will fill the world." In 1252 Thomas returned to Paris for graduate studies, eventually receiving the magistrate (doctorate) in theology in 1256.

On concluding his studies it seemed natural that Thomas would join the faculty of the University of Paris. However, scholars from the mendicant orders were held in suspicion by the regular faculty of the university. Along with the great Franciscan friar St. Bonaventure (1217–1274), Thomas was not allowed to teach in Paris until the pope himself intervened.

The rest of Thomas's life was spent teaching in France and Italy and writing extensively on philosophical and theological subjects. His complete works in Latin comprise twenty-five volumes. Thomas was also called upon to intervene in several disputes. In addition to defending his Dominican order, he was forced to articulate a middle position between those who rejected Aristotelian philosophy as anti-Christian and those who accepted Aristotle (or, rather, a version of Averroës' interpretation of Aristotle) too uncritically. Throughout his writings, Thomas negotiated a middle path of critical admiration for Aristotle.

Like other Christian thinkers, Thomas was concerned with the relation between reason and faith. Using basically Aristotelian categories, Thomas taught that natural reason could establish some of the truths of religion (such as the existence, unity, and goodness of God), but other truths were accessible only through faith. Contrary to some of the Latin Averroists, Thomas taught that there was no conflict between the teachings of philosophy and those of theology. To use a later analogy, Thomas believed that "the book of nature" (i.e., the created world) and the "Book of Scripture" were in perfect harmony.

In December 1273 Thomas suddenly stopped writing, apparently the result of a mystical experience. He reported to a friend that "all I have written seems like straw to me." A few months later he was called to a church council in Lyon, France. On the way there his health forced him to stop at Fossanova (south of Rome) where he died on March 7, 1274, at the age of forty-nine. Three years after his death, several of Thomas's teachings were condemned by the Bishop of Paris. However, the condemnation did not stand long, and in 1323 Saint Thomas Aquinas was canonized. In 1879 Pope Leo XII commended the study of Aquinas's philosophy in an encyclical, *Aeterni Patris*. This papal proclamation did not launch a revival of Thomism, as is often said, but it did lend an enormous prestige to the study of Thomas and his work. The encyclical praises the saint in the highest terms: "As far as man is concerned, reason can now hardly rise higher than she rose, borne up in the flight of Thomas; and Faith can hardly gain more helps from reason than those which Thomas gave her." Despite the encouragement of Leo XII and others, not all Catholic philosophers are by any means Thomists; many twentieth-century Catholic thinkers have shown more interest in existentialism and phenomenology. Today Thomas is studied and admired as much by Protestants and non-Christians as he is by Catholics.

*   *   *

Thomas's most famous work, the *Summa Theologica,* is one of the most comprehensive and systematic works of philosophy ever written. It has often been likened in its complexity and grandeur to a Gothic cathedral. This monumental classic is divided into four sections that, collectively, include 512 "Questions." Each Question raises a topic or area of investigation and is, in turn, made up of several "Articles" that explore specific concerns. These Articles range from abstract philosophical issues such as "Whether one can intend two things at the same time," to such minutiae of theology as "Whether one angel can speak to another in such a way that others will not know what he is saying." Each Article is examined in the same manner, beginning with a question, offering an answer that Thomas considers false, then supporting this answer with several "objections." At this point, a quotation or argument that contradicts the position taken thus far is introduced with the words "On the contrary *(sed contra).*" The dramatic tension between two opposing positions is then resolved by the author's concise and straightforward *Respondeo,* or "I answer that . . .," which introduces his own view. In presenting his answer, Thomas tries to avoid directly denying the preceding objections, seeing them instead as limited truths that his *Respondeo* supersedes. Finally, Thomas moves on to answer, one by one, each of the initial "objections." (The reader should keep in mind that the *first* things Thomas says about a subject are the *opposite* of the position he will subsequently defend.)

The extensive selections from the *Summa Theologica* given here include readings from Thomas's "Treatise on God" (including his famous "Five Ways" or five arguments for God's existence); "Treatise on Creation" (including his argument that the world was created in time); "Treatise on Man" (including a discussion of the nature of the soul and his theory of knowledge); "Treatise on Human Acts" (including his definition of happiness and his argument for free will); "Treatise on Habits" (with his presentation of the virtues); "Treatise on Law" (describing the kinds of law); and his argument for a just war. The translation is that of the Fathers of the English Dominican Province.

Two shorter works, *On the Principles of Nature,* translated by Vernon J. Bourke, and *Concerning Being and Essence,* translated by George G. Leckie, are given here complete. Both these treatises were written in Paris between 1252 and 1256 and show Thomas's original metaphysical thinking about questions of existence. They also demonstrate that while Thomas used Aristotelian categories, he was an original thinker, going beyond the work of his ancient Greek predecessor.

*   *   *

The best general introductions to Thomas Aquinas are F.C. Copleston, *Aquinas* (Baltimore, MD: Penguin Books, 1955), and Étienne Gilson, *The Christian Philosophy of St. Thomas Aquinas* (New York: Random House, 1956). Josef Pieper, *Guide to Thomas Aquinas* (New York: Pantheon, 1962); Ralph McInerny, *St. Thomas Aquinas* (Boston: Twayne, 1977); and Anthony Kenny, *Aquinas* (New York: Hill and Wang, 1980); and also provide useful overviews. James A. Weisheipl, *Friar Thomas D'Aquino: His Life, Thought, and Works* (Garden City, NY: Doubleday, 1974), offers a biography. G.K. Chesterton's impressionistic study, *St. Thomas Aquinas: The "Dumb Ox"* (1933; reprinted New York: Doubleday Image, 1956), is also a good place to become acquainted with Thomas. For an important collection of general essays, see Anthony Kenny, ed., *Aquinas: A Collection of Critical Essays* (Garden City, NY: Anchor Doubleday, 1969).

There are many studies on aspects of Thomas's thought. For example, a sampling of works on the "Five Ways" includes A.G.N. Flew, *God and Philosophy* (London: Hutchinson, 1966); Anthony Kenny, *The Five Ways: St. Thomas Aquinas' Proofs of God's Existence* (London: Routledge & Kegan Paul, 1969); Richard Swinburne, *The Existence of God* (Oxford: Clarendon Press, 1979); and J.L. Mackie, *The Miracle of Theism: Arguments for and against the Existence of God* (Oxford: Clarendon Press, 1982).

SUMMA THEOLOGICA (in part)

FIRST PART

Treatise on God

QUESTION 1: THE NATURE AND EXTENT OF SACRED DOCTRINE (In Ten Articles)

To place our purpose within proper limits, it is necessary first to investigate the nature and extent of this sacred doctrine. Concerning this there are ten points of inquiry:—

(1) Whether it is necessary? (2) Whether it is a science? (3) Whether it is one or many? (4) Whether it is speculative or practical? (5) How it is compared with other sciences? (6) Whether it is a wisdom? (7) What is its subject-matter? (8) Whether it is a matter of argument? (9) Whether it rightly employs metaphors and similes? (10) Whether the Sacred Scripture of this doctrine may be expounded in different senses?

FIRST ARTICLE

WHETHER, BESIDES PHILOSOPHY, ANY FURTHER DOCTRINE IS REQUIRED?

We proceed thus to the First Article:—

Objection 1. It seems that, besides philosophical science we have no need of any further knowledge. For man should not seek to know what is above reason: *Seek not the things that are too high for thee* (Ecclus. iii. 22). But whatever is not above reason is fully treated of in philosophical science. Therefore any other knowledge besides philosophical science is superfluous.

From St. Thomas Aquinas, *Summa Theologica,* Treatise on God (Part I, Q. 1 & 2; Q. 13, a. 2, 5); Treatise on Creation (Part I, Q. 46, a. 1, 2); Treatise on Man (Part I, Q. 75, a. 2; Q. 76, a. 2, 4; Q. 84, a. 5, 6; Q. 85, a. 1, 2; Q. 86. a. 1); Treatise on Human Acts (Part I–II, Q. 2, a. 8; Q. 3, a. 4, 5, 8; Q. 5, a. 5; Q. 10, a. 2; Q. 13, a. 6); Treatise on Habits (Part I–II, Q. 61, a. 1, 2; Q. 62, a. 1, 2, 3); Treatise on Law (Part I–II, Q. 94, a. 2, 4, 5; Q. 95, a. 1, 2; Q. 96, a. 2); Treatise on War (Part II–II, q. 40, a. 1), translated by the Fathers of the English Dominican Province (New York: Benziger Brothers, 1947). Reprinted by permission.

Obj. 2. Further, knowledge can be concerned only with being, for nothing can be known save what is true; and all that is, is true. But everything that is, is treated of in philosophical science—even God Himself, so that there is a part of philosophy called theology, or the divine science, as Aristotle has proved (*Metaph.* vi). Therefore, besides philosophical science, there is no need of any further knowledge.

On the contrary, It is written (2 Tim. iii. 16): *All Scripture inspired of God is profitable to teach, to reprove, to correct, to instruct in justice.* Now Scripture inspired of God is no part of philosophical science, which have been built up by human reason. Therefore it is useful that besides philosophical science there should be other knowledge—*i.e.,* inspired of God.

I answer that, It was necessary for man's salvation that there should be a knowledge revealed by God, besides philosophical science built up by human reason. Firstly, indeed, because man is directed to God as to an end that surpasses the grasp of his reason: *The eye hath not seen, O God, besides Thee, what things Thou hast prepared for them that wait for Thee* (Isa. lxvi. 4). But the end must first be known by men who are to direct their thoughts and actions to the end. Hence it was necessary for the salvation of man that certain truths which exceed human reason should be made known to him by divine revelation. Even as regards those truths about God which human reason could have discovered, it was necessary that man should be taught by a divine revelation; because the truth about God such as reason could discover would only be known by a few, and that after a long time, and with the admixture of many errors. Whereas man's whole salvation, which is in God, depends upon the knowledge of this truth. Therefore, in order that the salvation of men might be brought about more fitly and more surely, it was necessary that they should be taught divine truths by divine revelation. It was therefore necessary that, besides philosophical science built up by reason there should be a sacred science learned through revelation.

Reply Obj. 1. Although those things which are beyond man's knowledge may not be sought for by man through his reason, nevertheless, once they are revealed by God they must be accepted by faith. Hence the sacred text continues, *For many things are shown to thee above the understanding of man* (Ecclus. iii. 25). And in this sacred science consists.

Reply Obj. 2. Sciences are differentiated according to the various means through which knowledge is obtained. For the astronomer and the physicist both may prove the same conclusion—that the earth, for instance, is round: the astronomer by means of mathematics (*i.e.,* abstracting from matter), but the physicist by means of matter itself. Hence there is no reason why those things which may be learned from philosophical science, so far as they can be known by natural reason, may not also be taught us by another science so far as they fall within revelation. Hence theology included in sacred doctrine differs in kind from that theology which is part of philosophy.

SECOND ARTICLE

WHETHER SACRED DOCTRINE IS A SCIENCE?

We proceed thus to the Second Article:—

Objection 1. It seems that sacred doctrine is not a science. For every science proceeds from self-evident principles. But sacred doctrine proceeds from articles of faith which are not self-evident, since their truth is not admitted by all: *For all men have not faith* (2 Thess. iii. 2). Therefore sacred doctrine is not a science.

Obj. 2. Further, no science deals with individual facts. But this sacred science treats of individual facts, such as the deeds of Abraham, Isaac, and Jacob, and such like. Therefore sacred doctrine is not a science.

On the contrary, Augustine says (*De Trin.* xiv. 1), *to this science alone belongs that whereby saving faith is begotten, nourished, protected, and strengthened.* But this can be said of no science except sacred doctrine. Therefore sacred doctrine is a science.

I answer that, Sacred doctrine is a science. We must bear in mind that there are two kinds of sciences. There are some which proceed from a principle known by the natural light of the intelligence, such as arithmetic and geometry and the like. There are some which proceed from principles known by the light of a higher science: thus the science of perspective proceeds from principles established by geometry, and music from principles established by arithmetic. So it is that sacred doctrine is a science, because it proceeds from principles established by the light of a higher science, namely, the science of God and the blessed. Hence, just as the musician accepts on authority the principles taught him by the mathematician, so sacred science is established on principles revealed by God.

Reply Obj. 1. The principles of any science are either in themselves self-evident, or reducible to the conclusions of a higher science; and such, as we have said, are the principles of sacred doctrine.

Reply Obj. 2. Individual facts are treated of in sacred doctrine, not because it is concerned with them principally: but they are introduced rather both as examples to be followed in our lives (as in moral sciences), and in order to establish the authority of those men through whom the divine revelation, on which this sacred scripture or doctrine is based, has come down to us.

THIRD ARTICLE

WHETHER DOCTRINE IS ONE SCIENCE?

We proceed thus to the Third Article:—

Objection 1. It seems that sacred doctrine is not one science; for according to the Philosopher (*Poster.* i) *that science is one which treats only of one class of subjects.* But the creator and the creature, both of whom are treated of in sacred doctrine, cannot be grouped together under one class of subjects. Therefore sacred doctrine is not one science.

Obj. 2. Further, in sacred doctrine we treat of angels, corporeal creatures, and human morality. But these belong to separate philosophical sciences. Therefore sacred doctrine cannot be one science.

On the contrary, Holy Scripture speaks of it as one science: *Wisdom gave him the knowledge [scientiam] of holy things* (Wisd. x. 10).

I answer that, Sacred doctrine is one science. The unity of a faculty or habit is to be gauged by its object, not indeed, in its material aspect, but as regards the precise formality under which it is an object. For example, man, ass, stone agree in the one precise formality of being colored; and color is the formal object of sight. Therefore, because Sacred Scripture considers things precisely under the formality of being divinely revealed, whatever has been divinely revealed possesses the one precise formality of the object of this science; and therefore is included under sacred doctrine as under one science.

Reply Obj. 1. Sacred doctrine does not treat of God and creatures equally, but of God primarily; and of creatures only so far as they are referable to God as their beginning or end. Hence the unity of this science is not impaired.

Reply Obj. 2. Nothing prevents inferior faculties or habits from being differentiated by something which falls under a higher faculty or habit as well; because the
higher faculty or habit regards the object in its more universal formality, as the object of
the *common sense* is whatever affects the senses, including, therefore, whatever is visible or audible. Hence the *common sense,* although one faculty, extends to all the objects
of the five senses. Similarly, objects which are the subject-matter of different philosophical sciences can yet be treated of by this one single sacred science under one aspect precisely so far as they can be included in revelation. So that in this way sacred
doctrine bears, as it were, the stamp of the divine science, which is one and simple, yet
extends to everything.

FOURTH ARTICLE

WHETHER SACRED DOCTRINE IS A PRACTICAL SCIENCE?

We proceed thus to the Fourth Article:—

Objection 1. It seems that sacred doctrine is a practical science; for a practical
science is that which ends in action according to the Philosopher (*Metaph.* ii). But sacred doctrine is ordained to action: *Be ye doers of the word, and not hearers only* (Jas.
i. 22). Therefore sacred doctrine is a practical science.

Obj. 2. Further, sacred doctrine is divided into the Old and the New Law. But law
implies a moral science, which is a practical science. Therefore sacred doctrine is a
practical science.

On the contrary, Every practical science is concerned with human operations; as
moral science is concerned with human acts, and architecture with buildings. But sacred
doctrine is chiefly concerned with God, whose handiwork is especially man. Therefore
it is not a practical but a speculative science.

I answer that, Sacred doctrine, being one, extends to things which belong to different philosophical sciences, because it considers in each the same formal aspect,
namely so far as they can be known through divine revelation. Hence, although among
the philosophical sciences one is speculative and another practical, nevertheless sacred
doctrine includes both; as God, by one and the same science, knows both Himself and
His works. Still, it is speculative rather than practical, because it is more concerned with
divine things than with human acts; though it does treat even of these latter, inasmuch
as man is ordained by them to the perfect knowledge of God, in which consists eternal
bliss. This is a sufficient answer to the Objections.

FIFTH ARTICLE

WHETHER SACRED DOCTRINE IS NOBLER THAN OTHER SCIENCES?

We proceed thus to the Fifth Article:—

Objection 1. It seems that sacred doctrine is not nobler than other sciences; for
the nobility of a science depends on the certitude it establishes. But other sciences, the
principles of which cannot be doubted, seem to be more certain than sacred doctrine; for
its principles—namely, articles of faith—can be doubted. Therefore other sciences
seem to be nobler.

Obj. 2. Further, it is the sign of a lower science to depend upon a higher; as music depends upon arithmetic. But sacred doctrine does in a sense depend upon the philo-

sophical sciences; for Jerome observes, in his Epistle to Magnus, *that the ancient doc-tors so enriched their books with the ideas and phrases of the philosophers, that thou knowest not what more to admire in them, their profane erudition or their scriptural learning.* Therefore sacred doctrine is inferior to other sciences.

On the contrary, Other sciences are called the handmaidens of this one: *Wisdom sent her maids to invite to the tower* (Prov. ix. 3).

I answer that, Since this science is partly speculative and partly practical, it tran-scends all others speculative and practical. Now one speculative science is said to be nobler than another, either by reason of its greater certitude, or by reason of the higher worth of its subject-matter. In both these respects this science surpasses other specula-tive sciences; in point of greater certitude, because other sciences derive their certitude from the natural light of human reason, which can err; whereas this derives its certitude from the light of the divine knowledge, which cannot be misled: in point of the higher worth of its subject-matter, because this science treats chiefly of those things which by their sublimity transcend human reason; while other sciences consider only those things which are within reason's grasp. Of the practical sciences, that one is nobler which is ordained to a further purpose, as political science is nobler than military science; for the good of the army is directed to the good of the State. But the purpose of this science, in so far as it is practical, is eternal bliss; to which as to an ultimate end the purposes of ev-ery practical science are directed. Hence it is clear that from every standpoint it is no-bler than other sciences.

Reply Obj. 1. It may well happen that what is in itself the more certain may seem to us the less certain on account of the weakness of our intelligence, "which is dazzled by the clearest objects of nature; as the owl is dazzled by the light of the sun" (*Metaph.* ii. lect. i). Hence the fact that some happen to doubt about articles of faith is not due to the uncertain nature of the truths, but to the weakness of human intelli-gence; yet the slenderest knowledge that may be obtained of the highest things is more desirable than the most certain knowledge obtained of lesser things, as is said in *de Animalibus* xi.

Reply Obj. 2. This science can in a sense depend upon the philosophical sci-ences, not as though it stood in need of them, but only in order to make its teaching clearer. For it accepts its principles not from other sciences; but immediately from God, by revelation. Therefore it does not depend upon other sciences as upon the higher, but makes use of them as of the lesser, and as handmaidens: even so the master sciences make use of the sciences that supply their materials, as political of military science. That it thus uses them is not due to its own defect or insufficiency, but to the defect of our intelligence, which is more easily led by what is known through natural reason (from which proceed the other sciences), to that which is above reason, such as are the teachings of this science.

SIXTH ARTICLE

WHETHER THIS DOCTRINE IS THE SAME AS WISDOM?

We proceed thus to the Sixth Article:—

Objection 1. It seems that this doctrine is not the same as wisdom. For no doc-trine which borrows its principles is worthy of the name of wisdom; seeing that the wise man directs, and is not directed (*Metaph.* i). But this doctrine borrows its principles. Therefore this science is not wisdom.

Obj. 2. Further, it is a part of wisdom to prove the principles of other sciences. Hence it is called the chief of sciences, as is clear in *Ethic.* vi. But this doctrine does not prove the principles of other sciences. Therefore it is not the same as wisdom.

Obj. 3. Further, this doctrine is acquired by study, whereas wisdom is acquired by God's inspiration; so that it is numbered among the gifts of the Holy Spirit (Isa. xi. 2). Therefore this doctrine is not the same as wisdom.

On the contrary, It is written (Deut. iv. 6): *This is your wisdom and understanding in the sight of nations.*

I answer that, This doctrine is wisdom above all human wisdom; not merely in any one order, but absolutely. For since it is the part of a wise man to arrange and to judge, and since lesser matters should be judged in the light of some higher principle, he is said to be wise in any one order who considers the highest principle in that order: thus in the order of building he who plans the form of the house is called wise and architect, in opposition to the inferior laborers who trim the wood and make ready the stones: *As a wise architect I have laid the foundation* (1 Cor. iii. 10). Again, in the order of all human life, the prudent man is called wise, inasmuch as he directs his acts to a fitting end: *Wisdom is prudence to a man* (Prov. x. 23). Therefore he who considers absolutely the highest cause of the whole universe, namely God, is most of all called wise. Hence wisdom is said to be the knowledge of divine things, as Augustine says (*De Trin.* xii. 14). But sacred doctrine essentially treats of God viewed as the highest cause—not only so far as He can be known through creatures just as philosophers knew Him—*That which is known of God is manifest in them* (Rom. i. 19)—but also so far as He is known to Himself alone and revealed to others. Hence sacred doctrine is especially called wisdom.

Reply Obj. 1. Sacred doctrine derives its principles not from any human knowledge, but from the divine knowledge, through which, as through the highest wisdom, all our knowledge is set in order.

Reply Obj. 2. The principles of other sciences either are evident and cannot be proved, or are proved by natural reason through some other science. But the knowledge proper to this science comes through revelation, and not through natural reason. Therefore it has no concern to prove the principles of other sciences, but only to judge of them. Whatsoever is found in other sciences contrary to any truth of this science, must be condemned as false: *Destroying counsels and every height that exalteth itself against the knowledge of God* (2 Cor. x. 4, 5).

Reply Obj. 3. Since judgment appertains to wisdom, the twofold manner of judging produces a twofold wisdom. A man may judge in one way by inclination, as whoever has the habit of a virtue judges rightly of what concerns that virtue by his very inclination towards it. Hence it is the virtuous man, as we read, who is the measure and rule of human acts. In another way, by knowledge, just as a man learned in moral science might be able to judge rightly about virtuous acts, though he had not the virtue. The first manner of judging divine things belongs to that wisdom which is set down among the gifts of the Holy Ghost: *The spiritual man judgeth all things* (1 Cor. ii. 15). And Dionysius says (Div. Nom. ii.): *Hierotheus is taught not by mere learning, but by experience of divine things.* The second manner of judging belongs to this doctrine, which is acquired by study, though its principles are obtained by revelation.

SEVENTH ARTICLE

WHETHER GOD IS THE OBJECT OF THIS SCIENCE?

We proceed thus to the Seventh Article:—

Objection 1. It seems that God is not the object of this science. For in every science the nature of its object is presupposed. But this science cannot presuppose the essence of God, for Damascene says (*De Fid. Orth.* 1. iv): *It is impossible to define the essence of God.* Therefore God is not the object of this science.

Obj. 2. Further, whatever conclusions are reached in any science must be comprehended under the object of the science. But in Holy Writ we reach conclusions not only concerning God, but concerning many other things, such as creatures and human morality. Therefore God is not the object of this science.

On the contrary, The object of the science is that of which it principally treats. But in this science the treatment is mainly about God; for it is called theology, as treating of God. Therefore God is the object of this science.

I answer that, God is the object of this science. The relation between a science and its object is the same as that between a habit or faculty and its object. Now properly speaking the object of a faculty or habit is the thing under the aspect of which all things are referred to that faculty or habit, as man and stone are referred to the faculty of sight in that they are colored. Hence colored things are the proper objects of sight. But in sacred science all things are treated of under the aspect of God; either because they are God Himself; or because they refer to God as their beginning and end. Hence it follows that God is in very truth the object of this science. This is clear also from the principles of this science, namely, the articles of faith, for faith is about God. The object of the principles and of the whole science must be the same, since the whole science is contained virtually in its principles. Some, however, looking to what is treated of in this science, and not to the aspect under which it is treated, have asserted the object of this science to be something other than God—that is, either things and signs; or the works of salvation; or the whole Christ, as the head and members. Of all these things, in truth, we treat in this science, but so far as they have reference to God.

Reply Obj. 1. Although we cannot know in what consists the essence of God, nevertheless in this science we make use of His effects, either of nature or of grace, in place of a definition, in regard to whatever is treated of in this science concerning God; even as in some philosophical sciences we demonstrate something about a cause from its effect, by taking the effect in place of a definition of the cause.

Reply Obj. 2. Whatever other conclusions are reached in this sacred science are comprehended under God, not as parts or species or accidents, but as in some way related to Him.

EIGHTH ARTICLE

WHETHER SACRED DOCTRINE IS A MATTER OF ARGUMENT?

We proceed thus to the Eighth Article:—

Objection 1. It seems this doctrine is not a matter of argument. For Ambrose says (*De Fide,* 1): *Put arguments aside where faith is sought.* But in this doctrine faith especially is sought: *But these things are written that you may believe* (John xx. 31). Therefore sacred doctrine is not a matter of argument.

Obj. 2. Further, if it is a matter of argument, the argument is either from authority or from reason. If it is from authority, it seems unbefitting its dignity, for the proof from authority is the weakest form of proof. But if from reason, this is unbefitting its end, because, according to Gregory (*Homil.* 26), *faith has no merit in those things of which human reason brings its own experience.* Therefore sacred doctrine is not a matter of argument.

On the contrary, The Scripture says that a bishop should *embrace that faithful word which is according to doctrine, that he may be able to exhort in sound doctrine and to convince the gainsayers* (Tit. i. 9).

I answer that, As other sciences do not argue in proof of their principles, but argue from their principles to demonstrate other truths in these sciences: so this doctrine does not argue in proof of its principles, which are the articles of faith, but from them it goes on to prove something else; as the Apostle from the resurrection of Christ argues in proof of the general resurrection (1 Cor. xv). However, it is to be borne in mind, in regard to the philosophical sciences, that the inferior sciences neither prove their principles nor dispute with those who deny them, but leave this to a higher science; whereas the highest of them, viz., metaphysics, can dispute with one who denies its principles, if only the opponent will make some concession; but if he concede nothing, it can have no dispute with him, though it can answer his objections. Hence Sacred Scripture, since it has no science above itself, can dispute with one who denies its principles only if the opponent admits some at least of the truths obtained through divine revelation; thus we can argue with heretics from texts in Holy Writ, and against those who deny one article of faith we can argue from another. If our opponent believes nothing of divine revelation, there is no longer any means of proving the articles of faith by reasoning, but only of answering his objections—if he has any—against faith. Since faith rests upon infallible truth, and since the contrary of a truth can never be demonstrated, it is clear that the arguments brought against faith cannot be demonstrations, but are difficulties that can be answered.

Reply Obj. 1. Although arguments from human reason cannot avail to prove what must be received on faith, nevertheless this doctrine argues from articles of faith to other truths.

Reply Obj. 2. This doctrine is especially based upon arguments from authority, inasmuch as its principles are obtained by revelation: thus we ought to believe on the authority of those to whom the revelation has been made. Nor does this take away from the dignity of this doctrine, for although the argument from authority based on human reason is the weakest, yet the argument from authority based on divine revelation is the strongest. But sacred doctrine makes use even of human reason, not, indeed, to prove faith (for thereby the merit of faith would come to an end), but to make clear other things that are put forward in this doctrine. Since therefore grace does not destroy nature, but perfects it, natural reason should minister to faith as the natural bent of the will ministers to charity. Hence the Apostle says: *Bringing into captivity every understanding unto the obedience of Christ* (2 Cor. x. 5). Hence sacred doctrine makes use also of the authority of philosophers in those questions in which they were able to know the truth by natural reason, as Paul quotes a saying of Aratus: *As some also of your own poets said: For we are also His offspring* (Acts xvii. 28). Nevertheless, sacred doctrine makes use of these authorities as extrinsic and probable arguments; but properly uses the authority of the canonical Scriptures as an incontrovertible proof, and the authority of the doctors of the Church as one that may properly be used, yet merely as probable. For our faith rests upon the revelation made to the apostles and prophets, who wrote the canonical books, and not on the revelations (if any such there are) made to other doctors. Hence Augustine says (*Epist. ad Hieron.* xix. 1): *Only those books of Scripture which are called canonical have I learned to hold in such honor as to believe their authors have not erred in any way in writing them. But other authors I so read as not to deem anything in their works to be true, merely on account of their having so thought and written, whatever may have been their holiness and learning.*

NINTH ARTICLE

WHETHER HOLY SCRIPTURE SHOULD USE METAPHORS?

We proceed thus to the Ninth Article:—

Objection 1. It seems that Holy Scripture should not use metaphors. For that which is proper to the lowest science seems not to befit this science, which holds the highest place of all. But to proceed by the aid of various similitudes and figures is proper to poetry, the least of all the sciences. Therefore it is not fitting that this science should make use of such similitudes.

Obj. 2. Further, this doctrine seems to be intended to make truth clear. Hence a reward is held out to those who manifest it: *They that explain me shall have life everlasting* (Ecclus. xxiv. 31). But by such similitudes truth is obscured. Therefore to put forward divine truths by likening them to corporeal things does not befit this science.

Obj. 3. Further, the higher creatures are, the nearer they approach to the divine likeness. If therefore any creature be taken to represent God, this representation ought chiefly to be taken from the higher creatures, and not from the lower; yet this is often found in the Scriptures.

On the contrary, It is written (Osee xii. 10): *I have multiplied visions, and I have used similitudes by the ministry of the prophets.* But to put forward anything by means of similitudes is to use metaphors. Therefore this sacred science may use metaphors.

I answer that, It is befitting Holy Writ to put forward divine and spiritual truths by means of comparisons with material things. For God provides for everything according to the capacity of its nature. Now it is natural to man to attain to intellectual truths through sensible objects, because all our knowledge originates from sense. Hence in Holy Writ spiritual truths are fittingly taught under the likeness of material things. This is what Dionysius says (*Cæl. Hier.* i): *We cannot be enlightened by the divine rays except they be hidden within the covering of many sacred veils.* It is also befitting Holy Writ, which is proposed to all without distinction of persons—*To the wise and to the unwise I am a debtor* (Rom. i. 14)—that spiritual truths be expounded by means of figures taken from corporeal things, in order that thereby even the simple who are unable by themselves to grasp intellectual things may be able to understand it.

Reply Obj. 1. Poetry makes use of metaphors to produce a representation, for it is natural to man to be pleased with representations. But sacred doctrine makes use of metaphors as both necessary and useful.

Reply Obj. 2. The ray of divine revelation is not extinguished by the sensible imagery wherewith it is veiled, as Dionysius says (*Cæl. Hier.* i); and its truth so far remains that it does not allow the minds of those to whom the revelation has been made, to rest in the metaphors, but raises them to the knowledge of truths; and through those to whom the revelation has been made others also may receive instruction in these matters. Hence those things that are taught metaphorically in one part of Scripture, in other parts are taught more openly. The very hiding of truth in figures is useful for the exercise of thoughtful minds, and as a defence against the ridicule of the impious, according to the words *Give not that which is holy to dogs* (Matth. vii. 6).

Reply Obj. 3. As Dionysius says (*loc. cit.*), it is more fitting that divine truths should be expounded under the figure of less noble than of nobler bodies, and this for three reasons. Firstly, because thereby men's minds are the better preserved from error. For then it is clear that these things are not literal descriptions of divine truths, which might have been open to doubt had they been expressed under the figure of nobler bodies, especially for those who could think of nothing nobler than bodies. Secondly, because this is more befitting the knowledge of God that we have in this life. For what He is not is clearer to us than what He is. Therefore similitudes drawn from things farthest away from God form within us a truer estimate that God is above whatsoever we may say or think of Him. Thirdly, because thereby divine truths are the better hidden from the unworthy.

TENTH ARTICLE

WHETHER IN HOLY SCRIPTURE A WORD MAY HAVE SEVERAL SENSES?

We proceed thus to the Tenth Article:—

Objection 1. It seems that in Holy Writ a word cannot have several senses, historical or literal, allegorical, tropological or moral, and anagogical. For many different senses in one text produce confusion and deception and destroy all force of argument. Hence no argument, but only fallacies, can be deduced from a multiplicity of propositions. But Holy Writ ought to be able to state the truth without any fallacy. Therefore in it there cannot be several senses to a word.

Obj. 2. Further, Augustine says (*de util. cred.* iii) that *the Old Testament has a fourfold division as to history, etiology, analogy, and allegory.* Now these four seem altogether different from the four divisions mentioned in the first objection. Therefore it does not seem fitting to explain the same word of Holy Writ according to the four different senses mentioned above.

Obj. 3. Further, besides these senses, there is the parabolical, which is not one of these four.

On the contrary, Gregory says (Moral. xx. 1): *Holy Writ by the manner of its speech transcends every science, because in one and the same sentence, while it describes a fact, it reveals a mystery.*

I answer that, The author of Holy Writ is God, in whose power it is to signify His meaning, not by words only (as man also can do), but also by things themselves. So, whereas in every other science things are signified by words, this science has the property, that the things signified by the words have themselves also a signification. Therefore that first signification whereby words signify things belongs to the first sense, the historical or literal. That signification whereby things signified by words have themselves also a signification is called the spiritual sense, which is based on the literal, and presupposes it. Now this spiritual sense has a threefold division. For as the Apostle says (Heb. x. 1) the Old Law is a figure of the New Law, and Dionysius says (*Cæl. Hier.* i) *the New Law itself is a figure of future glory.* Again, in the New Law, whatever our Head has done is a type of what we ought to do. Therefore, so far as the things of the Old Law signify the things of the New Law, there is the allegorical sense; so far as the things done in Christ, or so far as the things which signify Christ, are types of what we ought to do, there is the moral sense. But so far as they signify what relates to eternal glory, there is the anagogical sense. Since the literal sense is that which the author intends, and since the author of Holy Writ is God, Who by one act comprehends all things by His intellect, it is not unfitting, as Augustine says (*Con-*

fess. xii), if, even according to the literal sense, one word in Holy Writ should have several senses.

Reply Obj. 1. The multiplicity of these senses does not produce equivocation or any other kind of multiplicity, seeing that these senses are not multiplied because one word signifies several things; but because the things signified by the words can be themselves types of other things. Thus in Holy Writ no confusion results, for all the senses are founded on one—the literal—from which alone can any argument be drawn, and not from those intended in allegory, as Augustine says (*Epist.* xlviii). Nevertheless, nothing of Holy Scripture perishes on account of this, since nothing necessary to faith is contained under the spiritual sense which is not elsewhere put forward by the Scripture in its literal sense.

Reply Obj. 2. These three—history, etiology, analogy—are grouped under the literal sense. For it is called history, as Augustine expounds *(loc. cit.),* whenever anything is simply related; it is called etiology when its cause is assigned, as when Our Lord gave the reason why Moses allowed the putting away of wives—namely, on account of the hardness of men's hearts; it is called analogy whenever the truth of one text of Scripture is shown not to contradict the truth of another. Of these four, allegory alone stands for the three spiritual senses. Thus Hugh of S. Victor *(Sacram.* iv. 4 *Prolog.)* includes the anagogical under the allegorical sense, laying down three senses only—the historical, the allegorical, and the tropological.

Reply Obj. 3. The parabolical sense is contained in the literal, for by words things are signified properly and figuratively. Nor is the figure itself, but that which is figured, the literal sense. When Scripture speaks of God's arm, the literal sense is not that God has such a member, but only what is signified by this member, namely, operative power. Hence it is plain that nothing false can ever underlie the literal sense of Holy Writ.

QUESTION 2: THE EXISTENCE OF GOD (In Three Articles)

Because the chief aim of sacred doctrine is to teach the knowledge of God, not only as He is in Himself, but also as He is the beginning of things and their last end, and especially of rational creatures, as is clear from what has been already said, therefore, in our endeavor to expound this science, we shall treat: (1) Of God; (2) Of the rational creature's advance towards God; (3) Of Christ, Who as man, is our way to God.

In treating of God there will be a threefold division:—

For we shall consider (1) Whatever concerns the Divine Essence; (2) Whatever concerns the distinctions of Persons; (3) Whatever concerns the procession of creatures from Him.

Concerning the Divine Essence, we must consider:—

(1) Whether God exists? (2) The manner of His existence, or, rather, what is *not* the manner of His existence; (3) Whatever concerns His operations—namely, His knowledge, will, power.

Concerning the first, there are three points of inquiry:—

(1) Whether the proposition "God exists" is self-evident? (2) Whether it is demonstrable? (3) Whether God exists?

FIRST ARTICLE

WHETHER THE EXISTENCE OF GOD IS SELF-EVIDENT?

We proceed thus to the First Article:—

Objection 1. It seems that the existence of God is self-evident. Now those things are said to be self-evident to us the knowledge of which is naturally implanted in us, as we can see in regard to first principles. But as Damascene says (*De Fid. Orth.* i. 1, 3), *the knowledge of God is naturally implanted in all.* Therefore the existence of God is self-evident.

Obj. 2. Further, those things are said to be self-evident which are known as soon as the terms are known, which the Philosopher (1 *Poster.* iii) says is true of the first principles of demonstration. Thus, when the nature of a whole and of a part is known, it is at once recognized that every whole is greater than its part. But as soon as the signification of the word "God" is understood, it is at once seen that God exists. For by this word is signified that thing than which nothing greater can be conceived. But that which exists actually and mentally is greater than that which exists only mentally. Therefore, since as soon as the word "God" is understood it exists mentally, it also follows that it exists actually. Therefore the proposition "God exists" is self-evident.

Obj. 3. Further, the existence of truth is self-evident. For whoever denies the existence of truth grants that truth does not exist: and if truth does not exist, then the proposition "Truth does not exist" is true: and if there is anything true, there must be truth. But God is truth itself: *I am the way, the truth, and the life* (John xiv. 6). Therefore "God exists" is self-evident.

On the contrary, No one can mentally admit the opposite of what is self-evident; as the Philosopher (*Metaph.* iv., lect. vi) states concerning the first principles of demonstration. But the opposite of the proposition "God is" can be mentally admitted: *The fool said in his heart, There is no God* (Ps. lii. 1). Therefore, that God exists is not self-evident.

I answer that, A thing can be self-evident in either of two ways; on the one hand, self-evident in itself, though not to us; on the other, self-evident in itself, and to us. A proposition is self-evident because the predicate is included in the essence of the subject, as "Man is an animal," for animal is contained in the essence of man. If, therefore the essence of the predicate and subject be known to all, the proposition will be self-evident to all; as is clear with regard to the first principles of demonstration, the terms of which are common things that no one is ignorant of, such as being and non-being, whole and part, and such like. If, however, there are some to whom the essence of the predicate and subject is unknown, the proposition will be self-evident in itself, but not to those who do not know the meaning of the predicate and subject of the proposition. Therefore, it happens, as Boethius says (*Hebdom., the title of which is: "Whether all that is, is good"),* "that there are some mental concepts self-evident only to the learned, as that incorporeal substances are not in space." Therefore I say that this proposition, "God exists," of itself is self-evident, for the predicate is the same as the subject; because God is His own existence as will be hereafter shown (Q. 3, A. 4). Now because we do not know the essence of God, the proposition is not self-evident to us; but needs to be demonstrated by things that are more known to us, though less known in their nature—namely, by effects.

Reply Obj. 1. To know that God exists in a general and confused way is implanted in us by nature, inasmuch as God is man's beatitude. For man naturally desires happiness, and what is naturally desired by man must be naturally known to him. This, however, is not to know absolutely that God exists; just as to know that someone is approaching is not the same as to know that Peter is approaching, even though it is Peter who is approaching; for many there are who imagine that man's perfect good which is happiness, consists in riches, and others in pleasures, and others in something else.

Reply Obj. 2. Perhaps not everyone who hears this word "God" understands it to signify something than which nothing greater can be thought, seeing that some have believed God to be a body. Yet, granted that everyone understands that by this word "God" is signified something than which nothing greater can be thought, nevertheless, it does not therefore follow that he understands that what the word signifies exists actually, but only that it exists mentally. Nor can it be argued that it actually exists, unless it be admitted that there actually exists something than which nothing greater can be thought; and this precisely is not admitted by those who hold that God does not exist.

Reply Obj. 3. The existence of truth in general is self-evident but the existence of a Primal Truth is not self-evident to us.

SECOND ARTICLE

WHETHER IT CAN BE DEMONSTRATED THAT GOD EXISTS?

We proceed thus to the Second Article:—

Objection 1. It seems that the existence of God cannot be demonstrated. For it is an article of faith that God exists. But what is of faith cannot be demonstrated, because a demonstration produces scientific knowledge; whereas faith is of the unseen (Heb. xi. 1). Therefore it cannot be demonstrated that God exists.

Obj. 2. Further, the essence is the middle term of demonstration. But we cannot know in what God's essence consists, but solely in what it does not consist; as Damascene says (*De Fid. Orth.* i. 4). Therefore we cannot demonstrate that God exists.

Obj. 3. Further, if the existence of God were demonstrated, this could only be from His effects. But His effects are not proportionate to Him, since He is infinite and His effects are finite; and between the finite and infinite there is no proportion. Therefore, since a cause cannot be demonstrated by an effect not proportionate to it, it seems that the existence of God cannot be demonstrated.

On the contrary, The Apostle says: *The invisible things of Him are clearly seen, being understood by the things that are made* (Rom. i. 20). But this would not be unless the existence of God could be demonstrated through the things that are made; for the first thing we must know of anything is, whether it exists.

I answer that, Demonstration can be made in two ways: One is through the cause, and is called *a priori,* and this is to argue from what is prior absolutely. The other is through the effect, and is called a demonstration *a posteriori;* this is to argue from what is prior relatively only to us. When an effect is better known to us than its cause, from the effect we proceed to the knowledge of the cause. And from every effect the existence of its proper cause can be demonstrated, so long as its effects are better known to us; because since every effect depends upon its cause, if the effect exists, the cause must pre-exist. Hence the existence of God, in so far as it is not self-evident to us, can be demonstrated from those of His effects which are known to us.

Reply Obj. 1. The existence of God and other like truths about God, which can be known by natural reason, are not articles of faith, but are preambles to the articles; for faith presupposes natural knowledge, even as grace presupposes nature, and perfection supposes something that can be perfected. Nevertheless, there is nothing to prevent a man, who cannot grasp a proof, accepting, as a matter of faith, something which in itself is capable of being scientifically known and demonstrated.

Reply Obj. 2. When the existence of a cause is demonstrated from an effect, this effect takes the place of the definition of the cause in proof of the cause's existence. This is especially the case in regard to God, because, in order to prove the existence of anything, it is necessary to accept as a middle term the meaning of the word, and not its essence, for the question of its essence follows on the question of its existence. Now the names given to God are derived from His effects; consequently, in demonstrating the existence of God from His effects, we may take for the middle term the meaning of the word "God."

Reply Obj. 3. From effects not proportionate to the cause no perfect knowledge of that cause can be obtained. Yet from every effect the existence of the cause can be clearly demonstrated, and so we can demonstrate the existence of God from His effects; though from them we cannot perfectly know God as He is in His essence.

THIRD ARTICLE

WHETHER GOD EXISTS?

We proceed thus to the Third Article:—

Objection 1. It seems that God does not exist; because if one of two contraries be infinite, the other would be altogether destroyed. But the word "God" means that He is infinite goodness. If, therefore, God existed, there would be no evil discoverable; but there is evil in the world. Therefore God does not exist.

Obj. 2. Further, it is superfluous to suppose that what can be accounted for by a few principles has been produced by many. But it seems that everything we see in the world can be accounted for by other principles, supposing God did not exist. For all natural things can be reduced to one principle, which is nature; and all voluntary things can be reduced to one principle, which is human reason, or will. Therefore there is no need to suppose God's existence.

On the contrary, It is said in the person of God: *I am Who am* (Exod. iii. 14).

I answer that, The existence of God can be proved in five ways.

The first and more manifest way is the argument from motion. It is certain, and evident to our senses, that in the world some things are in motion. Now whatever is in motion is put in motion by another, for nothing can be in motion except it is in potentiality to that towards which it is in motion; whereas a thing moves inasmuch as it is in act. For motion is nothing else than the reduction of something from potentiality to actuality. But nothing can be reduced from potentiality to actuality, except by something in a state of actuality. Thus that which is actually hot, as fire, makes wood, which is potentially hot, to be actually hot, and thereby moves and changes it. Now it is not possible that the same thing should be at once in actuality and potentiality in the same respect, but only in different respects. For what is actually hot cannot simultaneously be potentially hot; but it is simultaneously potentially cold. It is therefore impossible that in the same respect and in the same way a thing should be both mover and moved, *i.e.,* that it should move itself. Therefore, whatever is in motion must be put in motion by an-

a.

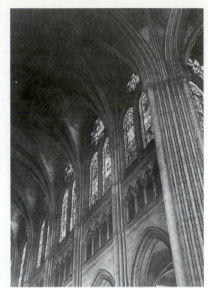

b.

c.

d.

The Gothic Cathedral

a. *The Cathedral of Notre Dame de Chartres,* Chartres, France, begun in the 1140s. The word "Gothic" was originally a perjorative term coined by Renaissance thinkers who considered this style to be a barbaric break from classical tradition. The two towers shown here, for example, are not symetrical. Even though the overall design of the cathedral may not be symmetrical, each of its elements was designed to reflect the harmony and beauty of God's creation. *(Lauros-Giraudon/Art Resource)*

b. *Interior, Chartres Cathedral.* By using pointed arches, it was possible to make soaring open spaces in the nave (main sanctuary) of the Gothic cathedral. The weight was shifted downward instead of outward. *(Bildarchiv Foto Marburg/Art Resource)*

c. *Flying Buttresses at Reims Cathedral,* ca. 1230–1235, by Villard De Honnecourt. To leave the interior unencumbered, the remaining outward stresses were often buttressed from outside the building. In some cathedrals exterior buttresses could not be built directly along the outside walls because of side aisles. Instead they were built outside the side aisles and connected to the pillars of the nave by stone ribs. These supporting ribs appear to "fly" over the side aisles. *(Villard de Honnecourt/Giraudon, Art Resource)*

d. *The Rose Window,* Notre Dame Cathedral, Paris, thirteenth century. By using pointed arches and flying buttresses, the walls of a cathedral did not have to bear the weight of the roof. Instead they could be used as screens for stained glass ornamentation such as this. *(Giraudon/Art Resource)*

other. If that by which it is put in motion be itself put in motion, then this also must needs be put in motion by another, and that by another again. But this cannot go on to infinity, because then there would be no first mover, and, consequently, no other mover; seeing that subsequent movers move only inasmuch as they are put in motion by the first mover; as the staff moves only because it is put in motion by the hand. Therefore it is necessary to arrive at a first mover, put in motion by no other; and this everyone understands to be God.

The second way is from the nature of the efficient cause. In the world of sense we find there is an order of efficient causes. There is no case known (neither is it, indeed, possible) in which a thing is found to be the efficient cause of itself; for so it would be prior to itself, which is impossible. Now in efficient causes it is not possible to go on to infinity, because in all efficient causes following in order, the first is the cause of the intermediate cause, and the intermediate is the cause of the ultimate cause, whether the intermediate cause be several, or one only. Now to take away the cause is to take away the effect. Therefore if there be no first cause among efficient causes, there will be no ultimate, nor any intermediate cause. But if in efficient causes it is possible to go on to infinity, there will be no first efficient cause, neither will there be an ultimate effect, nor any intermediate efficient causes; all of which is plainly false. Therefore it is necessary to admit a first efficient cause, to which everyone gives the name of God.

The third way is taken from possibility and necessity, and runs thus. We find in nature things that are possible to be and not to be, since they are found to be generated, and to corrupt, and consequently, they are possible to be and not to be. But it is impossible for these always to exist, for that which is possible not to be at some time is not. Therefore, if everything is possible not to be, then at one time there could have been nothing in existence. Now if this were true, even now there would be nothing in existence, because that which does not exist only begins to exist by something already existing. Therefore, if at one time nothing was in existence, it would have been impossible for anything to have begun to exist; and thus even now nothing would be in existence—which is absurd. Therefore, not all beings are merely possible, but there must exist something the existence of which is necessary. But every necessary thing either has its necessity caused by another, or not. Now it is impossible to go on to infinity in necessary things which have their necessity caused by another, as has been already proved in regard to efficient causes. Therefore we cannot but postulate the existence of some being having of itself its own necessity, and not receiving it from another, but rather causing in others their necessity. This all men speak of as God.

The fourth way is taken from the gradation to be found in things. Among beings there are some more and some less good, true, noble, and the like. But "more" and "less" are predicated of different things, according as they resemble in their different ways something which is the maximum, as a thing is said to be hotter according as it more nearly resembles that which is hottest; so that there is something which is truest, something best, something noblest, and, consequently, something which is uttermost being; for those things that are greatest in truth are greatest in being, as it is written in *Metaph.* ii. Now the maximum in any genus is the cause of all in that genus; as fire, which is the maximum of heat, is the cause of all hot things. Therefore there must also be something which is to all beings the cause of their being, goodness, and every other perfection; and this we call God.

The fifth way is taken from the governance of the world. We see that things which lack intelligence, such as natural bodies, act for an end, and this is evident from their acting always, or nearly always, in the same way, so as to obtain the best result. Hence it is plain that not fortuitously, but designedly, do they achieve their end. Now whatever lacks intelligence cannot move towards an end, unless it be directed by some being endowed with knowledge and intelligence; as the arrow is shot to its mark by the archer. Therefore some intelligent being exists by whom all natural things are directed to their end; and this being we call God.

Reply Obj. 1. As Augustine says (*Enchir.* xi): *Since God is the highest good, He would not allow any evil to exist in His works, unless His omnipotence and goodness were such as to bring good even out of evil.* This is part of the infinite goodness of God, that He should allow evil to exist, and out of it produce good.

Reply Obj. 2. Since nature works for a determinate end under the direction of a higher agent, whatever is done by nature must needs be traced back to God, as to its first cause. So also whatever is done voluntarily must also be traced back to some higher cause other than human reason or will, since these can change and fail; for all things that are changeable and capable of defect must be traced back to an immovable and self-necessary first principle, as was shown in the body of the *Article.*

* * *

QUESTION 13: THE NAMES OF GOD

*   *   *

SECOND ARTICLE

WHETHER ANY NAME CAN BE APPLIED TO GOD SUBSTANTIALLY?

We proceed thus to the Second Article:—

Objection 1. It seems that no name can be applied to God substantially. For Damascene says (*De Fid. Orth.* i. 9): *Everything said of God signifies not His substance, but rather shows forth what He is not; or expresses some relation, or something following from His nature or operation.*

Obj. 2. Further, Dionysius says (*Div. Nom.* i): *You will find a chorus of holy doctors addressed to the end of distinguishing clearly and praiseworthily the divine processions in the denomination of God.* Thus the names applied by the holy doctors in praising God are distinguished according to the divine processions themselves. But what expresses the procession of anything, does not signify its essence. Therefore the names applied to God are not said of Him substantially.

Obj. 3. Further, a thing is named by us according as we understand it. But God is not understood by us in this life in His substance. Therefore neither is any name we can use applied substantially to God.

On the contrary, Augustine says (*De Trin.* vi): *The being of God is the being strong, or the being wise, or whatever else we may say of that simplicity whereby His substance is signified.* Therefore all names of this kind signify the divine substance.

I answer that, Negative names applied to God or signifying His relation to creatures manifestly do not at all signify His substance, but rather express the distance of the creature from Him, or His relation to something else, or rather, the relation of creatures to Himself.

But as regards absolute and affirmative names of God, as *good, wise,* and the like, various and many opinions have been given. For some have said that all such names, although they are applied to God affirmatively, nevertheless have been brought into use more to express some remotion from God, rather than to express anything that exists positively in Him. Hence they assert that when we say that God lives, we mean that God is not like an inanimate thing; and the same in like manner applies to other names; and this was taught by Rabbi Moses. Others say that these names applied to God signify His relationship towards creatures: thus in the words, *God is good,* we mean, God is the cause of goodness in things; and the same rule applies to other names.

Both of these opinions, however, seem to be untrue for three reasons. First because in neither of them can a reason be assigned why some names more than others are applied to God. For He is assuredly the cause of bodies in the same way as He is the cause of good things; therefore if the words *God is good,* signified no more than, *God is the cause of good things,* it might in like manner be said that God is a body, inasmuch as He is the cause of bodies. So also to say that He is a body implies that He is not a mere potentiality, as is primary matter. Secondly, because it would follow that all names applied to God would be said of Him by way of being taken in a secondary sense, as healthy is secondarily said of medicine, forasmuch as it signifies only the cause of health in the animal which primarily is called healthy. Thirdly, because this is against the intention of those who speak of God. For in saying that God lives, they assuredly mean more than to say that He is the cause of our life, or that He differs from inanimate bodies.

Therefore we must hold a different doctrine—viz., that these names signify the divine substance, and are predicated substantially of God, although they fall short of a full representation of Him. Which is proved thus. For these names express God, so far as our intellects know Him. Now since our intellect knows God from creatures, it knows Him as far as creatures represent Him. Now it was shown above (Q. 4, A. 2) that God prepossesses in Himself all the perfections of creatures, being Himself simply and universally perfect. Hence every creature represents Him, and is like Him so far as it possesses some perfection: yet it represents Him not as something of the same species or genus, but as the excelling principle of whose form the effects fall short, although they derive some kind of likeness thereto, even as the forms of inferior bodies represent the power of the sun. This was explained above (Q. 4, A. 3), in treating of the divine perfection. Therefore the aforesaid names signify the divine substance, but in an imperfect manner, even as creatures represent it imperfectly. So when we say, *God is good,* the meaning is not, *God is the cause of goodness, or, God is not evil;* but the meaning is, *Whatever good we attribute to creatures, pre-exists in God,* and in a more excellent and higher way. Hence it does not follow that God is good, because He causes goodness; but rather, on the contrary, He causes goodness in things because He is good; according to what Augustine says (*De Doctr. Christ.* i. 32), *Because He is good, we are.*

Reply Obj. 1. Damascene says that these names do not signify what God is, forasmuch as by none of these names is perfectly expressed what He is; but each one signifies Him in an imperfect manner, even as creatures represent Him imperfectly.

Reply Obj. 2. In the significance of names, that from which the name is derived is different sometimes from what it is intended to signify, as for instance this name stone *(lapis)* is imposed from the fact that it hurts the foot *(lædit pedem),* but it is not imposed to signify that which hurts the foot, but rather to signify a certain kind of body; otherwise everything that hurts the foot would be a stone.* So we must say that these kinds of divine names are imposed from the divine processions; for as according to the diverse processions of their perfections, creatures are the representations of God, although in an imperfect manner; so likewise our intellect knows and names God according to each kind of procession; but nevertheless these names are not imposed to signify the procession themselves, as if when we say *God lives,* the sense were, *life proceeds from Him;* but to signify the principle itself of things, in so far as life pre-exists in Him, although it pre-exists in Him in a more eminent way than can be understood or signified.

Reply Obj. 3. We cannot know the essence of God in this life, as He really is in Himself; but we know Him accordingly as He is represented in the perfections of creatures; and thus the names imposed by us signify Him in that manner only.

* * *

*This refers to the Latin etymology of the word *lapis,* which has no place in English.

FIFTH ARTICLE

WHETHER WHAT IS SAID OF GOD AND OF CREATURES IS UNIVOCALLY PREDICATED OF THEM?

We proceed thus to the Fifth Article:—

Objection 1. It seems that the things attributed to God and creatures are univocal. For every equivocal term is reduced to the univocal, as many are reduced to one: for if the name *dog* be said equivocally of the barking dog, and of the dogfish, it must be said of some univocally—viz., of all barking dogs; otherwise we proceed to infinitude. Now there are some univocal agents which agree with their effects in name and definition, as man generates man; and there are some agents which are equivocal, as the sun which causes heat, although the sun is hot only in an equivocal sense. Therefore it seems that the first agent to which all other agents are reduced, is an univocal agent: and thus what is said of God and creatures, is predicated univocally.

Obj. 2. Further, there is no similitude among equivocal things. Therefore as creatures have a certain likeness to God, according to the word of Genesis (i. 26), *Let us make man to our image and likeness,* it seems that something can be said of God and creatures univocally.

Obj. 3. Further, measure is homogeneous with the thing measured. But God is the first measure of all beings. Therefore God is homogeneous with creatures; and thus a word may be applied univocally to God and to creatures.

On the contrary, Whatever is predicated of various things under the same name but not in the same sense, is predicated equivocally. But no name belongs to God in the same sense that it belongs to creatures; for instance, wisdom in creatures is a quality, but not in God. Now a different genus changes an essence. Since the genus is part of the definition; and the same applies to other things. Therefore whatever is said of God and of creatures is predicated equivocally.

Further, God is more distant from creatures than any creatures are from each other. But the distance of some creatures makes any univocal predication of them impossible, as in the case of those things which are not in the same genus. Therefore much less can anything be predicated univocally of God and creatures; and so only equivocal predication can be applied to them.

I answer that, Univocal predication is impossible between God and creatures. The reason of this is that every effect which is not an adequate result of the power of the efficient cause, receives the similitude of the agent not in its full degree, but in a measure that falls short, so that what is divided and multiplied in the effects resides in the agent simply, and in the same manner; as for example the sun by the exercise of its one power produces manifold and various forms in all inferior things. In the same way, as said in the preceding article, all perfections existing in creatures divided and multiplied, pre-exist in God unitedly. Thus, when any term expressing perfection is applied to a creature, it signifies that perfection distinct in idea from other perfections; as, for instance, by this term *wise* applied to a man, we signify some perfection distinct from a man's essence, and distinct from his power and existence, and from all similar things; whereas when we apply it to God, we do not mean to signify anything distinct from His essence, or power, or existence. Thus also this term *wise* applied to man in some degree circumscribes and comprehends the thing signified; whereas this is not the case when it is applied to God, but it leaves the thing signified as incomprehended, and as exceeding the signification of the name. Hence it is evident that this term *wise* is not applied in the same way to God and to man. The same rule applies to other terms. Hence no name is predicated univocally of God and of creatures.

Neither, on the other hand, are names applied to God and creatures in a purely equivocal sense, as some have said. Because if that were so, it follows that from creatures nothing could be known or demonstrated about God at all; for the reasoning would always be exposed to the fallacy of equivocation. Such a view is against the philosophers, who proved many things about God, and also against what the Apostle says: *The invisible things of God are clearly seen being understood by the things that are made* (Rom. 1. 20). Therefore it must be said that these names are said of God and creatures in an analogous sense, that is, according to proportion.

Now names are thus used in two ways: either according as many things are proportionate to one, thus for example *healthy* is predicated of medicine and urine in relation and in proportion to health of a body, of which the former is the sign and the latter the cause: or according as one thing is proportionate to another, thus *healthy* is said of medicine and animal, since medicine is the cause of health in the animal body. And in this way some things are said of God and creatures analogically, and not in a purely equivocal nor in a purely univocal sense. For we can name God only from creatures (A. 1). Thus, whatever is said of God and creatures, is said according to the relation of a creature to God as its principle and cause, wherein all perfections of things pre-exist excellently. Now this mode of community of idea is a mean between pure equivocation and simple univocation. For in analogies the idea is not, as it is in univocals, one and the same, yet it is not totally diverse as in equivocals; but a term which is thus used in a multiple sense signifies various proportions to some one thing; thus *healthy* applied to urine signifies the sign of animal health, and applied to medicine signifies the cause of the same health.

Reply Obj. 1. Although equivocal predications must be reduced to univocal, still in actions the non-univocal agent must precede the univocal agent. For the non-univocal agent is the universal cause of the whole species, as for instance the sun is the cause of the generation of all men; whereas the univocal agent is not the universal efficient cause of the whole species (otherwise it would be the cause of itself, since it is contained in the species), but is a particular cause of this individual which it places under the species by way of participation. Therefore the universal cause of the whole species is not an univocal agent: and the universal cause comes before the particular cause. But this universal agent, whilst it is not univocal, nevertheless is not altogether equivocal, otherwise it could not produce its own likeness, but rather it is to be called an analogical agent, as all univocal predications are reduced to one first non-univocal analogical predication, which is being.

Reply Obj. 2. The likeness of the creature to God is imperfect, for it does not represent one and the same generic thing (Q. 4, A. 3).

Reply Obj. 3. God is not the measure proportioned to things measured; hence it is not necessary that God and creatures should be in the same genus.

The arguments adduced in the contrary sense prove indeed that these names are not predicated univocally of God and creatures; yet they do not prove that they are predicated equivocally.

* * *

Treatise on Creation

QUESTION 46: OF THE BEGINNING OF THE DURATION OF CREATURES

* * *

FIRST ARTICLE

WHETHER THE UNIVERSE OF CREATURES ALWAYS EXISTED?

We proceed thus to the First Article:—

Objection 1. It would seem that the universe of creatures, called the world, had no beginning, but existed from eternity. For everything which begins to exist, is a possible being before it exists: otherwise it would be impossible for it to exist. If therefore the world began to exist, it was a possible being before it began to exist. But possible being is matter, which is in potentiality to existence, which results from a form, and to non-existence, which results from privation of form. If therefore the world began to exist, matter must have existed before the world. But matter cannot exist without form: while the matter of the world with its form is the world. Therefore the world existed before it began to exist: which is impossible.

Obj. 2. Further, nothing which has power to be always, sometimes is and sometimes is not; because so far as the power of a thing extends so long it exists. But every incorruptible thing has power to be always; for its power does not extend to any determinate time. Therefore no incorruptible thing sometimes is, and sometimes is not: but everything which has a beginning at some time is, and at some time is not; therefore no incorruptible thing begins to exist. But there are many incorruptible things in the world, as the celestial bodies and all intellectual substances. Therefore the world did not begin to exist.

Obj. 3. Further, what is unbegotten has no beginning. But the Philosopher (*Phys.* i, text. 82) proves that matter is unbegotten, and also (*De Cælo et Mundo* i, text. 20) that the heaven is unbegotten. Therefore the universe did not begin to exist.

Obj. 4. Further, a vacuum is where there is not a body, but there might be. But if the world began to exist, there was first no body where the body of the world now is; and yet it could be there, otherwise it would not be there now. Therefore before the world there was a vacuum; which is impossible.

Obj. 5. Further, nothing begins anew to be moved except through either the mover of the thing moved being otherwise than it was before. But what is otherwise now than it was before, is moved. Therefore before every new movement there was a previous movement. Therefore movement always was; and therefore also the thing moved always was, because movement is only in a movable thing.

Obj. 6. Further, every mover is either natural or voluntary. But neither begins to move except by some pre-existing movement. For nature always moves in the same manner: hence unless some change precede either in the nature of the mover, or in the movable thing, there cannot arise from the natural mover a movement which was not there before. And the will, without itself being changed, puts off doing what it proposes to do; but this can be only by some imagined change, at least on the part of time. Thus he who wills to make a house tomorrow, and not today, awaits something which will be tomorrow, but is not today; and at least awaits for today to pass, and for tomorrow to come; and this cannot be without change, because time is the measure of movement. Therefore it remains that before every new movement, there was a previous movement; and so the same conclusion follows as before.

Obj. 7. Further, whatever is always in its beginning, and always in its end, cannot cease and cannot begin; because what begins is not in its end, and what ceases is not in its beginning. But time always is in its beginning and end, because there is no time except now which is the end of the past and the beginning of the future. Therefore time cannot begin or end, and consequently neither can movement, the measure of which is time.

Obj. 8. Further, God is before the world either in the order of nature only, or also by duration. If in the order of nature only, therefore, since God is eternal, the world also is eternal. But if God is prior by duration; since what is prior and posterior in duration constitutes time, it follows that time existed before the world, which is impossible.

Obj. 9. Further, if there is a sufficient cause, there is an effect; for a cause to which there is no effect is an imperfect cause, requiring something else to make the effect follow. But God is the sufficient cause of the world; being the final cause, by reason of His goodness, the exemplar cause by reason of His wisdom, and the efficient cause, by reason of His power as appears from the above (Q. 44, AA. 2, 3, 4). Since therefore God is eternal, the world also is eternal.

Obj. 10. Further, eternal action postulates an eternal effect. But the action of God is His substance, which is eternal. Therefore the world is eternal.*On the contrary,* It is said (Jo. xvii. 5), *Glorify Me, O Father, with Thyself with the glory which I had before the world was;* and (Prov. vii. 22), *The Lord possessed Me in the beginning of His ways, before He made anything from the beginning.*

I answer that, Nothing except God can be eternal. And this statement is far from impossible to uphold: for it has been shown above (Q. 19, A. 4) that the will of God is the cause of things. Therefore things are necessary, according as it is necessary for God to will them, since the necessity of the effect depends on the necessity of the cause (*Metaph.* v, text. 6). Now it was shown above (Q. 19, A. 3), that, absolutely speaking, it is not necessary that God should will anything except Himself. It is not therefore necessary for God to will that the world should always exist; but the world exists forasmuch as God wills it to exist, since the being of the world depends on the will of God, as on its cause. It is not therefore necessary for the world to be always; and hence it cannot be proved by demonstration.

Nor are Aristotle's reasons (*Phys.* viii) simply, but relatively, demonstrative— viz., in order to contradict the reasons of some of the ancients who asserted that the world began to exist in some quite impossible manner. This appears in three ways. Firstly, because, both in *Phys.* viii and in *De Cælo* i, text. 101, he premises some opinions, as those of Anaxagoras, Empedocles and Plato, and brings forward reasons to refute them. Secondly, because wherever he speaks of this subject, he quotes the testimony of the ancients, which is not the way of a demonstrator, but of one persuading of what probable. Thirdly, because he expressly says (*Topic.* i. 9), that there are dialectical problems, about which we have nothing to say from reason, as, *whether the world is eternal.*

Reply Obj. 1. Before the world existed it was possible for the world to be, not, indeed, according to a passive power which is matter, but according to the active power of God; and also, according as a thing is called absolutely possible, not in relation to any power, but from the sole habitude of the terms which are not repugnant to each other; in which sense possible is opposed to impossible, as appears from the Philosopher (*Metaph.* v, text. 17).

Reply Obj. 2. Whatever has power always to be, from the fact of having that power, cannot sometimes be and sometimes not be; but before it received that power, it did not exist.

Hence this reason, which is given by Aristotle (*De Cælo* i, text. 120), does not prove simply that incorruptible things never began to exist; but that they did not begin by the natural mode whereby things generated and corruptible begin.

Reply Obj. 3. Aristotle (*Phys.* i, text. 82) proves that matter is unbegotten from the fact that it has not a subject from which to derive its existence; and (*De Cælo et Mundo* i, text. 20) he proves that heaven is ungenerated, forasmuch as it has no contrary from which to be generated. Hence it appears that no conclusion follows either way, except that matter and heaven did not begin by generation, as some said, especially about heaven. But we say that matter and heaven were produced into being by creation, as appears above (Q. 44, A. 1 ad 2).

Reply Obj. 4. The notion of a vacuum is not only *in which is nothing,* but also implies a space capable of holding a body and in which there is not a body, as appears from Aristotle (*Phys.* iv., text. 60). Whereas we hold that there was no place or space before the world was.

Reply Obj. 5. The first mover was always in the same state: but the first movable thing was not always so, because it began to be whereas hitherto it was not. This, however, was not through change, but by creation, which is not change, as said above (Q. 45, A. 2 ad 2). Hence it is evident that this reason, which Aristotle gives (*Phys.* viii), is valid against those who admitted the existence of eternal movable things, but not eternal movement, as appears from the opinions of Anaxagoras and Empedocles. But we hold that from the moment that movable things began to exist movement also existed.

Reply Obj. 6. The first agent is a voluntary agent. And although He had the eternal will to produce some effect, yet He did not produce an eternal effect. Nor is it necessary for some change to be presupposed, not even on account of imaginary time. For we must take into consideration the difference between a particular agent, that presupposes something and produces something else, and the universal agent, who produces the whole. The particular agent produces the form, and presupposes the matter; and hence it is necessary that it introduce the form in due proportion into a suitable matter. Hence it is correct to say that it introduces the form into such matter, and not into another, on account of the different kinds of matter. But it is not correct to say so of God Who produces form and matter together: whereas it is correct to say of Him that He produces matter fitting to the form and to the end. Now, a particular agent presupposes time just as it presupposes matter. Hence it is correctly described as acting in time *after* and not in time *before,* according to an imaginary succession of time after time. But the universal agent who produces the thing and time also, is not correctly described as acting now, and not before, according to an imaginary succession of time succeeding time, as if time were presupposed to His action; but He must be considered as giving time to His effect as much as and when He willed, and according to what was fitting to demonstrate His power. For the world leads more evidently to the knowledge of the divine creating power, if it was not always, than if it had always been; since everything which was not always manifestly has a cause; whereas this is not so manifest of what always was.

Reply Obj. 7. As is stated (*Phys.* iv., text. 99), *before* and *after* belong to time, according as they are in movement. Hence beginning and end in time must be taken in the same way as in movement. Now, granted the eternity of movement, it is necessary that any given moment in movement be a beginning and an end of movement; which need not be if movement has a beginning. The same applies to the *now* of time. Thus it appears that the idea of the instant now, as being always the beginning and end of time, presupposes the eternity of time and movement. Hence Aristotle brings forward this reason (*Phys.* viii., text. 10) against those who asserted the eternity of time, but denied the eternity of movement.

Reply Obj. 8. God is prior to the world by priority of duration. But the word *prior* signifies priority not of time, but of eternity.—Or we may say that it signifies the eternity of imaginary time, and not of time really existing; thus, when we say that above heaven there is nothing, the word *above* signifies only an imaginary place, according as it is possible to imagine other dimensions beyond those of the heavenly body.

Reply Obj. 9. As the effect follows from the cause that acts by nature, according to the mode of its form, so likewise it follows from the voluntary agent, according to the form preconceived and determined by the agent, as appears from what was said above (Q. 19, A. 4; Q. 41, A. 2). Therefore, although God was from eternity the sufficient cause of the world, we should not say that the world was produced by Him, except as preordained by His will—that is, that it should have being after not being, in order more manifestly to declare its author.

Reply Obj. 10. Given the action, the effect follows according to the requirement of the form, which is the principle of action. But in agents acting by will, what is conceived and preordained is to be taken as the form, which is the principle of action. Therefore from the eternal action of God an eternal effect did not follow; but such an effect as God willed, an effect, to wit, which has being after not being.

SECOND ARTICLE

WHETHER IT IS AN ARTICLE OF FAITH THAT THE WORLD BEGAN?

We proceed thus to the Second Article:—

Objection 1. It would seem that it is not an article of faith but a demonstrable conclusion that the world began. For everything that is made has a beginning of its duration. But it can be proved demonstratively that God is the effective cause of the world; indeed this is asserted by the more approved philosophers. Therefore it can be demonstratively proved that the world began.

Obj. 2. Further, if it is necessary to say that the world was made by God, it must therefore have been made from nothing, or from something. But it was not made from something; otherwise the matter of the world would have preceded the world; against which are the arguments of Aristotle (*De Cælo* i), who held that heaven was ungenerated. Therefore it must be said that the world was made from nothing; and thus it has being after not being. Therefore it must have begun.

Obj. 3. Further, everything which works by intellect, works from some principle, as appears in all kinds of craftsmen. But God acts by intellect: therefore His work has a principle. The world, therefore, which is His effect did not always exist.

Obj. 4. Further, it appears manifestly that certain arts have developed, and certain countries have begun to be inhabited at some fixed time. But this would not be the case if the world had been always. Therefore it is manifest that the world did not always exist.

Obj. 5. Further, it is certain that nothing can be equal to God. But if the world had always been, it would be equal to God in duration. Therefore it is certain that the world did not always exist.

Obj. 6. Further, if the world always was, the consequence is that infinite days preceded this present day. But it is impossible to pass through an infinite medium. Therefore we should never have arrived at this present day; which is manifestly false.

Obj. 7. Further, if the world was eternal, generation also was eternal. Therefore one man was begotten of another in an infinite series. But the father is the efficient cause of the son (*Phys.* ii., text. 29). Therefore in efficient causes there could be an infinite series, which is disproved (*Metaph.* ii., text. 5).

Obj. 8. Further, if the world and generation always were, there have been an infinite number of men. But man's soul is immortal: therefore an infinite number of human souls would actually now exist, which is impossible. Therefore it can be known with certainty that the world began, and not only is it known by faith.

On the contrary, The articles of faith cannot be proved demonstratively, because faith is of things *that appear not* (Heb. xi. 1). But that God is the Creator of the world: hence that the world began, is an article of faith; for we say, *I believe in one God,* etc. And again, Gregory says *(Hom.* i. *in Ezech.),* that Moses prophesied of the past, saying, *In the beginning God created heaven and earth:* in which words the newness of the world is stated. Therefore the newness of the world is known only by revelation; and therefore it cannot be proved demonstratively.

I answer that, By faith alone do we hold, and by no demonstration can it be proved, that the world did not always exist, as was said above of the mystery of the Trinity (Q. 32, A. 1). The reason of this is that the newness of the world cannot be demonstrated on the part of the world itself. For the principle of demonstration is the essence of a thing. Now everything according to its species is abstracted from *here* and *now;* whence it is said that universals are everywhere and always. Hence it cannot be demonstrated that man, or heaven, or a stone were not always. Likewise neither can it be demonstrated on the part of the efficient cause, which acts by will. For the will of God cannot be investigated by reason, except as regards those things which God must will of necessity; and what He wills about creatures is not among these, as was said above (Q. 19, A. 3). But the divine will can be manifested by revelation, on which faith rests. Hence that the world began to exist is an object of faith, but not of demonstration or science. And it is useful to consider this, lest anyone, presuming to demonstrate what is of faith, should bring forward reasons that are not cogent, so as to give occasion to unbelievers to laugh, thinking that on such grounds we believe things that are of faith.

Reply Obj. 1. As Augustine says (*De Civ. Dei* xi. 4), the opinion of philosophers who asserted the eternity of the world was twofold. For some said that the substance of the world was not from God, which is an intolerable error; and therefore it is refuted by proofs that are cogent. Some, however, said that the world was eternal, although made by God. For they hold that the world has a beginning, not of time, but of creation, so that in a certain hardly intelligible way it was always made. *And they try to explain their meaning thus (De Civ. Dei* x. 31): *for as, if the foot were always in the dust from eternity, there would always be a footprint which without doubt was caused by him who trod on it, so also the world always was, because its Maker always existed.* To understand this we must consider that the efficient cause, which acts by motion, of necessity precedes its effect in time; because the effect is only in the end of the action, and every agent must be the principle of action. But if the action is instantaneous and not successive, it is not necessary for the maker to be prior to the thing made in duration, as appears in the case of illumination. Hence they say that it does not follow necessarily if God is the active cause of the world, that He should be prior to the world in duration; because creation, by which He produced the world, is not a successive change, as was said above (Q. 45, A. 2).

Reply Obj. 2. Those who would say that the world was eternal, would say that the world was made by God from nothing, not that it was made after nothing, according to what we understand by the word creation, but that it was not made from anything; and so also some of them do not reject the word creation, as appears from Avicenna (*Metaph.* ix, text. 4).

Reply Obj. 3. This is the argument of Anaxagoras (as quoted in *Phys.* viii., text. 15). But it does not lead to a necessary conclusion, except as to that intellect which deliberates in order to find out what should be done, which is like movement. Such is the human intellect, but not the divine intellect (Q. 14, AA. 7, 12).

Reply Obj. 4. Those who hold the eternity of the world hold that some region was changed an infinite number of times, from being uninhabitable to being inhabitable and vice versa, and likewise they hold that the arts, by reason of various corruptions and accidents, were subject to an infinite variety of advance and decay. Hence Aristotle says (*Meteor.* i), that it is absurd from such particular changes to hold the opinion of the newness of the whole world.

Reply Obj. 5. Even supposing that the world always was, it would not be equal to God in eternity, as Boethius says (*De Consol.* v. 6); because the divine Being is all being simultaneously without succession; but with the world it is otherwise.

Reply Obj. 6. Passage is always understood as being from term to term. Whatever bygone day we choose, from it to the present day there is a finite number of days which can be passed through. The objection is founded on the idea that, given two extremes, there is an infinite number of mean terms.

Reply Obj. 7. In efficient causes it is impossible to proceed to infinity *per se*— thus, there cannot be an infinite number of causes that are *per se* required for a certain effect; for instance, that a stone be moved by a stick, the stick by the hand, and so on to infinity. But it is not impossible to proceed to infinity *accidentally* as regards efficient causes; for instance, if all the causes thus infinitely multiplied should have the order of only one cause, their multiplication being accidental, as an artificer acts by means of many hammers accidentally, because one after the other may be broken. It is accidental, therefore, that one particular hammer acts after the action of another; and likewise it is accidental to this particular man as generator to be generated by another man; for he generates as a man, and not as the son of another man. For all men generating hold one grade in efficient causes—viz., the grade of a particular generator. Hence it is not impossible for a man to be generated by man to infinity; but such a thing would be impossible if the generation of this man depended upon this man, and on an elementary body, and on the sun, and so on to infinity.

Reply Obj. 8. Those who hold the eternity of the world evade this reason in many ways. For some do not think it impossible for there to be an actual infinity of souls, as appears from the *Metaphysics* of Algazel, who says that such a thing is an accidental infinity. But this was disproved above (Q. 7, A. 4). Some say that the soul is corrupted with the body. And some say that of all souls only one will remain. But others, as Augustine says, asserted on this account a circuit of souls—viz., that souls separated from their bodies return again thither after a course of time; a fuller consideration of which matters will be given later (Q. 75, A. 6; Q. 76, A. 2; Q. 118, A. 6). But be it noted that this argument considers only a particular case. Hence one might say that the world was eternal, or at least some creature, as an angel, but not man. But we are considering the question in general, as to whether any creature can exist from eternity.

*　*　*

Treatise on Man

QUESTION 75: OF MAN WHO IS COMPOSED OF A SPIRITUAL AND A CORPOREAL SUBSTANCE: AND IN THE FIRST PLACE CONCERNING WHAT BELONGS TO THE ESSENCE OF THE SOUL

* * *

SECOND ARTICLE

WHETHER THE HUMAN SOUL IS SOMETHING SUBSISTENT?

We proceed thus to the Second Article:—

Objection 1. It would seem that the human soul is not something subsistent. For that which subsists is said to be *this particular thing*. Now *this particular thing* is said not of the soul, but of that which is composed of soul and body. Therefore the soul is not something subsistent.

Obj. 2. Further, everything subsistent operates. But the soul does not operate; for, as the Philosopher says (*De Anima* i. 4), *to say that the soul feels or understands is like saying that the soul weaves or builds.* Therefore the soul is not subsistent.

Obj. 3. Further, if the soul were subsistent, it would have some operation apart from the body. But it has no operation apart from the body, not even that of understanding: for the act of understanding does not take place without a phantasm, which cannot exist apart from the body. Therefore the human soul is not something subsistent.

On the contrary, Augustine says (*de Trin.* x. 7): *Whoever understands that the nature of the soul is that of a substance and not that of a body, will see that those who maintain the corporeal nature of the soul, are led astray through associating with the soul those things without which they are unable to think of any nature—i.e., imaginary pictures of the corporal things.* Therefore the nature of the human intellect is not only incorporeal, but it is also a substance, that is, something subsistent.

I answer that, It must necessarily be allowed that the principle of intellectual operation which we call the soul, is a principle both incorporeal and subsistent. For it is clear that by means of the intellect man can have knowledge of all corporeal things. Now whatever knows certain things cannot have any of them in its own nature; because that which is in it naturally would impede the knowledge of anything else. Thus we observe that a sick man's tongue being vitiated by a feverish and bitter humor, is insensible to anything sweet and everything seems bitter to it. Therefore if the intellectual principle contained the nature of a body it would be unable to know all bodies. Now every body has its own determinate nature. Therefore it is impossible for the intellectual principle to be a body. It is likewise impossible for it to understand by means of a bodily organ; since the determinate nature of that organ would impede knowledge of all bodies; as when a certain determinate color is not only in the pupil of the eye, but also in a glass vase, the liquid in the vase seems to be of that same color.

Therefore the intellectual principle which we call the mind or the intellect has the operation *per se* apart from the body. Now only that which subsists can have an operation *per se*. For nothing can operate but what is actual: wherefore a thing operates according as it is; for which reason we do not say that heat imparts heat, but that what is hot gives heat. We must conclude, therefore, that the human soul, which is called the intellect or the mind, is something incorporeal and subsistent.

Reply Obj. 1. *This particular thing* can be taken in two senses. Firstly, for anything subsistent; secondly, for that which subsists, and is complete in a specific nature. The former sense excludes the inherence of an accident or of a material form; the latter excludes also the imperfection of the part, so that a hand can be called *this particular thing* in the first sense, but not in the second. Therefore as the human soul is a part of human nature, it can indeed be called *this particular thing,* in the first sense, as being something subsistent; but not in the second, for in this sense, what is composed of body and soul is said to be *this particular thing.*

Reply Obj. 2. Aristotle wrote those words as expressing not his own opinion, but the opinion of those who said that to understand is to be moved, as is clear from the context. Or we may reply that to operate *per se* belongs to what exists *per se.* But for a thing to exist *per se,* it suffices sometimes that it be not inherent, as an accident or a material form; even though it be part of something. Nevertheless, that is rightly said to subsist *per se,* which is neither inherent in the above sense nor part of anything else. In this sense, the eye or the hand cannot be said to subsist *per se;* nor can it for that reason be said to operate *per se.* Hence the operation of the parts is through each part attributed to the whole. For we say that the man sees with the eye, and feels with the hand and, and, not in the same sense as when we say that what is hot gives heat by its heat; for heat, strictly speaking, does not give heat. We may therefore say that the soul understands, as the eye sees; but it is more correct to say that man understands through the soul.

Reply Obj. 3. The body is necessary for intellect, not as its origin of action, but on the part of the object; for the phantasm is to the intellect what color is to the sight. Neither does such a dependence on the body prove the intellect to be non-subsistent; otherwise it would follow that an animal is not subsistent, since it requires external objects of the senses in order to perform its act of perception.

*   *   *

QUESTION 76: OF THE UNION OF BODY AND SOUL

*   *   *

SECOND ARTICLE

WHETHER THE INTELLECTUAL PRINCIPLE IS MULTIPLIED ACCORDING TO THE NUMBER OF BODIES?

We proceed thus to the Second Article:—

Objection 1. It would seem that the intellectual principle is not multiplied according to the number of bodies, but that there is one intellect in all men. For an immaterial substance is not multiplied in number within one species. But the human soul is an immaterial substance; since it is not composed of matter and form, as was shown above (Q. 75, A. 5). Therefore there are not many human souls in one species. But all men are of one species. Therefore there is but one intellect in all men.

Obj. 2. Further, when the cause is removed, the effect is also removed. Therefore, if human souls were multiplied according to the number of bodies, it follows that the bodies being removed, the number of souls would not remain; but from all the souls there would be but a single remainder. This is heretical; for it would do away with the distinction of rewards and punishments.

Obj. 3. Further, if my intellect is distinct from your intellect, my intellect is an individual, and so is yours; for individuals are things which differ in number but agree in one species. Now whatever is received into anything must be received according to the condition of the receiver. Therefore the species of things would be received individually into my intellect, and also into yours: which is contrary to the nature of the intellect which knows universals.

Obj. 4. Further, the thing understood is in the intellect which understands. If, therefore, my intellect is distinct from yours, what is understood by me must be distinct from what is understood by you; and consequently it will be reckoned as something individual, and be only potentially something understood; so that the common intention will have to be abstracted from both; since from things diverse something intelligible common to them may be abstracted. But this is contrary to the nature of the intellect; for then the intellect would seem not to be distinct from the imagination. It seems, therefore, to follow that there is one intellect in all men.

Obj. 5. Further, when the disciple receives knowledge from the master, it cannot be said that the master's knowledge begets knowledge in the disciple, because then also knowledge would be an active form, such as heat is, which is clearly false. It seems, therefore, that the same individual knowledge which is in the master is communicated to the disciple; which cannot be, unless there is one intellect in both. Seemingly, therefore, the intellect of the disciple and master is but one; and, consequently, the same applies to all men.

Obj. 6. Further, Augustine (*De Quant. Animae* xxxii) says: *If I were to say that there are many human souls, I should laugh at myself.* But the soul seems to be one chiefly on account of the intellect. Therefore there is one intellect of all men.

On the contrary, The Philosopher says (*Phys.* ii. 3) that the relation of universal causes to universals is like the relation of particular causes to individuals. But it is impossible that a soul, one in species, should belong to animals of different species. Therefore it is impossible that one individual intellectual soul should belong to several individuals.

I answer that, It is absolutely impossible for one intellect to belong to all men. This is clear if, as Plato maintained, man is the intellect itself. For it would follow that Socrates and Plato are one man; and that they are not distinct from each other, except by something outside the essence of each. The distinction between Socrates and Plato would be no other than that of one man with a tunic and another with a cloak; which is quite absurd.

It is likewise clear that this is impossible if, according to the opinion of Aristotle (*De Anima* ii. 2), it is supposed that the intellect is a part or a power of the soul which is the form of man. For it is impossible for many distinct individuals to have one form, as it is impossible for them to have one existence, for the form is the principle of existence.

Again, this is clearly impossible, whatever one may hold as to the manner of the union of the intellect to this or that man. For it is manifest that, supposing there is one principal agent, and two instruments, we can say that there is one agent absolutely, but several actions; as when one man touches several things with his two hands, there will be one who touches, but two contacts. If, on the contrary, we suppose one instrument and several principal agents, we might say that there are several agents, but one act; for example, if there be many drawing a ship by means of a rope; there will be many drawing, but one pull. If, however, there is one principal agent, and one instrument, we say that there is one agent and one action, as when the smith strikes with one hammer, there is one striker and one stroke. Now it is clear that no matter how the intellect is united or coupled to this or that man, the intellect has the precedence of all the other things which appertain to man; for the sensitive powers obey the intellect, and are at its service. Therefore, if we suppose two men to have several intellects and one sense,—for instance, if two men had one eye,—there would be several seers, but one sight. But if there is one intellect, no matter how diverse may be all those things of which the intellect makes use as instruments, in no way is it possible to say that Socrates and Plato are otherwise than one understanding man. And if to this we add that to understand, which is the act of the intellect, is not affected by any organ other than the intellect itself; it will further follow that there is but one agent and one action: that is to say that all men are but one "understander," and have but one act of understanding, in regard, that is, of one intelligible object.

However, it would be possible to distinguish my intellectual action from yours by the distinction of the phantasms—that is to say, were there one phantasm of a stone in me, and another in you—if the phantasm itself, as it is one thing in me and another in you, were a form of the possible intellect; since the same agent according to divers forms produces divers actions; as, according to divers forms of things with regard to the same eye, there are divers visions. But the phantasm itself is not a form of the possible intellect; it is the intelligible species abstracted from the phantasm that is a form. Now in one intellect, from different phantasms of the same species, only one intelligible species is abstracted; as appears in one man, in whom there may be different phantasms of a stone; yet from all of them only one intelligible species of a stone is abstracted; by which the intellect of that one man, by one operation, understands the nature of a stone, notwithstanding the diversity of phantasms. Therefore, if there were one intellect for all men, the diversity of phantasms which are in this one and that one would not cause a diversity of intellectual operation in this man and that man. It follows, therefore, that it is altogether impossible and unreasonable to maintain that there exists one intellect for all men.

Reply Obj. 1. Although the intellectual soul, like an angel, has no matter from which it is produced, yet it is the form of a certain matter; in which it is unlike an angel. Therefore, according to the division of matter, there are many souls of one species; while it is quite impossible for many angels to be of one species.

Reply Obj. 2. Everything has unity in the same way that it has being; consequently we must judge of the multiplicity of a thing as we judge of its being. Now it is clear that the intellectual soul, by virtue of its very being, is united to the body as its form; yet, after the dissolution of the body, the intellectual soul retains its own being. In like manner the multiplicity of souls is in proportion to the multiplicity of bodies; yet, after the dissolution of the bodies, the souls retain their multiplied being.

Reply Obj. 3. Individuality of the intelligent being, or of the species whereby it understands, does not exclude the understanding of universals; otherwise, since separate intellects are subsistent substances, and consequently individual, they could not understand universals. But the materiality of the knower, and of the species whereby it knows, impedes the knowledge of the universal. For as every action is according to the mode of the form by which the agent acts, as heating is according to the mode of the heat; so knowledge is according to the mode of the species by which the knower knows. Now it is clear that common nature becomes distinct and multiplied by reason of the individuating principles which come from the matter. Therefore if the form, which is the means of knowledge, is material—that is, not abstracted from material conditions—its likeness to the nature of a species or genus will be according to the distinction and multiplication of that nature by means of individuating principles; so that knowledge of the nature of a thing in general will be impossible. But if the species be abstracted from the conditions of individual matter, there will be a likeness of the nature without those things which make it distinct and multiplied; thus there will be knowledge of the universal. Nor does it matter, as to this particular point, whether there be one intellect or many; because, even if there were but one, it would necessarily be an individual intellect, and the species whereby it understands, an individual species.

Reply Obj. 4. Whether the intellect be one or many, what is understood is one; for what is understood is in the intellect, not according to its own nature, but according to its likeness; *for the stone is not in the soul, but its likeness is,* as is said, *De Anima* iii. 8. Yet it is the stone which is understood, not the likeness of the stone; except by a reflection of the intellect on itself: otherwise, the objects of sciences would not be things, but only intelligible species. Now it happens that different things, according to different forms, are likened to the same thing. And since knowledge is begotten according to the assimilation of the knower to the thing known, it follows that the same thing may happen to be known by several knowers; as is apparent in regard to the senses; for several see the same color, according to different likenesses. In the same way several intellects understand one object understood. But there is this difference, according to the opinion of Aristotle, between the sense and the intelligence—that a thing is perceived by the sense according to the disposition which it has outside the soul—that is, in its individuality; whereas the nature of the thing understood is indeed outside the soul but the mode according to which it exists outside the soul is not the mode according to which it is understood. For the common nature is understood as apart from the individuating principles; whereas such is not its mode of existence outside the soul. But, according to the opinion of Plato, the thing understood exists outside the soul in the same conditions as those under which it is understood; for he supposed that the natures of things exist separate from matter.

Reply Obj. 5. One knowledge exists in the disciple and another in the master. How it is caused will be shown later on (Q. 117, A. 1).

Reply Obj. 6. Augustine denies a plurality of souls, that would involve a plurality of species.

* * *

FOURTH ARTICLE

WHETHER IN MAN THERE IS ANOTHER FORM BESIDES THE INTELLECTUAL SOUL?

We proceed thus to the Fourth Article:—

Objection 1. It would seem that in man there is another form besides the intellectual soul. For the Philosopher says (*De Anima* ii. 1), that *the soul is the act of a physical body which has life potentially.* Therefore the soul is to the body as a form of matter. But the body has a substantial form by which it is a body. Therefore some other substantial form in the body precedes the soul.

Obj. 2. Further, man moves himself as every animal does. Now everything that moves itself is divided into two parts, of which one moves, and the other is moved, as the Philosopher proves (*Phys.* viii. 5). But the part which moves is the soul. Therefore the other part must be such that it can be moved. But primary matter cannot be moved (*ibid.* v. 1), since it is a being only potentially; indeed everything that is moved is a body. Therefore in man and in every animal there must be another substantial form, by which the body is constituted.

Obj. 3. Further, the order of forms depends on their relation to primary matter; for *before* and *after* apply by comparison to some beginning. Therefore if there were not in man some other substantial form besides the rational soul, and if this were to inhere immediately to primary matter; it would follow that it ranks among the most imperfect forms which inhere to matter immediately.

Obj. 4. Further, the human body is a mixed body. Now mingling does not result from matter alone; for then we should have mere corruption. Therefore the forms of the elements must remain in a mixed body; and these are substantial forms. Therefore in the human body there are other substantial forms besides the intellectual soul.

On the contrary, Of one thing there is but one substantial being. But the substantial form gives substantial being. Therefore of one thing there is but one substantial form. But the soul is the substantial form of man. Therefore it is impossible for there to be in man another substantial form besides the intellectual soul.

I answer that, If we suppose that the intellectual is not united to the body as its form, but only as its motor, as the Platonists maintain, it would necessarily follow that in man there is another substantial form, by which the body is established in its being as movable by the soul. If, however, the intellectual soul be united to the body as its substantial form, as we have said above (A. 1), it is impossible for another substantial form besides the intellectual soul to be found in man.

In order to make this evident, we must consider that the substantial form differs from the accidental form in this, that the accidental form does not make a thing to be *simply,* but to be *such,* as heat does not make a thing to be simply, but only to be hot. Therefore by the coming of the accidental form a thing is not said to be made or generated simply, but to be made such, or to be in some particular condition—and in like manner, when an accidental form is removed, a thing is said to be corrupted, not simply, but relatively. Now the substantial form gives being simply; therefore by its coming a thing is said to be generated simply; and by its removal to be corrupted simply. For this reason, the old natural philosophers, who held that primary matter was some actual being—for instance, fire or air, or something of that sort—maintained that nothing is generated simply, or corrupted simply; and stated that *every becoming is nothing but an alteration,* as we read, *Phys.* i. 4. Therefore, if besides the intellectual soul there pre-existed in matter another substantial form by which the subject of the soul were made an actual being, it would follow that the soul does not give being simply; and consequently that it is not the substantial form: and so at the advent of the soul there would not be simple generation; nor at its removal simple corruption, all of which is clearly false.

Whence we must conclude, that there is no other substantial form in man besides the intellectual soul; and that the soul, as it virtually contains the sensitive and nutritive souls, so does it virtually contain all inferior forms, and itself alone does whatever the imperfect forms do in other things. The same is to be said of the sensitive soul in brute animals, and of the nutritive soul in plants, and universally of all more perfect forms with regard to the imperfect.

Reply Obj. 1. Aristotle does not say that the soul is the act of a body only, but *the act of a physical organic body which has life potentially;* and that this potentiality *does not reject the soul.* Whence it is clear that when the soul is called the act, the soul itself is included; as when we say that heat is the act of what is hot, and light of what is lucid; not as though lucid and light were two separate things, but because a thing is made lucid by the light. In like manner, the soul is said to be the *act of a body,* etc., because by the soul it is a body, and is organic, and has life potentially. Yet the first act is said to be in potentiality to the second act, which is operation; for such a potentiality *does not reject*—that is, does not exclude—the soul.

Reply Obj. 2. The soul does not move the body by its essence, as the form of the body, but by the motive power, the act of which presupposes the body to be already actualized by the soul: so that the soul by its motive power is the part which moves; and the animate body is the part moved.

Reply Obj. 3. We observe in matter various degrees of perfection, as existence, living, sensing, and understanding. Now what is added is always more perfect. Therefore that form which gives matter only the first degree of perfection is the most imperfect; while that form which gives the first, second, and third degree, and so on, is the most perfect: and yet it inheres to matter immediately.

Reply Obj. 4. Avicenna held that the substantial forms of the elements remain entire in the mixed body; and that the mixture is made by the contrary qualities of the elements being reduced to an average. But this is impossible, because the various forms of the elements must necessarily be in various parts of matter—for the distinction of which we must suppose dimensions, without which matter cannot be divisible. Now matter subject to dimension is not to be found except in a body. But various bodies cannot be in the same place. Whence it follows that elements in the mixed body would be distinct as to situation. And then there would not be a real mixture which is in respect of the whole; but only a mixture apparent to sense, by the juxtaposition of particles.

Averroës maintained that the forms of elements, by reason of their imperfection, are a medium between accidental and substantial forms, and so can be *more* or *less;* and therefore in the mixture they are modified and reduced to an average, so that one form emerges from them. But this is even still more impossible. For the substantial being of each thing consists in something indivisible, and every addition and subtraction varies the species, as in numbers, as stated in *Metaph.* viii. (Did. vii. 3); and consequently it is impossible for any substantial form to receive *more* or *less.* Nor is it less impossible for anything to be a medium between substance and accident.

Therefore we must say, in accordance with the Philosopher (*De Gener.* i. 10), that the forms of the elements remain in the mixed body, not actually but virtually. For the proper qualities of the elements remain, though modified, and in them is the power of the elementary forms. This quality of the mixture is the proper disposition for the substantial form of the mixed body; for instance, the form of a stone, or of any sort of soul.

* * *

QUESTION 84: HOW THE SOUL WHILE UNITED TO THE BODY UNDERSTANDS CORPOREAL THINGS BENEATH IT

* * *

FIFTH ARTICLE

WHETHER THE INTELLECTUAL SOUL KNOWS MATERIAL THINGS IN THE ETERNAL TYPES?

We proceed thus to the Fifth Article:—

Objection 1. It would seem that the intellectual soul does not know material thing in the eternal types. For that in which anything is known must itself be known more and previously. But the intellectual soul of man, in the present state of life, does not know the eternal types: for it does not know God in Whom the eternal types exist, but is *united to God as to the unknown,* as Dionysius says (*Myst. Theolog.* i). Therefore the soul does not know all in the eternal types.

Obj. 2. Further, it is written (Rom. i. 20) that *the invisible things of God are clearly seen . . . by the things that are made.* But among the invisible things of God are the eternal types. Therefore the eternal types are known through creatures and not the converse.

Obj. 3. Further, the eternal types are nothing else but ideas, for Augustine says (QQ. 83, qu. 46) that *ideas are permanent types existing in the Divine mind.* If therefore we say that the intellectual soul knows all things in the eternal types, we come back to the opinion of Plato who said that all knowledge is derived from them.

On the contrary, Augustine says (*Confess.* xii. 25): *If we both see that what you say is true, and if we both see that what I say is true, where do we see this, I pray? Neither do I see it in you, nor do you see it in me: but we both see it in the unchangeable truth which is above our minds.* Now the unchangeable truth is contained in the eternal types. Therefore the intellectual soul knows all true things in the eternal types.

I answer that, As Augustine says (*De Doctr. Christ.* ii. 11): *If those who are called philosophers said by chance anything that was true and consistent with our faith, we must claim it from them as from unjust possessors. For some of the doctrines of the heathens are spurious imitations or superstitious inventions, which we must be careful to avoid when we renounce the society of the heathens.* Consequently whenever Augustine, who was imbued with the doctrines of the Platonists, found in their teaching anything consistent with faith, he adopted it: and those things which he found contrary to faith he amended. Now Plato held, as we have said above (A. 4), that the forms of things subsist of themselves apart from matter; and these he called ideas, by participation of which he said that our intellect knows all things: so that just as corporeal matter by participating, the idea of a stone becomes a stone, so our intellect, by participating the same idea, has knowledge of a stone. But since it seems contrary to faith that forms of things should subsist of themselves, outside the things themselves and apart from matter, as the Platonists held, asserting that *per se* life or *per se* wisdom are creative substances, as Dionysius relates (*Div. Nom.* xi); therefore Augustine (QQ. 83, *loc. cit.*), for the ideas defended by Plato, substituted the types of all creatures existing in the Divine mind, according to which types all things are made in themselves, and are known to the human soul. When, therefore, the question is asked: Does the human soul know all things in the eternal types? we must reply that one thing is said to be known in another in two ways. First, as in an object itself known; as one may see in a mirror the images of things reflected therein. In this way the soul, in the present state of life, cannot see all things in the eternal types; but the blessed who see God, and all things in Him, thus know all things in the eternal types. Secondly, one thing is said to be known in another as in a principle of knowledge: thus we might say that we see in the sun what we see by the sun. And thus we must needs say that the human soul knows all things in the eternal types, since by participation of these types we know all things. For the intellectual light itself which is in us, is nothing else than a participated likeness of the uncreated light in which are contained the eternal types. Whence it is written (Ps. iv. 6, 7), *Many say: Who showeth us good things?* which question the Psalmist answers, *The light of Thy countenance, O Lord, is signed upon us,* as though he were to say: By the seal of the Divine light in us, all things are made known to us.

But since besides the intellectual light which is in us, intelligible species, which are derived from things, are required in order for us to have knowledge of material things; therefore this same knowledge is not due merely to a participation of the eternal types, as the Platonists held, maintaining that the mere participation of ideas sufficed for knowledge. Wherefore Augustine says (*De Trin.* iv. 16): *Although the philosophers prove by convincing arguments that all things occur in time according to the eternal types, were they able to see in the eternal types, or to find out from them how many kinds of animals there are and the origin of each? Did they not seek for this information from the story of times and places?*

But that Augustine did not understand all things to be known in their *eternal types* or in *the unchangeable truth,* as though the eternal types themselves were seen, is clear from what he says (QQ. 83, *loc. cit.*)—viz., that *not each and every rational soul can be said to be worthy of that vision,* namely, of the eternal types, but only those that are holy and pure, such as the souls of the blessed.

From what has been said the objections are easily solved.

SIXTH ARTICLE

WHETHER INTELLECTUAL KNOWLEDGE IS DERIVED FROM SENSIBLE THINGS?

We proceed thus to the Sixth Article:—

Objection 1. It would seem that intellectual knowledge is not derived from sensible things. For Augustine says (QQ. 83, qu. 9) that *we cannot expect to learn the fullness of truth from the senses of the body.* This he proves in two ways. First, because *whatever the bodily senses reach, is continually being changed; and what is never the same cannot be perceived.* Secondly, because, *whatever we perceive by the body, even when not present to the senses, may be present to the imagination, as when we are asleep or angry: yet we cannot discern by the senses, whether what we perceive be the sensible object or the deceptive image thereof. Now nothing can be perceived which cannot be distinguished from its counterfeit.* And so he concludes that we cannot expect to learn the truth from the senses. But intellectual knowledge apprehends the truth. Therefore intellectual knowledge cannot be conveyed by the senses.

Obj. 2. Further, Augustine says (*Gen. ad lit.* xii. 16): *We must not think that the body can make any impression on the spirit, as though the spirit were to supply the place of matter in regard to the body's action; for that which acts is in every way more excellent than that which it acts on.* Whence he concludes that *the body does not cause its image in the spirit, but the spirit causes it in itself.* Therefore intellectual knowledge is not derived from sensible things

Obj. 3. Further, an effect does not surpass the power of its cause. But intellectual knowledge extends beyond sensible things: for we understand some things which cannot be perceived by the senses. Therefore intellectual knowledge is not derived from sensible things.

On the contrary, The Philosopher says (*Metaph.* i. 1; *Poster.* ii. 15) that the principle of knowledge is in the senses.

I answer that, On this point the philosophers held three opinions. For Democritus held that *all knowledge is caused by images issuing from the bodies we think of and entering into our souls,* as Augustine says in his letter to Dioscorus (cxviii. 4). And Aristotle says (*De Somn. et Vigil.*) that Democritus held that knowledge is caused by a *discharge of images.* And the reason for this opinion was that both Democritus and the other early philosophers did not distinguish between intellect and sense, as Aristotle relates (*De Anima* iii. 3). Consequently, since the sense is affected by the sensible, they thought that all our knowledge is affected by this mere impression brought about by sensible things. Which impression Democritus held to be caused by a discharge of images.

Plato, on the other hand, held that the intellect is distinct from the senses: and that it is an immaterial power not making use of a corporeal organ for its action. And since the incorporeal cannot be affected by the corporeal, he held that intellectual knowledge is not brought about by sensible things affecting the intellect, but by separate intelligible forms being participated by the intellect, as we have said above (AA. 4, 5). Moreover he held that sense is a power operating of itself. Consequently neither is sense, since it is a spiritual power, affected by the sensible: but the sensible organs are affected by the sensible, the result being that the soul is in a way roused to form within itself the species of the sensible. Augustine seems to touch on this opinion (*Gen. ad lit.* xii. 24) where he says that the *body feels not, but the soul through the body, which it makes use of as a kind of messenger, for reproducing within itself what is announced from without.* Thus according to Plato, neither does intellectual knowledge proceed from sensible knowledge, nor sensible knowledge exclusively from sensible things; but these rouse the sensible soul to the sentient act, while the senses rouse the intellect to the act of understanding.

Aristotle chose a middle course. For with Plato he agreed that intellect and sense are different. But he held that the sense has not its proper operation without the co-operation of the body; so that to feel is not an act of the soul alone, but of the *composite.* And he held the same in regard to all the operations of the sensitive part. Since, therefore, it is not unreasonable that the sensible objects which are outside the soul should produce some effect in the *composite,* Aristotle agreed with Democritus in this, that the operations of the sensitive part are caused by the impression of the sensible on the sense: not by a discharge, as Democritus said, but by some kind of operation. For Democritus maintained that every operation is by way of a discharge of atoms, as we gather from *De Gener.* i. 8. But Aristotle held that the intellect has an operation which is independent of the body's co-operation. Now nothing corporeal can make an impression on the incorporeal. And therefore in order to cause the intellectual operation, according to Aristotle, the impression caused by the sensible does not suffice, but something more noble is required, *for the agent is more noble than the patient,* as he says (*ibid.* 5). Not, indeed, in the sense that the intellectual operation is effected in us by the mere impression of some superior beings, as Plato held; but that the higher and more noble agent which he calls the active intellect, of which we have spoken above (Q. 79, AA. 3, 4), causes the phantasms received from the senses to be actually intelligible, by a process of abstraction.

According to this opinion, then, on the part of the phantasms, intellectual knowledge is caused by the senses. But since the phantasms cannot of themselves affect the passive intellect, and require to be made actually intelligible by the active intellect, it cannot be said that sensible knowledge is the total and perfect cause of intellectual knowledge, but rather that it is in a way the material cause.

Reply Obj. 1. Those words of Augustine mean that we must not expect the entire truth from the senses. For the light of the active intellect is needed, through which we achieve the unchangeable truth of changeable things, and discern things themselves from their likeness.

Reply Obj. 2. In this passage Augustine speaks not of intellectual but of imaginary knowledge. And since, according to the opinion of Plato, the imagination has an operation which belongs to the soul only, Augustine, in order to show that corporeal images are impressed on the imagination, not by bodies but by the soul, uses the same argument as Aristotle does in proving that the active intellect must be separate, namely, because *the agent is more noble than the patient.* And without doubt, according to the above opinion, in the imagination there must needs be not only a passive but also an active power. But if we hold, according to the opinion of Aristotle, that the action of the imagination is an action of the *composite*, there is no difficulty; because the sensible body is more noble than the organ of the animal, in so far as it is compared to it as a being in act to a being in potentiality; even as the object actually colored is compared to the pupil which is potentially colored. It may, however, be said, although the first impression of the imagination is through the agency of the sensible, since *fancy is movement produced in accordance with sensation* (*De Anima* iii. 3), that nevertheless there is in man an operation which by synthesis and analysis forms images of various things, even of things not perceived by the senses. And Augustine's words may be taken in this sense.

Reply Obj. 3. Sensitive knowledge is not the entire cause of intellectual knowledge. And therefore it is not strange that intellectual knowledge should extend further than sensitive knowledge.

* * *

QUESTION 85: OF THE MODE AND ORDER OF UNDERSTANDING

* * *

FIRST ARTICLE

WHETHER OUR INTELLECT UNDERSTANDS CORPOREAL AND MATERIAL THINGS BY ABSTRACTION FROM PHANTASMS?

We proceed thus to the First Article:—

Objection 1. It would seem that our intellect does not understand corporeal and material things by abstraction from the phantasms. For the intellect is false if it understands an object otherwise than as it really is. Now the forms of material things do not exist as abstracted from the particular things represented by the phantasms. Therefore, if we understand material things by abstraction of the species from the phantasm, there will be error in the intellect.

Obj. 2. Further, material things are those natural things which include matter in their definition. But nothing can be understood apart from that which enters into its definition. Therefore material things cannot be understood apart from matter. Now matter is the principle of individualization. Therefore material things cannot be understood by abstraction of the universal from the particular, which is the process whereby the intelligible species is abstracted from the phantasm.

Obj. 3. Further, the Philosopher says (*De Anima* iii. 7) that the phantasm is to the intellectual soul what color is to the sight. But seeing is not caused by abstraction of species from color, but by color impressing itself on the sight. Therefore neither does the act of understanding take place by abstraction of something from the phantasm, but by the phantasm impressing itself on the intellect.

Obj. 4. Further, the Philosopher says (*De Anima* iii. 5) there are two things in the intellectual soul—the passive intellect and the active intellect. But it does not belong to the passive intellect to abstract the intelligible species from the phantasm, but to receive them when abstracted. Neither does it seem to be the function of the active intellect which is related to the phantasm, as light is to color; since light does not abstract any-thing from color, but rather streams on to it Therefore in no way do we understand by abstraction from phantasms.

Obj. 5. Further, the Philosopher (*De Anima* iii. 7) says that *the intellect under-stands the species in the phantasm;* and not, therefore, by abstraction.

On the contrary, The Philosophers says (*De Anima* iii. 4) that *things are intelligi-ble in proportion as they are separable from matter.* Therefore material things must needs be understood according as they are abstracted from matter and from material im-ages, namely, phantasms.

I answer that, As stated above (Q. 84, A. 7), the object of knowledge is propor-tionate to the power of knowledge. Now there are three grades of the cognitive powers. For one cognitive power, namely, the sense, is the act of a corporeal organ. And there-fore the object of every sensitive power is a form as existing in corporeal matter. And since such matter is the principle of individuality, therefore every power of the sensitive part can only have knowledge of the individual. There is another grade of cognitive power which is neither the act of a corporeal organ, nor in any way connected with cor-poreal matter; such is the angelic intellect, the object of whose cognitive power is there-fore a form existing apart from matter: for though angels know material things, yet they do not know them save in something immaterial, namely, either in themselves or in God. But the human intellect holds a middle place: for it is not the act of an organ; yet it is a power of the soul which is the form of the body, as is clear from what we have said above (Q. 76, A. 1). And therefore it is proper to it to know a form existing indi-vidually in corporeal matter, but not as existing in this individual matter. But to know what is in individual matter, not as existing in such matter, is to abstract the form from individual matter which is represented by the phantasms. Therefore we must needs say that our intellect understands material things by abstracting from the phantasms; and through material things thus considered we acquire some knowledge of immaterial things, just as, on the contrary, angels know material things through the immaterial.

But Plato, considering only the immateriality of the human intellect, and not its being in a way united to the body, held that the objects of the intellect are separate ideas; and that we understand not by abstraction, but by participating things abstract, as stated above (Q. 84, A. 1).

Reply Obj. 1. Abstraction may occur in two ways: First, by way of composition and division; thus we may understand that one thing does not exist in some other, or that it is separate therefrom. Secondly, by way of simple and absolute consideration; thus we understand one thing without considering the other. Thus for the intellect to abstract one from another things which are not really abstract from one another, does, in the first mode of abstraction, imply falsehood. But, in the second mode of abstraction, for the in-tellect to abstract things which are not really abstract from one another, does not involve falsehood, as clearly appears in the case of the senses. For if we understood or said that color is not in a colored body, or that it is separate from it, there would be error in this opinion or assertion. But if we consider color and its properties, without reference to the apple which is colored; or if we express in word what we thus understand, there is no er-ror in such an opinion or assertion, because an apple is not essential to color, and there-fore color can be understood independently of the apple. Likewise, the things which be-long to the species of a material thing, such as a stone, or a man, or a horse, can be thought of apart from the individualizing principles which do not belong to the notion of the species. This is what we mean by abstracting the universal from the particular, or the intelligible species from phantasm; that is, by considering the nature of the species apart from its individual qualities represented by the phantasms. If, therefore, the intellect is said to be false when it understands a thing otherwise than as it is, that is so, if the word *otherwise* refers to the thing understood; for the intellect is false when it understands a thing otherwise than as it is; and so the intellect would be false if it abstracted the species of a stone from its matter in such a way as to regard the species as not existing in matter, as Plato held. But it is not so, if the word *otherwise* be taken as referring to the one who understands. For it is quite true that the mode of understanding, in one who understands, is not the same as the mode of a thing in existing: since the thing understood is immaterially in the one who understands, according to the mode of the intellect, and not materially, according to the mode of a material thing.

Reply Obj. 2. Some have thought that the species of a natural thing is a form only, and that matter is not part of the species. If that were so, matter would not enter into the definition of natural things. Therefore it must be said otherwise, that matter is twofold, common, and *signate* or individual; common, such as flesh and bone; and individual, as this flesh and these bones. The intellect therefore abstracts the species of a natural thing from the individual sensible matter, but not from the common sensible matter; for example, it abstracts the species of man from *this flesh and these bones,* which do not belong to the species as such, but to the individual (*Metaph.* vii, Did. vi. 10), and need not be considered in the species: whereas the species of man cannot be abstracted by the intellect from *flesh and bones.*

Mathematical species, however, can be abstracted by the intellect from sensible matter, not only from individual, but also from common matter; not from common intelligible matter, but only from individual matter. For sensible matter is corporeal matter as subject to sensible qualities, such as being cold or hot, hard or soft, and the like: while intelligible matter is substance as subject to quantity. Now it is manifest that quantity is in substance before other sensible quantities are. Hence quantities, such as number, dimension, and figures, which are the terminations of quantity, can be considered apart from sensible qualities; and this is to abstract them from sensible matter; but they cannot be considered without understanding the substance which is subject to the quantity; for that would be to abstract them from common intelligible matter. Yet they can be considered apart from this or that substance; for that is to abstract them from individual intelligible matter. But some things can be abstracted even from common intelligible matter, such as *being, unity, power, act,* and the like; all these can exist without matter, as is plain regarding immaterial things. Because Plato failed to consider the twofold kind of abstraction, as above explained (*ad* 1), he held that all those things which we have stated to be abstracted by the intellect are abstract in reality.

Reply Obj. 3. Colors, as being in individual corporeal matter, have the same mode of existence as the power of sight: and therefore they can impress their own image on the eye. But phantasms, since they are images of individuals, and exist in corporeal organs, have not the same mode of existence as the human intellect, and therefore have not the power of themselves to make an impression on the passive intellect. This is done by the power of the active intellect which by turning towards the phantasm produces in the passive intellect a certain likeness which represents, as to its specific conditions only, the thing reflected in the phantasm. It is thus that the intelligible species is said to be abstracted from the phantasm; not that the identical form which previously was in the phantasm is subsequently in the passive intellect, as a body transferred from one place to another.

Reply Obj. 4. Not only does the active intellect throw light on the phantasm: it does more; by its own power it abstracts the intelligible species from the phantasm. It throws light on the phantasm, because, just as the sensitive part acquires a greater power by its conjunction with the intellectual part, so by the power of the active intellect the phantasms are made more fit for the abstraction therefrom of intelligible intentions. Furthermore, the active intellect abstracts the intelligible species from the phantasm, forasmuch as by the power of the active intellect we are able to disregard the conditions of individuality, and to take into our consideration the specific nature, the image of which informs the passive intellect.

Reply Obj. 5. Our intellect both abstracts the intelligible species from the phantasms, inasmuch as it considers the natures of things in universal, and, nevertheless, understands these natures in the phantasms, since it cannot understand even the things of which it abstracts the species, without turning to the phantasm, as we have said above (Q. 84, A. 7).

SECOND ARTICLE

WHETHER THE INTELLIGIBLE SPECIES ABSTRACTED FROM THE PHANTASM IS RELATED TO OUR INTELLECT AS THAT WHICH IS UNDERSTOOD?

We proceed thus to the Second Article:—

Objection 1. It would seem that the intelligible species abstracted from the phantasm is related to our intellect as that which is understood. For the understood in act is in the one who understands: since the understood in act is the intellect itself in act. But nothing of what is understood is in the intellect actually understanding, save the abstracted intelligible species. Therefore this species is what is actually understood.

Obj. 2. Further, what is actually understood must be in something; else it would be nothing. But it is not in something outside the soul: for, since what is outside the soul is material, nothing therein can be actually understood. Therefore what is actually understood is in the intellect. Consequently it can be nothing else than the aforesaid intelligible species.

Obj. 3. Further, the Philosopher says (1 *Peri Herm.* i) that *words are signs of the passions in the soul.* But words signify the things understood, for we express by word what we understand. Therefore these passions of the soul, viz., the intelligible species, are what is actually understood.

On the contrary, The intelligible species is to the intellect what the sensible image is to the sense. But the sensible image is not what is perceived, but rather that by which sense perceives. Therefore the intelligible species is not what is actually understood, but that by which the intellect understands.

I answer that, Some have asserted that our intellectual faculties know only the impression made on them; as, for example, that sense is cognizant only of the impression made on its own organ. According to this theory, the intellect understands only its own impression namely, the intelligible species which it has received, so that this species is what is understood.

This is, however, manifestly false for two reasons. First, because the things we understand are the objects of science; therefore if what we understand is merely the intelligible species in the soul, it would follow that every science would not be concerned with objects outside the soul, but only with the intelligible species within the soul; thus, according to the teaching of the Platonists all science is about ideas, which they held to be actually understood. Secondly, it is untrue, because it would lead to the opinion of the ancients who maintained that *whatever seems, is true,* and that consequently contradictories are true simultaneously. For if the faculty knows its own impression only, it can judge of that only. Now a thing seems, according to the impression made on the cognitive faculty. Consequently the cognitive faculty will always judge of its own impression as such; and so every judgment will be true: for instance, if taste perceived only its own impression, when anyone with a healthy taste perceives that honey is sweet, he would judge truly; and if anyone with a corrupt taste perceives that honey is bitter, this would be equally true; for each would judge according to the impression on his taste. Thus every opinion would be equally true; in fact, every sort of apprehension.

Therefore it must be said that the intelligible species is related to the intellect as that by which it understands: which is proved thus. There is a twofold action (*Metaph.* ix, Did. viii. 8), one which remains in the agent; for instance, to see and to understand; and another which passes into an external object; for instance, to heat and to cut; and each of these actions proceeds in virtue of some form. And as the form from which proceeds an act tending to something external is the likeness of the object of the action, as heat in the heater is a likeness of the thing heated; so the form from which proceeds an action remaining in the agent is the likeness of the object. Hence that by which the sight sees is the likeness of the visible thing; and the likeness of the thing understood, that is, the intelligible species, is the form by which the intellect understands. But since the intellect reflects upon itself, by such reflection it understands both its own act of intelligence, and the species by which it understands. Thus the intelligible species is that which is understood secondarily; but that which is primarily understood is the object, of which the species is the likeness. This also appears from the opinion of the ancient philosophers, who said that *like is known by like.* For they said that the soul knows the earth outside itself, by the earth within itself; and so of the rest. If, therefore, we take the species of the earth instead of the earth, according to Aristotle (*De Anima* iii. 8), who says *that a stone is not in the soul, but only the likeness of the stone;* it follows that the soul knows external things by means of its intelligible species.

Reply Obj. 1. The thing understood is in the intellect by its own likeness; and it is in this sense that we say that the thing actually understood is the intellect in act, because the likeness of the thing understood is the form of the intellect, as the likeness of a sensible thing is the form of the sense in act. Hence it does not follow that the intelligible species abstracted is what is actually understood; but rather that it is the likeness thereof.

Reply Obj. 2. In these words *the thing actually understood* there is a double implication:—the thing which is understood, and the fact that it is understood. In like manner the words *abstract universal* imply two things, the nature of a thing and its abstraction or universality. Therefore the nature itself to which it occurs to be understood, abstracted or considered as universal is only in individuals; but that it is understood, abstracted or considered as universal is in the intellect. We see something similar to this in the senses. For the sight sees the color of the apple apart from its smell. If therefore it be asked where is the color which is seen apart from the smell, it is quite clear that the color which is seen is only in the apple: but that it be perceived apart from the smell, this is owing to the sight, forasmuch as the faculty of sight receives the likeness of color and not of smell. In like manner humanity understood is only in this or that man; but that humanity be apprehended without conditions of individuality, that is, that it be abstracted and consequently considered as universal, occurs to humanity inasmuch as it is brought under the consideration of the intellect, in which there is a likeness of the specific nature, but not of the principles of individuality.

Reply Obj. 3. There are two operations in the sensitive part. One, in regard of impression only, and thus the operation of the senses takes place by the senses being impressed by the sensible. The other is formation, inasmuch as the imagination forms for itself an image of an absent thing, or even of something never seen. Both of these operations are found in the intellect. For in the first place there is the passion of the passive intellect as informed by the intelligible species; and then the passive intellect thus informed forms a definition, or a division, or a composition, expressed by a word. Wherefore the concept conveyed by a word is its definition; and a proposition conveys the intellect's division or composition. Words do not therefore signify the intelligible species themselves; but that which the intellect forms for itself for the purpose of judging of external things.

* * *

QUESTION 86: WHAT OUR INTELLECT KNOWS IN MATERIAL THINGS

* * *

FIRST ARTICLE

WHETHER OUR INTELLECT KNOWS SINGULARS?

We proceed thus to the First Article:—

Objection 1. It would seem that our intellect knows singulars. For whoever knows composition, knows the terms of composition. But our intellect knows this composition; *Socrates is a man:* for it belongs to the intellect to form a proposition. Therefore our intellect knows this singular, Socrates.

Obj. 2. Further, the practical intellect directs to action. But action has relation to singular things. Therefore the intellect knows the singular.

Obj. 3. Further, our intellect understands itself. But in itself it is a singular, otherwise it would have no action of its own; for actions belong to singulars. Therefore our intellect knows singulars.

Obj. 4. Further, a superior power can do whatever is done by an inferior power. But sense knows the singular. Much more, therefore, can the intellect know it.

On the contrary, The Philosopher says (*Phys.* i. 5), that *the universal is known by reason; and the singular is known by sense.*

I answer that, Our intellect cannot know the singular in material things directly and primarily. The reason of this is that the principle of singularity in material things is individual matter, whereas our intellect, as we have said above (Q. 85, A. 1), understands by abstracting the intelligible species from such matter. Now what is abstracted from individual matter is the universal. Hence our intellect knows directly the universal only. But indirectly, and as it were by a kind of reflection, know the singular, because, as we have said above (Q. 85, A. 7), even after abstracting the intelligible species, the intellect, in order to understand, needs to turn to the phantasms in which it understands the species, as is said *De Anima* iii. 7. Therefore it understands the universal directly through the intelligible species, and indirectly the singular represented by the phantasm. And thus it forms the proposition, *Socrates is a man.* Wherefore the reply to the first objection is clear.

Reply Obj. 2. The choice of a particular thing to be done is as the conclusion of a syllogism formed by the practical intellect, as is said *Ethic.* vii. 3. But a singular proposition cannot be directly concluded from a universal proposition, except through the medium of a singular proposition. Therefore the universal principle of the practical intellect does not save through the medium of the particular apprehension of a sensitive part, as is said *De Anima* iii. 11.

Reply Obj. 3. Intelligibility is incompatible with the singular not as such, but as material, for nothing can be understood otherwise than immaterially. Therefore if there be an immaterial singular such as the intellect, there is no reason why it should not be intelligible.

Reply Obj. 4. The higher power can do what the lower power can, but in a more eminent way. Wherefore what the sense knows materially and concretely, which is to know the singular directly, the intellect knows immaterially and in the abstract, which is to know the universal.

*   *   *

FIRST PART OF THE SECOND PART (I–II)

Treatise on Human Acts

QUESTION 2: OF THOSE THINGS IN WHICH MAN'S HAPPINESS CONSISTS

*   *   *

EIGHTH ARTICLE

WHETHER ANY CREATED GOOD CONSTITUTES MAN'S HAPPINESS?

We proceed thus to the Eighth Article:—

Objection 1. It would seem that some created good constitutes man's happiness. For Dionysius says (*Div. Nom.* vii) that Divine wisdom *unites the ends of first things to the beginnings of second things,* from which we may gather that the summit of a lower nature touches the base of the higher nature. But man's highest good is happiness. Since then the angel is above man in the order of nature, as stated in the First Part (Q. 111, A. 1), it seems that man's happiness consists in man somehow reaching the angel.

Obj. 2. Further, the last end of each thing is that which, in relation to it, is perfect: hence the part is for the whole, as for its end. But the universe of creatures which is called the macrocosm, is compared to man who is called the microcosm (*Phys.* viii. 2), as perfect to imperfect. Therefore man's happiness consists in the whole universe of creatures.

Obj. 3. Further, man is made happy by that which lulls his natural desire. But man's natural desire does not reach out to a good surpassing his capacity. Since then man's capacity does not include that good which surpasses the limits of all creation, it seems that man can be made happy by some created good. Consequently some created good constitutes man's happiness.

On the contrary, Augustine says (*De Civ. Dei* xix. 26): *As the soul is the life of the body, so God is man's life of happiness: of Whom it is written: "Happy is that people whose God is the Lord"* (Ps. cxliii. 15).

I answer that, It is impossible for any created good to constitute man's happiness. For happiness is the perfect good, which lulls the appetite altogether; else it would not be the last end, if something yet remained to be desired. Now the object of the will, *i.e.,* of man's appetite, is the universal good; just as the object of the intellect is the universal true. Hence it is evident that naught can lull man's will, save the universal good. This is to be found, not in any creature, but in God alone; because every creature has goodness by participation. Wherefore God alone can satisfy the will of man, according to the words of Ps. cii. 5: *Who satisfieth thy desire with good things.* Therefore God alone constitutes man's happiness.

Reply Obj. 1. The summit of man does indeed touch the base of the angelic nature, by a kind of likeness; but man does not rest there as in his last end, but reaches out to the universal fount itself of good, which is the common object of happiness of all the blessed, as being the infinite and perfect good.

Reply Obj. 2. If a whole be not the last end, but ordained to a further end, then the last end of a part thereof is not the whole itself, but something else. Now the universe of creatures, to which man is compared as part to whole, is not the last end, but is ordained to God, as to its last end. Therefore the last end of man is not the good of the universe, but God himself.

Reply Obj. 3. Created good is not less than that good of which man is capable, as of something intrinsic and inherent to him: but it is less than the good of which he is capable, as of an object, and which is infinite. And the participated good which is in an angel, and in the whole universe, is a finite and restricted good.

* * *

QUESTION 3: WHAT IS HAPPINESS

* * *

FOURTH ARTICLE

Whether, If Happiness Is in the Intellective Part, It Is an Operation of the Intellect or of the Will?

We proceed thus to the Fourth Article:—

Objection 1. It would seem that happiness consists in an act of the will. For Augustine says (*De Civ. Dei* xix. 10, 11), that man's happiness consists in peace; wherefore it is written (Ps. cxlvii. 3): *Who hath placed peace in thy end.* But peace pertains to the will. Therefore man's happiness is in the will.

Obj. 2. Further, happiness is the supreme good. But good is the object of the will. Therefore happiness consists in an operation of the will.

Obj. 3. Further, the last end corresponds to the first mover: thus the last end of the whole army is victory, which is the end of the general, who moves all the men. But the first mover in regard to operations is the will: because it moves the other powers, as we shall state further on (Q. 9, AA. 1, 3). Therefore happiness regards the will.

Obj. 4. Further, if happiness be an operation, it must needs be man's most excellent operation. But the love of God, which is an act of the will, is a more excellent operation than knowledge, which is an operation of the intellect, as the Apostle declares (1 Cor. xiii). Therefore it seems that happiness consists in an act of the will.

Obj. 5. Further, Augustine says (*De Trin.* xiii. 5) that *happy is he who has whatever he desires, and desires nothing amiss.* And a little further on (6) he adds: *He is almost happy who desires well, whatever he desires: for good things make a man happy, and such a man already possesses some good—i.e., a good will.* Therefore happiness consists in an act of the will.

On the contrary, Our Lord said (Jo. xvii. 3): *This is eternal life: that they may know Thee, the only true God.* Now eternal life is the last end, as stated above (A. 2 ad 1). Therefore man's happiness consists in the knowledge of God, which is an act of the intellect.

I answer that, As stated above (Q. 2, A. 6) two things are needed for happiness: one, which is the essence of happiness: the other, that is, as it were, its proper accident, *i.e.,* the delight connected with it. I say, then, that as to the very essence of happiness, it is impossible for it to consist in an act of the will. For it is evident from what has been said (AA. 1, 2; Q. 2, A. 7) that happiness is the attainment of the last end. But the attainment of the end does not consist in the very act of the will. For the will is directed to the end, both absent, when it desires it; and present, when it is delighted by resting therein. Now it is evident that the desire itself of the end is not the attainment of the end, but is a movement towards the end: while delight comes to the will from the end being present; and not conversely, is a thing made present, by the fact that the will delights in it. Therefore, that the end be present to him who desires it, must be due to something else than an act of the will.

This is evidently the case in regard to sensible ends. For if the acquisition of money were through an act of the will, the covetous man would have it from the very moment that he wished for it. But at that moment it is far from him; and he attains it, by grasping it in his hand, or in some like manner; and then he delights in the money got. And so it is with an intelligible end. For at first we desire to attain an intelligible end; we attain it, through its being made present to us by an act of the intellect; and then the delighted will rests in the end when attained.

So, therefore, the essence of happiness consists in an act of the intellect: but the delight that results from happiness pertains to the will. In this sense Augustine says (*Conf.* x. 23) that happiness is *joy in truth,* because, to wit, joy itself is the consummation of happiness.

Reply Obj. 1. Peace pertains to man's last end, not as though it were the very essence of happiness; but because it is antecedent and consequent thereto: antecedent, in so far as all those things are removed which disturb and hinder man in attaining the last end: consequent, inasmuch as, when man has attained his last end, he remains at peace, his desire being at rest.

Reply Obj. 2. The will's first object is not its act: just as neither is the first object of the sight, vision, but a visible thing. Wherefore, from the very fact that happiness belongs to the will, as the will's first object, it follows that it does not belong to it as its act.

Reply Obj. 3. The intellect apprehends the end before the will does: yet motion towards the end begins in the will. And therefore to the will belongs that which last of all follows the attainment of the end, viz., delight or enjoyment.

Reply Obj. 4. Love ranks above knowledge in moving, but knowledge precedes love in attaining: *for naught is loved save what is known,* as Augustine says (*De Trin.* x. 1). Consequently we first attain an intelligible end by an act of the intellect; just as we first attain a sensible end by an act of sense.

Reply Obj. 5. He who has whatever he desires, is happy, because he has what he desires: and this indeed is by something other than the act of his will. But to desire nothing amiss is needed for happiness, as a necessary disposition thereto. And a good will is reckoned among the good things which make a man happy, forasmuch as it is an inclination of the will: just as a movement is reduced to the genus of its terminus, for instance, *alteration* to the genus *quality.*

FIFTH ARTICLE

WHETHER HAPPINESS IS AN OPERATION OF THE SPECULATIVE, OR OF THE PRACTICAL INTELLECT?

We proceed thus to the Fifth Article:—

Objection 1. It would seem that happiness is an operation of the practical intellect. For the end of every creature consists in becoming like God. But man is like God, by his practical intellect, which is the cause of things understood, rather than by his speculative intellect, which derives its knowledge from things. Therefore man's happiness consists in an operation of the practical intellect rather than of the speculative.

Obj. 2. Further, happiness is man's perfect good. But the practical intellect is ordained to the good rather than the speculative intellect, which is ordained to the true. Hence we are said to be good, in reference to the perfection of the practical intellect, but not in reference to the perfection of the speculative intellect, according to which we are said to be knowing or understanding. Therefore man's happiness consists in an act of the practical intellect rather than of the speculative.

Obj. 3. Further, happiness is a good of man himself. But the speculative intellect is more concerned with things outside man; whereas the practical intellect is concerned with things belonging to man himself, viz., his operations and passions. Therefore man's happiness consists in an operation of the practical intellect rather than of the speculative.

On the contrary, Augustine says (*De Trin.* i. 8) that *contemplation is promised us, as being the goal of all our actions, and the everlasting perfection of our joys.*

I answer that, Happiness consists in an operation of the speculative rather than of the practical intellect. This is evident for three reasons. First because if man's happiness is an operation, it must needs be man's highest operation. Now man's highest operation is that of his highest power in respect of its highest object: and his highest power is the intellect, whose highest object is the Divine Good, which is the object, not of the practical, but of the speculative intellect. Consequently happiness consists principally in such an operation, viz., in the contemplation of Divine things. And since that *seems to be each man's self, which is best in him,* according to *Ethic.* ix. 8, and x. 7, therefore such an operation is most proper to man and most delightful to him.

Secondly, it is evident from the fact that contemplation is sought principally for its own sake. But the act of the practical intellect is not sought for its own sake but for the sake of action: and these very actions are ordained to some end. Consequently it is evident that the last end cannot consist in the active life which pertains to the practical intellect.

Thirdly, it is again evident, from the fact that in the contemplative life man has something in common with things above him, viz., with God and the angels, to whom he is made like by happiness. But in things pertaining to the active life, other animals also have something in common with man, although imperfectly.

Therefore the last and perfect happiness, which we await in the life to come, consists entirely in contemplation. But imperfect happiness, such as can be had here, consists first and principally in contemplation, but secondarily, in an operation of the practical intellect directing human actions and passions, as stated in *Ethic.* x. 7, 8.

Reply Obj. 1. The asserted likeness of the practical intellect to God is one of proportion; that is to say, by reason of its standing in relation to what it knows, as God does to what He knows. But the likeness of the speculative intellect to God is one of union and *information;* which is a much greater likeness.—And yet it may be answered that, in regard to the principal thing known, which is His Essence, God has not practical but merely speculative knowledge.

Reply Obj. 2. The practical intellect is ordained to good which is outside of it: but the speculative intellect has good within it, viz., the contemplation of truth. And if this good be perfect, the whole man is perfected and made good thereby: such a good the practical intellect has not; but it directs man thereto.

Reply Obj. 3. This argument would hold, if man himself were his own last end; for then the consideration and direction of his actions and passions would be his happiness. But since man's last end is something outside of him, to wit, God, to Whom we reach out by an operation of the speculative intellect; therefore man's happiness consists in an operation of the speculative intellect rather than of the practical intellect.

* * *

EIGHTH ARTICLE

WHETHER MAN'S HAPPINESS CONSISTS IN THE VISION OF THE DIVINE ESSENCE?

We proceed thus to the Eighth Article:—

Objection 1. It would seem that man's happiness does not consist in the vision of the Divine Essence. For Dionysius says (*Myst. Theol.* i) that by that which is highest in his intellect, man is united to God as to something altogether unknown. But that which is seen in its essence is not altogether unknown. Therefore the final perfection of the intellect, namely, happiness, does not consist in God being seen in His Essence.

Obj. 2. Further, the higher perfection belongs to the higher nature. But to see His own Essence is the perfection proper to the Divine intellect. Therefore the final perfection of the human intellect does not reach to this, but consists in something less.

On the contrary, It is written (1 Jo. iii. 2): *When He shall appear, we shall be like to Him; and we shall see Him as He is.*

I answer that, Final and perfect happiness can consist in nothing else than the vision of the Divine Essence. To make this clear, two points must be observed. First, that man is not perfectly happy, so long as something remains for him to desire and seek: secondly, that the perfection of any power is determined by the nature of its object. Now the object of the intellect is *what a thing is, i.e.,* the essence of a thing, according to *De Anima* iii. 6. Wherefore the intellect attains perfection, in so far as it knows the essence of a thing. If therefore an intellect know the essence of some effect, whereby it is not possible to know the essence of the cause, *i.e.* to know of the cause *what it is;* that intellect cannot be said to reach that cause simply, although it may be able to gather from the effect the knowledge that the cause is. Consequently, when man knows an effect, and knows that it has a cause, there naturally remains in man the desire to know about that cause, *what it is.* And this desire is one of wonder, and causes inquiry, as is stated in the beginning of the *Metaphysics* (i. 2). For instance, if a man, knowing the eclipse of the sun, consider that it must be due to some cause, and know not what that cause is, he wonders about it, and from wondering proceeds to inquire. Nor does this inquiry cease until he arrive at a knowledge of the essence of the cause.

If therefore the human intellect, knowing the essence of some created effect, knows no more of God than *that He is;* the perfection of that intellect does not yet reach simply the First Cause, but there remains in it the natural desire to seek the cause. Wherefore it is not yet perfectly happy. Consequently, for perfect happiness the intellect needs to reach the very Essence of the First Cause. And thus it will have its perfection through union with God as with that object, in which alone man's happiness consists, as stated above (AA. 1, 7; Q. 2, A. 8).

Reply Obj. 1. Dionysius speaks of the knowledge of wayfarers journeying towards happiness.

Reply Obj. 2. As stated above (Q. 1, A. 8), the end has a twofold acceptation. First, as to the thing itself which is desired: and in this way, the same thing is the end of the higher and of the lower nature, and indeed of all things, as stated above *(ibid.).* Secondly, as to the attainment of this thing; and thus the end of the higher nature is different from that of the lower, according to their respective habitudes to that thing. So then the happiness of God, Who, in understanding his Essence, comprehends It, is higher than that of a man or angel who sees It indeed, but comprehends It not.

*   *   *

QUESTION 5: OF THE ATTAINMENT OF HAPPINESS

*   *   *

FIFTH ARTICLE

WHETHER MAN CAN ATTAIN HAPPINESS BY HIS NATURAL POWERS?

We proceed thus to the Fifth Article:—

Objection 1. It would seem that man can attain Happiness by his natural powers. For nature does not fail in necessary things. But nothing is so necessary to man as that by which he attains the last end. Therefore this is not lacking to human nature. Therefore man can attain Happiness by his natural powers.

Obj. 2. Further, since man is more noble than irrational creatures, it seems that he must be better equipped than they. But irrational creatures can attain their end by their natural powers. Much more therefore can man attain Happiness by his natural powers.

Obj. 3. Further, Happiness is a *perfect operation,* according to the Philosopher *(Ethic.* vii. 13). Now the beginning of a thing belongs to the same principle as the perfecting thereof. Since, therefore, the imperfect operation, which is as the beginning in human operations, is subject to man's natural power, whereby he is master of his own actions; it seems that he can attain to perfect operation, *i.e.,* Happiness, by his natural powers.

On the contrary, Man is naturally the principle of his action, by his intellect and will. But final Happiness prepared for the saints, surpasses the intellect and will of man; for the Apostle says (1 Cor. ii. 9): *Eye hath not seen, nor ear heard, neither hath it entered into the heart of man, what things God hath prepared for them that love Him.* Therefore man cannot attain Happiness by his natural powers.

I answer that, Imperfect happiness that can be had in this life, can be acquired by man by his natural powers, in the same way as virtue, in whose operation it consists: on this point we shall speak further on (Q. 63). But man's perfect Happiness, as stated above (Q. 3, A.8), consists in the vision of the Divine Essence. Now the vision of God's Essence surpasses the nature not only of man, but also of every creature, as was shown in the First Part (Q. 12, A. 4). For the natural knowledge of every creature is in keeping with the mode of his substance: thus it is said of the intelligence (*De Causis;* Prop. viii.) that *it knows things that are above it, and things that are below it, according to the mode of its substance.* But every knowledge that is according to the mode of created substance, falls short of the vision of the Divine Essence, which infinitely surpasses all created substance. Consequently neither man, nor any creature, can attain final Happiness by his natural powers.

Reply Obj. 1. Just as nature does not fail man in necessaries, although it has not provided him with weapons and clothing, as it provided other animals, because it gave him reason and hands, with which he is able to get these things for himself; so neither did it fail man in things necessary, although it gave him not the wherewithal to attain Happiness: since this it could not do. But it did give him freewill, with which he can turn to God, that He may make him happy. *For what we do by means of our friends, is done, in a sense, by ourselves* (*Ethic.* iii. 3).

Reply Obj. 2. The nature that can attain perfect good, although it needs help from without in order to attain it, is of more noble condition than a nature which cannot attain perfect good, but attains some imperfect good, although it need no help from without in order to attain it, as the Philosopher says (*De Cælo* ii. 12). Thus he is better disposed to health who can attain perfect health, albeit by means of medicine, than he who can attain but imperfect health, without the help of medicine. And therefore the rational creature, which can attain the perfect good of happiness, but needs the Divine assistance for the purpose, is more perfect than the irrational creature, which is not capable of attaining this good, but attains some imperfect good by its natural powers.

Reply Obj. 3. When imperfect and perfect are of the same species, they can be caused by the same power. But this does not follow of necessity, if they be of different species: for not everything, that can cause the disposition of matter, can produce the final perfection. Now the imperfect operation, which is subject to man's natural power, is not of the same species as that perfect operation which is man's happiness: since operation takes its species from its object. Consequently the argument does not prove.

*   *   *

QUESTION 10: OF THE MANNER IN WHICH THE WILL IS MOVED

*   *   *

SECOND ARTICLE

WHETHER THE WILL IS MOVED, OF NECESSITY, BY ITS OBJECT?

We proceed thus to the Second Article:—

Objection 1. It seems that the will is moved, of necessity, by its object. For the object of the will is compared to the will as mover to movable, as stated in *De Anima* iii. 10. But a mover, if it be sufficient, moves the movable of necessity Therefore the will can be moved of necessity by its object.

Obj. 2. Further, just as the will is an immaterial power, so is the intellect: and both powers are ordained to a universal object, as stated above (A. 1 *ad* 3). But the intellect is moved, of necessity, by its object: therefore the will also, by its object.

Obj. 3. Further, whatever one wills, is either the end, or something ordained to an end. But, seemingly, one wills an end necessarily: because it is like the principle in speculative matters, to which principle one assents of necessity. Now the end is the reason for willing the means; and so it seems that we will the means also necessarily. Therefore the will is moved of necessity by its object.

On the contrary, The rational powers, according to the Philosopher (*Metaph.* ix. 2) are directed to opposites. But the will is a rational power, since it is in the reason, as stated in *De Anima* iii. 9. Therefore the will is directed to opposites. Therefore it is not moved, of necessity, to either of the opposites.

I answer that, The will is moved in two ways: first, as to the exercise of its act; secondly, as to the specification of its act, derived from the object. As to the first way, no object moves the will necessarily, for no matter what the object be, it is in man's power not to think of it, and consequently not to will it actually. But as to the second manner of motion, the will is moved by one object necessarily, by another not. For in the movement of a power by its object, we must consider under what aspect the object moves the power. For the visible moves the sight, under the aspect of color actually visible. Wherefore if color be offered to the sight, it moves the sight necessarily: unless one turns one's eyes away; which belongs to the exercise of the act. But if the sight were confronted with something not in all respects colored actually, but only so in some respects, and in other respects not, the sight would not of necessity see such an object: for it might look at that part of the object which is not actually colored, and thus it would not see it. Now just as the actually colored is the object of sight, so is good the object of the will. Wherefore if the will be offered an object which is good universally and from every point of view, the will tends to it of necessity, if it wills anything at all; since it cannot will the opposite. If, on the other hand, the will is offered an object that is not good from every point of view, it will not tend to it of necessity. And since lack of any good whatever, is a non-good, consequently, that good alone which is perfect and lacking in nothing, is such a good that the will cannot not-will it: and this is Happiness. Whereas any other particular goods, in so far as they are lacking in some good, can be regarded as non-goods: and from this point of view, they can be set aside or approved by the will, which can tend to one and the same thing from various points of view.

Reply Obj. 1. The sufficient mover of a power is none but that object that in every respect presents the aspect of the mover of that power. If, on the other hand, it is lacking in any respect, it will not move of necessity, as stated above.

Reply Obj. 2. The intellect is moved, of necessity, by an object, which is such as to be always and necessarily true: but not by that which may be either true or false—viz., by that which is contingent: as we have said of the good.

Reply Obj. 3. The last end moves the will necessarily, because it is the perfect good. In like manner whatever is ordained to that end, and without which the end cannot be attained, such as *to be* and *to live,* and the like. But other things without which the end can be gained, are not necessarily willed by one who wills the end: just as he who assents to the principle, does not necessarily assent to the conclusions, without which the principles can still be true.

*   *   *

QUESTION 13: OF CHOICE, WHICH IS AN ACT OF THE WILL WITH REGARD TO THE MEANS

*   *   *

SIXTH ARTICLE

WHETHER MAN CHOOSES OF NECESSITY OR FREELY?

We proceed thus to the Sixth Article:—

Objection 1. It would seem that man chooses of necessity. For the end stands in relation to the object of choice, as the principle of that which follows from the principles, as declared in *Ethic.* vii. 8. But conclusions follow of necessity from their principles. Therefore man is moved of necessity from (willing) the end to the choice (of the means).

Obj. 2. Further, as stated above (A. 1 ad 2), choice follows the reason's judgment of what is to be done. But reason judges of necessity about some things: on account of the necessity of the premises. Therefore it seems that choice also follows of necessity.

Obj. 3. Further, if two things are absolutely equal, man is not moved to one more than to the other; thus if a hungry man, as Plato says (cf. *De Cælo* ii. 13), be confronted on either side with two portions of food equally appetizing and at an equal distance, he is not moved towards one more than to the other; and he finds the reason of this in the immobility of the earth in the middle of the world. Now, if that which is equally (eligible) with something else cannot be chosen, much less can that be chosen which appears as less (eligible). Therefore if two or more things are available, of which one appears to be more (eligible), it is impossible to choose any of the others. Therefore that which appears to hold the first place is chosen of necessity. But every act of choosing is in regard to something that seems in some way better. Therefore every choice is made necessarily.

On the contrary, Choice is an act of a rational power; which according to the Philosopher (*Metaph.* ix. 2) stands in relation to opposites.

I answer that, Man does not choose of necessity. And this is because that which is possible not to be, is not of necessity. Now the reason why it is possible not to choose, or to choose, may be gathered from a twofold power in man. For man can will and not will, act and not act; again, he can will this or that, and do this or that. The reason of this is seated in the very power of the reason. For the will can tend to whatever the reason can apprehend as good. Now the reason can apprehend as good, not only this, viz., *to will or to act,* but also this, viz., *not to will* or *not to act.* Again, in all particular goods, the reason can consider an aspect of some good, and the lack of some good, which has the aspect of evil: and in this respect, it can apprehend any single one of such goods as to be chosen or to be avoided. The perfect good alone, which is Happiness, cannot be apprehended by the reason as an evil, or as lacking in any way. Consequently man wills Happiness of necessity, nor can he will not to be happy, or to be unhappy. Now since choice is not of the end, but of the means, as stated above (A. 3); it is not of the perfect good, which is Happiness, but of other particular goods. Therefore man chooses not of necessity, but freely.

Reply Obj. 1. The conclusion does not always of necessity follow from the principles, but only when the principles cannot be true if the conclusion is not true. In like manner, the end does not always necessitate in man the choosing of the means, because the means are not always such that the end cannot be gained without them; or, if they be such, they are not always considered in that light.

Reply Obj. 2. The reason's decision or judgment of what is to be done is about things that are contingent and possible to us. In such matters the conclusions do not follow of necessity from principles that are absolutely necessary but from such as are so conditionally; as, for instance, *If he runs, he is in motion.*

Reply Obj. 3. If two things be proposed as equal under one aspect, nothing hinders us from considering in one of them some particular point of superiority, so that the will has a bent towards that one rather than towards the other.

* * *

Treatise on Habits

QUESTION 61: OF THE CARDINAL VIRTUES

* * *

FIRST ARTICLE

WHETHER THE MORAL VIRTUES SHOULD BE CALLED CARDINAL OR PRINCIPAL VIRTUES?

We proceed thus to the First Article:—

Objection 1. It would seem that moral virtues should not be called cardinal or principal virtues. For *the opposite members of a division are by nature simultaneous* (Categor. x), so that one is not principal rather than another. Now all the virtues are opposite members of the division of the genus *virtue.* Therefore none of them should be called principal.

Obj. 2. Further, the end is principal as compared to the means. But the theological virtues are about the end; while the moral virtues are about the means. Therefore the theological virtues, rather than the moral virtues, should be called principal or cardinal.

Obj. 3. Further, that which is essentially so is principal in comparison with that which is so by participation. But the intellectual virtues belong to that which is essentially rational: whereas the moral virtues belong to that which is rational by participation, as stated above (Q. 58, A. 3). Therefore the intellectual virtues are principal, rather than the moral virtues.

On the contrary, Ambrose in explaining the words, *Blessed are the poor in spirit* (Luke vi. 20) says: *We know that there are four cardinal virtues, viz., temperance, justice, prudence, and fortitude.* But these are moral virtues. Therefore the moral virtues are cardinal virtues.

I answer that, When we speak of virtue simply, we are understood to speak of human virtue. Now human virtue, as stated above (Q. 56, A. 3), is one that answers to the perfect idea of virtue, which requires rectitude of the appetite: for such like virtue not only confers the faculty of doing well, but also causes the good deed done. On the other hand, the name virtue is applied to one that answers imperfectly to the idea of virtue, and does not require rectitude of the appetite: because it merely confers the faculty of doing well without causing the good deed to be done. Now it is evident that the perfect is principal as compared to the imperfect: and so those virtues which imply rectitude of the appetite are called principal virtues. Such are the moral virtues, and prudence alone, of the intellectual virtues, for it is also something of a moral virtue, as was clearly shown above (Q. 57, A. 4). Consequently, those virtues which are called principal or cardinal are fittingly placed among the moral virtues.

Reply Obj. 1. When a univocal genus is divided into its species, the members of the division are on a par in the point of the generic idea; although considered in their nature as things, one species may surpass another in rank and perfection, as man in respect of other animals. But when we divide an analogous term, which is applied to several things, but to one before it is applied to another, nothing hinders one from ranking before another even in the point of the generic idea; as the notion of being is applied to substance principally in relation to accident. Such is the division of virtue into the various kinds of virtue: since the good defined by reason is not found in the same way in all things.

Reply Obj. 2. The theological virtues are above man, as stated above (Q. 58, A. 3 ad 3). Hence they should properly be called not human, but *super-human* or godlike virtues.

Reply Obj. 3. Although the intellectual virtues, except in prudence, rank before the moral virtues, in the point of their subject, they do not rank before them as virtues; for a virtue, as such, regards good, which is the object of the appetite.

SECOND ARTICLE

WHETHER THERE ARE FOUR CARDINAL VIRTUES?

We proceed thus to the Second Article:—

Objection 1. It would seem that there are not four cardinal virtues. For prudence is the directing principle of the other moral virtues, as is clear from what has been said above (Q. 58, A. 4). But that which directs other things ranks before them. Therefore prudence alone is a principal virtue.

Obj. 2. Further, the principal virtues are, in a way, moral virtues. Now we are directed to moral works both by the practical reason, and by a right appetite, as stated in *Ethic.* vi. 2. Therefore there are only two cardinal virtues.

Obj. 3. Further, even among the other virtues one ranks higher than another. But in order that a virtue be principal, it needs not to rank above all the others, but above some. Therefore it seems that there are many more principal virtues.

On the contrary, Gregory says (*Moral.* ii): *The entire structure of good works is built on four virtues.*

I answer that, Things may be numbered either in respect of their formal principles, or according to the subjects in which they are: and either way we find that there are four cardinal virtues.

For the formal principle of the virtue of which we speak now is good as defined by reason; which good can be considered in two ways. First, as existing in the very act of reason: and thus we have one principal virtue, called *Prudence.*—Secondly, according as the reason puts its order into something else; either into operations, and then we have *Justice;* or into passions, and then we need two virtues. For the need of putting the order of reason into the passions is due to their thwarting reason: and this occurs in two ways. First, by the passions inciting to something against reason; and then the passions need a curb, which we call *Temperance.* Secondly, by the passions withdrawing us from following the dictate of reason, e.g., through fear of danger or toil: and then man needs to be strengthened for that which reason dictates, lest he turn back; and to this end there is *Fortitude.*

In like manner, we find the same number if we consider the subjects of virtue. For there are four subjects of the virtue we speak of now: viz., the power which is rational in its essence, and this is perfected by *Prudence;* and that which is rational by participation, and is threefold, the will, subject of *Justice,* the concupiscible faculty, subject of *Temperance,* and the irascible faculty, subject of *Fortitude.*

Reply Obj. 1. Prudence is the principal of all virtues simply. The others are principal, each in its own genus.

Reply Obj. 2. That part of the soul which is rational by participation is threefold, as stated above.

Reply Obj. 3. All the other virtues among which one ranks before another, are reducible to the above four, both as to the subject and as to the formal principle.

* * *

QUESTION 62: OF THE THEOLOGICAL VIRTUES

* * *

FIRST ARTICLE

WHETHER THERE ARE ANY THEOLOGICAL VIRTUES?

We proceed thus to the First Article:—

Objection 1. It would seem that there are not any theological virtues. For according to *Phys.* vii., text. 17, virtue is the disposition of a perfect thing to that which is best: and by perfect, I mean that which is disposed according to nature. But that which is Divine is above man's nature. Therefore the theological virtues are not virtues of a man.

Obj. 2. Further, theological virtues are quasi-Divine virtues. But the Divine virtues are exemplars, as stated above (Q. 61, A. 5), which are not in us but in God. Therefore the theological virtues are not virtues of man.

Obj. 3. Further, the theological virtues are so called because they direct us to God, Who is the first beginning and last end of all things. But by the very nature of his reason and will, man is directed to his first beginning and last end. Therefore there is no need for any habits of theological virtue, to direct the reason and will to God.

On the contrary, The precepts of the Law are about acts of virtue. Now the Divine Law contains precepts about the acts of faith, hope, and charity: for it is written (*Ecclus.* ii. 8, *seqq.*): *Ye that fear the Lord believe Him,* and again, *hope in Him,* and again, *love Him.* Therefore faith, hope, and charity are virtues directing us to God. Therefore they are theological virtues.

I answer that, Man is perfected by virtue, for those actions whereby he is directed to happiness, as was explained above (Q. 5, A. 7). Now man's happiness is twofold, as was also stated above (*ibid.,* A. 5). One is proportionate to human nature, a happiness, to wit, which man can obtain by means of his natural principles. The other is a happiness surpassing man's nature, and which man can obtain by the power of God alone, by a kind of participation of the Godhead, about which it is written (2 Pet. i. 4) that by Christ we are made *partakers of the Divine nature.* And because such happiness surpasses the capacity of human nature, man's natural principles which enable him to act well according to his capacity, do not suffice to direct man to this same happiness. Hence it is necessary for man to receive from God some additional principles, whereby he may be directed to supernatural happiness, even as he is directed to his connatural end, by means of his natural principles, albeit not without the Divine assistance. Such like principles are called *theological virtues:* first, because their object is God, inasmuch as they direct us aright to God: secondly, because they are infused in us by God alone: thirdly, because these virtues are not made known to us, save by Divine revelation, contained in Holy Writ.

Reply Obj. 1. A certain nature may be ascribed to a certain thing in two ways. First, essentially: and thus these theological virtues surpass the nature of man. Secondly, by participation, as kindled wood partakes of the nature of fire: and thus, after a fashion, man becomes a partaker of the Divine Nature, as stated above: so that these virtues are proportionate to man in respect of the Nature of which he is made a partaker.

Reply Obj. 2. These virtues are called Divine, not as though God were virtuous by reason of them, but because of them God makes us virtuous, and directs us to Himself. Hence they are not exemplar but exemplate virtues.

Reply Obj. 3. The reason and will are naturally directed to God, inasmuch as He is the beginning and end of nature, but in proportion to nature. But the reason and will, according to their nature, are not sufficiently directed to Him in so far as He is the object of supernatural happiness.

SECOND ARTICLE

WHETHER THE THEOLOGICAL VIRTUES ARE DISTINCT FROM THE INTELLECTUAL AND MORAL VIRTUES?

We proceed thus to the Second Article:—

Objection 1. It would seem that the theological virtues are not distinct from the moral and intellectual virtues. For the theological virtues, if they be in a human soul, must needs perfect it, either as to the intellective, or as to the appetitive part. Now the virtues which perfect the intellective part are called intellectual; and the virtues which perfect the appetitive part, are called moral. Therefore, the theological virtues are not distinct from the moral and intellectual virtues.

Obj. 2. Further, the theological virtues are those which direct us to God. Now, among the intellectual virtues there is one which directs us to God: this is wisdom, which is about Divine things, since it considers the highest cause. Therefore the theological virtues are not distinct from the intellectual virtues.

Obj. 3. Further, Augustine (*De Moribus Eccl.* xv) shows how the four cardinal virtues are the order of love. Now love is charity, which is a theological virtue. Therefore the moral virtues are not distinct from the theological.

On the contrary, That which is above man's nature is distinct from that which is according to his nature. But the theological virtues are above man's nature; while the intellectual and moral virtues are in proportion to his nature, as clearly shown above (Q. 58, A. 3). Therefore they are distinct from one another.

I answer that, As stated above (Q. 54, A. 2 *ad* 1), habits are specifically distinct from one another in respect of the formal difference of their objects. Now the object of the theological virtues is God Himself, Who is the last end of all, as surpassing the knowledge of our reason. On the other hand, the object of the intellectual and moral virtues is something comprehensible to human reason. Wherefore the theological virtues are specifically distinct from the moral and intellectual virtues.

Reply Obj. 1. The intellectual and moral virtues perfect man's intellect and appetite according to the capacity of human nature; the theological virtues, supernaturally.

Reply Obj. 2. The wisdom which the Philosopher (*Ethic.* vi. 3, 7) reckons as an intellectual virtue, considers Divine things so far as they are open to the research of human reason. Theological virtue, on the other hand, is about those same things so far as they surpass human reason.

Reply Obj. 3. Though charity is love, yet love is not always charity. When, then, it is stated that every virtue is the order of love, this can be understood either of love in the general sense, or of the love of charity. If it be understood of love, commonly so called, then each virtue is stated to be the order of love, in so far as each cardinal virtue requires ordinate emotions; and love is the root and cause of every emotion, as stated above (Q. 27, A. 4; Q. 28, A. 6 *ad* 2; Q. 41, A. 2 *ad* 1).—If, however, it be understood of the love of charity, it does not mean that every other virtue is charity essentially: but that all other virtues depend on charity in some way, as we shall show further on (Q. 65, AA. 2, 4; II–II, Q. 23, A. 7).

THIRD ARTICLE

WHETHER FAITH, HOPE, AND CHARITY ARE FITTINGLY RECKONED AS THEOLOGICAL VIRTUES?

We proceed thus to the Third Article:—

Objection 1. It would seem that faith, hope, and charity are not fittingly reckoned as three theological virtues. For the theological virtues are in relation to Divine happiness, what the natural inclination is in relation to the connatural end. Now among the virtues directed to the connatural end there is but one natural virtue, viz., the understanding of principles. Therefore there should be but one theological virtue.

Obj. 2. Further, the theological virtues are more perfect than the intellectual and moral virtues. Now faith is not reckoned among the intellectual virtues, but is something less than a virtue, since it is imperfect knowledge. Likewise hope is not reckoned among the moral virtues, but is something less than a virtue, since it is a passion. Much less therefore should they be reckoned as theological virtues.

Obj. 3. Further, the theological virtues direct man's soul to God. Now man's soul cannot be directed to God, save through the intellective part, wherein are the intellect and will. Therefore there should be only two theological virtues, one perfecting the intellect, the other, the will.

On the contrary, The Apostle says (1 Cor. xiii. 13): *Now there remain faith, hope, charity, these three.*

I answer that, As stated above (A. 1), the theological virtues direct man to supernatural happiness in the same way as by the natural inclination man is directed to his connatural end. Now the latter happens in respect of two things. First, in respect of the reason or intellect, in so far as it contains the first universal principles which are known to us by the natural light of the intellect, and which are reason's starting-point, both in speculative and in practical matters. Secondly, through the rectitude of the will which tends naturally to good as defined by reason.

But these two fall short of the order of supernatural happiness, according to 1 Cor. ii. 9: *The eye hath not seen, nor ear heard, neither hath it entered into the heart of man, what things God hath prepared for them that love Him.* Consequently in respect of both the above things man needed to receive in addition something supernatural to direct him to a supernatural end. First, as regards the intellect, man receives certain supernatural principles, which are held by means of a Divine light: these are the articles of faith, about which is faith.—Secondly, the will is directed to this end, both as to the movement of intention, which tends to that end as something attainable,—and this pertains to hope,—and as to a certain spiritual union, whereby the will is so to speak, transformed into that end,—and this belongs to charity. For the appetite of a thing is moved and tends towards its connatural end naturally; and this movement is due to a certain conformity of the thing with its end.

Reply Obj. 1. The intellect requires intelligible species whereby to understand: consequently there is need of a natural habit in addition to the power. But the very nature of the will suffices for it to be directed naturally to the end, both as to the intention of the end and as to its conformity with the end. But the nature of the power is insufficient in either of these respects, for the will to be directed to things that are above its nature. Consequently there was need for an additional supernatural habit in both respects.

Reply Obj. 2. Faith and hope imply a certain imperfection: since faith is of things unseen, and hope, of things not possessed. Hence faith and hope, in things that are subject to human power, fall short of the notion of virtue. But faith and hope in things which are above the capacity of human nature surpass all virtue that is in proportion to man, according to 1 Cor. i. 25: *The weakness of God is stronger than men.*

Reply Obj. 3. Two things pertain to the appetite, viz., movement to the end, and conformity with the end by means of love. Hence there must needs be two theological virtues in the human appetite, namely, hope and charity.

* * *

Treatise on Law

QUESTION 94: OF THE NATURAL LAW

* * *

SECOND ARTICLE

WHETHER THE NATURAL LAW CONTAINS SEVERAL PRECEPTS, OR ONE ONLY?

We proceed thus to the Second Article:—

Objection 1. It would seem that the natural law contains, not several precepts, but one only. For law is a kind of precept, as stated above (Q. 92, A. 2). If therefore there were many precepts of the natural law, it would follow that there are also many natural laws.

Obj. 2. Further, the natural law is consequent to human nature. But human nature, as a whole, is one; though, as to its parts, it is manifold. Therefore, either there is but one precept of the law of nature, on account of the unity of nature as a whole; or there are many, by reason of the number of parts of human nature. The result would be that even things relating to the inclination of the concupiscible faculty belong to the natural law.

Obj. 3. Further, law is something pertaining to reason, as stated above (Q. 90, A. 1). Now reason is but one in man. Therefore there is only one precept of the natural law.

On the contrary, The precepts of the natural law in man stand in relation to practical matters, as the first principles to matters of demonstration. But there are several first indemonstrable principles. Therefore there are also several precepts of the natural law.

I answer that, As stated above (Q. 91, A. 3), the precepts of the natural law are to the practical reason, what the first principles of demonstrations are to the speculative reason; because both are self-evident principles. Now a thing is said to be self-evident in two ways: first, in itself; secondly, in relation to us. Any proposition is said to be self-evident in itself, its predicate is contained in the notion of the subject: although, to one who knows not the definition of the subject, it happens that such a proposition is not self-evident. For instance, this proposition, *Man is a rational being,* is, in its very nature, self-evident, since who says *man,* says *a rational being:* and yet to one who knows not what a man is, this proposition is not self-evident. Hence it is that, as Boethius says *(De Hebdom.),* certain axioms or propositions are universally self-evident to all; and such are those propositions whose terms are known to all, as, *Every whole is greater than its part,* and, *Things equal to one and the same are equal to one another.* But some propositions are self-evident only to the wise, who understand the meaning of the terms of such propositions: thus to one who understands that an angel is not a body, it is self-evident that an angel is not circumscriptively in a place: but this is not evident to the unlearned, for they cannot grasp it.

Now a certain order is to be found in those things that are apprehended universally. For that which, before aught else, falls under apprehension, is *being,* the notion of which is included in all things whatsoever a man apprehends. Wherefore the first indemonstrable principle is that *the same thing cannot be affirmed and denied at the same time,* which is based on the notion of being and not-being: and on this principle all others are based, as is stated in *Metaph.* iv, text. 9. Now as being is the first thing that falls under the apprehension simply, so *good* is the first thing that falls under the apprehension of the practical reason, which is directed to action: since every agent acts for an end under the aspect of good. Consequently the first principle in the practical reason is one founded on the notion of good, viz., that *good is that which all things seek after.* Hence this is the first precept of law, that *good is to be done and pursued, and evil is to be avoided.* All other precepts of the natural law are based upon this: so that whatever the practical reason naturally apprehends as man's good (or evil) belongs to the precepts of the natural law as something to be done or avoided.

Since, however, good has the nature of an end, and evil, the nature of a contrary, hence it is that all those things to which man has a natural inclination, are naturally apprehended by reason as being good, and consequently as objects of pursuit, and their contraries as evil, and objects of avoidance. Wherefore according to the order of natural inclinations, is the order of the precepts of the natural law. Because in man there is first of all an inclination to good in accordance with the nature which he has in common with all substances: inasmuch as every substance seeks the preservation of its own being, according to its nature: and by reason of this inclination, whatever is a means of preserving human life, and of warding off its obstacles, belongs to the natural law. Secondly, there is in man an inclination to things that pertain to him more specially, according to that nature which he has in common with other animals: and in virtue of this inclination, those things are said to belong to the natural law, *which nature has taught to all animals,* such as sexual intercourse, education of offspring and so forth. Thirdly, there is in man an inclination to good, according to the nature of his reason, which nature is proper to him: thus man has a natural inclination to know the truth about God, and to live in society: and in this respect, whatever pertains to this inclination belongs to the natural law; for instance, to shun ignorance, to avoid offending those among whom one has to live, and other such things regarding the above inclination.

Reply Obj. 1. All these precepts of the law of nature have the character of one natural law, inasmuch as they flow from one first precept.

Reply Obj. 2. All the inclinations of any parts whatsoever of human nature, *e.g.,* of the concupiscible and irascible parts, in so far as they are ruled by reason, belong to the natural law, and are reduced to one first precept, as stated above: so that the precepts of the natural law are many in themselves, but are based on one common foundation.

Reply Obj. 3. Although reason is one in itself, yet it directs all things regarding man; so that whatever can be ruled by reason, is contained under the law of reason.

*   *   *

FOURTH ARTICLE

WHETHER THE NATURAL LAW IS THE SAME IN ALL MEN?

We proceed thus to the Fourth Article:—

Objection 1. It would seem that the natural law is not the same in all. For it is stated in the Decretals (*Dist.* i) that *the natural law is that which is contained in the Law and the Gospel.* But this is not common to all men; because, as it is written (Rom. x. 16), *all do not obey the gospel.* Therefore the natural law is not the same in all men.

Obj. 2. Further, *Things which are accordingly to the law are said to be just,* as stated in *Ethic.* v. But it is stated in the same book that nothing is so universally just as not to be subject to change in regard to some men. Therefore even the natural law is not the same in all men.

Obj. 3. Further, as stated above (AA. 2, 3), to the natural law belongs everything to which a man is inclined according to his nature. Now different men are naturally inclined to different things; some to the desire of pleasures, others to the desire of honors, and other men to other things. Therefore there is not one natural law for all.

On the contrary, Isidore says (*Etym.* v. 4): *The natural law is common to all nations.*

I answer that, As stated above (AA. 2, 3), to the natural law belongs those things to which a man is inclined naturally: and among these it is proper to man to be inclined to act according to reason. Now the process of reason is from the common to the proper, as stated in *Phys.* i. The speculative reason, however, is differently situated in this matter, from the practical reason. For, since the speculative reason is busied chiefly with necessary things, which cannot be otherwise than they are, its proper conclusions, like the universal principles, contain the truth without fail. The practical reason, on the other hand, is busied with contingent matters, about which human actions are concerned: and consequently, although there is necessity in the general principles, the more we descend to matters of detail, the more frequently we encounter defects. Accordingly then in speculative matters truth is the same in all men, both as to principles and as to conclusions: although the truth is not known to all as regards the conclusions, but only as regards the principles which are called common notions. But in matters of action, truth or practical rectitude is not the same for all, as to matters of detail, but only as to the general principles: and where there is the same rectitude in matters of detail, it is not equally known to all.

It is therefore evident that, as regards the general principles whether of speculative or of practical reason, truth or rectitude is the same for all, and is equally known by all. As to the proper conclusions of the speculative reason, the truth is the same for all, but is not equally known to all: thus it is true for all that the three angles of a triangle are together equal to two right angles, although it is not known to all. But as to the proper conclusions of the practical reason, neither is the truth or rectitude the same for all, nor, where it is the same, is it equally known by all. Thus it is right and true for all to act according to reason: and from this principle it follows as a proper conclusion, that goods entrusted to another should be restored to their owner. Now this is true for the majority of cases: but it may happen in a particular case that it would be injurious, and therefore unreasonable, to restore goods held in trust; for instance if they are claimed for the purpose of fighting against one's country. And this principle will be found to fail the more, according as we descend further into detail, e.g., if one were to say that goods held in trust should be restored with such and such a guarantee, or in such and such a way; because the greater the number of conditions added, the greater the number of ways in which the principle may fail, so that it be not right to restore or not to restore.

Consequently we must say that the natural law, as to general principles, is the same for all, both as to rectitude and as to knowledge. But as to certain matters of detail, which are conclusions, as it were, of those general principles, it is the same for all in the majority of cases, both as to rectitude and as to knowledge; and yet in some few cases it may fail, both as to rectitude, by reason of certain obstacles (just as natures subject to generation and corruption fail in some few cases on account of some obstacle), and as to knowledge, since in some the reason is perverted by passion, or evil habit, or an evil disposition of nature; thus formerly, theft, although it is expressly contrary to the natural law, was not considered wrong among the Germans, as Julius Caesar relates (*De Bello Gall.* vi).

Reply Obj. 1. The meaning of the sentence quoted is not that whatever is contained in the Law and the Gospel belongs to the natural law, since they contain many things that are above nature; but that whatever belongs to the natural law is fully contained in them. Wherefore Gratian, after saying that *the natural law is what is contained in the Law and the Gospel*, adds at once, by way of example, *by which everyone is commanded to do to others as he would be done by.*

Reply Obj. 2. The saying of the Philosopher is to be understood of things that are naturally just, not as general principles, but as conclusions drawn from them, having rectitude in the majority of cases, but failing in a few.

Reply Obj. 3. As, in man, reason rules and commands the other powers, so all the natural inclinations belonging to the other powers must needs be directed according to reason. Wherefore it is universally right for all men, that all their inclinations should be directed according to reason.

FIFTH ARTICLE

WHETHER THE NATURAL LAW CAN BE CHANGED?

We proceed thus to the Fifth Article:—

Objection 1. It would seem that the natural law can be changed. Because on Ecclus. xvii. 9, *He gave them instructions, and the law of life,* the gloss says: *He wished the law of the letter to be written, in order to correct the law of nature.* But that which is corrected is changed. Therefore the natural law can be changed.

Obj. 2. Further, the slaying of the innocent, adultery, and theft are against the natural law. But we find these things changed by God: as when God commanded Abraham to slay his innocent son (Gen. xxii. 2); and when he ordered the Jews to borrow and purloin the vessels of the Egyptians (Exod. xii. 35); and when He commanded Osee to take to himself *a wife of fornications* (Osee i. 2). Therefore the natural law can be changed.

Obj. 3. Further, Isidore says (*Etym.* v. 4) that *the possession of all things in common, and universal freedom, are matters of natural law.* But these things are seen to be changed by human laws. Therefore it seems that the natural law is subject to change.

On the contrary, It is said in the Decretals (*Dist.* v): *The natural law dates from the creation of the rational creature. It does not vary according to time, but remains unchangeable.*

I answer that, A change in the natural law may be understood in two ways. First, by way of addition. In this sense nothing hinders the natural law from being changed: since many things for the benefit of human life have been added over and above the natural law, both by the Divine law and by human laws.

Secondly, a change in the natural law may be understood by way of subtraction, so that what previously was according to the natural law, ceases to be so. In this sense, the natural law is altogether unchangeable in its first principles: but in its secondary principles, which, as we have said (A. 4), are certain detailed proximate conclusions drawn from the first principles, the natural law is not changed so that what it prescribes be not right in most cases. But it may be changed in some particular cases of rare occurrence, through some special causes hindering the observance of such precepts, as stated above (A. 4).

Reply Obj. 1. The written law is said to be given for the correction of the natural law, either because it supplies what was wanting to the natural law; or because the natural law was perverted in the hearts of some men, as to certain matters, so that they esteemed those things good which are naturally evil; which perversion stood in need of correction.

Reply Obj. 2. All men alike, both guilty and innocent, die the death of nature: which death of nature is inflicted by the power of God on account of original sin, according to 1 Kings ii. 6: *The Lord killeth and maketh alive.* Consequently, by the command of God, death can be inflicted on any man, guilty or innocent, without any injustice whatever.—In like manner adultery is intercourse with another's wife; who is allotted to him by the law emanating from God. Consequently intercourse with any woman, by the command of God, is neither adultery nor fornication.—The same applies to theft, which is the taking of another's property. For whatever is taken by the command of God, to Whom all things belong, is not taken against the will of its owner, whereas it is in this that theft consists.—Nor is it only in human things, that whatever is commanded by God is right; but also in natural things, whatever is done by God, is, in some way, natural, as stated in the First Part (Q. 105, A. 6 *ad* 1).

Reply Obj. 3. A thing is said to belong to the natural law in two ways. First, because nature inclines thereto: *e.g.,* that one should not do harm to another. Secondly, because nature did not bring in the contrary: thus we might say that for man to be naked is of the natural law, because nature did not give him clothes, but art invented them. In this sense, *the possession of all things in common and universal freedom* are said to be of the natural law, because, to wit, the distinction of possessions and slavery were not brought in by nature, but devised by human reason for the benefit of human life. Accordingly the law of nature was not changed in this respect, except by addition.

*   *   *

QUESTION 95: OF HUMAN LAW

*   *   *

FIRST ARTICLE

WHETHER IT WAS USEFUL FOR LAWS TO BE FRAMED BY MEN?

We proceed thus to the First Article:—

Objection 1. It would seem that it was not useful for laws to be framed by men. Because the purpose of every law is that man be made good thereby, as stated above (Q. 92, A. 1). But men are more to be induced to be good willingly by means of admonitions, than against their will, by means of laws. Therefore there was no need to frame laws.

Obj. 2. Further, as the Philosopher says (*Ethic.* v. 4), *men have recourse to a judge as to animate justice.* But animate justice is better than inanimate justice, which is contained in laws. Therefore it would have been better for the execution of justice to be entrusted to the decision of judges, than to frame laws in addition.

Obj. 3. Further, every law is framed for the direction of human actions, as is evident from what has been stated above (Q. 90, AA. 1, 2). But since human actions are about singulars, which are infinite in number, matters pertaining to the direction of human actions cannot be taken into sufficient consideration except by a wise man, who looks into each one of them. Therefore it would have been better for human acts to be directed by the judgment of wise men, than by the framing of laws. Therefore there was no need of human laws.

On the contrary, Isidore says (*Etym.* v. 20): *Laws were made that in fear thereof human audacity might be held in check, that innocence might be safeguarded in the midst of wickedness, and that the dread of punishment might prevent the wicked from doing harm.* But these things are most necessary to mankind. Therefore it was necessary that human laws should be made.

I answer that, As stated above (Q. 63, A. 1; Q. 94, A. 3), man has a natural aptitude for virtue; but the perfection of virtue must be acquired by man by means of some kind of training. Thus we observe that man is helped by industry in his necessities, for instance, in food and clothing. Certain beginnings of these he has from nature, viz., his reason and his hands; but he has not the full complement, as other animals have, to whom nature has given sufficiency of clothing and food. Now it is difficult to see how man could suffice for himself in the matter of this training: since the perfection of virtue consists chiefly in withdrawing man from undue pleasures, to which above all man is inclined, and especially the young, who are more capable of being trained. Consequently a man needs to receive this training from another, whereby to arrive at the perfection of virtue. And as to those young people who are inclined to acts of virtue, by their good natural disposition, or by custom, or rather by the gift of God, paternal training suffices, which is by admonitions. But since some are found to be depraved, and prone to vice, and not easily amenable to words, it was necessary for such to be restrained from evil by force and fear, in order that, at least, they might desist from evildoing, and leave others in peace, and that they themselves, by being habituated in this way, might be brought to do willingly what hitherto they did from fear, and thus become virtuous. Now this kind of training, which compels through fear of punishment, is the discipline of laws. Therefore, in order that man might have peace and virtue, it was necessary for laws to be framed: for, as the Philosopher says (Polit. i. 2), *as man is the most noble of animals if he be perfect in virtue, so is he the lowest of all, if he be severed*

Three Orders of Society, from *L'image du monde,* Franco-Flemish, late thirteenth century. This detail from an illustrated manuscript page shows the hierarchy of medieval society with monk, knight, and peasant. *(British Museum)*

from law and righteousness; because man can use his reason to devise means of satisfying his lusts and evil passions, which other animals are unable to do.

Reply Obj. 1. Men who are well disposed are led willingly to virtue by being admonished better than by coercion: but men who are evilly disposed are not led to virtue unless they are compelled.

Reply Obj. 2. As the Philosopher says (*Rhet.* i. 1), *it is better that all things be regulated by law, than left to be decided by judges:* and this for three reasons. First, because it is easier to find a few wise men competent to frame right laws, than to find the many who would be necessary to judge aright of each single case.—Secondly, because those who make laws consider long beforehand what laws to make; whereas judgment on each single case has to be pronounced as soon as it arises: and it is easier for man to see what is right, by taking many instances into consideration, than by considering one solitary fact.—Thirdly, because lawgivers judge in the abstract and of future events; whereas those who sit in judgment judge of things present, towards which they are affected by love, hatred, or some kind of cupidity; wherefore their judgment is perverted.

Since then the animated justice of the judge is not found in every man, and since it can be deflected, therefore it was necessary, whenever possible, for the law to determine how to judge, and for very few matters to be left to the decision of men.

Reply Obj. 3. Certain individual facts which cannot be covered by the law *have necessarily to be committed to judges,* as the Philosopher says in the same passage: for instance, *concerning something that has happened or not happened,* and the like.

SECOND ARTICLE

WHETHER EVERY HUMAN LAW IS DERIVED FROM THE NATURAL LAW?

We proceed thus to the Second Article:—

Objection 1. It would seem that not every human law is derived from the natural law. For the Philosopher says (*Ethic.* v. 7) that *the legal just is that which originally was a matter of indifference.* But those things which arise from the natural law are not matters of indifference. Therefore the enactments of human laws are not all derived from the natural law.

Obj. 2. Further, positive law is contrasted with natural law, as stated by Isidore (*Etym.* v. 4) and the Philosopher *(Ethic.* v, *loc. cit.).* But those things which flow as conclusion from the general principles of the natural law belong to the natural law, as stated above (Q. 94, A. 4). Therefore that which is established by human law does not belong to the natural law.

Obj. 3. Further, the law of nature is the same for all; since the Philosopher says (*Ethic.* v. 7) that *the natural just is that which is equally valid everywhere.* If therefore human laws were derived from the natural law, it would follow that they too are the same for all: which is clearly false.

Obj. 4. Further, it is possible to give a reason for things which are derived from the natural law. But *it is not possible to give the reason for all the legal enactments of the lawgivers,* as the jurist says. Therefore not all human laws are derived from the natural law.

On the contrary, Tully says (*Rhetor.* ii): *Things which emanated from nature and were approved by custom, were sanctioned by fear and reverence for the laws.*

I answer that, As Augustine says (*De Lib. Arb.* i. 5), *that which is not just seems to be no law at all:* wherefore the force of a law depends on the extent of its justice.

Now in human affairs a thing is said to be just, from being right, according to the rule of reason. But the first rule of reason is the law of nature, as is clear from what has been stated above (Q. 91, A. 2 ad 2). Consequently every human law has just so much of the nature of law, as it is derived from the law of nature. But if in any point it deflects from the law of nature, it is no longer a law but a perversion of law.

But it must be noted that something may be derived from the natural law in two ways: first, as a conclusion from premises, secondly, by way of determination of certain generalities. The first way is like to that by which, in sciences, demonstrated conclusions are drawn from the principles: while the second mode is likened to that whereby, in the arts, general forms are particularized as to details: thus the craftsman needs to determine the general form of a house to some particular shape. Some things are therefore derived from the general principles of the natural law, by way of conclusions; *e.g.,* that *one must not kill* may be derived as a conclusion from the principle that *one should do harm to no man:* while some are derived therefrom by way of determination; *e.g.,* the law of nature has it that the evil-doer should be punished; but that he be punished in this or that way, is a determination of the law of nature.

Accordingly both modes of derivation are found in the human law. But those things which are derived in the first way, are contained in human law not as emanating therefrom exclusively, but have some force from the natural law also. But those things which are derived in the second way, have no other force than that of human law.

Reply Obj. 1. The Philosopher is speaking of those enactments which are by way of determination or specification of the precepts of the natural law.

Reply Obj. 2. This argument avails for those things that are derived from the natural law, by way of conclusions.

Reply Obj. 3. The general principles of the natural law cannot be applied to all men in the same way on account of the great variety of human affairs: and hence arises the diversity of positive laws among various people.

Reply Obj. 4. These words of the Jurist are to be understood as referring to decisions of rulers in determining particular points of the natural law: on which determinations the judgment of expert and prudent men is based as on its principles; in so far, to wit, as they see at once what is the best thing to decide.

Hence the Philosopher says (*Ethic.* vi. 11) that in such matters, *we ought to pay as much attention to the undemonstrated sayings and opinions of persons who surpass us in experience, age and prudence, as to their demonstrations.*

* * *

QUESTION 96: OF THE POWER OF HUMAN LAW

* * *

SECOND ARTICLE

WHETHER IT BELONGS TO THE HUMAN LAW TO REPRESS ALL VICES?

We proceed thus to the Second Article:—

Objection 1. It would seem that it belongs to human law to repress all vices. For Isidore says (*Etym.* v. 20) that *laws were made in order that, in fear thereof, man's audacity might be held in check.* But it would not be held in check sufficiently, unless all evils were repressed by law. Therefore human law should repress all evils.

Obj. 2. Further, the intention of the lawgiver is to make the citizens virtuous. But a man cannot be virtuous unless he forbear from all kinds of vice. Therefore it belongs to human law to repress all vices.

Obj. 3. Further, human law is derived from the natural law, as stated above (Q. 95, A. 2). But all vices are contrary to the law of nature. Therefore human law should repress all vices.

On the contrary, We read in *De Lib. Arb.* i. 5: *It seems to me that the law which is written for the governing of the people rightly permits these things, and that Divine providence punishes them.* But Divine providence punishes nothing but vices. Therefore human law rightly allows some vices, by not repressing them.

I answer that, As stated above (Q. 90, AA. I, 2), law is framed as a rule or measure of human acts. Now a measure should be homogeneous with that which it measures, as stated in *Metaph.* x, text. 3, 4, since different things are measured by different measures. Wherefore laws imposed on men should also be in keeping with their condition, for, as Isidore says (*Etym.* v. 21), law should be *possible both according to nature, and according to the customs of the country.* Now possibility or faculty of action is due to an interior habit or disposition: since the same thing is not possible to one who has not a virtuous habit, as is possible to one who has. Thus the same is not possible to a child as to a full-grown man: for which reason the law for children is not the same as for adults, since many things are permitted to children, which in an adult are punished by law or at any rate are open to blame. In like manner many things are permissible to men not perfect in virtue, which would be intolerable in a virtuous man.

Now human law is framed for a number of human beings, the majority of whom are not perfect in virtue. Wherefore human laws do not forbid all vices, from which the virtuous abstain, but only the more grievous vices, from which it is possible for the majority to abstain; and chiefly those that are to the hurt of others, without the prohibition of which human society could not be maintained: thus human law prohibits murder, theft and such like.

Reply Obj. 1. Audacity seems to refer to the assailing of others. Consequently it belongs to those sins chiefly whereby one's neighbor is injured: and these sins are forbidden by human law, as stated.

Reply Obj. 2. The purpose of human law is to lead men to virtue, not suddenly, but gradually. Wherefore it does not lay upon the multitude of imperfect men the burdens of those who are already virtuous, viz., that they should abstain from all evil. Otherwise these imperfect ones, being unable to bear such precepts, would break out into yet greater evils: thus it is written (Prov. xxx. 33): *He that violently bloweth his nose, bringeth out blood;* and (Matth. ix. 17) that if *new wine,* i.e., precepts of a perfect life, *is put into old bottles,* i.e., into imperfect men, *the bottles break, and the wine runneth out,* i.e., the precepts are despised, and those men, from contempt, break out into evils worse still.

Reply Obj. 3. The natural law is a participation in us of the eternal law: while human law falls short of the eternal law. Now Augustine says (*De Lib. Arb.* i. 5): *The law which is framed for the government of states, allows and leaves unpunished many things that are punished by Divine providence. Nor, if this law does not attempt to do everything, is this a reason why it should be blamed for what it does.* Wherefore, too, human law does not prohibit everything that is forbidden by the natural law.

*   *   *

SECOND PART OF THE SECOND PART (II–II)

QUESTION 40: OF WAR

* * *

FIRST ARTICLE

WHETHER IT IS ALWAYS SINFUL TO WAGE WAR?

We proceed thus to the First Article:—

Objection 1. It would seem that it is always sinful to wage war. Because punishment is not inflicted except for sin. Now those who wage war are threatened by Our Lord with punishment, according to Matth. xxvi. 52: *All that take the sword shall perish with the sword.* Therefore all wars are unlawful.

Obj. 2. Further, whatever is contrary to a Divine precept is a sin. But war is contrary to a Divine precept, for it is written (Matth. v. 39): *But I say to you not to resist evil;* and (Rom. xii. 19): *Not revenging yourselves, my dearly beloved, but give place unto wrath.* Therefore war is always sinful.

Obj. 3. Further, nothing, except sin, is contrary to an act of virtue. But war is contrary to peace. Therefore war is always a sin.

Obj. 4. Further, the exercise of a lawful thing is itself lawful, as is evident in scientific exercises. But warlike exercises which take place in tournaments are forbidden by the Church, since those who are slain in these trials are deprived of ecclesiastical burial. Therefore it seems that war is a sin in itself.

On the contrary, Augustine says in a sermon on the son of the centurion [*Ep. ad Marcel.,* cxxxviii.]: *If the Christian Religion forbade war altogether, those who sought salutary advice in the Gospel would rather have been counselled to cast aside their arms, and to give up soldiering altogether. On the contrary, they were told: "Do violence to no man; . . . and be content with your pay."* [Luke iii. 14] *If he commanded them to be content with their pay, he did not forbid soldiering.*

I answer that, In order for a war to be just, three things are necessary. First, the authority of the sovereign by whose command the war is to be waged. For it is not the business of a private individual to declare war, because he can seek for redress of his rights from the tribunal of his superior. Moreover it is not the business of a private individual to summon together the people, which has to be done in wartime. And as the care of the common weal is committed to those who are in authority, it is their business to watch over the common weal of the city, kingdom or province subject to them. And just as it is lawful for them to have recourse to the sword in defending that common weal against internal disturbances, when they punish evil-doers, according to the words of the Apostle (Rom. xiii. 4): *He beareth not the sword in vain: for he is God's minister, an avenger to execute wrath upon him that doth evil;* so too, it is their business to have recourse to the sword of war in defending the common weal against external enemies. Hence it is said to those who are in authority (Ps. lxxxi. 4): *Rescue the poor: and deliver the needy out of the hand of the sinner;* and for this reason Augustine says (*Contra Faust.* xxii. 75): *The natural order conducive to peace among mortals demands that the power to declare and counsel war should be in the hands of those who hold the supreme authority.*

Secondly, a just cause is required, namely that those who are attacked, should be attacked because they deserve it on account of some fault. Wherefore Augustine says (QQ. *in Hept.,* qu. x, *super Jos.*): *A just war is wont to be described as one that avenges wrongs, when a nation or state has to be punished, for refusing to make amends for the wrongs inflicted by its subjects, or to restore what it has seized unjustly.*

Thirdly, it is necessary that the belligerents should have a rightful intention, so that they intend the advancement of good, or the avoidance of evil. Hence Augustine says *(De Verb. Dom.):* *True religion looks upon as peaceful those wars that are waged not for motives of aggrandizement or cruelty, but with the object of securing peace, of punishing evil-doers, and of uplifting the good.* For it may happen that the war is declared by the legitimate authority, and for a just cause, and yet be rendered unlawful through a wicked intention. Hence Augustine says (*Contra Faust.* xxii. 74): *The passion for inflicting harm, the cruel thirst for vengeance, an unpacific and relentless spirit, the fever of revolt, the lust of power, and such like things, all these are rightly condemned in war.*

Reply Obj. 1. As Augustine says (*Contra Faust.* xxii. 70): *To take the sword is to arm oneself in order to take the life of anyone, without the command or permission of superior or lawful authority.* On the other hand, to have recourse to the sword (as a private person) by the authority of the sovereign or judge, or (as a public person) through zeal for justice, and by the authority, so to speak, of God, is not to *take the sword,* but to use it as commissioned by another, wherefore it does not deserve punishment. And yet even those who make sinful use of the sword are not always slain with the sword, yet they always perish with their own sword, because, unless they repent, they are punished eternally for their sinful use of the sword.

Reply Obj. 2. Such like precepts, as Augustine observes (*De Serm. Dom. in Monte* i. 19), should always be borne in readiness of mind, so that we be ready to obey them, and, if necessary, to refrain from resistance or self-defense. Nevertheless it is necessary sometimes for a man to act otherwise for the common good, or for the good of those with whom he is fighting. Hence Augustine says (*Ep. ad Marcellin.* cxxxviii): *Those whom we have to punish with a kindly severity, it is necessary to handle in many ways against their will. For when we are stripping a man of the lawlessness of sin, it is good for him to be vanquished, since nothing is more hopeless than the happiness of sinners, whence arises a guilty impunity, and an evil will, like an internal enemy.*

Reply Obj. 3. Those who wage war justly aim at peace, and so they are not opposed to peace, except to the evil peace, which Our Lord *came not to send upon earth* (Matth. x. 34). Hence Augustine says (*Ep. ad Bonif.* clxxxix): *We do not seek peace in order to be at war, but we go to war that we may have peace. Be peaceful, therefore, in warring, so that you may vanquish those whom you war against, and bring them to the prosperity of peace.*

Reply Obj. 4. Manly exercises in warlike feats of arms are not all forbidden, but those which are inordinate and perilous, and end in slaying or plundering. In olden times warlike exercises presented no such danger, and hence they were called *exercises of arms* or bloodless wars, as Jerome states in an epistle.

ON THE PRINCIPLES OF NATURE

Observe that some things can exist though they do not exist, while other things do exist. That which can be is said to exist in potency; that which already exists is said to be in act. But there are two sorts of existence: the essential or substantial existence of a thing, for example, a man is, and this is to be in the unqualified sense; and the other is accidental existence, for example, a man is white, and this is to be in some qualified way.

Now, something may be in potency to either sort of existence. For it may be in potency to be a man, as is the case with male seed or the menstrual blood; or it may be in potency to be white, as is the case with a man. Both that which is in potency to substantial existence and that which is in potency to accidental existence may be called matter; as the seed in regard to man, and the man in regard to whiteness. But there is this difference: the matter that is in potency to substantial existence is called the matter *out-of-which;* while that which is in potency to be accidentally is called the matter *in-which.*

Again, properly speaking, that which is in potency to be substantially is called prime matter; but what is in potency to be accidentally is called the subject. So, we say that accidents are in a subject but not that the substantial form is in a subject. This is the difference between matter and a subject: the subject does not get its existence from that which comes to it; of itself it has complete existence. For example, a man does not get his existence from his whiteness. But matter does get existence from that which comes to it, for by itself it possesses incomplete existence. So, to speak without qualification, form gives existence to matter but an accident does not give existence to a subject, rather a subject gives existence to an accident. However, at times one is used for the other, that is, matter for subject, and the reverse.

Just as everything that is in potency can be called matter, so everything from which a thing gets existence, either substantial or accidental, may be called form. Thus a man, when potentially white, becomes actually white through whiteness; and the seed [sperma], when potentially man, becomes an actual man through the soul. Because the form makes something to be actually, the form is said to be an act. Now, that which makes substantial existence actual is called substantial form, and that which produces actual accidental existence is called accidental form.

Moreover, since generation is a movement toward a form, there are two kinds of generation corresponding to the two sorts of form. Generation terminating in accidental form is the qualified sense. In fact, when a substantial form is introduced, something is said to come into being without any qualification; thus, we say that a man comes to exist or is generated. However, when an accidental form is introduced, we do not say that a thing simply comes into existence but that it becomes this sort of thing; thus, when a man becomes white, we do not say that he comes into being or is generated in the unqualified sense, but that he becomes or is generated as a white man.

Again, two kinds of corruption stand in opposition to these two meanings of generation. Of course, generation and corruption in the unqualified sense occur only in the genus of substance. Yet, in the qualified sense generation and corruption occur in all the other genera, and since generation is a change from nonbeing to being, while conversely corruption moves from being to nonbeing, generation does not come about from merely any instance of nonbeing but from that nonbeing which is being in potency. Thus, a statue comes from the copper which is potentially, but not actually, a statue.

So, three items are needed in order that generation may occur: potential being, that is, matter; the fact that the product does not actually exist, and this is privation; and that through which it comes to be actually, namely the form. For example, when a statue is made from copper, the copper which is in potency to the form of the statue is the matter; the fact that it is shapeless or not structured is the privation; and the shape by which it is called a statue is the form—not the substantial form, of course, for the copper actually existed before the advent of this form, and its existence does not depend on this shape which is an accidental form. Indeed, all artificial forms are accidental. As a matter of fact, art operates only on that which is already established in existence by virtue of nature.

There are, then, three principles of nature, namely matter, form, and privation. One of these, form, is that toward which generation is directed; the other two are on the side of that from which generation begins. Consequently, matter and privation are identical in their subject but differ in meaning. Thus, the same thing which is bronze is also an unshaped thing prior to the incoming of the form; but it is called bronze for one reason, and shapeless for a different reason. Hence, privation is called a principle not essentially but accidentally, for it coincides with matter. In the same way, we say that a physician builds a house accidentally. For the fact that a physician builds is not because he is a doctor but rather because he is a builder and this coincides in one subject with the physician.

However, there are two sorts of accident: the necessary, which is inseparable from the thing, as the risible in man, and that which is not necessary but is separable, as whiteness is from man. Consequently, though privation is an accidental principle, it does not follow that it is unnecessary for generation, since matter is never stripped from privation. In fact, inasmuch as it exists under one form, it has privation for another, and conversely. For example, in fire there is a privation of air and in air a privation of fire.

We should note, further, that though generation starts from nonexistence, we do not say that negation is a principle, but rather privation, for negation does not determine its subject. The inability to see may be predicated even of non beings, as in the phrase "a chimera does not see"; and it can be predicated of beings not equipped by their origin to have sight, as in the case of a stone. But privation is predicated only of a subject that is determined, that is, one born to become so endowed, as blindness is attributed only to those that are born to see. Moreover, since generation does not come about from nonbeing in the unqualified sense but from the nonbeing which is in some subject—not just any subject but one of a determinate kind (for fire does not come about from just anything but from that kind of non fire that is by origin disposed to the form of fire)—therefore, we say that privation is a principle.

Yet, it differs from the other principles by the fact that the others are principles both in the act of being and in that of becoming. In order that a statue may come into being, there must be bronze and that which finally is the shape of the statue; and then, when the statue is already existing, these two principles must be present. Privation, on the other hand, is a principle in the act of becoming but not in that of being; because, while a statue is being made, it cannot as yet be a statue. If it were, then it could not come into being, since that which is becoming has no existence, except for items whose existence is successive, as are time and motion. But as soon as the statue is in existence there is no longer a privation of statue there, for affirmation and negation are not capable of coexistence, and likewise privation and possession. Privation is also an accidental principle, as explained above, while the other two are essential principles.

From what has been said, it is obvious that matter differs in meaning from form and privation. For matter is that in which form and privation are understood; thus, it is in regard to copper that shape and the shapeless are understood. Indeed, sometimes matter is denominated along with privation, and sometimes without privation. In the case of bronze, when it is the matter of a statue, then it does not imply a privation, for, from the fact that I say, "bronze," there is no suggestion that it is without structure or shape. On the other hand, flour, taken as matter in relation to bread, implies essentially a privation of the form of bread, for, from the fact that I say, "flour," there is signified a lack of disposition or an inordination opposed to the form of bread. And since matter or the subject endures throughout the process of generation, while privation does not, nor does the combination of matter and privation, therefore the matter that does not imply privation is enduring, but that which does imply it is transient.

Yet, we should note that in some cases, matter includes form in its composition; for instance, though bronze is matter in relation to a statue, nevertheless this very bronze is composed of matter and form. Thus, bronze is not called first matter, for it possesses a matter already. On the other hand, that matter which is understood without any form and privation but which is the subject of form and privation is called prime matter because there is no other matter prior to it. This is also called "hyle."

Now, since every definition and act of knowing depends on form, prime matter cannot be known or defined in itself but only in terms of the composite, as it may be said that prime matter is that which is related to all forms and privations as bronze is to the statue and to the shapeless. In this sense, it is called prime without qualification. Of course, it is possible for something to be called prime with respect to some definite genus, as water is prime matter in the genus of wet things. Yet, it is not prime in the simple sense, for it is composed of matter and form and consequently has a prior matter.

It should be noted, also, that prime matter, and form, too, are not generated or corrupted, because every generation is from something to something. Now, that from which generation takes place is matter, and that to which it is directed is form. So, if matter or form were generated, there would be matter for matter, and form for form, on to infinity. Hence, to speak strictly, there is generation of the composite only.

Observe, also, that prime matter is said to be numerically one in all things. Numerically one, of course, has two meanings: it may mean that which possesses one form which is numerically determined, as in the case of Socrates. Now, this is not the way in which prime matter is said to be numerically one, since it does not have in itself any form. Another meaning of numerically one is that which exists without dispositions making it numerically different. It is in this way that matter is said to be numerically one, for it is understood without any dispositions by which it is numerically differentiated.

Again, we should note that although prime matter includes no form or privation in its rational character, yet it is never stripped away from form and privation. Sometimes it exists under one form, sometimes under another. But it can never exist by itself because, since it has no form within its own rational character, it possesses no actual existence, for to be in act is impossible without a form; it is in potency only. So, whatever is in act cannot be called prime matter.

It is clear from the foregoing that there are three principles of nature, namely, matter, form, and privation. Yet, these are not enough for generation. In fact, that which is in potency cannot reduce itself to act. Thus, the copper which is potentially a statue does not make itself into a statue; it needs an operating agent to draw the form of the statue from potency into act. Now, the form cannot draw itself from potency into act— I am talking about the form of the product of generation, what we call the terminus of the process of generation. As a matter of fact, the form is not present except in that which actually exists: that which is being worked on is in the process of becoming, that is, while the thing is being made. So, beside the matter and form there must be some principle that acts and this is called a producer, a mover, or an agent, or that from which change takes its beginning.

Again, because everything that acts does so only by tending toward something, as Aristotle explains in the second book of the *Metaphysics* (II, text 8–9), there must be a fourth principle, namely, that which is intended by the agent. This is called the end. It should also be noted that although every agent both natural and voluntary intends an end, it does not follow that every agent knows its end or deliberates about its end. To know their end is necessary in the case of those agents whose actions are not determined but are open to opposite possibilities, as is true of voluntary agents. So, they must know their end, whereby they may determine their own actions. On the other hand, in the case of physical agents, their actions are determined; consequently, they do not have to choose the means to their end. Avicenna gives the example of a harpist (*Physics*, II, 10) who does not have to deliberate over each plucking of the strings, because the pluckings have become determinate in his case; otherwise, there would be a delay between the pluckings and that would not sound right.

Now, it is more obvious that the voluntary agent deliberates than that the physical agent does. So, there is greater force to the conclusion that if even the voluntary agent (in whose case deliberation is more evident) sometimes does not deliberate, therefore the physical agent does not. It is possible for the physical agent to tend towards its end without deliberation; and this intending is nothing but having a natural inclination toward something.

From the previous explanations, then, it is clear that there are four causes: material, efficient, formal, and final. Now, although "principle" and "cause" may be employed interchangeably (as is stated in the *Metaphysics,* V, 1, 1013a17), still, Aristotle in the *Physics* (I, 7, 191a20; II, 3, 195a15) gives four causes and three principles. He takes causes as extrinsic as well as intrinsic. Matter and form are said to be intrinsic to a thing, in the sense that they are constitutive parts of the thing. The efficient and final causes are called extrinsic because they are outside the thing. But he is taking principles as intrinsic causes only. Now, privation is not named among the causes because it is an incidental principle, as they say. So, when we speak of four causes, we mean essential *(per se)* causes, to which the incidental causes may be reduced; for everything that is incidental may be reduced to what is essential.

However, although in the first book of the *Physics* Aristotle speaks of principles as intrinsic causes, still (as is stated in the *Metaphysics,* XII, 4, 1070b22), "principle" is properly used of extrinsic causes and "element" of causes that are parts of the thing, that is, of intrinsic causes. However, "cause" is used for both; sometimes one of these terms is used for the other, since every cause may be called a principle and every principle a cause. Nevertheless, "cause" seems to add something to the usual way of speaking about a principle; for, whatever is first, whether the being of the consequent follows from it or not, can be called a principle. Thus, a metalworker is called the principle of a knife, because the existence of the knife is due to his work; but when something is changed from black to white, we also say that black is the principle of this change (and generally, everything from which a change takes its start is called a principle), yet black is not that from which the existence of the white flows as a consequent. Rather, we only use "cause" for that sort of first item from which the existence of the consequent follows. Hence, the statement is made that a cause is that from whose being another being follows. So, that first item from which motion takes its start cannot be called an essential cause, though it may be called a principle. For this reason, privation is placed among the principles and not among the causes; for privation is that from which generation takes its start. Of course, it can also be called an incidental cause, in the sense that it is coincident with matter, as has been explained above.

In the proper sense, "element" is used only in reference to the causes out of which the thing is composed, and these are properly the material ones. Again, this will not apply to every material cause but to that from which the primary composition takes place. Thus, we do not say that bodily members are elements of a man, because his members are also composed of other items. But we do say that earth and water are elements, for they are not composed of other bodies. Rather, the primary composition of natural bodies is made out of them.

As a result, Aristotle in the *Metaphysics* (V, 3, 1014a26) says that "element" means the primary component of a thing, immanent in it, and indivisible into other kinds of stuff. The meaning of the first phrase, "the primary component of a thing," is clear from what we have just said. The second phrase, "immanent in it," is included to differentiate "element" from matter that is wholly corrupted by generation. For example, food is the matter for blood, but blood is not produced unless the food is used up; hence, the food does not remain in the blood, and so, food cannot be called an element of blood. Of course, elements must remain in some way, for they are not completely corrupted, as is explained in the book *On Generation* (I, 10, 327b30). The third phrase, "and indivisible into other kinds of stuff," is included to differentiate "element" from things that have parts that are formally or specifically different; for instance, the hand, whose parts are flesh and bones which do differ in kind. But an element is not divisible into parts that differ in kind; water, for example, each part of which is water. It is not required that an element be indivisible quantitatively; it is enough if it be indivisible into different kinds of stuff. Of course, if it is also indivisible in all ways, it is called an element; thus, letters are called the elements of words. It is obvious, then, from what has been said that principle is as it were a more extensive term than cause, and cause more extensive than element. This is what the Commentator says in explaining Book V of the *Metaphysics* [Averroes, *Metaphysica,* Venice, 1552, fol. 50].

Having seen that there are four kinds of causes, we should next observe that it is not impossible for the same thing to have several causes. Thus, the cause of a statue is the copper and the sculptor, but the sculptor as efficient, the copper as matter. Nor is it impossible for the same thing to be the cause of contrary effects. For instance, a pilot may be the cause of saving or sinking a ship: of the former by his presence, of the latter by his absence.

It is even possible for one thing to be both cause and effect with regard to another item, but in a different fashion. Thus, walking, taken as efficient, is the cause of health; but health, as an end, is the cause of walking, for walking is sometimes done for the sake of health. So, too, the body is as matter to the soul; while the soul is as form to the body. In fact, the efficient is called a cause in relation to the end, since the end does not actually function without the activity of the agent. On the other hand, the end is called the cause of the agent, since the latter will not work unless it tend toward the end. Hence, the efficient is the cause of the fact that a certain item stands as an end, for instance, walking in order that there may be health; however, it does not cause the end to be an end, so it is not the cause of the causality of the end; it does not make the end a final cause. For example, a physician may make health to be present actually but he does not cause health to be an end. On the other hand, the end is not the cause of the fact that a given being is efficient but it is the cause of the fact that the agent is acting. Health does not make a physician exist as a physician (I am talking about the health that is produced by the physician's activity) but it does result in the fact that the physician is act-ing. Hence, the end is the cause of the causality of the agent, because it makes the agent to be an agent; likewise, it makes matter function as matter, and form as form. For mat-ter will not take on form except for the sake of an end; and form will not perfect matter except for the sake of an end. That is the reason for the statement: the end is the cause of causes, for it is the cause of the causality in all the causes.

Matter is also called the cause of the form, in the sense that the form does not ex-ist except in the matter. Likewise, the form is the cause of the matter, because the mat-ter has no actual being except by virtue of the form. In fact, matter and form are correl-atives, as is stated in the *Physics* (II, 2, 194b10). They are predicated of the composite as parts of the whole, and as the simple in relation to the complex.

Moreover, since every cause as cause is naturally prior to its effect, we should note that "prior" has two meanings, as Aristotle says in the treatise *On Animals* (XVI, 743a19–22). As a result of these different meanings, a thing can be called both prior and posterior in the same relationship, and the cause can be called the effect. Indeed, some-thing is said to be prior to another, (1) in generation and time, and (2) in substance and perfection. So, since a natural activity proceeds from the imperfect to the perfect, and from the incomplete to the complete, the imperfect is prior to the perfect according to generation and time; however, the perfect is prior to the imperfect in substance. Thus, one can say that the man is before the boy in substance and perfection, but the boy is be-fore the man in generation and time. However, although the imperfect is prior to the perfect, and potency is prior to act, in the order of generable things (considering the fact that in any one thing the imperfect is prior to the perfect and it is in potency before it is in act), yet, absolutely speaking, act and the perfect must be prior. For that which re-duces potency to act exists actually; and that which perfects the imperfect is something perfect. Matter, then, is prior to form in generation and time, for that to which some-thing happens is prior to the fact that it happens. But form is prior to matter in substance and complete being, for matter has no complete being without form. Likewise, the agent is prior to the end in generation and time, since motion toward the end comes from the agent. However, the end is prior to the agent, as agent in substance and perfec-tion, since the action of the agent is only completed by virtue of the end. And so, these two causes, material and efficient, are prior in the way of generation; but the form and the end are prior in the way of perfection.

Note, next, that necessity is twofold: namely, absolute and conditional. Absolute necessity is that which proceeds from causes that are prior in the way of generation, and these are the matter and the end. Such is the necessity of death; it results from matter, that is, from the disposition of its constituent contraries. This is called absolute because nothing impedes it. It is also called the necessity of matter. On the other hand, condi-tional necessity proceeds from causes that are posterior in the process of generation, that is, from the form and the end. Thus, we say that if a man is to be generated, there must be an act of conception. This kind is called conditional because in the absolute sense there is no necessity that this certain woman conceive, but only under this condi-tion, namely, if a human being is to be generated. This is also called the necessity of the end.

It is to be noted, too, that three of the causes can coincide: namely, form, end, and agent. This is illustrated in the production of fire. Indeed, fire generates fire, and thus fire is an efficient cause, inasmuch as it generates. Then, fire is a form, since it makes something that was previously in potency to be actually. Again, it is an end, in that the agent's activity terminates in it. Of course, the end is twofold: namely, the end of the process of generation and the end of the thing that is generated. This is evident in the production of a knife: the form of the knife is the end of the process of production, but cutting (which is the work of a knife) is the end of the thing itself that is produced, of the knife. Now, the end of the process of generation sometimes coincides with the two causes under discussion—that is to say, when generation takes place from a specifically similar being. For instance, when a man generates a man, or an olive produces an olive. But this does not apply to the end of the thing that is generated. Still, we should note that the end coincides with the form numerically; for numerically the same item that is the form of the thing generated is the end of the process of generation. However, this end does not coincide with the agent numerically but only specifically. It is impossible for the maker and his product to be numerically identical but they can be of the same species. For instance, when a man generates a man, the man generating and the one that is generated are numerically different but specifically the same. Matter, however, does not coincide with the other causes, for matter has the character of something imperfect because it is being in potency; while the other causes, since they are in act, have the character of something perfect. Now, the perfect and the imperfect do not coincide in the same subject.

Now that we have seen that there are four causes, the efficient, material, formal, and final, we should observe that each of these causes can be analyzed in many ways. We speak of something as a prior cause and of something else as a posterior cause. For instance, we say that art and the physician are the cause of health: art being the prior cause and the physician the posterior one. The same distinction applies to the formal and the other causes. Observe that we should always reduce a question to the primary cause. For example, if the question is: *Why is this man healthy?,* the answer should be: *Because a physician has cured him;* and again: *Why did the physician cure him? Because of the art of healing which he possesses.*

Note also that the so-called proximate cause is the same as the posterior cause; and the remote cause is the same as the prior cause. Hence, these two analyses of the causes—sometimes as prior and posterior, sometimes as remote and proximate causes—mean the same thing. Moreover, it is to be observed that, in all cases, that which is more general is called the remote cause, while that which is more special is the proximate cause. Thus, we say that man's proximate form is his definition, rational mortal animal, but "animal" is a more remote form, and "substance" is still more remote. Indeed, all higher things are as forms to lower things. Likewise, the proximate matter of a statue is bronze, the remote is metal, and still more remote is body.

Next, one kind of cause is essential (*per se*) and another incidental (*per accidens*). A cause is called essential when it is the cause of a certain thing as such. Thus, a builder is the cause of a house and wood is the material cause of a bench. An incidental cause means that which happens incidentally to an essential cause; for instance, when we speak of a grammarian who is building. In fact, the grammarian is called the cause of the building incidentally, not because he is a grammarian but because it is incidental to the builder that he is a grammarian. The same thing holds in the case of the other causes.

Again, some causes are simple and some are composite. A cause is called simple when it alone is assigned as cause to that of which it is the essential cause, or also when it alone is the incidental cause. Thus, we say that the builder is the cause of the house, and we may also say that the physician is the cause of the house. It is called composite when both are assigned as cause; thus we might say the physician-builder is the cause of the house. It is also possible to talk about simple cause in the way that Avicenna explains it (*Physics,* II, 8), as that which is a cause without the addition of anything else; thus is bronze for the statue (for the statue is made from bronze without the addition of any other matter). Similarly, we may say that the physician causes health, or that fire causes heating. Then, the composite cause means that several items must combine in order that there be a cause. For example, one man is not the cause of the motion of a ship but many are; and one stone is not the material cause of a house but many are.

Furthermore, some causes are in act and some in potency. A cause in act is one that is actually causing something; for example, the builder when he is building. Note that in speaking of causes in act, it is necessary for cause and effect to be simultaneous, in the sense that if one is, then the other is, too. In fact, if there is a builder in act, then he must be building; if the building process is in act, then there must be a builder in act. However, this is not required in the case of causes that are only in potency. Observe, too, that the universal cause is correlative with the universal effect, while a singular cause corresponds to a singular effect. Thus, we say that a builder is the cause of a house, and this builder of this house.

We should also note that in speaking about intrinsic principles, that is, matter and form, the points of resemblance or difference in the principles depend on the resemblance and difference of the consequents. Some are numerically the same, as Socrates and this man is, when we are pointing at Socrates. Others are numerically different but the same in species: for instance, Socrates and Plato, though alike in their human species, are nevertheless different in number. Still others differ specifically but are the same in their genus: thus, man and donkey agree in their animal genus. Of course, others are different generically and are the same only according to analogy: thus are substance and quantity, which do not agree in any genus but agree only according to analogy. Indeed, they agree only in the fact that each is a being; but being is not a genus, because it is not predicated univocally but analogically.

To understand this, we should observe that an item is predicable of several things in three ways: univocally, equivocally, and analogically. It is predicated univocally when the predication uses the same name and the same meaning or definition; thus is animal predicated of man and donkey. Both mean animal, and both mean an animate substance capable of sensing, since this is the definition of an animal. Predication is equivocal when the predication applies the same name to several things but with different meanings; thus we use "dog" to speak of a thing that barks and of a constellation in the heavens. They agree in name only and not in definition or signification. In fact, that which is signified by a name is the definition, as is stated in the *Metaphysics* (IV, 7, 1012a24). It is said to be predicated analogically when the predication applies to several items whose meanings are different but are attributed to some one meaning that is the same. For example, "healthy" is predicated of the animal body, of urine, and of a drink, but the meaning is not entirely the same in all the cases. It is predicated of urine as a sign of health, of a body as of its subject, of a drink as of its cause; nevertheless, all these meanings are attributed to one end, namely, health. Sometimes, items that agree analogically (that is, proportionally, comparatively, or by way of adaptation) are attributed to one end, as appears in the preceding example; and sometimes to one agent, as when "physician" is predicated of a person who practices by means of the art of medicine, and of one who practices without the art, like a midwife. And it may even be predicated of instruments, but by way of attribution to one basic item, as being is predicated of substance and of quantity, quality, and the other categories. For, the meaning whereby substance is being is not entirely the same as that for quantity and the others; but all are called being from the fact that they are attributed to substance, which is, indeed, the subject of the others. So, being is predicated primarily of substance and secondarily of the others. Thus, being is not the genus of substance and quantity, because no genus is predicated primarily and secondarily of its species, but being is predicated analogically. This is why we say that substance and quantity differ generically but are similar by way of analogy.

Of those items that are numerically the same, both form and matter are the same in a numerical unit, as in the example of Tully and Cicero [two names for the same man]. On the other hand, in things that are the same specifically but different numerically, the matter and form are also not the same in number but only in species: as in the case of Socrates and Plato. Similarly, for those things that are generically the same, the principles are also the same in their genus: thus the soul and body of a donkey and of a horse are different in species but the same in genus. Likewise, in those things that are in agreement by analogy only, the principles are the same by analogy only, or by proportion. For matter, form, and privation, or potency and act, are principles of substance and also of the other genera. Yet, the matter of substance and of quantity, and similarly their form and privation, differ generically but agree only by way of proportion—in the sense that just as the matter of substance is related to the substance according to the characteristic meaning of matter, so, too, is the matter of quantity related to quantity. However, as substance is the cause of the rest of the genera, so are the principles of substance principles for all the others.

CONCERNING BEING AND ESSENCE

INTRODUCTION

Because a small error in the beginning is a great one in the end, according to the Philosopher [i.e., Aristotle] in the first book of the *De Caelo et Mundo,* and since being and essence are what are first conceived by the intellect, as Avicenna says in the first book of his *Metaphysics,* therefore, lest error befall from ignorance of them (being and essence), in order to reveal their difficulty it should be said what is signified by the names being and essence, and how they are found in diverse things and how they are disposed with respect to *(se habeant ad)* logical intentions, namely, genus, species, and difference.

CHAPTER 1

Because indeed we must receive knowledge of the simple from the composite and arrive at what is prior from what is posterior, in order that beginning with the less difficult instruction may be made more suitably, we should proceed from the meaning of being to the meaning of essence.

Therefore one should know, as the Philosopher says in the fifth of the *Metaphysics,* that being by itself *(ens per se)* is said to be taken in two modes: in the one mode, that it is divided into ten genera; in the other, that it signifies the truth of proposi-

Reprinted from St. Thomas Aquinas, *Concerning Being and Essence,* translated by George G. Leckie (New York: Appleton-Century-Crofts, 1937).

tions. Moreover the difference between these is that in the second mode everything can be called being concerning which an affirmative proposition can be formed, even if it posits nothing in the thing *(in re);* by virtue of this mode privations and negations are likewise called beings, for we say that affirmation is the opposite of negation, and that blindness is in the eye. But in the first mode only what posits something in the thing can be called being; consequently, according to the first mode blindness and such are not beings. The name essence, therefore, is not taken from being in the second mode, for in this mode some things are said to have essence which have not being, as is evident in privations. But essence is taken from being only in the first mode; whence the Commentator [i.e., Averroës] says in the same place that "being in the first mode is said to be what signifies the essence of the thing." And because, as has been said, being in this mode is divided into ten genera, it follows that essence signifies something common to all natures by which diverse beings are disposed in different genera and species, as for instance humanity is the essence of man and so for others. And because that by means of which the thing is constituted in its proper genus or species is that which is signified by the definition indicating what the thing is, hence it is that the name essence has been changed by philosophers into the name quiddity. And this is what the Philosopher frequently calls *"quod quid erat esse,"* that is, that by virtue of which a thing (anything) has to be what it is (something). And indeed it is called form according as by means of form the certitude of any single thing is signified, as Avicenna remarks in the second part of his *Metaphysics.* This is called by another name, nature, accepting nature according to the first of the four modes assigned by Boethius in his book *De Duabus Naturis,* namely, according as nature is said to be all that which can be comprehended by the intellect in any mode whatsoever; for a thing is not intelligible except by virtue of its definition and essence. And thus also the Philosopher in the Fourth book of his *Metaphysics* says that every substance is a nature. But the name nature taken in this sense is seen to signify the essence of a thing inasmuch as it has a disposition *(ordinem)* towards an operation proper to the thing, since no thing is lacking in its proper operation. Indeed the name quiddity is taken from that which signifies the definition; but it is called essence according as by virtue of it and in it being has existence *(esse).*

But because being is asserted absolutely and primarily of substances and secondarily and as if in a certain respect *(secundum quid)* of accidents, hence it is that essence also exists truly and properly in substances, but exists in accidents in a certain mode and in a certain respect. Some substances indeed are simple and others are composite, and in both there is an essence. But essence is possessed by simple substances in a truer and more noble mode according as simple substances have a more exalted existence, for they are the cause of those which are composite,—at least the primary substance, which is God, is. But since the essences of these substances are more concealed from us, therefore we must begin from the essences of composite substances in order that instruction may be made more suitably from what is easier.

CHAPTER 2

In composite substances, therefore, matter and form are noted, as for instance in man soul and body are noted. Moreover it cannot be said that either of these alone is called essence. For it is evident that matter alone is not the essence of the thing, because it is by means of its essence that the thing is both known and ordered in its species and genus. But matter is not the principle of cognition, nor is anything determined as regards genus and species according to it (matter), but according to that by means of which something is in act. And furthermore neither can form alone be called the essence of composite substance, however much some attempt to assert this. From what has been said it is clear that essence is what is signified by the definition of the thing. But the definition of natural substances contains not only form but also matter; for otherwise natural definitions and mathematical definitions would not differ. Nor can it be said that matter is posited in the definition of a natural substance as an addition to its essence or as a being outside of its essence *(extra essentiam),* since this mode of definition is more proper to accidents which do not have a perfect essence; whence it follows that they must admit the subject into their definition, which (subject) is outside of their genus. It is clear, therefore, that essence comprehends matter and form. But it cannot be said that essence signifies a relation which is between matter and form, or that it is something superadded to them, since something superadded would of necessity be accidental or extraneous to the thing, nor could the thing be conceived by means of it, for everything is appropriate to its essence. For by the form, which is the actuality of matter, matter is made being in act and a this somewhat. Whence that which is superadded does not give existence *(esse)* in act simply to matter, but existence in act of such sort as likewise accidents make, as for instance whiteness makes something white in act. Wherefore whenever such form is acquired it is not said to be generated simply but in a certain respect *(secundum quid).* Hence it follows that in composite substances the name of essence signifies that which is composed of matter and form. And this agrees also with the opinion of Boethius in his commentary *Predicamentorum,* where he says that *ousia* signifies a composite. For *ousia* according to the Greeks is the same as essence according to us, as Boethius himself remarks in his book *De Duabus Naturis.* Avicenna also says that the quiddity of composite substances is itself a composition of matter and form. The Commentator also says concerning the seventh book of the *Metaphysics:* "The nature which species have in things capable of generation is something intermediate that is composed of matter and form." Reason also accords with this, because the existence of a composite substance is not the existence of form only, nor the existence of matter only, but of the composite itself; and indeed essence is that according to which a thing is said to exist. Whence it follows that the essence by virtue of which a thing is called being is not form alone, nor matter alone, but both; although in its mode the form is the cause of its existence. We discover it indeed thus in other things which are constituted from more than one principle, since a thing is not named from one of those principles alone, but from that which unites both. It appears thus in the case of tastes, because sweetness is caused from the action of warmth dissolving moisture, and although in this mode the warmth is the cause of the sweetness, yet a body is not called sweet from its warmth but from the taste which unites both the warmth and the moisture.

But because the principle of individuation is matter, it perhaps seems to follow from this that essence which unites in itself both matter and form would be only particular and not universal. From this it would follow that universals do not have definition, if essence is what is signified by means of the definition. One should therefore understand that matter in any mode whatsoever is not taken to be the principle of individuation, but only signated matter *(materia signata).* And I call signated matter that which is considered as under determinate dimensions. But now this matter is not posited in the definition of man inasmuch as he is man, but it would be posited in the definition of Socrates if Socrates were to have a definition. But in the definition of man non-signated matter is posited; for in the definition of man this certain flesh and this certain bone are not posited, but bone and flesh absolutely, which are the non-signated matter of man. Accordingly, it is clear that the essence of Socrates and the essence of man do not differ except according to signate and non-signate. Whence the Commentator remarks upon the seventh of the *Metaphysics:* "Socrates is nothing other than animality and rationality which are his quiddity." Thus also the essence of genus and of species differ according to signate and non-signate, although there is a different mode of designation for each of them, because the designation of the individual with respect to species is by means of matter determined by dimensions, whereas the designation of species in respect to genus is by means of the constitutive difference which is taken from the form of the thing.

This determination or designation, however, which is in the species in respect to genus is not by means of something existing in the essence of species, which is in no mode in the essence of genus; nay, whatever is in species is in genus as something undetermined. For if animal is not the whole of man, but part of him, it is not predicated of him, since no integral part is predicated of its whole.

But how this is related can be seen if one observes how body differs according as animal is posited as part or as genus; for it cannot be genus in the same mode in which it is an integral part. This name body, therefore, is taken in several senses. For body according as it is in the genus of substance is asserted of that which has a nature such that three dimensions can be designated in it; in truth the three designated dimensions themselves are body which is in the genus of quantity. But it happens in things that what has one perfection may also aim at further perfection; as for instance is clear in the case of man, since he has both a sensitive nature and further, intellectual nature. Likewise indeed beyond this perfection which is to have such a form that three dimensions can be designated in it, another perfection can be added, as life or something of this sort. This name body, therefore, can signify a certain thing which has a form such that from it follows the possibility of designating three dimensions in it, with this limitation, namely, that from that form no further perfection may follow, but if anything else is added it is beyond the significance of body thus spoken of. And in this mode body is an integral and material part of animal, because thus soul will be beyond what is signified by the name body and will be something added to (excelling) body itself in such wise that from these two, that is, from soul and body, the animal is constituted as from its parts. This name body can also be taken so as to signify a certain thing which has a form such that from the form three dimensions can be designated in it, whatsoever that form may be, and whether any further perfection can issue from it or not. And in this mode body is the genus of animal, because in animal nothing is taken which is not contained implicitly in body; for soul is not a form different from that by means of which three dimensions can be designated in that thing. And therefore when it was said that body is what has a form such that from the form three dimensions can be designated in the body, it was to be understood of whatever the form might be, whether animality or lapidity or any other. And so the form of animal is contained implicitly in the form of body, according as body is its genus. And such too is the habitude (relation) of animal to man. For if animal denoted only a certain thing which has a perfection such that it can feel and be moved by virtue of a principle existing in itself, to the exclusion of any further perfections, then whatever further perfection supervened to the thing, would be disposed in respect to *(haberet se ad)* animal by means of the partitive mode *(modum partis)* and not as if implicitly beneath (included in) the principle of animal, and thus animal would not be a genus. But animal is a genus according as it signifies a certain thing from the form of which can issue feeling and motion, whatsoever this form may be, whether it be the sensible soul alone or the sensible and rational together. Thus, therefore, genus signifies indeterminately all that which is in species, for it does not signify matter alone. Similarly, difference signifies the whole, but it does not signify form alone. And definition likewise signifies a whole, and also species does. But yet in diverse ways: because genus signifies a whole as a certain determination determining what is material in a thing, without the determination of the proper form. Whence genus is taken from matter, although it is not matter, as is evident in the instance of what is called body because it has a perfection such that three dimensions can be designated in it, which certain perfection is materially disposed towards further perfection. In truth, on the contrary, difference is taken determinately as a certain determination by form, for the reason that determined matter is involved in the primary conception of it, as appears when it is called animate or that which has soul; for what it is, whether body or something else, is not determined. Whence Avicenna says that genus is not intellected in difference as a part of essence, but only as a being beyond its essence *(extra essentiam),* just as a subject is in regard to the intellection of the passions. And therefore, likewise, speaking *per se,* genus is not predicated concerning difference, as the Philosopher remarks in the third of the *Metaphysics* and the fourth of the *Topics,* unless perchance as a subject is predicated of passion. But definition or species comprehends both, namely, determinate matter which the name of genus designates, and determinate form which the name of difference designates.

And from this the reason is clear why genus and species and difference are proportionally disposed towards *(se habeant ad)* matter and form and the composite in nature, although they are not the same as nature, since genus is not matter but taken from matter as signifying the whole, nor is difference form but taken from form as signifying the whole. Wherefore we call man a rational animal, not from the composite of animal and rational, as we say that he is composed of body and soul; for man is said to be composed of soul and body, just as from two things a third thing is truly constituted, which is neither of the two; for man is neither soul nor body. But if man can be said to be composed in some manner of animal and rational, it is not as a third thing from two things but as a third concept from two concepts; for the concept of animal is one expressing, without the determination of a special form, the nature of a thing, by that which is material in respect to its ultimate perfection. The concept, however, of the difference rational consists in the determination of a special form. And from the two concepts (animal and rational) is constituted the concept of the species or definition. And therefore just as a thing constituted from other things does not take the predication of those things, thus neither does the concept take the predication of those concepts from which it is constituted, for we do not say that the definition is genus or difference.

But, although genus signifies the whole essence of species, yet it does not follow that there is one essence of different species which have the same genus, because the unity of the genus proceeds from its very indetermination and indifference; not, however, because that which is signified by genus is one nature by number in different species to which supervenes something else which is the difference determining it, as for instance form determines matter which is numerically one; but because genus signifies some form, though not determinately this or that (form) which difference expresses determinately, which is none other than that (form) which is signified indeterminately through genus. And therefore the Commentator says in the twelfth book of the *Metaphysics* that prime matter is called one through the remotion of all forms *(scil.* pure potentiality in the order of substance), but genus is called one through the community of its signified form. Whence it is clear that by means of the addition of difference, which removes the indetermination which was the cause of the unity of genus, species remain different by virtue of essence.

And because, as has been said, the nature of species is indeterminate in respect to the individual, just as the nature of genus is indeterminate with respect to species, hence it is that, just as that which is genus according as it is predicated concerning species implies in its signification, although indistinctly, all that is determinate in species, thus likewise it follows that what is species, according as it is predicated of the individual, signifies all that which is in the individual essentially although indistinctly. And in this mode the essence of Socrates is signified by the name of man, and as a consequence man is predicated of Socrates. But if the nature of the species be signified with the exclusion of designated matter, which is the principle of individuation, it will thus be disposed *(se habebit)* as a part (by means of the partitive mode). And in this mode it is signified by the name humanity, for humanity signifies that in virtue of which man is man. But designated matter is not that in virtue of which man is man; and, therefore, in no mode is it contained among those things from which man possesses manness. Since therefore humanity includes in its concept only those things from which man possesses manness, it is clear that designated matter is excluded from or cut off from its signification. And since the part is not predicated of the whole, hence it is that humanity is not predicated either of man or of Socrates. Wherefore Avicenna says that the quiddity of a composite is not the composite itself of which it is the quiddity, although the quiddity itself is composite; as for instance humanity, although it is composite, still is not man. Nay rather, it must be received in something which is designated matter. But since, as has been said, the designation of species in respect to genus is by virtue of form, whereas the designation of the individual in respect to species is by virtue of matter, it follows therefore that the name signifying that whence the nature of genus is taken, with the exclusion of the determinate form perfecting the species, should signify the material part of the whole itself, as the body is the material part of man. But the name signifying that whence the nature of species is taken, with the exclusion of designated matter, signifies the formal part. And therefore humanity is signified as a certain form, and is spoken of as that which is the form of the whole; not indeed as if it were superadded to the essential parts, namely, to form and matter, as for instance the form of a house is superadded to its integral parts; but rather it is form that is the whole, that is, embracing form and matter, yet with the exclusion of those things by means of which matter is found to be designated. So, therefore, it is clear that the name man and the name humanity signify the essence of man, but in different modes, as has been said, since the name man signifies it as a whole, inasmuch as it does not exclude the designation of matter but contains it implicitly and indistinctly, as for instance it has been said that the genus contains the difference. And therefore the name man is predicated of individuals. But the name humanity signifies the essence as a part, since it does not contain in its signification anything except what is of man inasmuch as he is man, and because it excludes all designation of matter; whence it is not predicated of individual man. And for this reason likewise the name essence sometimes is found predicated of a thing, for Socrates is said to be an essence, and sometimes it is denied, as for instance it is said that the essence of Socrates is not Socrates.

CHAPTER 3

Having seen, therefore, what is signified by the name of essence in composite substances, we should see in what mode it is disposed towards *(se habeat ad)* the ratio of genus, species, and difference. Since, however, that to which the ratio of genus or species or difference applies is predicated concerning this signate singular, it is impossible that the ratio of the universal, namely, that of genus and of species, should apply to essence according as it is signified by means of the partitive mode, as for instance by the name humanity or animality. And therefore Avicenna says that rationality is not the difference, but the principle of difference. And for the same reason humanity is not species nor is animality genus. Similarly, also, it cannot be said that the ratio of genus or of species applies to essence according as essence is a certain thing existing apart from singulars, as the Platonists were accustomed to assert, since thus genus and species would not be predicated of this individual. For it cannot be said that Socrates is what is separated from him, nor again that the separated conduces to the cognition of a singular. And therefore it follows that the ratio of genus or species applies to essence according as it is signified in the mode of a whole, as for instance by the name of man or animal, according as it contains implicitly and indistinctly all that is in the individual.

But nature or essence taken thus can be considered in two ways. In one mode according to its proper ratio, and this is the absolute consideration of it, and in this mode nothing is true concerning it except what applies to it according to this mode, whence whatever else is attributed to it is a false attribution. For example, to man inasmuch as he is man rational and animal applies and the other things which fall within his definition. White or black, however, and whatsoever of this mode, which is not of the ratio of humanity, does not apply to man inasmuch as he is man. Accordingly, if it were asked whether this nature thus considered can be said to be one or more than one, neither ought to be conceded, because each is outside the concept of humanity, and either one can happen to it *(accidere)*. For if plurality were to belong to the concept of humanity, it could never be one although nevertheless it is one according as it is in Socrates. Similarly, if unity were to belong to its ratio, then would it be one and the same of Socrates and of Plato, nor could it be multiplied *(plurificari)* in many. It is considered in another mode according to the existence *(esse)* which it has in this or that, and in this mode something is predicated concerning it by means of accident *(per accidens),* by reason of that in which it is, as for instance it is said that man is white because Socrates is white, although this does not apply to man inasmuch as he is man.

But this nature has a twofold existence: having one existence in singulars and another in the soul, and according to both of the two, accident follows upon the nature spoken of, and in singulars also it has a manifold existence according to the diversity of the singulars. And nevertheless to this very nature according to its primary consideration, that is to say, its absolute one, none of these (existences) ought to belong. For it is false to say that the essence of man, inasmuch as he is man, has existence in this singular, because if existence in this singular applied to man as man, then (man) would never exist outside of this singular. Similarly, also, if it applied to man as man not to exist in this singular, (man) would never exist in it. But it is true to say that man as man does not have to be in this singular or in that or in the soul. Therefore it is clear that the nature of man absolutely considered abstracts from any sort of existence, yet in such wise that it does not exclude any of them. And this nature so considered is what is predicated of all individuals. Still it cannot be said that the ratio of universal applies to nature thus considered, because unity and community belong to the principle of the universal, whereas to human nature neither of these (two) applies according to its absolute consideration. For if community belonged to the concept of man, then in whatsoever humanity were found community would be found. And this is false because in Socrates there is not found any community, but whatever is in him is individuated. Similarly, also, it cannot be said that the ratio of genus or of species belongs to human nature according to the existence which it has in individuals, because human nature is not found in individuals according to its unity so that it is a one appropriate to all, which the ratio of the universal demands. It follows, therefore, that the ratio of species applies to human nature according to that existence *(esse)* which it has in the intellect. For human nature itself has an existence in the intellect abstracted from all individuations, and therefore it has a uniform ratio to all individuals which are outside the soul, according as it is equally the likeness *(similitudo)* of all and leads to the understanding of all inasmuch as they are men. And because it has such a relation to all individuals, the intellect discovers the ratio of species and attributes it to it (human nature). Whence the Commentator observes in the first book of the *De Anima* that intellect is what actuates *(agit)* universality in things. Avicenna also says this in his *Metaphysics*. Whence, although this intellectual nature has the ratio of universal according as it is compared to things which are outside of the soul because it is a single likeness of all, nevertheless according as it has existence in this intellect or that it is a certain particular intellected species. And therefore the error of the Commentator in book three on the *De Anima* is clear, seeing that he wished to conclude from the universality of the intellected form to the unity of the intellect in all men; because there is no universality of that form according to the existence which it has in the intellect, but according as it is referred to things as a likeness of things. Thus, too, if there were a single corporeal statue representing many men, it is clear that the image or species of the statue would have an existence singular and proper according as it existed in this matter, but it would have a ratio of community according as it were a common thing representing many. And because to human nature according to its absolute consideration belongs what is predicated of Socrates, and since the ratio of species does not belong to it according to its absolute consideration, but follows from accidents which issue from it according to the existence which it has in the intellect, therefore the name of species is not predicated of Socrates so that it is said that Socrates is a species, which would necessarily happen if the ratio of species belonged to man according to the existence which he has in Socrates, or according to man's absolute consideration, namely, inasmuch as he is man; for whatever applies to man inasmuch as he is man is predicated of Socrates. Yet to be predicated applies to genus by virtue of itself *(per se),* since it is posited in its definition. For predication is a certain thing which is perfected by means of the action of the intellect composing and dividing, having in the very thing as its foundation the unity of those things of which one is asserted of the other. Whence the ratio of predicability can be included in the ratio of this mode of intention which is genus, which, similarly, is perfected by means of an act of the intellect. Yet, nevertheless, that to which the intellect attributes the intention of predication, composing the one with the other, is not the very intention of genus but rather that to which the intellect attributes the intention of genus, as for instance what is signified by the name animal. Thus, therefore, it is clear how essence or nature is disposed towards *(se habet ad)* the ratio of species, because the ratio of species does not belong to those things which are appropriate to it according to its absolute consideration, nor likewise does it belong to the accidents which issue from it according to the existence which it has outside the soul, as whiteness or blackness. But it does belong to the accidents which issue from it according to the existence which it has in the intellect. And it is according to this mode that the ratio of genus and of difference also applies to it.

CHAPTER 4

Now it remains to see through what mode essence exists in separate substances, namely, in the soul, in intelligences and in the first cause. But although all grant the simplicity of the first cause, yet certain ones strive to introduce a composition of form and matter in intelligences and in the soul. The author of this position appears to have been

Avicebron, the writer of the book *Fons Vitae*. But this is opposed to what is commonly said by philosophers, seeing that they call them substances separated from matter and prove them to be devoid of all matter. The most powerful reason for the assertion is (taken) from the power *(virtute)* of understanding which is in them (separate substances). For we see that forms are not intelligible in act except according as they are separated from matter and its conditions, nor are they made intelligible in act except by the power *(per virtutem)* of intelligent substance, inasmuch as they are received in it and inasmuch as they are actuated by virtue of it. Whence it is necessary that in any intelligent substance there be entire immunity from matter in such wise that they neither have a material part to them nor yet exist as a form impressed in matter, as is the case respecting material forms. Nor can anyone say that intelligibility is not impeded by any sort of matter, but only by corporeal matter. For if this impediment were by reason of corporeal matter alone, since matter is not spoken of as corporeal except inasmuch as it stands under corporeal form, then it would follow necessarily that matter would impede intelligibility by means of its corporeal form. And this cannot be, because the very corporeal form also is intelligible in act, just as other forms are, inasmuch as it is abstracted from matter. Wherefore in the soul or in an intelligence there is in no way a composition of matter and form so that essence might be taken in them in the mode in which it is taken in corporeal substances. But there is there (in them) a composition of form and existence; whence it is said in the comment on the ninth proposition of the book *De Causis* that intelligence is having form and existence; and form is taken there for the very quiddity or simple nature.

But it is easy to see how this is. For whatever things are disposed towards *(se habent ad)* one another in such wise that one is the cause of the existence of the other, that which has the ratio of cause can possess existence without the other, but not conversely. But such is found to be the habitude of matter and form, because form gives existence to matter, and therefore it is impossible for matter to be without some form, yet it is not impossible for ally form, to exist without matter, for form inasmuch as it is form does not depend on matter. But if any forms should be discovered which cannot exist save in matter, this happens to them inasmuch as they are distant from the first principle which is the first and pure act. Whence those forms which have the greatest propinquity to the first principle are forms subsisting by virtue of themselves *(per se)* without matter. For form does not require matter according to its entire genus, as has been said, and forms of this sort are intelligences. And therefore it is not necessary that the essences or quiddities of these substances be anything save the very form. Therefore the essence of a composite substance and the essence of a simple substance differ in that the essence of a composite substance is not form alone but embraces form and matter, whereas the essence of a simple substance is form alone. And from this two other differences are derived. One is that the essence of a composite substance can be signified as a whole or as a part, which happens according to the designation of the matter, as has been stated. And therefore the essence of a composite thing is not predicated in any mode whatsoever of the composite thing itself; for it cannot be said that man is his quiddity. But the essence of a simple thing, which is its form, cannot be signified except as a whole, since there is nothing there except the form as form receiving, and, therefore, in whatever mode the essence of a simple substance is taken it is predicated of the substance. Whence Avicenna says that the quiddity of a simple (substance) is itself simple, because there is not anything else receptive of the quiddity. The second difference is that the essences of composite things, seeing that they are received in designated matter, are multiplied according to its division, whence it results that some things are the same in species and diverse numerically. But since the essence of simple substance is not received in matter, there cannot be there any such multiplication. And therefore it follows necessarily that in these substances more than one individual of the same species are not found, but however many individuals there are, just so many are the species, as Avicenna expressly says. (*scil.* "A species of this mode is one in number.")

And indeed substances of this sort, although they are forms alone without matter, still do not have an entire simplicity of nature so that they are pure act; on the contrary, they have a mixture of potency, which is evident thus: for whatsoever does not belong to the concept of essence or quiddity is something accruing from without and effecting a composition with the essence, since no essence can be conceived without those things which are parts of essence. But every essence or quiddity can be conceived aside from the condition that something be known concerning its existence, for I can conceive what a man or phoenix is and still not know whether it has existence in the nature of things. Therefore it is clear that existence is something other than essence or quiddity, unless perhaps there be something the quiddity of which is its very existence. And this thing can only be one and primary, because it is impossible that a multiplication of anything should be effected except by virtue of the addition of some difference, as the nature of genus is multiplied into species either by virtue of this, that the form is received in diverse matters, just as the nature of species is multiplied in diverse individuals, or by virtue of this, that it is one thing absolutely but another as received in something, as for instance if there were a certain separated heat it would be other than a non-separated heat from its very separation. But if some thing is posited which is existence alone such that the existence itself is subsisting, this existence does not receive an addition of difference, since then it would not be existence only but existence and beyond that some form; and much less does it receive an addition of matter because then it would be not a subsisting existence but a material existence. Wherefore it is clear that a thing such that it is its own existence cannot be except as one (unique). Whence it follows necessarily that in anything whatsoever except this (the unique) its existence must be one thing and its quiddity or nature or form another. Accordingly, in intelligences there is an existence over and beyond form, and therefore it has been said that an intelligence is form and existence.

But all that belongs to anything is either caused from principles of its nature, as for instance risibility in man, or accrues to it through some extrinsic principle, as for instance light in air from the influence of the sun. But it cannot be that existence itself should be caused by the form or quiddity of the thing, caused, I say, as by means of an efficient cause, because thus something would be the cause of itself and would bring its very self into existence, which is impossible. Therefore it follows that everything such that its existence is other than its nature has existence from another *(ab alio).* And because everything which exists by virtue of another is reduced to that which exists in virtue of itself *(per se),* as to its first cause, it follows that there must be something which is the cause of the existence *(causa essendi)* of all things, because it is very existence alone; otherwise the causes would proceed to infinity, since everything which is not existence alone would have a cause of its existence, as has been said. It is clear, therefore, that an intelligence is form and existence, and that it has its existence from the first being which is existence alone, and this is the first cause which is God. But everything which receives something from something *(aliquid ab aliquo)* is in potency in respect to that, and what is received in it is its act. Therefore it follows that the very quiddity or form which is the intelligence is in potency in respect to the existence which it receives from God, and that existence is received according to the mode of act. And thus potency and act are found in intelligences, yet not form and matter, except equivocally. Whence, too, to suffer, to receive, to be a subject and all things of this kind which are seen to belong to things by reason of matter, belong equivocally to intellectual substances and to corporeal substances, as the Commentator says in the third book of the *De Anima*. And because, as has been said, the quiddity of an intelligence is the intelligence itself, therefore its quiddity or essence is the same thing as itself, and its existence, received from God, is that by means of which it subsists in the nature of things. And for this reason substances of this sort are said by some to be composed of that by virtue of which it is *(quo est)* and that which it is *(quod est)*, or of that which it is and existence, as Boethius says.

And since potency and act are posited in intelligences it will not be difficult to find a multitude of intelligences, which would be impossible if there were no potency in them. Whence the Commentator says in the third book of the *De Anima*, that if the nature of the possible intellect were unknown we should not be able to discover multiplicity in separate substances. Therefore the distinction of these in regard to one another is according to their grade (measure) of potency and act, so that a superior intelligence which is more proximate to the first (being) has more of act and less of potency, and so for others. And this is fulfilled in the human soul which holds the lowest grade among intellectual substances. Whence its possible intellect is disposed towards *(se habet ad)* intelligible forms just as first matter, which holds the lowest grade in sensible existence, is disposed towards sensible forms, as the Commentator remarks in book three on the *De Anima*. And therefore the Philosopher compares it to a tablet upon which nothing is written, and for this reason among other intelligible substances it has more potency. Accordingly, it is made to be so close to material things that the material thing is drawn to participate in its existence, so that from soul and body results one existence in one composite, although that existence according as it pertains to soul is not dependent upon the body. And therefore after that form which is in the soul are discovered other forms having more potency and more propinquity to matter. In these, too, is found order *(ordo)* and grade (measure: *gradus*) all the way through to the first forms of elements which are in the greatest propinquity to matter. Accordingly, they do not have any operation except according to the exigency of active and passive qualities, and of the others by which matter is disposed to form.

CHAPTER 5

Having understood the above, one knows clearly how essence is found in different things. For there is a threefold way of having an essence in substances. One way is like God, whose essence is His very existence; and therefore some philosophers are found who say that God does not have a quiddity or essence, since His essence is none other than His existence. And from this it follows that God is not in a genus, since everything which is in a genus must have a quiddity in addition to its existence, seeing that the quiddity or nature of genus or species is not distinguished according to a principle of nature in those things of which it is genus and species, but existence is different in different things. And indeed if we say that God is existence alone it is not necessary that we fall into the error of those who said that God is that universal existence in which everything exists formally. For the existence which is God is of a condition such that no addition can be made to it. Whence by virtue of its very purity it is existence distinct from every other existence, as for instance a certain separated color would by its very separation be different from non-separated color. For this reason it is observed in the comment on the ninth proposition of the book *De Causis* that the individuation of the first cause which is existence alone is by means of its pure goodness. But common existence, just as it does not include an addition to its concept, so, too, does not include in its concept any exclusion of addition, because if this were so nothing could be conceived to exist in which something over and above were added to existence. Similarly, too, although a being be existence alone, it does not follow that it should be wanting in the rest of the perfections and nobilities. Indeed God has the perfections which are in all genera, and for this reason He is called perfect simply, as the Philosopher and Commentator say in the fifth book of the *Metaphysics,* but He has these (perfections) in a more excellent mode than other things, because in Him they are one, but in other things they have diversity. And this is because all of these perfections belong to Him according to his simple existence; just as, if someone were able by means of one quality to effect the operations of all qualities, in that one quality he would have all qualities, so God in His very existence has all perfections.

According to the second mode essence is found in created intellectual substances in which the essence is other than their existence, although their essence is without matter. Whence their existence is not absolute but received and therefore according to the capacity of the receiving nature, but their nature or quiddity is absolute and not received in any matter. And therefore it is said in the book *De Causis* that intelligences are infinite from beneath and finite from above. For they are finite in respect to their existence which they receive from above, but they are not finite from below, since their forms are not limited to the capacity of any matter receiving them. And therefore in such substances there is not found a multitude of individuals in one species, as has been said, except in the instance of the human soul because of the body which is united to it. And although its individuation depends on the body as its occasion inasmuch as its (that of the individuation) beginning is concerned, seeing that the soul does not acquire individuated existence except in a body of which it is the act, still it does not follow that, the body being removed, the individuation would perish; because, since it (the soul) has absolute existence from the time individuated existence is acquired, in that it is made the form of this body, that existence always remains individuated. And therefore Avicenna says that the individuation of souls and their multitude depends upon the body in respect to their beginning but not in respect to their end. And because in those substances quiddity is not the same as existence therefore they are capable of being ordered in a predicament (category) and for this reason genus, species, and difference are found in them, although their proper differences are hidden from us. For in sensible things likewise the essential differences themselves are unknown; hence they are signified by means of the accidental differences which arise from their essential differences, as a cause is signified by means of its effect, as for instance biped is posited as the difference of man. But the proper accidents of immaterial substances are not known to us, and accordingly their differences cannot be signified by us either by virtue of themselves or by virtue of their accidental differences.

Still one ought to know that genus and difference are not taken in the same mode in those substances and in sensible substances, because in sensible substances genus is taken from that which is material in the thing, but difference is taken from that which is formal in it. Whence Avicenna says in the beginning of his book *De Anima* that form in things composed of matter and form "is the simple difference of that which is constituted from it," not, however, so that the form itself is the difference, but because it is the principle of the difference, as he says in his *Metaphysics.* And such difference is called simple difference, because it is taken from what is a part of the quiddity of the thing, namely, from the form. But since immaterial substances are simple quiddities, difference in them cannot be taken from that which is a part of the quiddity but from the whole quiddity. And therefore in the beginning of the *De Anima* Avicenna says that "simple difference . . . is not possessed except in those species the essences of which are composed of matter and form." Similarly also in these substances genus is taken from the whole essence, yet in a different mode. For one separate substance agrees with others in immateriality, and these substances differ from one another in their grade of perfection according to their recession from potentiality and their accession to pure act. And therefore in them genus is appropriated from that which ensues from them inasmuch as they are immaterial, as intellectuality or something of this sort. Difference, however, is appropriated from that which ensues from the grade of perfection in them and this is unknown to us. And yet it is not necessary that these differences be accidental, because they are according to greater and less perfection which does not diversify species; for the grade of perfection in receiving the same form does not diversify species, just as more white and less white in participating in the same principle of whiteness (does not), but a different grade of perfection in the very forms or natures participated does diversify species, as for instance nature proceeds by grades from plants to animals through certain (levels) which are mediate between animals and plants, according to the Philosopher in the eighth book of the *De Animalibus.* Nor again is it necessary that the division of intellectual substances be always through two true differences, because it is impossible for this to happen in all things, as the Philosopher says in the eleventh book of the *De Animalibus.*

In the third mode essence is found in substances composed of matter and form, in which also existence is received and finite because they have existence from another, and again their nature or quiddity is received in signated matter. And therefore they are finite from above and below, and in them furthermore a multiplication of individuals in one species is possible, because of the division of signated matter. And how their essence is disposed towards *(se habeat ad)* logical intentions has been discussed above.

CHAPTER 6

It now remains to see how essence exists in accidents, for how it exists in all substances has been discussed. And because, as has been said, essence is what is signified by means of definition it is necessary that they (accidents) possess essence in the mode in which they have definition. But they have an incomplete definition because they cannot be defined unless a subject is posited in their definition; and this is because they do not have existence by virtue of themselves *(per se)* freed from *(absolutum)* the subject. But just as a substantial existence ensues from form and matter when composited, so, too, an accidental existence ensues from accident and subject when the accident advenes to the subject. And therefore neither has the substantial form itself complete essence, nor has matter; because likewise in the definition of substantial form it is necessary to posit that of which it is the form, and so its definition is by virtue of the addition of something which is outside its genus, as is also the definition of the accidental form. Whence in the definition of soul body is posited by the naturalist who considers the soul only inasmuch as it is the form of a physical body. But nevertheless there is a difference between substantial form and accidental form because, just as substantial form does not have an absolute existence by virtue of itself without that to which it advenes, so neither does that to which it advenes, namely, matter. And therefore from the conjunction of both ensues that existence in which the thing subsists by virtue of itself *(per se),* and from them is effected a unity by virtue of itself *(unum per se:* a substantial unity) for the reason that a certain essence ensues from their conjunction. Whence the form, although considered in itself *(in se)* it does not possess the complete ratio of essence, is nevertheless part of a complete essence. But that to which the accident advenes is a being complete in itself *(in se)*, subsisting in its own existence; which certain existence naturally precedes the accident which supervenes to it. And therefore the supervening accident, from its conjunction with that to which it advenes, does not cause that existence in which the thing subsists, through which the thing is a being by virtue of itself *(ens per se)*, but it causes a certain secondary existence, without which the subsisting thing can be conceived, as the first can be conceived without the second. Whence from an accident and a subject is not effected a unity by virtue of itself *(unum per se:* substantial unity), but a unity by virtue of accident *(unum per accidens:* accidental unity). And therefore from their conjunction a certain essence does not result, as from the conjunction of form with matter. For which reason an accident has neither the ratio of complete essence, nor is it a part of complete essence; but just as it is being in a certain respect *(secundum quid),* so also it has essence in a certain respect.

But because that which is in the greatest degree and most truly asserted in any genus whatsoever is the cause of those things which are posterior in that genus, as for instance fire which is the extreme of hotness is the cause of heat in hot things, as is also said in the second book of the *Metaphysics,* therefore substance, which is first in the genus of being, having essence most truly and in the greatest degree, is necessarily the cause of accidents which participate the principle of being only secondarily and, as it were, in a certain respect *(secundum quid).* This however happens in diverse ways. For since the parts of a substance are matter and form, therefore certain accidents principally follow upon form, and others upon matter. Moreover, some form is found the existence of which does not depend on matter, as the intellective soul does not; but matter, does not exist except by means of form. Whence in accidents which ensue from form there is something which has no communication with matter, as for instance to intellect, which is not by means of any corporeal organ, as the Philosopher proves in the third book of the *De Anima.* But some of the things ensuing from the form have communication with matter, as for instance to sense, and things of this sort; but no accident ensues from matter without communication with form. Yet in these accidents which ensue from matter there is found a certain diversity. For certain accidents ensue from matter according to an order which they have to a special form, as for instance masculine and feminine in animals, the diversity of which is reduced to matter, as is said in the tenth book of the *Metaphysics.* Whence the form of animal being removed, the accidents do not remain except equivocally. Certain (accidents) ensue from matter according to an order which it has to a general form, and therefore, the special form being removed, they still remain (in the matter), as for instance blackness of skin is in the Ethiopian from a mixture of elements and not by reason of his soul, and therefore remains in him after death. And because each and every thing is individuated from its matter and disposed in a genus or a species by virtue of its form, therefore accidents which ensue from matter are accidents of the individual, according to which individuals of the same species differ from one another. But the accidents which ensue from form are proper passions of the genus or of the species, whence they are found in all things participating in the nature of the genus or of the species, as for instance risibility in man ensues from the form, since a laugh arises from some apprehension in the soul of a man.

One should know, too, that accidents are sometimes caused by the essential principles according to perfect act, as for instance geat in fire which is always hot in act; but at times (they are caused) only according to an aptitude, with completion accruing to them from an exterior agent, as for instance transparency in the air which is completed by means of a lucid external body. And in such instances the aptitude is an inseparable accident, but the complement, which ensues to it from some principle which is outside the essence of the thing or which does not enter into its constitution, will be separable, as for instance to be moved and things of this sort.

One should know therefore that in accidents genus, species and difference are taken in a mode other than that in which they are taken in substances. For since in substances there is effected from the substantial form and the matter a unity by virtue of itself (*per se unum:* a substantial unity), a certain nature resulting from their conjunction which is properly placed in the predicament (category) of substance, therefore in substances the concrete names which signify the composite are properly said to be in a genus, whether species or genus, as man or animal. However, neither form nor matter is in a predicament (category) in this mode except through reduction, as the former is said to be in a genus. But a substantial unity (*unum per se*) is not effected from an accident and its subject, and therefore no nature results from their conjunction to which the intention of genus or species can be attributed. Accordingly, the accidental names expressing a concretion, as for instance white man or musician, are not placed in a predicament (category), either as species or as genus, except by reduction, for they can be placed in a predicament only according to what is signified in the abstract, as for instance white or musical. And because accidents are not composed of matter and form, therefore in them it is not possible to take the genus from the matter and the difference from the form as in composite substances. But the genus must be taken primarily from its very mode of being inasmuch as being is asserted in diverse modes of the ten predicamental genera (categories) in accordance with the (order of) prior and posterior. So likewise it is called quantity according as it is the measure of substance and quality inasmuch as it is said to be a disposition of substance, and likewise for the others (predicamental genera), as the Philosopher states in the fourth of the *Metaphysics*. Indeed, difference in accidents is taken from the diversity of the principles from which they are caused. And because proper passions are caused from proper principles of the subject, therefore a subject is posited in their definition in place of difference, if they are defined abstractly (*in absoluto*), according to which manner of definition they are properly in a genus, as for instance it is said that snub-nosedness is a curvature of the nose. But the converse would hold if their definition were taken concretely. For thus the subject would be posited in their definition as their genus, seeing that they would then be defined as composite substances are, in which the ratio of the genus is taken from matter, as we say that a snub-nose is a curved nose. If one accident be the principle of another accident, the case is similar to the above, as for instance the principle of relation is action and passion and quantity; and therefore according to this the Philosopher divides relation in the *Metaphysics*. But since the proper principles of accidents are not always manifest, therefore sometimes we take the difference of accidents from their effects, as condensing and dispersing are called differences of color, which are caused from the abundance or paucity of light from which the different species of color result.

Thus, therefore, it is clear in what mode essence is in substances and in accidents, and in what mode it is in composite substances and in simple substances, and after what manner universal logical intentions are found in all these; with the exception of the First which is the extreme of simplicity, and to which because of its simplicity neither the ratio of genus, nor of species, nor, consequently, definition applies.

In which may the end and consummation of this discourse be. Amen.

Late Medieval Philosophy

While Thomas Aquinas lived during a period of relative calm and well-being, the century and a half following his death was one of tumult and upheaval. As a part of the often vicious conflict between church and state, Philip IV of France captured Pope Boniface VIII in 1303 and soon thereafter moved the papal court to Avignon, France—the so-called Babylonian Captivity of the Church. Beginning in 1347 the Bubonic Plague, or "Black Death," struck Western Europe. Responses to the plague ranged from fanatical anti-intellectual apocalypticism to self-indulgent hedonism. Some even blamed the plague on intellectuals such as Thomas, saying they provoked divine wrath by explaining God's ways rationally; others simply counselled, "Let us eat, drink, and be merry, for tomorrow we die." Many turned to superstition or to scapegoating Jews. At the same time England and France were involved in the Hundred Years' War (1337–1453), which brought enormous casualties. Between the plague and the war, in the years from 1300 to 1450, the population of Western Europe was reduced by half—perhaps by as much as two-thirds. In 1378 the "Great Schism" divided the Catholic Church as the Italians reinstituted the papacy in Rome, while a second pope reigned in Avignon. For over thirty years rival popes condemned and excommunicated one another. In 1409 an attempt to end the schism with a compromise pope led only to a third pope and thus a third claimant to St. Peter's universal chair. Finally, in

1417 the church united around one pope ruling in Rome. But by now the power and prestige of the papacy had been severely diminished, and a hundred years later, in the Protestant Reformation, the church split decisively.

It is common to view the philosophy of this period in the light of these social upheavals, and, indeed, there does seem to be some connection. Thomas had harmonized philosophy and theology in a systematic way reflective of the relative peacefulness of the thirteenth century. Just as social stability—particularly in the relationship between church and state—deteriorated in the centuries following Thomas, so also the philosophies that developed during this period tended to separate reason and faith. In particular, thinkers became more skeptical about natural theology, that is, about the ability of reason to know truths concerning God. John Duns Scotus began this process as he tended to reduce the competence of theology to supernatural revelation alone, dismissing the natural theology of Thomas. William of Ockham took this tendency further, claiming philosophy and theology to be separate realms with separate rules. The transitional thinker Nicholas Cusanas claimed that knowledge was at best mere conjecture and that contradictories are compatible in reality: God, especially, incorporates all contradictions, all opposites, within Himself. In addition, mystics such as Meister Eckhart and Catherine of Siena argued for a nonrational way of knowing God. Clearly the coherent, rational synthesis of Thomas had unravelled.

But as Frederick Copleston has pointed out, there are other ways of understanding this transition. Instead of seeing late medieval/early Renaissance philosophy as destructive to a grand synthesis or as a reaction to societal chaos, "one can see . . . philosophy being reborn and growing up under the shadow and care of theology, reaching a more or less adult stage and then tending to go its own way and assert its independence" (*A History of Medieval Philosophy,* p. 314). While acknowledging the disintegration of the peculiarly Thomistic approach to synthesis, this view sees our period as a natural development of Western European thought.

*   *   *

For general surveys of medieval philosophy, which include the later period, see Maurice De Wulf, *History of Mediaeval Philosophy* (New York: Dover, 1952); Étienne Gilson, *History of Christian Philosophy in the Middle Ages* (New York: Random House, 1955); and Armand A. Maurer, *Medieval Philosophy* (New York: Random House, 1962). The following volumes of Frederick Copleston's *A History of Philosophy* deal with this period: *Volume II: Medieval Philosophy, Part II: Albert the Great to Duns Scotus* (1950; reprinted Garden City, NY: Image Doubleday, 1962); *Volume III: Late Medieval and Renaissance Philosophy, Part I: Ockham to the Speculative Mystics* and *Part II: The Revival of Platonism to Suárez* (both 1953; reprinted Garden City, NY: Image Doubleday, 1963); and the later single volume, *A History of Medieval Philosophy* (New York: Harper & Row, 1972). Ray C. Petry, ed., *Late Medieval Mysticism* (Philadelphia: Westminster Press, 1957); Gordon Leff, *The Dissolution of the Medieval Outlook: An Essay on Intellectual and Spiritual Change in the Fourteenth Century* (New York: New York University Press, 1976), and John Marenbon, *Later Medieval Philosophy (1150–1350): An Introduction* (London: Routledge & Kegan Paul, 1987), give surveys of the late medieval period, while Norman Kretzmann et al., eds., *The Cambridge History of Later Medieval Philosophy: From the Rediscovery of*

Aristotle to the Disintegration of Scholasticism 1100–1600 (Cambridge: Cambridge University Press, 1982), offers thematic essays.

For general studies of Renaissance thought, see Ernst Cassirer et al., eds., *The Renaissance Philosophy of Man* (Chicago: University of Chicago Press, 1948); Ernst Cassirer, *The Individual and Cosmos in Renaissance Philosophy,* translated by Mario Domandi (New York: Harper & Row, 1963); and Paul O. Kristeller, *Renaissance Thought and Its Sources* (New York: Columbia University Press, 1979).

John Duns Scotus
ca. 1265–1308

Not much is known about the early life of John Duns Scotus except that he was born in Scotland. He later became a Franciscan friar and taught at Cambridge, Oxford, and Paris. In 1303 he was banished from Paris because he sided with Pope Boniface VIII against King Philip IV. Within a year he was back in Paris and in 1305 became regent master of theology. Two years later he was transferred to Cologne, where he died in 1308.

Scotus managed to write a number of books during his short life—twelve Latin volumes in a seventeenth-century edition—though some work, previously thought his, is now believed to be that of his followers. Duns's abstract metaphysical speculations and technical terminology are extremely difficult to understand. It is not surprising, then, that later thinkers called him the "Subtle Doctor." The followers of John Duns Scotus were so intent on following his subtlety that Renaissance thinkers mocked them as "Dunsmen"—from which we get our word "dunce." Despite this epithet, there are those, such as the poet Gerard Manley Hopkins, who have found Scotus's thought penetrating and profound.

Scotus disagreed with Thomas Aquinas on a number of issues including the doctrine of analogy, the nature of individuation, and the limits of natural theology. But the most important difference between these two thinkers concerned the relative importance of intellect and will. A recent philosopher, Christopher Devlin, explains that for Thomas the mind is like a limpid and motionless pool in which both the nature of the surrounding objects and the movements of the heavens can be clearly discerned. Everything is reflected in a two-dimensional surface, and yet there is no mistaking the differences of depth and distance, there is no confusion between earth and heaven.

But, Devlin says, when Duns Scotus considers Thomas's understanding of the mind,

> He complains that if [the rational mind] is regarded as a closed circle sufficient unto itself, it does not adequately represent the human soul. The human soul is not co-extensive with reason or understanding . . . it is a mistake to regard the other powers of the soul simply as functions or adjuncts to understanding. There is a power of the soul which is below understanding, but which has better evidence of the soul's origin, and there is a power of the soul which is above understanding and which is more in touch with the soul's destiny. The secret entrance to the pool is the point where the unconscious begins to influence the conscious mind. The secret exit is the point where the soul finds that its intellectual powers extended to their fullest have still failed to satisfy it, and that it must bring a higher faculty into play. In this way he returns to, and hopes to reinstate St. Augustine's hierarchy of memory, understanding and will. He sees these powers as the one soul operating on different levels of consciousness. (Quoted in Fremantle, *The Age of Belief,* pp. 181–82.)

Our first selection, from *A Treatise on God as First Principle,* presents Scotus's argument for God's existence as the "one nature which is simply first." Here Scotus argues from possibility to a necessary being. Our second selection, from the Prologue to the *Ordinatio,* presents a discussion of the relationship between faith and reason. Following an exposition of reasoning to the contrary, Scotus argues for the necessity of revealed knowledge. In so doing, Scotus distances himself from the natural theology of Thomas and further separates reason and revelation. Both excerpts are translated by Allan B. Wolter.

* * *

For years, Charles R.S. Harris's *Duns Scotus,* 2 vols. (1927; reprinted New York: Humanities Press, 1959), was the standard work, but this study includes material now known to be unauthentic. For more recent work on Duns Scotus, see Efrem Bettoni, *Duns Scotus: The Basic Principles of His Philosophy,* translated by Bernardine Bonansea (Washington, DC: Catholic University of America Press, 1961), and Allan B. Wolter, *The Philosophical Theology of John Duns Scotus* (Ithaca, NY: Cornell University Press, 1990). For a collection of essays, see John K. Ryan and Bernardine M. Bonansea, eds., *John Duns Scotus* (Washington, DC: Catholic University of America Press, 1965). The Franciscan Institute Publications, Philosophy Series, includes several specialized studies on Duns Scotus, though they may prove difficult for the beginning student.

A TREATISE ON GOD AS FIRST PRINCIPLE (in part)

CHAPTER 3

3.1 The triple primacy of the First Principle.

3.2 O Lord, our God, you have proclaimed yourself to be the first and last. Teach your servant to show by reason what he holds with faith most certain, that you are the most eminent, the first efficient cause and the last end.

3.3 We would like to select three of the six essential orders referred to earlier, the two of extrinsic causality and the one of eminence and, if you grant us to do so, to demonstrate that in these three orders there is some one nature which is simply first. I say one "nature" advisedly, since in this third chapter these three ways of being first will be shown to characterize not a unique singular or what is but one in number, but a unique essence or nature. Numerical unity, however, will be discussed later.

3.4 (First conclusion) *Some nature among beings can produce an effect.*

3.5 This is shown to be so because something can be produced and therefore something can be productive. The implication is evident from the nature of correlatives. Proof of the antecedent: (1) Some nature is contingent. It is possible for it to exist after being nonexistent, not of itself, however, or by reason of nothing, for in both these cases a being would exist by reason of what is not a being. Therefore it is producible by another. (2) Some nature too is changeable or mobile, since it can lack some perfection it is able to have. The result of the change then can begin to be and thus be produced.

3.6 In this conclusion, as in some of those which follow, I could argue in terms of the actual thus. Some nature is producing since some nature is produced, because some nature begins to exist, for some nature is contingent and the result of motion. But I prefer to propose conclusions and premises about the possible. For once those about the actual are granted, those about the possible are also conceded, but the reverse is not the case. Also those about the actual are contingent, though evident enough, whereas those about the possible are necessary. The former concern the being as existing whereas the latter can pertain properly to a being considered even in terms of its essentials. The existence of this essence, of which efficiency is now established, will be proved later.

3.7 (Second conclusion) *Something able to produce an effect is simply first, that is to say, it neither can be produced by an efficient cause nor does it exercise its efficient causality in virtue of anything other than itself.*

3.8 It is proved from the first conclusion that something can produce an effect. Call this producer A. If A is first in the way explained, we have immediately what we seek to prove. If it is not such, then it is a posterior agent either because it can be produced by something else or because it is able to produce its effect only in virtue of some agent other than itself. To deny the negation is to assert the affirmation. Let us assume that this being is not first and call it B. Then we can argue of B as we did of A. Either we go on *ad infinitum* so that each thing in reference to what precedes it in the series will be second; or we shall reach something that has nothing prior to it. However, an infinity in the ascending order is impossible; hence a primacy is necessary because what-

Duns Scotus, *A Treatise on God as First Principle,* translated by Allan B. Wolter (Chicago: Franciscan Herald Press, 1969). Reprinted by permission.

ever has nothing prior is not posterior to anything posterior to itself, for the second conclusion of chapter two does away with a circle in causes.

3.9 An objection is raised here on the grounds that those who philosophize admit that an infinity is possible in an ascending order, as they themselves were wont to assume infinite generators of which none is first but each is second to some other, and still they assume no circle in causes. In ruling out this objection I declare that the philosophers did not postulate the possibility of an infinity in causes essentially ordered, but only in causes accidentally ordered, as is evident from Avicenna's *Metaphysics,* B. VI, chapter five, where he speaks of an infinity of individuals in a species.

3.10 But to show what I have in mind, I will explain what essentially ordered and accidentally ordered causes are. Here recall that it is one thing to speak of incidental causes *(causae per accidens)* as contrasted with those which are intended to cause a given effect *(causae per se)*. It is quite another to speak of causes which are ordered to one another essentially or of themselves *(per se)* and those which are ordered only accidentally *(per accidens)*. For in the first instance, we have merely a one-to-one comparison, [namely] of the cause to that which is caused. A *per se* cause is one which causes a given effect by reason of its proper nature and not in virtue of something incidental to it. In the second instance, two causes are compared with each other insofar as they are causes of the same thing.

3.11 *Per se* or essentially ordered causes differ from accidentally ordered causes in three respects. The first difference is that in essentially ordered causes, the second depends upon the first precisely in the act of causing. In accidentally ordered causes this is not the case, although the second may depend upon the first for its existence or in some other way. The second difference is that in essentially ordered causes the causality is of another nature and order, inasmuch as the higher cause is the more perfect, which is not the case with accidentally ordered causes. This second difference is a consequence of the first, since no cause in the exercise of its causality is essentially dependent upon a cause of the same nature as itself, for to produce anything one cause of a given kind suffices. A third difference follows, viz. that all essentially ordered causes are simultaneously required to cause the effect, for otherwise some causality essential to the effect would be wanting. In accidentally ordered causes this simultaneity is not required.

3.12 What we intend to show from this is that an infinity of essentially ordered causes is impossible, and that an infinity of accidentally ordered causes is also impossible unless we admit a *terminus* in an essentially ordered series. Therefore there is no way in which an infinity in essentially ordered causes is possible. And even if we deny the existence of an essential order, an infinity of causes is still impossible. Consequently in any case there is something able to produce an effect which is simply first. Here three propositions are assumed. For the sake of brevity, call the first A, the second B and the third C.

3.13 The proof of these: first, A is proved. (1) If the totality of essentially ordered causes were caused, it would have to be by a cause which does not belong to the group, otherwise it would be its own cause. The whole series of dependents then is dependent and upon something which is not one of the group. (2) [If this were not so], an infinity of essentially ordered causes would be acting at the same time (a consequence of the third difference mentioned above). Now no philosopher assumes this. (3) Thirdly, to be prior, according to Bk. V of the *Metaphysics,* a thing must be nearer the beginning. Consequently, where there is no beginning, nothing can be essentially prior to anything else. (4) Fourthly, by reason of the second difference, the higher cause is more perfect in its causality, therefore what is infinitely higher is infinitely more perfect, and hence of infinite perfection in its causing. Therefore it does not cause in virtue of another, because everything of this kind is imperfect in its causality, since it depends upon another to produce its effect. (5) Fifthly, inasmuch as to be able to produce something does not imply any imperfection—a point evident from conclusion eight of chapter two—it follows that this ability can exist in some nature without imperfection. But if every cause depends upon some prior cause, then efficiency would never be found without imperfection. Consequently, an independent power to produce something can exist in some nature and this is simply first. Therefore, such an efficient power is possible and this suffices for now, since we shall prove later from that that it exists in reality. And so A becomes evident from these five arguments.

3.14 Proof of B: If we assume an infinity of accidentally ordered causes, it is clear that these are not concurrent, but one succeeds another so that the second, though it is in some way from the preceding, does not depend upon it for the exercise of its causality. For it is equally effective whether the preceding cause exists or not. A son in turn may beget a child just as well whether his father be dead or alive. But an infinite succession of such causes is impossible unless it exists in virtue of some nature of infinite duration from which the whole succession and every part thereof depends. For no change of form is perpetuated save in virtue of something permanent which is not a part of that succession, since everything of this succession which is in flux is of the same nature. Something essentially prior to the series, then, exists, for everything that is part of the succession depends upon it, and this dependence is of a different order from that by which it depends upon the immediately preceding cause where the latter is a part of the succession. Therefore B is evident.

3.15 Proof of C: From the first conclusion, some nature is able to produce an effect. But if an essential order of agents be denied, then this nature capable of causing does not cause in virtue of some other cause, and even if we assume that in one individual it is caused, nevertheless in some other it will not be caused, and this is what we propose to prove to be true of the first nature. For if we assume that in every individual this nature is caused, then a contradiction follows if we deny the existence of an essential order, since no nature that is caused can be assumed to exist in each individual in such a way that it is included in an accidental order of causes without being at the same time essentially ordered to some other nature. This follows from B.

3.16 (Third conclusion) *If what is able to cause effectively is simply first, then it is itself incapable of being caused, since it cannot be produced and is independently able to produce its effects.*

3.17 This is clear from the second conclusion, for if such a being could cause only in virtue of something else or if it could be produced, then either a process *ad infinitum* or a circle in causes would result, or else the series would terminate in some being which cannot be produced and yet independently is able to produce an effect. This latter being I call "first," and from what you grant, it is clear that anything other than this is not first. Furthermore, it follows that if the first cannot be produced, then it has no causes whatsoever, for it cannot be the result of a final cause (from conclusion two of chapter two)—nor of a material cause (from the sixth conclusion of the same)—nor of a formal cause (from the seventh conclusion there). Neither can it be caused by matter and form together (from the eighth conclusion there).

3.18 (Fourth conclusion) *A being able to exercise efficient causality which is simply first actually exists, and some nature actually existing is capable of exercising such causality.*

3.19 Proof of this: Anything to whose nature it is repugnant to receive existence from something else, exists of itself if it is able to exist at all. To receive existence from something else is repugnant to the very notion of a being which is first in the order of efficiency, as is clear from the third conclusion. And it can exist, as is clear from the second conclusion. Indeed, the fifth argument there which seems to be less conclusive than the others established this much. The other proofs there can be considered in the existential mode—in which case they concern contingent, though manifest facts—or they can be understood of the nature, the quiddity and possibility, in which case the conclusions proceed from necessary premises. From all this it follows that an efficient cause which is first in the unqualified sense of the term can exist of itself, for what does not actually exist of itself is incapable of existing of itself. Otherwise a nonexistent being would cause something to exist; but this is impossible, even apart from the fact that in such a case the thing would be its own cause and hence could not be entirely uncaused. Another way to establish this fourth conclusion would be to argue from the impropriety of a universe that would lack the highest possible degree of being.

3.20 As a corollary of this fourth conclusion, note that not only is such a cause prior to all others, but that it would be contradictory to say that another is prior to it. And insofar as such a cause is first, it exists. This is proved in the same way as was the fourth conclusion. The very notion of such a being implies its inability to be caused. Therefore, if it can exist, owing to the fact that to be is not contradictory to it, then it follows that it can exist of itself and consequently that it does exist of itself.

3.21 (Fifth conclusion) *A being unable to be caused is of itself necessarily existent.*

3.22 Proof: By excluding every cause of existence other than itself, whether it be intrinsic or extrinsic, we make it impossible for it not to be. Proof: Nothing can be nonexistent unless something either positively or privatively incompatible with it can exist, for one of two contradictories is always true. But nothing can be either positively or privatively incompatible with a being which cannot be caused, because it would be either of itself or from another. Not the first way, for then it would exist of itself—from the fourth conclusion,—so that there would be two incompatible things, and for that reason neither would exist, since you admit that the uncausable is nonexistent because of this incompatible element and vice versa. Neither can the incompatible be from another, because nothing caused has a more intense or potent existence from a cause than an uncausable thing has of itself, since the former is dependent in existing whereas the uncausable is not. Furthermore the possibility of the causable being does not entail its actual existence as is the case with the uncausable. Nothing incompatible with what is already a being can come from a cause unless it receive from that cause a being more intense or powerful than is the being of that which is incompatible with it.

3.23 (Sixth conclusion) *It is the characteristic of but one nature to have necessary being of itself.*

3.24 This is proved thus: If two natures of themselves could be necessary being, then this necessity of existing would be a common feature. And this they would share by reason of some essential or generic kind of entity in addition to which they would differ by reason of their ultimate actual formalities. Now two inconsistencies follow from this. To begin with, each will be a necessary being first of all through that common nature which is the less actual, rather than through that distinctive nature which is the more actual. For were it necessary being also by reason of its distinctive nature, then it will be necessary being twice over, because that distinguishing nature does not formally include the common nature, even as a [specific] difference does not include the genus. It seems impossible however, that the less actual be the primary reason why something is necessary, and that it is neither primarily nor *per se* necessary by reason of what is more actual. The second impossibility is that neither of the two would necessarily exist by virtue of that common nature which is presumed to be the primary reason why each is necessary. For that nature is insufficient to account for the existence of either nature, since every nature is what it is by reason of its ultimate formal constituent. But it is precisely what—to the exclusion of all else—accounts for a thing's actual existence, that is the reason for its being necessary. If you say that the common nature suffices for existence apart from the distinguishing natures, then it follows that the common nature of itself exists actually and without any distinguishing features, and therefore cannot be distinguished, since the necessary being already existing is not in potency to being [different kinds of things] in an unqualified sense [in the way] that the generic being in a species is simply that *kind* of thing.

3.25 Besides, two natures included under a common class are unequal. Proof of this is to be found among the different kinds of things into which a genus is divided. But if the two such natures are unequal, one will be of a more perfect being than the other. Nothing however is more perfect than a being having necessary existence of itself.

3.26 Moreover, if there were two natures having necessary being of themselves, neither would depend upon the other for existence and consequently no essential order would exist between them. One of them, therefore, would not belong to this universe, for there is nothing in the universe which is not related by an essential order to the other beings, for the unity of the universe stems from the order of its parts. Here it is objected that inasmuch as each is related to the parts of the universe through the order of eminence, this suffices for unity. To the contrary: One is not so ordered to the other, for a more perfect existence characterizes the more eminent nature. Nothing however is more perfect than a being having necessary existence of itself. What is more, one of two is not ordered to the parts of the universe, because if the universe is one, then it is characterized by a single order and this obtains where there is but one first. Proof: If you assume there are two first natures, since there is a dual term of reference, the nature next to the first has no unique order or dependence and the same is true of each subsequent nature. And thus through the whole universe there will be two orders, and hence two universes. Or else where will be an order only to one necessary being, but not to the other. If one proceeds reasonably, then, it seems he ought not to postulate anything for no apparent need, or whose entity is not clearly revealed by reason of some order to other things,—for, according to *Physics,* Bk. I, more than one thing should not be postulated where one suffices. Now we show there is a necessary being in the universe from the uncausable, and this in turn from what is first in causing, and the latter from what is caused. But from these effects there is no apparent necessity for assuming several first causing natures; furthermore, this is impossible, as will be shown later in the fifteenth conclusion of this third chapter. Therefore it is not necessary to assume that there are several things which are uncaused and necessarily exist. With reason, then, they are not postulated.

3.27 Concerning the final cause I propose four conclusions similar to the first four in this chapter about a being able to produce an effect. They are also proved in a similar way. The first of these is this: (Seventh conclusion) *Among beings some nature is able to function as final cause.*

3.28 Proof: Since something is producible (from the proof of the first conclusion of this chapter), something is able to be ordered to an end. The implication is clear from the fourth conclusion of chapter two. That an essential order is involved is even more evident here than in the case of the efficient cause (from conclusion nine of chapter two).

3.29 (Eighth conclusion) *Something able to be an end is simply ultimate, that is to say, it can neither be ordained to something else nor exercise its finality in virtue of something else.*

3.30 This is proved by five arguments similar to those advanced for the second conclusion of this third chapter.

3.31 (Ninth conclusion) *Such an ultimate end cannot be caused in any way.*

3.32 This is proved from the fact that it cannot be ordained for another end; otherwise it would not be ultimate. It follows further that it cannot be caused by an efficient cause (from conclusion four of chapter two and also from what was said above in the proof for the third conclusion of the present chapter).

3.33 (Tenth conclusion) *The being which can be an ultimate end actually exists, and that this primacy pertains to some actually existing nature.*

3.34 The proof for this is like that used for the fourth conclusion of chapter three. Corollary: It is first to such an extent that it is impossible that anything should be prior to it. This is proved in the same fashion as the corollary to the fourth conclusion above.

PROLOGUE TO THE *ORDINATIO*

PART 1. THE NECESSITY OF REVEALED KNOWLEDGE. DOES MAN IN HIS PRESENT STATE NEED TO BE SUPERNATURALLY INSPIRED WITH SOME KNOWLEDGE?

1. The question is raised whether man in his present state needs to be supernaturally inspired with some special knowledge he could not attain by the natural light of the intellect.

[*The Pro and Con*]
That he needs none, I argue as follows:*

[Arg. 1] Every faculty which has something common as its primary object, is as competent by nature in regard to everything contained under this object as it is with regard to what is of itself the natural object. This is proved by the case of the primary object of vision and the other things contained under it. And thus we may proceed inductively with the other faculties and their primary objects. Reason also proves the same, for the primary object is that which is equal to the faculty in question. But if this notion, namely, of the primary object, were verified of something that is beyond the natural competency of the faculty, the object would not be equal to, but would exceed the faculty. The major then is evident. The natural primary object of our intellect is being qua being. Therefore, our intellect is able to know naturally any being whatsoever and consequently also any intelligible nonentity, for "affirmation explains denial." Therefore, etc. Proof of the minor: Avicenna in the first book of the *Metaphysics* says: "'Being' and 'thing' are impressed first upon the soul. Neither can they be revealed through other notions." But if the primary object of the intellect were anything other than these, then "being" and "thing" could be made known through this other notion. But this is impossible.

*For the refutation of these arguments see ¶90–94.

Translation by Allan B. Wolter. Reprinted from *Franciscan Studies*, Vol. XI, No. 3–4, 1951, by permission.

2. [Arg. 2] Furthermore, the sense needs no supernatural knowledge in its present state; therefore, neither does the intellect. The antecedent is evident. Proof of the consequence: "Nature leaves out nothing necessary" (*On the Soul,* III). Now, if this is true of things that are imperfect, all the more does it hold for things that are perfect. Consequently, if the inferior faculties lack nothing necessary for their function and the attainment of their end, all the more is this true of the higher faculty. Therefore, etc.

3. [Arg. 3] Furthermore, if some such knowledge were necessary, it would be so only because the faculty with its purely natural endowments is disproportionate to an object knowable only under such conditions. Therefore, an additional factor is required that the faculty may be made equal to the object. Now this other factor is either natural or supernatural. If natural, then the two combined are still disproportionate to the primary object. If this factor is supernatural, then the faculty is disproportionate to it; and so on *ad infinitum*. But since we cannot proceed to infinity according to *Metaphysics* II, it is necessary to stop with the first [viz. something natural], and admit that the intellective faculty is proportionate to everything that can be known and in any way in which it can be known. Therefore, etc.

4. *To the Contrary:*

"All doctrine divinely inspired is useful for arguing . . . etc." (*Tim.* 3).

Furthermore, it is said of wisdom: "No one can know its way, but He who knows all things knows it" (*Bar.* 3). Therefore, no other can have wisdom save from Him who knows all things. So much for the necessity of revelation. As to the fact thereof, he adds: "He [God] gave it to Jacob, His child, and to Israel, His beloved."—referring to the Old Testament—and the following: "After these things, He was seen on earth and talked with men."—referring to the New Testament.

[1. Controversy between the Philosophers and Theologians]

5. In this question we are faced with the controversy between the philosophers and theologians. The philosophers insist on the perfection of nature and deny supernatural perfection. The theologians, on the other hand, recognize the deficiency of nature and the need of grace and supernatural perfection.

[A. Opinion of the Philosophers]

The philosophers, then, would say that no supernatural knowledge is necessary for man in his present state, but that all the knowledge he needs could be acquired by the action of natural causes. In support of this, they cite from various places both the authority and the reasoning of the Philosopher.

6. [First argument]* The first is that passage in the third book *On the Soul,* where he [Aristotle] says that "the agent intellect is that by which [the intellect] makes all things; the possible intellect is that by which it becomes all things." From this I argue as follows. Once a natural agent and patient are put together and not impeded, action necessarily follows, for an action depends essentially only upon these factors as prior causes. But in regard to every intelligible object, the agent intellect is active and the possible intellect receptive. They are naturally in the soul and are not impeded. This is evident. By their natural power, then, an act of knowledge regarding any intelligible object whatsoever is possible.

7. [Second argument]** This is confirmed by reason. Every natural passive faculty has some corresponding natural agent. Otherwise the passive faculty would seem

---

*This argument is answered in ¶72.
**This argument is answered in ¶73–78.

to have no purpose in nature, since nothing in the realm of nature could reduce it to act. But the possible intellect is a passive faculty with regard to any intelligible object whatsoever. Some natural active power, consequently, corresponds to it. The thesis therefore follows. The minor is evident, since the possible intellect naturally seeks to know whatever can be known. Also it is naturally perfected by such knowledge. By nature then it is capable of receiving any knowledge whatsoever.

8. [Third argument]* Furthermore, speculative science is divided into mathematics, physics and metaphysics according to the *Metaphysics,* VI. And from the proof for this, which is given there, no other speculative science seems possible, since in these sciences the whole of being is considered, both in itself and in all its divisions. Now just as a speculative science other than these three would not be possible, neither is any practical science possible other than those acquired sciences that have to do with functional and productive activity. Consequently, practical acquired sciences suffice to perfect the practical intellect and speculative acquired sciences, the speculative intellect.

9. [Fourth argument]** Furthermore, anyone capable by nature of knowing a principle can know naturally the conclusions included in that principle. This I prove from the fact that the knowledge of the conclusions depends solely upon an understanding of the principle and the deduction of the conclusion from the principle, as is evident from the definition of "to know" in the *Posterior Analytics,* I. Now, the deduction is manifest of itself, as is clear from the definition of the perfect syllogism in the *Prior Analytics.* "Such a syllogism needs nothing either for being, or for appearing, evidently necessary." Consequently if the principles be known, everything needed for a knowledge of the conclusion is there. And so the major is clear.

10. Now we know naturally the first principles in which all conclusions are virtually contained. Hence, we can also know naturally all the conclusions that can be known.

Proof of the first part of the minor. Since the terms of the first principles are most common, it follows that they can be known naturally, for according to the first book of the *Physics,* we know first what is most common. But according to *Posterior Analytics,* I: "we know and understand principles in so far as we know their terms." We can know first principles then naturally.

11. Proof of the second part of the minor. Since the terms of the first principles are most common, when they are distributed, they are distributed in regard to all the concepts that fall under them. Now in first principles, such terms are taken universally and therefore they extend to all particular concepts. Consequently, they include the terms of all particular conclusions.

[B. Refutation of the Opinion of the Philosophers]

12. Three arguments can be raised against this opinion.† ([Marginal note by Scotus:] By natural reason nothing supernatural can be shown to exist in the wayfarer, nor can it be proved that anything supernatural is necessarily required for his perfection. Neither can one who has something supernatural know it is in him. Here then it is impossible to use natural reason against Aristotle. If one argues from beliefs, it is no argument against a philosopher since the latter does not concede a premise taken on faith. Hence, these reasons which are here urged against him have as one premise something

---

*This argument is answered in ¶79–82.
**This argument is answered in ¶83–89.
†Scotus actually adduces five arguments, but only accepts the first three as valid.

believed or proved from something believed. Therefore, they are nothing more than the-ological persuasions from beliefs to a belief.)

13. [First principal argument] The first way is this. Every agent who acts know-ingly needs a distinct knowledge of his destiny or end. I prove this, because every agent acting for the sake of an end, acts from a desire of the end. Now everything that is an agent in virtue of itself acts for the sake of an end. Therefore, every such agent seeks its end in a way proper to itself. Just as an agent that acts by its nature must de-sire the end for which it must act, so also the agent that acts knowingly. For the latter is also an agent in virtue of itself, according to the second book of the *Physics*. The major then is clear.

But man can have no definite knowledge of his end from what is natural; there-fore, he needs some supernatural knowledge thereof.

14. The minor is evident, first, because the Philosopher, following natural reason, maintained that perfect happiness consists in the acquired knowledge of the pure Spir-its, as he apparently wishes to say in the *Ethics,* book I and book X. Or if he does not categorically assert that this is our highest possible perfection, at least natural reason can argue to no other, so that on this basis alone, we will either err or be in doubt about our specific end. Hence, it is with some doubt in mind that he says in the first book of the *Ethics,* "If there be any gift of the gods, it is reasonable that it be happiness."

15. Secondly, the same minor is proved by reason. For we know the proper end only of such substances whose manifest actions show us that such an end is in accord with such a nature. Now of all the actions that we experience or know to exist in our na-ture at present, there are none that reveal that the vision of the pure Spirits is in accord with our nature. Naturally then we are unable to know definitely that this end is befitting our nature.

16. So much at least is sure, we cannot know definitely by natural reason certain conditions that make the end more desirable and cause us to seek it more fervently. For even granting that reason could prove that the face-to-face vision and enjoyment of God are the end of man, it still could not be inferred that these will be his forever or that they pertain to him as a whole, namely in body and soul, as will be pointed out in book IV, distinction 43. And yet the fact that such a good will never cease is something that ren-ders the end more attractive than if it were something transient. Also, it is more desir-able to possess this good with a complete [human] nature than with the soul apart from the body, as is clear from Augustine, *On Genesis,* XIII. It is necessary to know these and similar conditions associated with our end, if we are to seek it efficaciously. Still natural reason is insufficient in this regard. Therefore, supernaturally given knowledge is required.

17. [Second principal reason] The second argument runs in this fashion. Every-one who knowingly acts for the sake of an end, needs to know how and in what way such an end may be attained. In addition, he must know all that is necessary for this end. Thirdly, he must know that this is all that is required. The first is clear, because if one knows not how or in what way the end is to be attained, he is also ignorant of the way in which he must dispose himself in order to attain it. The second is proved, for if one does not know all that is necessary for the end, he could fail to reach it because he did not know that a certain action was necessary for its attainment. So also with the third. If these means were not known to be sufficient, the doubt that there might be some unknown yet necessary factor, would keep one from efficaciously doing what was necessary.

18. But by natural reason one in this life is unable to know these three points. Proof that the first cannot be known. Beatitude is granted as the reward of merits which

God accepts as worthy of such a reward. In consequence, beatitude does not follow with natural necessity from any kind of acts we may be able to perform, but is something that is freely given by God, who accepts as meritorious certain acts directed toward Him. Now, this is not something that can be known naturally, as is clear from the fact that the philosophers erred in this matter when they claimed everything God does immediately He does with necessity. The two other points, at least, are clear enough. For the fact that the divine will accepts just such and such things as worthy of eternal life, as well as the fact that just these things suffice, is not something that natural reason can know. This acceptance of what is only contingently related to it depends solely upon the divine will. Therefore, etc.

19. [Objections to the first two principal reasons] Objections are raised against these two reasons. To the first: Every created nature depends essentially upon anything that in virtue of itself causes such a nature. By reason of this dependence, it is possible to know and to demonstrate by a simple demonstration of fact any such cause of a given effect, once the latter is known. Now, since the nature of man can be known naturally by man—for it is not disproportionate to his cognitive power—it follows that once this nature is known, its destiny also could be known naturally.

20. This reason is confirmed. For if the destiny of a less perfect nature can be known from a knowledge of that nature, this is no less possible in our case, since what is destined for an end depends upon that end no less in the present case than it does in the others.

21. For this same reason, too, the proposition assumed in the proof of the minor, namely "the end of a substance is known only through the actions of that substance," would also seem to be false, since, by a demonstration of simple fact, the end of a nature could be known from a knowledge of that nature in itself.

22. And if it be maintained that reason infers only that man could know naturally his natural goal but not that which is supernatural, against this is Augustine's statement: "To be able to have faith, just as to be able to possess charity, pertains to the nature of men, although to have faith, just as to have charity, is due to the grace that is given to the faithful" *(On the Predestination of the Saints)*. Now, if the nature of man can be known naturally by man, then this ability in so far as it pertains to this nature, can also be known naturally. Consequently, it is also possible to know that such a nature can be ordained to an end for which charity and faith dispose it.

23. Likewise, man naturally seeks this goal which you call supernatural. Therefore, he is naturally ordained to it. This destiny, then, could be inferred from such an ordination just as it could be inferred from a knowledge of the nature ordained to such an end.

24. Also, according to Avicenna, it can be known naturally that *being* is the primary object of the intellect. And it is naturally knowable that this notion of being is verified most perfectly of God. The end of any power, however, is the very best of those things which come under its primary object, for only in such is there perfect rest and delight, according to the tenth book of the *Ethics*. Therefore, it can be known naturally that man according to his intellect is ordained to God as an end.

25. This reason is confirmed. For whoever can know any power naturally, is also able naturally to know what its primary object is. In addition he can know wherein the notion of this object is verified, as well as the fact that the most perfect of such things is the goal or end of this power. Now the mind knows itself, according to Augustine *(On the Trinity)*. Therefore, it knows what its primary object is, and it knows that God does not fall outside its scope, for otherwise God would not be intelligible to this mind in any way. Consequently, the mind knows that God is the very best of those things in which

the notion of its primary object is to be found, and thus it knows that God is the goal of this faculty.

26. Against the second reason the following argument is adduced. If one extreme is known through the other, the media are also known. But those things necessary for reaching the goal are media between the nature and the end to be attained. Now, since the end could be known from a knowledge of the nature, as has been proved above [¶19], it seems that the media necessary to this end can also be known in a similar way.

27. This reason is confirmed. For just as is the case with other things, so here also there seems to be a necessary connection of things with this end. But in other cases such a connection with the end serves to make other things known, for instance, such and such things are inferred to be necessary for health from the notion of health. Therefore, etc.

28. [Reply to the Objections] To the first of these [cf. ¶19–21], I say that even though the argument is based on the notion of an end which is a final cause and not that of an end to be attained through some action—a distinction of ends that will be treated later—nevertheless, to this objection as well as to what follows according to Augustine [cf. ¶22], and to the third objection regarding the power and its primary object [cf. ¶24], a single reply can be given. All these assume that our nature or our intellective power can be known naturally by us. Now this is false, if understood of that proper and special aspect by reason of which our nature is ordered to such an end, and in virtue of which it is capable of [receiving] the highest grace and has God as its most perfect object. For neither our soul nor our nature are known by us in our present state except under some general notion that can be abstracted from what the senses can perceive, as will be made clear later in distinction 3. And to be ordained to this end, or to be able to possess grace or to have God as its most perfect object is not something that pertains to our nature under such a general notion.

29. Now to the form [cf. ¶19]. It is stated that from the being which is ordained to this end, the end itself can be demonstrated by a demonstration of simple fact. Now I say this is true only if the being ordained to the end is known precisely according to that proper aspect in virtue of which it has such a destiny. And so the minor is false. And when they try to prove it on the grounds that there is no disproportion, I say that although the mind is identified with itself, nevertheless it is not proportionate to itself as object, except according to general notions which can be abstracted from what can be pictured in the imagination.

30. As to the confirmation [cf. ¶20], I say that even with other substances, their proper ends (namely, those which they have in virtue of their proper natures) remain unknown unless there be some manifest actions from which an ordination to such an end might be inferred.

31. And from this, the answer to what is added against the proof of the minor is clear [cf. ¶21]. The proposition: "The proper end of a substance is known to us only through its manifest actions," is not false. For this proposition does not mean that the end could not be known in some other way. Indeed, it is true that if the substance were known in its proper nature, from such knowledge one could ascertain what causes this substance in virtue of itself. But no substance is known to us at present in this way and therefore, in this life, we are unable to infer the proper end of any substance except through the evident actions of this substance, which substance is known only confusedly and in general. In our case, however, the end can be proved from a knowledge of neither the nature nor its acts. Although the proof of the minor touches but one way, namely our ignorance of its acts, it presupposes the other, namely, our ignorance of the nature in itself.

32. To the second argument based on Augustine [cf. ¶22] I say that this ability to possess charity, in so far as it disposes one to love God in himself under His proper nature, is something that pertains to man according to a special aspect and not as common to himself and to what is perceptible by the senses. In consequence, this ability is not something about man that can be known naturally in this life, even as man himself is not known under that peculiar aspect in virtue of which he possesses this ability. And in this way I reply to the objection in so far as it can be used to support the principal claim [of the philosophers], namely that the minor of the first argument [of the theologians] [cf. ¶14–15] is false. But in so far as it is leveled against the reply regarding the natural and supernatural end [cf. ¶22], I answer: I concede that God is the natural end of man, but an end that must be attained supernaturally and not naturally. And this is what the following reason concerning natural desire proves, which proof I concede.

33. As to the other argument [cf. ¶24], what it assumed must be denied, namely that it can be known naturally that being is the primary object of the intellect and this in so far as no restriction is made regarding a being that can be perceived by the sense and one that cannot. It must also be denied that Avicenna says this is something that can be known naturally, for he has mixed his religion—that of Mohammed—with philosophical matters, and some things he states as philosophical and proved by reason; others as in accord with his religion. Wherefore, he expressly assumes in the ninth book of the *Metaphysics,* chapter 7, that the disembodied soul knows immaterial substances in themselves, and therefore these have to be placed under the primary object of the intellect. But it was not so according to Aristotle. For him, the primary object of our intellect is, or seems to be, the quiddity of what can be perceived by the senses. And by this he means either what is in itself perceptible by the senses or what falls under this designation. The latter is the quiddity which can be abstracted from what is perceptible to the senses.

34. However, I reply to what is cited from Augustine in confirmation of the argument [cf. ¶25]. His statement, I say, should be understood of the first act which of itself is fully sufficient for the second act, but its activity is hindered at present. On account of this hindrance, the second act in the present life is not elicited from the first. But more of this later.

35. Some may object to this answer on the grounds that man in the state of original justice could have known his nature, and therefore the destiny of this nature, as the argument for the first objection claims [cf. ¶19]. Therefore, this knowledge is not supernatural.

36. Also, the reply to the last reason might be questioned [cf. ¶33]. For if we are ignorant of what the primary object of the intellect is because the intellect is not known under each proper aspect according to which it regards such an object, it follows that we cannot know that any given thing is intelligible, because the power is not known under every proper aspect according to which it could consider any given thing as an intelligible object.

37. I reply: To the first [cf. ¶35]. It is necessary to point out what kind of knowledge man had in his original state, a topic which may be put off until later. But at least so far as man in his present state is concerned, it is called supernatural knowledge, because it exceeds man's natural power—natural, I understand, according to his fallen state.

38. As to the second [cf. ¶36], I concede that at present our knowledge of the soul or of some of its faculties is not so distinct that such knowledge could be used to ascertain that some intelligible object corresponds to it. But from the act which we experience, we conclude that the power and the nature to which this act belongs regards as its

object that which we perceive to be attained through the act in question. Hence, we do not infer the object of the faculty from a knowledge of the faculty in itself, but from the knowledge of the act we experience. But of a supernatural object we have neither kind of knowledge, and in consequence neither method of knowing the proper end of this nature is to be had.

39. The answer to the objection against the second reason is clear [cf. ¶26]. For the argument assumes something that has already been denied [cf. ¶28–29]. To the confirmation of this argument [cf. ¶27] I say that when the end follows naturally those things that lead to the end, and demands them naturally as prerequisites, then, such things could be inferred from the end. But in this case, these things do not follow naturally, but only in virtue of a [voluntary] acceptance on the part of the divine will, which reckons these merits as worthy of such an end.

40. [Third principal reason] A third main argument is raised against the opinion of the philosophers. The knowledge of pure Spirits is the most noble, because it has to do with the noblest class (*Metaphysics,* IV). Hence, the knowledge of their proper attributes is noblest and most necessary. For their proper attributes are more perfectly knowable than those attributes they have in common with objects perceptible to the senses. But these proper attributes cannot be known merely from what is purely natural. For, in the first place, if these properties were found to be treated in any science possible to us at present, it would be in metaphysics. But it is not possible for us naturally to have a science of the proper attributes of these pure Spirits, as is evident. And this is what the Philosopher maintains when he says in the first book of the *Metaphysics* that it is necessary for the wise man to know all things in some way, and not in particular. And he adds: "For he who knows universals, knows in a sense all things." Here he calls the metaphysician the "wise man," just as he calls philosophy "wisdom."

41. I prove the same thing in a second way. These properties are not known by a science or knowledge that gives the reason for the facts unless their proper subjects are known, for only the subjects give the reason for such proper attributes. Now the proper subjects of these attributes cannot be known naturally by us. Therefore, etc.

Neither can we know these properties from their effects by a demonstration of the simple fact. Proof: the effect leaves the intellect in doubt with regard to these properties or even leads it into error. This is clear with regard to the properties of the First Spiritual Substance itself, for it is a property of this [divine] Substance that it can be shared with three [Divine Persons]. But the effects [*viz.* creatures] do not reveal this property, because they are not from this Substance in so far as it is a Trinity. And if one were to argue from the effects to the cause, one would rather conclude the very opposite and so be in error. For in no effect is one nature associated with more than one *supposit*. It is also a property of this nature, in its external relations, to cause [its effects] contingently. And the effects lead one to infer the opposite view and to fall into error, as is evident from the opinion of philosophers who held that the First Cause causes necessarily whatever it produces. As to the properties of the other pure Spirits [*viz.* the angels or Intelligences], clearly the same holds. For effects rather lead one to conclude that they are necessary and everlasting beings, according to the philosophers, instead of contingent beings, which have come into existence after being non-existent. Again, these philosophers also seem to conclude on the basis of movement that the number of these pure Spirits corresponds with the number of movements of the heavenly bodies. Again, [they held that] these pure Spirits were naturally beatified and incapable of sin—all of which is absurd.

42. [Objection to the third principal reason] Against this reason I argue that whatever necessary knowledge regarding these pure Spirits we may have at present by

faith or what is commonly revealed could also be had by a knowledge that is natural. And I prove it in this way. We can comprehend naturally any necessary truths whose terms we can know naturally. Now we know naturally the terms of all necessary revealed truths. Therefore, etc.

43. Proof of the major. These necessary truths are either mediately or immediately [evident]. If immediately, then, they are known once the terms are known, according to the first book of the *Posterior Analytics*. If they are mediate truths, then we can conceive the middle term between them, since we can know the extremes. By joining this middle term with the two extremes, we have either mediate or immediate premises. If immediate, we argue as before. If mediate, the process of conceiving the middle term between the extremes and joining it with the latter continues until we come to truths that are immediately evident. In the last analysis, then, we shall arrive at necessary and immediate propositions, which are known from their terms and from which all other necessary truths follow. Hence, these mediate truths could be known naturally by us through those which are immediate.

44. Proof of the minor. If one who has faith contradicts one who has no faith, the two do not contradict each other in word only but according to the conceptual meaning, as is evident when the philosopher and theologian contradict each other regarding the proposition: "God is triune." Here, one denies and the other affirms not only the same name but also the same concept. Consequently, every simple concept that the theologian has, the philosopher also has.

45. [Reply to the objection] To this, I reply. There are certain truths about the pure Spirits that are immediate. Now I take one such primary and immediate truth, let us call it "a." In it are included many mediate truths, for instance, all those which affirm in particular what is common to the predicate of those things which are common to the subject, let us call them "b" and "c." These mediate truths are evident only through some immediate truth. Therefore, the former cannot be known unless the immediate truth is understood. If therefore some intellect could grasp the terms of "b" and combine them with one another in a proposition, but could not understand the terms of "a" nor, in consequence, the proposition "a" itself, then so far as this intellect is concerned, "b" would be a neutral proposition. It is known neither through itself, nor through the immediate proposition [*viz.* "a"], since in our assumption the latter remains unknown. And so it is with us. For we have certain concepts common to material and immaterial substances, and these we can put together into propositions. But these latter are not evident except through those immediate truths which concern the proper and special character of these quiddities. Now we do not conceive these quiddities under this aspect and therefore, neither do we know those general truths which involve the universal concepts.

46. For example: if someone were able to conceive a triangle not according to its proper notion as a triangle but only under the notion of "figure" abstracted from a quadrangle, it would be impossible for him to grasp that property by which a triangle is the first [of plane geometrical figures], because this property could be conceived only if it were abstracted from a triangle itself. He could, however, abstract the notion of "first" from other things that are first, e.g. of numbers. Although his intellect could form the proposition: "Some figure is first," because it could grasp the terms involved, still such a proposition would be neutral to him, because it is a mediate proposition included in this immediate proposition: "A triangle is first in this way." But he would be unable to know this immediate proposition because he cannot grasp its terms. Therefore, he is not able to understand the mediate proposition, which can be known from the immediate proposition alone.

47. Applying this to the argument [cf. ¶42], I deny the major. To the proof, I say that these necessary truths are mediately evident propositions. And when you say, "Therefore, we can conceive a medium between these extremes," I deny the consequence, because the medium between the extremes is at times essentially ordered, for example, when it is the essence of the extreme or is a prior attribute with regard to one that is posterior. Now a middle term through which one extreme can universally be inferred from the other is of this kind. I concede, therefore, that whoever can grasp the extremes can grasp such a middle term between them, because its concept is included in, or is the same as, that of the other extreme. But if the middle term is particular, and is contained under the other extremes and is not essentially related to these extremes, then it is not necessary that one who can conceive universal extremes, could conceive a means which is particular in regard to these extremes. So it is here. For the quiddity under its proper and particular aspect has some immediate attribute inhering in it, and is a middle term that is less universal than the common concept of which this attribute, conceived in general, is predicated. Therefore, it is not a medium for universally inferring the attribute of the common concept, but only in a particular case. This is evident in the above example [cf. ¶46], because it is not necessary that one who can conceive a figure in general and the general notion of being first, can conceive a triangle in particular, for a triangle is a medium contained under figure—a medium, I say, for concluding that a particular figure is first.

48. ([Note] This third argument [cf. ¶40] holds above all of the first immaterial substance [*viz.* God], for it is especially necessary to know God as a beatific object. Now the reply to the objection brought against it supposes that we conceive God naturally in the present life only in a concept that is common to Him and to what can be perceived by the senses, which is explained later in the first question of the third distinction. But even if this assumption were denied, it would still be necessary to maintain that any concept of God we could derive from creatures is imperfect, whereas that which could be had in virtue of His essence in itself would be perfect. Hence, what was said regarding the universal and particular notions [cf. ¶47], would also be valid for the perfect and imperfect notions in this other view.)

49. [Fourth principal reason] A fourth argument is this. Whatever is ordered to some end toward which it is not disposed, must be gradually disposed for this end. Man is ordered to a supernatural end toward which he is of himself indisposed. Therefore he needs to be gradually disposed to possess this end. This takes place by reason of some imperfect supernatural knowledge, which is maintained to be necessary. Therefore, etc.

50. But if it be objected that a perfect agent can remove any imperfection immediately and can act immediately, I reply that even if it could do so by its absolute power, still it is more perfect to make the creature active in attaining its perfection than to deprive it of any such activity. But man could have some activity in the attainment of his final perfection. Hence, it is more perfect that such be given him. But this could not be done without imparting some imperfect knowledge which precedes that perfect knowledge which he is ultimately destined to possess.

51. [Fifth principal argument] A fifth argument is this. Any agent that makes use of an instrument in acting, cannot in virtue of this instrument perform any action which exceeds [in perfection] the nature of the instrument. The light of the agent intellect, however, is an instrument which the soul at present uses to understand things naturally. In consequence, the soul, using this light, is not capable of any action that would exceed this light. Therefore, the soul is incapable of any knowledge that it does not attain in this way. But this light of itself is limited to knowledge by way of the senses. Now the knowledge of many other things, however, is necessary for us at present. Therefore, etc.

52. This reason seems to militate against the position of the one who advanced it.* For according to this line of reasoning, the Uncreated Light would be unable to make use of the agent intellect as an instrument in producing a knowledge of pure truth. For such truth, according to him, cannot be ours through the senses without some special illumination. And so it follows that in knowing pure truth the light of the agent intellect plays no part at all, which seems hardly possible inasmuch as this illumination [by the agent intellect] is the most perfect of all intellectual activity. Consequently, the most perfect intellectual power in the soul should in some way concur with this action.

53. [Evaluation of the fourth and fifth reasons] These last two reasons [cf. ¶49–51] do not seem to be very efficacious. For the first would hold, if it were proved that man was destined for supernatural beatitude (the proof of which pertains to the questions of beatitude), and if, in addition, it were shown that natural knowledge does not dispose one sufficiently in our present state for the attainment of supernatural knowledge. The second reason begs two points, namely, that a knowledge of certain things unknowable by way of the senses, is necessary, and that the light of the agent intellect is limited to things that can be known by way of the senses.

54. The first three reasons appear to be more probable.

[C. Objection to the opinion of the Theologians]

That no such knowledge, however, is necessary for salvation, I prove: Let us assume that someone is not baptized. When he grows up, he has no one to teach him. The affections [of his will], such as he is capable of, are good and in accord with what his natural reason tells him is right. What reason reveals to him as evil, he avoids.

Although God could visit such a one, teaching him the common law by man or angel even as He visited Cornelius, still let us assume that such an individual is taught by no one. Nevertheless, he will be saved. And even if he should be instructed later, before such instruction he is just and consequently, worthy of eternal life. For, by willing what is good, even before he is instructed, he merits grace which renders him just. And still he has no theology, not even in regard to the primary truths of faith. His is purely natural knowledge. Consequently, nothing that pertains to theology is, absolutely speaking, necessary for salvation.

55. [Reply] It could be said that such an individual, by willing what is good in general, merits *de congruo*** to be justified from original sin, and God does not deprive such a one of this gift of His liberality. Hence, He gives him the first grace without using the sacrament [i.e., baptism], because God is not constrained to make use of the sacraments. But grace is not [ordinarily] given without the habit of faith. Hence, such an individual actually possesses the habit of theology, even though this habit could not be reduced to act. Neither could such an individual be baptized unless first instructed. And even though it would not be a contradiction [for God] to give grace without faith, for these are distinct habits and reside in different faculties, nevertheless, just as in baptism these two are infused simultaneously, so, for the same reason, they could be given together in this case. For God is no less gracious toward one whom He justifies without the sacraments, because of merit *de congruo,* than He is toward one whom He justifies through the reception of the sacrament without any merit on this individual's part. And thus it is possible for God by his absolute power to save anyone, and to enable him to merit glory without infused faith—if God were to give grace without faith—for once

*[Namely, Scotus's chief adversary, Henry of Ghent]
**[A reward which is fitting even though there is no strict obligation in justice.]

such an individual possessed grace, he could use it properly to will what he knew by natural reason and acquired faith (or by natural reason alone without acquired faith, if no one were to teach him). Nevertheless, according to God's usual way of acting, He does not give grace without first giving the habit of faith, for grace is not assumed to be infused unless faith is also infused. But this is not because of any necessity, as if grace without faith would not be sufficient, but because of the divine liberality which reforms the whole [soul, *viz.* intellect and will]. Then, too, many would be less perfectly inclined to assent to certain truths without infused faith.

56. Now, I say, there is a similar relation in the case of the habit of theology, which, when perfect, includes both an infused and an acquired faith of the articles [of the Creed] and of other things revealed by God in Scripture, so that there is not just infused faith, or just acquired faith, but both together. Hence, if we are speaking of the more fundamental or prior habit which theology includes, *viz.* infused faith, it is true, according to the usual way in which God acts, that theology is necessary for all, as a general rule. But it is not true that theology is necessary for all, if we understand by theology the second habit which it includes, *viz.* acquired faith. But if we speak of the necessity based on God's usual way of acting. Perhaps it is necessary for an adult who could have and is able to understand a teacher, that he have an acquired faith with regard to certain general truths.

[*II. Solution to the Question*]

57. To the question, then, I reply first by distinguishing in what sense something may be called supernatural. For a capacity to receive may be compared to the act which it receives or to the agent from which it receives [this act]. Viewed in the first way, this potentiality is either natural or violent or neither natural nor violent. It is called natural, if it is naturally inclined toward the form it receives. It is violent, if what it suffers is against its natural inclination. It is neither the one nor the other, if it is inclined neither to the form which it receives nor to its opposite. Now from this viewpoint, there is no supernaturality. But when the recipient is compared to the agent from which it receives the form, then there is naturalness if the recipient is referred to an agent which is naturally ordained to impress such a form in such a recipient. Supernaturalness is had, however, when the recipient is referred to an agent which does not impress this form upon this recipient naturally.

58. Before this distinction is applied to the case at hand, several arguments are brought to bear against it, first on the grounds that the distinction of "natural" and "violent" is based upon the recipient's relation to the agent and not merely to the form, and secondly on the count that the distinction of "natural" and "supernatural" is based upon the recipient's relation to the patient and not to the agent exclusively. I will not cite the arguments for these points here.

59. Nevertheless, the solution seems reasonable, because a cause which causes anything in virtue of itself is that cause whose presence is followed by the effect even when all other factors are excluded or varied. Now even though a form contrary to the inclination is induced only by means of some agent which does violence to the recipient, and even though a supernatural agent acts supernaturally only by inducing some form, still the precise character of "violent" arises by virtue of the relation of the recipient to the form, whereas that of "supernatural" arises precisely in virtue of the relation of the recipient to the agent. This is proved from the fact that as long as the recipient and form remain what they are (*viz.* that the form can be received, but only contrary to the inclination of the recipient), then no matter how the agent is varied, violence is still done to the recipient. Similarly, when the agent and recipient are so related to each

other that the recipient is altered only by an agent that does not act naturally (I say "only" to exclude any preparation by a natural agent), whatever be the form such an agent induces, it will be supernatural with regard to the recipient.

A second proof that such is the case is based not only on the induction [of the form] but on its permanency. A form which does violence to the recipient may remain in it without any external action, but not for a long time. Another remains naturally and for some time. [Hence, the external agent need not be taken into consideration.] Again, one form that endures is natural; another supernatural, but only by reason of the agent, so that if the latter were not taken into consideration, the form could not be called supernatural. But it might be called natural, because it perfects naturally, if the relation of the form to the recipient alone is considered.

60. Applying this to the question at issue, I say that if the possible intellect be compared to the knowledge that is actualized in it, no knowledge is supernatural to it, because the possible intellect is perfected by any knowledge whatsoever and is naturally inclined toward any kind of knowledge. But according to the second way of speaking, that knowledge is supernatural which is generated by some agent which by its very nature is not ordained to move the possible intellect in a natural manner.

61. In our present state, however, the possible intellect, according to the Philosopher, is ordained to be moved to knowledge by the agent intellect and the phantasm. Therefore, that knowledge alone is natural to it which is impressed by these agencies.

In virtue of these, however, all conceptual knowledge which one has in this life according to the common law, can be obtained, as is evident from the objections raised against the third principal reason [cf. ¶84]. Consequently, even though God by way of revelation could cause some special knowledge, as for instance, when one is rapt in ecstasy, still such supernatural knowledge is not necessary according to the common law.

62. It is different, however, with the truth of propositions, because as has been shown by the three reasons adduced against the first opinion [cf. ¶13ff.], even when the agent intellect and sense image are fully active, many propositions we need to know remain unknown or neutral. The knowledge of such propositions must be given to us in a supernatural manner, because no one could naturally discover them and teach them to others, for on natural grounds alone, if they are neutral to one, they are to all. The question of whether it would be possible, once such knowledge was originally imparted, for another to assent to these propositions on purely natural grounds will be discussed in book III, distinction 23. The original transmission of such knowledge, however, is called revelation. It is supernatural, therefore, since it is due to an agent that does not naturally move our intellect in its present state.

63. Another way in which an action or knowledge could be called supernatural would be because it is from an agent which takes the place of a supernatural object. For that object which is able to cause such propositions as "God is triune" and the like, is the divine essence known in its proper nature. Knowable in this way, it is a supernatural object. Whatever agent, then, causes some knowledge of truths which such an object would be able to make evident when known in its own nature, such an agent [I say] takes the place of this object. And if this agent would cause as perfect a knowledge of those truths as the object would cause if known in itself, then such an agent would substitute perfectly for the object. But no matter how imperfect the knowledge caused by such an agent would be, it is still virtually contained in that perfect knowledge which the object would cause if known in itself.

64. And so it is in this case. For one who reveals that "God is triune" causes in the mind some knowledge of this truth, obscure though it be, a knowledge which concerns an object unknown in its proper nature. If this object were known properly, it

would be able to produce a clear and perfect knowledge of this truth. In so far as this knowledge is obscure and is included eminently in the clear knowledge, as the imperfect is included eminently in the perfect, to that extent, then, the agent which reveals or causes the obscure truth, takes the place of the object that could cause a clear knowledge of the same. This is true especially when the agent could cause a knowledge of a certain truth only by taking the place of a certain object, and when it would be unable to make known a truth about this object by taking the place of some less perfect object that could naturally move our intellect. For no such inferior object virtually includes any knowledge of these truths, be it clear or obscure knowledge. Hence, it is necessary that the agent somehow take the place of a supernatural object, even when causing this obscure knowledge.

65. The difference between these two ways in which revealed knowledge is called supernatural is apparent if we consider each separately. Thus, if a supernatural agent would cause a knowledge of some natural object, for example, if it infused the knowledge of geometry in someone, this would be supernatural in the first way but not in the second. What is supernatural in the second way, however, is supernatural in both ways, for the second way implies the first, but not vice versa. However, where there is only the first type of supernatural [e.g. infused geometry], it is not impossible that what is supernatural could have been produced naturally [under other conditions]. Where something is supernatural in the second way, however, it is necessary that it be produced supernaturally, since it could not possibly be produced naturally.

[III. Concerning the three principal reasons against the philosophers]

66. The three reasons upon which this solution is based are confirmed by arguments from authority. The first [cf. ¶13–16] is confirmed by the statement of Augustine in the *City of God,* XVIII, Chapter 41: "The philosophers, not knowing to what end these things were to be referred, were able to see some truth among the false things they asserted."

67. The second argument [cf. ¶17–18] is confirmed by Augustine in the *City of God,* XI, Chapter 2: "What good is it to know where one must go if one does not know how to get there?" In this the philosophers erred, for even though they handed on some truths regarding virtues, still their teaching was tainted with error, as he points out in the text quoted above. This is clear from their books. For Aristotle criticizes the polities devised by many another (*Politics* II), and yet his own polity is not without reproach, since he teaches that the gods are to be honored. "It is fitting," he says (*Politics* VII. ch. 7), "that honor be shown to the gods," and in the same book, Chapter 5: "There ought to be a law . . . that no deformed child shall be nursed."

68. The third argument [cf. ¶40–41] is confirmed by Augustine in the *City of God,* XI, Chapter 3: "We need the testimony of others concerning objects that lie beyond the reach of our own senses, since we cannot know them by our own testimony." And this confirms our main solution throughout [cf. ¶5765], for those propositions which the argument declares to be neutral so far as we are concerned [cf. ¶40–41], cannot be believed by anyone on the basis of his own testimony, but he must needs have the testimony of someone who is above the whole of mankind.

69. It is doubtful just how this first revelation or imparting of such knowledge actually did or could have taken place. Was it by some interior or by some exterior communication, together with such signs as would suffice to cause assent? For the problem at hand, it is enough to point out that such knowledge could be supernaturally revealed in either way. But in neither way could it be imparted without error by man right from the beginning.

70. The objection is raised that these three reasons [cf. ¶¶13–41] refute themselves, for whatever they reveal as necessary to know is something that is true, since we can really know only what is true. Consequently, whatever these arguments reveal to be necessary for us to know—for example, that the end of man is the enjoyment of God in himself (first argument); that the manner of reaching Him is by way of merits which God accepts as worthy of such a reward (second argument); that God is triune and causes things contingently, etc. (third argument)—all these are shown to be true. Consequently, these reasons either are based solely on faith or a conclusion is drawn from them which is the very opposite of what they actually prove.

71. I reply that natural reason merely shows us that it is necessary for us to know definitely one part of this contradiction: "The enjoyment [of God] is [our] end; this enjoyment is not our end." In other words, our intellect must not remain in doubt or ignorance on this problem of whether such enjoyment is our end, for such would keep us from seeking the end. But natural reason does not reveal just which part we must know. In this way, then, the aforementioned reasons in so far as they are natural, reveal that one part of the contradiction must be true. Either it is this or it is that. But a definite answer is possible only from what we believe.

[IV. Reply to the arguments of the philosophers]

72. As to the arguments for the opinion of Aristotle, I say to the first [cf. ¶6] that knowledge depends upon the soul knowing and the object known, for according to Augustine (*On the Trinity,* IX, last chapter): "Knowledge is born of the knower and the known." Hence, even though the soul may possess sufficient active and passive faculties so far as its own activity in knowing is concerned, still it does not have in itself active powers that would suffice to take the place of the object's action for it is like a blank writing-tablet, as the third book, *On the Soul* tells us. Hence to say that the agent intellect is that by which [the mind] makes all things [known], is true only in so far as this "making" something known is an action of the soul and not in so far as it involves an action on the part of the object.

73. To the confirmation by reason [cf. ¶7], I say to the major that "nature" at times is taken in the sense of an intrinsic principle of movement and rest—as is described in the second book of the *Physics*—at other times, for a naturally active principle, in so far as nature is distinguished from art and deliberate intention on the basis of the different ways these proceed from their principle. In this latter sense, "nature" may or may not be intrinsic, just so long as it is natural [i.e. not deliberate or the result of art]. According to the first meaning of "nature," the major is not true, because not everything that is naturally passive has a corresponding intrinsic active principle or nature, for many things lack an intrinsic active power to produce some act they are able to receive naturally. If nature be taken in the second sense, the major is also false in certain instances, namely when a nature because of its excellence is naturally ordained to receive a perfection so eminent that it could be caused by an agent that is natural in the second sense. And so it is in our case.

74. To the proof given for the major, I say that the passive potency is not in vain for even though it could not be reduced to act by a natural agent as the principal cause, still a natural agent can dispose it for such an act. And there is some agent in nature, i.e., in the universe as a whole, that can completely reduce it to act, namely the First or Supernatural Agent.

75. Someone may object that to be incapable of attaining its perfection through what is natural devaluates [our] nature, for according to the second book *On the Heavens and Earth:* "The more noble nature, the less it should lack." I reply: if our happiness

consisted in the highest speculation that is naturally attainable, the Philosopher would not say our nature lacked anything necessary. But I admit that we can naturally possess such perfection at present. But I go further when I say that there is another higher form of speculation that can be received naturally. Consequently, nature in this regard is honored even more than if one were to claim that the highest possible perfection it could receive is that which is naturally attainable. Nor is it surprising that some nature has the ability to receive a perfection greater than that which lies within the reach of its own active causality.

76. The above citation from the second book *On the Heavens and Earth* is not to the point, because the Philosopher is speaking here of organs corresponding to the power of movement, if this be present in the stars. Now I concede universally that nature gives an organ to everything to which it gives an organic power (I am speaking of things that are not deformed). In our case, however, it is a question of giving a non-organic power, and still not giving naturally all the other requisites for the act. From the Philosopher's statement here, then, it can be said that if a nature can be ordained for a certain act or object, this nature has a natural faculty for the act and also a corresponding organ, if the faculty is organic. But the same cannot be said of the other requisites for the act.

77. The major [cf. ¶7] could be answered in another way, namely that it is true if one speaks of a natural passive potency with respect to an active power, but it is false if passive potency is taken with respect to the act received. The difference between these two is clear from the first part of the solution to this question [cf. ¶57].

78. The minor [cf. ¶7] is true in the second way [*viz.* if the possible intellect is taken in respect to the act received], but not in the first. There is a third and easy way of answering the minor, namely: to deny it. For even though absolutely speaking the possible intellect is naturally receptive of this intellection, this is not so in its present state. The reason for this, however, will be explained later in distinction 3.

79. To the third reason [cf. ¶8] see Thomas' reply in the *Summa* I, Question 1 where he says: "Sciences are diversified according to the diverse nature of their knowable objects. For both the astronomer and the physicist demonstrate the same conclusion, for example, that the earth is round. The astronomer does so by means of mathematics (i.e. abstracting from matter), but the physicist does so by means of the matter considered. Hence, there is no reason why the same things treated by the philosophical sciences inasmuch as they can be known by the light of natural reason, may not also be treated by another science inasmuch as they are known by the light of divine revelation."

To the contrary: If the knowledge of those things which can be known in theology is, or can be, treated in other sciences, even though it be in another light, it follows that theological knowledge of such things is unnecessary. The consequence is evident from his own example, for anyone who knows that the earth is round by means of physics has no absolute need of a mathematical knowledge [of the same].

80. This reply [of Thomas], to the third argument, however, is explained in this way. Habit is both a form and a habit. In so far as it is a habit, it is distinguished by reason of the object. In so far as it is a form, however, it can be distinguished by reason of the active principle. Now principles are the efficient causes of a habit of knowledge. Consequently, even though the same object of knowledge (for example, that the earth is round), is not distinguished by reason of the object, there is still a distinction by reason of the different principles which the mathematician and physicist use to prove this. And so there will be a distinction of habits in so far as they are forms, but not in so far as they are habits.

81. To the contrary: Form is a common [or generic term] with reference to habit. Now it is impossible that anything be distinct by reason of some superior classification and yet not be distinct by reason of some subordinate classification. Therefore, it is impossible that anything be distinct by reason of form (and hence distinct in form) and still not be distinct by reason of habit. This is like saying that certain things differ as animals but not as men. Furthermore, he assumes that principles distinguish habits according to some other type of causality than as efficient principles, which is false. For if the distinguishing causes have any relation to habits, it is none other than as efficient causes. Furthermore, the [basic] reason always holds, for no matter how cognitive habits may be distinguished, so long as other habits are possible, there would still be no need of any one habit [e.g. theology], in the sense that without it knowledge would be impossible.

82. Therefore, I reply to the argument that even though these speculative sciences [*viz.* physics, mathematics and metaphysics] treat of all speculative things, they still do not exhaust all that can be known about these objects, for they fail to treat of what is proper to them, as has been made clear in the third argument against the first opinion. See above [cf. ¶40ff.].

83. The fourth argument [cf. ¶9] is answered in this way. First principles cannot be applied to any conclusions other than those which deal with what can be perceived by the senses, both because their terms are abstracted from sensible objects and so partake of their nature, and because the agent intellect, through which this application [of principles] takes place, is limited to objects that can be perceived by the senses.

84. To the contrary: The intellect is certain that these first principles are true not only of what can be perceived by the senses, but also of what cannot be so perceived. For the intellect has no doubt that contradictories cannot be simultaneously true of spiritual things any more than of material things. And there is no value in the statement that the term of the first principle is the "being" which is divided into the ten categories and does not apply to theological objects. For we have not the slightest doubt that contradictories are not simultaneously verified about God (e.g. God is happy; God is not happy, etc.) any more than of something white.

85. Another solution is offered, namely, that the conclusions follow from the major premises only when the latter are combined with a minor premise. But the minors to which they must be joined are not naturally evident.

To the contrary: The minors subsumed under the first principles predicate of the things subsumed, the subject terms of the first principles. But the terms of the first principles are known to be predicated about everything, for these terms are most common, therefore, etc.

86. Therefore, I reply that the second part of the minor [cf. ¶10] is false, *viz.* that all the conclusions that can be known are virtually included in the first principles. To the proof, I say that just as the subject terms are common, so also are those of the predicate. Therefore, when the subject terms, since they are distributed, stand for [supposit for] all things, they stand for them only in regard to the predicate terms, which are most common. In virtue of such principles, then, only the most common predicates are known of those things which fall under such principles.

87. This is evident from reason, because the middle term cannot give the reason why any attribute inheres in its respective subject, unless the attribute in question is included virtually in the notion of the middle term. But the notion of the subject of a most common principle includes the reason for the inherence of only the most universal attributes and not those which are particular. Therefore, it is only under this most general aspect that such a subject can be the means or the reason why anything is known. But in

addition to the most general attributes, there are many other attributes that can be known. Because these are not included in the attributes of the first principles, however, the latter will yield no knowledge of them. Consequently there are many things that can be known which are not included in the first principles.

This is clear from an example. Although the proposition: "Every whole is greater than its part," includes "A quarternion is greater than a binary" and other similar propositions with the same predicate, it does not include these: "A quarternion is twice as much as a binary" or "A ternary is one and a half times a binary," for these propositions would require some special middle terms which include them.

88. The third proof is from logic [cf. ¶86–87]. Although it is licit to descend from a universal affirmative subject, it is not licit to do so from the predicate. Now there are many predicates contained under the predicates of the first principles that can be known of those things which fall under the subjects of these principles. Therefore, these predicates are not known of these subjects through the first principles.

89. Against this it is objected: "Anything can be either affirmed or denied, but nothing can be both affirmed and denied." It follows: "Therefore, this is white or not white," so that it is permissible in this case to descend both from the predicate and from the subject.

I reply that this principle, "Anything can be affirmed or denied, etc. . . ." is equivalent to this: "Concerning anything one part of any contradiction is true and the other is false," where there is a double distribution [*viz.* "concerning anything" and "of any contradiction"], and it is lawful to descend from both distributed terms: "Therefore, of this thing, [one part] of this contradiction [is true, the other false; of that thing, one part of this contradiction is true, etc.; of that thing, one part of that contradiction is true, etc.] etc. But it is not lawful to descend [distributively] from a predicate with confused supposition," because it does not follow "Concerning everything, one part of every contradiction [is true and the other false], therefore, this part [is true and the other false]." And so it is with other principles. The predicate of a universal affirmative proposition always has only confused supposition, whether there is a double or only one distribution of the subject.

And in the example proposed it is clear that this still holds true. For it can be known of man that he is risible. From this principle "Of anything, etc. . . ." we can never infer anything more than: "Therefore, man is either risible or not risible." Hence, the other part of this disjunctive predicate will never be known of the subject through this principle. On the contrary another special principle is required such as the definition of the subject or the attribute, which is in truth a means and reason for knowing definitely that man is risible.

[Solution of the initial arguments]

90. To the arguments at the beginning.—To the first [cf. ¶1]: I distinguish natural objects. For a natural object can mean one which the faculty can attain naturally, i.e. by the action of causes that are naturally active, or it may mean an object toward which the faculty is naturally inclined, whether such an object can be naturally attained or not. The major, then, could be denied if natural is taken in the first sense, for the first object is equal to the faculty, and therefore this object is abstracted from everything concerning which the faculty is able to function. Still it does not follow necessarily that just because the intellect could know such a common object naturally, it could know everything contained under it, because the knowledge of some of the things contained is much more perfect than the confused knowledge of the common object itself. And so, even granting the minor in either sense of natural knowledge, the intended conclusion

about what can be naturally attained does not follow, for the major is not true of the object that can be naturally attained.

91. Against this answer, I contend that it destroys itself. For according to him [Henry of Ghent], the primary object is one that is equal to the power. Now this is true: a power regards as its object [a] only those things of which the notion of its first object is verified and [b] anything of which this notion is verified. Therefore, it is impossible that something should be the primary natural object without everything of which it is verified being of itself a natural object. For grant the opposite and then the object is not naturally adequate but exceeds [the faculty] and something inferior is adequate and therefore the first object.

The reason given for [Henry's] answer, however, is a fallacy of figure of speech. For although, in so far as "being" is something that can be grasped by the intellect in a single act (as "man" can be grasped in one intellectual act), "being" can be known naturally (for this one concept of being in so far as it is a concept of one object is something natural), still it cannot be maintained that "being" is the primary object naturally attainable. For "being" is the first object in so far as it is included in all objects known of themselves, and as such it would be naturally attainable only if each of these objects were naturally attainable. Therefore, he [Henry] interchanges "this something," [without qualification], with "of a certain kind" when he argues: "Being is naturally knowable; therefore, being in so far as it is the first (i.e. adequate) object of the intellect, is naturally attainable." For the antecedent is true in so far as "being" is one single intelligible [object], e.g. a white thing, but the consequent makes a conclusion about being in so far as it is included in every intelligible object, and not "being" as conceived without this qualification.

92. To the argument, therefore, there is another, a real, answer, namely, the minor is false in regard to the object naturally attainable, but it is true in the other sense (namely the object to which the power is naturally ordered or inclined). In this way the quotation from Avicenna must be understood. (It will be pointed out later in distinction 3 what must be held to be the first object naturally attainable.) This answer is confirmed by Anselm in Chapter 4, *On Free Will:* "We have no power, I believe, which alone suffices for an act." By "power" he means what we commonly call a faculty, as is evident from his example about sight. Therefore, it is not unfitting that a power should be naturally ordered to an object which it cannot attain naturally by natural causes, any more than it is for a power or faculty to be ordained by its very nature [for an act] and nevertheless be unable to produce this act by itself alone.

93. As to the second argument [cf. ¶2], I deny its consequence. What is to be said of its proof, is clear from the reply given the second argument for the opinion of the Philosopher [cf. ¶73–74], because superior natures are ordained passively to receive something greater than they can actively produce. Consequently, their perfection cannot be achieved except by some supernatural agent. But this is not so with the perfection of less perfect things whose ultimate perfection could fall under the action of inferior agents.

94. As to the third [cf. ¶3], I say some of the propositions we must firmly hold to be true, are disproportionate to the possible intellect, that is to say, the intellect is not equal to being moved [to know them] by what can be known from sense images and the natural light of the agent intellect.

When you argue: "Therefore, the intellect becomes proportionate by means of something else," I concede that there is something else—both something that moves it (for, moved supernaturally by the one revealing, the intellect assents to this truth), and something else in the sense of a form (for there is the assent produced in the intellect, which is a kind of inclination in the intellect toward this object which brings the intellect into proportion with the latter).

But when you press further, "Is this 'something else' natural or supernatural?" I reply that it is supernatural, and this is so whether you understand this "something else" in the sense of agent or form.

When you infer: "Therefore, the intellect is disproportionate to it and must be made proportionate through something else," I declare that the intellect by its very nature is in obediential potency toward the agent, and thus is sufficiently proportionate to it to the extent that it can be moved by this agent. Also of itself, the intellect is capable of the act of assent caused by such an agent and this capability is natural. Hence, it is not necessary that it be proportioned by something in order that it be able to receive this assent.

Therefore, we stop not with the first [*viz.* something natural] but with the second [*viz.* something supernatural]. For this revealed truth of itself is insufficient to incline the intellect to assent to it, and hence neither the agent nor the patient is proportionate to this truth. But a supernatural agent suffices to incline the intellect toward this truth by causing in it the act of assent which makes the intellect proportionate to this truth. Hence, an additional something is not required to make the intellect proportionate to such an agent or to the form it impresses, in the same way that something is required in addition to the intellect that it be made proportionate to such an object in the twofold manner mentioned above.

William of Ockham
ca. 1285–1349

William of Ockham was born in Ockham, Surrey, near London, between 1280 and 1290. As a young man he joined the Franciscan order. In 1309 or 1310 he went to Oxford, where his studies included the work of Duns Scotus. Despite his success as a student and, later, as a student lecturer, Ockham was denied a license to teach. The chancellor of the university accused him of heresy, even going to the papal court in Avignon, France, in 1323 to press charges. The following year Ockham was summoned to Avignon by Pope John XXII. The affair dragged on for four years. Meanwhile, Ockham kept writing and came into conflict with the pope again when he joined the general of his Franciscan order in advocating apostolic poverty.

In 1328 Ockham was forced to flee Avignon when the pope was prepared to condemn the Franciscan position on poverty. He eventually found refuge in Munich under the protection of Emperor Ludwig of Bavaria, who was angry with the pope for not recognizing his crown. Ockham reportedly told the emperor, "Defend me with your sword, and I will defend you with my pen."

Over the next twenty years, Ockham did indeed defend the emperor, arguing that imperial power flows from God through the people, not through the pope—a position that anticipated later political theories. Following Ludwig's death in 1347, Ockham sought reconciliation with the pope (now Clement VI), and a document of submission was drawn up. We do not know whether Ockham ever signed the document, for he died in 1349, apparently from the plague.

Ockham's philosophy reflects his times: He is much less optimistic than was Thomas Aquinas about the ability of human reason to understand the things of God. Ockham criticized the proofs for God's existence, arguing that theological truth can be known only by revelation, not reason. In so arguing he separated philosophy from theology and reason from faith more completely than had any of his predecessors.

Ockham is probably best known for his "Law of Parsimony," or "Ockham's Razor." This principle has often been formulated as *entia non sunt multiplicanda praeter necessitatem,* "entities are not to be multiplied beyond necessity," though none of Ockham's known works contains that exact phrase.* Essentially this principle holds that we should always seek the simplest explanation, a principle still used by philosophers and scientists. Ockham was not the first to enunciate this principle: It can be found earlier in the writings of Thomas Aquinas,** Duns Scotus, and even, in embryonic form, in Aristotle. But the skill with which Ockham wielded this "razor" ensured its association with his name.

Ockham was especially effective in using his razor on the question of universals. Contrary to the moderate realism dominant in his day, Ockham saw no need to posit universals as real entities beyond individual things. This critique is clear in the selections on universals given here. Following some defining of terms, Ockham argues against the realist position and, with great care, against the position of the "Subtle Doctor," Duns Scotus. Ockham asserts that "in a particular substance there is nothing substantial except the particular form, the particular matter, or the composite of the two"—that is, there is no real universal apart from the particular thing. These selections conclude with Ockham's presentation of a position he later rejected and a restatement of his final understanding of universals.

In addition, representative passages on being, essence, and existence; on God and predestination; and on politics are included. The reading on predestination represents this volume's conclusion to the issues of God and foreknowledge first raised by Boethius. The reading on politics—with its strong, though guarded, antipapal polemic—represents a marked departure from the political theory of John of Salisbury.

*   *   *

Marilyn McCord Adams's *William Ockham,* two vols. (Notre Dame, IN: University of Notre Dame Press, 1987), is the definitive introduction to Ockham, while Meyrick Heath Carré, *Realists and Nominalists* (London: Oxford University Press, 1946), and Gordon Leff, *William of Ockham: The Metamorphosis of Scholastic Discourse* (Manchester: Manchester University Press, 1975), provide helpful overviews. Specialized studies include E.A. Moody, *The Logic of*

---

*Ockham's extant writings do include the phrases *pluralitas non est ponenda sine necessitate,* "plurality is not to be posited without necessity," and *frustra fit per plura quod potest fieri per pauciora,* "what can be explained by the assumption of fewer things is vainly explained by the assumption of more things." Perhaps applying his principle to its own formulation, we should say, "Why use many if few will do?"

**See his *Summa Theologica,* Part I, Q. 2, a. 3, obj. 2—page 341 in this volume.

Plague Victim, from *Das Buch der Cirurgia,* 1497, by Hieronymus Brunschwig. Beginning in 1347 the Bubonic Plague, or "Black Death," struck Western Europe. Transmitted by flea bite, the disease was characterized by enormous swelling or "buboes" in the groin or armpits. The patient in this woodcut has a large buboe on his armpit—a sure sign that he will be dead within two or three days. Apparently William of Ockham met such a fate in 1349. *(Library of Congress)*

William of Ockham (1935; reprinted New York: Russell and Russell, 1965); Damascene Webering, *The Theory of Demonstration According to William Ockham* (St. Bonaventure, NY: Franciscan Institute, 1953); Herman Shapiro, *Motion, Time and Place According to William Ockham* (St. Bonaventure, NY: Franciscan Institute, 1957); and Arthur Stephen McGrade, *The Political*

Thought of William of Ockham: Personal and Institutional Principles (London: Cambridge University Press, 1974). For an important collection of essays, see Philotheus Bohner, ed., *Collected Articles on Ockham* (St. Bonaventure, NY: Franciscan Institute, 1958).

ON UNIVERSALS (selections)

SUMMA LOGICAE, PART I

Chapter 14: On the Universal

It is not enough for the logician to have a merely general knowledge of terms; he needs a deep understanding of the concept of a term. Therefore, after discussing some general divisions among terms we should examine in detail the various headings under these divisions.

First, we should deal with terms of second intention and afterwards with terms of first intention. I have said that "universal," "genus," and "species" are examples of terms of second intention. We must discuss those terms of second intention which are called the five universals, but first we should consider the common term "universal." It is predicated of every universal and is opposed to the notion of a particular.

First, it should be noted that the term "particular" has two senses. In the first sense a particular is that which is one and not many. Those who hold that a universal is a certain quality residing in the mind which is predicable of many (not suppositing for itself, of course, but for the many of which it is predicated) must grant that, in this sense of the word, every universal is a particular. Just as a word, even if convention makes it common, is a particular, the intention of the soul signifying many is numerically one thing a particular; for although it signifies many things it is nonetheless one thing and not many.

In another sense of the word we use "particular" to mean that which is one and not many and which cannot function as a sign of many. Taking "particular" in this sense no universal is a particular, since every universal is capable of signifying many and of being predicated of many. Thus, if we take the term "universal" to mean that which is not one in number, as many do, then, I want to say that nothing is a universal. One could, of course, abuse the expression and say that a population constitutes a single universal because it is not one but many. But that would be puerile.

Therefore, it ought to be said that every universal is one particular thing and that it is not a universal except in its signification, in its signifying many things. This is what Avicenna means to say in his commentary on the fifth book of the *Metaphysics*. He says, "One form in the intellect is related to many things, and in this respect it is a universal; for it is an intention of the intellect which has an invariant relationship to anything you choose." He then continues, "Although this form is a universal in its relationship to individuals, it is a particular in its relationship to the particular soul in which it resides; for it is just one form among many in the intellect." He means to say that a universal is an intention of a particular soul. Insofar as it can be predicated of many things not for itself but for these many, it is said to be a universal; but insofar as it is a particular form actually existing in the intellect, it is said to be a particular. Thus "particular" is predicated of a universal in the first sense but not in the second. In the same way we say that the sun is a universal cause and, nevertheless, that it is really and truly a particular or individual cause. For the sun is said to be a universal cause because it is the cause of many things (i.e., every object that is generable and corruptible), but it is said to be a particular cause because it is one cause and not many. In the same way the intention of the soul is said to be a universal because it is a sign predicable of many things, but it is said to be a particular because it is one thing and not many.

But it should be noted that there are two kinds of universals. Some things are universal by nature; that is, by nature they are signs predicable of many in the same way that the smoke is by nature a sign of fire; weeping, a sign of grief; and laughter, a sign of internal joy. The intention of the soul, of course, is a universal by nature. Thus, no substance outside the soul, nor any accident outside the soul is a universal of this sort. It is of this kind of universal that I shall speak in the following chapters.

Other things are universals by convention. Thus, a spoken word, which is numerically one quality, is a universal; it is a sign conventionally appointed for the signification of many things. Thus, since the word is said to be common, it can be called a universal. But notice it is not by nature, but only by convention, that this label applies.

Chapter 15: That the Universal Is Not a Thing Outside the Mind

But it is not enough just to state one's position; one must defend it by philosophical arguments. Therefore, I shall set forth some arguments for my view, and then corroborate it by an appeal to the authorities.

That no universal is a substance existing outside the mind can be proved in a number of ways:

No universal is a particular substance, numerically one; for if this were the case, then it would follow that Socrates is a universal; for there is no good reason why one substance should be a universal rather than another. Therefore no particular substance is a universal; every substance is numerically one and a particular. For every substance is either one thing and not many or it is many things. Now, if a substance is one thing and not many, then it is numerically one; for that is what we mean by "numerically one." But if, on the other hand, some substance is several things, it is either several particular things or several universal things. If the first alternative is chosen, then it follows that some substance would be several particular substances; and consequently that some substance would be several men. But although the universal would be distinguished from a single particular, it would not be distinguished from several particulars. If, however, some substance were to be several universal entities, I take one of those universal entities and ask, "Is it many things or is it one and not many?" If the second is the case then it follows that the thing is particular. If the first is the case then I ask, "Is it several particular things or several universal things?" Thus, either an infinite regress will follow or it will be granted that no substance is a universal in a way that would be incompatible with its also being a particular. From this it follows that no substance is a universal.

Again, if some universal were to be one substance existing in particular substances, yet distinct from them, it would follow that it could exist without them; for everything that is naturally prior to something else can, by God's power, exist without that thing; but the consequence is absurd.

Again, if the view in question were true, no individual would be able to be created. Something of the individual would pre-exist it, for the whole individual would not take its existence from nothing if the universal which is in it were already in something else. For the same reason it would follow that God could not annihilate an individual substance without destroying the other individuals of the same kind. If He were to annihilate some individual, he would destroy the whole which is essentially that individual and, consequently, He would destroy the universal which is in that thing and in others of the same essence. Consequently, other things of the same essence would not remain, for they could not continue to exist without the universal which constitutes a part of them.

Again, such a universal could not be construed as something completely extrinsic to the essence of an individual; therefore, it would belong to the essence of the individual; and, consequently, an individual would be composed of universals, so that the individual would not be any more a particular than a universal.

Again, it follows that something of the essence of Christ would be miserable and damned, since that common nature really existing in Christ would be damned in the damned individual; for surely that essence is also in Judas. But this is absurd.

Many other arguments could be brought forth, but in the interests of brevity, I shall dispense with them. Instead, I shall corroborate my account by an appeal to authorities.

First, in the seventh book of the *Metaphysics,* Aristotle is treating the question of whether a universal is a substance. He shows that no universal is a substance. Thus, he says, "it is impossible that substance be something that can be predicated universally."

Again, in the tenth book of the *Metaphysics,* he says, "Thus, if, as we argued in the discussions on substance and being, no universal can be a substance, it is not possible that a universal be a substance in the sense of a one over and against the many."

From these remarks it is clear that, in Aristotle's view, although universals can supposit for substances, no universal is a substance.

Again, the Commentator in his forty-fourth comment on the seventh book of the *Metaphysics says,* "In the individual, the only substance is the particular form and matter out of which the individual is composed."

Again, in the forty-fifth comment, he says, "Let us say, therefore, that it is impossible that one of those things we call universals be the substance of anything, although they do express the substances of things."

And, again, in the forty-seventh comment, "It is impossible that they (universals) be parts of substances existing of and by themselves."

Again, in the second comment on the eighth book of the *Metaphysics,* he says, "No universal is either a substance or a genus."

Again, in the sixth comment on the tenth book, he says, "Since universals are not substances, it is clear that the common notion of being is not a substance existing outside the mind."

Using these and many other authorities, the general point emerges: no universal is a substance regardless of the viewpoint from which we consider the matter. Thus, the viewpoint from which we consider the matter is irrelevant to the question of whether something is a substance. Nevertheless, the meaning of a term is relevant to the question of whether the expression "substance" can be predicated of the term. Thus, if the term "dog" in the proposition "The dog is an animal" is used to stand for the barking animal, the proposition is true; but if it is used for the celestial body which goes by that name, the proposition is false. But it is impossible that one and the same thing should be a substance from one viewpoint and not a substance from another.

Therefore, it ought to be granted that no universal is a substance regardless of how it is considered. On the contrary, every universal is an intention of the mind which, on the most probable account, is identical with the act of under standing. Thus, it is said that the act of understanding by which I grasp men is a natural sign of men in the same way that weeping is a natural sign of grief. It is a natural sign such that it can stand for men in mental propositions in the same way that a spoken word can stand for things in spoken propositions.

That the universal is an intention of the soul is clearly expressed by Avicenna in the fifth book of the *Metaphysics,* in which he comments, "I say, therefore, that there are three senses of 'universal.' For we say that something is a universal if (like 'man') it is actually predicated of many things; and we also call an intention a universal if it could be predicated of many." Then follows the remark, "An intention is also called a universal if there is nothing inconceivable in its being predicated of many."

From these remarks it is clear that the universal is an intention of the soul capable of being predicated of many. The claim can be corroborated by argument. For every one agrees that a universal is something predicable of many, but only an intention of the soul or a conventional sign is predicated. No substance is ever predicated of anything. Therefore, only an intention of the soul or a conventional sign is a universal; but I am not here using the term "universal" for conventional signs, but only for signs that are universals by nature. That substance is not capable of functioning as predicate is clear; for if it were, it would follow that a proposition would be composed of particular substances; and, consequently, the subject would be in Rome and the predicate in England which is absurd.

Furthermore, propositions occur only in the mind, in speech, or in writing; therefore, their parts can exist only in the mind, in speech, and in writing. Particular substances, however, cannot themselves exist in the mind, in speech, or in writing. Thus, no proposition can be composed of particular substances. Propositions are, however, composed of universals; therefore, universals cannot conceivably be substances.

Chapter 16: Against Scotus' Account of the Universal

It may be clear to many that a universal is not a substance outside the mind which exists in, but is distinct from, particulars. Nevertheless, some want to claim that the universal is, in some way, outside the soul and in particulars; and while they do not want to say that a universal is really distinct from particulars, they say that it is formally distinct from particulars. Thus, they say that in Socrates there is human nature which is contracted to Socrates by an individual difference which is not really, but only formally, distinct from that nature. Thus, while there are not two things, one is not formally the other.

I do not find this view tenable:

First, in creatures there can never be any distinction outside the mind unless there are distinct things; if, therefore, there is any distinction between the nature and the difference, it is necessary that they really be distinct things. I prove my premise by the following syllogism: the nature is not formally distinct from itself; this individual difference is formally distinct from this nature; therefore, this individual difference is not this nature.

Again, the same entity is not both common and proper, but in their view the individual difference is proper and the universal is common; therefore, no universal is identical with an individual difference.

Again, opposites cannot be attributed to one and the same created thing, but *common* and *proper* are opposites; therefore, the same thing is not both common and proper. Nevertheless, that conclusion would follow if an individual difference and a common nature were the same thing.

Again, if a common nature were the same thing as an individual difference, there would be as many common natures as there are individual differences; and, consequently, none of those natures would be common, but each would be peculiar to the difference with which it is identical.

Again, whenever one thing is distinct from another it is distinguished from that thing either of and by itself or by something intrinsic to itself. Now, the humanity of Socrates is something different from the humanity of Plato; therefore, they are distinguished of and by themselves and not by differences that are added to them.

Again, according to Aristotle things differing in species also differ in number, but the nature of a man and the nature of a donkey differ in species of and by themselves; therefore, they are numerically distinguished of and by themselves; therefore, each of them is numerically one of and by itself.

Again, that which cannot belong to many cannot be predicated of many; but such a nature, if it really is the same thing as the individual difference, cannot belong to many since it cannot belong to any other particular. Thus, it cannot be predicable of many; but, then, it cannot be a universal.

Again, take an individual difference and the nature which it contracts. Either the difference between these two things is greater or less than the difference between two particulars. It is not greater because they do not differ really; particulars, however, do differ really. But neither is it less because then they would admit of one and the same definition, since two particulars, can admit of the same definition. Consequently, if one of them is, by itself, one in number, the other will also be.

Again, either the nature is the individual difference or it is not. If it is the difference I argue as follows: this individual difference is proper and not common; this individual difference is this nature; therefore this nature is proper and not common, but that is what I set out to prove. Likewise, I argue as follows: the individual difference is not formally distinct from the individual difference; the individual difference is the nature; therefore, the nature is not formally distinct from the individual difference. But if it be said that the individual difference is not the nature, my point has been proved; for it follows that if the individual difference is not the nature, the individual difference is not really the nature; for from the opposite of the consequent follows the opposite of the antecedent. Thus, if it is true that the individual difference really is the nature, then the individual difference is the nature. The inference is valid, for from a determinable taken with its determination (where the determination does not detract from or diminish the determinable) one can infer the determinable taken by itself; but "really" does not express a determination that detracts or diminishes. Therefore, it follows that if the individual difference is really the nature, the individual difference is the nature.

Therefore, one should grant that in created things there is no such thing as a formal distinction. All things which are distinct in creatures are really distinct and, therefore, different things. In regard to creatures modes of argument like the following ought never be denied: this is A; this is B; therefore, B is A; and this is not A; this is B; therefore, B is not A. Likewise, one ought never deny that, as regards creatures, there are distinct things where contradictory notions hold. The only exception would be the case where contradictory notions hold true because of some syncategorematic element or similar determination, but in the same present case this is not so.

Therefore, we ought to say with the philosophers that in a particular substance there is nothing substantial except the particular form, the particular matter, or the composite of the two. And, therefore, no one ought to think that in Socrates there is a humanity or a human nature which is distinct from Socrates and to which there is added an individual difference which contracts that nature. The only thing in Socrates which can be construed as substantial is this particular matter, this particular form, or the composite of the two. And, therefore, every essence and quiddity and whatever belongs to substance, if it is really outside the soul, is just matter, form, or the composite of these or, following the doctrine of the Peripatetics, a separated and immaterial substance.

* * *

ORDINATIO, D. II, Q. VIII, PRIMA REDATIO

A Universal Is a Thought-object*

Another theory [different from those opinions concerning the nature of universals previously criticised by Ockham] could be advanced. I maintain that a universal is not something real that exists in a subject [of inherence], either inside or outside the mind, but that it has being only as a thought-object in the mind. It is a kind of mental picture which as a thought-object has a being similar to that which the thing outside the mind has in its real existence. What I mean is this: The intellect, seeing a thing outside the mind, forms in the mind a picture resembling it, in such a way that if the mind had the power to produce as it has the power to picture, it would produce by this act a real outside thing which would be only numerically distinct from the former real thing. The case would be similar, analogously speaking, to the activity of an artist. For just as the artist who sees a house or building outside the mind first pictures in the mind a similar house and later produces a similar house in reality which is only numerically

---

*[Ockham's first opinion, later abandoned.]

distinct from the first, so in our case the picture in the mind that we get from seeing something outside would act as a pattern. For just as the imagined house would be a pattern for the architect, if he who imagines it had the power to produce it in reality, so likewise the other picture would be a pattern for him who forms it. And this can be called a universal, because it is a pattern and relates indifferently to all the singular things outside the mind. Because of the similarity between its being as a thought-object and the being of like things outside the mind, it can stand for such things. And in this way a universal is not the result of generation, but of abstraction, which is only a kind of mental picturing.

I shall first show that something exists in the mind whose being is that of an object of thought only, without inhering in the mind as an independent subject.

This is clear from the following: According to the philosophers, existence is primarily divided into existence in the mind and existence outside the mind, the latter being subdivided into the ten categories. If this is admitted, then I ask "What is understood here by 'existence in the mind'?" It means either existence as a thought-object, and then we have our intended thesis, or it means existence as in a subject. The latter, however, is not possible; for, whatever exists truly in the mind as a subject, is contained under existence that is divided into the ten categories, since it falls under quality. For an act of intellect, and indeed in general every accident or form of the mind, is a true quality, like heat or whiteness, and hence does not fall under the division of existence that is set over against existence in the ten categories. [Consequently the main distinction of the philosophers would be futile.]

Furthermore, fictions have being in the mind, but they do not exist independently, because in that case they would be real things and so a chimera and a goatstag and so on would be real things. So some things exist only as thought-objects.

Likewise, propositions, syllogisms, and other similar objects of logic do not exist independently; therefore they exist only as thought-objects, so that their being consists in being known. Consequently, there are beings which exist only as thought-objects.

Again, works of art do not seem to inhere in the mind of the craftsman as independent subjects any more than the creatures did in the divine mind before creation.

Likewise, conceptual relations are commonly admitted by the [scholastic] doctors. If this is conceded, then I ask "Do they exist only in a subject?" In that case they will be genuine things and real relations. Or do they exist only as thought-objects? In that case we have our intended thesis.

Again, according to those who think differently, the term "being" means a univocal concept, and nevertheless does not mean a distinct reality.

Likewise, practically all men distinguish second intentions from first intentions, and they do not call the second intentions real qualities of the mind. Since they are not in reality outside the mind, they can only exist as thought-objects in the mind.

Secondly, I maintain that this mental picture is what is primarily and immediately meant by the concept "universal," and has the nature of a thought-object, and is that which is the immediate term of an act of intellection having no singular object. This mental picture, in the manner of being that a thought-object has, is just whatever the corresponding singular is, in the manner of being proper to a subject; and so by its very nature it can stand for the singulars of which it is in a way a likeness. . . .

I maintain, therefore, that just as a spoken word is universal and is a genus or a species, but only by convention, in the same way the concept thus mentally fashioned and abstracted from singular things previously known is universal by its nature.

*   *   *

EXPOSITIO SUPER LIBRUM PERIHERMENIAS

A Universal Is an Act of the Intellect*

There could be another opinion, according to which a concept is the same as the act of knowing. This opinion appears to me to be the more probable one among all the opinions which assume that these concepts really exist in the soul as a subject, like true qualities of the soul; I shall first explain this opinion in its more probable form.

I maintain, then, that somebody wishing to hold this opinion may assume that the intellect apprehending a singular thing performs within itself a cognition of this singular only. This cognition is called a state of mind, and it is capable of standing for this singular thing by its very nature. Hence, just as the spoken word "Socrates" stands by convention for the thing it signifies, so that one who hears this utterance, "Socrates is running," does not conceive that this word, "Socrates," which he hears, is running, but rather that the thing signified by this word is running; so likewise one who knew or understood that something was affirmatively predicated of this cognition of a singular thing would not think that the cognition was such and such, but would conceive that the thing to which the cognition refers is such and such. Hence, just as the spoken word stands by convention for a thing, so the act of intellect, by its very nature, and without any convention, stands for the thing to which it refers.

Beside this intellectual grasp of a singular thing the intellect also forms other acts which do not refer more to one thing than to another. For instance, just as the spoken word "man" does not signify Socrates more than Plato, and hence does not stand more for Socrates than Plato, so it would be with an act of intellect which does not relate to Socrates any more than to Plato or any other man. And in like manner there would be also a knowledge whereby this animal is not more known than that animal; and so with other notions.

To sum up: The mind's own intellectual acts are called states of mind. By their nature they stand for the actual things outside the mind or for other things in the mind, just as the spoken words stand for them by convention. . . .

. . . By such a common or confused intellection, singular things outside the mind are known. For instance, to say that we have a confused intellection of man, means that we have a cognition by which we do not understand one man rather than another, but that by such a cognition we have cognition of a man rather than a donkey. And this amounts to saying that such a cognition, by some kind of assimilation, bears a greater resemblance to a man than to a donkey, but does not resemble one man rather than another. In consequence of the aforesaid, it seems necessary to say that an infinity of objects can be known by such a confused cognition. Still this seems no more untenable than that an infinity of objects can be liked or desired by the same act of liking or desiring. Yet the latter does not seem to be untenable. For a man may like all the parts of a continuous thing, which are infinite in number, or he may desire that all these parts remain in existence. Now in such a case, what was desired would simply be a part of the continuous thing, but not one part rather than another; therefore all parts must be de-

*[Second opinion, finally held by Ockham.]

sired; these parts, however, are infinite in number. Likewise, somebody can desire the existence of all men who can exist. Now these are infinite in number, since an infinity of men can be generated.

And so it could be said that one and the same cognition refers to an infinite number of singulars without being a cognition proper to any one of them, and this is so because of some specific likeness between these individuals that does not exist between others. However, no singular thing can be distinguished from another by such a cognition.

*   *   *

SUMMA LOGICAE, PART II

Chapter 2: What Is Required for the Truth of a Singular Non-Modal Proposition

. . . We will first discuss singular non-modal present-tense propositions whose subjects and predicates are both in the nominative case and which are not equivalent to hypothetical propositions.

On this point it should be noted that for the truth of such a singular proposition which is not equivalent to several propositions it is not required that the subject and predicate be really identical, or that the predicate be in reality in the subject or that it really inhere in the subject, or that the predicate be united to the subject itself outside the mind. Thus, for the truth of "This is an angel" it is not required that the common term "angel" be really identical with what is posited as the subject, or that it be really in that subject, or anything of this sort. Rather, it is sufficient and necessary that the subject and predicate supposit for the same thing. And, therefore, if in "This is an angel" the subject and predicate supposit for the same thing, the proposition will be true. Thus, it is not asserted that this thing has angelhood or that angelhood is in it—or anything of this sort. Rather, it is asserted that this thing is truly an angel—not, indeed, that it is the predicate, but that it is that for which the predicate supposits.

Similarly, by means of propositions like "Socrates is a man" and "Socrates is an animal" it is not asserted that Socrates has humanity or animality. Nor is it asserted that humanity or animality is in Socrates, or that man or animal is in Socrates, or that animal is part of the quidditative concept of Socrates. Rather, it is asserted that Socrates is truly a man and is truly an animal. Nor, indeed, is it asserted that Socrates is the predicate "man" or the predicate "animal." Rather, it is asserted that he is a thing for which the predicate "man" or the predicate "animal" stands or supposits. For both of these predicates stand for Socrates.

From this it is clear that, literally speaking, all propositions such as these are false: "Man is of the quiddity of Socrates," "Man is of the essence of Socrates," "Humanity is in Socrates," "Socrates has humanity," "Socrates is a man in virtue of humanity"—and many other such propositions which are considered true, it seems,

From *Ockham's Theory of Propositions: Part II of the Summa Logicae* by William of Ockham, translated by Alfred J. Freddoso and Henry Schuurman. Copyright © 1980 by University of Notre Dame Press. Reprinted by permission.

by everyone. Their falsity is obvious. For I take one of them, namely, "Humanity is in Socrates," and I ask: what does "humanity" stand for? Either for a thing or for an intention, i.e. by means of this proposition it is asserted either that a real extramental thing is in Socrates or that an intention of the soul is in Socrates. If it supposits for a thing, then I ask: for which thing? Either for Socrates, or for a part of Socrates, or for a thing which is neither Socrates nor a part of Socrates. If for Socrates, then the proposition is false, since nothing which is Socrates is in Socrates—for Socrates is not in Socrates, even though Socrates is Socrates. And in the same way humanity is not in Socrates but is Socrates, if "humanity" supposits for a thing which is Socrates. On the other hand, if "humanity" stands for a thing which is a part of Socrates, then the proposition is false, because anything which is a part of Socrates is either matter or form or a composite of matter and form—and just one human form and not another— or it is an integral part of Socrates. But humanity is no such part, as is clear inductively. For humanity is not an intellective soul. For if it were, then real humanity would have remained in Christ in the tomb, and humanity would have been really united to the Word in the tomb, and, consequently, he would really have been a man—which is false. Similarly, humanity is not matter. Nor is humanity the body of Socrates or his foot or his head, and so on for the other parts of Socrates. For no part of Socrates is humanity—rather, it is only a part of humanity. As a result, "humanity" cannot supposit for a part of Socrates. If it supposits for a thing which is neither Socrates nor a part of Socrates, then, since such a thing could only be an accident or some other thing which is not in Socrates, "humanity" would supposit for an accident of Socrates or for some other thing which is neither Socrates nor a part of Socrates— and it is clear that that is false. If, moreover, "humanity" supposits for an intention of the soul, then the proposition is clearly false. For an intention of the soul is not in Socrates. And so it is clear that "Humanity is in Socrates" is false no matter how it is understood.

One can argue in the same way with respect to all the other propositions noted above. For if man or humanity is of the essence of Socrates, I then ask: what does "man" or "humanity" supposit for? Either for Socrates, in which case it would be asserted that Socrates is of the essence of Socrates—which is not true. Or if it supposits for a thing other than Socrates, then it supposits either for a part of Socrates—but this cannot be, since no part of Socrates is a man or humanity—or for something else which is neither Socrates nor a part of Socrates—but it is clear that no such thing is a man or humanity unless it is Plato or John or some other man. And it is manifest that no man other than Socrates is of the essence of Socrates. On the other hand, if it supposits for an intention of the soul or for a spoken word, it is clear that in that case it is not of the essence of Socrates. And so it is obvious that all such propositions are literally false.

Now someone might claim that humanity is in Socrates and is of the essence of Socrates, and that, nevertheless, it is neither Socrates, nor matter, nor form, nor an integral part—rather, it is a common nature which enters into a composition with the individual difference of Socrates. Hence, it is a part of Socrates but neither matter nor form.

I argue against this view at length in several places, namely, in my commentaries on the first book of the *Sentences,* on the book of Porphyry, and on the *Categories.* At present I will offer some arguments against it.

The first is this. If humanity were something different from singular things and of the essence of singulars, then the same thing, while remaining unchanged, would be in many singular things. And so the same thing, while remaining naturally unchanged, would be in many distinct places without a miracle. But it is obvious that this is false.

Similarly, in that case the same thing, while remaining unchanged, would be damned in Judas and saved in Christ. And so there would be something miserable and damned in Christ—which is absurd.

Likewise, in that case God would not be able to annihilate an individual unless he annihilated or destroyed every individual of the same genus. For when something is annihilated, nothing of it remains and, as a result, such a common nature does not remain. Consequently, no individual in which it is remains, and so each individual would be annihilated or destroyed.

Further, I take that humanity which you posit in Socrates and in every other man, and the donkeyhood which you posit in every donkey. And let that humanity be called *A*, so that *A* stands just for that humanity; and let that donkeyhood be called *B*, so that *B* stands just for that donkeyhood. Then I ask: are *A* and *B* just two things, or more than two things, or not more than one thing? It cannot be said that they are not more than one thing. For in that case necessarily either they are one thing, or neither *A* nor *B* is a thing, or *A* is not a thing, or *B* is not a thing. It is clear, even according to those who hold this position, that the first answer cannot be given. Nor can the second answer be given, since these same people deny it when they claim that humanity is a real thing and, likewise, donkeyhood. Nor can the third answer be given, since there is no more reason for claiming that *B* is not a thing than for claiming that *A* is not a thing, and conversely. Therefore, it is absolutely necessary to say that *A* and *B* are more than one thing. Further, it cannot be claimed that they are more than two things. For if they are more than two things and if they are not more than two universal things, then they are more singular things. And, as a result, they are not distinguished absolutely from singular things. Therefore, the only remaining alternative is that they are two things and no more. Consequently, each of them is one in number, since each will be one thing in such a way that it is not many things. And this is what it is to be one in number, namely, to be one thing and not many. For that ought to be the description of being one in number. For if this were to be denied, I might just as easily claim that Socrates is not numerically one thing even if he is one thing and not many things.

Hence, it is the opinion of the Philosopher as well as the truth that the predicate "is one in species" or "is one or the same in genus" is never predicated except of an individual or individuals, each of which is one in number. Thus, "Socrates and Plato are one in species" and "Socrates and this donkey are one in genus" are true. And nothing other than individuals is one in species or in genus. And so it is the case that that humanity which is posited in every man is one thing and not more than one thing and, consequently, that it is one in number. From this it follows that numerically one thing would be in every man.

Moreover, I think that in other places I have sufficiently responded to arguments which seem to contravene the view I have set forth.

Nor does it help to claim that the humanity of Socrates is only formally distinct—and not really distinct—from Socrates. For such a distinction should not be posited in creatures, although it can in some sense be posited in the divinity. This is so because among creatures it is impossible to find any numerically one thing which is really more than one thing and is each of those things, as is the case with God. For in God the divine essence is three persons and it is each of those persons, and yet one person is not another. For to say that the essence and a person are formally distinguished, in the true sense, is nothing other than to say that the essence is three persons and a person is not three persons. Similarly, I understand the proposition, "The essence and the Paternity are formally distinguished" to mean nothing other than the proposition "The essence is the Filiation and the Paternity is not the Filiation and yet the essence is the Paternity." Likewise, to say that the Paternity and the Active Procession are formally distinguished is nothing other than to say that the Paternity is not the Filiation and that the Active Procession is the Filiation and yet that the Paternity is the Active Procession.

And so, generally, when two things are truly said to be formally distinguished, this is nothing other than to say that something is truly affirmed of the one and truly denied of the other, and yet that one of those two things is truly affirmed of the other—without any variation or equivocation or verification for different things, as happens in particular and indefinite propositions. But this can never occur except when one simple thing is more than one thing, as a single divine essence is three persons and as a single Active Procession is the Paternity and the Filiation. And since it cannot happen among creatures that one thing is more than one thing and is each of them, a formal distinction ought not be posited in creatures. And so it is clear that it should not be claimed that the humanity of Socrates is formally—but not really—distinguished from Socrates. The same holds for propositions like "Animality is distinguished from a man," and so on for the others. In the commentary on the first book of the *Sentences,* distinction two I proved, moreover, that such a formal distinction must not be posited in creatures.

ON BEING, ESSENCE, AND EXISTENCE
(selections)

SUMMA LOGICAE, PART I

Chapter 38: On Being

Having dealt with terms of second intention and second imposition we shall turn our attention to those terms of first intention that are called the categories. But first we shall consider some expressions that are common to all things, both signs and things that are not signs. "Being" and "one" are terms of this sort.

It should first be noted that the term "being" has two senses. In one sense the term is used to correspond to one concept that is common to all things and is predicable *in quid* of everything in the way in which a transcendental is capable of being predicated *in quid.*

One can prove that there is one common concept predicable of everything in the following way: if there is no one such common concept, then there are different concepts for different things. Let us suppose that there are two such concepts, *A* and *B.* Following out this supposition, I can show that some concept more general than *A* and

B is predicable of an object, *C*. Just as we can form the verbal propositions *"C is B," "C is A,"* and *"C is something,"* we can form three corresponding mental propositions. Two of these are dubious and one is certain; for someone can doubt which of the first two is true, while knowing that the third is true. If this is granted, I argue as follows: two of the propositions are dubious and one is certain. The three propositions all have the same subject; therefore, they have different predicates. Were it not so, one and the same proposition would be both certain and dubious; for in the present case the first two are dubious. But if they have different predicates, the predicate in *"C is something"* is not the predicate in either *"C is B"* or *"C is A."* It is, we can conclude, a different predicate. But it is clear that the relevant predicate is neither less general nor convertible with either *A* or *B*. It must therefore be more general. But this is what we set out to prove—that some concept of the mind, different from those that are logically subordinated to it, is common to everything. That must be granted. Just as one word is capable of being truly predicated of everything, there is some one concept of the mind that can be truly predicated of every object or of every pronoun referring to an object.

But while there is one concept common to everything, the term "being" is equivocal because it is not predicated of the items logically subordinated to it according to just one concept; several different concepts correspond to the term as I have indicated in my commentary on Porphyry.

Further, it should be noted that, as the Philosopher says in the fifth book of the *Metaphysics,* "Being is said both essentially and accidentally." In drawing this distinction the Philosopher should not be understood to mean that some things are beings *per se* and others, beings *per accidens.* What he is doing on the contrary is pointing to the different ways in which one thing can be predicated of another through the mediation of "to be." This is clear from the examples he uses. As he notes, we say that the musical is *per accidens* just, that the musical is *per accidens* a man, and that the musical is *per accidens* a builder. It should be clear from these examples that he is only distinguishing the different ways of predicating one thing of another, viz., *per accidens* and *per se.* It is clear that there are not two kinds of being, the *per se* and the *per accidens.* Everything is either a substance or an accident, but both substances and accidents are beings *per se.* This point holds even though we have *per se* and *per accidens* predication.

Similarly, being is divided into being in potency and being in act. This should not be understood to mean that there are two kinds of beings, those which do not exist in nature but could and those which actually exist in nature. By dividing being into potency and act in the fifth book of the *Metaphysics,* Aristotle means to show that the term "being" is predicated of some things by means of *de inesse* propositions and not by means of propositions equivalent to propositions of possibility. Thus "Socrates is a being" and "Whiteness is a being." Of other things, Aristotle wants to say, "being" is predicated only by means of a proposition of possibility or by a proposition equivalent to such. Thus "The Anti-Christ can be" and "The Anti-Christ is a being in potency." He wants to say that being like knowledge and sleep, can be predicated both potentially and actually. But note: things do not sleep or have knowledge except actually.

We will talk about the other divisions in being elsewhere. In the interests of brevity these remarks will suffice for the present.

*   *   *

SUMMA LOGICAE, PART III, II

Chapter 27: The Distinction Between Existence and Essence

Since we have touched upon "existence," we shall make a digression for a while and consider how the existence of a thing is related to the thing, i.e. whether the existence of a thing and its essence are two entities extra-mentally distinct from each other. It appears to me that they are not two such entities, nor does "existence" signify anything different from the thing itself. For if there were something distinct, then it would be either a substance or an accident. But it is not an accident, because in that case the existence of a man would be a quality or a quantity, which is manifestly false, as can be shown by considering cases. Nor can it be a substance, because every substance is either matter or form, or a composition of matter and form, or a separated substance. But it is manifest that none of these can be called the existence of a thing, if existence is a thing distinct from the essence of the thing itself.

Furthermore, if essence and existence were two things, then either they would constitute something that is intrinsically one, or they would not. If they did, then the one must be actuality and the other potentiality; hence the one would be matter and the other form; but that is absurd. If, however, they did not constitute something that is intrinsically one, then they would be one as an aggregate is one, i.e. they could constitute some one thing only incidentally. From this, however, it would follow that the one is an accident of the other.

Furthermore, if they were two things, then no contradiction would be involved if God preserved the essence of a thing in the world without its existence, or vice versa, its existence without its essence; both of which are impossible.

We have to say, therefore, that essence and existence are not two things. On the contrary, the words "thing" and "to be" signify one and the same thing, but the one in the manner of a noun and the other in the manner of a verb. For that reason, the one cannot be suitably substituted for the other, because they do not have the same function. Hence the verb "to be" can be put between two terms by saying "Man is an animal," but the same cannot be done with the noun "thing" or "essence." Hence "existence" signifies the thing itself. Now, it signifies the first simple cause, when it is predicated of this cause without signifying that it depends on something else. However, when it is predicated of other things, it signifies them in their dependence on, and subordination to, the first cause. And this is so, because these things are things only in as much as they are dependent on and ordered towards the first cause, just as it is only thus that they exist. Hence, just as a man does not exist when he is not depending on God, so likewise he is not, in that case, a man.

Therefore there is no more reason to imagine that essence is indifferent in regard to being and non-being, than that it is indifferent in regard to being an essence and not being an essence. For as an essence may exist and may not exist, so an essence may be an essence and may not be an essence. For this reason the following arguments are invalid: "Essence may exist and may not exist, therefore existence is distinct from essence"; "Essence can come under the opposite of existence, therefore essence differs from existence." Just as the following ones are not valid: "Essence may be or may not be an essence, therefore essence differs from essence"; "Essence can come under the opposite of essence, therefore essence differs from essence." Hence, there is no more reason for essence and existence to be two things, than for essence and essence to be two things. Therefore existence is not a thing different from the essence of a thing.

This is the teaching of the Lincolnian [Robert Grosseteste], when he says on the second book of the *Posterior Analytics:* "When 'it exists' is said of the first cause, what is predicated is just the absolutely simple essence of the first cause; but when 'it exists' is said of other things, what is predicated only is just their order and dependence on the first being, which exists of itself. And this ordering or dependence does not add anything to the dependent essence. For that reason, the question whether or not a thing exists does not figure among the demonstrative questions, whether it be raised about the first being or about a being dependent on the first being."

The reason why the saints and others say that God is His very existence is this. God exists in such a manner that He cannot not exist; in fact, He exists necessarily; and He is not from something else. A creature, on the other hand, exists in such a manner that it does not necessarily exist, just as it is not necessarily a thing; and it is from something else, just as it is a thing on account of something else as its efficient cause. For that reason, there is no distinction in God between "that which is" and "that in virtue of which it is," because there is not anything different from God in virtue of which God is. But in a creature there is a distinction, because that which a creature is and that in virtue of which a creature is are simply distinct, just as God and a creature are distinct.

ON GOD AND PREDESTINATION
(selections)

QUODLIBETA, PART I

Question 1: Can It Be Proved by Natural Reason That There Is Only One God?

It can be proved: For one world has only one ruler, as is stated in the 12th book of the *Metaphysics;* but it can be proved by natural reason that there is only one world, according to Aristotle in the first book of the *De Caelo;* therefore by natural reason it can be proved that there is only one ruler; but this ruler of the world is God, therefore, etc.

To the contrary: An article of faith cannot be evidently proved; but that there is only one God is an article of faith; therefore, etc.

As regards this question, I shall first explain what is meant by the name "God"; secondly I shall answer the question.

Concerning the first point I say that the name "God" can have various descriptions. One of them is: "God is some thing more noble and more perfect than anything else besides Him." Another is: "God is that than which nothing is more noble and more perfect."

Concerning the second point, I maintain that if we understand "God" according to the first description, then it cannot be demonstratively proved that there is only one God. The reason for this is that it cannot be evidently known that God, understood in this sense, exists. Therefore it cannot be evidently known that there is only one God. The inference is plain. The antecedent is proved in this way. The proposition "God exists" is not known by itself, since many doubt it; nor can it be proved from propositions known by themselves, since in every argument something doubtful or derived from faith will be assumed; nor is it known by experience, as is manifest.

Secondly I maintain: If it could be evidently proved that God exists—"God" being understood in the present sense—then the unicity of God could be evidently proved. The reason for this is the following: If there were two Gods, let us call them *A* and *B*, then in virtue of our description God *A* would be more perfect than anything else, therefore God *A* would be more perfect than God *B*, and God *B* would be more imperfect than God *A*. But God *B* would also be more perfect than God *A*, because according to our assumption God *B* would be God. Consequently God *B* would be more perfect and more imperfect than God *A*, and God *A* than God *B*, which is a manifest contradiction. If, therefore, it could be evidently proved that God exists—"God" being understood in the present sense—then the unicity of God could be evidently proved.

Thirdly I maintain that the unicity of God cannot be evidently proved if we understand "God" according to the second description. Yet this negative proposition, "The unicity of God cannot be evidently proved," cannot be proved demonstratively either. For it cannot be demonstrated that the unicity of God cannot be evidently proved, except by rebutting the arguments to the contrary. For instance, it cannot be demonstratively proved that the stars make up an even number, nor can the Trinity of Persons be demonstrated. Nevertheless, these negative propositions, "It cannot be demonstrated that the stars make up an even number," "The Trinity of Persons cannot be demonstrated," cannot be evidently proved. We must understand, however, that it can be proved that God exists, if we understand "God" according to the second description. For otherwise we could go on *ad infinitum,* if there were not some one among beings to which nothing is prior or superior in perfection. But from this it does not follow that it can be demonstrated that there is only one such being. This we hold only by faith.

The answer to the main objection is clear from the aforesaid.

* * *

PREDESTINATION, GOD'S FOREKNOWLEDGE, AND FUTURE CONTINGENTS

Question I

A. Regarding the subject of predestination and foreknowledge, it should be observed that those who suppose that passive predestination and passive foreknowledge are real relations in the [person who is] predestinate and foreknown have necessarily to admit contradictories.

Proof of the claim: I take someone—*A*—who is now predestinate, and I ask whether or not *A* can commit the sin of final impenitence.

If he cannot, then necessarily he will be saved, which is absurd.

If he can, then suppose that he does commit [that] sin. On this supposition "*A* is reprobate" is true. And then I ask whether or not the real relation of predestination has been destroyed.

If it has not been destroyed, then it remains in *A* when *A* is reprobate. Consequently *A* will be at one and the same time both reprobate and predestinate, since if such a relation is a relation really existing in *A*, *A* can be denominated by it.

If it is destroyed, then at any rate it will always be true to say afterwards that there was such a relation in *A*, since according to the Philosopher in Book VI of the *Ethics* [Ch. 2, 1139b10–11], "in this alone is God deprived: to make undone things that have been done." (This is to be understood in the following way. If some assertoric proposition merely about the present that is not equivalent to one about the future is true now, so that it is true of the present, then it will always be true of the past. For if the proposition "this thing is"—some thing or other having been indicated—is true now, then "this thing was" will be true forever after, nor can God in His absolute power bring it about that this proposition be false.) Therefore, since "this relation is in *A*" was true at some time, "this relation was in *A*" will always be true. Therefore "*A* was predestinate" will always be true, nor can it be false as the result of any power whatever. And then this follows further: he is reprobate now; therefore "he was reprobate" will always be true after this instant. Thus at one and the same instant "*A* was predestinate" and "*A* was reprobate" will be true. Further, he was therefore predestinate and not predestinate, reprobate and not reprobate.

There is no way in which this argument can be resolved as long as one supposes that predestination and foreknowledge are real relations.

B. There are, nevertheless, some objections to what has been said so far.

[Objection] 1. The conclusion seems to be opposed as much to those who deny as to those who suppose [that they are real] relations. For I take someone existing in divine acceptance—the same is predestinate—and then I ask whether or not charity can be destroyed; and the conclusion deduced earlier follows whether it can or cannot be destroyed.

[Reply.] I maintain that what he assumes is false, for "everyone existing [in a state of] charity is predestinate" is false, just as "everyone who commits mortal sin is reprobate" is false. For Peter and Paul committed mortal sin but were never reprobate;

similarly, Judas sometimes performed a meritorious act but was not then predestinate. For these propositions [*viz.,* "everyone existing in a state of charity is predestinate" and "everyone who commits mortal sin is reprobate"] are equivalent to some about the future, since they are equivalent [respectively] to these: "God will give these [existing in a state of charity] eternal life" and "God will give those [having committed mortal sin] eternal punishment." [But corresponding propositions about the future—*viz.,* "God will give Peter eternal life" and "God will give Peter eternal punishment"] do not follow [respectively] from "Peter is in [a state of] charity" and "Peter has committed mortal sin." Therefore, if no one could be in [a state of] charity without having been predestinate, the conclusion of the argument would be opposed as much to those who deny as to those who suppose [that they are real] relations. But that is false, and so the conclusion is not [of that sort].

C. [Objection] 2. Every proposition about the present that is true at some time has [corresponding to it] a necessary proposition about the past. For example, if "Socrates is seated" is true, "Socrates was seated" will be necessary forever after. But suppose "Peter is predestinate" is now true; in that case "Peter was predestinate" will always be necessary. Then I ask whether or not he can be damned. If he can be so, suppose that he is. Then "Peter is reprobate" is true of the present; therefore "Peter was reprobate" will always be necessary of the past. Thus "Peter was predestinate" and "Peter was reprobate" would be true at one and the same time.

[Reply.] I maintain that the major premiss is false (as is clear from Assumption 3); for that proposition that is about the present in such a way that it is nevertheless equivalent to one about the future and its truth depends on the truth of the one about the future does not have [corresponding to it] a necessary proposition about the past. On the contrary, the one about the past is contingent, just as is its [corresponding proposition] about the present. All propositions having to do with predestination and reprobation are of this sort (as is clear from Assumption 4), since they all are equivalently about the future even when they are verbally about the present or about the past. Therefore "Peter was predestinate" is contingent just as is "Peter is predestinate."

And when you ask whether Peter can be damned, I reply that he can be so and that we can suppose that he is. In that case, however, "Peter is reprobate and Peter was predestinate" will be false, since if one of a pair of contradictories is posited—i.e., if it is posited that it is true—the other will be false. But "Peter was predestinate" and "Peter was reprobate" include contradictories—*viz.,* "God will give eternal life to Peter" and "God will not give eternal life to Peter." Therefore if one is true the other is false, and vice versa.

D. [Objection] 3. If someone predestinate can be damned, [he can be so] only as a result of an act of a created will. Consequently an act of the divine will can be obstructed by such an act [—which is absurd].

[Reply.] I grant the premiss, but I reject the inference. An act of the divine will is not obstructed by an act of a created will, unless something opposed to a standing divine ordinance were to occur as a result of some other will, in which case "God has predestinated Peter" and "Peter is damned as a result of an act of his own will" would be true at one and the same time. But they cannot hold good at one and the same time, since if "Peter is damned because of an evil act of his own will" is true, then "Peter is predestinate" was never true. Similarly, if "Peter is damned" is true, then "Peter was preordained to eternal life" was never true.

[Objection 3a.] The argument is supported in the following way. Suppose God has determined Peter to be saved. I ask whether or not in that case Peter's will would follow necessarily the determination of the divine will. If not, the divine will is obstructed. If so, the thesis [that someone predestinate cannot be damned] is established.

[Reply.] I maintain that a created will follows a divine ordinance or determination not necessarily but freely and contingently. But it does not follow further from the previously stated argument that the divine will can be obstructed, since the truth of "God predestinated Peter" is inconsistent with the truth of "Peter is damned."

E. [Objection] 4. The proposition "God predestinated Peter" was true from eternity. Therefore it cannot be false. Therefore it is necessary.

[Reply.] I reject the inference, since many propositions were true from eternity that are false now. For example, "the world does not exist" was true from eternity and nevertheless is false now. Thus I maintain that even if "God predestinated Peter" will have been true from eternity, it can nevertheless be false and it can fail ever to have been true.

F. [Objection] 5. Since everything that is God or is in God is necessary, divine predestination is necessary. Therefore, necessarily He predestinated Peter. Therefore Peter necessarily is predestinate, and so not contingently.

[Reply.] I maintain that "predestination is necessary" can be understood in two different ways. In one way [it can be understood as the claim] that that which is principally signified by the noun "predestination" is necessary. [Understood] in this way, I grant it, since that [which is principally signified] is the divine essence, which is necessary and immutable. In another way [it can be understood as the claim that that which is secondarily signified by the noun "predestination"—*viz.,*] that someone is predestinated by God [—is necessary]. [Understood] in this way, [predestination] is not necessary, for just as everyone who is predestinate, contingently is predestinate, so God contingently predestinates everyone [who is predestinate].

And when it is said that divine predestination is immutable and therefore absolutely necessary, I maintain that what is immutable and real is necessary. When, however, we are speaking of an immutable complex—["mutable" and "immutable"] in the sense in which one complex can change from truth to falsity and vice versa and another complex cannot change in that way—then not everything immutable is necessary. For there is some contingent proposition that cannot be first true and afterwards false and vice versa, so that it is [not] true to say of it "this proposition is true now but was false earlier" and vice versa, and yet [this proposition] is not necessary but contingent. The reason for this is that although by hypothesis [the proposition] is true and will have been true, it is nevertheless possible that it is not true and that it will never have been absolutely true. For example, "God knows that this person will be saved" is true and yet is possible that He will never have known that this person will be saved. And so that proposition is immutable and is nevertheless not necessary but contingent.

[Objection 5a.] On the contrary: every proposition that is true now and can be false can change from truth to falsity. But suppose that the proposition "Peter is predestinate" is true now and can be false (as is consistent); therefore ["Peter is predestinate" can change from truth to falsity].

[Reply.] I maintain that the major premise is false, since more is required—i.e., that the proposition that will be false or will be capable of being false was true at some time. Therefore, although the proposition "Peter is predestinate" is true now and can be false, nevertheless when it will be false, it will be true to say that it never was true. Therefore it cannot change from truth to falsity.

G. [Objection] 6. When opposites are related to each other in such a way that the one cannot succeed the other, then if one of them is posited the other cannot be posited—as is clear regarding blindness and vision. But to be predestinate and to be damned are [opposites] of this kind. Therefore [if one of them is posited the other cannot be posited].

[Reply.] I maintain that this is not true as regards such opposites as those to which future contingents correspond—opposites such as to be predestinate and to be reprobate. Therefore, although they could not succeed each other, still it does not follow that if one obtains the other cannot obtain.

[Objection 6a.] On the contrary: concerning everyone of whom it is true to say today that he is predestinate and nevertheless that he can be reprobate tomorrow, "predestinate" and "reprobate" can be successively verified of him. Therefore [these opposites can succeed each other].

[Reply.] I deny it, unless it could be truly said when he is reprobate that he was at some time predestinate. Therefore, since this cannot be said in the case put forward, they are not successively verified of one and the same person, nor can they be.

H. [Objection] 7. One whom God predestinated from eternity He cannot not predestinate, for otherwise He could change [—which is absurd]. Therefore if God predestinated Peter from eternity, then from eternity He cannot not predestinate him. As a consequence, necessarily he will be saved.

[Reply.] I maintain that the first proposition is false, since all such [propositions] as "God predestinated Peter from eternity" and "Peter was predestinated from eternity" are contingent, since they can be true and they can be false—not *successively,* however, so that they are true after they were false, or vice versa. Therefore, even though "God predestinated Peter from eternity" and [other propositions] of that kind are true now, before Peter is granted supreme blessedness, they can nevertheless be false. If he should in fact be damned, then [that proposition] is false in fact (or [such propositions] are false in fact). [Such propositions,] therefore, are just as contingent with the phrase "from eternity" as without it. Nor do they present any difficulty other than that presented by those that are verbally about the present.

J. [Objection] 8. I ask regarding the things that have been revealed by the Prophets whether or not necessarily they come to pass as they have been revealed. If so, then since such things are future, it follows that their opposite cannot come to pass. On the other hand, if not, then "this is revealed"—where some such thing is indicated—was true at some time and therefore was ever afterwards necessary. Now it was not revealed as false, for the Prophets did not say what is false. Therefore it was revealed as true. Therefore it is necessary that what is revealed come to pass, since otherwise what is false could form the basis of a prophecy.

[Reply.] I maintain that no revealed future contingent comes to pass necessarily; rather, contingently. I grant that "this is revealed" was true at some time and that its [corresponding proposition] about the past was ever afterwards necessary. I grant also that it was not revealed as false, but as true and contingent (rather than as true and necessary). Consequently it could have been and can be false. Nevertheless the Prophets did not say what is false, since all prophecies regarding any future contingents were conditionals. But the condition was not always expressed. Sometimes it was expressed—as in the case of David and his throne—and sometimes it was understood—as in the case of [the prophecy of] the destruction of Nineveh by the prophet Jonah: "Yet forty days, and Nineveh shall be overthrown"—i.e., unless they would repent; and since they did repent, it was not destroyed.

ASSUMPTIONS

K. In order to resolve these objections I first make certain assumptions. Once these are seen, the resolution of the arguments will be clear.

Assumption 1. Neither active predestination nor active reprobation is a real thing distinct in some way or other from God or the divine Persons. Nor is passive predestination something absolute or relative distinct in some way from the person who is predestinate. But the noun "predestination" (or the concept), whether taken in the active or in the passive sense, signifies not only God Himself who will give eternal life to someone but also the person to whom it is given. Thus it signifies three things: God [who will give eternal life to someone], eternal life, and the person to whom it is given. Similarly, "reprobation" signifies God who will give eternal punishment to someone, [eternal punishment, and the person to whom it is given].

L. Assumption 2. All propositions having to do with predestination and reprobation are contingent whether they are of present tense—e.g., "God predestinates Peter" and "Peter is predestinate"—or of past tense, or of future tense. If any [such proposition] were necessary, it would be one about the past. But "Peter was predestinate," for example, is neither a necessary proposition nor a proposition *de necessario*. For I ask whether or not Peter could be damned. If not, then necessarily he will be saved, and in that case there would be no need to deliberate or to take trouble—which is absurd. If he can be damned, suppose that he is so in fact. Then "Peter is damned" is true. Therefore after this instant "Peter was damned" will always be true. But according to you "Peter was predestinate" is necessary. Therefore "Peter was predestinate" and "Peter was reprobate" will be true at one and the same time; and contradictories follow from these [propositions], as is clear. (Scotus, too, maintains this conclusion.)

M. Assumption 3. Some propositions are about the present as regards both their wording and their subject matter. Where such [propositions] are concerned, it is universally true that every true proposition about the present has [corresponding to it] a necessary one about the past—e.g., "Socrates is seated," "Socrates is walking," "Socrates is just," and the like.

Other propositions are about the present as regards their wording only and are equivalently about the future, since their truth depends on the truth of propositions about the future. Where such [propositions] are concerned, the rule that every true proposition about the present has [corresponding to it] a necessary one about the past is not true. And this is not remarkable, since there are true propositions about the past and about the future that have no true [proposition] about the present [corresponding to them]. For example, "what is white was black" and "what is white will be black" are true while their [corresponding proposition] about the present—"what is white is black"—is false.

N. Assumption 4. All propositions having to do with predestination and reprobation, whether they are verbally about the present or about the past, are nevertheless equivalently about the future, since their truth depends on the truth of propositions formally about the future. But Assumption 3 shows that such true [propositions] about the present do not have a necessary one about the past [corresponding to them] but rather one that is merely contingent, just as the one about the present is contingent. From these [considerations] it follows that no proposition about the present having to do with predestination and reprobation has a necessary one about the past [corresponding to it].

O. Assumption 5. From the Philosopher's point of view God does not know one part of a contradiction [to be true] any more than [He knows] the other, not only as regards future contingents but also as regards those [propositions] about the present and about the past that are equivalent to propositions about the future. On the contrary, according to him neither [part of the contradiction] is known by God, since according to him in Book One of the *Posterior Analytics* [Ch. 2, 71b26] nothing is known unless it is true. But as regards these [propositions] truth is not determinate, since according to him no reason can be given why one part is true rather than the other. Consequently both parts will be true or neither will be true. But it is not possible that both parts be true. Therefore neither is true. Therefore neither is known.

P. Assumption 6. It must be held beyond question that God knows with certainty all future contingents—i.e., He knows with certainty which part of the contradiction is true and which false. (Nevertheless all such propositions as "God knows that this part— or that part—of the contradiction is true" are contingent, not necessary, as has been said before.)

It is difficult, however, to see how He knows this [with certainty], since one part [of the contradiction] is no more determined to truth than the other. The Subtle Doctor maintains that the divine intellect, insofar as it is in some respect prior to the determination of the divine will, apprehends those complexes as neutral with respect to itself, and then the divine will determines that one part [of the contradiction] is true for some instant, willing that the other part is false for that same instant. After the determination of the divine will is effected, however, the divine intellect sees the determination of its own will, which is immutable. It sees clearly that one part is true with certainty—viz., that part which its own will wills to be true.

I argue against this opinion, however, for [in the first place] it does not seem to preserve the certainty of God's knowledge in respect of future things that depend absolutely on a created will. For I ask whether or not the determination of a created will necessarily follows the determination of the divine will. If it does, then the will necessarily acts [as it does], just as fire does, and so merit and demerit are done away with. If it does not, then the determination of a created will is required for knowing determinately one or the other part of a contradiction regarding those [future things that depend absolutely on a created will]. For the determination of the uncreated will does not suffice, because a created will can oppose the determination [of the uncreated will]. Therefore, since the determination of the [created] will was not from eternity, God did not have certain cognition of the things that remained [for a created will to determine].

Secondly, when something is determined contingently, so that it is still possible that it is not determined and it is possible that it was never determined, then one cannot have certain and infallible cognition based on such a determination. But the determination of the divine will in respect of future contingents is such a determination, both according to him [Scotus] and in truth. Therefore God cannot have certain cognition of future contingents based on such a determination.

[The argument] is supported as follows. All such propositions as "God from eternity willed this part of the contradiction to be true" and "God from eternity determined this" are contingent, as is clear from Assumption 2. Consequently they can be true and [they can be] false. Therefore one will have no certain cognition based on such a determination.

For that reason I maintain that it is impossible to express clearly the way in which God knows future contingents. Nevertheless it must be held that He does so, but contingently. That must be held because of the pronouncements of the Saints, who say that

God does not know things that are becoming in a way different from that in which [He knows] things that have already occurred.

Despite [the impossibility of expressing it clearly], the following way [of knowing future contingents] can be ascribed [to God]. Just as the [human] intellect on the basis of one and the same [intuitive] cognition of certain noncomplexes can have evident cognition of contradictory contingent propositions such as "*A* exists," "*A* does not exist," in the same way it can be granted that the divine essence is intuitive cognition that is so perfect, so clear, that it is evident cognition of all things past and future, so that it knows which part of a contradiction [involving such things] is true and which part false.

Suppose it is said that that which is not true in itself cannot be known by anyone, but that [the proposition] that I shall sit down tomorrow is of that sort.

In that case I maintain that [that proposition] is true, so that [it is] not false, but *contingently* true, since it *can* be false.

On the contrary: each part of this [contradiction] "I shall sit down tomorrow," "I shall not sit down tomorrow," can, indifferently, be true. Therefore one part is not more true than the other. Hence either neither is now true or both [are now true]. Not both; therefore neither.

I maintain that one part is now determinately true, so that [it is] not false, since God wills the one part to be true and the other to be false. Nevertheless He wills contingently. Therefore He can not will the one part and He can will the other part, inasmuch as the other part can come to pass.

Q. Assumption 7. In connection with the subject of predestination and reprobation the verb "to know" is taken either broadly—i.e., for the cognition of anything whatever—and in that sense God knows all things, non-complexes as well as complexes, necessary, contingent, false, and impossible; or strictly, and in that sense it is the same as to know what is true. It is in this sense that the Philosopher says in Book One of the *Posterior Analytics* [Ch. 2, 71b26] that nothing is known unless it is true.

R. Assumption 8. Some propositions having to do with predestination and reprobation are to be distinguished with respect to composition and division, such as those in which a mode is posited together with a clause in indirect discourse. The result is that what is indicated in the sense of composition is that the mode is predicated of the prejacent of the clause in indirect discourse, or of the proposition belonging to that clause. What is indicated in the sense of division, however, is that the predicate belonging to the clause in indirect discourse or to the proposition belonging to that clause, is predicated together with such a mode of that for which the subject of the clause supposits, as is shown in logic. This shows that "the predestinate can be damned" and [propositions] like it are not to be distinguished with respect to composition and division.

S. Assumption 9. For present purposes "cause" is taken in two ways. In one way for a real thing having another real thing as its effect. That from whose existence something else follows is called the cause, for when it is posited the effect is posited, and when it is not posited [the effect] cannot be posited.

It is used in another way when it means the priority of one proposition over another with respect to an inference. We say, for instance, that when there is a natural inference from one proposition to another and not vice versa, the antecedent is the cause of the consequent and not vice versa.

Once these [assumptions] have been seen one can respond to the arguments that have been propounded, proving that the predestinate can be damned, and also to other [arguments] propounded for other questions concerning God's knowledge in respect of future contingents.

ON POLITICS (selections)

EIGHT QUESTIONS ON THE POWER OF THE POPE

Question 2: The Origin of the Supreme Civil Power

Chapter 1

In the second place, the question is raised whether the supreme lay power derives the character strictly proper to it immediately from God. On this question there are two contrary opinions. According to one, the supreme lay power does not derive the power strictly proper to it immediately from God, because it derives it from God through the mediation of papal power. For the pope possesses the fullness of power in temporal and spiritual matters alike, and therefore no one possesses any power save from him. The things alleged above [in Question I, Chapter 2] can be put forward in support of this opinion, and other reasons can also be offered. For it seems to some that, even though the pope did not have the fullness of power of this sort in temporal matters, it should still be said that the imperium* comes from him. From this it can be concluded that the supreme lay power—namely, the imperial power—derives the power proper to it from the pope, and not immediately from God, since it derives the power proper to it from him from whom it receives the imperium.

It remains to be proved, then, that the imperium comes from the pope, and this can be demonstrated in many ways. For the imperium comes from him to whom the keys of heavenly and earthly imperium were given; but the keys of heavenly and earthly imperium were given to Peter, and consequently to his successors, and therefore imperium comes from the pope. To state the point more fully, imperium comes from him who, by the ordinance of God (in whose power imperium most perfectly lies), is the first head and supreme judge of all mortals. Now by God's ordinance the pope, and not the emperor, is the first head and the judge of all mortals; the imperium, therefore, comes from the pope. Again, the imperium is derived from him who can depose the emperor; but the pope can depose the emperor, and therefore the imperium comes from the pope. Again, the imperium comes from him who can transfer the imperium from one nation to another; but the pope can do this and therefore the imperium is derived from the pope. Again, the imperium comes from him by whom the emperor, once elected, is examined, anointed, consecrated, and crowned. Now the emperor is examined, anointed, consecrated, and crowned by the pope; therefore, the imperium comes from the pope. Again, the imperium comes from him to whom the emperor takes an oath like a vassal; but the emperor executes an oath of fidelity and subjection to the pope, like a vassal of the latter and therefore the imperium comes from the pope. Again, the imperium comes from him who holds both swords, that is, the material and the spiritual. Now the pope possesses both swords, and therefore the imperium is derived from the

---

*["Empire," "imperial authority," "dominion," etc.]

From *A Scholastic Miscellany: Anselm to Ockham,* edited and translated by Eugene R. Fairweather (Volume X: The Library of Christian Classics). First published in MCMLV by SCM Press Ltd., London and The Westminster Press, Philadelphia. Used by permission of Westminster/John Knox Press.

pope. This seems to be Innocent IV's meaning when in a certain decretal he asserts that "the two swords of both administrations are held concealed in the bosom of the faithful Church"; for this reason, if anyone is not within that Church, he possesses neither. "Thus," he goes on, "both rights are believed to belong to Peter, since the Lord did not say to him, with reference to the material sword, 'Cast away,' but rather, 'Put up again thy sword into thy scabbard,' meaning, 'Do not employ it by thyself.'" Here he significantly expresses the name of the second, because this power of the material sword is implicit with the Church, but is made explicit by the emperor who receives it.

Again, the imperium is derived from him to whom the emperor stands in the relation of a son to his father, of a disciple to his master, of lead to gold, of the moon to the sun. Now the emperor stands in these relations to the pope; the imperium, therefore, comes from the pope. Again, the imperium is derived from him to whom the emperor is obliged to bow his head; but the emperor is bound to bow his head to the pope and therefore the imperium comes from the pope. Again, the imperium comes from him by whom, on his own authority and not by the ordinance of the emperor or of some other man, it ought to be ruled during a vacancy; but the pope does this when the imperium is vacant, and therefore the imperium is derived from the pope.

[*Chapters 2, 3 have to do with different forms of the papal theory, Chapters 4 to 6 with different arguments for the imperial position.*]

* * *

Chapter 7

Now that the above opinions have been considered, a reply should be made in accordance with them to the arguments alleged on the other side, and first to the points put forward above (in Chapter 1) against the view last stated. In answer to these, it is said that the imperium does not come from the pope, since after Christ's advent the imperium was derived from the same person as before; but before Christ's advent the imperium was not derived from the pope (as was alleged above), and therefore it has never afterward come from the pope.

But in reply to the first argument to the contrary, to the effect that, according to Pope Nicholas, Christ gave or committed to blessed Peter the rights of heavenly and earthly imperium together, it is said that Pope Nicholas' words are really to be expounded against the interpretation which at first glance appears to be proper, lest they seem to savor of heresy. The same holds for certain other things said by the same pope in the same chapter—for instance, when he says, "He alone established and founded and erected that Church," namely, the Roman, "on the rock of the faith just springing up," and when he says, "The Roman Church instituted all primates, whether the supreme dignity of any patriarch or the primacies of metropolitan sees, or the chairs of episcopates, or, for that matter, the dignity of churches of any order." Unless these words are somewhat discreetly interpreted, they seem to be contrary to the divine Scriptures and the writings of the holy Fathers, because Christ did not found the Roman Church upon the rock of the faith just springing up, since the Roman Church was not founded at the beginning of the faith, nor did it found all the other Churches. For many churches were founded before the Roman Church, and many were raised up to ecclesiastical dignities even before the foundation of the Roman Church, for before the Roman Church existed blessed Matthias was elected to the dignity of apostleship (Acts 1:15–26). Seven deacons also were chosen by the apostles before the Roman Church began (Acts 6:1–6); also, before the Roman Church existed they "had peace throughout all Judea, and Galilee, and Samaria" (Acts 9:31). Before the Roman Church existed blessed Paul and Barnabas were raised to the apostolic dignity by God's command (Acts 13:1–3); before the Roman Church had the power of appointing prelates, Paul and Barnabas appointed presbyters throughout the several churches (Acts 14:22). Before the Roman Church had any authority, the apostles and elders held a general council (Acts 15:6ff.); also, before the Roman Church had the power of instituting prelates, blessed Paul said to the elders whom he had called from Ephesus (as we are told in Acts 20:17, 28): "Take heed to yourselves, and to the whole flock, wherein the Holy Ghost hath placed you bishops, to rule the church of God." Before the Roman Church held the primacy, the churches of Antioch were so multiplied that the disciples of Christ were first called Christians there (Acts 11:26); for this reason also blessed Peter had his see there before Rome, and thus he instituted churches and ecclesiastical dignities in the Antiochene church before he did so in the Roman. It is necessary, then, to attach a sound interpretation to the words of Pope Nicholas given above, lest they openly contradict the divine Scriptures. And, likewise, his other statements that follow, concerning the rights of heavenly and earthly imperium alike committed to blessed Peter, must be soundly expounded, lest they seem to savor of manifest heresy. For if they are construed as they sound at first hearing, two errors follow from them.

According to the first error, heavenly imperium comes from the pope, because Pope Nicholas says that Christ committed the rights of heavenly as well as earthly imperium to Peter. But it is certain that heavenly imperium does not come from the pope, particularly in the way in which some say, on account of that authoritative statement of Pope Nicholas, that earthly imperium is derived from the pope—namely, so that he who possesses the earthly imperium holds it as a fief from the pope—since it would be heretical to say that anyone held the heavenly imperium from the pope as a fief. Nor does the heavenly imperium come from the pope as its lord, as they claim that the earthly imperium comes from the pope as its lord, since the pope is merely in some sense the key bearer of the heavenly imperium, and in no sense its lord.

The second error which follows from Nicholas' words, understood as certain people understand them, is to the effect that all kingdoms are derived from the pope. It is recognized that this principle works to the disadvantage of all kings who do not pay homage to the pope for their kingdoms. For the king of France seems to err dangerously in faith when he makes no acknowledgment of a superior in temporal affairs.

These say, then, that the aforesaid words of Nicholas are to be interpreted in another way than their sound suggests. Thus they say that, just as according to Gregory, in the homily for the Common of virgins, the "kingdom of heaven" must sometimes be understood to refer to the Church Militant, so also the "heavenly imperium" can be understood to refer to the spiritually good in the Church Militant. Therefore, the spiritually evil in the Church can also be designated by the term, "earthly imperium," and the aforesaid words of Nicholas should be interpreted as meaning that Christ committed to blessed Peter some power over the good and over the evil in the Church. Or else, some say that by the "heavenly imperium" Pope Nicholas understands the "spirituals," whose "conversation is in heaven," and by the "earthly imperium" the "seculars," wrapped up in earthly business, and that he means that the pope has power over both.

Or else it is said that Christ committed to Peter the rights of heavenly imperium, in so far as in spiritual things he has power over wayfarers predestined to the heavenly imperium, and that he also committed to him the rights of earthly imperium, in so far as he made him superior in spiritual things to the earthly emperor, whom on occasion he can even coerce. Yet just as no one holds the heavenly imperium from the pope in fief, so also no one holds the earthly imperium in fief from him.

Meister Eckhart
ca. 1260–ca. 1328

The medieval mystic Johannes Eckhart was born at Hochheim in Thuringia, central Germany. As a young man he entered the Dominican monastery at nearby Erfurt where he began his studies for the priesthood. Over the next several years he studied in Cologne and Paris. He received the degree of Master in Sacred Theology (hence the title "Meister") and taught at the University of Paris. From 1294 Eckhart held a number of administrative positions within the Dominican Order, eventually becoming Provincial of Saxony and Vicar of Bohemia. These administrative positions required numerous meetings, extensive travel, and voluminous correspondence. Despite his workload, Eckhart found time for writing a book of advice *(Counsels on Discernment),* several speculative volumes (such as the *Book of Divine Comfort*), and a major theological work *(Opus Tripartitum,* most of which has been lost).

Eckhart was also a popular preacher, delivering a number of sermons as he travelled through Germany. Many of these sermons were preached in German rather than Latin. According to some scholars, by presenting his ideas in the vernacular, Eckhart did for German what Dante did for Italian: He gave the vernacular stature and prestige. In his most famous German sermon, reprinted here in the Raymond Bernard Blakney translation, Eckhart describes union with God in the core of the human soul. According to Eckhart, this core of the soul is the source of the soul's "agents": the intel-

479

lect, the memory, and the will. Because they are only agents of the soul and not the soul itself, neither the intellect nor the will can adequately present God to us. Neither ideas *about* God nor willingness to accept God can bring union with God. Instead, we must withdraw from all agents and prepare a place of silence for God to enter. Once God has entered the core of the soul, human beings are divinized.

While talk of "communion" with God is orthodox in Christian theology, teaching "union" with God has sometimes been considered to be immodest. Traditional Christian theology wants to maintain a respectful distinction between Creator and creation. Talk of union with God violates this tact. A later work (falsely) attributed to Eckhart indicates what the church feared: "Sir, rejoice with me, I have become God!" Eckhart's sermons eventually led to trouble with church authorities. Eckhart himself admitted that some of the ideas in his vernacular sermons were ill-expressed and that in translating theological ideas from Latin to German he may have made errors. But the Archbishop of Cologne felt the problem was deeper than mistranslation: Eckhart was a heretic. Eckhart's last years were spent fighting heresy charges. As Eckhart succinctly put it, "I am able to be in error, but I cannot be a heretic, for the first [i.e., error] belongs to the intellect, the second [i.e., heresy] to the will." Though he protested innocence until his death (around 1328), in 1329 Pope John XXII declared eleven of Eckhart's teachings suspect and seventeen heretical. Despite this papal condemnation, Eckhart's thought and writings continued to be influential in the later Middle Ages and are still consulted today.

* * *

For general works on mysticism, see the suggested readings in the introduction to Hildegard of Bingen (p. 194). For a study of mystics in the late Middle Ages, see Ray C. Petry, *Late Medieval Mysticism* (Philadelphia: Westminster Press, 1957).

There are several anthologies of Eckhart's writings with commentary, including Meister Eckhart, *Meister Eckhart: An Introduction to the Study of His Works with an Anthology of His Sermons,* edited and translated by James M. Clark (London: Thomas Nelson and Sons, 1957), and Meister Eckhart, *Meister Eckhart: Mystic and Philosopher,* translated with commentary by Reiner Schürmann (Bloomington: Indiana University Press, 1978). For readings that explore Eckhart's work in the context of German mysticism, see James Midgley Clark, *The Great German Mystics, Eckhart, Tauler and Suso* (1949, reprinted New York: Russell & Russell, 1970); Jeanne Ancelet-Hustache, *Master Eckhart and the Rhineland Mystics,* translated by Hilda Graef (New York: Harper Torchbooks, 1957); and Oliver Davies, ed., *The Rhineland Mystics: Writings of Meister Eckhart, Johannes Tauler, and Jan van Ruusbroec and Selections from the Theologia Germanica and the Book of Spiritual Poverty* (New York: Crossroad, 1990). Specialized studies of various aspects of Eckhart's thought include C.F. Kelley, *Meister Eckhart on Divine Knowledge* (New Haven, CT: Yale University Press, 1977), and Frank J. Tobin, *Meister Eckhart: Thought and Language* (Philadelphia: University of Pennsylvania Press, 1986).

SERMON #1

This is Meister Eckhart from whom God hid nothing

For while all things were wrapped in peaceful silence and night was in the midst of its swift course . . .

—Wisdom of Solomon 18:14

Because the same One, who is begotten and born of God the Father, without ceasing in eternity, is born today, within time, in human nature, we make a holiday to celebrate it. St. Augustine says that this birth is always happening. And yet, if it does not occur in me, how could it help me? Everything depends on that.

We intend to discuss, therefore, how it does occur in us, or how it is made perfect in a good soul, for it is in a good soul that God the Father is speaking his eternal word. What I shall say applies to that perfect person who has turned to the way of God and continues in it, and not to the natural undisciplined person who is far from this birth and ignorant of it. This, then, is the saying of the wise man: "While all things were wrapped in peaceful silence . . . a secret word leaped down from heaven, out of the royal throne, to me." This sermon is to be on that word.

Three points are, then, noteworthy. The first is: where does God the Father speak his word in the soul, or where does this birth take place—or what part of the soul is susceptible to this act? It must be in the purest, noblest, and subtlest element the soul can provide. Truly, if God could give the soul anything rarer out of his omnipotence, and if the soul could have received into its nature anything nobler from him, he must have awaited its coming to be born. Therefore the soul in which this birth is to happen must have purity and nobility of life, and be unitary and self-contained; it must not be dissipated in the multiplicity of things, through the five senses. What is more, it must continue to be self-contained and unitary and of the utmost purity, for that is its station and it disdains anything less.

The second part of this sermon will discuss what one should do about this act of God, this inward utterance, this birth: whether it is necessary to co-operate in some way to merit and obtain the birth. Should one construct an idea in his mind and thinking-process and discipline himself by meditating upon it, to the effect that God is wise, almighty, and eternal? Or should one withdraw from all thought and free his mind of words, acts, and ideas, doing nothing but being always receptive to God and allowing him to act? How shall one best serve the eternal birth?

The third part [of this sermon will discuss] the profitableness of this birth and how great it is.

In the first place, please note that I shall support what I have to say by citations from nature, which you may check for yourselves. Even though I believe more in the Scriptures than I do in myself, I shall follow [this policy] because you will get more out of arguments based on evidence.

Let us take first the test: "Out of the silence, a secret word was spoken to me." Ah, Sir!—what is this silence and where is that word to be spoken? We shall say, as I have heretofore, [it is spoken] in the purest element of the soul, in the soul's most exalted

Meister Eckhart: A Modern Translation, translated by Raymond Bernard Blakney (New York: Harper & Row, 1941). Reprinted by permission.

place, in the core, yes, in the essence of the soul. The central silence is there, where no creature may enter, nor any idea, and there the soul neither thinks nor acts, nor entertains any idea, either of itself or of anything else.

Whatever the soul does, it does through agents. It understands by means of intelligence. If it remembers, it does so by means of memory. If it is to love, the will must be used and thus it acts always through agents and not within its own essence. Its results are achieved through an intermediary. The power of sight can be effectuated only through the eyes, for otherwise the soul has no means of vision. It is the same with the other senses. They are effectuated through intermediaries.

In Being, however, there is no action and, therefore, there is none in the soul's essence. The soul's agents, by which it acts, are derived from the core of the soul. In that core is the central silence, the pure peace, and abode of the heavenly birth, the place for this event: this utterance of God's word. By nature the core of the soul is sensitive to nothing but the divine Being, unmediated. Here God enters the soul with all he has and not in part. He enters the soul through its core and nothing may touch that core except God himself. No creature enters it, for creatures must stay outside in the soul's agents, from whence the soul receives ideas, behind which it has withdrawn as if to take shelter.

When the agents of the soul contact creatures, they take and make ideas and likenesses of them and bear them back again into the self. It is by means of these ideas that the soul knows about eternal creatures. Creatures cannot approach the soul except in this way and the soul cannot get at creatures, except, on its own initiative, it first conceives ideas of them. Thus the soul gets at things by means of ideas and the idea is an entity created by the soul's agents. Be it a stone, or a rose, or a person, or whatever it is that is to be known, first an idea is taken and then absorbed, and in this way the soul connects with the phenomenal world.

But an idea, so received, necessarily comes in from outside, through the senses. Thus the soul knows about everything but itself. There is an authority who says that the soul can neither conceive nor admit any idea of itself. Thus it knows about everything else but has no self-knowledge, for ideas always enter through the senses and therefore the soul cannot get an idea of itself. Of nothing does the soul know so little as it knows of itself, for lack of means. And that indicates that within itself the soul is free, innocent of all instrumentalities and ideas, and that is why God can unite with it, he, too, being pure and without idea, or likeness.

Whatever skill a master teacher may have, concede that skill to God, multiplied beyond measure. The wiser and more skillful a teacher is, the more simply, and with less artifice, he achieves his ends. Man requires many tools to do his visible work and, before he can finish it as he has conceived it, much preparation is required. It is the function and craft of the moon and sun to give light and they do it swiftly. When they emit their rays, all the ends of the world are filled with light in a moment. Higher than these are the angels who work with fewer instruments and also with fewer ideas. The highest seraph has only one. He comprehends as unity all that his inferiors see as manifold. But God needs no idea at all, nor has he any. He acts in the soul without instrument, idea, or likeness. He acts in the core of the soul, which no idea ever penetrated—but he alone—his own essence. No creature can do this.

How does God beget his Son in the soul? As a creature might, with ideas and likenesses? Not at all! He begets him in the soul just as he does in eternity—and not otherwise. Well, then, how? Let us see.

God has perfect insight into himself and knows himself up and down, through and through, not by ideas, but of himself. God begets his Son through the true unity of the divine nature. See! This is the way: he begets his Son in the core of the soul and is made One with it. There is no other way. If an idea were interposed, there could be no true unity. Man's whole blessedness lies in that unity.

Now you might say: "Naturally! But there is nothing to the soul but ideas." No! Not at all! If that was so, the soul could never be blessed, for even God cannot make a creature in which a perfect blessing is found. Otherwise, God himself would not be the highest blessing, or the best of ends, as it is his nature and will to be—the beginning and the end of everything. A blessing is not a creature nor is it perfection, for perfection [that is, in all virtues] is the consequence of the perfecting of life, and for that you must get into the essence, the core of the soul, so that God's undifferentiated essence may reach you there, without the interposition of any idea. No idea represents or signifies it-self. It always points to something else, of which it is the symbol. And since man has no ideas, except those abstracted from external things through the senses, he cannot be blessed by an idea.

The second point [of this sermon] is this: What should a man do to secure and de-serve the occurrence and perfection of this birth in his soul? Should he co-operate by imagining and thinking about God, or should he keep quiet, be silent and at peace, so that God may speak and act through him? Should he do nothing but wait until God does act? I repeat, as I have said before, that this exposition and this activity are for those good and perfect persons only, who have so absorbed the essence of virtue that virtue emanates from them without their trying to make it do so, and in whom the useful life and noble teachings of our Lord Jesus Christ are alive. Such persons know that the best life and the loftiest is to be silent and to let God speak and act through one.

When all the agents [of the soul] are withdrawn from action and ideation, then this word is spoken. Thus he said: "Out of the silence, a secret word was spoken to me." The more you can withdraw the agents of your soul and forget things and the ideas you have received hitherto, the nearer you are to [hearing the word] and the more sensitive to it you will be. If you could only become unconscious of everything all at once and ignore your own life, as St. Paul did when he could say: "Whether in the body, or out of it, I cannot tell. God knoweth!" His spirit had so far withdrawn all its agents that the body was forgotten. Neither memory nor intellect functioned, nor the senses, nor any [of the soul's] agents which are supposed to direct or grace the body. The warmth and energy of the body were suspended and yet it did not fail during the three days in which he neither ate nor drank. It was also this way with Moses, when he fasted forty days on the mountain and was none the worse for it. He was as strong on the last day as on the first. This is the way a man should diminish his senses and introvert his faculties until he achieves forgetfulness of things and self. So one authority said to his soul: "Draw back from the unrest of external actions," and also: "Fly from the storm of visible works and inward thoughts and hide yourself, for they only make turmoil."

Therefore, if God is to speak his word to the soul, it must be still and at peace, and then he *will* speak his word and give himself to the soul and not a mere idea, apart from himself. Dionysius says: "God has no idea of himself and no likeness, for he is intrinsic good, truth, and being." God does all that he does within himself and of himself in an instant. Do not imagine that when God made heaven and earth and all the creatures, that he made one today and another tomorrow. To be sure, Moses describes it thus, but he knew much better! He put it this way on account of the people who could neither un-derstand nor conceive it otherwise. God did nothing more about it than just this: he willed and they were! God acts without instrumentality and without ideas. And the freer you are from ideas the more sensitive you are to his inward action. You are nearer to it in proportion as you are introverted and unself-conscious.

It was to this point that Dionysius instructed his disciple Timothy, saying: "My dear son Timothy, you should soar above self with untroubled mind, above all your faculties, characteristics, and states, up into the still, secret darkness, so that you may come to know the unknown God above all gods. Forsake everything. God despises ideas."

But now, perhaps you say: "What can God do in the core and essence [of the soul] without ideas?" I couldn't possibly know, for the agents of the soul deal only in ideas, taking things and naming them, each according to its own idea. A bird is not known [as such] on the human idea [pattern], and thus, since all ideas come from the outside, [what God is doing in the core of my soul] is hidden from me and that is a great benefit. Since the soul itself does not know, it wonders and, wondering, it seeks, for the soul knows very well that something is afoot, even though it does not know how or what. When a person learns the cause of anything, he soon grows tired of it and looks for something else to work out, and is constantly uneasy until he knows all about that, and thus he lacks steadfastness. Only this unknown knowledge keeps the soul steadfast and yet ever on the search.

The wise man said: "In the middle of the night, while all things were wrapped in silence, a secret word was spoken to me." It came stealthily, like a thief. What does he mean by a word that is secret or hidden? It is the nature of a word to reveal what is hidden. "It opened and shone before me as if it were revealing something and made me conscious of God, and thus it was called 'a word.' Furthermore it was not clear to me what it was, because it came with stealth like a whisper trying to explain itself through the stillness." See! As long as it is concealed, man will always be after it. It appears and disappears, which means that we shall plead and sigh for it.

St. Paul says that we are to hunt it and track it down and never give up till we get it. Once he was caught up into the third heaven of the knowledge of God and saw everything. When he came back he had forgotten nothing but it had so regressed into the core of his soul that he could not call it up to mind. It was covered up. Thus he felt constrained to pursue it within [his soul] and not without. It is always within and never outside—but always inward. When he was convinced of that, he said: "I am persuaded that neither death . . . nor any affliction can separate me from what I find within me."

One heathen authority once said something fine about this to another: "I am aware of something in myself whose shine is my reason. I see clearly that something is there, but what it is I cannot understand. But it seems to me that, if I could grasp it, I should know all truth." To which the other authority replied: "By all means keep after it! For if you do grasp it, you will possess the totality of all goods and life eternal!" St. Augustine also has something to say about this: "I am aware of something in myself, like a light dancing before my soul, and if it could be brought out with perfect steadiness, it would surely be life eternal. It hides, and then again, it shows. It comes like a thief, as if it would steal everything from the soul. But since it shows itself and draws attention, it must want to allure the soul and make the soul follow it, to rob the soul of self." One of the prophets also has something to say about this: "Lord, take from them their spirit and give them instead thy spirit!" This is what that loving soul meant when she said: "When Love said that word, my soul melted and flowed away. Where he comes in, I must go out!" That is also what Christ meant, when he said: "Whosoever shall forsake anything for my sake, shall receive again a hundredfold and whosoever will have me, must deny himself of everything and whosoever will serve me must follow me and not seek his own."

Now perhaps you are saying: "My dear sir! You are trying to reverse the natural course of the soul. It is the soul's nature to take things in through the senses and convert them into ideas. Do you want to reverse that sequence?"

No! But how do you know what precious things God has stored up in nature which have not yet been described—things still hidden? Those who write about the aristocracy of the soul can get no further than their natural intelligence will take them. They cannot get into the core and therefore much must remain hidden from them and unknown. The prophet said: "I will sit and be silent and listen to what God shall say in me." That this word comes "at night and in the darkness" is expressive of its hiddenness. St. John says: "The light shone in the darkness. It came unto its own. And to as many as received it, to them power was given to become the Sons of God."

See now the profit and fruit of this secret word and this darkness. Not only the Son of the heavenly Father is born in the darkness which is his own, but you, too, are born there, a son of the same heavenly Father, and to you also he gives power. Now see how great the profit is! For all the truth the authorities ever learned by their own intelligence and understanding, or ever shall learn up to the last of days, they never got the least part of the knowledge that is in the core [of the soul]. Let it be called ignorance or want of knowledge, still it has more in it than all wisdom and all knowledge without it, for this outward ignorance lures and draws you away from things you know about and even from yourself. That is what Christ meant when he said: "Whosoever forsaketh not himself and mother and father and all that is external is not worthy of me." It was as if he would say: "Whosoever will not depart from the externality of creatures cannot be born or received in this divine birth." By robbing yourself of self and all externalities you are admitted to the truth.

And I really believe it, and am sure that the person who is right in this matter will never be separated from God by any mode [of action] or anything else. I say that there is no way he can fall into deadly sin. He would rather suffer the most shameful death than commit the least of mortal sins, as did the saints. I say that he could not commit even a venial sin nor consent to one in himself or other people, if it could be prevented. He is so strongly attracted and drawn and accustomed to this way of life that he would not turn to another. All his mind and power are directed to this one end.

May God, newly born in human form, eternally help us, that we frail people, being born in him, may be divine. Amen.

Catherine of Siena

ca. 1347–1380

Saint Catherine was born in the central Italian city of Siena, the twenty-fourth of twenty-five children. Despite her family's expectations, Catherine was uninterested in marriage. Instead, she spent much of her youth in the nearby Dominican church, eventually receiving the Dominican habit at age eighteen. For the next three years she was a recluse in her parents' home, leaving her room only for mass. Although she had no formal schooling, during this time she somehow learned to read. At twenty-one she reentered the world and began a lifelong practice of caring for the poor and ill. On several occasions she ministered to those who had the plague, putting her life at great danger. In 1370 she had an ecstatic union with God, which she described as her "mystical death." But rather than leading to further isolation, this experience led her to deeper involvement in church reform and in church–state politics.

For the rest of her short life, Catherine acted as emissary for the pope in disputes with various city-states in Italy. While travelling on diplomatic missions, she also heard confessions and as a woman was given the rare privilege by Pope Gregory XI that those whom she confessed were absolved. She also found time to write a number of letters, which convey her basic ideas. During a break from church diplomacy in 1377, Catherine had another intense mystical experience, which led to her writing the *Dialogues*. The last years of her life were spent in a disappointing attempt to organize a new crusade to the Holy Land. In 1461 Catherine was canonized and in 1970 she and the Spanish mystic St. Teresa of Avila (1515–1582) were the first women given the title, "Doctor of the Church."

Among the many letters she wrote, the one reprinted here, translated by Suzanne Noffke, shows Catherine's emphasis on love. Catherine explains that God loves us only because God chooses to love us—there is no necessity in divine charity. Our highest calling is to love God and show our love by loving others. In propounding this doctrine of love, Catherine hints at the necessity of free will as a prerequisite for such love. Elsewhere she clearly asserts the importance of free will, claiming that while God "created us without our help, he will not save us without our help" (*Dialogues,* 23). This notion of free will is clearly quite different from that of Augustine and Thomas Aquinas.

Some have argued that the mystics are not really philosophers and should not be included in a study of philosophic classics. It is true that the mystics often used different forms of discourse to make their points—this is why I have included a vision from Hildegard, a sermon from Eckhart, and a letter from Catherine. It is also true that they often held unusual perspectives on the issues. But mystics such as Catherine address many of the classic philosophical questions of epistemology, metaphysics, and ethics and so can provide correctives to more rationalist colleagues.

*   *   *

For brief overviews of Catherine of Siena's thought, see the introduction to Catherine of Siena, *The Dialogue,* translated and introduced by Suzanne Noffke (New York: Paulist Press, 1980), and Cornelia Wolfskeel, "Catherine of Siena" in Mary Ellen Waithe, *A History of Women Philosophers, Volume II: Medieval, Renaissance and Enlightenment Women Philosophers, 500–1600* (Dordrecht, The Netherlands: Kluwer Academic Publishers, 1989). There are a number of biographies of Catherine of Siena, beginning with Raymond of Capua, 1330–1399, *The Life of St. Catherine of Siena,* translated by George Lamb (New York: P.J. Kennedy, 1960). Studies in this century include Edmund G. Gardner, *Saint Catherine of Siena: A Study in the Religion, Literature, and History of the Fourteenth Century in Italy* (London: J.M. Dent, 1907); Augusta Theodosia Drane, *The History of St. Catherine of Siena and Her Companions,* 4th ed. (London: Longmans, Green and Co., 1915); Johannes Jørgensen, *Saint Catherine of Siena,* translated by Ingeborg Lund (London: Longmans, Green and Co., 1939); Arrigo Levasti, *My Servant, Catherine,* translated by Dorothy M. White (Westminster, MD: Newman Press, 1954); Igino Giordani, *Catherine of Siena: Fire and Blood,* translated by Thomas J. Tobin (Milwaukee, WI: Bruce Publishing Co., 1959); and Joseph Marie Perrin, *Catherine of Siena,* translated by Paul Barrett (Westminster: Newman Press, 1965).

LETTER #58

To Monna Melina, wife of Bartolomeo Barbani of Lucca

In the name of Jesus Christ crucified and of gentle Mary, mother of God's Son.

My daughter in Christ Jesus,

I Caterina, servant and slave of the servants of Jesus Christ, am writing to encourage you in his precious blood. I long to see you so transformed and fused into the fire of divine charity that nobody and nothing will ever separate you from it. You know, my dear beloved daughter, that to join two things together there must be nothing between them or there cannot be a perfect fusion. Now realize that this is how God wants our soul to be, without any selfish love of ourselves or of others in between, just as God loves us without anything in between. Freely and generously he loved us, gratuitously and not because he had to: he loved us without being loved. For us it is impossible to love the way God does. We are always obligated in duty to love since we are constantly being given a share in God's goodness and blessings. So we have to love with this second sort of love. But let this love be so clean and free that we love no one, nothing, spiritually or temporally, apart from God.

And if you say to me, "How can I have this sort of love?" I tell you, daughter, that we cannot have it or draw it from any source but the fountain of First Truth. At this fountain you will discover your soul's dignity and beauty. You will see the Word, the slain Lamb who gave himself as your ransom and as your food. And he was moved only by the fire of his charity and not by any service he could have received from us, from whom he had received nothing but offense. I am saying, then, that when we gaze into this fountain thirsty and hungry for virtue, we begin at once to drink. We do not see or love ourselves or anything else selfishly, because we see everything in the fountain of God's goodness. In him we love what we love, and we love nothing without him.

Now how could the soul who has seen such immeasurable goodness on God's part do anything but love? This, it seems, is what gentle First Truth invited us to when he cried out with heartfelt earnestness in the temple: "Let anyone who is thirsty come to me and drink, for I am the fountain of living water!" You see, daughter, it is the thirsty who are invited. He does not say, "anyone who is not thirsty," but "anyone who is thirsty." So God insists that we bring with us the vessel of our free will, with a thirst and willingness to love. Let's go, then, to the fountain of God's sweet goodness. There we shall discover the knowledge of ourselves and of God. And when we dip our vessel in, we shall draw out the water of divine grace, powerful enough to give us everlasting life.

But remember: we wouldn't be able to make any progress if we were burdened with a heavy load. This is why I don't want you to clothe yourself with love for me or anyone else, but to be clothed only in love for God. I'm telling you this because I know from your letter the pain you suffered at my departure. I want you to learn from gentle First Truth. Neither attachment to his mother nor to any of his disciples kept him from running like one in love to the shameful death of the cross, leaving Mary and his disci-

The Letters of St. Catherine of Siena, Vol. I, Medieval & Renaissance Texts and Studies, vol. 52 (Binghamton, NY 1988), pp. 180–83. Copyright, Center for Medieval and Early Renaissance Studies, State University of New York at Binghamton.

ples behind. Yet he loved them immensely. And later on they left one another for the greater honor of God and other people's salvation, because their concern was not for themselves. They gave up their own consolations for God's praise and glory, as people who eat and savor souls. You must believe that when they were so distressed they would gladly have stayed with Mary, whom they loved so much. Yet they all left. For they did not love themselves or their neighbors or God selfishly. No, they loved God because he was supremely good and worthy of love, and themselves and their neighbors and everything else they loved in God.

Now this is how I want you and the others to love. Look at me only in terms of giving honor to God and your best efforts to your neighbors. For though we may feel a certain sadness when someone we love leaves us, still we accept it graciously if our love is true, rooted only in God's honor and concerned more for the salvation of souls than for ourselves. Now then, don't let me see any more sadness, because this would be an interference that would hinder your being conformed and united with Christ. It is because I think God asks us to give ourselves freely, as he did, that I said I want you and my other dear daughters to be transformed in and united with God by love, getting rid of any medium, anything that gets in between—except divine charity, which is a sweet and glorious medium that doesn't separate but unites.

Really, it seems just like the master mason. He gathers many stones and fits them together, and the result is called both "stones" and "a wall." He does this by using mortar as his medium. Without the medium the stones would fall apart more scattered and broken than ever. So now imagine how our soul has to gather all people and be united with them in love and desire for their salvation, so that they may be sharers in the blood of the Lamb. So here this wall stands—many people, yet they are one. This, it seems, is what Saint Paul was inviting us to when he said that many run the race, but only one wins, and the winner is the one who has used this medium, divine charity. But you could say to me what the disciples said to Christ when he said, "A little while and you shall not see me, and again a little while and you shall see me." They said, "What is he going to do, that he says, 'A little while and you shall not see me, and again a little while and you shall see me'?" So you could say, "First you tell us that God doesn't want anything between us and him, and now you tell us to put something in between!" My answer is that you must use the medium that doesn't put anything between us and God, the fire of divine charity, which becomes one with [God] as wood put into the fire. Would you say the wood remains wood? No, it becomes one with the fire. But if you were to use as medium your selfish love for yourself, you would be using a medium that would separate you from God, even though it is nothing (because sins have their root in nothing but selfish love and pleasure and enjoyment apart from God). For just as all virtue proceeds from charity, which gives it life, so all vice proceeds from selfish love, which deals death and eats away every virtue in the soul. This is why I said that God doesn't want anything between himself and us, and that any love not set in the true medium [of divine charity] does not last.

Run, my beloved daughters! Let's sleep no longer! I've felt sorry about your pain, and this is why I am giving you this remedy of loving God without anything between you and him. But if you still want poor wretched me as intermediary, I want to show you where to find me without being separated from this true love. Go with the dear loving Magdalen to the most sweet venerable cross. There you will find the Lamb and me, and there you can graze and feed and fulfill your desires. This is the way I want you to seek me and every created thing; let this cross be your standard and comfort. And don't imagine, because I am physically far away from you, that my affection and my concern for your salvation are far away. No, I am even closer than when I am there physically.

Don't you know that the holy disciples had a greater awareness and knowledge of the Master after he had left them than before? They had been so taken up with his humanity that they hadn't looked beyond it. But after his departure they began to know and understand his goodness. This is why First Truth said, "I have to go; otherwise the Paraclete will not come to you." So I say I had to leave you so you would begin to seek God in truth and not through any intermediary. I tell you, you will be better off than before, if you enter into yourselves to ponder the words and teaching you have been given. In this way you will receive the fullness of grace by the very grace of God. I'll write no more, because I have no more time for writing.

I'm sending this letter primarily to you, Melina, and then to Caterina, Monna Chiara, Monna Bartolomea, Monna Lagina, and Monna Colomba. Warm greetings from all of us!

Keep living in God's holy and tender love.

Nicholas Cusanas
1401–1464

Nicholas Cusanas (or "Nicholas of Cusa") was born in Cusa (or Kues) on the Moselle River in Germany. As a boy he studied with the Brothers of the Common Life in Deventer, Holland, a group that put special emphasis on piety and humility. From there he went on to study philosophy at Heidelberg (1416), canon (or church) law at Padua (1417–1423), and theology at Cologne (1425). He received a doctorate in canon law at Padua and was ordained a priest in 1426. Soon after his ordination, Nicholas became involved in a number of legal matters related to church reform. He first supported the "conciliar" movement, which advocated the primacy of church councils over the pope. But disillusionment with the Council of Basel's inability to reform the church led him to side with the pope. He was sent by the Holy See on various missions, including the (temporarily) successful negotiations on reunification with the Eastern Church in Byzantium. For his efforts he was rewarded by being made a cardinal in 1448 and being given the bishopric of Brixen in 1450, positions he held until his death in 1464.

In his attempt at a synthesis between reason and faith, Nicholas returned to the Neoplatonic tradition of the early Middle Ages and the mysticism of Meister Eckhart. In particular, he was taken by the Neoplatonic mystical belief that there is a faculty of intuition or intelligence that is above reason. The Aristotelian understanding of reason, which his predecessors had used, begins with the law of non-contradiction. This law states that contradictories cannot be true of the same thing at the same time. But Nicholas claimed that this law is not true; there is a "coincidence of opposites" in all particular entities, but especially in God. Using language that would later be echoed by the German philosopher Hegel, Nicholas claimed that reason cannot grasp the divine Absolute. We need to recognize the "ignorance" of reason and "see incomprehensively" by means of the higher faculty of intuition.

Nicholas develops this idea in his most famous work, *On Learned Ignorance*. There he argues that God's essence is paradoxical and cannot be known. In the opening chapters of this work, given here, Nicholas asserts that God is both Absolute Maximum and Absolute Minimum and draws out the implications of this position. He goes on to say that while God is beyond our reason, as we cannot comprehend the Absolute Maximum, we can have an ignorance about God that is "learned" and "sacred." Our selection ends with the last chapter from Book I, where Nicholas emphasizes the *via negativa,* the way of negation, which gives us incomprehensible truth about God by telling us what God is not. I am pleased to offer the outstanding new translation of Jasper Hopkins.

* * *

Henry Bett, *Nicholas of Cusa* (London: Methuen, 1932), provides the classic study of Nicholas, while Jasper Hopkins, *A Concise Introduction to the Philosophy of Nicholas of Cusa,* 2nd ed. (Minneapolis: University of Minnesota Press, 1980), and Pauline Moffitt Watts, *Nicolaus Cusanus, A Fifteenth-Century Vision of Man* (Leiden, Netherlands: Brill, 1982), give more recent introductions. For specialized studies see Paul E. Sigmund, *Nicholas of Cusa and Medieval Political Thought* (Cambridge, MA: Harvard University Press, 1963); James E. Biechler, *The Religious Language of Nicholas of Cusa* (Missoula, MT: Scholars Press, 1975); and Ronald Levao, *Renaissance Minds and Their Fictions: Cusanus, Sidney, Shakespeare* (Berkeley: University of California Press, 1985). For a recent collection of essays, see Gerald Christianson and Thomas M. Izbicki, eds., *Nicholas of Cusa, in Search of God and Wisdom* (Leiden: E. J. Brill, 1991).

ON LEARNED IGNORANCE (in part)

Chapter 1: How It Is That Knowing Is Not-Knowing.

We see that by the gift of God there is present in all things a natural desire to exist in the best manner in which the condition of each thing's nature permits this. And [we see that all things] act toward this end and have instruments adapted thereto. They have an innate sense of judgment which serves the purpose of knowing. [They have this] in order

Reprinted, by permission, from Jasper Hopkins, *Nicholas of Cusa on Learned Ignorance: A Translation and an Appraisal of De Docta Ignorantia,* Chaps. 1–4, 26 (Minneapolis: Banning Press, 2nd edition, 2nd printing, 1990).

that their desire not be in vain but be able to attain rest in that [respective] object which is desired by the propensity of each thing's own nature. But if perchance affairs turn out otherwise, this [outcome] must happen by accident—as when sickness misleads taste or an opinion misleads reason. Wherefore, we say that a sound, free intellect knows to be true that which is apprehended by its affectionate embrace. (The intellect insatiably desires to attain unto the true through scrutinizing all things by means of its innate faculty of inference.) Now, that from which no sound mind can withhold assent is, we have no doubt, most true. However, all those who make an investigation judge the uncertain proportionally, by means of a comparison with what is taken to be certain. Therefore, every inquiry is comparative and uses the means of comparative relation. Now, when, the things investigated are able to be compared by means of a close proportional tracing back to what is taken to be [certain], our judgment apprehends easily; but when we need many intermediate steps, difficulty arises and hard work is required. These points are recognized in mathematics, where the earlier propositions are quite easily traced back to the first and most evident principles but where later propositions [are traced back] with more difficulty because [they are traced back] only through the mediation of the earlier ones.

Therefore, every inquiry proceeds by means of a comparative relation, whether an easy or a difficult one. Hence, the infinite, qua infinite, is unknown; for it escapes all comparative relation. But since comparative relation indicates an agreement in some one respect and, at the same time, indicates an otherness, it cannot be under-

La Primavera ("The Allegory of Spring"), ca. 1482. Botticelli (1445–1510) shows the eternal spring of Venus's garden of Hesperides. Like Nicholas Cusanas, Botticelli was heavily influenced by Neoplatonism and his paintings are usually interpreted in Neoplatonic terms. (For example, there are nine figures in this work just as there are nine Enneads of Plotinus.) *(Alinari/Art Resource)*

stood independently of number. Accordingly, number encompasses all things related comparatively. Therefore, number, which is a necessary condition of comparative relation, is present not only in quantity but also in all things which in any manner whatsoever can agree or differ either substantially or accidentally. Perhaps for this reason Pythagoras deemed all things to be constituted and understood through the power of numbers.

Both the precise combinations in corporeal things and the congruent relating of known to unknown surpass human reason—to such an extent that Socrates seemed to himself to know nothing except that he did not know. And the very wise Solomon maintained that all things are difficult and unexplainable in words. And a certain other man of divine spirit says that wisdom and the seat of understanding are hidden from the eyes of all the living. Even the very profound Aristotle, in his First Philosophy, asserts that in things most obvious by nature such difficulty occurs for us as for a night owl which is trying to look at the sun. Therefore, if the foregoing points are true, then since the desire in us is not in vain, assuredly we desire to know that we do not know. If we can fully attain unto this [knowledge of our ignorance], we will attain unto learned ignorance. For a man even one very well versed in learning—will attain unto nothing more perfect than to be found to be most learned in the ignorance which is distinctively his. The more he knows that he is unknowing, the more learned he will be. Unto this end I have undertaken the task of writing a few things about learned ignorance.

Chapter 2: Preliminary Clarification of What Will Follow.

Since I am going to discuss the maximum learning of ignorance, I must deal with the nature of Maximality. Now, I give the name "Maximum" to that than which there cannot be anything greater. But fulness befits what is one. Thus, oneness—which is also being—coincides with Maximality. But if such oneness is altogether free from all relation and contraction, obviously nothing is opposed to it, since it is Absolute Maximality. Thus, the Maximum is the Absolute One which is all things. And all things are in the Maximum (for it is the Maximum); and since nothing is opposed to it, the Minimum likewise coincides with it, and hence the Maximum is also in all things. And because it is absolute, it is, actually, every possible being; it contracts nothing from things, all of which [derive] from it. In the first book I shall strive to investigate—incomprehensibly above human reason—this Maximum, which the faith of all nations indubitably believes to be God. [I shall investigate] with the guidance of Him "who alone dwells in inaccessible light."

Secondly, just as Absolute Maximality is Absolute Being, through which all things are that which they are, so from Absolute Being there exists a universal oneness of being which is spoken of as "a maximum deriving from the Absolute [Maximum]"—existing from it contractedly and as a universe. This maximum's oneness is contracted in plurality, and it cannot exist without plurality. Indeed, in its universal oneness this maximum encompasses all things, so that all the things which derive from the Absolute [Maximum] are in this maximum and this maximum is in all [these] things. Nevertheless, it does not exist independently of the plurality in which it is present, for it does not exist without contraction, from which it cannot be freed. In the second book I will add a few points about this maximum, viz., the universe.

Thirdly, a maximum of a third sort will thereafter be exhibited. For since the universe exists-in-plurality only contractedly, we shall seek among the many things the one maximum in which the universe actually exists most greatly and most perfectly as in its goal. Now, such [a maximum] is united with the Absolute [Maximum], which is the universal end; [it is united] because it is a most perfect goal, which surpasses our every capability. Hence, I shall add some points about this maximum, which is both contracted and absolute and which we name *Jesus,* blessed forever. [I shall add these points] according as Jesus Himself will provide inspiration.

However, someone who desires to grasp the meaning must elevate his intellect above the import of the words rather than insisting upon the proper significations of words which cannot be properly adapted to such great intellectual mysteries. Moreover, it is necessary to use guiding illustrations in a transcendent way and to leave behind perceptible things, so that the reader may readily ascend unto simple intellectuality. I have endeavored, for the purpose of investigating this pathway, to explain [matters] to those of ordinary intelligence as clearly as I could. Avoiding all roughness of style, I show at the outset that learned ignorance has its basis in the fact that the precise truth is inapprehensible.

Chapter 3: The Precise Truth Is Incomprehensible.

It is self-evident that there is no comparative relation of the infinite to the finite. Therefore, it is most clear that where we find comparative degrees of greatness, we do not arrive at the unqualifiedly Maximum; for things which are comparatively greater and lesser are finite; but, necessarily, such a Maximum is infinite. Therefore, if anything is posited which is not the unqualifiedly Maximum, it is evident that something greater can be posited. And since we find degrees of equality (so that one thing is more equal to a second thing than to a third, in accordance with generic, specific, spatial, causal, and temporal agreement and difference among similar things), obviously we cannot find two or more things which are so similar and equal that they could not be progressively more similar *ad infinitum.* Hence, the measure and the measured—however equal they are—will always remain different.

Therefore, it is not the case that by means of likenesses a finite intellect can precisely attain the truth about things. For truth is not something more or something less but is something indivisible. Whatever is not truth cannot measure truth precisely. (By comparison, a noncircle [cannot measure] a circle, whose being is something indivisible.) Hence, the intellect, which is not truth, never comprehends truth so precisely that truth cannot be comprehended infinitely more precisely. For the intellect is to truth as [an inscribed] polygon is to [the inscribing] circle. The more angles the inscribed polygon has the more similar it is to the circle. However, even if the number of its angles is increased ad infinitum, the polygon never becomes equal [to the circle] unless it is resolved into an identity with the circle. Hence, regarding truth, it is evident that we do not know anything other than the following: viz., that we know truth not to be precisely comprehensible as it is. For truth may be likened unto the most absolute necessity (which cannot be either something more or something less than it is), and our intellect may be likened unto possibility. Therefore, the quiddity of things, which is the truth of beings, is unattainable in its purity; though it is sought by all philosophers, it is found by no one as it is. And the more deeply we are instructed in this ignorance, the closer we approach to truth.

Chapter 4: The Absolute Maximum, with Which the Minimum Coincides, Is Understood Incomprehensibly.

Since the unqualifiedly and absolutely Maximum (than which there cannot be a greater) is greater than we can comprehend (because it is Infinite Truth), we attain unto it in no other way than incomprehensibly. For since it is not of the nature of those things which can be comparatively greater and lesser, it is beyond all that we can conceive. For whatsoever things are apprehended by the senses, by reason, or by intellect differ both within themselves and in relation to one another—[differ] in such way that there is no precise equality among them. Therefore, Maximum Equality, which is neither other than nor different from anything, surpasses all understanding. Hence, since the absolutely Maximum is all that which can be, it is *altogether* actual. And just as there cannot be a greater, so for the same reason there cannot be a lesser, since it is all that which can be. But the Minimum is that than which there cannot be a lesser. And since the Maximum is also such, it is evident that the Minimum coincides with the Maximum. The foregoing [point] will become clearer to you if you contract maximum and minimum to quantity. For maximum quantity is maximally large; and minimum quantity is maximally small. Therefore, if you free *maximum* and *minimum* from *quantity*—by mentally removing *large* and *small*—you will see clearly that maximum and minimum coincide. For *maximum* is a superlative just as *minimum* is a superlative. Therefore, it is not the case that absolute quantity is maximum quantity rather than minimum quantity; for in it the minimum is the maximum coincidingly.

Therefore, opposing features belong only to those things which can be comparatively greater and lesser; they befit these things in different ways; [but they do] not at all [befit] the absolutely Maximum, since it is beyond all opposition. Therefore, because the absolutely Maximum is absolutely and actually all things which can be (and is so free of all opposition that the Minimum coincides with it), it is beyond both all affirmation and all negation. And it is not, as well as is, all that which is conceived to be; and it is, as well as is not, all that which is conceived not to be. But it is a given thing in such way that it is all things; and it is all things in such way that it is no thing; and it is maximally a given thing in such way that it is it minimally. For example, to say "God, who is Absolute Maximality, is light" is [to say] no other than "God is maximally light in such way that He is minimally light." For Absolute Maximality could not be actually all possible things unless it were infinite and were the boundary of all things and were unable to be bounded by any of these things—as, by the graciousness of God, I will explain in subsequent sections. However, the [absolutely Maximum] transcends all our understanding. For our intellect cannot, by means of reasoning, combine contradictories in their Beginning, since we proceed by means of what nature makes evident to us. Our reason falls far short of this infinite power and is unable to connect contradictories, which are infinitely distant. Therefore, we see incomprehensibly, beyond all rational inference, that Absolute Maximality (to which nothing is opposed and with which the Minimum coincides) is infinite. But "maximum" and "minimum," as used in this [first] book, are transcendent terms of absolute signification, so that in their absolute simplicity they encompass—beyond all contraction to quantity of mass or quantity of power—all things.

*   *   *

Chapter 26: Negative Theology.

The worshipping of God, who is to be worshipped in spirit and in truth, must be based upon affirmations about Him. Accordingly, every religion, in its worshipping, must mount upward by means of affirmative theology. [Through affirmative theology] it worships God as one and three, as most wise and most gracious, as Inaccessible Light, as Life, Truth, and so on. And it always directs its worship by faith, which it attains more truly through learned ignorance. It believes that He whom it worships as one is All-in-one, and that He whom it worships as Inaccessible Light is not light as is corporeal light, to which darkness is opposed, but is infinite and most simple Light, in which darkness is Infinite Light; and [it believes] that Infinite Light always shines within the darkness of our ignorance but [that] the darkness cannot comprehend it. And so, the theology of negation is so necessary for the theology of affirmation that without it God would not be worshipped as the Infinite God but, rather, as a creature. And such worship is idolatry; it ascribes to the image that which befits only the reality itself. Hence, it will be useful to set down a few more things about negative theology.

Sacred ignorance has taught us that God is ineffable. He is so because He is infinitely greater than all nameable things. And by virtue of the fact that [this] is most true, we speak of God more truly through removal and negation—as [teaches] the greatest Dionysius, who did not believe that God is either Truth or Understanding or Light or anything which can be spoken of. (Rabbi Solomon and all the wise follow Dionysius.) Hence, in accordance with this negative theology, according to which [God] is only infinite, He is neither Father nor Son nor Holy Spirit. Now, the Infinite qua Infinite is neither Begetting, Begotten, nor Proceeding. Therefore, when Hilary of Poitiers distinguished the persons, he most astutely used the expressions "Infinity in the Eternal," "Beauty in the Image," and "Value in the Gift." He means that although in eternity we can see only infinity, nevertheless since the infinity which is eternity is negative infinity, it cannot be understood as Begetter but [can] rightly [be understood as] eternity, since "eternity" is affirmative of oneness, or maximum presence. Hence, [Infinity-in-the-Eternal is] the Beginning without beginning. "Beauty in the Image" indicates the Beginning from the Beginning. "Value in the Gift" indicates the Procession from these two.

All these things are very well known through the preceding [discussion]. For although eternity is infinity, so that eternity is not a greater cause of the Father than is infinity: nevertheless, in a manner of considering, eternity is attributed to the Father and not to the Son or to the Holy Spirit; but infinity is not [attributed] to one person more than to another. For according to the consideration of oneness infinity is the Father; according to the consideration of equality of oneness it is the Son; according to the consideration of the union [of the two it is] the Holy Spirit. And according to the simple consideration of itself infinity is neither the Father nor the Son nor the Holy Spirit. Yet, infinity (as also eternity) is each of the three persons, and, conversely, each person is infinity (and eternity)—not, however, according to [the simple] consideration [of itself], as I said. For according to the consideration of infinity God is neither one nor many. Now, according to the theology of negation, there is not found in God anything other than infinity. Therefore, according to this theology [God] is not knowable either in this world or in the world to come (for in this respect every created thing is darkness, which cannot comprehend Infinite Light), but is known only to Himself.

From these [observations] it is clear (1) that in theological matters negations are true and affirmations are inadequate, and (2) that, nonetheless, the negations which remove the more imperfect things from the most Perfect are truer than the others. For example, it is truer that God is not stone than that He is not life or intelligence; and [it is truer that He] is not drunkenness than that He is not virtue. The contrary [holds] for affirmations; for the affirmation which states that God is intelligence and life is truer than [the affirmation that He is] earth or stone or body. All these [points] are very clear from the foregoing. Therefrom we conclude that the precise truth shines incomprehensibly within the darkness of our ignorance. This is the learned ignorance we have been seeking and through which alone, as I explained, [we] can approach the maximum, triune God of infinite goodness—[approach Him] according to the degree of our instruction in ignorance, so that with all our might we may ever praise Him, who is forever blessed above all things, for manifesting to us His incomprehensible self.

Epilogue: Giovanni Pico della Mirandola

1463–1494

In the late 1300s some Italian thinkers began to talk about a rebirth or "renaissance." They wrote in a disparaging manner of the "Middle" or "Dark Ages," depicting it as a period of barbarian ignorance from which they had just emerged. They saw themselves as awakening to their classical past and continuing the civilizing work of the ancient Greeks and Romans.

While there are few scholars today who would not modify this self-characterization, there does seem to have been something different about the late medieval/early modern period. While the medievals had access to some classical texts, the Renaissance thinkers had a wide, and often contradictory, variety of ancient Greek and Roman works. While the philosophers of the Middle Ages tended to use ancient materials to reinforce their Christian beliefs, the early modern thinkers found new uses for these ancient texts. But most importantly, while the Middle Ages tended to be vertically oriented, focusing on God and God's Kingdom, the early modern period became more and more horizontally oriented, examining the created world and celebrating its most important inhabitants, human beings.

The person who most typifies this use of ancient texts to express the importance and "dignity of man" is Count Giovanni Pico della Mirandola. Pico was born in Mirandola, near Ferrara, northern Italy. The son of a minor Italian prince, his education included a variety of subjects and a diversity of institutions. In 1477 he went to the University of Bologna to study cannon (church) law. After two years he moved to study philosophy at the universities of Ferrara and Padua. Finally in 1482 he concluded his studies by examining Hebrew and Arabic thought while in Florence and Paris.

Pico believed it was possible to reconcile the seeming contradictions among the various systems of thought he had studied. Drawing out what he considered the best in each thinker and system he encountered, he developed a philosophy known as "syncretism." Syncretism holds that all schools of philosophy have some truth and so should be examined and defended, but no system of thought has all the truth, and so one must also expose the errors in each scheme.

Applying his philosophy of syncretism, in 1486 Pico drew up a list of nine hundred true theses (or propositions) using various Greek, Arabic, Hebrew, and Roman thinkers who summarized his views. He invited scholars from all over Europe to come to Rome where he would defend his positions against all challengers. However, the disputation never occurred. Pope Innocent VIII suspended the debate and appointed a commission to investigate the nine hundred theses. Seven of the propositions were subsequently declared unorthodox and six more held to be dangerous. Pico publicly protested the decision by publishing a defense of his positions, succeeding only in infuriating the pope. The pope condemned all nine hundred propositions, reportedly commenting, "That young man wants someone to burn him." Pico fled to France but was arrested there by papal envoys. Through the intervention of friends in Italy, Pico was released by the French king. He spent the rest of his short life in Florence under the protection of the powerful Lorenzo de Medici.

The *Oration on the Dignity of Man* was intended as an introductory speech for the proposed Rome debate. In the selection reprinted here, translated by Elizabeth Livermore Forbes, Pico exhibits his syncretistic willingness to draw from many different sources. Quoting from a wide variety of writings, he argues that God has given all creatures besides humans a unique, fixed nature. They have a certain kind of being that they cannot change. But we as human beings do not have a given being—we alone have the freedom to choose what we will become. While we can choose to become animals or "couch potatoes" or angelic philosophers, it is the ability to *choose* that gives us dignity.

*   *   *

Pico's life was chronicled by his nephew in the difficult to find Giovanni Francesco Pico, *Giovanni Pico della Mirandola: His Life by His Nephew Giovanni Francesco Pico,* translated by Sir Thomas More, edited by J.M. Rigg (London: D. Nutt, 1890). For a general overview of Pico, see William G. Craven, *Giovanni Pico della Mirandola, Symbol of His Age: Modern Interpretations of a Renaissance Philosopher* (Geneve: Droz, 1981).

For collections of primary source readings in Renaissance philosophy, see Ernst Cassirer, Paul O. Kristeller, and John H. Randall, Jr., eds., *The Renaissance Philosophy of Man* (Chicago: University of Chicago Press, 1948), and Arturo B. Fallico and Herman Shapiro, eds., *Renaissance Philosophy,* 2 vols. (New York: Random House, 1967–1969). For general studies of Renaissance thought, see Ernst Cassirer, *The Individual and Cosmos in Renaissance Philosophy,* translated by Mario Domandi (New York: Harper & Row, 1963); and Paul O. Kristeller, *Renaissance Thought and Its Sources* (New York: Columbia University Press, 1979).

ORATION ON THE DIGNITY OF MAN
(in part)

I have read in the records of the Arabians, reverend Fathers, that Abdala the Saracen [probably the cousin of Mohammed], when questioned as to what on this stage of the world, as it were, could be seen most worthy of wonder, replied: "There is nothing to be seen more wonderful than man." In agreement with this opinion is the saying of Hermes Trismegistus: "A great miracle, Asclepius, is man." But when I weighed the reason for these maxims, the many grounds for the excellence of human nature reported by many men failed to satisfy me—that man is the intermediary between creatures, the intimate of the gods, the king of the lower beings, by the acuteness of his senses, by the discernment of his reason, and by the light of his intelligence the interpreter of nature, the interval between fixed eternity and fleeting time, and (as the Persians say) the bond, nay, rather, the marriage song of the world, on David's testimony but little lower than the angels (Ps. 8:5). Admittedly great though these reasons be, they are not the principal grounds, that is, those which may rightfully claim for themselves the privilege of the highest admiration. For why should we not admire more the angels themselves and the blessed choirs of heaven? At last it seems to me I have come to understand why man is the most fortunate of creatures and consequently worthy of all admiration and what precisely is that rank which is his lot in the universal chain of Being—a rank to be envied not only by brutes but even by the stars and by minds beyond this world. It is a matter past faith and a wondrous one. Why should it not be? For it is on this very account that man is rightly called and judged a great miracle and a wonderful creature indeed.

    2. But hear, Fathers, exactly what this rank is and, as friendly auditors, conformably to your kindness, do me this favor. God the Father, the supreme Architect, had already built this cosmic home we behold, the most sacred temple of His godhead, by the laws of His mysterious wisdom. The region above the heavens He had adorned with Intelligences, the heavenly spheres He had quickened with eternal souls, and the excrementary and filthy parts of the lower world He had filled with a multitude of animals of every kind. But, when the work was finished, the Craftsman kept wishing that there were someone to ponder the plan of so great a work, to love its beauty, and to wonder at its vastness. Therefore, when everything was done (as Moses and Timaeus bear witness), He finally took thought concerning the creation of man. But there was not among His archetypes that from which He could fashion a new offspring, nor was there in His treasure-houses anything which He might bestow on His new son as an inheritance, nor was there in the seats of all the world a place where the latter might sit to contemplate the universe. All was now complete; all things had been assigned to the highest, the middle, and the lowest orders. But in its final creation it was not the part of the Father's power to fail as though exhausted. It was not the part of His wisdom to waver in a needful matter through poverty of counsel. It was not the part of His kindly love that he who was to praise God's divine generosity in regard to others should be compelled to condemn it in regard to himself.

Giovanni Pico della Mirandola, *Oration on the Dignity of Man,* 1–7, translated by Elizabeth Livermore Forbes, from *The Renaissance Philosophy of Man,* edited by Ernst Cassirer, Paul Oskar Kristeller, and John Herman Randall, Jr. (Chicago: The University of Chicago Press, 1948). Copyright © 1948 The University of Chicago Press. Reprinted by permission.

3. At last the best of artisans ordained that that creature to whom He had been able to give nothing proper to himself should have joint possession of whatever had been peculiar to each of the different kinds of being. He therefore took man as a creature of indeterminate nature and, assigning him a place in the middle of the world, addressed him thus: "Neither a fixed abode nor a form that is thine alone nor any function peculiar to thyself have we given thee, Adam, to the end that according to thy longing and according to thy judgment thou mayest have and possess what abode, what form, and what functions thou thyself shalt desire. The nature of all other beings is limited and constrained within the bounds of laws prescribed by Us. Thou, constrained by no limits, in accordance with thine own free will, in whose hand We have placed thee, shalt ordain for thyself the limits of thy nature. We have set thee at the world's center that thou mayest from thence more easily observe whatever is in the world. We have made thee neither of heaven nor of earth, neither mortal nor immortal, so that with freedom of choice and with honor, as though the maker and molder of thyself, thou mayest fashion thyself in whatever shape thou shalt prefer. Thou shalt have the power to degenerate into the lower forms of life, which are brutish. Thou shalt have the power, out of thy soul's judgment, to be reborn into the higher forms, which are divine."

4. O supreme generosity of God the Father, O highest and most marvelous felicity of man! To him it is granted to have whatever he chooses, to be whatever he wills. Beasts as soon as they are born (so says Lucilius) bring with them from their mother's womb all they will ever possess. Spiritual beings, either from the beginning or soon thereafter, become what they are to be for ever and ever. On man when he came into life the Father conferred the seeds of all kinds and the germs of every way of life. Whatever seeds each man cultivates will grow to maturity and bear in him their own fruit. If they be vegetative, he will be like a plant. If sensitive, he will become brutish. If rational, he will grow into a heavenly being. If intellectual, he will be an angel and the son of God. And if, happy in the lot of no created thing, he withdraws into the center of his own unity, his spirit, made one with God, in the solitary darkness of God, who is set above all things, shall surpass them all. Who would not admire this our chameleon? Or who could more greatly admire aught else whatever? It is man who Asclepius of Athens, arguing from his mutability of character and from his self-transforming nature, on just grounds says was symbolized by Proteus in the mysteries. Hence those metamorphoses renowned among the Hebrews and the Pythagoreans.

5. For the occult theology of the Hebrews sometimes transforms the holy Enoch into an angel of divinity whom they call "Mal'akh Adonay Shebaoth," and sometimes transforms others into other divinities. The Pythagoreans degrade impious men into brutes and, if one is to believe Empedocles, even into plants. Mohammed, in imitation, often had this saying on his tongue: "They who have deviated from divine law become beasts," and surely he spoke justly. For it is not the bark that makes the plant but its senseless and insentient nature; neither is it the hide that makes the beast of burden but its irrational, sensitive soul; neither is it the orbed form that makes the heavens but their undeviating order; nor is it the sundering from body but his spiritual intelligence that makes the angel. For if you see one abandoned to his appetites crawling on the ground, it is a plant and not a man you see; if you see one blinded by the vain illusions of imagery, as it were of Calypso, and, softened by their gnawing allurement, delivered over to his senses, it is a beast and not a man you see. If you see a philosopher determining all things by means of right reason, him you shall reverence: he is a heavenly being and not of this earth. If you see a pure contemplator, one unaware of the body and confined to the inner reaches of the mind, he is neither an earthly nor a heavenly being; he is a more reverend divinity vested with human flesh.

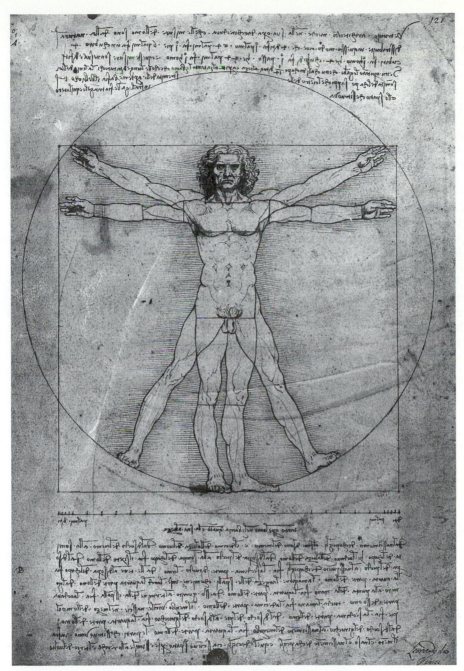

Study of Human Proportions, by Leonardo da Vinci (1452–1519). Like Pico, Leonardo enjoyed the patronage of Lorenzo de Medici; and also like Pico, Leonardo celebrated the "dignity of man" and exuberantly exhibited his own ability. (© *1991 Archivi Alinari/Art Resource*)

6. Are there any who would not admire man, who is, in the sacred writings of Moses and the Christians, not without reason described sometimes by the name of "all flesh," sometimes by that of "every creature," inasmuch as he himself molds, fashions, and changes himself into the form of all flesh and into the character of every creature? For this reason the Persian Euanthes, in describing the Chaldaean theology, writes that man has no semblance that is inborn and his very own but many that are external and foreign to him; whence this saying of the Chaldaeans: "Hanorish tharah sharinas," that is, "Man is a being of varied, manifold, and inconstant nature." But why do we emphasize this? To the end that after we have been born to this condition—that we can become what we will—we should understand that we ought to have especial care to this, that it should never be said against us that, although born to a privileged position, we failed to recognize it and became like unto wild animals and senseless beasts of burden, but that rather the saying of Asaph the prophet should apply: "Ye are all angels and sons of the Most High," and that we may not, by abusing the most indulgent generosity of the Father, make for ourselves that freedom of choice He has given into something harmful instead of salutary. Let a certain holy ambition invade our souls, so that, not content with the mediocre, we shall pant after the highest and (since we may if we wish) toil with all our strength to obtain it.

7. Let us disdain earthly things, despise heavenly things, and, finally, esteeming less whatever is of the world, hasten to that court which is beyond the world and nearest to the Godhead. There, as the sacred mysteries relate, Seraphim, Cherubim, and Thrones hold the first places; let us, incapable of yielding to them, and intolerant of a lower place, emulate their dignity and their glory. If we have willed it, we shall be second to them in nothing.